ALL • IN • ONE

Nortel Networks™ Support Specialist and Expert Certification

E X A M   G U I D E

Zeecil M. Kimmel

Eric S. Renkoff

Osborne / McGraw-Hill
New York • Chicago • San Francisco • Lisbon
London • Madrid • Mexico City • Milan • New Delhi
San Juan • Seoul • Singapore • Sydney • Toronto

McGraw-Hill/Osborne
2600 Tenth Street
Berkeley, California 94710
U.S.A.

To arrange bulk purchase discounts for sales promotions, premiums, or fund-raisers, please contact McGraw-Hill/Osborne at the above address. For information on translations or book distributors outside the U.S.A., please see the International Contact Information page immediately following the index of this book.

Nortel Networks™ Support Specialist and Expert Certification All-in-One Exam Guide

1234567890 DOC DOC 0198765432

Book p/n 0-07-213035-0 and CD p/n 0-07-213034-2
parts of
ISBN 0-07-213036-9

Publisher
Brandon A. Nordin

Vice President & Associate Publisher
Scott Rogers

Editorial Director
Gareth Hancock

Project Manager
Jenn Tust

Acquisitions Coordinator
Jessica Wilson

Technical Editors
Yitzy Kimmel
James Edwards

Composition
MacAllister Publishing Services, LLC

Cover Design
Greg Scott

This book was composed with QuarkXPress™.

DEDICATION

I would like to dedicate this book to my husband and soul mate Mordeachai Gholian. Without his encouragement, support, and help, there would be no book. Mordeachai, this book was your idea; you urged me to finish it, agreed to eat leftovers while I was busy with it, and did the dishes to give me more time to work on it. Thank you and here it is! May we share many more successes together for all the years to come.

Zeecil Kimmel

ACKNOWLEDGMENTS

It is very difficult to properly thank the many people that influenced my life in the past few years and really helped to make this book happen. I would just like to mention a few individuals by name. Firstly I would like to thank God, for without Him I would not have the talents, knowledge, or strength to complete this project. Secondly I would like to thank my parents and in laws for their unconditional support and love. Lastly I would like to thank Nortel Networks and my managers, past and present, for giving me the opportunity to learn and grow and have a job that I really love.

Zeecil Kimmel

I would like to give thanks to all of the people who worked on this project with me for all that they did to help get this book out. I would like to thank Zeecil for including me on this project. I would especially like too thank all of the teachers that I have had since entering this field. I know that I have learned from some of the best. Most of all I would like to thank my wife for her support and love, as well as my children for their patience while I was writing this book. I would also like to thank the writer of RFC 1925 for all the inspiration that particular piece of work provided.

Eric Renkoff

ABOUT THE AUTHORS

Zeecil M. Kimmel is a Rapid Response Engineer for Nortel Networks, a worldwide communications and networking hardware corporation. She works in the Global Customer Care Service Group as a level-three engineer, responding to technical support issues at customer sites. Zeecil supports a myriad of different hardware products including routers with BayRS, Passport layer 3 switches, and the OPTera Metro.

In the past Ms. Kimmel's career has included working as a consultant and providing customer solutions with both Nortel Networks hardware and Microsoft networking software. She has also taught certification classes for both technologies all over the United States. She is also the coauthor of *Nortel Networks Layer 3 Switching*.

Zeecil holds a Bachelor's degree in computer science from Maalot Institute in Jerusalem as well as her NNCI (Nortel Networks Certified Instructor), NNCSS (Nortel Networks Certified Support Specialist), MCT (Microsoft Certified Trainer), and MCSE (Microsoft Certified Systems Engineer) certifications.

Zeecil Kimmel can be reached at Zeecil.kimmel@verizon.net.

Eric S. Renkoff began his career as an instructor at Westcon Services teaching Novell Netware. He was encouraged by his managers to pursue certification as a Nortel Networks Certified Instructor (then Bay Networks Certified Instructor) to fill an organizational need at Westcon. Along the way Eric became a Nortel Networks Certified Support Specialist (NNCSS), a Nortel Networks Certified Support Expert (NNCSE), a Nortel Networks Certified Instructor, and he also is a CCNA and CNE. He is certified to teach Hub Connectivity, Centillion 100, Optivity Campus and Optivity NMS 9.X, Frame Switching and Interroperability, Accellar (now Passport) 1xxx, and the Router classes. He has taught classes for Westcon, Nortel, PricewaterhouseCoopers, IMS, Global Knowledge, and many others. Eric attended the University of Maryland (College Park) and received a Bachelor of Arts in English literature in 1989.

Eric is currently an employee of Nortel Networks as a resident engineer at a premium account.

ABOUT THE REVIEWERS

Yitzy Kimmel has a B.S. in Computer Science from Brooklyn College. He has taught numerous computer courses at Brooklyn College, and is currently a senior technical consultant at American Healthware Systems in Brooklyn, NY.

James Edwards, NNCSS, NNCDS, NNCSE is a Senior Network Support Engineer at Nortel Networks. He has been involved in network design and network support for the past several years. Mr. Edwards is also the co-author of *Nortel Networks: A Beginners Guide*.

CONTENTS

INTRODUCTION

If you are a member of the IT community and are looking to get certified in Nortel Networks products, here is the place to start. This book explains the different certifications available from Nortel Networks to help you find the right certification for you. Use this book as a study guide for learning different technologies that are part of the certification requirements of Nortel Networks. This book is also valuable for learning how to set up and configure equipment and understanding technologies used in a day-to-day IT job.

Of course this book cannot replace experience. It is absolutely essential to gain access to hardware in order to gain a truer understanding of networking equipment and its functionality. Nortel Networks recommends at least three to six months of experience working with products before attempting to take an exam. This book can be used in conjunction with a lab that contains hardware. Many exercises and commands are provided to take advantage of live equipment.

This book also includes a CD of test questions that can help you get into the mindset for a Nortel Networks exam. Definitely use this CD before registering for an exam to verify knowledge of hardware and exam preparedness.

Updates to this book will be published from time to time at www.osborne.com. Please visit the web site for the latest and greatest information. Also visit the Nortel Networks certification web site for current information on Nortel Certification programs that do change over time. That website is www.nortelnetworks.com/servsup/certification.

For those attempting to take exams: Good luck! For those who love their jobs and just want to learn more: Knowledge is power! For everyone reading this book: May you gain that which you desire from this book!

PART I

Certification Overview

The Certification Process

Welcome to the *Nortel Networks Support Specialist and Expert Certification All-in-One Exam Guide*. The goal of this book is to help the reader understand the different certifications available from Nortel Networks in order to prepare candidates for getting certified. Additionally, we hope to share knowledge that will help make people become more sought-after employees.

Not every certification is for everyone, but through this chapter we hope to assist candidates in finding the proper certification as well as the path to getting that certification. The book helps candidates achieve their desired certification by describing the exams required for certification and discussing in depth the materials necessary to pass the exams. This chapter explains the different certification programs that exist within Nortel Networks, how to prepare for those certifications, and how this book can be used as supplemental knowledge when striving to achieve certification. The rest of this book discusses protocols, hardware, and software at the level of knowledge and understanding needed to certify and pass the Nortel Networks certification tracks. All chapters, except this one, include valuable test questions for review purposes.

NOTE   It is extremely important to get hands-on experience with Nortel Networks equipment in addition to using this guide when studying for exams.

Before we discuss certification, let us begin with some history of Nortel Networks, which will help us understand the company's certification program and its evolution.

3

In the beginning, there were two companies: Synoptics, a maker of hubs and network management products, which was headquartered in Santa Clara, California, and Wellfleet, a maker of routers, which was headquartered in Billerica, Massachusetts. The two companies joined to form Bay Networks (representing the two headquarters in the Bay of California and the Bay of Massachusetts). Bay Networks was a data company that mainly focused on the enterprise customer. They produced products for networking like hubs, switches, routers, and Asynchronous Transfer Mode (ATM) devices. They also produced network management products to monitor their products in a local area network (LAN) or wide area network (WAN) environment.

On August 31, 1998, Nortel (Northern Telecom) acquired Bay Networks. They were a Canadian-based telephony company whose primary focus was voice for the carrier-class customer. The combination of the two companies led to great advances in products like voice over IP and optical switches for both the carrier and enterprise customer.

Bay Networks had a certification program that was based on their products. They offered a base-level specialist certification that required a base level of proficiency in a single product. Bay Networks also offered an expert-level certification that required advanced levels of knowledge with the same product and required the candidate to pass a lab practical of setting up, installing, and fully configuring one specific product. The focus was entirely on Enterprise data, and their exams tested for proficiency with specific products. The newly expanded Nortel Networks certification, as we will explain in depth, includes proficiency with data and voice products as well as Carrier and Optical Internet products. This creates a greater diversity of products to choose from when going for certification. The certification is also expanded to create certified professionals who have knowledge of more than one product, protocol, or expertise.

NOTE   Individuals already certified by Bay Networks are automatically grandfathered into the new certification framework.

Previous Certification Title	New Certification Title
Bay Networks Certified Specialist	Nortel Networks Certified Support Specialist
Bay Networks Certified Expert	Nortel Networks Certified Support Expert

NOTE   Although currently certified individuals may not have any immediate testing requirements, they may still be subject to any future recertification requirements.

The goal of this chapter, as we said, is to provide an in-depth discussion of the Nortel Networks certification tracks; however, first we will discuss the general benefits of certification and how it can help in building careers.

The Benefits of Certification

In an industry where standardization is very crucial, certification gives the measuring stick with which to judge knowledge level. Employers look for certification to make their hiring decisions, and employees want certification to obtain better salaries. Certification is another step towards industry standardization. Companies are demanding more of their employees, and in times when the job market is tight, the expectations are higher. Certification leads to industry recognition. The program is aimed at helping people become experts in the field of networking and have proof of their expertise. Nortel Networks certified individuals are recognized throughout the industry as highly qualified network solutions professionals. There are tremendous benefits of certification to the employee, employer, and industry.

For the employee, the benefits may be the greatest. After all, certification belongs to the individual and not the company, so the individual will ultimately benefit the most. Certification can be used as a validation of job skills, and proof of learning and the ability to apply knowledge. This leads to increased credibility with customers, increased productivity and proficiency, and improved skills. Pursuing certification forces an employee to develop skills that enhance his or her market value in the industry, which can lead to new and exciting career paths. Certification also provides individual, personalized certificates and plaques (fancy pens), greater access to technical information, and the ability to use the certification logo on business cards or web sites to represent the candidate's expertise level.

Companies that offer their employees certification benefits promote employee loyalty, which in turn promotes customer loyalty and satisfaction. Having employees that are certified can lead to increased business efficiencies, which brings increased revenue for the company and its business partners.

For the industry, certification provides an increase in the pool of qualified talent, growth, and new revenue opportunities. Previously, for example, the Optical Internet industry did not have a certification program. This hampered the growth of the optical market because there were no methods available to verify whether people had the necessary skills required to sell, design, deploy, and support Optical Internet networks. To solve this industry problem, Nortel Networks created various certifications, which we will mention later. These help to create certified individuals who can implement optical solutions and help the optical market grow.

Because of the tremendous benefits of becoming certified, some people decide to gain certification through reading books, and then taking exams without even gaining any experience with products. In the industry, this is known as *paper certification*. It is a derogatory term that implies that the person certified has no real-world experience. In reality, people achieving certification may use this to gain a job, which would then give the individual the opportunity to work with the equipment and gain experience. This can be very useful in providing people with opportunities that they might not have had otherwise. The value of becoming certified varies depending on each candidate's perspective and objectives. Candidates using certification to gain additional knowledge and experience are valuable to the networking community.

The Nortel Networks Certification Program (NNCP)

In this era of high-performance Internet and networking, Nortel Networks recognizes the importance of developing expertise to help meet the demands for qualified resources that are the result of the explosive growth in the industry. Nortel Networks' goal is to deliver an industry-leading global certification program that sets the standard for selling, designing, installing, and supporting Nortel Networks solutions.

The Nortel Networks Certification Program takes a unique approach to building and developing data networking skills in the areas of sales, design, and support. Its approach combines networking education and experience with the ability to understand and resolve complex networking scenarios. Certifications include sales, network design, and technical support for a broad range of Nortel Networks voice, data, and Internet products. Each of these areas has designations designed for different professionals who perform a variety of job functions.

Participation in the Nortel Networks Certification Program helps candidates meet the challenges presented by an ever-changing technology landscape. The certification program offers a range of proficiencies to meet specific certification needs, from specialist to expert to architect. There are many different types of certification that you can achieve through the Nortel Networks certification track. Individual certifications are detailed under the specific Enterprise, Optical, and Instant Internet (Carrier) tracks.

NOTE This book mainly covers the Enterprise data track.

Enterprise Solutions certification is appropriate for anyone who supports, installs, or designs Enterprise solutions, for anyone reselling or purchasing Nortel Networks Enterprise solutions, or for anyone involved or interested in a career in Enterprise solutions.

Intelligent Internet certification is appropriate for anyone who supports, installs, or designs Intelligent Internet solutions, for anyone reselling or purchasing Nortel Networks Intelligent Internet solutions, or for anyone involved or interested in a career in Intelligent Internet.

 NOTE Intelligent Internet is the new name for Carrier networking.

Nortel Networks recently added its Optical certification. It is the first company in the industry to offer a multifaceted program designed to verify a candidate's knowledge and skills in various aspects of the Optical Internet. All designations verify that candidates have an understanding of generic Optical Internet terms and a fundamental knowledge of optical networking. In addition, each of the optical pieces of the certification track verifies additional different skills and knowledge.

The new Nortel Networks Certification Program is modular as well, which enables candidates to choose the certification that best meets their individual and business needs. This certification framework offers candidates a progressive development path as they gain experience and increase their skill set.

Finally, the expanded certification program offers new certification opportunities and skills-based testing for additional quality. By utilizing performance-based solutions-oriented exams, Nortel Networks strives to measure real-world skills. By increasing the use of web-based exams, the new certification program strives for greater test accessibility.

 NOTE The program does not discriminate against anyone from becoming certified, and anyone is eligible to become certified.

Steps to Certification

The following are the recommended steps to follow to achieve Nortel Networks certification:

1. Select a certification designation track by choosing the product and area in which to certify. Nortel Networks offers certifications that are targeted at people in different job functions with different skill levels. The specific requirements for obtaining a Nortel Networks certification depends on which specific certification the candidate is seeking. Review the requirements and targeted skills for the chosen certification designation and determine the skills that need further development.

2. Once the appropriate certification track is determined, the next step is to become familiar with the associated exams and prerequisites. Although training is not mandatory to become certified, Nortel Networks offers specific curriculum tracks to help prepare for the certification exams. Each candidate should create a personal development plan that identifies the training activities he or she needs to enhance his or her skill sets, and set target dates for the training activities and certification test. If a candidate chooses to take training, he or she should schedule his or her training by contacting the training provider for classroom training or scheduling time for self-directed learning (readings, video courses, and hands-on exercises).

3. Candidates should be constantly reassessing their knowledge as they progress through their development plan, making sure to compare their evolving skill sets against the skill requirements for the chosen certification designation. Candidates should make sure to practice what they have learned using Nortel Networks equipment whenever possible. For some certifications, Nortel Networks recommends at least three months of product and on-the-job experience before attempting the exams. For more challenging certification exams, Nortel Networks recommends at least 6 to 12 months of on-the-job experience prior to taking the test. When the candidate has gained the required knowledge and practiced what he or she has learned, then the candidate is ready to take the exam.

4. Register, take, and pass the exam. Nortel Networks uses a variety of testing methodologies for certification exams. Testing methodologies are applied as appropriate across the certification levels and across the product lines within Nortel Networks. Registration is mandatory for all web-based and Prometric-proctored exams.

Certification Tracks

Choosing to become certified requires a candidate to first decide which area he or she is going to focus on to achieve certification. Obviously, the candidate will choose an area for certification where he or she can most easily fulfill the qualifications for certification. Let us examine those qualifications for Nortel Networks certification.

Nortel Networks offers account, design, field, and support specialist designations as well as expert designations. Most of these designations offer certification for Enterprise data and voice, Optical networks, and Intelligent Internet. This book focuses mainly on the Enterprise data support specialist and support expert certifications, but it also covers information for the Instant Internet Support Specialist exam.

NOTE   The specific tracks defined within the certification designations, mentioned in the following sections, represent the currently available certification options. As the Internet market continues to grow and change, additional tracks within these designations will be added and some will no longer be available.

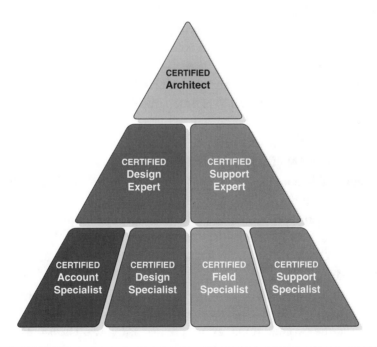

Figure I-I   Triangle of certification

Specialist Certifications

The specialist level is for candidates with a basic level of technical proficiency to support Nortel Networks solutions.

 NOTE Beginning January 2002, all certifications will require the completion of a fundamentals exam and at least one product/solution exam. The fundamental exam requirement will be added to each designation as it is released.

Nortel Networks Certified Account Specialist (NNCAS)

This certification is designed for entry- and mid-level sales representatives and is available for the Enterprise and Optical tracks. This certification recognizes a fundamental level of knowledge with products, solutions, and technology. Candidates attempting this certification should be able to recognize customers needs and identify Nortel Networks equipment that can be positioned in the customer market.

The requirement for this certification is the passing of two exams. The exams include one fundamentals exam and one Unified Solutions exam. The fundamentals exam can be a Sales Fundamentals exam (Enterprise track) or an Optical Fundamentals exam (Optical Track Metro designation), and the Unified Solutions exam can include topics on sales solutions for a LAN, WAN, VPN, small business, or metro network.

Nortel Networks Certified Design Specialist (NNCDS)

This certification is designed for the entry- to mid-level technical sales and system engineers. It is ideal for candidates who have the skills and knowledge required for designing and deploying Enterprise solutions or Intelligent Internet products. Additionally, this certification is available for the Optical Internet networks with an emphasis on Nortel Networks OPTera Metro or an OPTera Long-Haul solution and will verify the skills and knowledge associated with designing basic Optical Internet networks.

The requirement for this certification is the passing of two or three exams. There is one fundamental exam for Voice, Data IP, or Optical Networks Fundamentals. For the Enterprise track, the two additional exams are necessary: two Unified exams on LAN, WAN, Ethernet, ATM, or VPN. For the Optical track, those two additional exams are the Optical Network Design Principles exam and the Optical Metro Solutions, or the Optical Long-Haul Solutions exam. For the Instant Internet designation only, one additional exam is necessary: the Design Specialist exam for the Passport 8600 or the Passport 7000/15000, or the CVX 1800 exam.

Nortel Networks Certified Field Specialist (NNCFS)

This designation is aimed at entry- to mid-level candidates with the ability to operate as a field technician and contract firms looking to deploy Nortel Networks products. These candidates may be working with Nortel Networks Optical, Instant Internet (Carrier), and Enterprise data products. Candidates should have the ability to install, commission, and provision equipment at a customer site including cable racks and wiring. This requires an understanding of power, inventory, site housekeeping, the use of tools, wire wrapping, and fiber handling. They should also be able to perform first-line maintenance, basic troubleshooting, system-level acceptance testing, and link equalization. Additionally, candidates should have knowledge of the basic terminology, be able to apply guidelines for safety and quality, and be able to locate information in Nortel Networks documentation.

Requirements for the Optical certification called the OPTera Metro 5000 Multiservice Platform Series includes the Optical Networks Fundamentals exam and either the Field Installation and Commissioning exam or the First-Line Maintenance exam. The Instant Internet certification requires only one exam called the Physical Installation exam, whereas the requirement for the Enterprise data track includes two fundamental exams: Data IP and Voice, and one product-specific exam of Business Communication Manager (BCM) 2.5, MPS 100, Meridian IP Enabled/Succession CSE 1000, or Symposium Portfolio.

Nortel Networks Certified Support Specialist (NNCSS)

The target audience for this certification is the entry- to mid-level technical support, help desk, and field support personnel. A specialist is someone who provides day-to-day technical support for the networking equipment in a company. Someone with at least a fundamental level of technical expertise on a single Nortel Networks product line might choose to become certified for that product. For example, a network engineer who supports routers or switches may choose to become a router or switch specialist.

NOTE A support specialist generally has complete support knowledge of a specific product family.

The support certification designations verify that candidates have the proper skills and knowledge to support Nortel Networks products and solutions. A candidate going for this certification should be able to deploy, operate, and troubleshoot Nortel Networks hardware and possess at least a fundamental level of technical support to implement, configure, and maintain a live system. Some of the skill sets and requirements that are questioned on exams and are necessary for certification include the following: product and network installation, using standard information resources, configuration using default parameters, performance basics and troubleshooting, maintenance of network operations, monitoring network status, problem identification, provisioning, upgrades, initial configuration, operations, and administration.

The specialist designation is available for all the tracks including the Enterprise solutions, Intelligent Internet (Carrier), and Optical Internet tracks. Each track has slightly different requirements.

Requirements after January 1, 2002 include the completion of two exams. The first exam is a fundamental exam, which candidates can choose from the Data IP Fundamentals, Voice Fundamentals, Optical Networks Fundamentals, Sales Fundamentals, or Wireless Fundamentals exams. Fundamental exams are used to validate the candidate's ability to apply knowledge and skills in a particular technology. Additionally, candidates must choose one technology exam.

Technology exams include the Hubs and Shared Media Core Technology exam, Router Core Technology exam, Switching Core Technology exam, Multiservice Access Core Technology exam, IP Telephony Core Technology exam, BCM 2.0 Core Technology exam, Support Specialist OPTera Metro 3000 exam, Support Specialist OPTera Metro 5000 exam, Contivity VPN Switch exam, Passport 15000 exam, Passport 7000 exam, and CVX 1800 exam.

The Core Technology exams are Prometric-proctored electronic exams for service professionals. The exams are a mix of technology-oriented topics as well as some basic product installation and configuration topics. Each exam has optional courses or self-paced study materials.

NOTE Technology areas and exams are subject to change; visit the Web for the most current information and selections.

For Optical networks, candidates are also expected to provide a Support Experience Validation Record. The support experience validation requirements have been modeled from existing recognized professional associations, such as the engineering profession. Nortel Networks believes that this experience validation requirement is essential in the support specialist certification to ensure that anyone practicing and providing professional carrier-grade support to high-capacity, multiservice Optical Internet networks holds the necessary qualifications, professionalism, experience, and responsibility to safeguard the interest of a client's Optical Internet network.

 NOTE   Certified specialist designations require renewal every two years. Requirements include taking the current versions of any tests that may have expired. Candidates will receive notification 30 days prior to certification expiration. To maintain certification status, candidates may recertify at the same level or certify at a higher level.

Expert Designations

Expert designations are created for those people with the skills required in advanced networking situations.

Design Expert

This certification is designed for mid- to senior-level system engineers, professional services, and network consultants. Candidates should possess the ability to apply design principles and plan Enterprise solutions using Nortel Networks products.

A prerequisite requirement for this certification is the design specialist designation. The expert certification also requires the successful completion of two exams: one product exam and one solution exam. The product exams include the WAN/Advanced IP Configuration exam, Network Management with Optivity exam, and Meridian Database exam. The solution exams include the Network Design Essentials for Routers and Switches exam and the Centillion (V4.0) exam.

Nortel Networks Certified Support Expert (NNCSE)

The target audience for this level of certification is someone who is mid- to senior-level technical support, help desk, field support, global support, operations and deployment personnel, and the network manager. This certification was created for someone who works with many different pieces of Nortel Networks hardware. An expert is a person within a company who will be called upon to provide advanced operational network support.

NOTE The support expert generally has in-depth knowledge of multiple product families.

The Nortel Networks support expert designation recognizes an advanced level of technical expertise to implement, configure, support, troubleshoot, and optimize Nortel Networks products and solutions. The required skills necessary to achieve this certification include setting up complex network configurations, sustaining network operations throughout the life cycle of the network, advanced troubleshooting, and problem resolution. Additionally, this certification tests for an increased level and range of product expertise demonstrated in a lab environment including maintaining a live system, problem identification, provisioning, upgrades, initial configurations, operations, administration, and maintenance.

Requirements for Enterprise support expert certification include the prerequisite of the support specialist certification plus an additional three exams: two core technology exams as explained previously in the support specialist track and one advanced product exam.

NOTE Because becoming an NNCSS is a prerequisite to becoming an NNCSE, the Core Technology exams will be familiar by the time the candidate is ready to become an expert.

Advanced product exams are Prometric-proctored electronic exams and they include the WAN/Advanced IP Configuration exam, the Centillion Switching V4.0 exam, and the Network Management with Optivity exam. Typically, these exams include topics for advanced installation, configuration, troubleshooting, and monitoring related to specific products. There are additional expert exams that are available to 3C distributors only. They include the Meridian 1 Call Center Expert, Meridian 1 Core Expert, and Meridian Messaging Expert exams.

Expert exams for the Intelligent Internet certification are the Passport 7000 ATM, Passport 7000 Frame Relay, Passport 7000 ILS, and Passport 7000 exams. These exams are administered at Nortel Networks certification test centers. They include a comprehensive hands-on lab scenario in a 7.5-hour combination written and hands-on test. The test is based on Passport Release 5.0.

Before registering for a Passport expert-level exam, candidates must have passed the related specialist exam: the NNCSS Passport exam, which is the mandatory prerequisite for all NNCSE Passport exams. To register for an expert test, the test request form must be filled in and submitted online. The test center requires a minimum of ten working days to schedule a test. The test is scheduled during the next available test interval and confirmation of the schedule is sent to the candidate via e-mail.

NOTE Certified expert designation must be renewed every two years by the candidate's anniversary date. Requirements will be to take the current test. Notification will be sent 30 days prior to expiration of certification.

Nortel Networks Certified Network Architect (NNCNA)

The Nortel Networks Certified Network Architect designation recognizes a highly advanced level of technical, design, and analytical expertise used for implementing complex Nortel Networks solutions. It is designed to assess real-world networking capability by including requirements for education, experience, and evidence of proficiency in solving networking problems. Some of the required skills to achieve certification include being able to interpret customer business drivers, influence customer decision making, influence network architecture and product direction, have expert-level knowledge in multiple technological disciplines, integrate Nortel Networks solutions in a multivendor environment, have advanced knowledge of competitor products, and have the ability to develop network evolution strategy.

The target audience for this certification includes senior networking consultants, network architects, design engineers, and network engineers. The ideal candidate for this certification possesses an advanced level of consulting, technical, and design expertise. The architect is the person within a company who has a lot of professional experience with Nortel Networks equipment as well as other vendors and is called upon for integration and advanced troubleshooting.

To become a Nortel Networks Certified Network Architect, candidates must first meet the minimum education and experience requirements via providing the documentation of related work experience, industry-recognized certifications, and formal education.

Candidates trying to achieve this certification must also pass a rigorous portfolio assessment, a highly regarded method for certifying advanced-level practitioners, which enables candidates to illustrate and document significant dimensions of their professional life. Peers who have already achieved the status of NNCNA will grade portfolios. When viewed in its totality, the portfolio provides a verification of the professional preparation and achievements of the candidate.

The NNCNA program uses a portfolio assessment mechanism to give credentials to the NNCNA as it allows for the documentation and validation of professional experience.

NNCNA Portfolio Assessment

To become an NNCNA, candidates are required to submit a portfolio that documents their professional accomplishments. The Nortel Networks Certified Network Architect actually uses a two-part portfolio assessment. Each part of the portfolio must be submitted at a specific time in accordance with the cycle provided on the Nortel Networks web site www.nortelnetworks.com/servsup/certification.

Part 1 In Part 1, candidates document their education and relevant experience. To meet the minimum requirements for network architect consideration, candidates must be experienced, with at least five years of networking work experience. Two of these years must have provided the candidate with experience in network design or architecture. In addition, candidates must provide documentation of five network architecture projects. Candidates must show evidence of involvement in the following major network architecture consulting areas: planning, design, implementation, operations, and tuning/optimization. Documentation must demonstrate the breadth and depth of the candidate's expertise as well as his or her business insight.

The application for Part 1 must be completed and signed and include all forms. Forms should include the documentation of five major network design projects including a description of the project scope, such as the candidate's role in the planning, design, implementation, operations, and/or optimization of the project. A current resume should be included that documents five years of networking experience with two years of being in network design specifically. A copy of the achieved degrees should be provided if applicable such as industry-recognized certifications, experience, and education with copies of score reports and certificates.

 NOTE An advanced degree is not required.

In addition to the requirements previously stated, candidates must demonstrate supplementary experience and education. Fulfillment of this requirement is shown by the accumulation of at least 500 points through experience, formal education, and industry certifications. Points are awarded for each additional year of networking experience beyond five years, which should be documented on the candidate's resume. In addition, formal degrees such as an associate's degree, bachelor's degree, master's degree, or doctorate give candidates additional points.

NOTE Only the highest degree attained counts toward a candidate's total point structure. For example, an NNCNA candidate with a Master's degree does not receive additional credit for having attained a Bachelor's degree.

Finally, points are accumulated through industry certifications that are currently recognized by the NNCNA program. These certifications include the following:

- **Nortel Networks** Certified account specialist, support specialist, design specialist, support expert, and design expert

- **Cisco** CCNA, CCNP, design professional, and CCIE

- **Ascend** Certified Technical Expert

- **3Com** Xylan Certified Switching Specialist (XCSS) and (XCSE)

- **Network General** Certified Network Expert (CNX)

- **Microsoft** MCP and MCSE

- **Novell** CNA, CNE, and Master CNE

NOTE Only the highest certification attained within each category counts toward a candidate's total point structure.

NOTE A minimum of 150 points must be achieved through Nortel Networks certifications.

The addition of the Optical Internet certification track only further enhances the multidisciplinary nature of the network architect. After the Optical Internet expert certification designations become available, the Nortel Networks Architect certification will evolve to include Optical Internet content in addition to the existing content. This further enhances the value of the multidiscipline, multitechnology aspect of a Nortel Networks Certified Architect.

Candidates must then return the completed Part 1 Portfolio to Nortel Networks in the time specified for the cycle on the certification web site. There is a fee of $1,000 associated with this certification.

 CAUTION Materials should be sent to Nortel Networks by a delivery service so that the candidate can verify and track all materials sent. All Part 1 Portfolio materials must be sent in one packet. Incomplete Part 1 applications will be returned to candidates. Nortel Networks is not responsible for lost or misdirected mail.

Part 1 Portfolio submissions are documented and scored by qualified Nortel Networks staff based on the program guidelines. Candidates are notified of the status of their portfolios. Candidates who pass Part 1 are sent Part 2. Candidates who fail to meet the strict criteria of Part 1 are notified of deficiencies in the documentation of experience and education. They may resubmit Part 1 within one calendar year for no additional fee or they may appeal the decision. The NNCNA Program Manager reviews appeals.

Part 2   In Part 2, candidates respond to one of two networking case studies presented in the Part 2 Portfolio Application. Case studies are based on actual customer scenarios, prepared by senior networking professionals working in the field of network architecture. Most case studies involve multivendor scenarios:

- Candidates have six weeks to respond to Part 2.
- The estimated time for candidates to complete a response is 40 hours.
- The solution response must meet specific format requirements.
- Portfolios must be received by the date noted on the NNCNA timeline or they will not be accepted.
- Candidates are required to provide a telephone number where they can be reached during the specified grading period. If needed, candidates could be contacted to provide additional insights or clarification to their response.

- Candidates will have their NNCNA status updated in the CertManager Database within two weeks (see http://www.galton.com/~nortel/).

 NOTE A sample case study is available on the certification web site and the CD supplied with this book.

The candidate's response to the Part 2 networking case study reflects his or her depth of knowledge and experience in the field of network architecture and design. Responses to the case study must be presented in an organized fashion and the candidate must communicate his or her ideas clearly. A team of currently certified NNCNA consultants scores Part 2 Portfolio submissions. "Blind" judges who do not know the identity of candidates grade candidate responses. The case study is scored per topic. One point is awarded if the response is adequate and two points if the response is complete and thorough. No points are rewarded if the response is considered inadequate. The sections are weighted and include whether the ideas and diagrams are communicated clearly, whether the response is presented in an organized manner, whether there are assumptions that facilitate a working design and coincide with the case study documented, and whether decision criteria are documented. Judges examine whether the candidate's response demonstrates knowledge of IP and routing protocols, physical and logical network topology, LAN/WAN technologies constraints and characteristics, security policies, network management, remote access, and scalability. Additionally, the candidate's response should meet customer requirements and financial constraints, solve the problems presented, and present the appropriate migration strategy where necessary. Nortel Networks' staff may contact candidates to set up a teleconference to elicit clarification of their solution. All ratings will be subjected to rigorous statistical analysis to detect bias or differences in grader severity.

Candidates who fail Part 2 may retake Part 2 within one calendar year for no additional charge; however, candidates will have to wait one grading period. In addition, candidates who retake Part 2 will only receive one networking case study. Candidates will not have a choice of case studies, nor will they receive the same networking case study that they received in a prior attempt. Candidates may also appeal the decision if they choose. In the case of an appeal, the portfolio submissions will be reviewed by a different set of judges than those who originally reviewed the Part 2 Portfolio submission. Candidates must submit an appeal within 30 days of the receipt of the notification of failure for Part 2. There is no charge for appeals submitted within this time period.

Candidates who pass are awarded the NNCNA credential. An official notification and NNCNA Welcome Kit will be sent to all new NNCNAs. The Welcome Kit includes a Nortel Networks Certified Network Architect confirmation letter, a computer bag/portfolio, a plaque, a crystal recognition piece, and a logo sheet.

 NOTE Any misrepresentation provided to Nortel Networks may result in expulsion from the Nortel Networks Professional Certification program.

Security of the Portfolio Assessment

Each candidate is responsible for maintaining the security of all portfolio materials. The materials should be kept in a secure location at all times. No part of the portfolio should be shared or transmitted in any form or by any means (except for purposes of required verification). Candidates are required to sign the NNCNA Agreement and Release. Violations of confidentiality may result in the revocation of the NNCNA certification. Once in its possession, Nortel Networks keeps all portfolio materials secure. No candidate response or application information will be shared with other organizations or individuals. No part of the portfolio will be transmitted in any form or by any means (except for purposes of required verification) by Nortel Networks. All application materials will be kept in a secure location within the premises of Nortel Networks.

 NOTE The Nortel Networks Certified Network Architect certification is valid for three years from the date of issue. Candidates who want to maintain their NNCNA status will submit a new case study according to templates to be provided.

Recertification

Recertification requires fulfilling the original certification requirements and selecting different product/solution exams than the ones already completed per the specific certification. Completing a higher level of certification (expert or architect) before the current certification expires fulfills the recertification requirements. Recertification in any designation uses the latest NNCP testing material and testing process.

These recertification guidelines are implemented to ensure that Nortel Networks Certified individuals are adding to the knowledge pool of network consulting and keeping current with evolving issues and problems in this field. Currently, Nortel Networks Certified Network Architects will automatically be sent a recertification application.

Training and Preparing for Exams

New training courses have been added to all designations, especially the Optical certification track. Courses include fundamental as well as technical and expert-level courses as options for anyone who might want to go through training prior to taking an exam. For all certifications, it is beneficial to read all of Nortel Networks standard product documentation. It is helpful to read the chapters in this or any other guide that can give additional information on the exam as well. There is also a new book for optical networking called *Optical Networking Crash Course*, by Steven Shepard, which is published by McGraw-Hill (ISBN: 0071372083). A new optical course that is recommended but not required is the Fundamentals of Optical Networking course that is available in instructor-led or web-based training forms. Many new courses have been added for the first-line maintenance designations as well.

 NOTE Although training is highly recommended, any candidate who believes he or she has the knowledge and skills required may take the certification exam without any recommended training.

Fundamental Exams

Data IP Fundamentals Exam

Exam number: 920-901
Time: 4 hours
 # questions: 96
Passing score: 75 percent
Topics: Internetworking and IP history, IP addressing and masking (subnetting and supernetting, broadcast, multicast, and unicast packet types, and IPv6), OSI model and layers, media types (twisted pair, fiber, and coaxial), switching, bridging and routing

fundamentals, data link types (ATM, Ethernet, and Token Ring), WAN concepts and terminology, introduction to routing protocols (RIP, OSPF, and BGP), internet standards (IETF and RFCs), TCP/IP Protocol Suite (TCP, UDP, DHCP, and ARP), quality of service (QoS), traffic management, and tunneling technologies (IPSec and NAT).

Recommended Training

There are two courses recommended as preparation for this exam. They are available as self-paced study courses from Nortel Networks' training partners. They are the IP Fundamentals and the Introduction to Internetworking courses. Additionally, Chapters 2, 3, 4, 5, 6, and 7 of this guide can be used to study for this exam.

 NOTE Training associated with each exam is not required; however, if a candidate is unable to perform the stated exam objectives, he or she should consider the suggested training in preparation for the exam.

Core Technology Exams

The Core Technology exams are a mix of technology-oriented topics as well as some basic product installation and configuration topics. Select one exam from the six exams currently available.

Hubs and Shared Media Core Technology Exam

Exam number: 920-013
Time: 75 minutes
 # questions: 60
Passing score: 70 percent
Topics: All the Baystack Ethernet hubs, System 3000, 5000, and 5005 chassis, hub and network management, Ethernet design and troubleshooting, and Token Ring design and troubleshooting. Further details on this exam are available in Chapter 10.

Recommended Training

Most of the training for this exam includes generally recommended prerequisites that are available as self-paced study courses from Nortel Networks' training partners. The one classroom prerequisite is not given in the United States anymore because the demand for new hub training is very limited as most companies are replacing their shared media hubs with faster switches. The self-study classes are Token Ring Basics, Ethernet Basics, Introduction to Internetworking, Fundamentals of SNMP, and Fundamentals of IP Networking. The instructor-led training is a course called Hub Connectivity, which runs for four days.

Experience

Before taking this exam, a candidate should have three months of on-the-job experience with Nortel Networks hubs and shared media.

Switching Core Technology Exam

Exam number: 920-016
Time: 60 minutes
 # questions: 73
Passing score: 70 percent
Topics: Networking, bridging, frame, and cell-switching concepts as well as an in-depth knowledge of the Baystack switches 303/304, 350, and 450. Further details on this exam are available in Chapter 11.

Recommended Training

To prepare for this exam, Nortel Networks recommends some prerequisites that are available as self-paced study courses from Nortel Networks' training partners. These include Fundamentals of SNMP, Fundamentals of IP Networking, High-Speed Networking Solutions, and Introduction to ATM. There are two recommended instructor-led courses available to prepare for this exam: the Frame Switching Interoperability and Implementation class, which runs for four days, and an optional ATM Technical Tutorial course, which runs for two days.

Experience

Candidates are recommended to have some hands-on experience before taking this exam. The experience should include installing and configuring Nortel Networks switches in a LAN environment, having knowledge of the Windows operating system environment, and understanding data communications.

Router Core Technology Exam

Exam number: 920-014
Time: 90 minutes

questions: 60

Passing score: 60 percent

Topics: Router hardware, software and management, knowledge of the Technical Interface (TI) and Site Manager, and IP and bridging concepts. Further details on this exam are available in Chapter 14.

Recommended Training

To prepare for this exam, Nortel Networks recommends some prerequisites that are available as self-paced study courses from Nortel Networks' training partners. They are Fundamentals of IP Networking and Introduction to Internetworking. There are also two courses that are specifically focused on the exam materials. They are available as two instructor-led courses or one accelerated version of the two courses that is available for more advanced users. The two courses are Router Installation and Basic Configuration, which runs for three days, and the Router Configuration and Management course, which runs for four days. The accelerated course that incorporates both these courses is the Accelerated Router Configuration course that runs for five days. Technicians going for certification can take both the Installation and Configuration and the Configuration and Management courses, or the Accelerated Router Configuration course.

Experience

Before taking this exam, a candidate should have experience with installing and configuring Nortel Networks routers, know how to use Site Manager, and have experience in an MS-DOS and Windows LAN environment. An in-depth understanding of data communications is recommended for this exam as well.

Multiservice Access Core Technology Exam (Passport 4400)

Exam number: 920-020

Time: 75 minutes

questions: 72

Passing score: 60 percent

Topics: Telephony basics, private branch exchange (PBX) concepts, voice fundamentals and switching, and Passport 4400 basics, operations, and network configurations.

Recommended Training

To prepare for this exam, Nortel Networks recommends some prerequisites that are available as self-paced study courses from Nortel Networks' training partners: the Fundamentals of IP Networking course and the Voice Fundamentals course. There are two instructor-led courses available for this exam as well: the Passport 4400 for Small-to-Medium Enterprise Networks, which runs for five days, and the Internetworking Fundamentals for LAN/WAN Technologies course, which runs for four days.

Experience

Candidates seeking to take this exam should have experience installing, configuring, and operating the Passport 4400 as well as have a working knowledge of TCP/IP, LAN, and WAN technology, and analog and digital voice technology.

Contivity VPN Switch Exam

Exam number: DX0-231
Time: 90 minutes
 # questions: 69
Passing score: 63 percent
Topics: The entire Contivity Portfolio (including the Instant Internet products), fundamentals of VPN technology, designing and integrating Contivity systems into existing networks, using LDAP and RADIUS, and provisioning a Contivity system. More details are provided in Chapter 16.

Recommended Training

To prepare for this exam, Nortel Networks recommends some prerequisites that are available as documentation from the Nortel web site. These include Nortel Networks Contivity VPN Switching Portfolio and the Contivity VPN Switching Portfolio Document Library. Additionally, a course called Contivity Technical Overview is available as a self-paced CD-ROM from Nortel Networks' training partners. This course is a prerequisite to the instructor-led training course Contivity VPN Switch Configuration and Management, which can also be used to prepare for this exam.

Experience

Candidates seeking to take this exam should have experience installing, configuring, and operating the entire Contivity product line as well as have a working knowledge of VPN technology and LAN and WAN environments.

Advanced Product Exams

The Advanced Product exams are high-end technical exams that are product focused. Topics related to the specific products include advanced installation, configuration, troubleshooting, and monitoring.

WAN/Advanced IP Configuration Exam

Exam number: 920-015
Time: 60 minutes
 # questions: 65
Passing score: 55 percent
Topics: An overview of the WAN, Frame Relay, protocol prioritization, Point-to-Point Protocol (PPP), dial services, as well as Routing Information Protocol (RIP), Open Shortest Path First (OSPF), and Border Gateway Protocol version 4 (BGPv4) concepts. Further details on this exam are available in Chapters 6, 7, and 9.

Recommended Training

There are two instructor-led courses available for preparation for this exam. They are the WAN Protocol Implementation course, which runs for four days, and the Advanced IP Routing course, which runs for four days.

Experience

Additionally, candidates should have three months of experience installing and configuring Nortel Networks routers in a complex networked environment, have experience with LANs, MS-DOS, and Windows environments, and understand data communications.

Centillion Switching (V4.0) Exam

Exam number: 920-023
Time: 75 minutes
 # questions: 74
Passing score: 62 percent
Topics: Bridging, switching, and VLANs, Centillion switching, Command Line Interface (CLI), SpeedView, ATM, LANE, and PNNI concepts. Further details on this exam are available in Chapters 5, 8, and 14.

Recommended Training

Four general self-paced introductory courses are recommended for preparing for this exam. They are Introduction to ATM, Ethernet Basics, Token Ring Basics, and ATM Technical Tutorial. There is one classroom instructor-led course called Centillion Switching, which runs for four days.

Experience

A candidate should additionally have at least three months of experience installing and configuring Centillion switches in a complex network environment. The candidate should also have experience with MS-DOS- and Windows-based LAN and internetworking.

Network Management with Optivity Exam

Exam number: 920-019

Time: 75 minutes

 # questions: 64

Passing score: 65 percent

Topics: Network management, discovering and documenting the network, baselining, performance, fault and configuration management, as well as an overview of NetArchitect. Further details on this exam are available in Chapter 15.

Recommended Training

One self-paced introductory course is recommended for preparing for this exam. This course is called Introduction to Network Management and is available from Nortel Networks' training partners. There is also one classroom instructor-led course called Optivity Enterprise for Unix, which runs for four days.

Experience

A candidate should additionally have at least three months of experience working with Optivity, and DOS and Windows networks.

Registering and Taking Exams

Here are some helpful reminders when taking certification exams. Identify the exam number that is needed for certification. Exams may be available in an online format or at a Prometric location. All exams are closed book, so candidates should be prepared when taking exams. Remember that Nortel Networks uses performance-based tests to demonstrate the skill sets and level of expertise for a specific designation. Candidates must achieve the passing score to be awarded certification status.

Candidates who will be taking computer-based exams at authorized Prometric centers should be aware that the centers will ask for two pieces of identification, one of which must have a picture. Candidates should keep the printout of their exam results for future reference or validation if needed.

Scheduling an Exam

To schedule a Prometric exam, call (800) 791-EXAM in the United States/Canada/Puerto Rico or visit them on the Web at www.2test.com.

Information Resources

For more information on the Nortel Networks Certification Program, see the following:

Web site http://www.nortelnetworks.com/servsup/certification/index.html

E-mail certprog@nortelnetworks.com

Call center hotline Call (877) 662-5669 (toll-free, North America).

Web-based test access http://nortel.etest.prometric.com/

Prometric testing centers http://www.2test.com

Tracking—database access To track certification progress, visit the certification database at http://www.galton.com/~nortel/.

The previous link accesses the Nortel Networks CertManager Data Access Service. This enables candidates to track their progress toward Nortel Networks certifications. It is available as soon as a candidate has taken one or more certification exams. Any candidate who has taken a web-based certification exam on the Prometric web site can use their permanent username and password as a valid login and password for CertManager. Any candidate who has registered for an exam through Prometric can use their Candidate ID (most commonly the candidate's social security number) on the Prometric Examination Score Report to access the site and obtain a password. CertManager has the following services:

- Updating personal information

- Viewing personal exam history for certification exams

- Viewing progress towards a Nortel Networks certification

- Submitting an online help request to customer service

 NOTE It will take at least four business days for exam records to update on CertManager.

Summary

The role of the Nortel Networks Certification Program is to provide a consistent approach and structure for all the certification programs across all of the Nortel Networks product lines. It focuses development on the technical knowledge and skills that are critical to success in specific functional disciplines, provides parallel certification paths for account management, network design, field specialist, and network support, and incorporates three certification levels: specialist, expert, and architect. In this book, we will specifically cover the Enterprise data track for the support, expert, and architect designations. Additionally, one Intelligent Internet Support exam (Contivity) will be covered.

PART II

Networking Technologies

Data Link Layer

Objectives

- Learn about the Open Systems Interconnection (OSI) model and the layers of the model

- Learn the basic responsibilities of the Layer 2 protocols

- Learn Ethernet, Fast Ethernet, and Gigabit Ethernet fundamentals

- Learn Token Ring fundamentals

- Learn the difference between the Media Access Control (MAC) and Logical Link Control (LLC) sublayers

- Learn the difference in the responsibilities of the Data Link and Physical layers

- Learn the purpose of addressing and link management

- Learn about the fundamentals of transmission, reception, error control, and congestion management

- Learn about network topologies

- Learn about the difference between a physical topology and a logical topology

- Learn about the different types of topologies

Introduction

The second layer of the OSI model, the Data Link layer, is very important to your understanding of how networking occurs. Although all of the layers of the model are important for a network to exist, for an administrator of routers, hubs, and switches you do not need to be very much concerned (at this time) with the layers above the third layer. You will concentrate on the upper layers when your focus is more on actual application design and issues. Although the Physical layer is incredibly important for a network to function (ever try building a house *on* thin air, with thin air?), we are only going to cover it in an introductory manner because it is a very complex topic that should be dealt with in detail as part of an engineering degree (i.e., electrical engineering). We will, therefore, in this book focus on Layer 2 (Data Link) and Layer 3 (Network/Internet). There is no exam in the Nortel Networks Certification track that is dedicated to the testing of your knowledge of the second layer of the OSI model and its protocols. There is, however, in every exam the expectation and understanding that you do have a firm grasp of the basics of the OSI model, the Data Link layer, and how some of its protocols (that is, Ethernet and Token Ring) function.

The OSI Model

The OSI model was developed in order to help provide an overall framework so that different developers would be able to develop systems that could interact. By providing a common framework (the model) for understanding the responsibilities for different pieces of the network, different developers would be able to develop pieces of software/hardware that would have the responsibilities of particular layers. Other vendors could independently develop other components that would interact together as an integrated system. This modularity of design also leads to a division of responsibilities within a network. Certain people can be responsible for maintaining the first three layers of the network while other people are responsible for the higher layers. This enables for specialization of the administrators that may be able to provide for a smoother running network (though that was not the purpose of the model).

The model (developed by the International Standards Organization in 1974) is divided into seven layers as follows (see Figure 2-1).

The layers are numbered from the bottom up like the floors of a building, and like a building all of the bottom layers are necessary to support the higher layers, but each layer can be considered separately. Each layer of the model represents ideas of how networking may be implemented, but they do not define the rules for that implementa-

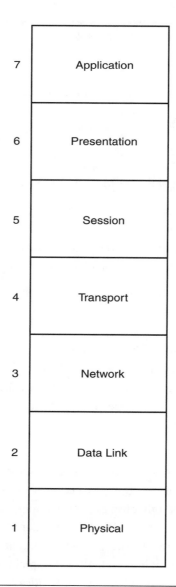

Figure 2-1   Seven layers of the OSI model

tion. That is the task of protocols. For example, there is a topic for debate today: should students be required to wear school uniforms? This is an example of an idea that is defined at a layer of the model. Requiring students to follow a dress code would be a protocol. When school X enforces the rule, this is an example of an implementation.

NOTE   Remember, protocol means rule.

The Seven Layers

Let's take a brief look at each of the seven layers and some of the ideas that they define.

Layer 1: Physical

The Physical layer defines issues like how 0's and 1's are transmitted and received on the network medium. It also defines the network medium. Hubs are an example of a Layer 1 device.

Layer 2: Data Link

This defines issues like addressing, the media access method, error checking, flow control, connection-oriented or connectionless services, the forwarding of traffic to hosts on the same network, and other topics. Bridges and switches are the devices that best exemplify what is called a *Layer 2 device*. We will be looking at this layer in detail in this chapter.

Layer 3: Network

This layer defines how traffic is forwarded between stations on different networks. It also defines addressing, error checking, flow control, connection-oriented or connectionless services, routing, and other topics. Some of these topics also appear at Layer 2. This is not a contradiction. It is possible for two similar ideas to be dealt with at different layers. Remember that we are talking about ideas that need to be considered. It is up to the developers to decide what ideas actually get implemented when the protocols are developed. It is also possible to implement similar ideas at more than one layer of the model. Addressing is a topic that exists at most layers of the model. In some layers the address defines individual stations, while at other layers the address defines a service on a particular host. Routers and routing switches are examples of Layer 3 devices.

Layer 4: Transport

This defines whether or not (and how) end-to-end communication may occur between stations. It defines connection-oriented or connectionless services between the stations.

Layer 5: Session

This layer deals with the opening and closing of communications between two stations.

Layer 6: Presentation

This layer deals with the form with which data is transferred (such as, ASCII or EBCDIC) and encryption.

Layer 7: Application

This defines network applications. These are the actual tools that the end user interacts with. Examples of TCP/IP Application layer applications are Telnet, File Transfer Protocol (FTP), and Simple Mail Transfer Protocol (SMTP).

The Data Link Layer

The Data Link layer (Layer 2) is further divided into two sublayers, the MAC sublayer and the LLC sublayer.

The MAC sublayer deals with

- Addressing

- Media access method

- Framing

Addressing

Devices communicate with each other by sending data to and from addresses (regardless of what name you give your computers). The MAC address is the address used when two devices on the same network communicate with each other (see Figure 2-2).

When device MAC A wants to communicate with device MAC B, they communicate using MAC addresses because they are both on the same network. Every network node that communicates has a MAC address. The size and type of address is determined by the Layer 2 protocol (Ethernet, Token Ring, Fiber Distributed Data Interface [FDDI], and Frame Relay). For our purposes we will center our discussions on Ethernet and Token Ring (because they are by far the most common Layer 2 protocols), and we will assume a 6-byte address. MAC addresses are expressed as hexadecimal (0X) numbers (0-F). You will usually see the address expressed as shown in Figure 2-3.

Sometimes the dashes (-) are replaced with periods (see Figure 2-4).

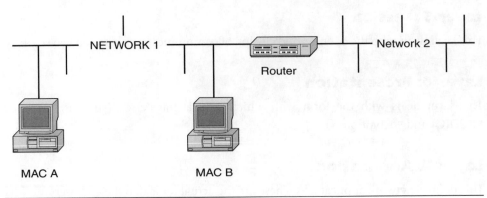

Figure 2-2   Devices on the same network

00-00-81-B4-33-F1

Figure 2-3   MAC address with dash separators

00.00.81.B4.33.F1

Figure 2-4   MAC address with period (.) separators

Sometimes the bytes are simply put together with no separators between the bytes of the address (see Figure 2-5).

The first six digits (3 bytes, 24 bits) are called the Organizationally Unique Identifier (OUI), and it identifies the manufacturer of the device (NIC card, router port, and so on). These OUIs are registered with the IEEE and are reserved for the use of the body that owns the registration. Some of the better known OUIs are

- Bay Networks (Nortel Networks)   00-00-81
- 3com Corp   00-01-02
- IBM Corp   00-02-55
- Cabletron Systems   00-E0-3A

The remaining six digits (3 bytes, 24 bits) are sequentially assigned in order of manufacture at the factory. This whole scheme is designed to ensure that all MAC addresses are unique. This is a requirement for devices on a network to communicate.

000081B433F1

Figure 2-5   MAC address with no separators

> **NOTE**   It is possible, in some cases, for devices with the same MAC address to communicate if they are on separate networks and attached to separate routers, but it is a bad network design that uses duplicate MAC addresses.

The address is assigned at the factory at the time that the device is manufactured, and the address is a physical part of the card. This is the reason that sometimes MAC addresses are referred to as physical addresses.

> **NOTE**   It is possible to change a device's MAC address using software. This is sometimes done for management purposes. It is important to remember that *all* MAC addresses on the same network must be unique. Duplicate addresses will cause network communications problems. If you duplicate the MAC address of a router, you could be in for some interesting problems.

In every message transmitted there are two MAC addresses. One address is the Destination Address (DA), and it is the address of the intended recipient. The second address is the Source Address (SA), and it signifies the device transmitting the message. Devices on the network view the transmitted message (hereafter called a *frame*) and examine the DA. If the DA and the station's MAC address match, the station copies the frame and processes it. If the DA and the station's MAC address do not match, the station ignores the frame. The inclusion of the SA in the frame tells the receiving station the MAC address of the device to reply to.

Media Access Method

The media access method is the rule for transmitting data on the network. Just like when you want to speak in a classroom or cross a street you cannot just start speaking (if you are not the teacher) nor can you just run into the street blindly whenever you want. Either of these two examples would be considered either rude or suicidal. Regardless what you call it, it is in violation of the protocols set up and understood for how to conduct yourself in these situations. The same goes for networking protocols. When two devices attempt to communicate at the same time (on a shared network segment), their communications end up colliding with each other. This creates a condition in which both messages are corrupted. What is needed is a method for keeping this from happening and/or a method of recovering communications once this does occur. We will be discussing two media access methods:

- Contention
- Token passing

NOTE Although we will be looking at Ethernet and Token Ring in this section, we will be looking at it very briefly. More attention will be given later in the chapter.

Contention

As an example of the contention media access method, we will use the Carrier Sense Multiple Access/Collision Detection (CSMA/CD) Ethernet protocol. Ethernet (designated as 802.3 by the IEEE) is a contention-based protocol. In such a protocol all devices are able to transmit at any given time without waiting for any special event to occur. The only restriction is that transmission may occur only if no other device is transmitting at that moment. This is like first-come, first-served. In Ethernet this is done by listening to the network prior to transmission (carrier sense) and transmitting only if there is no other transmission going on at the same time. (No other stations are permitted to transmit once another station has started transmitting.) This is similar to looking both ways before crossing the street. It is not a bad method, but it is not perfect. There is the probability that, eventually, some other device will listen to the network at the same time as your device, and when both devices hear a quiet network, both devices will attempt transmission simultaneously. When this occurs we get a collision. Collisions are detected when data is received while in the act of transmitting (collision detection). When this occurs, both stations involved in the collision are required to send out jam packets to alert other stations that a collision has occurred and enter the back-off algorithm. The back-off algorithm requires both devices to choose a random period of time and wait for that time to expire before attempting retransmission.

This method is good in that it has very little overhead, because no intensive monitoring or management functions exist, and that it is reliable. The disadvantage is that there is no guarantee as to the amount of access that any one device will get to the network medium in any given period of time. For this reason this protocol is referred to as a *probabilistic protocol*. Also, there is a limit to the practical amount of utilization of the network bandwidth before so many collisions occur that very little actual data ever gets through. The average peak utilization of a CSMA/CD network is about 33 percent. Much more than that, and the number of collisions start to increment at a huge rate.

Token Passing

The Token Passing (as used in Token Ring and FDDI) media access method requires the station to wait to capture a Token frame before it is able to begin transmitting. This is similar to a technique used in classrooms by teachers when the class gets difficult to manage. The teacher declares that no one may talk unless they hold the token (usually a blackboard eraser or some such object). The teacher then gives the token to a student, and that student may talk. In a Token Passing network protocol, the token is a frame that is generated by a device on the network called the *active monitor*. This token goes around the ring from station to station. When a station needs to transmit, it waits until it receives the token. It then claims the token (by changing the bits in the frame that identify the frame as a token) and appends the data that it needs to transmit to the frame. The frame is then transmitted onto the ring. Each station receives the frame and retransmits it back onto the ring. When the frame reaches the station that is specified in the DA portion of the frame, the station copies and processes the frame. It also alters the frame before retransmitting the frame onto the ring. The frame carries information that tells devices on the network the status of the message on the ring. This information is in two parts:

- Address recognized
- Frame-copied

The address recognized bits tell network devices if the device specified as the DA has received the frame. (A device on the network signals that it has recognized its own MAC address as the DA of the frame.) The frame-copied bits tell if the data in the frame was successfully copied by the DA. (The DA device sets these bits to indicate successful reception of the frame's data.) These are the bits in the frame that the DA alters before transmitting the frame back onto the ring. The frame continues traveling on the ring until it reaches the SA device. The only device that is allowed to remove a frame from the ring is the SA device. The SA device examines the frame to verify that it was successfully received by the DA device. If this is the case, then the data contained in the frame is removed (stripped), and the token is restored to its original state and placed back onto the ring. Because there may be only one token on a ring at any given moment and because the token is released after it has been used, it is possible to mathematically determine the minimum and maximum amount of access that any given station will have over a given amount of time (very civilized behavior). For this reason Token Ring is referred to as a *deterministic protocol*.

Framing

A picture's borders are marked by its frame. In a very similar fashion, data transmitted over the network is also held by a frame.

Looking back to our OSI model (refer to Figure 2-1), we see the application that generates data at the top of the model. The data generated is ultimately destined for the peer Application layer protocol on a target device. Every layer of the OSI model has a corresponding peer layer on a target device. In Figure 2-6, we see Device A and Device B and the layers of the OSI model. Let's assume that Device A is a workstation using a web browser (HTTP client) and that Device B is a web server. These two entities are peer applications at the Application layer (Layer 7) of the model. They communicate with each other. They do not, however, communicate directly. For the HTTP browser to send a request to the HTTP server, the message must be passed down the model from Layer 7 to Layer 6 and so on until the message reaches the Physical layer where it is finally transmitted to the peer Physical layer on the HTTP server. From there it is passed up through the model until it reaches the HTTP server for final processing. The protocols that the request uses from Layer 7 through Layer 1 are referred to as the *protocol stack*. Imagine that you want to send information to a friend by means of a letter. You use your pen to write the letter (unless you are a true geek like me who has atrocious penmanship and is forced to type all letters). The information in the letter is what is important, and it is meant for your friend. Because the message is for your friend, the next step is to place the message in an envelope. We assume that it is not possible to communicate directly with your friend by placing the paper with the message in his or her hand, so you have to use the services of the mail. Just like in our HTTP example, it is impossible for the HTTP request to go directly to the HTTP server; we need to use the services of lower layers. What we see here is that the upper layers of the model are dependent on the lower layers for networks to function properly.

Getting back to our letter analogy, the post office cannot take a piece of paper and deliver it without the proper steps being taken first. The letter must be placed in a package (envelope), and information must be included on the package to tell how to process it. This is called *encapsulation*. The data from the upper layer (referred to as the Protocol Data Unit or PDU) is surrounded with packing and processing information. The form of this information is called a *header* (at the front of the PDU), and sometimes a *trailer* (at the back of the PDU) is also used. The form of the header and trailer is determined by the protocol at that layer of the model being used. The headers and

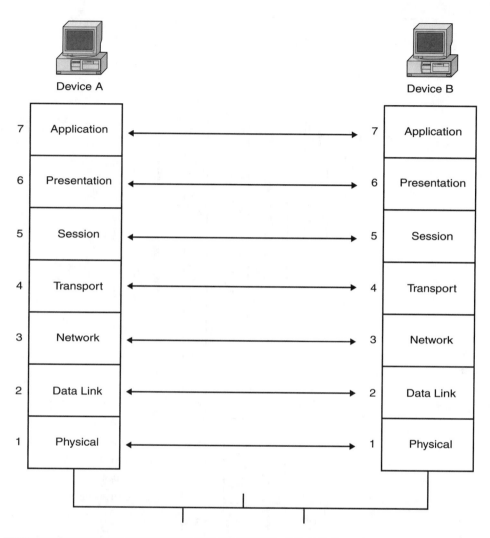

Figure 2-6   Peer layers

trailers are added as the data passes down the stack and are stripped off as they are processed at the destination as they go up the stack, as we can see in Figure 2-7.

For the sake of clarity, PDUs are given names that identify the layer that they were created at. PDUs from the Data Link layer are referred to as *frames*. PDUs from the Network layer are referred to as *datagrams*. PDUs from the Transport layer are referred to as *segments*. PDUs from the Session and Presentation layers are referred to as *packets*, and PDUs from the Application layer are called *messages*. Many people who do not care to be very descriptive when they discuss these matters simply call all PDUs packets.

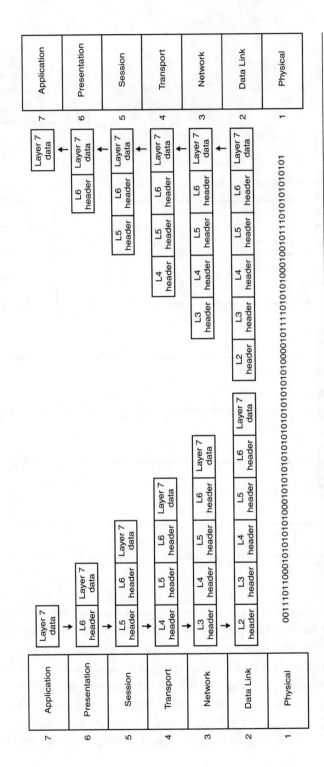

Figure 2-7 Headers and trailers being added and removed

44

As an example of a header, let's look at an Ethernet header. What we will be examining is an Ethernet II frame, which displays the Ethernet header encapsulating an IP datagram. What we are looking at in Figure 2-8 is the display of data captured from the network using Network Associates Sniffer®. It displays network data in a raw but user-friendly manner to facilitate network troubleshooting and diagnostics. What we see in the upper portion of the display is the Data Link Connection (DLC) header (in this case, an Ethernet header).

NOTE For reasons that I will not go into, there is more than one type of Ethernet frame and, therefore, more than one type of Ethernet header. They all have in common the first 12 bytes of the frame. As we will see, these bytes represent the DA and the SA. It is in these fields that we see a difference in the frame's design. We will discuss these differences later and for now use the Ethernet II (2) frame as our guide because it has the simplest design (see Figure 2-8).

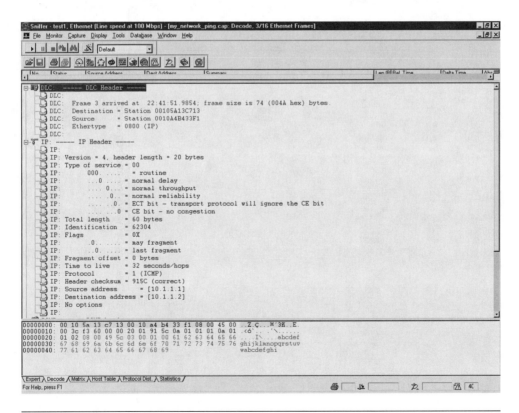

Figure 2-8 Ethernet II header

What we see here highlighted towards the top of Figure 2-9 is the DA of the frame. We know that this is the DA because it falls in the position reserved for this purpose. A position that has been reserved for a purpose is referred to as a field. The DA field is the first six bytes (bytes zero through five) of an Ethernet frame. In this example the DA is 00105A13C713. The DA, as we remember, is the device that the frame is being transmitted to. Notice at the bottom of the figure there is a highlighted portion that represents the six bytes as they appear in hexadecimal in the frame without being decoded for us. This is the raw form of the data. What appears in the upper portion of the figure represents the explanation of the data.

In Figure 2-10, we see the SA highlighted. The SA field is the second six bytes (bytes 6 through 11) of the Ethernet frame. In this example the SA is 0010A4B433f1. This represents the address of the device that transmitted this particular packet.

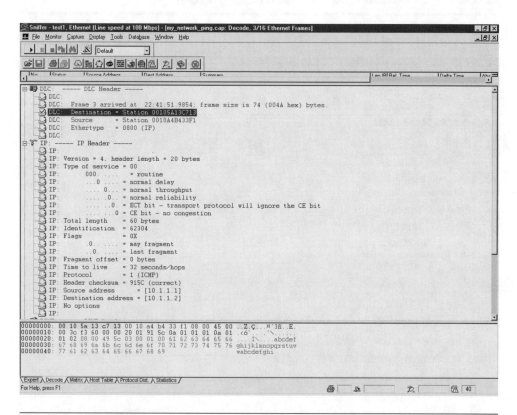

Figure 2-9 The DA

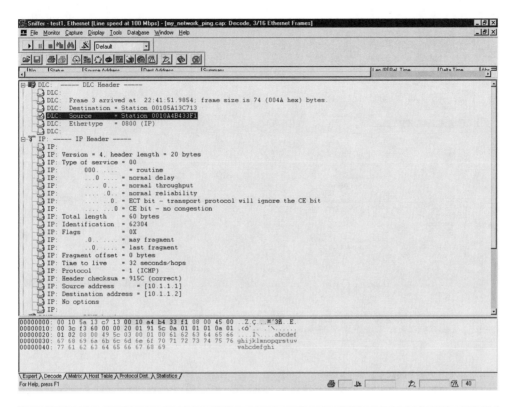

Figure 2-10 The SA

Following the SA is the Ethertype field (see Figure 2-11). In this example the Ethertype is set to 0800. The purpose of the Ethertype field is to tell the receiving device what protocol stack to forward this frame to. The Ethertype value 0800 is reserved for IP. In other words, the datagram (contained in the data portion of the frame right after the header) is an IP datagram and is to be processed by the IP stack on the target machine.

The first 14 bytes of an Ethernet II frame make up the Ethernet header. This is the data that is appended to the front of the datagram that has been passed down from the network layer. At the end of the datagram is also a field called the Frame Check Sequence (FCS), which is a value computed based on the value of the bits in the frame. Upon reception of a frame, the FCS is checked by running the same formula against the frame as that which generated the FCS on the source device. If the FCS does not match, the frame is determined to have been corrupted in transit and is discarded. If the FCS does match, the frame is copied and processed. In this manner Ethernet devices have a basic form of error detection.

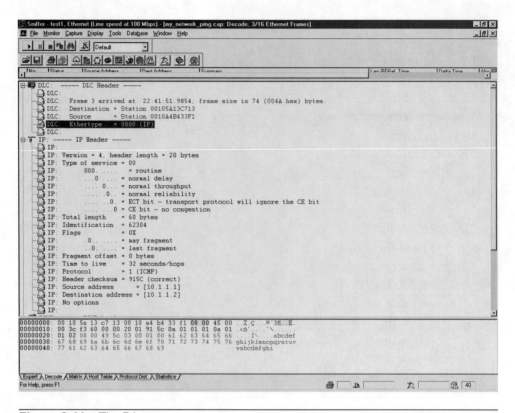

Figure 2-11 The Ethertype

NOTE There are actually bits transmitted in front of the DA. These eight bytes make up what is called the *preamble*. The job of the preamble is to alert stations on the network that a frame is following. They are not displayed by the sniffer and not considered when numbering the byte positions of fields within the frame.

Other Frame Types

There are three other frame types that we need to be concerned with:

- Novell Raw
- 802.3
- 802.3 SNAP

Novell Raw is the frame type that was developed by Novell prior to the IEEE committee defining an official standard frame type. The Novell Raw frame header is the same size as the Ethernet II frame (14 bytes). The frame (see Figure 2-12) has a 6-byte DA in the first six bytes of the header and the SA in the second six bytes of the header. The third field of the header is a 2-byte field, as in the Ethernet II header, but instead of an Ethertype this field is the length field. The length field of the Novell Raw header tells the length (in bytes) of the data portion of the frame. Valid values for the length are 0x0000–0x05dc (0–1500).

802.3 is the frame type that the IEEE standardized in 1985 (see Figure 2-13). The first three fields are the same as that of the Novell Raw frame (6-byte DA, 6-byte SA, and 2-byte length). Following the length field is a new header called the Logical Link Control (LLC) header. The first two fields of the LLC header are the Destination Service Access Point (DSAP) and the Source Service Access Point (SSAP). A Service Access Point points to a Layer 3 protocol (much in the way an Ethertype does in the Ethernet II header). The Service Access Point for IP is 0x06 (6). The third field of the LLC header is the control field. Following that are the data field, which contains the data handed down from the upper layers, and, finally, the FCS.

802.3 SNAP is the frame type that remains (see Figure 2-14). The reason for the 802.3 SNAP frame is that in the 802.3 frame, the Service Access Points field is just 1 byte

Preamble 8 bytes	DA 6 bytes	SA 6 bytes	Length 2 bytes (0x0000-0x05DC)	Data 0-1500 bytes	FCS 4 bytes

Figure 2-12   Novell Raw

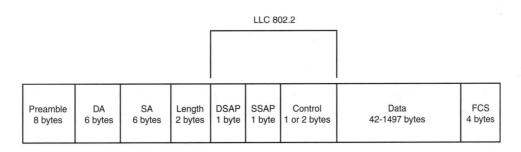

Preamble 8 bytes	DA 6 bytes	SA 6 bytes	Length 2 bytes	DSAP 1 byte	SSAP 1 byte	Control 1 or 2 bytes	Data 42-1497 bytes	FCS 4 bytes

Figure 2-13   The 802.3 frame

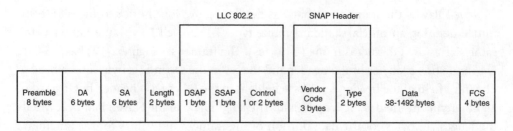

Figure 2-14   802.3 SNAP frame

in length. Added to that fact, many of the values of the SAP are reserved, which means that there were only a few (relatively) available SAPs that could be registered with the IEEE. The SNAP header (see Figure 2-14) maintains a field following the Control field that is the Vendor Code and Type field. That field is 5 bytes long. Three of these bytes are used to register individual vendors. This means that there are a great many more available values for vendors to register. The remaining two bytes following the Vendor Code field are used for the Type field. This field is used by the vendor to subdivide his Vendor Code field to define the protocol types that the vendor will use. To identify the 802.3 SNAP frame (which appears very similar to the 802.3 frame), the LLC header uses the reserved Destination Service Access Point (DSAP) and Source Service Access Point (SSAP) of 0xAA (170), which is the reserved SAP for SNAP.

Network Topologies

A network has both physical and logical components that define how communication occurs. These components define how the network functions. The topology of a network is like a map. It depicts the geography of the network. There are two different categories of topologies:

- Physical topology
- Logical topology

The physical topology defines how the actual equipment and cabling are laid out. The logical topology defines how communication occurs on the network medium.

Physical Topology

The physical topology is defined by the Layer 2 protocols being used. Certain Layer 2 protocols require specific physical topologies. Other Layer 2 protocols are more flexible and enable a number of different physical topologies. The protocols determine details like

- Cable type
- Cable length
- Equipment
- Environment

There are four different types of topologies:

- Bus
- Ring
- Star
- Cell

Bus Topology

The physical bus topology uses a single physical cable (the bus) that is laid throughout the network (see Figure 2-15). All devices attach to the bus in order to be a part of the network. The manner in which devices attach will be discussed later. Information on the bus (typically) travels in both directions, and all devices on the bus see the data. Data is processed in the manner defined by the Layer 2 protocol. Cable faults on a bus

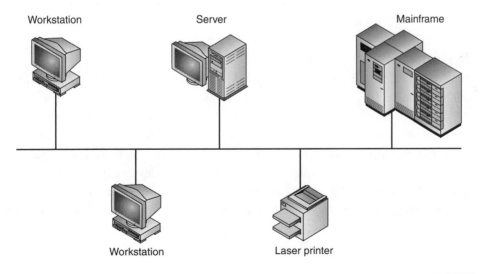

Figure 2-15   Physical bus topology

are difficult to locate because they affect all network devices on the bus. The advantage to such a physical topology is ease of installation. Disadvantages are that faults affect all devices, and reconfiguration (if devices need to be added or moved) is very difficult. Also, because this type of physical topology is no longer widely (if ever) used, it is difficult to find replacement equipment.

Physical Ring

The physical ring (see Figure 2-16) uses a cable to connect Device 1 to Device 2, a cable to connect Device 2 to Device 3, from Device 3 to Device 4, and from Device 4 back to Device 1 to form a complete circuit. All traffic on a ring travels in the same direction. Frames transmitted from Device 1 to Device 2 go directly to Device 2. The reply from Device 2 to Device 1, however, goes by way of Device 3 and from Device 3 to Device 4 before returning to Device 1. This requires all devices on the ring to receive every transmission, examine it, and retransmit it onto the ring. This requires every station on the ring to (at least partially) process the packet, whereas devices on a bus may ignore packets not transmitted to them.

Advantages of such a topology are that they are relatively easy to install and that faults are easy to troubleshoot because the protocols that use such a topology employ various features that help to identify faults. Also, rings are usually designed in such a manner that a fault in the cabling may not bring down the ring because the ring may be able to recover by wrapping, or a second ring may be employed. (We will look closer at these ideas when we examine Token Ring later.)

Disadvantages in such a topology are that it is difficult to reconfigure, and the equipment is relatively expensive.

Physical Star

The physical star topology uses a centrally located device (originally a hub, but today switches are usually employed in the same role) to which all devices attach (see Figure 2-17). Picture a bicycle wheel's central hub to which all spokes attach, and you'll get the idea. The difference between the physical star and the physical bus is that the hub device used in a star topology is contained in a single location while the physical bus must extend throughout the entire network. Also, the hub device employs an integrated repeater and (optionally) management functions that are not present in a bus topology.

Disadvantages to the physical star topology are that installing is relatively more expensive and possibly more time consuming because two devices (even two devices right next to each other) each require a separate run of cable that goes back to the same central hub.

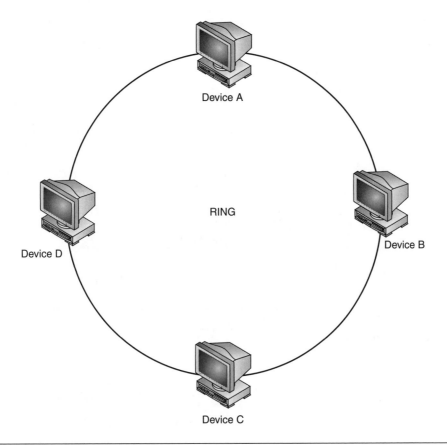

Figure 2-16   Physical ring topology

An advantage to such a topology is that a cable fault only affects a single device. Reconfiguration and stations' moves/additions are simple because all that needs to be done is to run a single new cable. Almost every current and new networking technology uses such a topology.

Cell Topology

The physical cell topology (see Figure 2-18) is employed by cableless networking technologies like infrared and radio-based technologies. A cell is an area within which a device may communicate, and cells may overlap to provide seamless coverage throughout the network. Advantages of such a topology are that moves and additions require no work at all. Disadvantages are that extensive planning may be required, and cost may be considerable. Also, environmental conditions may cause problems.

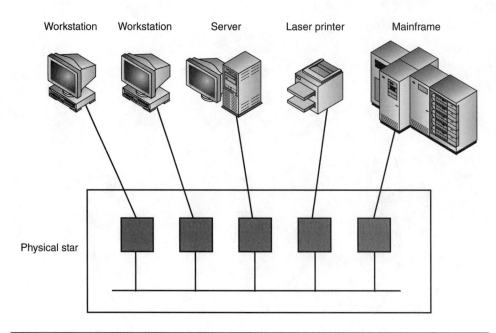

Figure 2-17 Physical star topology

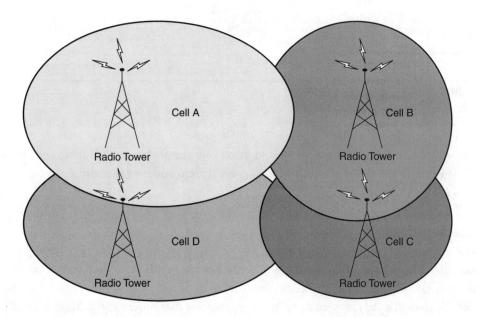

Figure 2-18 Cell topology

Logical Topologies

The logical topology defines how communication occurs on the network medium. It tells the devices how to think that they are connected and how the signal should travel. This communication in a logical form may occur in a form that does not match the physical topology. There are two logical topologies:

- Logical bus
- Logical ring

The Logical Bus

In the logical bus topology all devices receive all frames transmitted and only respond to the ones that are destined for them. Think of it as if you were standing at the front of an actual city bus. If you yell to your friend at the back of the bus, everyone hears you, but only your friend (the intended recipient) responds to your shouting. Ethernet is an example of a Layer 2 protocol that employs a logical bus. The physical topology most often employed with Ethernet is the physical star. This is not a contradiction. The hub device acts as if it were actually a bus. The bus is maintained within the confines of the hub device and is extended to every attached device. Frames transmitted by a device attached to a port are repeated to every other port. The reason for this is that all ports attach to the bus within the hub (see Figure 2-19).

 NOTE Do not test the shouting-on-the-bus example on a real city bus as it may have consequences that we do not consider in a book on networking. Technically speaking, shouting on a city bus may be a violation of the how-to-act-in-public protocol.

Logical Ring

In the logical ring topology, devices are physically attached in a star configuration, much as in Ethernet. However, in the logical ring, frames received on a port are retransmitted to the next port on the ring (empty ports are bypassed). The device on that port receives the frame and retransmits it back to the hub, which then retransmits it to the next port, and so on until the frame returns to the device that originated the transmission. This is because all of the ports on this type of hub are attached to a ring within the confines of the hub (see Figure 2-20). This is the logical topology employed by Token Ring and FDDI.

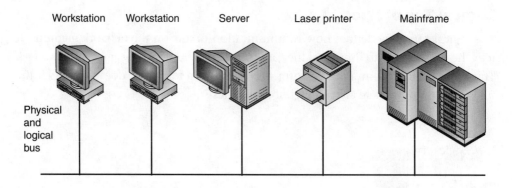

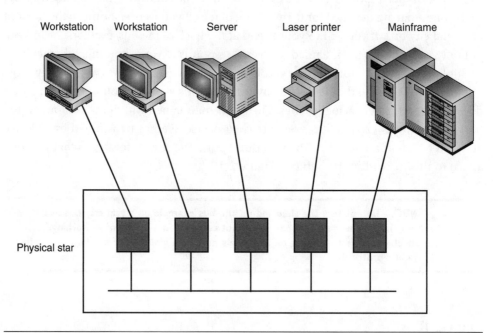

Figure 2-19   Physical versus logical bus

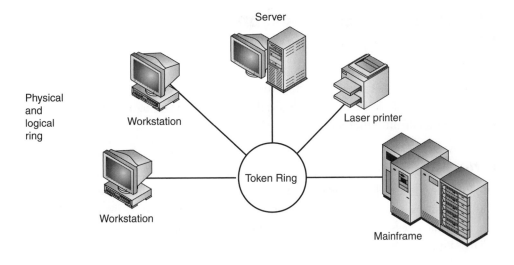

Physical
and
logical
ring

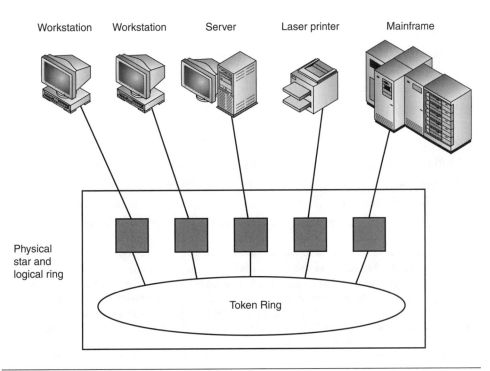

Physical
star and
logical ring

Figure 2-20   Physical versus logical ring

Ethernet, Fast Ethernet, and Gigabit Ethernet

Although there are some differences between the Ethernet, Fast Ethernet, and Gigabit Ethernet protocols, as their names infer, there are also a great many similarities. We will examine Ethernet in some detail here and then go on to examine the differences in Fast Ethernet and Gigabit Ethernet.

Ethernet

The Ethernet protocol is a low-overhead, easy-to-understand-and-implement protocol that has gained a huge market share since it was first invented. It uses a contention-based media access method and some very simple to implement rules of design. There are five Ethernet protocols:

- 10BASE-5

- 10BASE-2

- 10BASE-T

- 10BASE-F

- 10BROAD-36

We will examine the first four of these five protocols because there is very little installed base (if any) of the fifth.

10BASE-5

The 10BASE-5 standard was developed in the early 1970s, standardized in the early 1980s, and was the original 802.3 standard. It uses a very thick (10mm diameter) 50 ohm coaxial cable and for this reason was dubbed *thicknet*. It makes use of baseband technology, and a single segment of thicknet can be 500 meters in length.

 NOTE The numbers and words that make up the naming of the different Ethernet protocols have a purpose. The first part of the nomenclature defines the speed of the protocol, in this case 10 Mbps. The second part of the name defines the type of technology, baseband or broadband. The third part describes the characteristics of the physical medium either in length (that is, 5 stands for 500 meter segments or a letter that describes which medium is used).

Up to 100 stations may exist on a single segment. Up to five segments may be connected together via up to four repeaters, and up to three of these segments may be populated. These numbers became known as the *5-4-3 rule*. This means that the network diameter (the maximum distance from one end of the network to the other) of a 10BASE-5 network is 2,500 meters and may have up to 300 devices attached. To go beyond these numbers you need to add a new network and route between.

Devices attach to the network via an Attachment Unit Interface (AUI) cable that runs from the network device's (workstation or other) Network Interface Card (NIC) to the transceiver. The transceiver is a separate, external device that attaches to the coaxial cable by actually running a screw through the covering of the cable until the core is reached. These devices are usually called *vampire taps* because of the method of attachment. The maximum length of cable from the tap to the network device is five meters, and taps may not be closer than 2.5 meters from each other. (The cable is marked at 2.5 meter intervals.) The bus must be terminated at both ends with 50 ohm terminating resistors. These terminators absorb the signals when they reach the end of the cable and prevent them from being reflected back and causing collisions. One end of the bus must be grounded.

10BASE-2

The 10BASE-2 standard (1984) was developed as a less expensive, easier to work with alternative to 10BASE-5. It uses a thinner 50 ohm coax cable, which is easier to work with because it is more flexible than thicknet cable and less expensive to manufacture because it is not as high quality. Due to the thinner cable the standard was destined to be called *thinnet*. The lesser-quality cable also had other effects besides cost on the design of an Ethernet network. The cable for thinnet had less resistance to attenuation than did the thicknet cable, so the segment length of a thinnet segment was reduced to 185 meters.

 NOTE The 2 in 10BASE-2 does not stand for 200 meters. What it does stand for I have not been able to determine.

The maximum number of stations per segment is 30 when using 10BASE-2. The 5-4-3 rule still applies. This makes the maximum diameter of a single 10BASE-2 network 925 meters.

Another major difference between 10BASE-5 and 10BASE-2 is that 10BASE-2 uses a transceiver that is integrated to the NIC. Connections to the network are made using BNC connectors. The cable segment runs from one device to the next; the device connects using a BNC connector attached to a T connector, and the next cable segment goes to the next device (see Figure 2-21).

> **NOTE** I have heard two different stories that both appear to be credible for the meaning of the acronym BNC. One states that the BNC connector was developed by the British Navy, and therefore the acronym stands for British Navy (or Naval) Connector. The other story states that the connector is called the Bayonet Connector because the thin cable that extends from the end of the connector seems like a bayonet. (It also hurts if you stick yourself with it.) I make no claims to believe one story over the other. My technical editor informs me that the BNC connector was invented by Engineer Carl Concelman and Paul Neill and stands for Bayonet Neill Concelman (see http://www.marvac.com/funpages/rf_information.htm). So I'm adding his comments for completeness.

The bus must be terminated at both ends with 50 ohm terminating resistors. These terminators absorb the signals when they reach the end of the cable and prevent them from being reflected back and causing collisions. One end of the bus must be grounded.

10BASE-T

The 10BASE-T standard uses Unshielded Twisted-Pair (UTP) cable. UTP is made up of thin copper wires, each wire insulated in a color-coded sheath. The wires are in pairs, and the pairs are twisted around each other to help offset the affects of signal leakage.

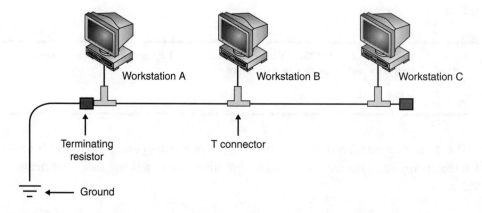

Figure 2-21 10BASE-2 physical connections

The cable is terminated with an RJ-45 connector and is similar to the RJ-11 connector used by your telephone but with room for four pairs instead of two. The transceiver is built in to the NIC just like in 10BASE-2. 10BASE-T uses a physical star topology (10BASE-5 and 10BASE-2 use a physical bus topology). Each segment is a maximum of 100 meters. This means that the cable that goes from the network node to the repeater (hub) or from one repeater to the next may be no longer than 100 meters. There may be no more than five segments connected by four repeaters between any two devices communicating with one another.

The UTP cable used in 10BASE-T networks is cheaper and much easier to work with than the coaxial cable used in 10BASE-5 and 10BASE-2 networks. The physical star topology has many advantages over the physical bus. The development of this technology sounded the death toll for 10BASE-5 and 10BASE-2. It also has many features in common with Fast Ethernet and Gigabit Ethernet.

10BASE-F

10BASE-F represents the standards that were developed for Ethernet transmission over fiber-optic cable. Fiber-optic cable has many advantages over copper. Fiber-optic cable (here on referred to as fiber) has an extremely high immunity from attenuation and Electro-Magnetic Interference (EMI). Because attenuation is so low and signal fidelity is so high, cable distances can be much longer than those of copper, up to 20 kilometers. Because it resists EMI so well it is perfect for use in environments that are noisy (have lots of EMI emitting devices) like factories and elevator shafts, near florescent lights, and so on. Another advantage of fiber is that it enables newer and faster technologies to develop faster because of the high quality of its signal. There are two major drawbacks to fiber:

- Cost

- Ease of installation

Both of these factors are tied to each other. Fiber is expensive because it is difficult to manufacture and has limited use (you do not make dishwashers using fiber), whereas copper has many industrial uses, which enables it to be manufactured cheaply in great quantities. Fiber is also difficult to terminate and is fragile, requiring time and skill to install (which simply adds to the cost of acquisition).

Frame Sizes

The Ethernet protocol defines a frame as having a minimum frame size of 64 bytes (12 bytes address, 48 bytes data) and a maximum frame size of 1,518 bytes. Today you may see Ethernet maximum frame sizes of 1,522 bytes. This is to support something called *VLAN tagging* in which a VLAN ID is inserted into the header of the Ethernet frame as it leaves a switch to tell the receiving switch which VLAN the frame belongs to.

CSMA/CD

The basis for how Ethernet functions is the CSMA/CD MAC. It defines the rules for transmission. Remembering that Ethernet is a contention-based system and is therefore subject to collisions, there need to be rules for detecting and recovering from collisions.

Step 1: Ready-to-Send

We begin with the device being ready to transmit. This means that data has been passed down from the upper layers and is ready to be transferred to the network medium for transportation to the destination.

Step 2: Carrier Sense

In this step the station that is ready to send data senses the network medium for the presence of other transmissions. Another way of putting this is to say that the station listens to the network to see if anyone else is talking. The station listens to detect quiet (a lack of other transmissions) for a time equal to the interpacket gap. The interpacket gap is the minimum distance enabled between frames. When a station that is ready to send detects quiet on the network for this period of time, it assumes that the network is free and moves to step 3. If the network is busy, the station returns to step 2.

Step 3: Transmit and Sense

The station begins to transmit its data. While this is occurring, the station is required to continue listening for the presence of other transmissions. If another transmission is detected while the original transmission is still in progress, a collision has occurred and we go to step 4. If no collision is detected and the transmission had been completed, the transmission has been successful and the station returns to step 1.

Step 4: Jam

Once a collision has been detected, the stations involved in the collision send a jam signal. The purpose of this signal is to alert other stations to the presence of the collision. After the jam signal, the stations move to step 5.

Step 5: Backoff

The stations choose a random number and wait that amount of time before returning to step 1. Because the number is random, this helps to ensure that the two stations will not again attempt to transmit at the same time.

Collisions and Their Domains

Collisions are an interesting thing. Devices need to listen for them, but where does a device need to be in order for a collision to affect it? The answer is simple. A device is affected by a collision if it exists within the same collision domain as the collision. What does that mean? A collision domain is the shared media segment that the collision occurs on up to the next router or switch. A router or switch/bridge does not pass a collision from one interface to another. A router and a switch/bridge can detect packets that were involved in a collision and drop them. This limits the area of affect that a collision has. This area of affect is the collision domain. Hubs do not have the capability to selectively drop or forward frames, so all frames, even corrupted ones, get forwarded. Therefore, if two devices are separated by hubs only, they are part of the same collision domain.

Broadcast Domains

A broadcast domain is the area in which a broadcast frame is seen. A broadcast frame is one that carries the broadcast address (ff.ff.ff.ff.ff.ff for Ethernet) in the DA field of the header. Devices that are connected by hubs and switches are part of the same broadcast domain because switches will forward broadcast traffic. A router will not forward broadcast traffic, so the boundary of a broadcast domain is a router. We will examine this idea further in Chapter 3.

Fast Ethernet

Although 10BASE-T and 10BASE-F were great steps forward for Ethernet, there was still one minor problem; it still was not as fast as Token Ring. 10Mb Ethernet was slower than 16Mb Token Ring even before the realization that, of your 10 Mb, you could only hope to get about 30 percent utilization before your performance started to degrade due to excessive collisions. 16Mb Token Ring could deliver around 60 percent without breaking a sweat. Sixty percent of 16 is much more than 30 percent of 10. So although pricing and ease of installation were far better, Ethernet still could not compete with Token Ring in the performance arena, until someone developed Fast Ethernet.

Similarities

Fast Ethernet functions at 100 Mbps. It maintained the same physical star topology, and in most cases your 10BASE-T wiring was still perfectly good. Fast Ethernet NICs were more expensive than their slower brothers, but that still put them on the market cheaper than most Token Ring cards.

Fast Ethernet (IEEE 802.3U) comes with a few different Physical layer standards for flexibility and has many of the same features found in 10BASE-T Ethernet:

- Same contention-based CSMA/CD MAC

- Same star-wired topology

- Same MAC addressing scheme

- Same framing

- Same minimum (64 bytes) and maximum (1,518 bytes) frame size

Differences

The major difference between Ethernet and Fast Ethernet is the length of a bit, measured in microseconds. In Ethernet the bit time (the time it takes to transmit 1 bit) is 9.6 microseconds. In Fast Ethernet the bit time is .96 microseconds, or 10 times less. This means that 10 times as much data can be sent in the same amount of time as with Ethernet. Many people make the mistake of assuming that the difference between Ethernet and Fast Ethernet is that the individual bits move faster in Fast Ethernet. This is not true. A way has been developed to make a bit smaller and still retain its meaning. This means that the same amount of bits can be shipped in less time because it takes less time to transmit them. (It takes less time to say a short word than it does a long word even if both the words mean the same thing.)

An individual bit cannot be made to move any faster because the rate of propagation of a signal along a copper wire (how fast the bit goes from one end to the other) is a function of the resistance of the copper and the speed of light in a vacuum. Because we cannot increase the speed of light (unless it is an amber traffic light about to turn red), the only thing to do is make the bit smaller. That is what was accomplished in Fast Ethernet. The technology existed to create and receive a signal that was 10 times smaller than the 10BASE-T signal without the value of the signal becoming corrupted.

Another addition to the Fast Ethernet standard is the capability to function in full-duplex mode. 10Mb Ethernet was only capable of functioning in half-duplex (one station talks, then another). This was defined by the CSMA/CD protocol. It was discovered, however, that it is possible for more than one device to talk at a time and still not cause a collision. If two devices are connected by a single Category 5 (four-pair) cable, one pair is used for transmit, and one pair is used for receive. This means that it is impossible for two transmissions to collide because the transmit (TX) pair of one device is only connected to the receive (RX) of the other device (see Figure 2-22). When this dedicated connection exists, the CD part of the CSMA/CD protocol is unnecessary. This type of connection is precisely what occurs when devices are attached to a switch. Switches create dedicated paths from device to device, making collisions impossible. Therefore, a method of making full-duplex communication was decided upon. Simply turn off the CD of the CSMA/CD protocol. This is a simple matter in most NIC cards; there is a configuration parameter that enables the user to choose either full- or half-duplex operation available with most 10/100 Ethernet cards today.

Yet another feature of Fast Ethernet is auto-detection. This enables the NIC card or other network device to test the device that it is connected to so it can determine whether it is functioning at 10 or 100 Mbps. Auto-negotiation enables two devices to vote on how they will communicate (10 or 100, full-duplex or half-duplex). Please remember that full duplex is available only when the bandwidth between two devices is dedicated. This means that one of two conditions must exist:

- The connection between the two devices must be a single cable with no other devices attached.

- The connection between the two devices must be a switch capable of supporting full-duplex.

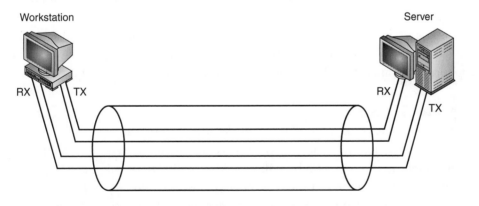

Figure 2-22   Full-duplex operation

The moment that there is a hub between two devices, it is impossible to use full-duplex communication because by definition a hub is a shared media device and offers no dedicated bandwidth.

Fast Ethernet Standards

There are three physical standards for 802.3U Fast Ethernet:

- 100BASE-TX
- 100BASE-T4
- 100BASE-FX

100BASE-TX This is the most widely used physical standard. It specifies 100Mb communication over four-pair Category 5 (Cat 5) UTP cable. This is the cable used in most Ethernet installations so it made migration fairly simple by negating the need for a huge cable upgrade. It supports cable lengths of up to 100 meters (just like 10BASE-T).

100BASE-T4 This standard was developed to meet the needs of customers who had installed large quantities of inferior four-pair Cat 3 cable and were not able to afford large-scale cable upgrades. This standard will work over Cat 3 cable if only four pairs were installed. It does not support two-pair Cat 3 cable, and it does not support full-duplex communication. For this reason it was not widely popular.

100BASES-FX This standard supports Fast Ethernet over fiber. Using multimode fiber, the connection between two devices running full duplex can be 2,000 meters (2 kilometers) in length (in half duplex only 412 meters). If single-mode fiber is used in the same scenario, the distance can be up to 20 kilometers in length. Not all vendors support single-mode fiber for Fast Ethernet because it was not a part of the standard.

Repeater Types

There are two classes, or types, of repeaters defined for Fast Ethernet; they are the Class I (translational) repeater and the Class II (transparent) repeater. The translational (Class I) repeater supports both 100BASE-TX/100BASE-FX signaling and 100BASE-T4 signaling. Because 100BASE-TX and 100BASE-FX use the same signaling method (125 MHz with 4B/5B encoding), it is easy to implement both physical standards into one repeater. 100BASE-T4 uses a different signaling, however. It uses 25 MHz with 8B/6T encoding. Therefore, there needs to be a translation (hence the term *translational repeater*) from the signaling used by 100BASE-TX/100BASE-FX and 100BASE-T4 if they are both to be supported in the same repeater at the same time. All Nortel Networks' Fast Ethernet hubs (repeaters) are of this type.

The transparent repeater will support only one signaling system, either 125 MHz with 4B/5B encoding or 25 MHz with 8B/6T. This type of repeater is not supported by Nortel Networks.

There is a side effect created by the existence of two types of repeaters. The translational repeaters, because of the translation being provided, are capable of supporting a single repeater hop only in a collision domain. The transparent repeaters (because they do not translate) are capable of supporting two repeater hops per collision domain (see Figure 2-23). This limitation of Class I repeaters is mitigated by the capability to stack hubs (making them a single repeater hop) and the capability to connect hubs via switches (creating multiple collision domains). See Chapter 10 for more details on this subject.

Gigabit Ethernet

In 1998, the IEEE standardized the next leap forward. Gigabit became the 802.3z standard. The ideas for the development of the Gigabit Ethernet protocol were to create a protocol that functioned the same as Ethernet, just faster. This means that the intentions were to create a faster protocol with the same

- 802.3 frame format

- Capability to operate in full- or half-duplex

- CSMA/CD MAC

This was a great idea. It would mean that engineers would already have most of the requisite knowledge to work with the protocol and very few new decisions would need to be made while standardizing it. All of these desires were met to some extent.

The desire to keep the same 802.3 frame format was partially met. The fields of the frame are the same except for one little detail. The minimum Ethernet frame size is 64 bytes. The minimum Gigabit Ethernet frame size is 512 bytes. We have to remember that the minimum frame size has an effect on the maximum network diameter.

Let's consider why the Ethernet (10 Mb) minimum frame size is 64 bytes (512 bits). Ethernet devices are required to transmit for at least as long as it takes for the first bit of the frame to travel to the end of the network and back again. This is so that when collisions occur under the worst case scenario (when the two colliding devices are at the farthest ends of the network), the notification of the collision will get back to the devices that transmitted the colliding frames. The network diameter for an Ethernet network (10BASE-5) is 2,500 meters; therefore, the frame must be at least 5,000 meters long.

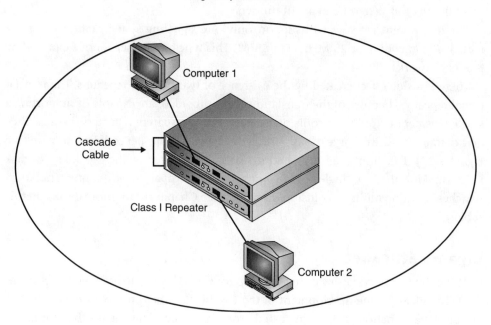

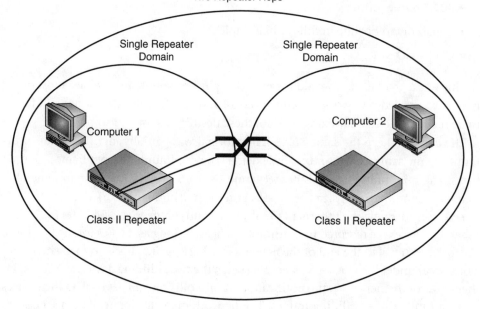

Figure 2-23   Fast Ethernet repeater types and hop limitations

The bits are transmitted at a rate of 10 Mbps (10,000,000 bits). The individual bits move (propagate) approximately 200,000,000 meters per second (or 200,000 thousand kilometers per second). If you divide the speed (200,000,000 meters/second) by the rate (10,000,000 bits/second), you get the length of a bit on copper cable, 20 meters. Because for a collision to be sensed, the bits have to be transmitted from one end of the network to the other, collide, and have that collision be noticed back at the source of the transmission that directly affects the maximum network diameter. For a network of 2,500 meters in length to have a valid collision occur at the farthest end means that the first bit of the transmission has to travel 2,500 meters, collide, and travel 2,500 meters back (5,000 meters total) for the collision to have any effect on the CSMA/CD protocol. This is referred to as the *round trip delay*. The minimum frame size is 64 bytes long because a 64-byte frame is 10,240 meters long (64 bytes is 512 bits multiplied by 20 meters is 10,240 meters) to account for the delay (and to give extra room in case future developments of innovations increased the maximum network diameter) or else the CD algorithm will be useless for detecting and preventing additional collisions. Networks where the diameter is out of spec (longer than the maximum diameter permits) suffer from late collisions.

For Gigabit Ethernet, the numbers change. The 200,000,000 meters per second propagation rate for a bit on copper stays the same (it is a constant), but the rate of transmission is now 1,000 Mbps (1,000,000,000 bps). If you divide 200,000,000 meters per second by 1,000,000,000 bps you get a bit that is .2 meters in length; 512 bits multiplied by .2 meters is a 102.4 meters, which, when divided by two, gives us a network diameter of approximately 50 meters from end to end. This is a fairly short and very impractical network diameter. Therefore, the minimum frame size was extended to 512 bytes (4,096 bits).

How does this affect the Ethernet frame? In order to fill out the minimum required frame size for frames without the necessary amount of data, a field was added to the Gigabit Ethernet frame after the 4-byte FCS. This is called the Carrier Extension (CE) field. Any frame size that is missing from the frame is made up here.

The CSMA/CD MAC was also partially kept. I am not familiar with any Gigabit Ethernet implementations where half-duplex transmission is being used. All Gigabit networking devices are routers and switches; there are no Gigabit hubs. If half-duplex is not being used, neither is the CD.

Physical Standards

We will examine here three different Physical layer standards for Gigabit Ethernet:

- 1000BASE-SX
- 1000BASE-LX
- 1000BASE-T

The 1000BASE-SX standard defines how Gigabit Ethernet is transmitted over multi-mode fiber using short-wave transmissions and it supports cable lengths of 220 to 550 meters.

The 1000BASE-LX standard defines how Gigabit Ethernet is transmitted over multi-mode or single-mode fiber using long-wave transmissions and it supports cable lengths of 5,000 meters when using single-mode fiber.

The 1000BASE-T standard defines how Gigabit Ethernet is transmitted over Cat 5 or better, four pair copper cable supporting up to 100 meters of cable.

Token Ring

Token Ring (IEEE 802.5) is a token-passing Layer 2 protocol developed by IBM. A station that has data to transmit must wait to claim the token (only one token per ring) before it is enabled to transmit. This means that Token Ring does not have collisions. You might say that Token Ring is a polite protocol because every station waits its turn before speaking. Also, every station gets equal opportunity to speak. These are ideas that are alien to Ethernet. Token Ring exists in two speeds, 4 Mbps and 16 Mbps.

 NOTE There is a movement to standardize Fast Token Ring at 100 Mbps, but it does not appear to have a very large following and is losing support.

Framing

The Token Ring frame is similar in a few ways to the Ethernet frame (it does contain a DA and an SA) but different in many others (see Figure 2-24). Token Ring frames can be as large as 18,000 bytes long (though normally, we see 4,544 bytes as the maximum), so they have the potential to be more efficient than the smaller Ethernet frames.

Starting Delimiter 1 byte	Access Control 1 byte	Frame Control 1 byte	Destination Address 2 or 6 bytes	Source Address 2 or 6 bytes	Routing Information Field 2-18 bytes	DSAP 1 byte	SSAP 1 byte	Control Field 1 or 2 bytes	Data	FCS	Ending Delimiter 1 byte	Frame Status

Figure 2-24   Token Ring frame

On the other side, the Token Ring protocol has a lot more management overhead, as we will see later.

The fields of the Token Ring frame are as follows:

- Starting Delimiter (SD)
- Access Control (AC)
- Frame Control
- Destination Address (DA)
- Source Address (SA)
- Routing Information Field (RIF)
- DSAP
- SSAP
- Control field
- Data
- Frame Check Sequence (FCS)
- Ending Delimiter
- Frame Status

Starting Delimiter
The SD uses a special value to indicate the start of a frame. It is a one-byte field.

Access Control
The AC field (one byte) is actually subdivided into four parts:

- Priority (3 bits)
- Reservation (3 bits)
- Token (1 bit)
- Monitor (1 bit)

As a token goes from station to station, stations wanting to grab the token and use it must examine the priority bits. The station must have a priority equal or greater than the present priority of the token (0–7) before the station can take possession of the token. If a station wants a token but it does not have a high-enough priority, it can set the reservation bits to its priority. This will cause the next token generated to have a priority equal to that of the station. (When the next token is generated, the station that generates the token sets the priority bits equal to the reservation bits and then sets the reservation bits to 0.) The next bit is the Token bit. When set to 0, it indicates that this frame is in fact a token. If it is set to 1, then the frame is a frame with data in it or a MAC frame for ring management and not a token. The last bit in the Access Control field is the Monitor bit. This bit is set to 0 by the station that generated the frame and set to 1 by the active monitor (a role filled on a Token Ring network by a workstation or network device). The active monitor does this so it can tell if the frame passes by it again. If the frame passes the active monitor, it indicates that the frame was not removed by the station that generated it, which is a sign of a problem. The active monitor will then remove the frame from the ring and produce a new token.

Frame Control

These bits areused to differentiate between a frame that contains data and a frame containing MAC management information. If the frame is identified as the latter, then the type of MAC management frame is identified.

Destination Address (DA)

The DA is the address of the device that the frame is intended for.

Source Address (SA)

The SA is the address of the device that originated the packet. The first bit of the SA is the Routing Information Indicator (RII). If this bit is set to 1, it indicates that there is an optional Routing Information Field (RIF) present in the frame. The RIF is used for making forwarding decisions in a Source Route Bridged network (see Chapter 3 for more information on Source Route Bridging [SRB]).

DSAP, SSAP, and the Control Fields

These fields are part of the optional LLC frame.

Data

The Data field is where the information transmitted by the upper-layer protocols is stored.

Frame Check Sequence (FCS)

This field is used to check for transmission errors in the frame as it travels around the ring.

Ending Delimiter

The Ending Delimiter field marks the end of the frame. It is also used to notify stations if an error was detected when computing the FCS. Every station checks the FCS as it receives the frame and may set the error bit in the ending delimiter. There is also a bit in the field that is used to indicate whether or not there are more frames to follow.

Frame Status

The Frame Status field lets other stations on the ring know a number of things. One is if the frame was received by the destination device (A bit set to 1). This is known as the *address recognized bit*. There is also a bit that indicates if the frame was copied by the destination device. This is the frame-copied bit (C bit set to 1).

Entering the Ring

Unlike Ethernet, Token Ring stations go through an elaborate process when they attach to the network media, known as *entering the ring*. There is a 5-step process (referred to as *phases*) that a Token Ring station goes through when it attempts to enter a ring. If any of the phases fails to complete successfully, the station does not enter the ring, and the NIC card becomes disabled.

Phase 0

In this phase the Token Ring controller (the NIC) tests the cable that attaches the controller to the multiaccess unit (MAU). At the MAU the port is looped. The cable (called a *lobe cable*) does not attach to the ring yet; any frames transmitted by the station will be sent back to the station without being seen on the ring. This is how the controller tests the lobe cable; it transmits frames and waits to see if they come back.

Phase 1

In this phase the controller sends the phantom current to the MAU. This current trips the relay that keeps the port looped and connects the port to the ring; this is known as *insertion*. This causes a ring error to occur; all data currently on the ring is lost, and the ring enters a stage of recovery. Every time a station insets onto the ring or leaves a ring this occurs. During this phase, a ring speed check is performed. A station is not enabled to insert into a ring at the wrong speed.

Phase 2

In this phase the station checks to see if any other device on the ring is using the same MAC address as itself. This is due to the fact that many Token Ring implementations use MAC address other than the ones burned into the card. The Locally Administered Address (LAA) is just fine, provided that no human error causes an address on the ring to be duplicated. When the station checks for duplicate addresses, it transmits a frame onto the ring with the DA and the SA set to their own MAC address. When the frame returns to the workstation it checks to see if the address recognized bit is set. If not, then the workstation knows that there are no other devices on the ring using the same MAC address. If it is set, then we have a duplicate address and the workstation (the one performing the check) removes itself from the ring.

Phase 3

In this phase the station identifies the Nearest Active Upstream Neighbor (NAUN). This is the station on the ring immediately before the workstation. Remember that traffic on the ring is unidirectional. Therefore, there is an upstream device (the device we receive frames from) and a downstream device (the device we transmit frames to). In this phase we also identify ourselves to the downstream neighbor. The workstations maintain this list of neighbors in order to help locate a fault domain should a ring error occur.

Phase 4

In this phase the station waits for information from the Ring Parameters Server (RPS). The RPS is a device that maintains ring parameters for the workstations. If no RPS is present, the station uses default parameters.

Grabbing the Token

We know that Token Ring uses a token-passing MAC protocol. This means that in order to transmit on the ring the station wanting to transmit must first capture the token. A station may capture a token when it recognizes a token with a lower or equal priority than its own. Once the station has the token, it appends the data to the token, flips the token bit to a frame, and sends the frame onto the ring. What happens next depends on the configuration of the devices on the ring. Normally, the device waits for the frame to be copied by the destination device and return. The source device then strips the data from the frame, sets the token bit back to token, and places the token on the ring. There is another option called Early Token Release (ETR). Rather than wait for the frame to return the device that has just transmitted, the frame releases a new token onto the ring immediately. This does not violate the basic rule of Token Ring that there be only one token on a ring at any given time. With ETR there is a single token and a single frame on the ring simultaneously. This increases the rate at which transmission can occur because it reduces the amount of time that a downstream device needs to wait for the token.

Review Questions

1. What is the purpose of the OSI model?
   A. To develop a tool for programming network device drivers
   B. To confuse students of networking
   C. To provide a framework to help developers design compatible networking components

2. How many layers are there to the OSI model?
   A. 5
   B. 6
   C. 7
   D. 4

3. Which layer is the second layer of the OSI model?
   A. Presentation
   B. Data Link
   C. Network
   D. Session

4. What are the two sublayers of the Data Link layer?
   A. MAC
   B. LCP
   C. MAT
   D. LLC

5. The address applied to devices at the Data Link layer of the OSI model is called the
   A. Logical address
   B. MAC address
   C. OUI
   D. LLC address

6. What do the first 3 bytes of a 6-byte MAC address represent?
   A. Function
   B. Serial number
   C. SSAP
   D. Manufacturer

7. What happens when two devices attempt simultaneous communication on a shared media network segment?
   A. A collision occurs.
   B. A token is generated.
   C. An abend.
   D. An exception.

8. What is a method of recognizing and recovering from the effects of a collision?
   A. Token passing
   B. CSMA/CD
   C. Full-duplex
   D. Half-duplex

9. How do token-passing protocols deal with the effects of collisions?
   A. By backing off and retransmitting
   B. By increasing the strength of the transmission
   C. By leaving the ring
   D. None of the above

10. Which of the following are different Ethernet frame types?
    A. Ethernet II
    B. 802.3
    C. 802.3 SNAP
    D. Novell RAW
    E. All of the above

11. In the Ethernet II frame, what does the Ethertype field denote?
    A. The frame type
    B. The upper-layer protocol the message comes from
    C. The lower-layer protocol to use to transmit the frame
    D. The speed of transmission

12. True/False
    The physical topology defines the actual path that the frame follows.

13. The 10BASE-5 protocol specifies
    A. Ethernet transmission over thinnet coax cable with cable segment lengths of 185 meters in a physical bus
    B. Ethernet transmission over UTP cable with cable segment lengths of 100 meters and wired in a physical star topology

   C. Ethernet transmission over thicknet coax cable with cable segment lengths of
      500 meters in a physical bus topology
   D. Ethernet transmission over thicknet coax cable with cable segment lengths of
      500 meters in a physical star topology

14. The minimum Ethernet frame size is
   A. 48 bytes
   B. 64 bytes
   C. 1,518 bytes
   D. 1,522 bytes

15. What does an Ethernet device do before transmitting data on the network?
   A. It listens to sense if any other devices are transmitting.
   B. It captures a token.
   C. It verifies the integrity of the data.
   D. Nothing.

16. Once an Ethernet device has determined that it has been involved in a collision,
   what is the first thing that it does?
   A. Continue to transmit.
   B. Unload and reload its network drivers.
   C. Send a jam signal.
   D. All of the above.

17. Which devices do collisions not pass through to affect the network segments on
   the other side? (Choose all that apply.)
   A. Switch
   B. Bridge
   C. Router
   D. Hub

18. Which devices do broadcasts not pass through to reach the network segments on
   the other side? (Choose all that apply.)
   A. Switch
   B. Bridge
   C. Router
   D. Hub

19. Which of the following devices may never be involved if full-duplex communica-
   tion is to take place?
   A. Switch
   B. Bridge

    C. Router

    D. Hub

20. On a Token Ring segment, which devices may remove a frame from the ring? (Choose all that apply.)

    A. The source device

    B. The destination device

    C. The active monitor

    D. The ring leader

Answers

1. C.

2. D.

3. B. The Data Link layer is the second layer of the OSI model. Remember that the layers of the model are numbered from the bottom up like the floors of a building.

4. A, D. The Media Access Control (MAC) is the sublayer that determines how the network is accessed, addressed, and framed. The Logical Link Control (LLC) is the sublayer that controls connection-oriented or connectionless communication.

5. B. The address applied to devices at the Data Link layer of the OSI model is the MAC address. The MAC address is usually 6 bytes (48 bits) long and is divided into two parts that combine to make a single unique address.

6. D. The first three bytes of a 6-byte MAC address represent the manufacturer of the hardware. It is called the Organizationally Unique Identifier (OUI) and is registered with the IEEE.

7. A. When two devices attempt to talk at the same time a collision occurs. The results of a collision are similar to two or more people talking on a CB radio and attempting to transmit at the same time. Multiple communications attempting to use a channel designed to support a single communication at a time cause all the transmitted data becomes garbled and unrecognizable.

8. B. CSMA/CD is a contention-based protocol that enables the occurrence, recognition of, and recovery from the effects of collisions.

9. **D.** There are no collisions in token-passing protocols, so there is no need or method for dealing with their effects.

10. **E.** Ethernet II, 802.3, 802.3 SNAP, and Novell RAW are all valid Ethernet frame types.

11. **B.** The Ethertype tells the receiving station the upper layer protocol contained in the data field of the frame.

12. **False.** The physical topology defines the type of cabling used as well as specifications of how to make network connections, what type of devices to use, the maximum number of connections, and so on.

13. **C.** The 10BASE-5 protocol specifies how Ethernet transmissions occur over thicknet coax cable with cable segment lengths of 500 meters in a physical bus topology. It also specifies the 5-4-3 rule for network design. It has a maximum network length of 2,500 meters.

14. **B.** The minimum size for an Ethernet frame is 64 bytes: 48 bytes for the data and 12 bytes for the source and destination address; 1,518 represents the maximum size for an Ethernet frame that does not include 802.1Q VLAN tagging information. 1,522 represents the maximum size for an Ethernet frame that does include 802.1Q VLAN tagging information.

15. **A.** Ethernet is a contention-based protocol. This means that it has to compete for network bandwidth. Because network bandwidth is allocated on a first-come, first-served basis with no other means of controlling the bandwidth other than the good behavior of the network devices, collisions do occur. In order to reduce the number of collisions that do occur, devices are required to listen to the network first to determine if the bandwidth is available.

16. **C.** Once an Ethernet device determines that it has become involved in a collision, it sends a jam signal to alert all other devices that there has been a collision on the network.

17. **A, B, C.** Collisions do not pass through switches, bridges, or routers. These devices perform an FCS check on all frames before forwarding them. Frames that do not pass the FCS are dropped. Hubs, on the other hand, do not perform any testing of the frame and forward all traffic received, including collisions.

18. **C.** Broadcast frames are not forwarded from one port on a router to another. A switch, bridge, and hub will forward broadcasts from one port to another.

19. **D.** A hub may never be involved in full-duplex communication because it does not supply dedicated bandwidth, which is a requirement for full-duplex.

20. **A, C.** The only devices on a Token Ring network that may remove a frame are the station that transmitted it (the source device) and the active monitor. The active monitor may only remove a frame that the source device fails to remove.

Bridging, Switching, and VLANs

This chapter will cover some bridging and switching fundamentals that are essential to understanding networking. We will discuss the necessity of different types of bridges, how bridges work, and their associated algorithms. We will also discuss switches and how they evolved from bridges. Our final discussion will cover virtual local area networks (VLANs) and how they enhance a network. This chapter will cover information that is part of the Data IP Fundamentals exam. As was mentioned in the first chapter, this exam is a necessary prerequisite to becoming Nortel Networks certified. Each of the technologies discussed here may appear on at least one other product specific exam and, in some cases, correlate directly to an exam objective. As we discuss specific exam objectives in later chapters, we will refer to what is written here.

Bridging Fundamentals

Bridges are data link layer relay devices that connect two or more networks. Bridging occurs in the second layer of the OSI model—the data link layer (see Figure 3-1). Because bridges make their decision at layer 2, they work with separate physical LANs that are on the same network and have the same network ID. This provides lower processing overhead. Bridges use the Media Access Control (MAC) source and destination addresses to relay frames between connected networks. They are not dependent on upper layer protocols. Because bridges operate at layer 2, they are concerned only with MAC layer addresses and are not involved with upper layer protocols. Therefore, bridges must be locally attached to the destination workstation they will forward packets to. They cannot be involved in any routing to forward data.

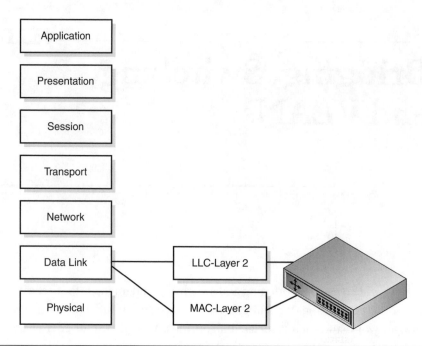

Figure 3-1 The OSI reference model and the position of the bridge/switch at the data link layer, layer 2

Bridges are advantageous when dividing large networks into manageable segments. The advantages of bridges include the following:

- Limiting collisions by separating segments from crossing over the bridge. This enables the administrator to isolate specific network areas, giving users less exposure to network outages.

- Communication between more internetworking devices than supported on a single LAN without a bridge. We will discuss this more fully in later parts of the chapter.

The function of a bridge is to segment the network and enable communication between the segments. This type of segmentation is at the collision domain level.

Collision Domains

A *collision domain* is defined as the part of the network that includes cable segments, attached devices, and hubs/switches arranged so that any two devices share the wire. All workstations in the same hub group are part of a single collision domain (see Fig-

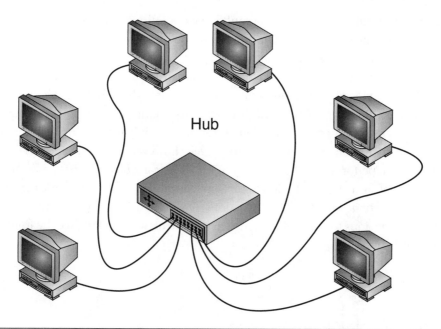

Figure 3-2   Workstations that share the same physical media are part of the same collision domain.

ure 3-2). The function of a bridge is to separate networks into different collision domains and to connect workstations on separate collision domains into one logical broadcast domain.

A discussion of Ethernet and Carrier Sense Multiple Access with Collision Detection (CSMA/CD) is important to understanding bridging more completely. A collision domain is the creation of the protocol Ethernet that is a CSMA/CD protocol. The nature of Ethernet is that of a contention-based network where every device can transmit whenever it needs to send information. For communication to occur, each workstation "listens" on the wire to see if it can transmit data. The wire is shared by all workstations in the same hub group or on the same port of a switch. If the line is quiet, the workstation will transmit. This is known as carrier sensing. If two or more workstations think it is okay to transmit at the same time, the result is a collision. In a collision scenario, all workstations back off the wire and jamming signals of garbage are sent for a period of time. This is the collision detection portion. Each workstation will wait and try to transmit again.

The problem with Ethernet is that the more workstations in the collision domain, the more likely collisions will occur. The increased number of workstations waiting to send data can cause more mistakes of multiple workstations sending at the same time. If we do not segment the network, it can be slow and inefficient.

On the other hand, this type of networking practice is very simple to manage because workstations can actually send data without overhead and without waiting to be told it is their turn to transmit. Therefore, actual user data throughput is high at a lower level of traffic. Plus, the ratio of bandwidth utilized to overhead is very high because no bandwidth is used for permission to send information (only for sending signals to find out if it is okay to transmit). At high traffic levels, however, collisions and retransmissions diminish performance dramatically. It is theoretically possible that collisions can be so frequent at higher traffic levels that no station has a clear chance to transmit. More than a certain number of workstations sharing the same media will cause the number of collisions to rise and the efficiency of the network to fail (see the following illustration).

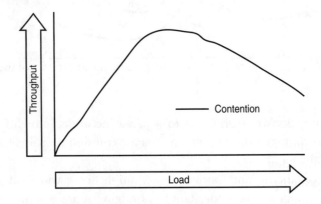

Because each workstation must be able to hear transmissions from all other workstations in the collision domain, there is a physical limitation of 100 meters using standard 10MB Ethernet. This is important to keep in mind when creating networks, because it determines how far workstations can be from the nearest bridge or other networking device.

These characteristics of Ethernet were the reason for separating networks into different segments. A bridge can be used to separate networks into smaller collision domains that seem to the end stations like one domain. This represents a separation at the layer 2 or MAC layer of the OSI model. This reduces network traffic because the bridge only forwards the data if the destination is on the other side. This isolates the local traffic to one of the collision domains or segments.

NOTE All network communication occurs at layer 2 by means of MAC addresses. The MAC address is unique for each and every workstation. The Address Resolution Protocol (ARP) is involved in mapping IP addresses to the MAC address for network communication. We will discuss this further in the next chapter.

Bridges are used to minimize collisions in a single domain. Bridges should be able to function as a forwarding device and to filter data that should not be forwarded. To do this, a bridge needs to maintain address tables to determine where each device is located. How do bridges do their jobs?

Transparent Bridging

The first type of bridge we will discuss is the transparent bridge. This bridge was first developed by DEC for use in Ethernet networks. It is also referred to as a learning bridge. Transparent bridging provides interconnections of LANs transparent to stations communicating across the bridge. Transparent bridges make no changes to the packet data link address. They provide network connections to LANs that employ identical protocols at the data link and physical layers. Transparent bridging is used in IEEE 802.3/Ethernet LANs or IEEE 802.5/token ring LANs. It is used to connect networks of the same layer 2 protocol, like Ethernet to Ethernet or Token Ring to Token Ring. The ultimate source and destination must have the same data link address format.

Transparent bridging requires that the bridge dynamically maintain a source address database. Each bridge interface operates in promiscuous mode for any frame on the LAN that is received and processed. The source address for each frame is saved in the database. The database is then searched to determine whether the destination address of the frame is located in the database. If it is, the frame is forwarded to the LAN segment. If both the source and destination stations are on the same LAN, the frame is discarded. If, however, the frame destination is not found in the database, the bridge forwards the frame to all other LAN segments. This decision process is a type of broadcasting called flooding. This process is transparent to the end station (hence the name). A station communicates with any other station in the network as though both stations are on the same LAN.

In short, when a bridge performs transparent bridging, it provides the following services:

- It learns the addresses of end stations on connected networks.

- It forwards or drops frames based upon the acquired forwarding tables (or user-configured filters).

The transparent bridge creates a forwarding table that stores MAC addresses and ports numbers. It also enables broadcast traffic to cross to other segments.

 NOTE A broadcast packet is one in which the destination MAC address is all Fs or binary ones.

The Transparent Bridging Process

Transparent bridges connect LANs using the same data link protocol. The transparent bridge receives and examines every frame transmitted on the network to which it is attached. It learns about the end stations on each LAN by reading the source MAC address of every received packet and noting on which interface the frame was received. The bridge then enters this information into a data structure known as a forwarding table, which the bridge constantly updates.

An individual workstation transmits information onto the LAN addressing the data to another node. The bridge's function is to first note the source address of the communication and place the MAC address into its forwarding table for that port. Then it forwards the frame if the destination is not on the same cable as the source. The bridge performs its function using the MAC address and a lookup table to determine if the destination is local or remote. If the device is local, the bridge does not need to do anything; if the address is remote, the bridge forwards the packet to the destination LAN.

Bridges use a built-in table to determine how to handle traffic. As a bridge builds a table, it knows whether to drop, forward, or broadcast a packet (see Figure 3-3). A transparent bridge learns all the MAC addresses on all nodes on all ports of the bridge. It does this by examining all packets and learning information based on the sender or source address. The bridge will consider four scenarios:

- **The source and destination on the same segment** It drops the packet—the workstation already received it.

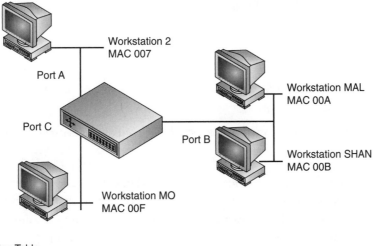

Figure 3-3   The transparent bridge and its forwarding table

- **The source and destination on different segments**   It forwards the packet to the destination segment.

- **Destinations unknown**   It floods the packet to all segments attached to the bridge *except* the source segment. (If the source and destination are on the same segment, the destination workstation will have received the packet already.)

- **Broadcast MAC address**   It forwards the packet to all segments except the source segment.

   NOTE   A transparent bridge builds a forwarding table using source addresses and makes forwarding decisions based on destination addresses.

Quick Quiz I

Look at the diagram and the bridge's forwarding table.

1. What would this bridge do if it received a data packet destined for workstation MAL?

2. What would this bridge do if it received a data packet with a destination address of all Fs?

Answers

1. The bridge would forward the packet for MAL out of port B unless that port has the source station on it.

2. The bridge would forward a packet of all Fs out all ports except the port it received the packet from.

Bridges rely heavily on broadcasting. If a packet contains no bridging information, the packet must be sent everywhere. When a bridge is first brought up onto the network, in fact, it will broadcast all packets because it has no forwarding table and no bridging information. This is one of bridging's severe limitations because this method of data delivery is inefficient and can trigger broadcast storms. In networks with low-speed links, broadcasting can introduce costly overhead. Especially problematic is a scenario where a bridge is unstable and can be brought up and down. The bridge needs to broadcast until it has built a forwarding table, and then if it goes down, it needs to rebuild the table when it comes up again.

What happens when an end station's location is changed, perhaps to a different segment of a port on the bridge? The bridge updates its forwarding table with the new address of the workstation when it sees the first packet sent from this workstation. It notices the source address moved and places a new entry for this MAC into its forwarding table. Until this workstation transmits data, the bridge does not know of the segment change. This is critical to note when moving workstations from one segment to another. As soon as this workstation *transmits* its first packet, the bridge knows about this workstation's move and adds the appropriate entry into the table. Until that transmission, the bridge continues to forward packets to the workstation at its old location.

What happens in a network configured with parallel bridges, such as the network in Figure 3-4? In a topology where more than one bridge may be connected to a LAN (for fault tolerance perhaps), data packets can bounce back and forth between the bridges. This causes redundant traffic and a phenomenon known as looping.

To understand the looping process firsthand, Figure 3-5 includes some fake MAC addresses for workstations sending data across bridges that are in parallel.

Why is the forwarding table in Figure 3-5 on bridges Mord and Chai all messed up? Here is what has taken place in this network. Workstation 2 sent a packet across the network to workstation B. Bridge Mord did not have an entry for workstation B in its forwarding table, so it flooded the data packet out of ports 2 and 3 (creating two data packets out of the one workstation 2 originally sent). Bridge Chai received information that workstation 2 was on port B (sent from port 3 by bridge Mord) but did not know where work-

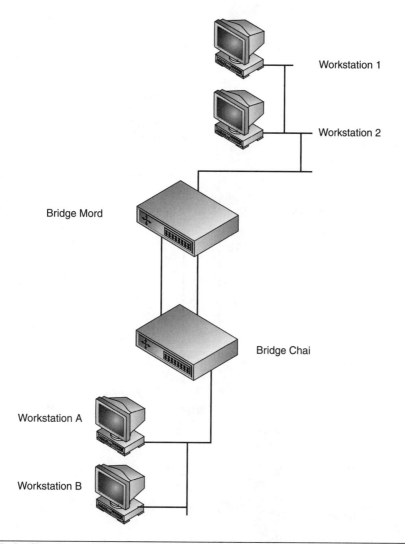

Figure 3-4 This figure shows bridges configured in a loop. For better understanding, it is a simplified picture of a network.

station B was—so it flooded the data packet out of port C and port A (creating two more data packets). While bridge Chai was in the process of flooding out these packets, it received the data packet that bridge Mord flooded out of port 2. Thinking that workstation 2 had moved, bridge Chai flooded the data packet out of ports B and C. Bridge Mord meanwhile received the data packet from bridge Chai saying that workstation 2 was located on port 2. Thinking that workstation 2 had moved, it also began flooding more packets out onto the network. Eventually, all these data packets that began with one packet from workstation 2 to workstation B would cause the network to go down.

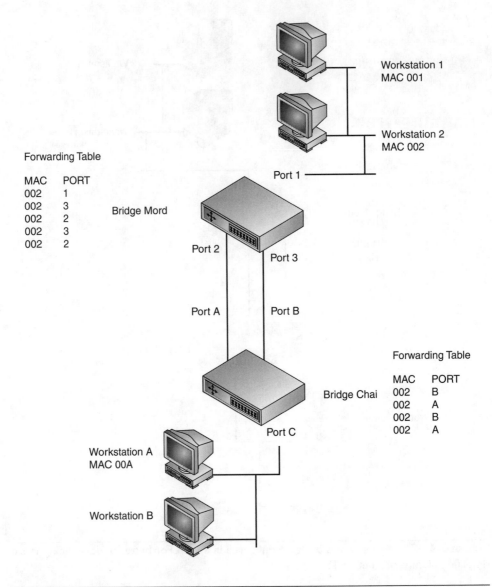

Figure 3-5 Transparent bridges in parallel mode cause a network loop because the bridges do not know how to forward packets.

Looping can occur in a network with bridges placed in parallel for the purpose of fault tolerance. When loops occur in the network, the administrator must reconfigure the LAN to remove the spare hardware. But how can we have fault tolerance in our network? With spanning tree, a self-configured algorithm that enables any bridge to be added to the topology dynamically without creating loops. When a new bridge is added, the spanning tree reconfigures all bridges on the LAN into a single loop-free network. What is spanning tree?

Spanning Tree Algorithm

The spanning tree algorithm was developed to overcome problems cause by redundant links (loops) in the LAN. It is defined as the IEEE 802.1D standard. The Spanning Tree Protocol detects and eliminates logical loops in a bridged/switched network. When physical path redundancy exists, the spanning tree algorithm configures the network so the bridge (or switch) uses only one most efficient path. If that path fails, the protocol automatically reconfigures the network to make another path active, but never enables redundant paths to be active at the same time because that would cause a loop (refer to Figure 3-5).

The spanning tree algorithm produces and maintains a loop-free topology in a bridged network that may contain loops in its physical design. The spanning tree algorithm provides this loop-free topology by enabling a single path through the extended network. The algorithm produces a logical tree topology of any physical arrangements of bridges. Redundant links are unused in a network with loops. The spanning tree algorithm provides a high degree of fault tolerance by enabling the automatic reconfiguration of the spanning tree topology around a failed bridge or data path. Once the spanning tree bridges have converged, all devices on the extended network can still communicate with one another. The spanning tree algorithm is initiated automatically when bridges are powered on or when a change in the topology affects the tree. Spanning tree works with active and passive routes, thereby eliminating data loops on each bridge. The algorithm determines which ports to use to forward packets. Some ports are blocked to form a loop-free topology. Spanning tree also provides loop detection, the backup of data paths, and user-configured and seamless interoperability.

The Spanning Tree Protocol has some disadvantages. All the forwarding tables are cleared every time the spanning tree is reconfigured, causing a broadcast storm as the tables are being reconstructed. In a network of bridges that are unstable, spanning tree can disable the network by constantly broadcasting for updates to recreate the spanning tree.

NOTE Spanning tree never has more than one active data route between two end stations.

For each bridge, the spanning tree algorithm determines which ports to use to forward data and which ports to block to form a loop-free topology.

The spanning tree features are as follows:

- **Loop detection**   Detects and eliminates physical data loops in the LAN.
- **Backup data paths**   When a primary path fails, the algorithm can respan to discover redundant paths and enable those paths to become the forwarding path.
- **User configurability**   Many of the spanning tree parameters can be adjusted to create a more efficient network path for data. Some factors used to determine the root ports and designated LANs that can be configured are bridge priority, port costs, and path cost. We will discuss these later in further detail. Using the spanning tree algorithm allows a bridge to be added anywhere in a LAN without creating a loop.

The Spanning Tree Protocol works with Bridge Protocol Data Units (BPDUs). Each bridge sends out BPDUs at startup (see Figure 3-6).

The fields in the BPDU are as follows:

- **Flags**   Used to indicate a topology change.
- **Root ID**   A number composed of the assigned bridge priority and the bridge MAC address of the root bridge.
- **Root Cost**   The cost of the total path to the root bridge from the bridge sending the BPDU.
- **Bridge ID**   The ID of the bridge sending the BPDU, composed of the bridge priority (2 bytes) and the bridge MAC address (6 bytes).
- **Port ID**   Made up of the configured port priority and the interface number (the order of circuit creation).

35 Bytes

Protocol ID	Version	Message Type	Flags	Root ID	Root Cost	Bridge ID	Port ID	Message Age	Max Age	Hello Time	Forward Delay
2 Bytes	1 Byte	1 Byte	1 Byte	8 Bytes	4 Bytes	8 Bytes	2 Bytes	2 Bytes	2 Bytes	2 Bytes	2 Bytes
				Bridge Priority 2 MAC address 6		Bridge Priority 2 MAC address 6	Port Priority Interface #				

Figure 3-6   The 35-byte BPDU that bridges participating in the Spanning Tree Protocol will send out

- **Message Age**   Timers used for message aging and other configuration information.

- **Max Age**   The message age value at which the stored configuration in the message is considered too old and is discarded.

- **Hello Time**   The time that elapses between the sending of configuration messages by a bridge that assumes itself to be the root bridge.

- **Forward Delay**   A parameter that prevents a bridge from temporarily forwarding data packets to and from a link until news of a topology change has spread to all parts of a bridged network. This represents the transition period to give all links that need to go into the blocking state time to turn off before new links are turned on.

The first step in the operation of the spanning tree algorithm is the election of the root bridge. The bridge with the lowest priority value becomes the root. The root bridge will be at the top of the logical tree bridge topology. When spanning tree is initialized in a bridge network, all bridges declare themselves to be the root by issuing BPDUs (refer to Figure 3-6). At the time the BPDU is first sent out, the root bridge and the bridge ID are the same for all bridges trying to declare themselves the root bridge. The BPDU also contains the bridge priority and MAC address of the bridge. Bridge priority is an assigned parameter (assigned by the administrator) and is the primary factor in determining which bridge becomes the root bridge. The bridge with the lowest priority will be the root bridge (the administration can set the priority). If bridges have equal priority, the bridge with the lowest MAC address will be elected root. (Be careful, because this may be the oldest bridge on the network.)

The first time a bridge sees a BPDU from a bridge with a lower priority than its own, it stops generating all BPDU packets and forwards only the received BPDU from that bridge. After the election is complete, only the root bridge generates BPDUs; all other bridges in the network update and forward packets they receive. The bridges propagate BPDUs to all other bridges and out to all interfaces. Each subsequent bridge that receives the BPDU adds its interface-assigned path cost to the root cost in the BPDU and propagates it out to ports where it is the designated bridge. BPDUs are *only* originated by the root bridge; all that other bridges do is to forward out the BPDU generated by the root bridge.

After the root bridge has been determined, the next step is to eliminate the loops in the topology. This task is done by enabling only one path to the root from each bridge. All the bridges will determine a least-cost path to the root bridge by reading the root cost field in the BPDU (refer to Figure 3-6) received on all bridge interfaces and choosing the best offer. All bridges listen to the BPDUs received on all their ports. Each BPDU contains a path cost to the route (root cost). The bridge has a path cost assigned to each port, which it adds to the root cost contained within the incoming BPDU. This defines the new root cost (the cost to the root). The interface receiving the lowest cumulative cost to the root bridge becomes the root port. The port that has the lowest-cost path to the root is put in the forwarding state.

When the root bridge generates a BPDU, the initial cost is zero. A bridge that receives a BPDU from the root bridge adds its interface-assigned path cost to the BPDU and propagates it out to all interfaces.

 NOTE The interface cost is configurable. A formula like 100,000/speed of the port is recommended to assign the highest-speed links the lowest cost. Failure to configure the port cost may result in lower-speed links becoming primary in the spanning tree configuration.

Each subsequent bridge to receive that BPDU adds its interface-assigned path cost to the root cost in the BPDU and propagates it out to all interfaces. The cumulative root cost values of the BPDUs received on all bridged interfaces are compared, and the interface that received the lowest root cost becomes the root port. After each bridge has chosen its root port, a bridge must be selected as the designated bridge for each LAN segment. The designated bridge is responsible for accepting traffic from that segment and forwarding to the root bridge. It is the only bridge that forwards data to that LAN segment. The designated bridge is the bridge with the lowest cost path to the root bridge. The ports on the bridge responsible for forwarding data are called the designated LAN ports. All bridges on the LAN (even those not designated) continue to receive BPDUs. This is essential because all bridges need to know if there is to be a topology change.

The final step is to break loops that exist in the network topology by causing bridges to block redundant ports. Any port that is not the root port or a port designated to a LAN is blocked. Blocked ports will not forward traffic to or accept traffic from a LAN segment. Blocked ports are held in reserve to be used as redundant paths, which provide fault tolerance. All designated bridges enable and place in the forwarding state the following ports:

- **Root port** The single port that offers the lowest path cost to the root
- **Designated port** Any port connected to a LAN and for which the bridge offers the best path to the root

The steps in the spanning tree algorithm are as follows.

1. A root bridge is selected by comparing the bridge IDs of each bridge in the network. The bridge with the lowest ID (the best priority and/or MAC address) wins.

2. The spanning tree algorithm then selects the designated bridge for each LAN. If more than one bridge is connected to the same LAN, the bridge with the lowest path cost to the root is selected as the designated bridge. In case of duplicate path costs, the bridge with the lowest bridge ID is selected as the designated bridge.

3. The nondesignated bridges on the LANs put each port that has not been selected as a root port into a blocked state. In the blocked state, a bridge still listens to hello BPDUs so that it can act on any changes made in the network (if a designated bridge fails) and change its state from blocked to forwarding data.

Through this process, the spanning tree algorithm reduces a bridged LAN network of arbitrary topology into a single spanning tree. With the spanning tree, no more than one active data path exists between any two end stations, thus eliminating data loops.

Each circuit involved in the spanning tree will be in one of the following states:

- **Listening** During this intermediate state, the port is listening to BPDUs to determine who the root is and whether this port goes into a blocking or forwarding state.

- **Learning** During this intermediate state, the bridge forwarding tables are being built.

- **Forwarding** This state enables data to be received or transmitted through the port.

- **Blocked** This state prevents ports from sending or receiving data. BPDUs are being forwarded.

 NOTE At the initialization of the spanning tree algorithm, all ports are blocked. At the conclusion of the spanning tree algorithm, all bridge ports are in either the blocking or forwarding state.

In the event of a logical change, the spanning tree algorithm may change the state of some ports. Decisions are always native based on incoming port information; tiebreakers always look for the lowest number. The order is as follows: lowest cost, lowest bridge priority, lowest MAC address, lowest port priority, and finally, lowest port index (see Table 3-1).

Changes in topology cause traffic to stop while the setup is rearranged. The root bridge is always a forwarding position and is not involved in topology changes. It can continuously forward traffic. Even during topology changes, however, BPDUs are still received. In fact, all ports generate BPDUs until the loops in the topology have been eliminated. Root bridges continuously send BPDUs every two seconds even after the topology changes have been completed. The root bridge does not block any of its ports when the spanning tree algorithm has completed.

Table 3-1 The Fields Used in the Event of a Tie to Determine the Root Port

Bridge priority	The port that received a BPDU from a bridge with the lowest priority becomes the root port.
	If bridge priorities are equal:
MAC address	The port that received a BPDU from a bridge with the lowest MAC address becomes the root port.
	If bridge priority and MAC address are equal:
Port priority	The port that received a BPDU from the port with the lowest priority becomes the root port.
	If the port priorities are equal:
Interface number	If everything else is equal then, the interface number contained within the BPDU is used as the tiebreaker.

NOTE A bridge that has a blocked port cannot be the root bridge.

This new configuration is bounded by a time factor. If the designated bridge fails or is physically removed, other bridges on the LAN detect this situation when they do not receive hello BPDUs within the maximum age time (refer to Figure 3-6). This event triggers a new configuration process in which a new bridge is selected as the designated bridge. A new configuration is also created if the root bridge fails.

Transparent bridging overall gives the engineer a powerful tool that does not require host reconfiguration or changes to packet formats. Transparent bridging has addressing requirements and can provide a quick fix to certain network performance problems. When spanning tree uses its default settings, the spanning tree algorithm generally provides acceptable results. The algorithm, however, may sometimes produce a tree with poor network performance. In this case, the administrator must adjust the bridge priority, port priority, and path cost as necessary to shape the tree to meet network performance expectations.

A transparent bridge with spanning tree enabled offers the following advantages:

- Because the bridge is responsible for forwarding packets, no changes are required at the end station, and all sections of the bridged network appear as one layer 2 LAN (one broadcast domain).

- Network changes, like moving a workstation from segment to segment, are made easily because the transparent bridge notes the new location of a workstation or resource.

- The spanning tree algorithm automatically reconfigures new paths between LANs if the primary path goes down.

The transparent bridge has the following disadvantages:

- Transparent bridges do not enable parallel or multiple paths.

- The backup paths are idle during normal operation, wasting network bandwidth.

- No provision for load balancing exists in the case of congested paths or bridges. Alternate paths are used only if a link failure occurs.

- Network management is more difficult because the transparent bridge uses all network components as part of one large, flat network.

In a token ring environment, a second type of bridge may also be used. In addition to the typical header and address information, a field called the routing information field is added. This routing information field is used to determine the specific techniques of a bridge between token rings. The source route bridge is also a MAC layer bridge.

Source Route Bridge

The source route bridge was developed by IBM for transporting frames in a token ring network. The bridge does not maintain forwarding tables; it relies on information within packets that are received to determine which port to forward packets to. The burden of route discovery and router retention in this environment is placed on the end station. A source route bridge passes information that it is told to pass by reading the packet to determine what to do. The source creates packets with path information inside its token ring frame.

Source routing bridges are not considered transparent because they rely on the end stations for determining the route the packet should take through the network. A process called route discovery is used to find the cost of all paths for the communication session. Through this process, the route is discovered using broadcast packets (discovery packets) sent between the source and the destination end station.

Source route bridging is used in token ring environments. A source route bridge links token ring LANs and provides the software needed to move a frame between the rings.

The characteristics of source route bridging include source station responsibility for determining the path that a bridge frame will use to reach a destination. The source station has the capability to perform a route discovery to learn all the potential paths between itself and the desired destination.

The end station is responsible for maintaining routing tables that define its route to all nodes with which it must communicate. If no route information is available, the end station must implement route discovery.

A typical discovery process might go as follows. The source node determines the destination is not on the local ring. The source then checks its routing table for route information to the destination node. Route information consists of ring/bridge pair identifiers. If the source node does not know the route, the source node sends an explorer frame on the network.

NOTE   The token ring end station will go out on the local ring to make sure the station is not there.

The source route bridge accepts the explorer frame and adds the following routing information: the number of the ring from which the frame came, its assigned bridge number, and the number of the ring to which the frame is being copied. The bridge then forwards the frame to all adjacent rings except the ring from which the frame came. Each bridge along a path adds its bridge number and the number of the ring to which the frame is copied (forwarded).

Once at the destination node, the frame contains the route it took to get there. The destination node returns the frame with a bit set indicating that this route information should be read in reverse.

Each source route bridge that receives the frame uses the route information contained within the frame to forward to the next ring.

When the source node receives the response to its explorer frame, it updates its routing tables and uses that route information for all subsequent communication with that node.

In a token ring network, more than one route could exist between two nodes (see Figure 3-7).

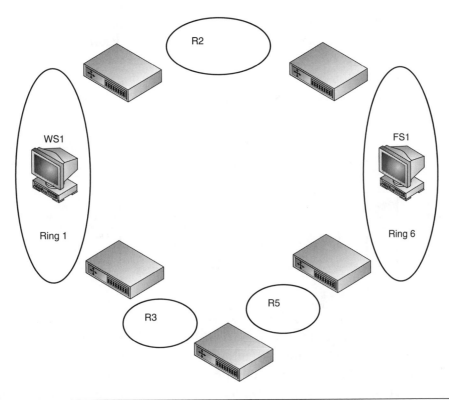

Figure 3-7   For workstation 1 on ring 1 to get to file server 1 on ring 6, it can choose one of two paths: either it could go through ring 3 and ring 5 or it may decide to go through ring 2. This is different from a transparent bridge, where this configuration could cause looping. In a token ring environment, an end station must choose one path to direct its traffic over.

Source route frames have a routing information field (RIF) in the packet headers, essentially a list of bridges that a packet should traverse to reach its destination. For source route purposes, the most important part of the frame is the RIF. Each bridge interface is represented by a routing designator (RD), the 2-byte number used in the RIF. This field contains the routing information needed by the bridge to forward a frame. The RIF, however, is an optional field. It is needed only if the frame is going to leave the ring. The RIF, when used, is actually placed at the beginning of the frame data field. The source route bridge must be able to quickly determine the presence of the RIF field. It examines the first bit of the source address to do so.

If the bit is set to zero, the frame does not contain routing control information and is not a candidate for bridging. It is only forwarded on the ring it arrived from. If the bit is set to one, the frame contains routing control information and should be examined by the bridge. The following illustration is a simple token ring frame with the first bit of the source address set to zero. No RIF is present.

Standard Token ring Frame

Start Delimeter (SD)	Access Control (AC)	Frame Control (FC)	Destination Address (DA)	Source Address (SA) First bit of SA set to zero	Destination Service Access (DSAP)	Source Service Access (SSAP)	Control	Info	Frame Check Sequence (FCS)	End Delimeter (ED)	Frame Status (FS)

Three types of source route frames exist:

- The all routes broadcast (ARB), also referred to as all routes explorer (ARE) or all paths explorer (APE), is forwarded through every path in the network. Bridges add their RDs to the RIF field and use this information to prevent loops by never crossing the same RD twice. When the ARB arrives at the destination from a source, the RIF contains a RD path through the bridges. Flipping the RIF direction bit turns the RIF into a path from destination to source.

- Single route broadcast (SRB), also known as spanning tree explorer (STE).

- Specifically routed frame (SRF).

The RIF is subdivided into the following two sections: routing control fields and RDs (see Figure 3-8).

Routing Control Fields

The fields within the routing control are defined as follows:

- Routing type:

    0xx for SRF

    10x for ARE

    11x for STE

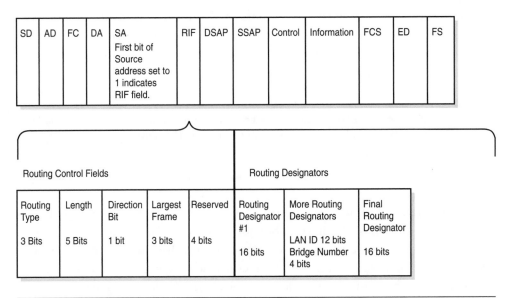

Figure 3-8   This is a token ring source route frame with routing information included.

- **Length**   A 5-bit field indicates the total length of the RIF in bytes. Values are from 2 to 30 bytes.

- **Direction bit**   One bit that shows the direction of the frame source to destination or destination to source. If it is set to one in an SRF, the route designators should be read in reverse. In an SRB and ARE, it is always set to zero.

- **Largest frame size**   A 3-bit field representing the maximum-size packet that all devices can accept. A device may need to decrement this field, but it cannot be incremented.

- **Reserved**   Four bits reserved for future use.

Routing Designators (RDs)

RDs are 16 bits in length and consist of a LAN ID and a bridge number. The LAN ID is a 12-bit field that specifies the network ring number. Each ring in the network must have a unique LAN ID. The bridge number is a 4-bit field that specifies a particular bridge in the token ring environment. It does not have to be unique except when two bridges are connected to the same rings (parallel bridges). The last bridge designator will always be zero because the bridges on the next ring are unknown. (There is always one more ring than bridge, so the final bridge is represented by a zero.)

One or more route designators define the path from source to destination. The source route bridge specification indicates that the RIF field can contain a maximum of 14 designators. However, token ring chip manufactures reduced that number to a maximum of eight rings (seven bridges).

 NOTE Nortel Network equipment enables only seven rings and six bridges in its source route bridge implementation on the BayRS routers.

Token ring uses the RD field in this manner. Each ring is assigned a unique ring number, and each bridge has a bridge number. Together they form the routing designator. When an ARB frame is forwarded, each bridge that is involved in forwarding the frame adds its bridge number and the ring number it is forwarding the frame to. When a bridge receives a frame to forward, it looks in the RIF field at the RDs and examines the type of frame (ARB, SRB, or SRF).

If the ring the bridge wants to forward the frame on is already in the RIF field of an ARB or SRB frame, the bridge discards the frame because it has already circled the target ring. This helps to avoid loops, as frames do not recircle rings they have already been on.

If the next ring the bridge wants to forward the frame to is not in an ARB or SRB frame, the bridge adds its RD (bridge number and next ring number) to the frame's RIF and forwards it to that ring.

If a ring number, bridge number, and ring number combination match is in a non-broadcast frame, the bridge forwards the frame to the indicated ring.

If no ring number, bridge number, or ring number combination match is in the non-broadcast frame, the bridge discards the frame.

In general, application software running at the end station determines what combination of the previous frame types will be used. Source route bridges can be configured to pass only specific types of frames and block certain frames—especially SRB frames, which are used in a source route bridge/spanning tree combination network. Blocking SRB frames means that no spanning tree frames will enter the token ring portion of the network.

Five scenarios can occur in determining a route:

- Source node sends an ARB and uses the first ARB to come back.

- Source node sends an ARB and uses the first SRF to come back.

- Source node sends an SRB and uses the first SRB to come back.

- Source node sends an SRB and uses the first SRF to come back.

- Source node sends an SRB and uses an ARB for return.

Vendors must consider the following when developing source route bridging capabilities in their devices:

- Token ring specifications and limitations. The original specifications called for two-port bridges only. Now each implementation needs to compensate for multiport bridges.

- IBM imposed a seven-hop limit (eight rings and seven bridges). Bridges compatible with the IBM standards must keep this in mind.

- Vendors must make sure their devices can interoperate with all source route specifications.

- Vendors must make sure that the source route bridge is tolerant of loops in the topology.

Source route bridging has its problems. It is even more broadcast-intensive than transparent bridging because each host must send out broadcasts to find paths to other nodes, rather than just the bridge broadcasting for the entire network. In addition, some method within the host software must be able to manage the RIF fields. Good client software has some way of maintaining multiple paths to remote hosts and getting rid of paths to hosts that are no longer active. Few hosts, however, have such software; in most cases, a reboot is required if a bridge fails and the network topology changes.

On the other hand, to segment a token ring network, SRB is just about the only choice. Like transparent bridging, it enables the engineer to improve network performance by allowing traffic areas to be segmented and bridged.

Translational Bridging

One type of transparent bridge, the translational bridge, can provide network connections between layers of different protocols at the physical and data link layer. It converts the frame formats of one media type into the frame format of another media type—for example, from token ring to Ethernet, or Ethernet to FDDI.

The process flow for the translation of token frame to Ethernet is as follows. When a token ring frame arrives at the translational bridge, the RIF field is removed. A new field called frame length is added. The destination and source address are converted to canonical form. The routing information bit of the source address is cleared (the beginning of the source address was set to one to indicate the presence of RIF fields). The data fields are not changed. A similar process occurs in reverse when an Ethernet frame arrives at the bridge destined for the token ring network.

Forwarding Tables, RIF Tables, and Table Management

As discussed earlier, when a transparent bridge (and, as we will see, a switch) is brought onto the network, it begins to build forwarding tables based on source MAC addresses from packets that are sent onto the LAN. These bridges associate MAC addresses with the ports that received these data frames. Once they have built a table, they can forward frames based on information in the forwarding table. Until the forwarding table is built, bridges flood all frames out of all ports.

NOTE When a bridge first comes up, it does not provide any advantages until it can build a forwarding table.

If a workstation or MAC address is moved from one port of the bridge (or switch) to another port, the bridge does not know of this change until it receives a packet with the source MAC coming in from another port. In this situation, the bridge merely writes a new entry into the forwarding table for this MAC address and its new port association. Because the forwarding table is read in a Last In, First Out (LIFO) manner, the latest entry for this MAC address is the only one the bridge sees.

Part of table maintenance is a technique called aging. Aging is the process of removing addresses from the table if they have not been accessed for a period of time. The administrator can set the time allocation, after which the addresses should be purged from the table. This frees up space in the bridge for new entries. Some vendors (including Nortel Networks) do not age out the forwarding table by default. In these cases, it is essential to make sure that enough space is allocated in the bridge's memory to hold all addresses on the network (generally, the amount of memory allocated is a configurable parameter). Any time an address cannot fit into the forwarding table (or perhaps has been purged from the table) and the bridge fails on lookup for it, the bridge needs to broadcast all packets going to the address. This can cause excessive broadcasts on the network, which is not desirable at all.

RIF tables, on the other hand, are maintained by client software running on token ring end stations. These end stations are responsible for sending out broadcast packets to find paths to every other node they want to communicate with in the token ring network (as discussed in detail previously). The reliability and capabilities of client software on these end stations differ. Better software is able to recover from faults and maintain multiple paths to single destination addresses. Other software may need to be rebooted if bridges or paths to end stations become unavailable.

Source route bridges do not maintain any type of tables. They merely forward packets based on the information in the RIF field. However, Nortel Networks BayRS router software can be configured to maintain token ring tables and support token ring end stations within the router/bridge itself. These routers, acting in a bridging mode, can send out token ring broadcast packets and maintain tables to all destination nodes. This is known as token ring end station support and is one of the configuration options for a BayRS router.

Switching Fundamentals

Switches are multiport devices that create paths to send packets on directly from specific sources to the proper destinations. Sounds like a bridge, doesn't it? When separating networks into different collision domains in the past, bridges were used. Early bridges had only two ports, so a single network could be separated only into two collision domains.

NOTE Ever notice the switching symbol and wonder where it came from? In the past, switches were only two-port devices, as shown in the following illustrations. Now, doesn't the latter illustration look like the universal-switching symbol (χ)?

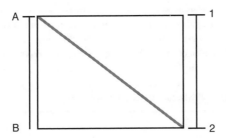

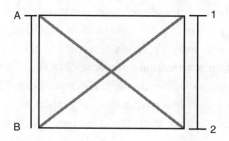

Then along came switches. Switches work with bridging technology; however, they are faster and have many ports that can even be of different speeds. Switches are capable of multiple conversations at once and also enable VLANs. We will discuss VLANs at the end of this chapter. In a switch, only all workstations connected to the same port are considered one collision domain. This separates workstations on different ports into separate collision domains. To achieve maximum speed and throughput, each workstation could have its own port and every workstation would be in its own collision domain.

When bringing up ports on switches, the Spanning Tree Protocol must be used when loops in the network topology occur. This forces the ports to come up in a blocked mode, and it takes about a minute (that is the specification—one minute) for the listening and learning state until the port actually comes up. This is not an error; it is the way the Spanning Tree Protocol works. Many manufacturers offer a fast start option that enables the ports to come up forwarding, but if they receive a BPDU from an upstream switch (indicating a possible spanning tree loop), they immediately go into the listening learning mode and run the complete Spanning Tree Protocol algorithm.

CAUTION In an environment where workstations are directly connected to switches, spanning tree should be disabled on workstation ports. Because only a workstation is connected to the port, we are not concerned with loops. Failure to disable the Spanning Tree Protocol can cause these workstations to fail when first booting up. The minute or so it takes for the spanning tree algorithm to run may cause a Dynamic Host Configuration Protocol (DHCP) failure.

By using switching technologies, designers can build high-speed, flexible networks. Multiple switches in a single LAN configuration can help to overcome distance limitations caused by Ethernet and enable users in different parts of the building to be part of the same broadcast domain.

NOTE   Remember Ethernet and Cat 5 cabling have a limit of 100 meters after which a repeater is necessary. This means that users in older networks can be only 100 meters away from each other at maximum. With the advent of VLANs, users could still be only 100 meters from a switch or repeater, but with inter-switch connections, users all over the campus network can be in the same broadcast domain.

Older technology limited the number of workstations in a LAN. There can be more workstations in a LAN when using switching.

Switch Types

Two major types of switches exist: the frame switch and the cell switch. Nortel has many products that fall into each of these two categories. As we get further into specific technologies later in this book we will review each of them.

In general, however, frame switches connect each node or workstation directly to one port on the switch. The use of a dedicated switch port eliminates collision. Each port of the frame switch must integrate MAC layer functionality because the port must be capable of examining the incoming frame and extracting the destination address. Frame switches are used with conventional LAN frames to increase performance and enable VLANs. Nortel Networks has a range of frame switch products, including the BayStack product line and the Passport layer three switches. These will be discussed in more detail in the product section of this book.

Cell-switched networks use fast and efficient hardware-based switching nodes to provide high throughput. These networks operate over very low-error-rate, high-speed digital links. The short length of cells simplifies the switching hardware because the queues within the switching nodes contain only cells of the same length. The short, fixed-length cells reduce the variation in network transit delays that can result from data blocks of irregular length, which take inconsistent lengths of time to process and to transmit in the queues. Small cells also shorten the transit delay through the network. ATM products use this type of switching by converting Ethernet packets to cells and then back again. Cell switches are the future of voice and video by providing ultimate scalability, performance, and virtualization. They offer optimal mixed-application support. More information about cell switching will be presented in the technology-specific chapter about the Centillion switches and ATM.

Switch Forwarding Technologies

Two different technologies are used in forwarding packets through a switch: the cut-through method and the store and forward method. A cut-through switch starts to transmit the packet before it has completely received the entire packet. In fact, the cut-through switch begins transmission to the end point as soon as it determines the destination MAC address. The advantage of cut-through switches is low latency; however, because cut-through switches do not check for the integrity of the entire frame before starting transmission, they can propagate bad packets and send out corrupted frames. The store and forward switch receives the entire frame into its buffer before forwarding it. By waiting to read the entire frame, a store and forward can make more involved routing decisions and can also filter out bad packets and protect destination LANs from corrupt frames. One disadvantage of the store and forward switch is latency.

Virtual LANs (VLANs)

As we mentioned before, in a traditional shared media network, traffic generated by a station is propagated to all other stations on the local segment. For all given stations on shared Ethernet, the local segment is considered the collision domain because traffic on the segment has the potential to cause an Ethernet collision. The local segment is also the broadcast domain because any broadcast is sent to all stations on the local segment.

Broadcast Domain

What exactly is a *broadcast domain*? It is a segment of the network onto which broadcasts will be propagated. A broadcast domain can be composed of many collision domains. Usually, a router defines the boundary of the broadcast domain because broadcasts do not cross the router (see Figure 3-9). Although Ethernet bridges and switches divide a network into smaller collision domains, they do not affect the broadcast domain.

A VLAN is a collection of switch ports that make up a single broadcast domain. A *VLAN* can be defined for a single switch, or it can span multiple switches. VLANs are logical entities created in the software configuration to control traffic flow. Membership in workgroup segments can be determined logically instead of by user location and adds, moves, and changes can be easily configured as the network evolves. In simple terms, a VLAN can be thought of as a mechanism to fine-tune broadcast domains.

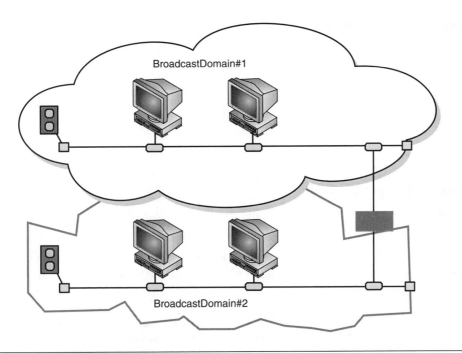

Figure 3-9 Broadcast domains separated by a router

VLANs enable boundaries of a broadcast domain to be defined through software and by users' needs. Administrators are no longer bound by hardware to define which workstations are part of which broadcast domains. The very definition of a VLAN is a flexible, software-defined boundary, independent of physical media. A VLAN can be created in a switch according to the specific needs of each organization. Just like in any LAN, there will be low latency and wire speed communications between the members of the VLAN. Administrators choose which ports in the switch should be part of this virtual LAN. Workstations attached to the ports may become part of the VLAN if they meet certain criteria. VLANs can support network segmentation in many different ways because they enable more flexibility in choosing users to be part of the VLAN. Several ports of the same switch or ports from multiple switches can be part of a single VLAN. Two ports on the same switch physically next to each other can be part of separate VLANs—or members of entirely separate networks.

Types of VLANs

Two major types of VLANs are used to segment users based on different administrative needs:

- Port-based VLANs
- Policy-based VLANs

Port-Based VLANs

The first type of VLAN, the port-based VLAN, is the simplest and most common. In a port-based VLAN, membership is based on explicitly configured ports. Once a port is a member of the VLAN, all workstations, hubs, and so on plugged into that port become a member of that VLAN. When creating a port-based VLAN on a switch, you assign a VLAN identification number (VID) and specify which ports belong to the VLAN.

 NOTE A VID is used to coordinate VLANs across multiple switches.

Port-based VLANs can carry any type of data frame. Membership for the data frame in a port-based VLAN is a function of the port on which the traffic came into the switch (the ingress port). The MAC address of the port is directly connected to the VLAN.

The advantage of this VLAN is that it is simple to configure. The disadvantage, however, is that because workstations are not VLAN-aware, it would be necessary to reconfigure ports to move workstations to another port in a switch.

Figure 3-10 shows two port-based VLANs: one for authors and one for editors. Ports are assigned to each port-based VLAN. For an editor (Lisa, for example) to become part of the author VLAN, the port the editor is attached to (in this example, port 2/4) is moved from the editor VLAN to the author VLAN. Moving the port affects all workstations attached to this port. The other option is to use move the user to another port that is already part of the author's port-based VLAN. This may not always be a viable option.

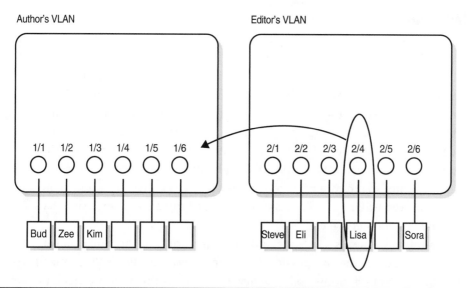

Figure 3-10   Two port-based VLANs. Moving Lisa from the editor's VLAN to the author's VLAN requires that she change ports.

Policy-Based VLANs

The second type of VLAN, the policy-based VLAN, uses the type information in a packet to determine membership in the VLAN. Frames are associated with the VLAN based on frame content. A policy-based VLAN can span multiple ports. Specifically, membership in a policy-based VLAN is determined by examining the Protocol Type field of the frame and by determining the VID on that value. A given port may be a member of policy-based VLANs in addition to being a member of IP-subnet VLANs and port-based VLANs. A port's membership in a VLAN is determined by traffic coming into the port. A policy-based VLAN enables ports to be dynamically added to the VLAN based on traffic coming into the port.

The three criteria that can change port membership represent three subtypes of the policy-based VLAN. They are as follows:

- MAC VLAN
- Protocol-based VLAN
- IP subnet VLAN

MAC VLANs

MAC-based VLANs offer the network manager the capability of defining a VLAN composed of specific end stations. It is a subset of policy-based VLANs, using a source MAC address in the frame to associate the frames with the VLAN. In a MAC-based VLAN, the MAC address of the workstation itself determines the membership in the VLAN. Traffic is sent to all workstations that have MAC addresses defined as members of this specific VLAN. Members are associated only if the end station MAC address is contained in a predefined list of allowed MAC addresses. MAC-based VLANs are used primarily for security. By combining MAC-based VLANs with other policy-based VLANs, certain users can be permitted to access specific services that may be granted or denied to other users. This is true even when multiple users are connected to a single switch port via a shared media hub or another switch.

The advantages of this VLAN include a high level of security. Moving a workstation to a different port in the switch does not change the workstation's VLAN membership. When the workstation boots up in the new port, it finds the correct VLAN based on its MAC address. This also allows for ease of administration when making changes to the network and switch. It can be tedious to set up because the administrator must statically configure the table with all the MACs; however, this is really the most secure. Some hardware implementations use MAC-based VLANs that enable workstations to boot up and identify themselves and get included in the VLAN. Nortel Networks does not enable this dynamic MAC VLAN configuration.

Figure 3-11 could represent an educational environment in which teachers must have access to all files and servers, while students should not be able to make changes in the administrative environment. A MAC-based VLAN can be defined for teachers, which gives them access to resources such as administrative file servers. The network manager can also define a different MAC-based VLAN for students, with no access to administrative file servers. Switches enable multiple MAC-based VLANs to overlap on the same switch ports.

Protocol VLANs

In a protocol-based VLAN, traffic is determined to be part of the VLAN based on its layer 3 protocol. These VLANs are used to pass protocols through the switch without needing a router. The protocols include IP, IPX, AppleTalk, DECnet, NetBIOS, and so on, as well as user-defined protocols. There can be an IP, AppleTalk, and IPX VLAN associated with any port or ports in the switch. IPX traffic, for example, flows to all ports that are associated with the IPX VLAN. Ports associated with other protocols do not see that traffic.

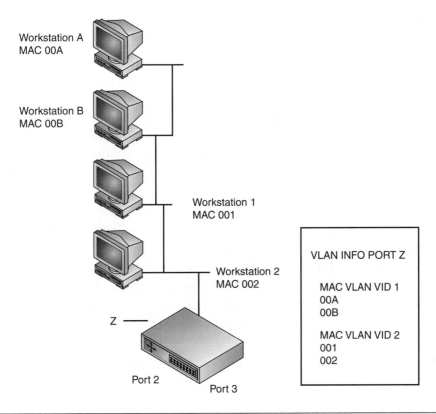

Figure 3-11   This figure demonstrates two MAC-based VLANs associated with a single port. MAC addresses of all the workstations on the network have been defined and placed into one of the two VLANs.

A network administrator can create an IPX protocol VLAN and place ports carrying substantial IPX traffic into this new VLAN. This arrangement localizes traffic and ensures that only ports associated with the IPX VLAN receive this traffic.

An administrator must be careful when creating protocol VLANs to create only one of the same type of VLAN per port. If an AppleTalk VLAN is on the port, there can only be one AppleTalk VLAN. Otherwise, a frame will not know which policy VLAN to belong to. If the administrator created two AppleTalk-based VLANs on a single port, AppleTalk frames would not know which AppleTalk VLAN to associate with. That is called a leaky bucket port because packets do not know to which VLAN they belong. Of course, there can also be an IPX VLAN and an IP VLAN. This is because those are two different protocol types. When moving a workstation to a different port on the switch, care must be taken to ensure that a protocol-based VLAN has been defined at that port.

IP Subnet VLANs

An IP subnet VLAN is a subset of a protocol VLAN. VLAN membership is determined by the IP subnet. Examination is made to the layer 3 protocol portion of the packet entering the switch. However, subsequent packet examination is necessary, as an IP subnet is based on the source IP address of the packet. Workstations become members of this VLAN if their IP address is part of the VLAN IP subnet. Traffic is determined to be part of the VLAN based on the source IP address. This type of VLAN is most similar to actual IP subnets and classical network subdivisions. The IP VLAN enables imitations of actual network subnets without physical boundaries because workstations can be on the same subnet anywhere within the campus network of switches.

More specifically, IP subnet VLANs enable network managers to create VLANs based on IP address prefixes. A frame's membership in a subnet-based VLAN is based on the IP source address associated with a mask. Using source IP subnet-based VLANs, multiple workstations on a single port can belong to different subnets. There can also be multiple IP subnet VLANs on a single port because packet membership in the VLAN is determined by the source IP so there will be no leaky bucket and packets that do not know which VLAN to be part of. This type of subnet VLAN is most similar to traditional subnetted networks. An administrator who does not want to reconfigure the network can take the current subnets and create subnet VLANs. However, this is not the most efficient way for a network to operate. Figure 3-12 shows an example of an IP Subnet VLAN.

The whole point of VLANs is to create new criteria to determine which workstation/traffic flow is part of the broadcast domain and which is not. Physical switch and workstation locations are no longer boundaries that we must consider.

To extend VLANs across switches, however, we must have some way to identify packets sent between multiple switches as part of a specific VLAN that exists on all the switches. Furthermore, each switch must recognize parameters like VIDs from other switches to be able to place incoming data packets into the appropriate VLAN. These functions are enabled through VLAN tagging (also called trunking in some other vendor implementations).

802.1Q VLAN Tagging/Trunking Standard

The IEEE 802.1Q is the specification for standards-based frame tagging (see Figure 3-13). The specification defines a method for coordinating VLANs across multiple switches, even in a multivendor environment. In the specification, an additional 4-byte (octet) header is inserted into a frame after the source address and before the frame type.

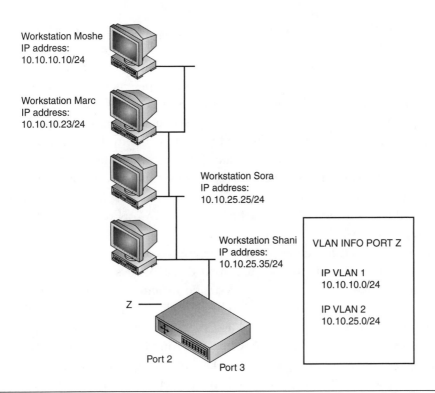

Figure 3-12   This figure shows two IP subnet VLANs on Port Z. One is of the IP subnet 10.10.10.0 and one is the IP subnet 10.10.25.0. Workstation Moshe and Marc will be in IP subnet VLAN 1, while workstations Sora and Shani will be in IP subnet VLAN 2.

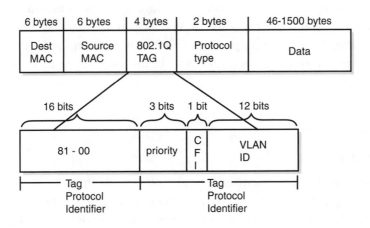

Figure 3-13   A packet constructed with the 802.1Q protocol standard

The tag contains the VID with which the frame is associated. By coordinating VIDs across multiple switches, VLANs can be extended to multiple switches.

Two 2-byte fields are used in the standard for a tag. The first set of two bytes is for the tag protocol identifier (TPID). The second two bytes represent the tag control information (TCI). The TPID field is not used yet and has the value of 8100 in all Nortel Networks' products. The TCI field (2 bytes = 16 bits) contains a priority field of 3 bits for queuing packets in a switch according to high or low priority. It also contains one bit that is used for the canonical field indicator (for token ring), and the final 12 bits are the VID. The VID is most essential because it represents the VLAN as a shared VLAN among different switches. If there was a VID #9 representing IPX VLAN on switch A, there would have to be a VID #9 defined as an IPX VLAN on switch B to have the VLANs spanning switches.

Whether or not tagged frames are sent or received is configured at the port level. Tagging is set as true or false for the port and applied to all VLANs on the port. Tagged ports trunk any number of port-based VLAN traffic to another switch. A tagged frame received on a trunk port is considered to be an explicitly tagged frame. VLAN association is derived from the tag. An implicitly tagged frame is received without a tag. The switch associates the frame with a VLAN based upon the data content of the frame or receiving port. Because no tag is present, VLAN membership is implied from the type field of the packet itself. If the packet is an IPX packet and it comes into a port with an IPX VLAN, the packet is mapped to that IPX VLAN. If the packet has an IP address associated with an IP subnet VLAN, it is placed into that VLAN. This is an extremely important concept and will be discussed in further detail in the later chapter discussing the passport switching technology. In all cases, data frames should be able to cross multiple switches and remain in the correct VLAN. Tagging helps to extend VLANs across switches and lessen our limitations and dependence on hardware even further. Tagged ports were formally called trunk ports in Nortel Networks terminology. Because of a new terminology called multilink trunking (to be discussed later), these ports are now called tagged ports.

Summary

In conclusion, we discussed many important topics in this chapter. First, we discussed general bridging technologies and followed this with specific descriptions of different types of bridging. Those included transparent bridging, source route bridging, translational bridging, and the Spanning Tree Protocol. We then discussed switching, which is based on bridging technologies. We ended the chapter with a discussion of VLANs, an enhancement available to us only with switches. For the testing of knowledge purposes, the following questions-and-answer keys have been provided.

Bridging and VLAN Study Questions

1. How does a transparent bridge build a forwarding table?
   A. It reads the source MAC address of every received frame, noting which interface the frame was received on.
   B. It reads the destination MAC address of every received frame, noting which interface the frame was received on.
   C. It reads the source network address of every received frame, noting which interface the frame was received on.
   D. It reads the destination network address of every received frame, noting which interface the frame was received on.

2. If a transparent bridge receives a frame but it has no match for the frame in its forwarding table, what does the bridge do?
   A. Drop the frame.
   B. Flood the frame.
   C. Broadcast the frame out of all interfaces.
   D. Forward the frame.

3. In the spanning tree algorithm, what comprises the bridge ID?
   A. Bridge priority and serial number
   B. Bridge priority and port priority
   C. Bridge priority and MAC address
   D. Bridge priority and interface number

4. If the bridge priorities of two bridges are equal, what is the tiebreaker to determine the root bridge in the spanning tree algorithm?
   A. The bridge with the lowest MAC address
   B. The bridge with the highest MAC address
   C. The bridge with the lowest port priority
   D. The bridge with the highest port priority

5. In the spanning tree algorithm, a bridge that forwards traffic on behalf of the LAN is called the _____.
   A. Root bridge
   B. Chosen bridge
   C. Source route bridge
   D. Designated bridge

6. In a source route bridge environment, what is responsible for determining the path that an SRB uses?
   A. Source route bridge
   B. Destination station
   C. Source station
   D. Repeater

7. What are the two sections of the RIF field in an SRB?
   A. Routing management and routing designators
   B. Routing management and routing path
   C. Routing management and routing hops
   D. Routing control and routing designators
   E. Routing control and routing path
   F. Routing control and routing hops

8. Which layer of the OSI model does the transparent bridge operate at?
   A. Physical
   B. Data Link
   C. Network
   D. Session

9. Which bridge connects similar media?
   A. Transparent bridge
   B. Source route bridge
   C. Translational bridge
   D. Source route translational bridge

10. What type of frame does the Spanning Tree Protocol use to elect a root bridge?
    A. Bridge Protocol Data Units
    B. Bridge hello packets
    C. Bridge packet updates
    D. Root Bridge Election Packets

11. What is contained in a transparent bridge's forwarding table?
    A. RIF
    B. MAC address
    C. Port ID
    D. Spanning tree ID

12. What are two major advantages of the store-and-forward method of switching? (Choose two.)
    A. It can filter out bad packets.
    B. There is low latency.
    C. It begins transmitting a packet as soon as it determines the location of the destination.
    D. It protects end stations from receiving corrupt frames.

13. Which two of the following statements is true of cell switching? (Choose two.)
    A. Cell switching connects each workstation directly to one port on the switch.
    B. Cell switching networks use extremely fast hardware to provide high throughput.
    C. Cell switching uses short, fixed-length cells to reduce the variation in transit delays.
    D. Cell switching integrates MAC layer functionality into the port itself because the port must examine each incoming packet and extract the destination address.

14. Which type of VLAN defines the traffic using the MAC address as the only determining factor?
    A. Port-based
    B. Policy-based
    C. MAC layer-based
    D. IP address based

15. Which type of VLAN defines the traffic using the type field as a determining factor?
    A. Port-based
    B. Policy-based
    C. MAC layer-based
    D. IP address-based

16. Which three statements are true about the 802.1Q standard?
    A. It provides a standardized approach to VLAN expansion.
    B. It sets the rules for VLAN definition.
    C. It supports frame prioritization.
    D. It defines the tagging rules for ports.
    E. It does not enable extending VLANs to end stations.

17. Which bridge connects dissimilar media at Layer 2?
    A. Transparent bridge
    B. Source route bridge
    C. Designated bridge
    D. Translational bridge

18. Which is *not* a benefit of transparent bridging?
    A. Minimizing collision
    B. Minimizing broadcasts
    C. Segmenting traffic
    D. Connecting segments into a single LAN

19. If a workstation moved to a different segment in a transparent bridged network, what would happen?
    A. The bridge's forwarding table will always have to flood information destined to that workstation.
    B. The bridge will never learn of the move.
    C. When the workstation sends out a packet, the bridge will see the source address and update its table.
    D. When another workstation sends a packet destined to the moved station, the bridge will learn of the station's move.

20. Which protocol prevents loops in a bridged environment?
    A. Open Shortest Path First (OSPF)
    B. Dijkstra's algorithm
    C. Spanning tree algorithm
    D. Border Gateway Protocol (BGP)

21. Bridges forward packets based on which type of address?
    A. IP address
    B. MAC address
    C. Gateway address
    D. Network Service Access Point (NSAP) address

22. What is a bridge?
   A. A device that connects modems to end user systems
   B. A device that connects LAN segments to WAN devices
   C. A device that connects and passes packets between two LAN segments
   D. A device that connects different types of networks using different LAN protocols

23. What does the bridge use the destination MAC address to determine?
   A. Which interface to forward the packet to
   B. How to route a packet across a network
   C. The interface the packet was received from
   D. The total throughput statistics for data traffic analysis

24. Which two are switching techniques? (Choose two.)
   A. Cut through
   B. ROM buffering
   C. Data fragmentation
   D. Store and forward

Here is a real challenger. Use Figure 3-14 to answer the next three questions.

25. Based on Figure 3-14 and your knowledge of spanning tree, which bridge will become the root bridge?
   A. Bridge A
   B. Bridge B
   C. Bridge C
   D. Bridge D

26. Based on Figure 3-14 and your knowledge of spanning tree, assuming all port costs are equal, which two ports will be forwarding? (Choose two.)
   A. Bridge A port ID 8002
   B. Bridge A port ID 8003
   C. Bridge B port ID 8002
   D. Bridge B port ID 8001

27. Based on Figure 3-14 and your knowledge of spanning tree, assuming all port costs are equal, which two ports will be blocked? (Choose two.)
   A. Bridge A port 8002
   B. Bridge D port 8001
   C. Bridge B port 8002
   D. Bridge B port 8001

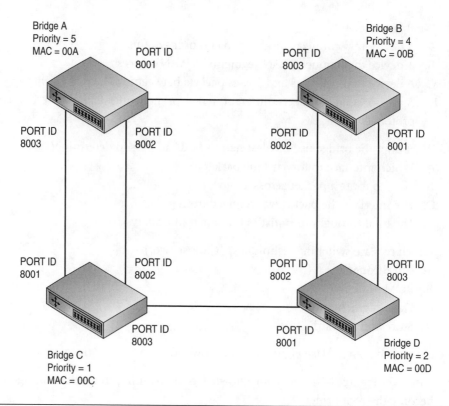

Figure 3-14 Use the information in this figure and your knowledge of the spanning tree algorithm to answer questions 25 to 27.

Answer Key

1. A. Bridges work with source MAC addresses.

2. B. A bridge floods the frame on every port except the one that the frame was received on.

3. C.

4. A.

5. D.

6. C. In source routing, it is not the bridge that controls the routing, but it is the source station. Bridges are unintelligent devices that forward packets based on the RIF.

7. **D.**

8. **B.** All bridges operate at the MAC layer of the OSI model.

9. **A.**

10. **A.**

11. **B.** A bridge's forwarding table contains MAC addresses associated with ports for forwarding purposes.

12. **A, D.** The store-and-forward method examines each packet before forwarding it. This causes latency, but prevents bad packets from getting out onto the LAN segment.

13. **B, C.** Cell switching uses extremely fast hardware and short fixed-length cells to provide excellent throughput.

14. **C.**

15. **B.** The type field is used in a Protocol VLAN to determine VLAN membership for packets.

16. **A, C, D.**

17. **D.**

18. **B.** Bridges cannot control broadcasts because they are part of layer 3 networking. That is the job of the router.

19. **C.** When a workstation moves segments, the bridge only learns of the move when the workstation sends out a packet, and the bridge records the MAC address and associates it with a new port.

20. **C.**

21. **B.**

22. **C.** A bridge works at layer 2 and connects/separates LAN segments.

23. **A.** Destination MAC addresses are used to determine where to forward packets.

24. **A, D.**

25. **C.** Bridge C has the lowest priority and will therefore become the root bridge.

26. **B, C.**

27. **A, D.**

TCP/IP

Introduction

In the previous chapter we discussed different types of layer 2 bridging and switching and their benefits. In this chapter we will begin to discuss the Transmission Control Protocol/Internet Protocol (TCP/IP) (a layer 3 addressing scheme), how it works, and its benefits. Furthermore, we will discuss different protocols that enhance the workings of TCP/IP and give us the full use of our network and the Internet.

The technologies discussed in this chapter are an essential part of the Data IP Fundamentals exam. Passing this exam, as we explained previously, is a prerequisite to achieving some of the Nortel Networks certifications, including Nortel Networks Certified Specialist and Certified Expert. In many cases the materials discussed here will give the basis for technologies and objectives for product specific exams as well.

Why TCP/IP?

TCP/IP is an industry-standard suite of protocols. This protocol was developed when the U.S. Department of Defense developed DARPA, the precursor to the Internet. TCP/IP is a standard routable networking protocol and the most complete and accepted protocol available. All modern systems offer TCP/IP support, and most large networks rely on TCP/IP for most of their network traffic because of its versatility and capability to be routed.

TCP/IP is a fat protocol that is robust, scalable, and offers a cross-platform client server framework. TCP/IP is also a technology for connecting dissimilar systems because it includes a suite of protocols (like FTP and Telnet) and works across many operating systems. TCP/IP therefore became the post facto default for the Internet, which consists of thousands of networks worldwide, including private research facilities, universities, libraries, government agencies, and private companies, all running TCP/IP.

The TCP/IP protocol was established through a series of Requests For Comments (RFCs) and is continuously evolving. Any TCP/IP user can suggest features that should be included in the protocol. New suggestions that are accepted become new RFCs and may eventually bring new features to inclusion in the protocol.

The protocol also has many utilities that we will discuss in more detail later in the book. They include the File Transfer Protocol (FTP) and the Trivial File Transfer Protocol (TFTP), used for transferring data from one machine to another in a TCP/IP network. A utility called *Telnet* provides a terminal emulation to a piece of hardware running a Telnet server. Another utility called the *Simple Network Management Protocol* (SNMP) enables the management of different types of hardware on the network through the use of the Management Information Base (MIBs).

TCP/IP also has utilities that are useful for troubleshooting. The *Packet InterNet Groper* (PING) enables the user to check connectivity to a remote workstation. *IPCONFIG* and *WINIPCFG* are utilities that enable users within the Windows operating system to view their IP information. Also, a *Route* command enables users to view their routing tables and a *Tracert* command enables users to see the path (through the networks) that a packet travels to get from the local workstation to a remote workstation. Finally, the *Address Resolution Protocol* (ARP) enables the mapping of IP addresses to MAC addresses.

Internet Protocol (IP)

The IP in TCP/IP, the *Internet protocol*, is a connectionless protocol primarily responsible for addressing and routing packets between hosts. IP is responsible for transmitting blocks of datagrams received from its upper-layer protocols. IP does not establish a session with the destination before transmitting its data, classifying it as a connectionless service. IP is therefore unreliable and delivery is not guaranteed.

IP will always make a best-effort attempt to deliver a packet. Along the way a packet might be lost, delivered out of sequence (not in the correct order), duplicated, or delayed. Additionally, an acknowledgement is not required when the packet is received. This means that IP attempts to deliver the packet, but does not make up for the fault encountered in its attempts. If an error occurs in the delivery of the datagram, the IP layer does not inform anyone. The upper-layer protocols must provide error discovery and recovery. Sequencing and reliability are also left to the functions of upper-layer protocols, such as TCP. This makes IP more versatile to integrate into a variety of hardware. Upper-layer protocols can add levels of reliability, as needed by the application.

IP provides four main functions: 1) serves as a basic unit for transfer; 2) provides protocol addressing; 3) routes datagrams or packets; and 4) enables the fragmentation of datagrams. The primary function of IP is to accept data from higher-level protocols like TCP and the User Datagram Protocol (UDP) on a source host; create a datagram; and route the datagram through the network to a destination host. The secondary functions of IP include the fragmentation and reassembly of datagrams if necessary and packet lifetime control.

IP is mostly used in conjunction with upper-layer protocols, which provide additional upper-layer functions like the guaranteed delivery of datagrams. The Internet protocol has its own four-layer model that maps to the seven-layer OSI model, as shown in Table 4-1.

IP is not concerned with the type of data in the packet either. All IP is concerned about is applying its control information to the segment received from the upper-layer protocol, presumably TCP or UDP. This control information is called an IP header, which is used to deliver the datagram to some station on the network or Internet. The IP provides a means of control on how the hosts and router should process transmitted and received packets, or when an error should be generated and when an IP packet should be discarded. The IP datagram contains an IP header and the data from upper-layer protocols (see Figure 4-1). The IP header is designed to accommodate the features of the IP layers.

Table 4-1 Mapping the IP Protocol to the Seven Layers of the OSI Model

OSI Model	Sample Protocols		IP Model
Layers 5–7 (Session, Presentation, and Application)	FTP, Telnet	SNMP, TFTP	Application
Layer 4 (Transport)	TCP	UDP	Transport
Layer 3 (Network)	IP ICMP	ARP/RARP	Internet
Layers 1–2 (Physical and Data Link)	Ethernet	Token Ring	Network Interfaces

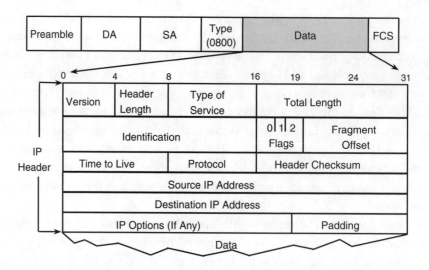

Figure 4-1 An IP datagram. Notice it is considered the data portion packaged inside an Ethernet frame header (or some other frame header on another network type).

The fields in an IP header include version, header length, type of service, total length, identification, flags, fragment offset, time to live, protocol, header checksum, source IP address, destination IP address, IP options, and padding:

- **Version**   A 4-bit field indicating IP4 or IP6. Most applications currently use IP4.

- **Header length**   A 4-bit field indicating header length.

- **Type of service**   Never implemented, it was supposed to be for indicating a packet priority of special handling in the network. This field is now being used for DiffServ and Quality of Service to indicate high or low priority for queuing.

- **Total length**   The length of the IP datagram.

- **Identification**   Uniquely identifies each datagram. It is important when datagrams are fragmented to find all the packets of the same datagram for reassembly.

- **Flags**   A 3-bit field used for fragmentation. The first bit is reserved and set to 0. The second bit indicates whether a packet can be fragmented. If it is set to 1, the packet cannot be fragmented. The last bit is used to indicate when the last fragment of a single datagram arrives. If the bit is set to 1, there are more segments; if the bit is set to 0, it indicates no more fragments.

- **Fragment offset**   Specifies an offset for each fragment and is used to reassemble the datagram.

- **Time to live (TTL)**   The number of seconds a packet is allowed to remain on the network before it is discarded. This prevents packets from looping around end-lessly on the network (unlike a bridged packet, which can loop around infinitely). Routers decrement this TTL by at least one each time the datagram passes through the router, or more than one if there is a time delay in the router. If this counter reaches 0, the datagram is discarded and an ICMP message is sent back to the station sending the datagram. The default TTL in a Nortel Networks implementation is 32.

- **Protocol**   Defines the upper-layer protocol, usually TCP or UDP.

- **Header checksum**   A mathematical calculation used to verify that the header of the packet arrived intact (not the data inside the packet).

- **IP options**   Primarily used in testing networks. This field will be used in trace functions for routers that pass the packet to record their IP addresses.

- **Padding**   Used to ensure that packets are a minimum length.

How does IP route packets? To route a packet, IP checks if the destination address is local (on the same network as the sending station—we will discuss how IP determines this based on the subnet mask). If the packet is local, IP sends the packet out of the local interface. If the destination IP address is identified as a remote address (on a different network than the source station), IP checks the local routing table for a route to the remote host. If a route is found, IP sends the packet using that route. If no specific route is found, IP attempts to send the packet to the default gateway or router advertising a default route to all networks (see Figure 4-2).

TCP/IP can be configured either manually or by using the Dynamic Host Configuration Protocol (DHCP). We will discuss how DHCP works and its benefits later. For now, we will assume we are statically configuring users with IP addresses to discuss properties of TCP/IP and its parameters. On the main tab of the TCP/IP properties (refer to Figure 4-2) are three parameters:

- **IP Address**   This is a logical 32-bit address used to identify this host. It must be unique for every host on the network. See the following section to learn more about this address.

- **Subnet Mask**   This is used to identify to the router whether another workstation is remote or local to this workstation. Every workstation that wants to communicate with TCP/IP must have at least a proper IP address and correct subnet mask. For communication out of your local network, a default gateway must be configured (see Figure 4-3).

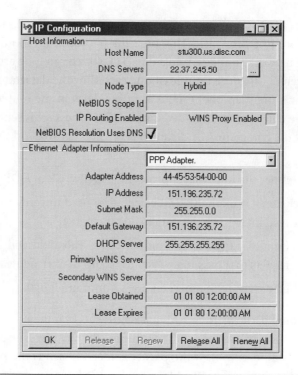

Figure 4-2 The results of a Windows (95/98) *Winipcfg* command using the *more info* extension

- **Default Gateway** Also known as the router, this is where a host sends its packets that are destined for other networks (remote packets). This parameter is not necessary for local communication within a single subnetwork.

Exercise One: Manually Configuring TCP/IP Using a Windows Operating System

To configure TCP/IP, open the TCP/IP properties. This can be done in one of two ways. The first is to go to the Network Neighborhood icon; right-click; choose Properties from the menu; and go to the TCP/IP properties of your NIC. The second way is to go to the Start menu; choose Settings, Control panel; open the network neighborhood icon from inside the Control panel; and go to the TCP/IP properties of your NIC.

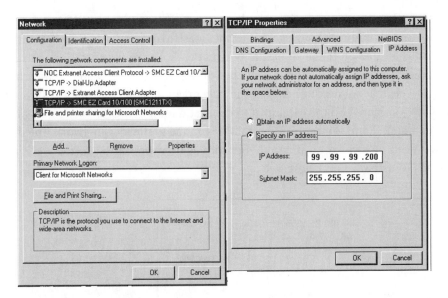

Figure 4-3   The network properties of a Windows 95 workstation and the specific TCP/IP configurations of the Network Interface Card (NIC)

IP Addressing

Each TCP/IP host is identified by a logical IP address. An *IP address* is a logical 32-bit address used to identify a host. It must be unique for every host on the network. The IP address identifies a system's location on the network, just as a street address identifies a house on a city block. Each IP address has two parts: a network ID and a host ID. The *network ID* identifies the network to which this address belongs or which systems are located on the same subnet. All systems on the same subnet must have the same network ID. This network ID must be unique to the intranetwork. Information is routed based on this portion of the IP address. If the network portion of the IP address is set to all 0's, a parameter called zero subnet enabled must be enabled.

A *host ID* identifies a workstation, server, router, or other hosts within a segment. The host ID must be unique for the specific network. The host ID is the portion of the address that identifies the individual host on the destination network. It is not used until the destination network is reached. The host ID portion of the IP address cannot be all 1's or all 0's. A host ID of all 1's represents a broadcast, while a host ID of all 0's represents a network address.

Every host on the network that wants to communicate must have at least an IP address and a subnet mask. The subnet mask is used to block out a portion of the IP address so that TCP/IP can distinguish the network ID from the host ID. When TCP/IP hosts try to communicate, they use this subnet mask to determine whether the destination host is located on the local or a remote network. For communication with a host on another network, an IP address must be configured with a default gateway. TCP/IP sends packets that are destined for remote networks to the default gateway if no other routes are configured on the local host to the destination network. If a default gateway is not configured, the communication may be limited to the local network. The default gateway must be located on the same network as the workstation so the workstation can reach its gateway (see Figure 4-4).

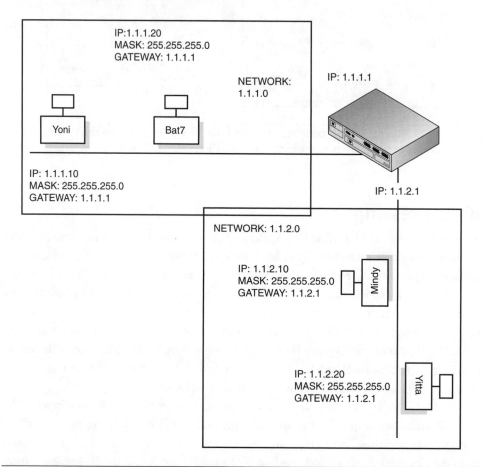

Figure 4-4 This figure shows two networks that have workstations on them. Yoni and Bat7 both have IP addresses local to network 1.1.1.0 and the same subnet mask; they also use the router at 1.1.1.1 for remote communications. Workstations Mindy and Yitta have addresses on the 1.1.2.0 network; they also have the same subnet mask; and they use 1.1.2.1 as the router for their remote communications.

NOTE Communication will fail if multiple devices use the same IP address.

IP Addresses Explained

To understand the 32-bit IP address in greater detail, it is important to understand that the IP address is composed of four 8-bit fields called octets (bytes), separated by periods. Each octet (8 bits) can be converted into a decimal number between 0 and 255. The IP address is represented as four decimal integers, with each integer corresponding to one byte/octet. This format is called *dotted decimal notation*.

To convert the octet to a decimal value, it is important to understand that each position in an octet has an assigned decimal value. A bit data set to 0 has a 0 value. A bit set to 1 can be converted to a decimal value. The total value of the decimal conversion is all the bits that are set to 1 and their bit location. The high-order bit represents a decimal value of 128. The highest value of an octet is 255, when all the bits are set to 1 (see Table 4-2).

Table 4-2 Binary Conversion to Decimal

0	0	0	0	0	0	0	1	= 1
0	0	0	0	0	0	1	0	= 2
0	0	0	0	0	1	0	0	= 4
0	0	0	0	1	0	0	0	= 8
0	0	0	1	0	0	0	0	= 16
0	0	1	0	0	0	0	0	= 32
0	1	0	0	0	0	0	0	= 64
1	0	0	0	0	0	0	0	= 128
1	0	1	0	1	0	1	0	=?
1	1	1	1	1	1	1	1	=?

Quick Quiz I

Fill in the chart

1. What should be the calculation for rows nine and ten?

Answer

Row nine: $128 + 32 + 8 + 2 = 170$

Row ten: $128 + 64 + 32 + 16 + 8 + 4 + 2 + 1 = 255$

The Internet community has defined five address classes that take into consideration networks of varying sizes. Four primary classes of IP addresses exist. The high-order bits of the IP address identify the class. Each class allocates a different number of bits to the network and to the host portion of the address. A natural mask is implied by the address class and is used to determine the network and the host portion of the IP address. For each address class, the Internet community defines the default or natural mask (see Table 4-3).

Class A addresses have the first bit set to 0; the address therefore falls between 0 and 127 (00000000 to 01111111). The network ID is the first octet and the last three octets are left for host IDs. That leaves a possibility of more than 16 million hosts ($2^{24} - 2$). Very few Class A addresses exist, actually less than 126; because the 0 is not a valid network address, the ten network address is used for private network addressing and the entire 127 network is used for loopback testing. (PINGing 127.0.0.1 actually sends an ICMP echo request to the local NIC.)

Class B addresses have the first bit set to 1 and the second bit set to 0 for a range of addresses between 128 and 191 (10000000 to 1011111). The first two octets represent the network ID and the last two octets are left for host bits. A Class B network can accommodate more than 64,000 hosts per network ($2^{16} - 2$). Approximately 16,000

Table 4-3 Internet Default Classification of IP Addresses

Class	Range	Sample Address	Mask & Number of Bits	Network Portion	Number of Hosts
Class A	0–127	10.10.10.10	255.0.0.0 or /8 bits	10.0.0.0	16,777,214
Class B	128–192	176.15.41.37	255.255.0.0 or /16 bits	176.15.0.0	65,534
Class C	193–223	200.200.200.200	255.255.255.0 or /24 bits	200.200.200.0	254
Class D	224–239	224.0.0.5	No mask defined	N/A	N/A

Class B networks are available. Because the first two octets are significant, an address of 173.10.10.10 is on a different network than 173.76.10.10.

Class C addresses are used for small LANs. The three high-order bits in a Class C address are set to binary 110 and fall in the range of 192 to 223 (1100000 to 1101111). The first three octets represent the network ID. The remaining octet (8 bits) is left for host bits. This enables only 254 hosts per network ($2^8 - 2$). Approximately 2 million Class C networks are available because the first three octets are significant. Therefore, the address 200.200.200.200 is on a different network than the address 200.200.40.0 (see Figure 4-5).

Class D addresses are used for multicasting. A Class D address has the form of the first 4 bits of the first octet that is set to 1110 and falls between 224 and 239 (11100000 to 11101111). No specific networks or hosts are used in multicasting; the entire address is significant. Multicasts work with hosts participating in a multicast group that all have the same IP multicast address. When hosts send packets using multicasts, the source and destination address are the same. Several hosts may respond to the packet (all RIP 2 routers, for example), all having the same multicast address.

What is the difference between unicast, broadcast, and multicast? A unicast is when a host sends a directed packet to another specific host and specifies the source and destination addresses. This type of packet is the least network-intensive, as all hosts look at the packet, see the MAC address is not theirs, and disregard the packet. The broadcast

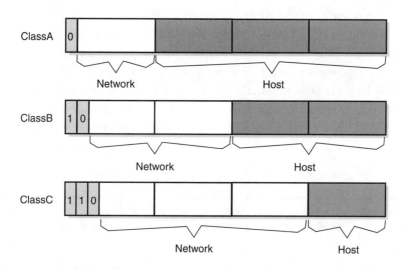

Figure 4-5 A pictorial view of the addresses and address spaces for the three major address classes

packet is the most network-intensive because it is sent to an old broadcast MAC address (FFFFFFFF). Every host on the network must process the packet until it figures out whether the packet is for them or not. Broadcast requests like DHCP require processing the packet until the host determines if it is a DHCP server and if it should process the packet (all the way up to the port level). A multicast packet is a directed broadcast to several stations. The MAC address is a multicast MAC in the case of Ethernet, so all stations that are part of the multicast group recognize the MAC address and all other hosts on the network drop the packet. It is as efficient as a unicast packet with a destination to multiple hosts.

A Class E address is available in the form of the first octet being 1111. This is not currently implemented and is still considered experimental.

A unique IP address must be assigned to each physical connection of a host to a network. A host having more than one connection to a network is *multihomed* (as in the case of a dual NIC server) and will have one IP address for each NIC. The host ID must be unique to the subnet. Every router interface has a unique network ID. A router's function is to route between networks; it can do so only by having different network IDs to route between.

Subnet Masks Explained

IP datagrams are routed based on the network portion of the address. For IP to know which portion of the address belongs to the network and which portion belongs to the host, IP depends on the subnet mask. A *subnet mask* is a 32-bit address that specifies the portion of the IP address that is going to be used to define IP networks and subnetworks (as opposed to hosts). In a mask, any bit set to a 1 defines the network address. Any bit set to 0 defines the host address. Because subnet masks are important in determining whether the destination host's IP address is located on a local or a remote network, each host on a TCP/IP network must have a subnet mask. A host has either a default mask or a custom mask, which is used when the network is divided into subnets.

NOTE   The key to understanding subnet masking is this: In a mask, any bit set to 1 defines the network address. Any bit set to 0 defines the host address.

*AND*ing is the specific process that IP uses to determine whether a packet is destined for a local or remote host. The host's address is ANDed with the subnet mask and the local network is determined. Then whenever the host tries to send a packet, the destination address of the packet is ANDed with the same mask. If both results match, the packet is destined for a local host. If the results do not match, the packet must be sent to a router or gateway.

To perform the AND process, all dotted decimal addresses and masks are changed into binary format. IP then compares the binary IP address with the binary subnet mask. The math for ANDing is as follows: Only 1 and 1 equal 1; anything else is 0. So, if a 0 is in either the address or the mask, the result will be a binary 0.

Subnetting

Subnet addressing is an extension of the Internet address scheme that enables a site to subdivide a single Internet address for use across multiple physical networks. This addressing is especially useful because only a limited number of IP network addresses are left for allocation from the network information center (InterNIC). Subnet addressing takes a portion of the Internet address and uses it to define networks within networks, or subnetworks. Defining a subnet enables an administrator to build many physical networks while using one Internet address. Subnetting uses part of the host ID to create different networks. Each subnet has a different IP address.

Subnetworks are implemented by extending the natural mask and changing some of the bits that are set to 0 (host bits) to 1 (network bits). The mask is entered when the address is configured. IP masks are entered in dotted decimal notation, and all the 1's must be successive (follow each other with no 0's in between). Subnets are important to limit the number of hosts in a single broadcast domain and for reducing network congestion by reducing broadcasting hosts.

The more bits allocated for subnets, the less bits available for hosts. Be careful when subnetting to leave the correct number of bits for host expansion. The opposite is true as well; the more bits used for hosts, the less bits are available for subnets. This may leave the network unable to accommodate new networks. Planning is essential for proper subnet assignment.

NOTE **The more bits allocated for the subnet mask, the more subnets are available, however, fewer hosts are available per subnet.**

The most crucial part in subnetting is to plan what the resulting network will look like. Figuring out the proper subnet for a network being planned requires some essential steps:

1. Determine the number of networks or hosts that are needed.

2. Determine the number of bits required to achieve that number of networks or hosts.

3. Determine the subnet mask based on the number of bits.

4. Determine the networks that are created based on that mask.

5. Determine the host addresses that are available for the newly created networks.

Once the administrator has determined that it is necessary to subnet the network, the administrator must decide the number of networks and hosts per subnet. When planning the network, the administrator must always keep in mind room for future network growth. It is then necessary to determine the number of bits needed to obtain this configuration. The number of bits needed (for host IDs or subnets) is determined by using the simple formula of $2^n - 2$ where n equals the number of bits necessary to achieve the number of subnets or hosts (see Table 4-4). For example, if we need ten subnets, at least 4 bits are required ($2^4 - 2 = 14$). This same formula is used to determine the number of bits necessary for hosts. So, if we need six hosts per subnet, we must leave at least 3 bits for host IDs. We must subtract two because a subnet or host address of all 0's or all 1's is not allowed.

Nortel Networks enables a subnet of all 0's and all 1's with a parameter called zero subnet enabled. If it is enabled on routers and switches, there is no need to subtract two networks from the formula, and every network can be utilized. This can save hundreds of host addresses that would otherwise be unusable.

Once the administrator determines the number of bits, he or she can make a new subnet mask for the network. Three items are important to note. First, the new subnet mask will begin *after* the default mask is applied. Therefore, if we are subnetting a Class A address, the subnet will be 255. Secondly, all masks are contiguous, so once we determine that we require four new network bits for our new mask, they will be the next 4 bits after the default mask. Host bits fall after the mask is complete. Lastly, network bits are set to 1; host bits are set to 0. If we require four additional network bits, they will take the form of 11110000 to fill the octet and the mask will be 240.

Table 4-4 provides an example of subnet masking. If one has a Class A address, up to three octets can be subnetted and this table could go on.

Table 4-4 Subnet Masking in Action

Number of Subnets	Number of Bits	Binary Mask	Decimal Mask
2	2 ($2^2 - 2 = 2$)	11000000	192
6	3 ($2^3 - 2 = 6$)	11100000	224
14	4 ($2^4 - 2 = 14$)	11110000	240
30	5 ($2^5 - 2 = 30$)	11111000	248
62	6 ($2^6 - 2 = 62$)	11111100	252
126	7 ($2^7 - 2 = 126$)	11111110	254
254	8 ($2^8 - 2 = 254$)	11111111	255
510	9 ($2^9 - 2 = 512$)	11111111.10000000	255.128
1022	10 ($2^{10} - 2 = 1022$)	11111111.11000000	255.192
2046	11 ($2^{11} - 2 = 2046$)	11111111.11100000	255.224

Exercise Two

For additional practice, create a table like the one above but one that goes to three octets. It is sometimes useful to understand what subnet masks look like in binary.

Table 4-4 shows that more than one entire octet can be used for subnetting. This is true only if the user has at least a Class B network. For a Class C network, a maximum of 6 bits may be subnetted. A Class C network with a 6-bit subnet enables only two hosts on the network (255.255.255.252).

NOTE It is only possible to subnet up to 30 bits. The created mask is 255.255.255.252. This mask leaves only two hosts per network and is commonly associated with a point-to-point network.

NOTE Binary calculators are very useful items. The Microsoft operating system has a built-in binary calculator.

A trick formula determines the network numbers of the newly created subnet: 256 − subnet mask = the first network ID and the increment to the next network ID. The subnet mask minus the network increment is the final network. In the case of a subnet mask of 240, where 14 networks have been created, take 256 − 240 to obtain the first network ID of 16, which is also the network increment. Therefore, the next network is 32, 48, 64, and so on, and the final network is the network (240 − 16) = 224. (The network 240 is considered a network ID of all 1's and would be allowed together with the zero network only in a case where the zero subnet enabled parameter was enabled.)

The administrator then determines the host IDs on the newly created networks. The first host on the network is the network ID + 1. The last host on the network is the next network ID − 2. The host before the next network ID is considered the broadcast for the newly created network.

To understand how this works, let's take a sample network with subnetting requirements and work through an example.

Exercise Three

An administrator would like to subnet his network. He has an address of 141.9.0.0 with the default mask. He needs to have 80 new subnets.

To approach this problem, let's go through the five steps, solve each step, and learn some new things in the process.

1. There are 80 networks needed. (That wasn't too hard.)

2. The number of bits required is 7 (looking at the chart in Table 4-4). Using 7 bits, the administrator has the availability of 126 networks, which leaves ample room to grow. This also leaves 9 bits for hosts, which allows 510 hosts per network.

3. Now this gets a bit tricky. Before determining the new subnet mask, the administrator must examine the old mask for inclusion. The administrator began with a Class B address. That means there was a 16-bit mask by default or a mask of 255.255.0.0. Now 7 bits have been added (looking at the chart in Table 4-4) or another octet containing 254. The resulting mask is 255.255.254.0 or /23 bits.

4. (This is fun.) The networks created are (using the trick formula of 256 − mask) 141.9.2.0, 141.9.4.0, 141.9.6.0, and 141.9.8.0 through 141.9.252.0. The networks of 141.9.0.0 and 141.9.254.0 are valid networks in the case of zero subnet being enabled.

5. The hosts on the network would vary. This gets a little complicated, so let's take each new network individually and look at some sample hosts. On the newly created network of 141.9.2.0, that is the network ID, so that address in itself is not a valid address. The first host on this network is 141.9.2.1. The last host on the network is 141.9.3.254. The host 141.9.3.255 is the broadcast address for this network.

Quick Quiz II
Is the address 141.9.2.255/23 valid?

Quick Quiz III
Is the address 141.9.3.0 valid?

Answer
The answer is yes to both. It is important to note that on this newly created network with the 23-bit mask we have created, the host addresses of 141.9.2.255 and 141.9.3.0 are both valid.

How is it that these two seemingly invalid addresses are actually fine? The ANDing process that the router would use proves that these are valid addresses. Taking the address 141.9.2.255 and turning it into a binary address, it becomes 10001101. 00001001.00000010.11111111. The 23-bit mask becomes 11111111.11111111.11111110. 00000000. Looking at the mask in comparison to the address, 9 bits are used for host addresses. Of those 9 bits, the first bit is a 1 and the last 8 bits are 0's. That is a perfectly valid host address because it is a combination of 1's and 0's.

Exercise Four
Do the same binary check done in the previous note for the address of 141.9.3.0 to see clearly that it too is a valid address.

Now it is clear that the same would apply to each newly created network. For the network with the ID of 141.9.4.0, that address is the network address. The address of 141.9.4.1 is the first host on the network, and the address of 141.9.5.254 is the last host. The address of 141.9.5.255 is the broadcast ID (see Figure 4-6).

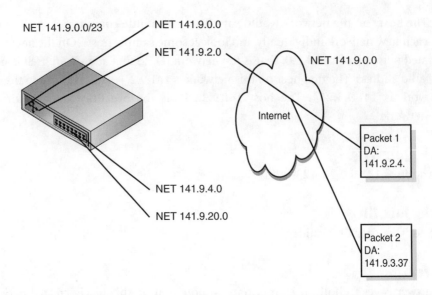

Figure 4-6 A router is routing packets to the newly created subnets (example three). The router performs the ANDing process to determine that hosts 141.9.2.4 and 141.9.3.37 are both on the same network (Network 141.9.2.0).

Exercise Five

Practice your new skills by creating 17 networks for the 201.26.7.0 network (answers are at the end of the chapter).

NOTE The five step formula is also used in cases where the network administrator is concerned with the number of hosts per subnet.

Quick Quiz IV

If an administrator has an IP address, 145.26.0.0, and would like to subnet his network so that each subnet has 70 hosts, how many subnets could he make?

Answer

In this scenario, we have to analyze the fact that the administrator requires 70 hosts per subnet. That means that 7 bits are required for host IDs (Table 4-4 the same table we use for the number of mask bits.) If 7 bits are used for host IDs and this is a natural

Class B network with 16 available bits, this leaves 11 bits for networks. So, if we go back and examine our five-step process, we find the following:

1. We need 70 hosts.

2. This requires 7 bits.

3. This leaves 11 bits for networks, therefore our mask is 255.255.255.224. The first portion is from the natural Class B network and 255.224 is our new subnet mask.

4. The networks created are therefore 145.26.1.32, 145.26.1.64, and 145.26.1.96, all the way up to 145.26.255.192.

5. Hosts on the network 145.26.1.32 would include all workstations with IP addresses between 145.26.1.33 and 145.26.1.63.

When using RIP version 1 (which will be further explained in Chapter 6), the same mask must be applied throughout the physical network that shares the same network address. All devices connected to the networks that compose the subnet must have the same mask.

Variable Length Subnet Mask (VLSM)

Variable Length Subnet Mask (VLSM) enables the better use of addressing space when an organization is using a single network ID. Using only one subnet mask that has a large number of hosts per subnet for a network with only a few hosts wastes an entire subnet. Take the previous example where a single network had 510 hosts. What happens when an administrator needs to create a network for just two hosts (a point-to-point network)? Using one of the networks created previously means that more than 500 host addresses have been lost for a network with two nodes. VLSM enables subnetting for a single network ID into many different network IDs, each with their own mask, allowing for different numbers of hosts on each network. Administrators using VLSM must be careful and understand that once a network has been included in an address, it cannot be reused or resubnetted.

Example

Let's take an example of Network 141.9.0.0. Using VLSM enables the creation of these different networks in one address space (see Table 4-5).

Table 4-5   The Subnetting of the Address 141.9.0.0 into Smaller and Smaller Networks

NET ID: 141.9.1.0	NET ID: 141.9.1.0	NET ID: 141.9.1.0
Subnetted to 24 bits	Subnetted again to 28 bits	Subnetted again to 30 bits
Mask of 255.255.255.0	Mask of 255.255.255.240	Mask of 255.255.255.252
256 subnets/254 hosts each	Additional 16 subnets/14 hosts	Additional 4 subnets/2 hosts
Sample Networks	**Sample Networks**	**Sample Networks**
141.9.1.0	141.9.1.16	141.9.1.16
141.9.2.0	141.9.1.32	141.9.1.20
141.9.3.0	141.9.1.48	141.9.1.24
141.9.4.0	141.9.1.64	141.9.1.28
141.9.5.0	141.9.1.80	
141.9.6.0	141.9.1.96	

NOTE   In this example, network 141.9.1.0 and network 141.9.1.16 cannot be used except with the longest mask of 255.255.255.252.

RIPv1 enables the use of only one fixed-length subnet mask per network number. As we will explain in the next chapter, RIPv1 does not advertise subnet masks and therefore cannot distinguish between two networks with the same network number that have different masks. If another routing protocol that understands VLSM receives a packet for a network that has two different masks, the routing protocol always forwards the packet to the network with the longest mask, as that is considered the most specific network (see Figure 4-7).

Supernetting/Classless InterDomain Routing (CIDR)

Supernetting permits the grouping of smaller subnet address spaces to make one larger supernet. With today's flat networks using super-fast switches, administrators may need to create networks with a large number of workstations. Supernetting enables this by enabling the aggregation of contiguous IP network numbers beyond the class boundary, in other words, shortening the subnet mask to leave more bits for workstations. Supernetting works by borrowing bits from the network ID and masking them into

ROUTE TABLE:

DEST:	NEXT HOP:	TYPE:	PROTOCOL
141.9.0.0	10.1.1.90	Indirect	RIP
141.9.5.0	10.1.32.1	Indirect	OSPF
141.9.10.0	10.1.32.1	Indirect	OSPF
10.10.10.10	10.1.1.90	Direct	Local

Figure 4-7 The router sends the packet destined for 141.9.5.53 out of the interface with the 24-bit mask. This is more specific and therefore considered more correct.

host ID bits for more efficient routing. Supernetting is the opposite of subnetting, which takes host bits and uses them to create networks. Supernetting is also used to overcome the small address space limitation associated with Class C addressing—only 255 hosts per segment—and enables networks to be created more efficiently.

Classless Inter-Domain Routing (CIDR) enables supernetting and in general makes all IP addressing combinations legal. CIDR also enables an IP subnet structure that ignores the normal position dependencies associated with standard IP addressing. A former Class C address, 199.1.1.0, which had a mask of at least 24 bits (255.255.255.0), can now be aggregated with other Class C addresses (199.1.2.0 through 199.1.255.0) and have a 16-bit mask (255.255.0.0)—a former Class B mask—to represent this group of addresses. Using conventional routing with these Class C addresses would cause an additional 255 routes to be added to the routing table. To prevent this, CIDR is used to collapse all of these addresses into the single route with a 16-bit mask. Just as in subnetting, supernetting uses the AND procedure to route packets to the correct destination network. CIDR notation is the commonly used notation of /# of bits (such as 141.17.0.0 /16), where the number of bits represents the subnet mask instead of including a full mask (255.255.0.0).

NOTE Supernetting and subnetting are temporary solutions for IP addressing issues. The Internet community has been working on a new protocol, IP version 6 (IPV6), which has more than enough addresses for every resource in the universe. Once IPV6 becomes the commonly used protocol, temporary solutions will become unnecessary.

In Chapter 6, we will discuss network summarization, which is based on CIDR. It is important to understand that through CIDR notation, many single networks can be grouped into one network and represented with a single routing statement.

Network Address Translation (NAT)

Another means of avoiding addressing issues is by using private addressing. Many networks today use an address of some form of the ten (or another private) network (10.10.5.0/24, for example). The only issue in using private addressing is with users trying to gain access to the Internet and other public domains. Because the 10 network is considered a private network, it is not considered a valid source or destination address on the Internet. The solution for most networks is Network Address Translation (NAT). Using NAT, an administrator can set up an entire network with a private address, and then have a router or switch translate addresses to public Internet addresses if necessary. (Nortel Networks routers running BayRS and Contivity Extranet Switches used for VPN tunneling both allow for NAT.)

Three NAT types exist:

- **Static NAT**   Provides a one-to-one relationship between a private address and a public Internet address. An administrator creates a table for each address that needs to be translated into a public address. Once the table has been created on the device, a user can send a packet with a private address, and the hardware device changes the address to a public address and sends it to the Internet. All packets that arrive at the device with a destination address of this public address are readdressed to the private address before being sent to that workstation. Static NAT is the only type of NAT that allows bidirectional access with incoming packets using a public address being mapped back to a private address in the intranet (see Figure 4-8).

- **Pooled NAT**   This type of dynamic NAT allows for translation from the private intranet to the Internet, but not from the Internet back. A characteristic of pooled NAT is a many-to-many relationship between private and public addresses. If a private address reaches the NAT device and a public address is available from the pool, the device dynamically assigns a public address. If no available addresses are in the pool, the private packet is dropped. Pooled NAT is used in a situation in which a limited number of public Internet addresses are available and an unlimited number of workstations are using private IP addresses. Not all the stations are able to access the Internet at one time in this situation. (Port NAT is the better solution in the case of limited public addresses.)

- **Port NAT**   Like pooled NAT, port NAT is a dynamic type of NAT that also enables translation only from the private intranet to the Internet. Port NAT is a many-to-one mapping situation. Every private address is mapped to the same public address, but each address is given a specific port mapping (this is how source addresses are translated [using that port]). When a private address reaches the NAT

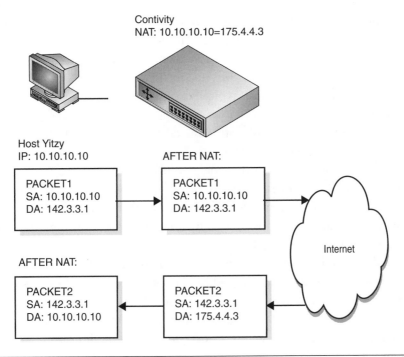

Figure 4-8 Static NAT is in action. The Contivity switch is translating the private address of workstation Yitzy to a valid public IP address and allowing bidirectional communication between the workstation and Internet.

device, and there is a mapping for it, the device maps the next available port for this address and puts the mapping in its table.

NAT will be mentioned again when the Contivity Extranet Switch is discussed in detail in Chapter 16.

A corporation using NAT could use any subnet mask it chose and customize its network to a very strong degree.

Address Resolution Protocol (ARP)

IP addresses are assigned to hosts at layer 3 level and are logically independent of their physical addresses, which reside at layer 2. The higher-layer software must depend on the data link layer to deliver data to a host on the same physical network. Therefore, the IP address (L3) must be mapped to the physical address (L2) of the host. Hosts must know each other's hardware addresses to communicate on an Ethernet network. *Address*

Resolution Protocol (ARP) is used to resolve a layer-3 address to a layer-2 MAC address. It works by broadcasting a packet to all hosts attached to the LAN. The packet contains the IP address that the sender is interested in communicating with. Most hosts ignore the packet. The target machine recognizes that the IP address inside the packet matches its own and returns an answer. Hosts typically keep a cache of ARP responses, based on the assumption that the IP-to-MAC hardware mapping rarely changes.

ARP is responsible for obtaining hardware addresses of TCP/IP hosts on broadcast-based networks. Ethernet LANs are broadcast-based. (This protocol will not work in an Asynchronous Transfer Mode [ATM] wide area network [WAN] environment or any other network that does not support broadcasting.) A node uses ARP with another node when it determines that the destination address is on a directly attached network. The node can determine if the host is local by comparing the network portion (including the subnet mask) of its own address with the target address. ARP uses a local broadcast of the destination IP address to acquire the hardware address of the destination host or gateway. Once the hardware address is obtained, both the IP address and hardware address are stored as a single entry in the ARP cache. The ARP cache is always checked first for an IP address/MAC address mapping before an ARP request is sent out. An ARP request is initiated every time a host tries to communicate with another host (see Figure 4-9).

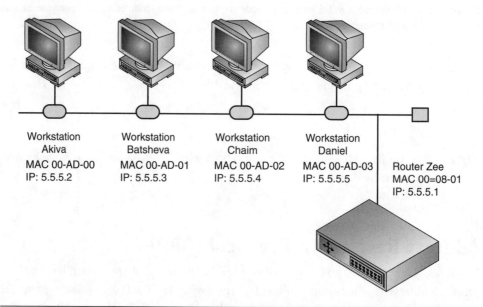

Figure 4-9 In an IP network, such as this, workstations will send out ARP requests for their neighbor's MAC address.

Hosts Akiva and Daniel are on the same physical network. Each has an assigned network address. Each has a physical address. Host Akiva wants to send a packet to host Daniel. When IP determines that the address is for the local network, the source checks its own ARP cache for the destination host. Host Akiva knows only the IP address of host Daniel.

Host Akiva broadcasts an ARP request packet on the physical network. This packet requests a response from any host with the IP address of host Daniel. All hosts receive the broadcast request and look into the IP portion of the datagram. Each host checks for a match to its own IP address. If a host does not find a match, it ignores the request. (In more sophisticated ARP implementations, some workstations create a cache from broadcast requests sent on the network mapping sender workstations with their MAC addresses.) Only host Daniel will respond to host Akiva. The ARP response packet contains host Daniel's hardware address and is sent directly to host Akiva, not through a broadcast. Host Akiva maps the host Daniel IP address to the physical MAC address and saves the results in the cache for future use (by default, a Nortel networks router does not age out its cache). Microsoft workstations age out their ARP cache after two minutes if the host is not accessed again or after ten minutes if the host is accessed (see Figure 4-10).

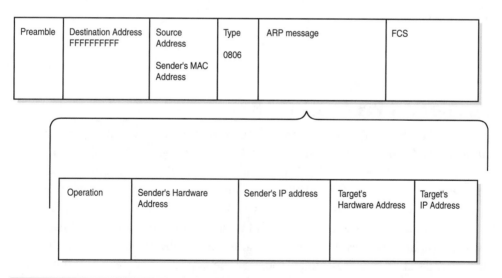

Figure 4-10   An ARP request packet. Notice the destination MAC is a broadcast.

An ARP message is carried across the network in the data portion of the frame. It is not encapsulated within IP an datagram. The type field of 0806 identifies a frame carrying an ARP message. The operation field is set to 1 if the frame is an ARP request and set to 2 if the frame is an ARP response.

ARP is transparent to bridges but not to routers. Bridges propagate ARP broadcasts like any other Ethernet broadcast and transparently bridge their replies. A router does not propagate broadcasts, because the router is a network layer-3 device.

What happens if the workstation is located on a remote network? If host A wants to send a packet to host D and IP determines that the packet is for a remote network, the next step is to find the route to that destination network. Often the workstation sends all remote packets to the default gateway or router. In this case, the workstation checks its cache for the MAC address of the default gateway. If it does not have the address of the router in its cache, the workstation sends out an ARP request for the router's MAC address. Once the workstation obtains the MAC address of the router, it uses that MAC to map to all addresses on the remote network. It sends packets with the IP of the remote destination station and the MAC of the local router. When the router receives the packet destined for the remote network, it ARPs out for that workstation from its local port that represents that remote network. It then forwards the packet to the remote network using the MAC address of the workstation mapped to the destination network's IP address.

Reverse Address Resolution Protocol (RARP)

Reverse Address Resolution Protocol (RARP) is used to obtain an IP address from a MAC address. It is used most often by diskless workstations. When this type of station boots, it requests an IP address from a server so that the workstation can be downloaded with an operating image. Like ARP, RARP is implemented in the data link layer. It uses the same packet format, but the type field is 8035. When enabling RARP support, the administrator defines a static mapping of MAC addresses to IP addresses to ensure that each workstation receives the correct operating image. RARP works very similarly to ARP. A workstation broadcasts to all nodes on the same physical network a frame containing a RAPR request that contains the workstation data link (MAC address). The server that has RARP enabled views its RARP table and finds the containing data link address and IP address pair. Upon finding the match, the server responds with a RARP reply that contains the workstation IP address. The workstation receives the reply from the server and now knows which IP address to use.

Proxy ARP

Proxy ARP is used primarily when some hosts on a network do not support subnet masking. The terms *proxy ARP*, *promiscuous ARP*, and *ARP* hack refer to the technique in which a router responds to an ARP request received on one interface that is for a host on another interface by supplying its own physical address. Proxy ARP enables the administrator to maintain a logical presentation of a single network and enables hosts to communicate as though they were directly attached. Proxy ARP simulates regular ARP for workstations that are not network-aware. When these workstations attempt to send ARP broadcast requests directly to remote workstations, the router responds with its own MAC, which enables normal connectivity for the end station. Proxy ARP enables a router to respond to an ARP request from a locally attached workstation for a remote destination. It does so by sending an ARP response back to the local host with its own MAC address of the router interface for the subnet on which the ARP request was received. The reply is generated only if the switch has an active route to the destination network (see Figure 4-11).

Hosts Benjy and Ruthie are on the same network but on separate subnets. Host Benjy does not understand subnetting (it has no subnet mask). Router Aryeh connects the two networks; it knows which hosts belong to which physical network. Host Benjy wants to send a packet to host Ruthie. Host Benjy broadcasts an ARP request asking the IP address to respond with its physical address. Router Aryeh captures the ARP request from host Benjy. Router Aryeh responds to host Benjy with its own MAC/hardware address (00-0A) using host Ruthie's IP address (37.79.47.25). Host Benjy maps host Ruthie's IP address to the router's hardware address. Host Benjy sends the packets to host Ruthie using the MAC address of the router.

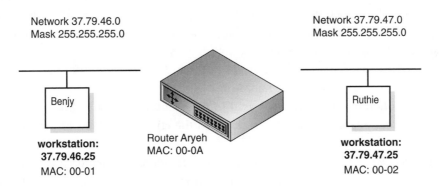

Figure 4-11   If enabled, the router can perform proxy ARP to enable two hosts on different subnets to communicate with each other.

A workstation that is network-aware would send an ARP request to the router to find a host that is attached to a remote network. In Figure 4-11, if workstation Benjy needs to reach workstation Ruthie, he consults his routing table. Because Ruthie is a host on a remote network, the ARP request (MAC broadcast) could not be sent directly to it. (Broadcasts cannot cross the router.) All packets destined for Ruthie must go to the router Aryeh. In reality, workstation Benjy does not need workstation Ruthie's MAC address because it will never communicate directly with Ruthie. Workstation Benjy uses the router's MAC address in an ARP reply to router Aryeh and then forwards all IP packets destined to workstation Ruthie to router Aryeh. When addressing packets to workstation Ruthie, workstation Benjy uses Ruthie's IP address, with the MAC address of router Aryeh's.

Dynamic Host Configuration Protocol (DHCP)

Dynamic Host Configuration Protocol (DHCP) (and the Bootstrap Protocol [BootP], as we shall soon see) is a feature of the IP addressing protocol. It is used to dynamically provide end stations with configuration information. Because all workstations that are running IP must have an address and subnet mask (and a default gateway—if they need to leave their local network), having a server on the network that can dynamically assign these addresses is very beneficial.

DHCP centralizes and manages the allocation of TCP/IP configuration information by automatically assigning IP addresses to computers configured to use DHCP. Implementing DHCP eliminates some configuration problems associated with manually configured TCP/IP. Each time a DHCP client starts, it issues a request for IP addressing information from a DHCP server, including IP address, subnet mask, and optional values such as the default gateway, DNS, and Windows Internet Naming Service (WINS). When a DHCP server receives a request, it selects IP addressing information from a pool of addresses defined in its database and offers it to the DHCP client. If the client accepts the offer, the IP address is leased to the client for a specified period. If no IP addresses are available in the pool to lease to the client, the client cannot initialize TCP/IP.

Issues related to the manual configuration of IP addresses include users randomly picking IP addresses or workstations moving from one network to another. This can lead to incorrect addresses and networking problems. An incorrect IP address, mask, or

PART II

gateway can lead to problems ranging from trouble communicating to duplicate IP addresses. If a computer is moved from one subnet to another with a static configuration, the IP addresses for the workstation must be manually reconfigured. This gives the administrator additional overhead. These are some of the reasons for implementing DHCP.

Using DHCP also means that users no longer need to acquire an IP address from an administrator. The DHCP server supplies all necessary configuration information to the DHCP clients. That may mean providing an IP address, a subnet mask, and a default gateway. The DHCP server may also be called upon to provide the address of a WINS server, a DNS server, or many other configuration parameters. Correct configuration information ensures network connectivity and eliminates most of the network problems.

DHCP uses a four-phase process to configure a client:

1. **IP lease request** The client initializes with a limited version of TCP/IP and broadcasts a request for the location of the DHCP server and IP addressing information.

2. **IP lease offer** All DHCP servers that have valid IP address information available send an offer to the client.

3. **IP selection** The client selects IP address information from the first offer it receives and broadcasts a message requesting to lease the IP address and information in the offer.

4. **IP lease acknowledgment** The DHCP server that made the offer responds to the message, and all other DHCP servers withdraw their offers. The IP addressing information is assigned to the client and an acknowledgment is sent. The client finishes initializing and binding the TCP/IP protocol.

Once the automatic configuration process is complete, the client can use all TCP/IP services and utilities for normal networking communications and connectivity to other IP hosts.

This process is also known as Discover, Offer, Request, Acknowledgment (DORA): Discover—a discovery packet from the workstation looks for a DHCP server; Offer—an offer from the server or several servers is made for an IP address for the workstation; Request—a second request from the workstation is made for a specific address offered by one of the servers; Acknowledgment—a final acknowledgement is made from the server that offered the IP address together with defined parameters of how long the address is valid and perhaps other information like the default router.

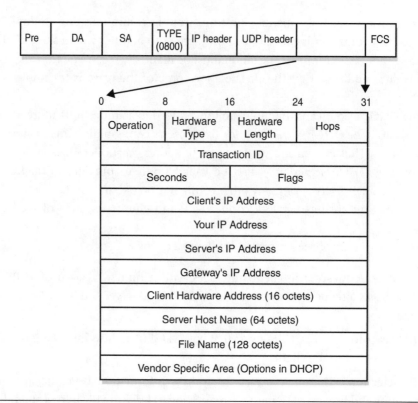

Figure 4-12   A DHCP packet. The same packet is used in all four phases of the DHCP process. Different information is available inside the packet for each phase.

Most DHCP messages are sent by broadcast (see Figure 4-12). For DHCP clients to communicate with a DHCP server on a remote network, the IP routers must support forwarding DHCP broadcasts. We will discuss this in further detail later in the chapter.

The fields in a DHCP packet that are important include operation, client IP address, your IP address, server IP address, client IP address, server host name, and vendor-specific area:

- **Operation**   This field specifies whether this is a request (1) or reply (2) message.

- **Client IP address**   If a client knows its IP address (and this is a renewal request), the client can put its IP address in this field. Otherwise, this field is 0.

- **Your IP address**   If the client IP address field is 0, the server will return an IP address in this field.

- **Server IP address**   When a client knows the specific server's address, these fields will be filled in (by a request packet).

- **Client hardware address** The MAC address of the client. This is especially necessary if there is a reservation for an IP address for this MAC address.

- **Server host name** The name of the server the client wants to get an address from.

- **Vendor-specific area** This contains optional information that is passed from the server to the client. In DHCP, this field can be up to 312 octets and contains information such as the default gateway and DNS and WINS server addresses.

In the first two phases, the client requests a lease from a DHCP server, and a DHCP server offers an IP address to the client. The first time the client initializes, it requests to lease an IP address by broadcasting a request to all DHCP servers. Because the client has no IP address and does not know the IP address of the DHCP server, it uses 0.0.0.0 as the source address and 255.255.255.255 as the destination address. The request for a lease is sent in the DHCP discover message. This message also contains the hardware address of the client and computer name, so that the DHCP server knows which client sent the request. The IP lease process is used when TCP/IP is initialized for the first time on a DHCP client. It also occurs if the client requests an IP address and is denied, possibly because the DHCP server dropped the lease or the client has moved to another subnet.

All DHCP servers that received the request and have a valid configuration for the client broadcast an offer. This offer contains the client's MAC address, an offered IP address, a subnet mask, the length of the lease, and a server identifier (the IP address of the offering DHCP server). A broadcast is used because the client does not yet have an IP address. The offer is sent as a DHCP offer message. The DHCP server reserves the IP address so it will not be offered to another client unless this client refuses the address. The DHCP client waits one second for an offer. If an offer is not received, it rebroadcasts the request three more times. If an offer is not received after four requests, the clients will retry every five minutes. As we said in the previous chapter, when using a switch directly attached to a workstation using DHCP, the switch port should be configured in FastStart mode for the Spanning Tree Protocol method so the DHCP client does not time out waiting for the port to come up.

For the last two phases, the client selects an offer and the DHCP server acknowledges the lease. After the client receives an offer from at least one DHCP server, it broadcasts to all DHCP servers that it has made a selection and accepted an offer. The broadcast is sent in a DHCP request message and includes a server identifier (IP address) of the server whose offer was accepted. All other DHCP servers then retract their offers so that those IP addresses are available for the next IP lease requests. IP lease acknowledgement occurs when the DHCP server with the accepted offer broadcasts a successful acknowledgement in the form of a DHCP ACK message. This message contains a valid lease for an IP address and possibly other configuration information (DNS, Windows, default gateway). When the DHCP client receives the acknowledgment, TCP/IP is completely initialized. Once bound, the client can use TCP/IP to communicate on the intranetwork and Internet (see Figure 4-13).

A client may receive a DHCP NACK—a negative acknowledgement—if the client is trying to lease a previous IP address that is no longer available, or the client moved to another subnet and the previous address is no longer valid. The client that receives a NACK goes through the DHCP process again.

All DHCP clients attempt to renew their lease when 50 percent of the lease is expired. Renewing a lease takes only two packets: a request message followed by an acknowledgement from the original server that gave the station its lease. If the client does not

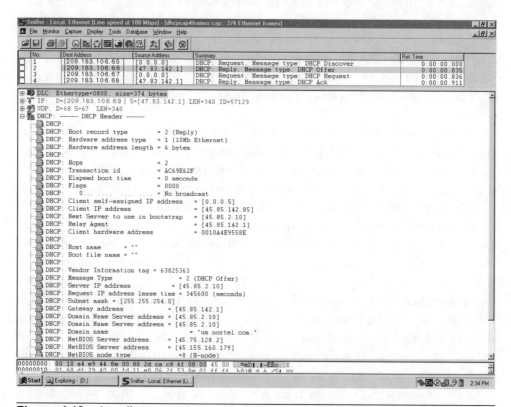

Figure 4-13 A sniffer trace of the complete DHCP client requesting process (DORA). Note that all destination addresses are 255.255.255.255 for the broadcast address. The destination address for packets to the client is 0.0.0.0. The DHCP offer is highlighted, and it is possible to see that the workstation received an IP address, a default gateway, a DNS server, and a WINS server as well.

receive an acknowledgement, it can continue to use its lease until the lease expires. If it expires, the client must go through the entire four-step DHCP process again.

> **NOTE** Using DHCP does not preclude using static addresses for devices whose addresses should never change, such as routers, servers, and switches.

To configure DHCP, the server itself must have a static IP address and a scope defined with a range of IP addresses, a subnet mask, and any additional parameters necessary. If the DHCP server services many subnets, it should have a scope for each subnet. Additionally, if the administrator is using static addresses for printers, servers, Extranet clients, or anything else, those addresses should not be included in the range. Including those addresses will cause network issues because of duplicate addresses.

DHCP is also very useful in a network with limited IP addresses. A client can be leased an address for a specified time. If that lease expires because the client is no longer online or has not renewed the address, it becomes available again in the pool. DHCP also makes configuration easier because if a client moves, it automatically receives a new address for its new network. Additionally, if a router's address changes, making the change on the DHCP server makes the change on the client machines when they next go to renew their lease.

> **NOTE** A client configured with anything static will override DHCP. This includes a static WINS server, DNS server, or default gateway.

Bootstrap Protocol (BootP)

The *Bootstrap Protocol* (BootP) process is also a means for assigning IP addresses dynamically. In fact, BootP is the originator of DHCP and uses the same packet type. The BootP process, however, consists of only two steps: 1) a request from a workstation, and 2) an acknowledgement from a BootP server. With BootP, the lease for the address of the workstations does not expire, and the workstation cannot obtain any additional configuration parameters. Just like DHCP, the BootP client issues a broadcast request. The server responds by mapping the source address in the BootP packet to a configuration file location. It then issues a BootP reply containing an IP address and pointers to the configuration file the client needs. The client can then use the Trivial File Transfer Protocol (TFTP) to download the configuration file.

BootP is used mainly to enable diskless workstations to receive an IP address from a server without using the data link protocol that RARP uses. BootP is more flexible than RARP because it uses UDP as its transport protocol.

DHCP/BootP Relay Agents

To enhance network management, administrators find it useful to configure a small number of DHCP/BootP servers in a central location. However, it is essential to understand one issue. The DHCP/BootP process consists of workstations that send out a request packet for an IP address. Because these workstations have no address, the destination of these packets is to the broadcast address (IP address: 255.255.255.255; MAC address: FF-FF-FF-FF), and the source address is all 0's. Responses from the server giving out the IP address are broadcasts as well. A DHCP host on a subnet that does not include a DHCP server may not get an IP address, because the UDP broadcasts are by default not forwarded to the server on a different subnet. Both DHCP and BootP rely on broadcasts to communicate configuration information between clients and servers in the network.

NOTE Routers do not normally forward broadcasts.

This seems to indicate that there must be a DHCP or BootP server on every subnet containing clients that need to receive dynamic IP addresses. This can cause several network and administrative issues. Fortunately, Nortel Networks routers and switches (some Microsoft servers as well) have implemented a feature called the BootP/DHCP relay agent. This agent can receive broadcasts destined for a BootP/DHCP server and forward them to the network that has a BootP/DHCP server. Some implementations of the relay agent even repackage the broadcast requests for the BootP/DHCP into directed packets addressed to the BootP/DHCP server. This saves on the amount of broadcast traffic that is seen on the LAN. (And we all know that broadcast traffic must be processed by each and every NIC to make sure the data is not for the local workstation.)

Internet Control Message Protocol (ICMP)

Internet Control Message Protocol (ICMP) is a required companion to the IP protocol and must be included in every IP implementation. ICMP's basic function is to provide feedback about problems that occur in a communications environment. ICMP reports errors and control messages on behalf of IP. The higher-level protocols that use IP must implement their own reliability procedures. ICMP is a messaging service that enables a destination device to notify a source about problems or conditions in the network.

Some sample ICMP messages include time exceeded TTL, destination unreachable, source quench, and echo (request)/echo reply:

- **Time exceeded TTL**   A router sends this message any time it is forced to discard a packet because its TTL field was set to 0. This happens when the hop count for the packet exceeded the network limit.

- **Destination unreachable**   This message can be issued for several reasons. Network unreachable, which is returned by a router, states that no route in its routing table gets to that network. Host unreachable also comes from a router and is the result of the router being unable to reach a destination station.

- **Source quench**   If a TCP/IP host is sending packets to a router at a rate that is saturating the link between them, the router may send a source quench message. This may occur because the router's buffer is full and cannot accept more packets. This source quench message asks the sending station to slow down transmission.

- **Echo (request)/echo reply**   These messages are used in the PING utility.

ICMP is used in both PING and traceroute to get network information. In the PING application, the goal is to test the capability to reach a remote device on the network. PING uses echo request to ask a target host to transmit an echo reply, which is then reported back to the requesting station with the time information.

Every PING request issues four echo requests and expects the return of four echo replies (see Table 4-6). In Figure 4-14, one of the echo replies is highlighted. It is possible to see the IP source and destination addresses in the trace. It is also interesting to note that in the hexadecimal portion of the trace you can see the data that is sent from the source to the destination during a PING command. The source station sends an echo containing the alphabet ABCDEF . . . , and it is replied with an echo reply containing the same information.

Table 4-6 Results of a PING

Alive	The system received an ICMP echo response from the target device within the timeout period.
Does not respond	The system does not receive a response from the target device within the allowed time period.
ICMP host unreachable	The local router or a remote router cannot forward the PING request along the path any further because there is no route to the IP address of the device.

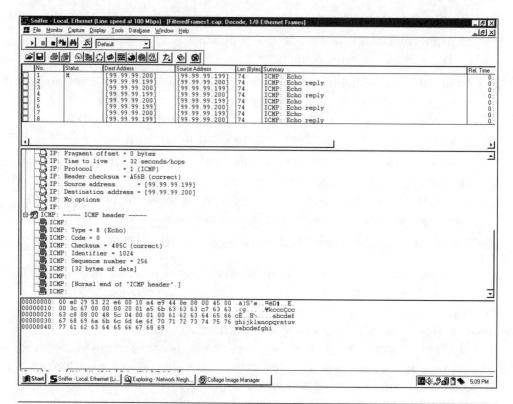

Figure 4-14 This is a sniffer trace capturing a PING command from workstation 99.99.99.199 to workstation 99.99.99.200 (PING 99.99.99.200).

Traceroute is another utility that uses ICMP to send back control messages to a user. The traceroute utility verifies the route that a packet takes to reach its destination. This is useful to find out if a router has failed or if one of the routers along the way is slow. The response time is returned in the output (see Figure 4-15).

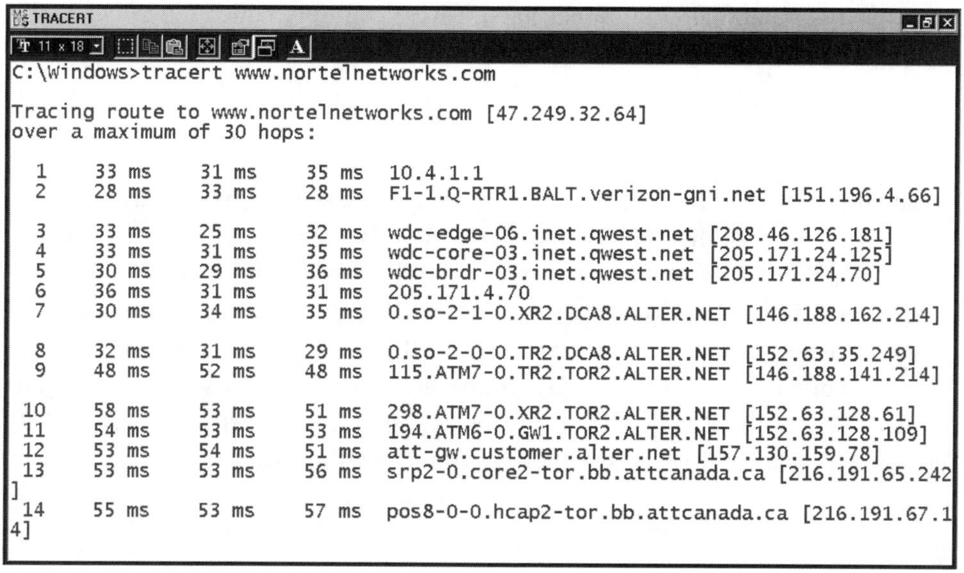

```
TRACERT                                                          _ 回 ×
 T 11 x 18   □ 🖻 🖻  🖾  🗗🗐  A
C:\Windows>tracert www.nortelnetworks.com

Tracing route to www.nortelnetworks.com [47.249.32.64]
over a maximum of 30 hops:

  1    33 ms    31 ms    35 ms   10.4.1.1
  2    28 ms    33 ms    28 ms   F1-1.Q-RTR1.BALT.verizon-gni.net [151.196.4.66]

  3    33 ms    25 ms    32 ms   wdc-edge-06.inet.qwest.net [208.46.126.181]
  4    33 ms    31 ms    35 ms   wdc-core-03.inet.qwest.net [205.171.24.125]
  5    30 ms    29 ms    36 ms   wdc-brdr-03.inet.qwest.net [205.171.24.70]
  6    36 ms    31 ms    31 ms   205.171.4.70
  7    30 ms    34 ms    35 ms   0.so-2-1-0.XR2.DCA8.ALTER.NET [146.188.162.214]

  8    32 ms    31 ms    29 ms   0.so-2-0-0.TR2.DCA8.ALTER.NET [152.63.35.249]
  9    48 ms    52 ms    48 ms   115.ATM7-0.TR2.TOR2.ALTER.NET [146.188.141.214]

 10    58 ms    53 ms    51 ms   298.ATM7-0.XR2.TOR2.ALTER.NET [152.63.128.61]
 11    54 ms    53 ms    53 ms   194.ATM6-0.GW1.TOR2.ALTER.NET [152.63.128.109]
 12    53 ms    54 ms    51 ms   att-gw.customer.alter.net [157.130.159.78]
 13    53 ms    53 ms    56 ms   srp2-0.core2-tor.bb.attcanada.ca [216.191.65.242
]
 14    55 ms    53 ms    57 ms   pos8-0-0.hcap2-tor.bb.attcanada.ca [216.191.67.1
4]
```

Figure 4-15   This figure was obtained by going to the command prompt on a Windows station and using the Microsoft TRACERT utility. It is part of the results of a TRACERT from a local workstation to the www.nortelnetworks.com Web server. One can see the different Web routers that the packet goes through to reach the destination network.

Transmission Control Protocol (TCP)

Transmission Control Protocol (TCP) is a layer-4 transport protocol that IP relies on to be transported through the network. TCP is a reliable, connection-oriented delivery service. A session must be created and acknowledged between the source and destination stations before any data is transmitted. Data is transmitted in segments. Reliability is further maintained through assigning sequence numbers to each segment transmitted. Acknowledgements are used to verify that data was received by the remote host. For each segment, the sending station must receive an acknowledgement within a certain period of time or the data will be retransmitted. The station will not send an acknowledgement if the packet is received damaged, so the source station will also retransmit in that situation.

A TCP session is established through a three-way handshake. The steps in this session establishment are as follows:

1. The initiating host requests a session by sending out a segment with the synchronization flag set (SYN).

2. The receiving host acknowledges the request by sending back a flag with the synchronization flag, a sequence number to indicate the numbering for the segments

it will send, and an acknowledgement (ACK) with the sequence number of segments it expects to receive.

3. The initiating/requesting host sends back a segment with the acknowledged sequence numbers.

The purpose of this handshake is to synchronize the sending and receiving of segments, to inform the other station of the amount of data the station is able to receive at once (called the TCP window size), and to establish a virtual connection.

TCP uses a similar process to end a connection. This guarantees that both hosts have finished transmitting and all the data was received.

Applications that use TCP are often connection-oriented applications that require the dependency of TCP to function. They include HyperText Transfer Protocol (HTTP), File Transfer Protocol (FTP), and Telnet, which will be discussed shortly.

User Datagram Protocol (UDP)

Like TCP, *User Datagram Protocol* (UDP) is a layer-4 transport protocol that IP also uses to be transported through the network. UDP provides a connectionless datagram service that offers best-effort delivery. UDP is used by applications that do not require an acknowledgement and typically send small amounts of data at once. Some examples of applications using UDP include Trivial File Transfer Protocol (TFTP) and Simple Network Management Protocol (SNMP).

Ports

Applications identify themselves within a computer by using a port number. Services also use port numbers to advertise and gain recognition by other workstations. TCP and UDP use port numbers to pass data to specific upper-layer applications. Some applications use well-known port numbers and are universal. Well-known ports are between 1 and 1024. These port numbers are used as source and destination addresses in TCP and UDP. Applications that use well-known port numbers include FTP, TFTP, HTTP, SNMP, and Telnet (discussed in the following section). To see the port numbers of some well-known applications, find the Ports file on any computer running a Windows-based operating system.

It is important to note that applications do no need to use these well-known ports. In fact, for security purposes, an administrator may hide applications in different ports to prevent outside users from accessing these services. If the administrator changes the port of an application, all programs that must access that application must be informed of this port change and be able to use the new port to access the application. If an administrator is changing port numbers, it should be to a port number above 1024.

TCP Applications, Layer Seven: FTP, Telnet, and HTTP

FTP is an application used for transferring data across the network. When a client initiates a session with the FTP server, the session establishes two separate connections between the host and the server. One is a control session for sending a command request or response that uses port 21. The second is a data connection for transferring data that uses port 20. A user that has the FTP client software (which comes standard with most operating systems and TCP/IP implementations) can transfer a file from his or her workstation to a server or a host running the FTP server software. Using FTP, the client can view directories and transfer files.

FTP requires a username and also has anonymous user access with no password. Security and permissions can be assigned based on usernames. FTP offers commands that include *ls* to look at directories on the FTP host and *mdir* to make a new directory.

Two commands used for transferring files are also available for TFTP: the GET and PUT commands. The *GET* command transfers a file to the local host from the remote host. The *PUT* command puts a file from the local host to the remote host.

Exercise Six

If one has access to an FTP server, it is possible to practice using FTP. A sample listing of FTP commands are shown in Figures 4-16 and 4-17.

Telnet is another TCP-based application that uses TCP port 23. Telnet is used to provide terminal emulation to a remote router or server running the Telnet host. Most Nortel Networks devices allow Telnet access for users to connect to a command prompt for remote command line capabilities and management. For local terminal emulation to a Nortel Networks device, administrators can use HyperTerminal or another terminal application through the serial Com port. That also gives users a command line interface.

```
FTP                                                                    _ 日 X
 Auto    ▾                      A
Microsoft(R) Windows 98
    (C)Copyright Microsoft Corp 1981-1999.

C:\Windows\Desktop>ftp
ftp> open
To 99.99.99.199
Connected to 99.99.99.199.
220 3Com FTP Server Version 1.1
User (99.99.99.199:(none)): anonymous
331 User name ok, need password
Password:
230 User logged in
ftp> ?
Commands may be abbreviated.  Commands are:

!              delete        literal       prompt        send
?              debug         ls            put           status
append         dir           mdelete       pwd           trace
ascii          disconnect    mdir          quit          type
bell           get           mget          quote         user
binary         glob          mkdir         recv          verbose
bye            hash          mls           remotehelp
cd             help          mput          rename
close          lcd           open          rmdir
ftp>
```

Figure 4-16   A Windows 98 user using FTP. First, the user performs an *open* command to connect to the server located at 99.99.99.199. Then the user logs on to the FTP server using the default *anonymous* account and password. The user then requests help. One can see a listing of different commands that are possible using FTP.

```
MS-DOS Prompt                                                          _ 日 X
 Auto    ▾                      A
220 3Com FTP Server Version 1.1
User (99.99.99.199:(none)): anonymous
331 User name ok, need password
Password:
230 User logged in
ftp> ls
200 PORT command successful.
150 File status OK ; about to open data connection
.
..
WinIPCfg.Txt
config.cfg2
config.txt
JETA1D3.TMP
226 Closing data connection
ftp: 59 bytes received in 0.11Seconds 0.54Kbytes/sec.
ftp> get config.txt
200 PORT command successful.
150 File status OK ; about to open data connection
226 File transfer successful.
ftp: 841 bytes received in 0.11Seconds 7.65Kbytes/sec.
ftp> bye
221 Service closing control connection

C:\Windows\Desktop>
```

Figure 4-17   An FTP client on a Windows 98 workstation connected to an FTP server. The user performs an *ls* command to view a listing of the files in the FTP directory of the FTP server. Then the user performs a *GET command* for the file config.txt. Finally, the user types in *bye* to exit the FTP program.

HTTP uses TCP port 80. This protocol is used for Web browsing and other Web services. When we open a Web browser (such as Internet Explorer or Netscape) and type in a URL (such as www.yitta.com), we are actually using HTTP port 80. The actual command that is executed is the HTTP command of http://www.yitta.com:80.

UDP Applications, Layer Seven: TFTP and SNMP

TFTP uses UDP port 69 to transfer data from one node to another across the network. Like FTP, a station is required to act as a TFTP server so other clients can receive data from this station. Most of Nortel Network's hardware can utilize TFTP services to get configuration files upon startup. This enables administrators to make changes to configuration files and keep them updated at central server locations. The central servers must be running the TFTP server service so that routers and switches running TFTP client software can get their remotely managed configuration files.

SNMP is used in TCP/IP to remotely monitor and control network devices. SNMP provides the means for the communication of network management information across a network. It is a simple protocol by which management information for a network device can be remotely inspected or altered.

SNMP has two components. A management station can configure, monitor, and receive trap messages from network devices that are configured as SNMP agents. An SNMP agent is the process running on a device that responds to SNMP SET and GET requests and sends trap messages. SNMP works with communities for security. There are different types of communities based on network access: Read only specifies members that can view configuration and performance information, while Read/write specifies members that can view as well as change configuration information.

SNMP also works with the GET and SET commands. A GET command enables the administrator to see and monitor hardware information. A SET command enables a user to make changes to the configuration of the device. SNMP devices receive all messages at UDP port 161 except for trap messages that are received at UDP port 162. The agent issues traps to the client to report a fault or other condition.

SNMP works based on the *Management Information Bases* (MIB) structure, which is a primitive database that sits on the agent. In concept, it is a tree-like structure, with a root and branches off the root. Some parts of the MIB database are defined by the Internet community and are standard (that is considered the root of the MIB tree), while other parts are vendor-specific (and viewed as the branches of the structure). When a user issues a SNMP GET request, the user is actually asking the SNMP agent to retrieve a MIB variable.

Most of the graphical tools that Nortel Networks uses for device management are really based on SNMP and use MIB GETs and SETs. Site Manager for routers, Device Managers for switches, and Speedview for Centillion switches all use SNMP GETs and SETs to manage and make changes to the hardware configuration. These are not the only way to access MIBs on Nortel Networks devices. Most devices enable direct MIB access to knowledgeable administrators directly through the command-line applications.

Computer Names

Human beings have a hard time remembering TCP/IP addresses when attempting to access different computers and services. To make life easier, names were introduced to be mapped to IP addresses for easier resource access. There are several types of computer names and methods of resolving them to addresses. We will discuss NetBIOS names commonly used in Microsoft networks, names for computers, and services (such as printers) being referred to as prntfl1rma (printer floor 1 room a) instead of 5.5.5.5. We will also discuss host names commonly used in native TCP/IP applications (such as www.zeecilismyname.com) that are used on the Internet and with PING that are more easily memorable than IP addresses like 194.37.26.4.

NETBIOS and Windows Internet Name Service (WINS)

NetBIOS provides a standard protocol that functions at the session/transport layer. NetBIOS provides support for network name registration. A NetBIOS name is a unique name used to identify a resource on the network and services that the resource may offer (a domain browser or a NetBIOS name server). This type of name is commonly used in the Microsoft networking environment to identify computers on the network. Microsoft computers register NetBIOS names, and all Windows commands (Explorer or net use commands) use NetBIOS names to access these services. In this environment, NetBIOS uses TCP/IP as the transport protocol (specifically UDP).

The registration process for using a NetBIOS name can occur using a broadcast or through a WINS server. The name each computer uses must be unique. A computer that tries to register a name already in use receives a NACK and is not be able to register the name.

Computers in the NetBIOS environment have to resolve names to TCP/IP addresses (and then to MAC addresses) to communicate on the network. Some of the methods for name resolution include cache, broadcast, WINS server, and LMHOST files, as well as the Internet standard methods of DNS and HOST files. The proper order for name resolution is cache, WINS, broadcast, and then LMHOST, DNS, and HOST files. Cache is the local cache containing recently resolved NetBIOS names.

Exercise Seven

To see the local name cache on a Windows machine, go to the Dos prompt and type **NBTSTAT -c**. This will give you all the recently resolved NetBIOS names.

Windows Internet Name Service (WINS) provides resolution for registered names. WINS assumes that all workstations will register with a WINS server so their IP address can be resolved to names.

A workstation can broadcast on the local network for an address-to-name resolution. This resolution will only work if the name is registered to a LOCAL resource. The reason for this is that routers generally do not forward broadcast requests. Because broadcasts effectively remain on the local segment, the name resolution will only work if the name is being utilized for a resource on the local network.

The LMHOSTS file is a static file that provides name resolution for NetBIOS names to IP addresses. Static text files need to be manually configured and changed on each machine to work.

WINS is designed to eliminate the need for broadcasting to resolve names to IP addresses. For this service to work properly, when a client boots, the computer must register its names and services with WINS. The client must be configured with the IP address of the WINS server either statically (in the TCP/IP properties) or through the DHCP server (as one of the optional parameters that the DHCP server can supply to DHCP clients). Once the client registers with the WINS server and other clients do the same, the client can go back to the server and submit through a directed WINS request the IP address of any NetBIOS workstation on the network.

The client must have the address of the WINS server to communicate with NetBIOS. The client can have either a static WINS server configured (see Figure 4-18) or get a WINS server address from the DHCP server (refer to Figure 4-13).

Clients that do not have the address for the WINS server will have to broadcast for all NetBIOS name resolutions. This can cause a lot of network traffic.

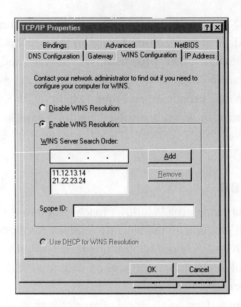

Figure 4-18   A client with a static WINS server configuration

Domain Naming Service (DNS)

A TCP/IP host uses a standard host or domain name to be accessed in the Internet/intranet. Just like a NetBIOS name, this host name is mapped to an IP address. A host name is an alias assigned to a TCP/IP host. It does not have to match the Net-BIOS name and can be a string of up to 256 characters. It is used for easier reference to TCP/IP hosts. A host name can be used with TCP/IP utilities such as PING, FTP, and others. A host name always corresponds to an IP address. The resolution for the name to the address can be found in either a HOSTS file or a DNS server.

Host name resolution is different from NetBIOS name resolution because there is no registration. Nevertheless, a host name must be resolved to an IP address, which can then be resolved to a hardware address. TCP/IP can use the following methods to resolve host names. First, check to see if the host name matches the local host name, then check the HOSTS file, and finally look for a DNS server. Unlike NetBIOS, a TCP/IP workstation never uses a broadcast to resolve a host name.

The static HOST file provides resolution for host names to IP addresses. Like LMHost files, any changes made to the host names must be changed in all the static files in all the workstations on the network.

The DNS server is a centralized online database used to resolve Fully Qualified Domain Names (FQDNs) and other host names to IP addresses. All host names must be statically configured in this database, as hosts generally do not register their names dynamically (see Figure 4-19).

DNS is used not only for resolving host names to IP addresses for the local network. DNS is also the protocol for mapping host names to IP addresses throughout the Internet. At first, when the Internet consisted of just a few hundred computers, all host name resolution was contained in a static text file called Host.txt, which was maintained on a few computers around California. Now that the Internet is a large, growing community with hundreds of computers joining all the time, a static file no longer works.

The current DNS system consists of a hierarchical naming structure contained in a distributed database. In the DNS system, clients are called resolvers and servers are called name servers. Name servers take requests from resolvers and resolve Internet names to IP addresses. If the name server is not able to resolve the request, it may forward the request to a name server that can resolve it. The name servers are grouped in different levels called domains. In the DNS system, there are root-level domains, top-level domains, and second-level domains. Root domains are the servers that point off to other resolvers down the list. Top-level domains resolve com, gov, edu, org, and

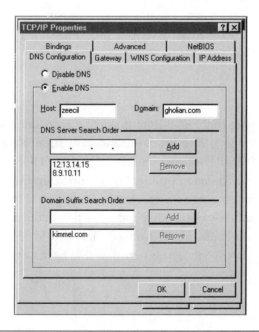

Figure 4-19 DNS properties on a Windows 95 workstation. The host name is zeecil and the domain name is gholian.com.

those types of inquiries. Second-level domains are private companies or institutions that may have subdomains (Nortel Networks.com and Training.Nortel Networks.com). Adding the host name gives the FQDN. An example is support.Nortel Networks.com.

In the example of www.NortelNetworks.com, www is the host name. Nortel Networks is the second-level domain name, and com is the top-level domain. A hidden period at the end of the FQDN represents the root servers.

The process of resolving names is called an iterative query. What actually happens is a many-step process: A resolver can send a request to find the IP address of a universal resource locator (URL) like www.Zeecil.com. The request is sent to a local name server, which may not know this domain name. This DNS server then sends a query to the com server. The com server sends back a response directing this request to the Zeecil server. The local server then sends a request to the Zeecil.com server to find the address of www.Zeecil.com. When that server responds, the final IP address is returned to the workstation, which can now communicate with the remote host.

If an organization wants to connect to the Internet, it must register a domain name with the InterNIC and provide the addresses of at least two DNS servers that will be used in its domain. This process ensures that the organization's domain name gets registered in the upper-level DNS servers.

The user of a network must have access to a DNS server. The user can have static mappings to a DNS server (as shown in Figure 4-18) or receive a DNS server's address from the DHCP server (as shown in Figure 4-13).

Summary

In this chapter we discussed the TCP/IP protocol in great detail. We learned how to perform IP addressing on a network and how to identify subnets using the subnet mask. We discussed static TCP/IP configurations and dynamic TCP/IP using DHCP. We also mentioned many of the different utilities, applications, and services available in this protocol, including naming services with DNS or WINs and file transfer protocols like TFTP and FTP. To completely utilize all of these utilities on the network, we will need to further understand how traffic moves from one location to another. In Chapter 6, we will look at routing TCP/IP data across networks that have workstations and servers in various locations.

Review Questions

1. IP is a
   A. Connection-oriented protocol
   B. Connectionless protocol
   C. Application layer protocol
   D. Media Access Control protocol

2. Which protocol provides a reliable delivery service?
   A. IP
   B. UDP
   C. TCP
   D. ARP

3. Which protocol resolves IP addresses to MAC addresses?
   A. RIP
   B. ARP
   C. UDP
   D. TCP

4. The splitting of datagrams into smaller units is called:
   A. Routing
   B. Fragmentation
   C. Encapsulation
   D. Padding

5. What is the natural (default) class for the IP address 11.11.11.11?
   A. Class A
   B. Class B
   C. Class C
   D. Class D
   E. Class E

6. Which parameters are required for a Windows NT-based computer running TCP/IP to communicate in a WAN environment? (Choose three.)
   A. IP addresses
   B. Default gateway
   C. Subnet mask
   D. DNS
   E. WINS

7. Which protocol is used to inform a client that a destination network is unreachable?

   A. DNS

   B. WINS

   C. TCP

   D. UDP

   E. ICMP

8. Which two applications use UDP? (Choose two.)

   A. RARP

   B. FTP

   C. TFTP

   D. SNMP

9. Which two applications use TCP? (Choose two.)

   A. FTP

   B. Telnet

   C. TFTP

   D. SNMP

10. Which two methods are used to resolve Internet names to IP addresses? (Choose two.)

    A. ARP

    B. LMHOSTS files

    C. HOSTS files

    D. DNS

    E. WINS

11. What are the two primary objectives of the network layers? (Choose two.)

    A. Move information between multiple independent networks.

    B. Deliver data to all devices attached to a single network.

    C. Hide the intricacies of the network structure from the upper-layer processes.

    D. Organize the physical-layer bits into frames.

12. A user attempting to access a terminal server might use which protocol?

    A. FTP

    B. TFTP

    C. UDP

    D. RARP

    E. Telnet

13. What is the function of RARP?

   A. To resolve a MAC address to an IP address

   B. To resolve an IP address to a MAC address

   C. To resolve a NetBIOS name to an IP address

   D. To resolve a host name to an IP address

14. Which protocol is used to resolve IP addresses to MAC addresses?

   A. ARP

   B. RARP

   C. DHCP

   D. WINS

   E. DNS

15. The administrator attempts to connect to www.mordeachai.com but cannot do so. Which service may not be working in the network?

   A. FTP

   B. SNMP

   C. DNS

   D. WINS

   E. Telnet

16. A workstation is not configured with the address of a WINS server. What will happen if that workstation attempts to browse the network?

   A. The workstation will be able to see all network resources local and remote.

   B. The workstation will be able to see all local resources.

   C. The workstation will be unable to see any resources.

   D. The workstation will be able to see all network resources, but it will take a very long time.

17. A workstation is not configured with the address of a DNS server. What will happen when this user attempts to view Web pages using URLs?

   A. The name resolution will take longer.

   B. The name resolution will fail and the user will not be able to reach the Web site.

   C. The name resolution will use a broadcast to reach the DNS server.

   D. Name resolution is unnecessary in this situation; the user can reach the Web site directly through our browser.

18. Which two resources require a subnet mask? (Choose two.)
    A. A TCP/IP host
    B. A bridge
    C. A router
    D. A client running IPX

19. Which is not a valid host ID?
    A. 125.13.255.0 /16
    B. 125.13.4.255 /24
    C. 125.13.0.7 /16
    D. 10.13.0.0 /8

20. What is the default class for the IP address 196.196.196.196?
    A. Class A
    B. Class B
    C. Class C
    D. Class D
    E. Class E

21. What is the natural class for the IP address 191.191.191.191?
    A. Class A
    B. Class B
    C. Class C
    D. Class D
    E. Class E

22. Which IP address is a multicast address?
    A. 127.0.0.1
    B. 224.224.224.224
    C. 0.0.0.0
    D. 255.255.255.255
    E. 223.255.255.255

23. Given the IP address 198.198.198.57/30, which statement is true?
    A. There are 30 hosts on this network.
    B. There are 30 bits in the subnet mask.
    C. The network number is 198.198.198.0.
    D. This is an example of a standard Class C address.

24. Given a network address with a Class C natural mask, how many hosts are available per network?

    A. 0

    B. 64

    C. 128

    D. 254

25. At which layer of the OSI model does IP function?

    A. Layer 1

    B. Layer 2

    C. Layer 3

    D. Layer 4

    E. Layer 7

26. Which protocol works at layer 4 of the OSI model?

    A. IP

    B. TCP

    C. ICMP

    D. ARP

27. What is the definition of the acronym RFC?

    A. Request for Comments

    B. Request for Communications

    C. Routing Functionality Committee

    D. Routing Fundamentals Committee

28. Which protocol is able to recover from errors?

    A. UDP

    B. FTP

    C. TCP

    D. Telnet

29. Which statement about TCP and UDP is true?

    A. TCP and UDP are both layer 4 protocols.

    B. TCP and UDP are connectionless layer 3 protocols.

    C. TCP and UDP are connection-oriented layer 4 protocols.

    D. UDP is a layer 3 protocol and TCP is a layer 4 protocol.

30. Which statement is true?

    A. TCP is considered less reliable than UDP.

    B. TCP uses acknowledgments when setting up connections.

    C. UDP uses acknowledgments when setting up connections.

    D. UDP uses flow control mechanisms to maintain a connection.

31. What is SNMP used for?

    A. Viewing Web pages

    B. Managing remote network nodes

    C. Transferring files across the network

    D. Sending e-mail messages through the network

32. What is SNMP?

    A. Simple Node Management Protocol

    B. Standard Node Management Protocol

    C. Simple Network Management Protocol

    D. Standard Network Monitoring Protocol

33. What is HTTP used for?

    A. Viewing Web pages

    B. Acquiring an IP address

    C. Monitoring remote network nodes

    D. Transferring files across the network

34. Which Internet Control Message Protocol (ICMP) message type is used to indicate that a buffer is full?

    A. retransmit

    B. source quench

    C. packet redirect

    D. fragmentation required

35. What does the Internet Control Message Protocol (ICMP) message "time exceeded TTL" indicate?

    A. A connection has timed out.

    B. A user has been logged in too long.

    C. A packet has exceeded the Maximum Hop number.

    D. A packet cannot be routed in the maximum time allowed.

36. Given the IP address 15.15.15.15/16, what is the broadcast address?

    A. 15.15.15.0

    B. 15.15.15.255

    C. 15.15.255.255

    D. 15.255.255.255

37. Which statement about ARP is true?
    A. It relates an IP address to a hardware address.
    B. It routes packets efficiently to a destination node.
    C. It is used by routers to maintain IP address tables.
    D. It is used to assign IP addresses to new nodes on a network.

Answer Key

1. **B.**

2. **C.** Reliable service is a characteristic of TCP.

3. **B.** ARP is the protocol that maps IP to MAC addresses.

4. **B.** Splitting datagrams is called fragmentation.

5. **A.** 11.11.11.11 falls in the range of Class A addresses between 0 and 127.

6. **A, B,** and **C.** For connectivity in any TCP/IP network, an address and mask are required. If the user also wants connectivity to the WAN, then a default gateway is required as well.

7. **E.** Internet Control Message Protocol (ICMP) is the protocol that sends back messages to alert users when destination networks are unavailable.

8. **C, D.**

9. **A, B.**

10. **C, D.** For Internet name resolution, the operating system uses DNS and host files.

11. **A, C.**

12. **E.** Telnet is used for access to terminal servers.

13. **A.** RARP is MAC-to-IP address resolution and is the reverse of ARP.

14. **A.**

15. **C.** DNS is always used in Internet names; www is an Internet name.

16. **B.** Even without WINS, users can broadcast for computer name resources (like browsing). However, broadcasts only work for the local network; therefore, computers can browse only the local network.

17. **B.** URLs and Internet names will fail if DNS is not working. Internet names cannot be resolved with Broadcasts.

18. **A, C.** Only routers and workstations need subnet masks. Bridges are Layer 2 devices and do not need IP.

19. **B.** With a 24-bit mask, 125.13.4.0 would be the network address and 255 would be the host, but this is not a valid host ID.

20. **C.** 196.196.196.196 is a default Class C address as it falls in the range of 192 to 223.

21. **B.** 191.191.191.191 is a default class b as it falls in the range of 128 to 191.

22. **B.** 224.224.224.224 is a multicast address as it falls in the range of 224 to 239.

23. **C.** /30 is the CIDR notation for 30 bits in the subnet mask.

24. **D.** A natural Class C network has a possibility for 254 workstations.

25. **C.** IP operates at Layer 3.

26. **B.** TCP operates at Layer 4.

27. **A.**

28. **C.** Only TCP can recover from errors because of its connection-oriented properties.

29. **A.** TCP and UDP are both Layer 4 protocols.

30. **B.** TCP uses acknowledgements when establishing connections.

31. **B.** SNMP is used for management of remote nodes.

32. **C.**

33. **A.** HTTP is used for viewing Web pages.

34. **B.** A source quench ICMP message tells the sending network node that the receiving nodes buffers are full and that sending further packets will only saturate the network.

35. **C.** A time-exceeded ICMP message indicates that the packet has spent *too long* on the network and its hop count has exceeded the maximum hop count.

36. **C.** For the address 15.15.15.15 with a 16-bit mask, the broadcast address would be 15.15.255.255

37. **A.**

Answer to Exercise Five

Using the five-step approach:

1. There are 17 networks that are required.

2. For 17 networks, 5 bits are necessary, leaving only 3 bits for hosts or six hosts per subnet.

3. Five bits gives us an additional 248 to our natural Class C network resulting in a mask of 255.255.255.248.

4. The new networks are 201.26.7.8, 201.26.7.16, 201.26.7.24, 201.26.7.32, 201.26.7.40, all the way up to 201.26.7.240. If zero subnet enabled is enabled, then 201.26.7.0 and 201.26.7.248 would both be valid subnets.

5. The new hosts for the network 201.26.7.8 will be 201.26.7.9 to 201.26.7.14. 201.26.7.8 is the network ID and 201.26.7.15 is the broadcast host on the network.

ATM

Asynchronous Transfer Mode (ATM) is a technology that is the subject of numerous books all by itself. The material in this chapter is meant to be a brief overview of some of the topics that you may need to familiarize yourself with to work with ATM and Centillion switches. This chapter is by no means intended to be a one-stop-shopping place for all your ATM learning needs. Topics like Private Network Node Interface (PNNI) will be covered in Chapter 8, while other items will be covered in Chapter 13's discussion of the Centillion ATM switches. In this chapter we will examine some of the benefits of ATM, how it differs from legacy (Ethernet and Token Ring) LAN technologies, and how ATM resolves some of these differences to allow for a smooth integration.

ATM Basics

ATM is a set of standards and its purpose is to supply great amounts of bandwidth, a flexibility of management, and Quality of Service (QoS) to better support the explosion of network-based applications and high-speed access to the Internet. It also provides the capability to guarantee levels of service necessary to support applications that require very strict end-to-end latency (such as real time video) over the same network infrastructure that supports high-bandwidth applications with very little latency concerns (such as file transfers and e-mail).

Multiplexes Data

ATM switches multiplex data. Multiplexing is taking data from separate sources and combining the data for transfer across a single physical link (see Figure 5-1) as it travels

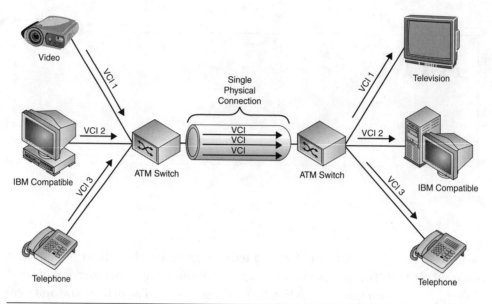

Figure 5-1   Multiplexing

towards separate destinations. When combined with ATM's QoS capabilities, this can greatly increase the efficiency of the network.

High Bandwidth

Even without the need for QoS, the bandwidth requirements of current applications dictate a need for more speed. Although the earliest ATM standards provide for data transfer rates of 25 Mbps, current standards enable rates of 2.4 Gbps.

Quality of Service (QoS)

In most modern businesses, three networks (at a minimum) need to be installed at every location: a network for the computer system and its applications and devices (e-mail and servers), a separate and unique network for the telephone system and its applications and equipment (voice mail, audio conferencing, and pbx), and a video network for cameras and monitors (not solely restricted to security applications). This is driven by the needs of the applications. Video and audio have absolute requirements for guaranteed throughput but not necessarily much bandwidth. Computer networks use high bandwidth, and applications have varying susceptibility to latency. Until ATM there was no way to guarantee that all the different applications could get the access to the media required for acceptable operation. ATM standards include the capability to exchange QoS parameters between ATM nodes to help the network make intelligent decisions that guarantee service levels.

Use of Fixed-Length Cells

One of the great advances in the function of the ATM switch was the decision to use fixed-length units (cells) to transfer data, rather than variable-length frames (such as in Ethernet and Token Ring). The fixed length of the cell enables memory to be allocated for maximum efficiency from the moment of manufacture. This enables a much higher level of efficiency and performance.

Addressing

ATM addressing does take a little getting used to. Let's look back at other familiar addressing schemes. IP addressing takes 32 zeroes and ones (bits) and breaks them down into four separate bytes that we refer to by their decimal equivalent for greater ease (see Figure 5-2). We refer to this as dotted decimal notation. Ethernet MAC addresses are six bytes long (48 bits), which are referred to by 12 hexadecimal numbers (see Figure 5-3). People do not even try to remember these addresses because other protocols mask them from the users' point of view.

The ATM address is 20 bytes (160 bits) long (see Figure 5-4). Thankfully, they are carefully broken down and handed out in such a manner as to be manageable.

The first 13 bytes of the ATM address are called the prefix. The governing body that issues the address controls the prefix. This leaves six bytes for the user to implement (a seventh byte called the selector is left over and is reserved for functions running on the switch). Because one of the goals of ATM addressing is to be strictly hierarchical, try to picture a network design that lends itself to such a structure. Remembering that there are 2^{48} unique addresses in six bytes (281,474,976,710,656 addresses), we can steal a few bytes to define regions. If we steal two bytes, that enables us to define 65,536 regions. We are left with four bytes. We can now use one of those bytes for cities (256 cities/region), one byte for buildings (256 buildings/city), and one byte for floors (256 floors/building). That leaves us with one byte to define individual switches/devices (256/floor). This is just one way of breaking down the address structure. You are free to alter it to your satisfaction and/or needs (and we still have the one byte selector left over).

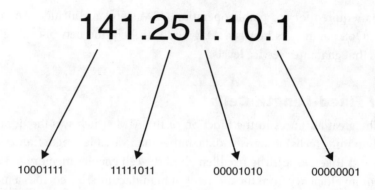

Figure 5-2   IP address

00-10-A4-B4-33-F1

00000000   00010000 10100100 10110100 00110011 11110001

Figure 5-3   MAC address

37:00:40:34:21:01:B1:A2:A4:FF:21:07:13:00:55:08:06:04:02:01

Figure 5-4   ATM address

Layers

In keeping with familiar concepts, the ATM model has a layered form that can be roughly compared to layers two (Data Link) and three (Network) of the OSI model (see Figure 5-5).

ATM Adaptation Layer (AAL Layer)

The AAL layer of the model specifically helps the higher-layer applications and protocols adapt to the ATM world. There are two sublayers at this level: the Segmentation and Reassembly (SAR) sublayer and the Convergence Sublayer (CS).

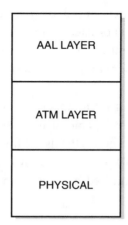

Figure 5-5   Layers of the ATM model

The SAR (for data that is being transmitted) takes the data from the higher layers and fragments (segments) it into 48-byte chunks. The SAR also (for data that is being received) takes the received 48-byte chunks and puts them back together (reassembly) to form the original message.

The CS dictates how to segment the higher-layer Protocol Data Unit (PDU) so it can set the Constant Bit Rate (CBR) or Variable Bit Rate (VBR) timing according to the needs of the higher-layer application. To accommodate different service requirements, different payload structures (AAL types) were created. Some AAL types in practice do not match their published specifications and have fallen into disuse.

DEFINITIONS   **PDU refers to any data passed from one layer of the OS model to another. As an example, an IP datagram is considered a PDU to the MAC layer. To the Network layer, a UDP packet is considered a PDU.**

CBR refers to the need of applications, such as real-time voice applications, to have a strict timing relationship between the source and destination. CBR applications typically do not require large amounts of bandwidth, but they do require regular intervals. CBR ensures those intervals are kept.

VBR refers to the need of applications, such as packetized video applications, to have a strict timing relationship between the source and destination, but not as strict as CBR applications. Watching a training video online is an example of an application that can make use of VBR. To ensure steady viewing, the destination must always have data ready to display, but that data does not need to arrive at regular intervals. VBR applications usually buffer large amounts of data. As long as the next chunk of data arrives before the buffer is empty, the application will function properly. VBR ensures that the network provides the proper amount of bandwidth when necessary to support the VBR application.

The Available Bit Rate (ABR) is a service that supports applications that do not have any time-sensitivity issues but are capable of increasing performance when enough bandwidth is available. The ABR requires the use of flow control mechanisms.

The Unspecified Bit Rate (UBR) requires no flow control mechanisms. It is a best-effort service. When there is unutilized bandwidth in a circuit, it is offered to UBR service.

AAL Types

This section will outline the various AAL types and how they are meant to be used.

Type 1

Type 1 has been created for applications that require CBR, such as real-time video. It essentially takes the 48-byte payload and fills it with 46 or 47 bytes of user data. The remaining one or two bytes of the payload are used for sequencing, so cells delivered out of order can be dropped.

Type 2

This is meant for use with applications that require VBR, such as compressed voice or video. It takes the 48-byte payload and fills up to 45 bytes with user data. The remaining three bytes are used for the connection identifier.

Type 3 and Type 4

The Type 3 and Type 4 AAL existed separately at one point but were combined into the Type 3/4 AAL.

Type 3/4

This type is also meant for VBR traffic. It can be connection-oriented or connectionless. It uses four bytes of the payload for connection information and leaves 44 bytes for user data. The four bytes taken from the payload are used for the segment type (ST, 2 bits), the Sequence Number (SN, 4 bits), the Multiplex ID (MID, 10 bits) in front of the PDU, the Length Indicator (LI, 6 bits) and the Cyclic Redundancy Check (CRC, 10 bits) at the tail end of the PDU.

Type 5

Type 5 is the most widely used AAL type. It can be used with VBR, UBR, and ABR traffic. The entire 48-byte payload is left intact.

ATM Layer

The ATM layer adds a five-byte header to each payload. All we need to do is examine the header fields to realize the importance of this layer. It is responsible for determining the path through the network and placing the identifiers of that path into the appropriate (VPI/VCI) fields of the header. The other fields of the header enable us to identify higher-layer protocols and perform error checking and basic flow control. The switch multiplexes and demultiplexes data at the ATM level. There are two types of headers: the User to Network Interface (UNI) and the Network to Network Interface (NNI). The UNI is used when user devices or edge devices connect to the ATM switch. The NNI is used when ATM switches in the network connect to each other.

The UNI Header

The UNI header has six fields totaling five bytes (see Figure 5-6):

- Generic Flow Control (GFC) (4 bits)
- Virtual Path Identifier (VPI) (8 bits)
- Virtual Channel Identifier (VCI) (16 bits)
- Payload Type Identifier (PTI) (3 bits)
- Cell Loss Priority (CLP) (1 bit)
- Header Error Check (HEC) (8 bits)

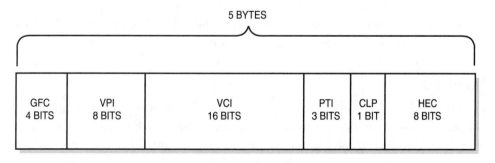

Figure 5-6   The UNI header

Generic Flow Control (GFC)

The GFC field is where flow control schemes are implemented. It is a 4-bit field.

Virtual Path Identifier (VPI)

This 8-bit field is part of how point-to-point connections are identified. A VPI is made up of one or more VCIs. It is based on the combination of the VPI/VCI values that cells are multiplexed across a point-to-point link.

Virtual Channel Identifier (VCI)

This 16-bit field is where the channel of a point-to-point connection is identified. It is a subset of a VPI. It is based on the combination of the VPI/VCI values where cells are multiplexed across a point-to-point link.

Payload Type Identifier (PTI)

This 3-bit field identifies upper-layer protocols (what is actually in the cell payload).

Cell Loss Priority (CLP)

This 1-bit field is similar to the Discard Eligible (DE) bit in Frame Relay (FR). It tells the receiving ATM device if this cell should be dropped before other high-priority cells in the event of congestion.

Header Error Check (HEC)

HEC is an error check run against the cell header. The receiving side checks the value against its own computations and tries to correct any errors it finds, if possible.

The NNI Header

The NNI adds a five-field (five bytes) header (see Figure 5-7). The difference between the NNI and the UNI header is the exclusion of the GFC field in the NNI. The 4 bits from the GFC are added to the VPI field. The remaining fields are the same.

Physical

The Physical layer is made up of the Transmission convergence (TC) sublayer and the Physical layer Medium dependant (PMD) sublayer. The TC sublayer is responsible for framing as specified by the physical transport layer (SONET) and converting the cells into bits. The PMD sublayer is responsible for timing of the bit transmission over the physical media.

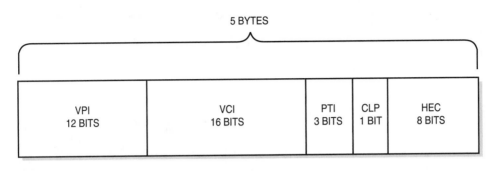

Figure 5-7 The NNI header

Signaling

Signaling, in part, is how routes through the ATM network are created automatically when using Switched Virtual Circuits (SVCs). Additionally, manually created routes through the ATM network are called Permanent Virtual Circuits (PVCs). These routes are static; because they are manually configured, they require no signaling. Both methods have advantages and disadvantages, as well as circumstances in which one method is preferable to the other.

REMEMBER   In this case, signaling refers to the point-to-point connection between two devices (see Figure 5-10 later). Also in the ATM world is end-to-end signaling, which we will examine later.

PVCs are practical and useful in either small networks or in special cases where a network administrator needs complete control over what path particular nodes use to communicate. Circumstances also may exist in which devices are incapable of creating SVCs (incompatible signaling method support) and PVCs can enable us to connect to otherwise incompatible devices. Because PVCs are manually configured, they are not subject to signaling failures. The values of the path identifiers (see VPI/VCI) are known, so they can be easily singled out in trace files for troubleshooting. If we want to create a full mesh configuration (where a direct route is defined between every device) in even a moderate-sized network (15 ATM switches), we need to create at least 105 $[n\times(n-1)/2]$ PVCs (see Figure 5-8). This requires quite a bit of planning.

SVCs are practical in moderate to large networks because they require far less planning. The route determination is dynamic. Although this can make troubleshooting more difficult, it certainly makes initial configuration and implementation much simpler.

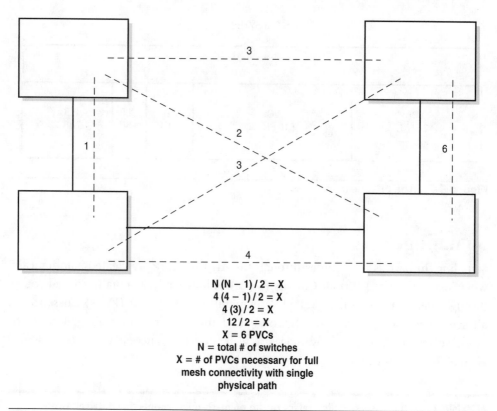

$$N(N - 1) / 2 = X$$
$$4(4 - 1) / 2 = X$$
$$4(3) / 2 = X$$
$$12 / 2 = X$$
$$X = 6 \text{ PVCs}$$
$$N = \text{total \# of switches}$$
$$X = \text{\# of PVCs necessary for full}$$
mesh connectivity with single
physical path

Figure 5-8   Circuit calculation

Before we examine signaling, we must learn a few terms used in ATM to describe the paths taken through the network (see Figure 5-9).

We begin with the Transmission Path (TP). The TP is the sum of the point-to-point links between the ATM devices. For example, in Figure 5-10, the TP from device 1 to device 4 may include link 101 and link 102.

The TP is further divided into Virtual Paths (VPs) and Virtual Circuits (VCs). If we compare this system to a system of roads, the ATM cloud would be analogous to the infrastructure of roads in North America. A particular set of roads (such as roads from Massachusetts to Florida that we take driving from Boston to Orlando) would be the TP. Although this generally indicates the path our trip will take, it does not mention other specifics, such as which tube to take in larger tunnels, or which lane to drive in (left, center, or right).

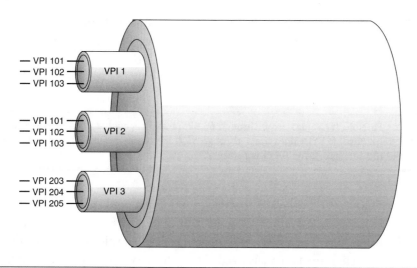

Figure 5-9   Paths

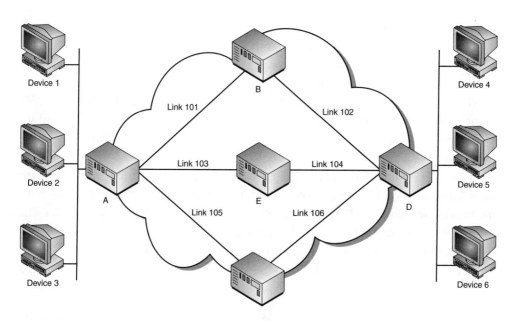

Figure 5-10   The TP includes link 101 and 102.

The TP is made up of one or more VPs. VPs are uniquely identified by their Virtual Path Identifier (VPI). VPs are made up of one or more VCs. VCs are uniquely identified by their Virtual Channel Identifier (VCI). When combined, they yield the VPI/VCI value that absolutely specifies a path from source to destination across a point-to-point link.

BY THE WAY Possible VCI values are 0 through 65,536, but 0 through 31 are reserved for special functions. Possible VPI values are 1 through 55 (for the UNI interface) and 1 through 4095 (for the NNI interface). The 0 VPI is reserved.

In Figure 5-11, 1/101 (VPI/VCI) specifies a uni-directional path from switch A to switch C. The path from switch C to switch E may be across 2/202. The end devices involved in the conversation do not determine the VPI/VCI values. They are either pre-set (in PVCs) or determined on an as-needed basis from switch to switch for individual connections (in the case of SVCs).

UNI Signalling

Now that we have learned some of the terminology and concepts associated with paths in an ATM world, let's examine the UNI signaling. The UNI defines the interface where the user device (like a server with an ATM NIC or, more often, an edge device such as a switch acting as a LEC, which we will address in this chapter when we discuss LANE) connects to the ATM network. Although the upper-layer protocols may require end-to-end connections, the UNI signaling creates a series of point-to-point connections (see Figure 5-12).

When a device needs to communicate with another device, a call setup is initiated across the UNI. Step 1 is the call/connection request in which the source device initiates the call by sending a SETUP message. The NETWORK device responds with a CALL PROCEDING message (Step 2). It is important to note that the network device responds, not the destination device. The call setup is point-to point. The source device needs to be concerned only with its connection to the network device. The network

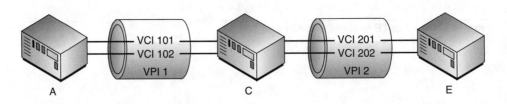

Figure 5-11 Point-to-point connections

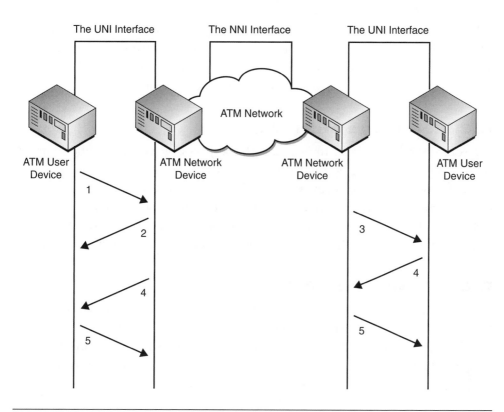

Figure 5-12 The UNI and the call setup

devices in the ATM network will also (transparently) make their connections along the path to the destination.

In Step 3, the network has forwarded the SETUP message to the destination device. In Step 4, the destination device responds with a CONNECT message. The CONNECT message is forwarded to the source device. Step 5 consists of the source device sending a CONNECT ACKNOWLEDGE, which is forwarded to the destination device.

Classical IP Routing

Although it is true (or at least can be argued) that ATM has some functions associated with layer 3, it is primarily a layer 2 set of protocols. Because the world as we know it lives and breathes over IP, there has to be a way of marrying the IP protocol stack with ATM. This is referred to as Classical IP over ATM.

In classical IP over ATM, all ATM devices have both an ATM address and an IP address. This is not a new concept. Ethernet devices have both Ethernet (MAC) addresses and IP addresses. The issue that arises is address resolution. How do we equate (resolve) an IP address to an ATM address? We know of two ways.

RFC 1293 Inverse ARP (PVC)

The source station sends an Inverse ARP (InARP) message containing the source IP address over a PVC. The station at the far side of the PVC sees the message and notes that the station with IP address X (the source station) is reachable via PVC 1 (the PVC over which the message was received). The receiving station then responds to the InARP message with its IP address so that the source station can learn the IP address of the station at the far end of the PVC. This is similar to how inverse ARP functions in Frame Relay.

RFC 1577 ATMARP (SVC)

ATMARP requires the use of an ATMARP server. The server provides address resolution by registering an ATM device's IP address when the device first contacts the server. The ATM device requests an ATM address for an IP device by issuing an ATMARP request. The ATMARP server responds with the ATM address that it has stored in its tables when the target device registered (prior to the current request). It acts as an ARP proxy.

Routing

So far, we have talked about addressing and address resolution. After this has been accomplished, the rest is a piece of cake. Routing takes place as it always has. You attach a router with an ATM and an IP address on its interface and let it route. Address resolution occurs for non-routed cells, and routing occurs for cells whose destination is off the local subnet.

There is more than one way to attach a router to a network (why make things easy?). The traditional way is for the router to use (at least) two interfaces, one per IP subnet. The result is similar to what you see in Figure 5-13. The other way is sometimes referred to as "one-armed routing." In this scenario, a single physical interface is used and two IP subnets are bound to it. Even though there may be a more direct physical path between two devices on separate IP subnets in this scenario, the devices are required to forward traffic to the router for handling (see Figure 5-14).

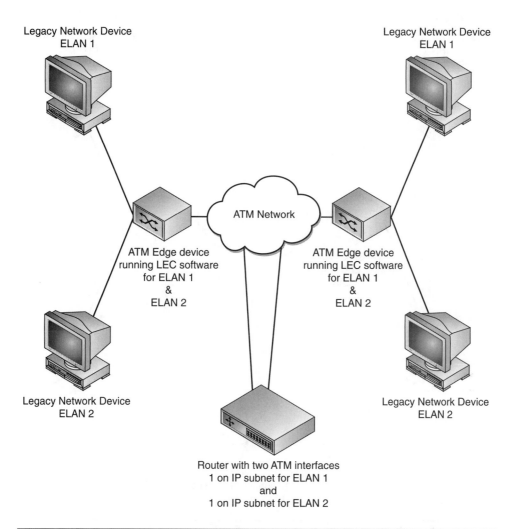

Figure 5-13   Traditional configuration routing

LAN Emulation (LANE)

LAN Emulation (LANE) is a method for extending the services of an ATM network to legacy (Ethernet and Token Ring) network devices without the need for a layer 3 device (Router or Gateway) to provide translation from one networking standard to another. In fact, LANE does not translate legacy protocols to ATM; rather, it transports legacy protocols through an ATM network without actually converting the whole frame to ATM. It does this by taking the variable length frames and segmenting them so that they can fit inside the 48-byte payload of an ATM cell (AAL Type 5). Then LANE appends the

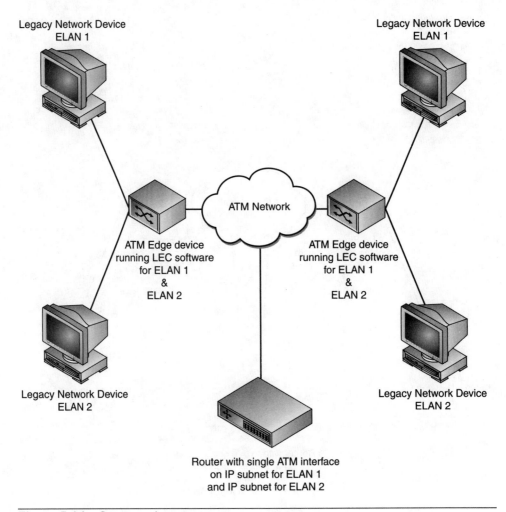

Figure 5-14 One-armed routing

typical five-byte ATM header to the payload, creating the 53-byte ATM cell, and transports the encapsulated frame through the ATM network. The original frame is reconstructed at the point of egress from the ATM network.

Things other than just the size of the frame should be considered as well. There needs to be a method for resolving (mapping) legacy MAC addresses to ATM addresses so a destination legacy device can be located through the ATM network. Also, there is no inherent broadcast capability in ATM. Because legacy LAN protocols make use of these broadcasts, a method of providing broadcast capability to ATM networks is necessary.

LANE enables clients in an Emulated LAN (ELAN) to communicate with one another across an ATM network. An ELAN is very much like connecting geographically separate VLANs together. All of the devices are a part of the same IP subnet. Because the devices are all in the same IP subnet, they are in the same Broadcast Domain (BD).

REMEMBER   A Broadcast Domain (BD) is bounded by routers/layer 3 devices. It defines the extent to which broadcasts are propagated. Broadcast frames are typically propagated through hubs and bridges/switches, but not through routers. Address resolution occurs differently for devices within a BD than for devices in separate BDs.

This means that broadcasts propagate throughout the entire ELAN and to all devices attached to it, even though ATM does not have an inherent broadcast capability (we will address this issue later in the chapter).

LANE enables devices to be part of the same BD regardless of their physical location. The devices can be separated by a cubicle, floor, building, or continent—it does not matter. Two ATM switches (and their attached clients) can converse without the need for (and the latency associated with) layer 3 routing. A physical device with an appropriate WAN interface may be necessary, and this device may be encased in a box that is usually called a router. However, no routing is performed across the interface for two clients of the same ELAN to communicate (see Figure 5-15). Because no routing takes place, we will not incur the latency associated with such software-based functions running on general-purpose processors. Instead, only layer 2 functions running on dedicated pieces of hardware need to be invoked. These dedicated hardware-based functions occur much faster than the layer 3 functions and the latency normally associated with a router is eliminated.

We will, however, have a need for layer 3 (router) devices eventually. When two devices are not in the same ELAN, they are not in the same IP subnet and therefore not in the same BD. When two devices that are not in the same IP subnet want to communicate with each other, they must use the services of a router. These are the rules of IP. These same rules apply equally to VLANs and ELANs. Even if the two devices that want to communicate are physically attached to the same switch and are on adjacent ports, when they are not in the same ELAN they must use a router to communicate with each other.

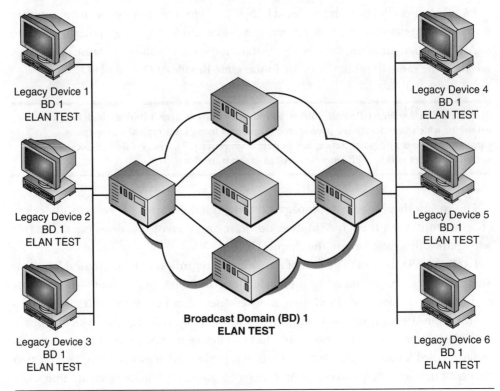

Figure 5-15 Broadcast domains and ELANS

Components

There have been many complaints (both in the workplace by my coworkers and in class by my students) that the ATM standard is so full of Three-Letter Acronyms (TLAs) that it is impossible to make heads or tails of any of it. Those complaints are fully justified, and their root is right here. The following are the components that make up a LANE network or Emulated LAN (ELAN):

- LAN Emulation Configuration Server (LECS) (optional)
- LAN Emulation Client (LEC) (required)
- LAN Emulation Server/Broadcast Unknown Server (LES/BUS) (required)

LAN Emulation Configuration Server (LECS)

The LECS helps the LEC locate the LANE Server and the Broadcast Unknown Server (BUS). The function that LECS provides to a LANE environment is similar to what a

Dynamic Host Configuration protocol (DHCP) server provides to an IP subnet. Just as an IP device boots up and requests IP parameters (address and gateway) from the DHCP server, a LEC can request required information (the address of the LES/BUS, the name of the ELAN, or the MTU size) from a LECS (see what I mean about TLAs).

LAN Emulation Client (LEC)

Please take careful note here. Many instances of LEC will be called LECs—note the lower case "s." This stands for LAN Emulation Clients. Do not confuse them with the single entity LECS—note the capital "S." The LECS stands for LAN Emulation Configuration Server (see the previous section). For a painful experience, gather a roomful of people who do not understand LANE. Try to explain the components of LANE to them. Try to get them to understand the difference between LECS and LECs without using your hands and without writing the words for them to look at. (I tried it once, before I knew better. I still have not yet fully recovered, and neither have my students.)

The LEC is the software that enables the legacy device to access the ATM network (see Figure 5-16). The LEC runs on an ATM device. It cannot run on an Ethernet or Token Ring workstation. ATM devices that run the LEC software can join the ELAN (see the following section). Once a member of the ELAN, the ATM device can extend services to the ELAN. The LEC typically runs on what we call an edge device. The edge device sits at the boarder of an ATM network (where the ATM world meets the legacy protocols).

The edge device provides the access to the services (address resolution, frame fragmentation, and encapsulation) that makes it possible for LANE to function. In a way, the LEC proxies requests for the legacy client. Legacy devices belong to an ELAN because their LEC is a client of that ELAN. From the point of view of the legacy device, the LEC and its functions are transparent. The ingress LEC receives the data from the source legacy device, and from that point the LEC is responsible for address resolution, fragmentation and encapsulation, transmission into the ATM network (including route selection), reception, de-encapsulation, reassembly, and transmission out to the destination legacy device in the same format as it was originally transmitted by the source legacy device.

Remember that the LEC is a process running in RAM. It can run on a switch and associate certain ports (and their attached devices) with an ELAN, or it can run on a file server with an ATM NIC. Note that no restriction says that only one LEC can be present at a time. A single ATM device can belong to multiple ELANs by running multiple LECs on it simultaneously, one LEC per ELAN to join.

In the case of a switch, ports A through M can be associated with LEC 1 and ports N through Z can be associated with LEC 2. In the case of a file server, all of the processes on the server can be associated with both LECs at the same time, therefore belonging to

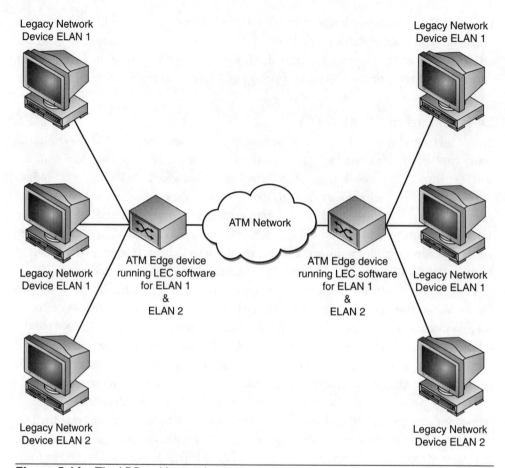

Figure 5-16   The LEC and legacy devices

both ELANs at the same time. Such a device can communicate among the ELANs that it belongs to without the services of a router.

LAN Emulation Server/Broadcast Unknown Server (LES/BUS)

The LES and the BUS are two separate entities providing two unique functions. However, because they are usually implemented in the same device (I have yet to see them separated from each other), they are referred to as the LES/BUS pair. It is the job of the LES to register each LEC as it joins the ELAN. It also maps MAC addresses to ATM addresses and assists in the location of legacy devices that have yet to be discovered.

It is the job of the BUS to add the broadcast capabilities to the ATM network that the legacy devices need to function and to locate devices that the LES could not discover. These entities are normally implemented on a switch (such as a Centillion). A single switch can support multiple LES/BUSes for multiple ELANs (one LES/BUS per ELAN). Exactly how many LES/BUSes you put on a single device depends on that device's capabilities and your network design. There can also be more than one LES/BUS per ELAN.

Fault tolerance and load balancing can be added to an ELAN by creating additional LES/BUSes for ELAN. The LES/BUSes synchronize with each other so, in the event of a failure, the second takes over, providing services for the ELAN. We call these entities co-operating LES/BUS pairs.

REMEMBER Nothing says that any two (or more) of the mentioned components cannot be implemented in a single physical device. The LES and the BUS are always two logical components in the same physical device. The LECS can also run in the same physical device as the LES/BUS. A LEC can, and usually does, run on each device that has either a LECS or a LES/BUS on it (see Figure 5-17).

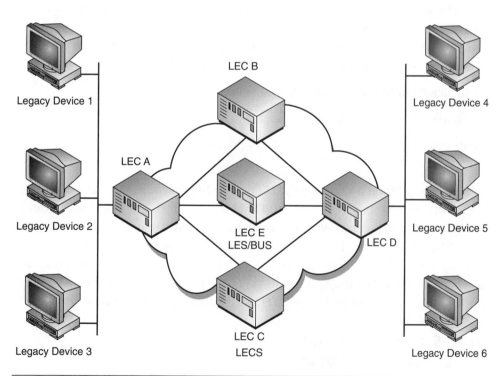

Figure 5-17 ELAN components

Joining an ELAN

When an LEC (edge device, router, or server) wants to join an ELAN, it must connect to a LES/BUS. There are two methods of locating a LES/BUS. The first is to use the services of the LECS. The second is by having the address of the LES/BUS statically preconfigured on the LEC. Both of these methods have their advantages and disadvantages that we will examine here.

Using the LECS

Using the LECS is much like a computer using a DHCP server to gain an IP address and other related information so it can gain access to an IP network. The LECS can give (upon request) the address of the LES/BUS that services the ELAN that the LEC requests. The LECS can provide other parameters (some are required; some are optional). Using this method to locate a LES/BUS has many of the same benefits as using a DHCP server to provide an IP parameter assignment to a workstation. There is a single device to manage, which makes setting up and implementing changes easier. You can have multiple LECS for a single ELAN to provide fault tolerance and load balancing (a single LECS can also service multiple ELANs as well). Four methods of locating a LECS are available.

The first method for locating the LECS is a well-known address. The ATM forum has defined two addresses that are reserved for use by the LECS:

C500790000000000000000000000-00A03E000001-00

If that one does not work, the second one

470079000000000000000000000000-00A03E000001-00

will be tried.

The second method for locating the LECS is the Integrated Local Management Interface (ILMI). ILMI uses the reserved VPI/VCI value 0/16. The LEC simply issues a Config Request over the well-known VCC (0/16) and a LECS will respond.

The third method for locating the LECS is by preconfiguring the LEC with the address of the LECS (this address does not have to be the well-known reserved address for a LECS as defined by the ATM forum. A LECS can be given any valid ATM address).

The fourth method for locating the LECS is by using the well-known VPI/VCI 0/17.

Preconfiguring the LEC with the Address of the LES/BUS

Just as an IP workstation can be manually configured with an IP address or a default gateway, an LEC can be preconfigured with the address of the LES/BUS. The advantage here is that the administrator has complete control over the environment. With good documentation, this can ease the troubleshooting process. The problem is that if the address of the LES/BUS changes, every LEC needs to be manually updated. Some LEC implementations may not support more than one manually configured LES/BUS per ELAN. This would eliminate the possibility of fault-tolerant or load-balancing LES/BUS pairs.

If the LEC Is Configured to Use the LECS

The LEC creates a Configure Direct VCC to the LECS and sends a LE_CONFIGURE_ REQUEST control frame to request the LECS configuration information. The LECS responds with a LE_CONFIGURE_RESPONSE control frame over the Configure Direct VCC that was built by the LEC. After the LECS responds, the VCC from the LEC to the LECS can be torn down. That VCC is not used again during the membership of the LEC to the ELAN, and the ATM forum standards do not require that it be maintained. Once the LEC has the address of the LES, it may attempt to join the ELAN.

The LEC now builds a Control Direct (bidirectional point-to-point) VCC to the LES. The LEC sends a LE_JOIN_REQUEST to the LES. The request contains parameters that the LEC requests (some required, some optional), which the LES examines and uses to determine if the LEC should be allowed to join the ELAN. The LES sends a LE_JOIN_ RESPONSE (either positive or negative) to the LEC either over the Control Direct VCC or over the Control Distribute (unidirectional point-to-multipoint) that the LES constructs. If the response from the LES is positive, the VCCs that were constructed are maintained throughout the membership of the LEC to the ELAN. The membership is not yet complete.

The LEC still needs to connect to the BUS. The LEC issues an LE_ARP_REQUEST. The request contains the all-ones MAC address (0X ffffffffffff). Because the LES does not resolve broadcast addresses for the ELAN, it hands to the LEC the address of the BUS (which does) in an LE_ARP_RESPONSE. The LEC contacts the BUS by creating a Multicast Send (point-to-point bidirectional) VCC, and the BUS responds by creating a Multicast Forward (point-to-multipoint unidirectional) VCC. At this point, the LEC has fully joined the ELAN.

How It Works

A legacy device wants to communicate with another legacy device across an ATM network. If both devices are in the same ELAN, what happens?

The first device does what it normally does (broadcast or unicast) when it attempts to initiate communication. The LEC sees the request and checks its tables to see if it has registered an ATM address to the destination MAC address in the frame. If not, the ingress LEC sends an LE_ARP request to the LES to see if there is a registered address for the destination. If the LES has registered the destination address, it can send it to the LEC. If the LES has not registered the address, it can send LE_ARP requests to the other LECs in the ELAN to see if any other LECs have registered the address. If no LEC has registered the address, the ingress LEC can send the data to the BUS. The BUS then sends the data to every LEC in the ELAN. The LECs will send the data to all of the stations connected to them.

When the data reaches its destination and responds, the LEC attached to it registers the address. When the response reaches the ingress LEC, it registers the address. The ingress LEC now has enough information to build a Data Direct VCC to the LEC that services the destination. The LEC servicing the destination MAC device will also register the address with the LES so that in future communications, other LECs will not have to use the services of the BUS.

Multiprotocol Over ATM (MPOA)

MPOA addresses issues with the inefficiency of ELAN implementation related to layer 3 routing (among other things). We have explored how efficiency can be increased by placing devices that are geographically remote in the same ELAN. By placing the devices in the same ELAN, we place them in the same Logical IP Subnet (LIS). As we know from IP, when two devices exist in the same LIS and they need to talk to each other, they perform local address resolution (like ARP) and then send unicast messages. In this example, no layer 3 device gets involved in the conversation, and therefore we do not incur the latency usually associated with such devices.

The drawback, or flip side, of this equation is when devices are geographically local to each other but in separate ELANs. When the devices are in separate ELANs, they are in separate LISs and therefore need to use a router to forward messages between each other. Even in the case of one-arm routing (when both LISs exist on the same physical interface of the router and therefore do not need to cross the router backplane), the router exists in the data path and must process the packets. This takes time and adds latency to the network. This may even cause packets to cross many switches just to get to a router to route a packet to a device that is just one port away on the same switch as the source.

MPOA addresses exactly this issue. By placing MPOA-capable routers in the network along with MPOA clients, routing can be done in a distributed fashion and in such a way as to eliminate the router from the data path altogether. The MPOA router learns routes just as any router does, but it can distribute the information to MPOA clients. These clients are then capable of determining the actual location of devices in separate ELANs (LISs) and build short-cuts that take the data on a path that may not traverse the router at all. The MPOA clients are capable of creating the SVCs that will connect the source with the destination without the data ever traversing the router (if the network design allows). MPOA uses the Next Hop Resolution Protocol (NHRP) for routing and LANE for bridging.

As an example of how MPOA works, let's examine a possible conversation between two devices in separate ELANs. In Figure 5-18, assume that workstation 2 and workstation 6 are in separate ELANS and want to communicate. If not for MPOA, that conversation would need to traverse four switches and one router (switch A, E, the router, switch F, and D). In an MPOA environment, the conversation may traverse three switches only (Switch A, C, and D) without ever crossing the router.

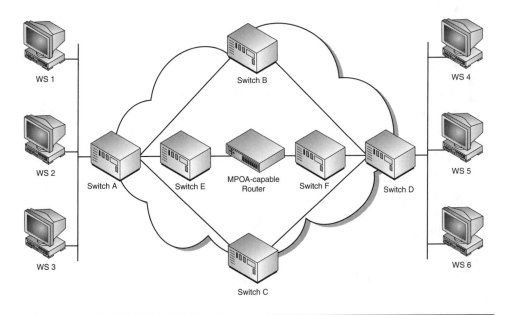

Figure 5-18 MPOA

Review Questions

1. What is one of the major benefits of ATM?
   A. Support for QoS.
   B. It requires the use of separate physical links for different data types.
   C. It is a set of proprietary protocols that enables single-vendor solutions.
   D. For efficiency, it uses variable-length frames.

2. Fixed-length cells have which of the following advantages?
   A. They require more processing power.
   B. They enable hardware and protocols to be designed more efficiently to handle cells of known lengths.
   C. They move faster than variable-length cells.

3. An ATM address is how many bytes in length?
   A. 6
   B. 4
   C. 16
   D. 20

4. True/False: ATM addresses are expressed in decimal.
   A. True
   B. False

5. The SAR function is a feature of what layer of the ATM model?
   A. AAL Type 5
   B. AAL
   C. ATM
   D. PMD

6. SAR stands for
   A. Stop and Resend
   B. Segmentation and Reassembly
   C. Supply and Record
   D. Snmp and Rmon

7. The SAR on the source ATM device is responsible for
   A. Retransmission of unacknowledged cells
   B. Buffering of cells over the CIR
   C. Fragmentation of large variable-length PDUs into 48-byte payloads
   D. Network management and monitoring

8. True/False

A protocol data unit (PDU) is data received from a higher layer.

   A. True

   B. False

9. AAL Type 1 is meant for use with

   A. UBR traffic

   B. VBR traffic

   C. ILMI

   D. CBR traffic

10. What is the most widely used AAL type?

   A. AAL Type 1

   B. AAL Type 2

   C. AAL Type 3

   D. AAL Type 4

   E. AAL Type 3/4

   F. AAL Type 5

11. The ATM layer adds a ____-byte header to each payload.

   A. 5

   B. 6

   C. 7

   D. 20

12. The UNI header has _____ fields.

   A. three

   B. four

   C. five

   D. six

13. The length of the VPI field in the UNI header is

   A. 8 bits

   B. 12 bits

   C. 16 bits

   D. 4 bits

14. An interface would be defined as UNI between what two devices?

   A. Two switches in an ATM cloud

   B. An edge device and an ATM switch

15. Which of the following diagrams depicts an NNI header?

A.

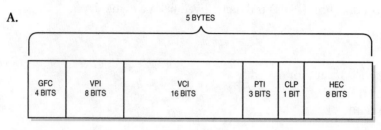

B.

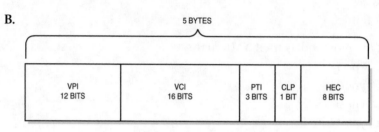

16. Signalling is used to create
   A. PVCs
   B. SVCs
   C. LLCs
   D. PMDs

17. Which of the following are advantages of SVCs in large networks? (Choose two.)
   A. They require less planning than PVCs.
   B. They require more planning than PVCs.
   C. They are easy to troubleshoot.
   D. They require less setup time when configuring the switch.

18. Which of the following statements are true regarding Virtual Paths and Virtual Circuits? (Choose two.)
   A. A Virtual Path can be made up of one or more Virtual Circuits.
   B. A Virtual Circuit can be made up of one or more Virtual Paths.
   C. A user can manually assign a VPI/VCI value of 0/16 to a PVC.
   D. VPI/VCI values identify a conversation between two nodes.

19. True/False
   VPI/VCI values absolutely specify a path from source to destination from end to end.
   A. True
   B. False

20. When a connection request SETUP message is sent by the source node, the (Choose two.)

    A. Destination node responds with a CALL PROCEEDING message.

    B. Ingress network device responds with a CALL PROCEEDING message.

    C. SETUP message is forwarded to the destination by the network.

    D. Ingress network device responds with a CONNECT message.

21. Two concerns of Classical IP routing are

    A. Addressing

    B. Cell inversion

    C. DLCI

    D. Address resolution

22. Which of the following are components of a LANE environment? (Choose two.)

    A. LEC

    B. LES

    C. CLP

    D. DHCP server

23. The device responsible for giving the LEC the ATM address of the LES is the

    A. DHCP server

    B. BUS

    C. FECN

    D. LECS

24. LANE is a method of

    A. Converting legacy protocols such as SNA to IP

    B. Enabling legacy protocols such as Ethernet or Token Ring to be transported across an ATM network

    C. Segmenting and reassembling upper-layer PDUs

    D. Converting Ethernet to Token Ring

25. A single ELAN is characterized by

    A. Being a single IP subnet

    B. Being multiple IP subnets that can be geographically separated

    C. Being able to contain devices that are geographically separate

    D. Being a single broadcast domain

26. To communicate between two ELANs, there must be a
    A. Hub
    B. Bridge
    C. Switch
    D. Router
    E. Terminal server

27. True/False
    The LECS is responsible for registering LECs as they join the ELAN.
    A. True
    B. False

28. True/False
    The LEC can run on a workstation with an Ethernet card provided that there is a supported driver.
    A. True
    B. False

29. The two methods by which a LEC can obtain the address of the LES are by
    A. Receiving the information from a DHCP server
    B. Listening for LE_LES_ADVERTISEMENTs
    C. Being statically configured with the LES address
    D. By receiving the information from a LECS

30. ARP requests attempt to resolve known IP addresses to unknown MAC addresses. What do LE_ARP requests attempt to resolve?
    A. Known LANE addresses with unknown MAC addresses
    B. Known MAC addresses with unknown IP addresses
    C. Known IP addresses with unknown ATM addresses
    D. Known ATM addresses with unknown IP addresses
    E. Known SAP addresses with unknown MAC addresses

Answers

1. **A.** ATM supports Quality of Service (QoS). Requiring separate physical links and using proprietary protocols would not be beneficial. Variable length frames are not a feature of ATM.

2. **B.** When the variable length of the cell is removed from the equation, the hardware and software that drives it become easier to design. Because the flexibility to

deal with variable length cells is not an issue, the hardware can take over more of the processing. Therefore, B is the correct answer. A is incorrect because requiring more processing power is not an advantage. C is incorrect because all data over a given medium travels at the same speed regardless of the size of its cell (frame).

3. **D.** An ATM address is 20 bytes long.

4. **False.** ATM addresses are expressed as Hexacecimal numbers where each byte is separated by a ".".

5. **B.** The ATM Adaptation Layer (AAL) provides the Segmentation and Re-assembly (SAR) function. AAL Type 5 is not a correct answer because it is not a layer of the ATM model. ATM is not the correct answer because the ATM layer does not provide this function. PMD is incorrect because it is a sublayer of the physical layer and is responsible for the details of transmitting the raw bits after the SAR function has been performed (or for receiving the raw bits before the SAR function has been performed).

6. **B.** Segmentation and Reassembly is the correct answer. It takes the variable-length PDU that is handed down from upper layers (for transmitting nodes) and converts it into smaller pieces that can fit into the payload of an ATM cell. For receiving nodes, it takes the data found in ATM cell payloads and recreates the original data PDU that was sent by the transmitting node. A and C are incorrect because I made them up.

7. **C.** See previous answer.

8. **True.** The PDU refers to data received from another layer.

9. **D.** AAL Type 1 provides the connection-oriented data transfer and strict timing relationships that make Constant Bit Rate (CBR) traffic possible over nondedicated connections. Variable Bit Rate (VBR) is used with AAL Type 2. Unspecified Bit Rate (UBR) is used with AAL Type 5.

10. **F.** AAL Type 5 is the most widely used AAL Type.

11. **A.** The ATM Layer adds the five-byte header to the 48-byte payload to create the 53-byte cell. The five-byte header contains the VPI/VCI values that are required to switch cells in an ATM network.

12. **D.** The six fields in the UNI header are the GFC, VPI, VCI, PT, CLP, and HEC. The NNI header has one less field for a total of five.

13. **A.**

14. B. The UNI interface defines communications between a user device and a network device. An edge device acts as a user device in this definition; therefore, the interface between an edge device and an ATM switch matches the definition of a UNI interface. The interface between two switches in an ATM cloud would be an NNI.

15. B. The difference between Figure B (the correct answer) and Figure A (the incorrect answer) is that Figure B has only five fields in the header. The NNI header has one field less that the UNI header.

16. B. Signalling is used to create Switched Virtual Circuits (SVCs). Permanent Virtual Circuits (PVCs) are created manually on the switches by the administrator and do not require any protocol for their dynamic creation.

17. A, D. Switched Virtual Circuits are advantageous because they are created dynamically as needed and therefore do not need to be planned or configured as PVCs do.

18. A, D. The correct answers are that a Virtual Path can be made up of one or more Virtual Circuits and that the VPI/VCI values identify a conversation between nodes. Virtual Circuits are subdivisions of a Virtual Path similar to lanes on a highway. In order to be entirely specific about a route or conversation, both the Path and the Circuit need to be identified. B is incorrect because it reverses the relationship between the Virtual Path and the Virtual Circuit. C is incorrect because the VPI/VCI 0/16 is reserved by the ATM Forum for the ILMI function.

19. False. The VPI/VCI value absolutely specifies the path from source to destination across a specific point-to-point link. The VPI/VCI value is only recognized locally (between two switches, for example) in much the same fashion that DLCIs have only local significance. The VPI/VCI value along the next point-to-point link of any given path may be different than that of the previous values.

20. B, C. Remembering that the communications between the source and destination are actually made up of a series of individual point-to-point connections with signaling that occurs independently, we can see that the network responds to the initiator's request long before the message reaches the destination node. The network device that receives the SETUP message then must forward the message to the destination device. D is incorrect because the ingress network device does not send the CONNECT message until the destination node agrees to a connection.

21. A, D. The conversion and resolution of an ATM address to an IP address and vice versa are the major concerns of classical IP routing. C is incorrect because it deals with Frame Relay and B is incorrect because I made it up.

22. **A, B.** The LAN Emulation Client (LEC) is a component that runs on any ATM device that needs to join an ELAN or on the edge device that provides the service for legacy devices. The LAN Emulation Server is the component of LANE that provides for management of the ELAN, including address registration and address resolution.

23. **D.** The LAN Emulation Configuration Server (LECS) is the device responsible for giving the LEC the address of the LES.

24. **B.** LANE is a method of enabling legacy protocols such as Ethernet or Token Ring to be transported across an ATM network. Transporting SNA over IP is a service provided by DLSW. Segmenting and reassembling upper-layer PDUs is provided by the SAR. Converting Ethernet to Token Ring is a service called Translational Bridging.

25. **A, C, D.** Being a single IP subnet and a single broadcast domain are both characteristics of an ELAN. The fact that an ELAN can contain devices that are geographically separate is not only a characteristic, but one of the purposes of LANE.

26. **D.** To communicate between two ELANs, there must be a Router. Remembering that one of the characteristics of an ELAN is that each ELAN is a separate IP subnet, we can determine that to communicate between IP subnets we need a Layer 3 device. A router fulfils this need. Hubs, switches, and bridges provide communication to devices in the same IP subnet. Terminal servers provide communication to devices not accessible through in-band communication.

27. **False.** The LAN Emulation Server (LES) is responsible for registering LECs as they join the ELAN. The LAN Emulation Configuration Server (LECS) is responsible for delivering the address of the LES to the LECs as they request it.

28. **False.** The LEC can only run on an ATM device.

29. **C, D.** Being statically configured with the LES address and receiving the information from a LECS are both methods for a LEC to obtain the address of a LES.

30. **C.** LE_ARP requests attempt to resolve known IP addresses with unknown ATM addresses.

## CHAPTER 6

TCP/IP Routing

This chapter will cover routing and how routers discover the network. We will focus primarily on a distance vector routing protocol called the Routing Information Protocol (RIP). We will discuss the benefits and limitations of RIP as well as the two versions of RIP currently in wide use in networks around the world. This chapter, like the previous ones, contains material that appears in the Data IP Fundamentals exam for the first portion of the Nortel Networks Support Specialist designation. Additionally, the material discussed here will appear on at least one product specific exam (Routers and Passport). In some cases what is discussed here will correlate directly to an exam objective and then we will refer back to what is written here.

Routing

Routing is the process that every node on a network uses to choose a path to send packets to destination nodes. As we discussed in Chapter 4, routers are used to forward packets from one physical network to another. Routers are also referred to as gateways (as in default gateways) and operate at layer 3 of the OSI model, the networking layer. Because routers are layer 3 devices, they can connect different networks to each other.

When a packet is received at a router, IP will decrement the Time To Live (TTL) of the packet by one or remove the packet from the network if the TTL is zero. IP may have to fragment the packet if it is too large (this will cause changes to the flag, fragment ID, and fragment offset fields that were discussed in Chapter 4). IP will also change the packet's checksum information based on routing decisions that will be made for the packet.

For every packet on the network, a routing decision of where to send the packet is made based on source and destination IP address. The IP layer of every IP host on the network makes these decisions (as we discussed in Chapter 4) based on the subnet mask. When a host attempts to communicate with another host, the IP layer first checks to see if the destination host is local or remote.

NOTE Local packets result in an ARP request to find the destination MAC, whereas remote packets are forwarded to the router or gateway.

If the destination is remote, IP checks the routing table for a route to the host. If no explicit route is found, IP can use a default gateway or default route if one is available. When a router is involved in routing decisions, the IP layer consults a routing table stored in memory. A routing table contains entries with the IP addresses of networks to which the router can communicate.

This process occurs at each hop along the path from source to destination. The final router on the destination host's network sends out an ARP request to the destination station and sends the packet directly there.

NOTE The router looks for the most specific route for packets. This is the entry with the longest mask. A default route is used only if no specific route is available to the destination network.

Nortel Networks provides routing tables and forwarding tables for every IP routing interface of a router or routing switch. The routing table is stored in the memory of the router and is the same for all interfaces on the router/routing switch. The routing table is created by the routing table manager (RTM), which chooses the best route available to each destination network and submits them to the routing table. For greater efficiency the administrator can preallocate memory for the routing table. This ensures that all the memory used for the routing table is contiguous. If not enough memory is preallocated by the administrator, the router automatically adds memory to the routing table as needed.

The forwarding table, on the other hand, is different for each interface. It is actually a subset of the larger routing table and contains an interface's last-accessed routes. It acts as a fast cache to make finding routes faster, because if the route appears in the forwarding table, the interface does not have to hash the larger routing table.

Routers within a single company's network (also known as the Autonomous System, or AS) generally have the complete set of routes to all addresses. If the destination node address does not appear in the routing table, the address is not a valid destination address. When the address is invalid, the router sends back a message that the network is unreachable. But how do routes get into the routing table?

Static and Dynamic Routing Methods

Static routing requires that all routing tables on all routers be updated manually. If routes change, static routers do not inform each other of the change or exchange information with each other. Static routes are manually configured routes that specify the next hop in the transmission path of the datagram. An administrator may create a static route to control paths that the datagram follows. When building a static route, an administrator must make sure to build the route on both ends of the routers and networks, so that the routers can communicate with each other and the data has the capability to find the destination station and come back.

A static router can communicate only with networks for which it has a configured interface. To route IP in a static network, each router must be configured with an entry in each router's routing table for each network in the internetwork or a default gateway address of another router's local interface. Entries in the routing table should include a network address, a netmask, and a gateway address (see Figure 6-1).

```
route add 20.4.4.0 mask 255.255.255.0 10.1.1.112 metric 1
route add 20.4.5.0 mask 255.255.255.0 10.1.1.112 metric 1
route add 20.4.6.0 mask 255.255.255.0 10.1.1.112 metric 1
route add 21.4.4.4 mask 255.255.255.255 100.1.1.112 metric 1
```

Figure 6-1 This figure shows the adding of static routes into the Microsoft routing table. The networks 20.4.4.0, 20.4.5.0, and 20.4.6.0 with a 24-bit mask are all being directed out of the interface 10.1.1.112. Additionally, a static route has been added for the workstation 21.4.4.4 (hence the 32-bit mask representing this station only) mapped to the interface 100.1.1.112.

Default Route

The address 0.0.0.0 in a routing table can be interpreted to mean any network that the router does not know how to get to. It is often used to represent a default route, and it points to a default gateway. It can be used on a workstation for communicating to other networks. It can also be used on a router to forward requests for unknown networks to a gateway router. A default route is a type of static route that can be created to point to some type of gateway router. This gateway router may even be the network's entry to the Internet. To use a default route, the administrator must first define this route. The administrator chooses which router is the destination for traffic that is not on a known network. All routers forward their nonspecified network traffic to this defined default route.

 NOTE A default route is a static route that an administrator must define.

Routers that route to the Internet do not have a complete set of routes and rely on default routes to handle node addresses they do not understand. Using default routes in the AS or within a local network has issues. Local routing errors go unnoticed because a workstation may send a packet that is forwarded to the Internet because of the default route. On the other hand, having default routes could mean that the routing update messages are smaller because the routing tables can be smaller as well.

EXERCISE On a Microsoft workstation, go the Command prompt and type in Route Print. What are the entries in the routing table? Notice the default route and the specific route for the workstation. Notice the multicast route and the loopback route (see Figure 6-2).

The disadvantages of static routes are obvious. They cannot accommodate rapid growth or change. In rapidly changing environments, administrators cannot respond to changes fast enough to handle problems. If there are multiple paths in a static network, the administrator also has to manually choose to create only one path. If that path becomes unavailable, the routers will not know about an alternate path, even if one exists.

Dynamic routing is a function of routing protocols, such as the Routing Information Protocol (RIP) and Open Shortest Path First (OSPF). We will discuss RIP in this chapter and OSPF in Chapter 7. Routing protocols periodically exchange routing information about known networks with other dynamic routers. That way, if a route changes,

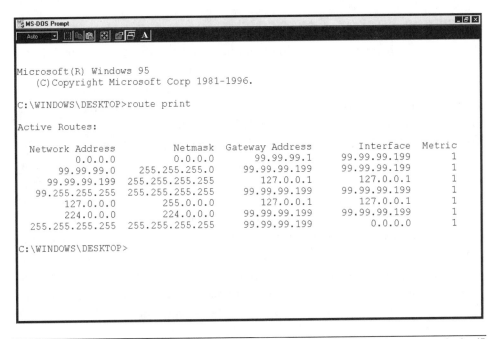

Figure 6-2 The result of a Route Print command on a Microsoft workstation with the IP address of 99.99.99.199 and the default gateway of 99.99.99.1

other routers are automatically informed of the change. They also eliminate the need to create static routing tables. Dynamic routing makes more sense in larger networks because the administrator needs to do much less configuration.

There are two types of routing protocols: the Interior Gateway Protocol (IGP) and the Exterior Gateway Protocol (EGP). A single company's network (which may consist of multiple LANs and WANs) is called an AS. An AS is a collection of routers and hosts that belong to a single company. Multiple ASs from many different companies worldwide make up the global Internet. Routers inside an AS tend to use IGPs to communicate and exchange network topology information with each other. This is because a company needs to share all known routes with all routers within the AS or company network. Two IGPs are commonly used: RIP and OSPF. Routers in separate ASs, on the other hand, use EGPs to communicate with other companies' routers. When different companies communicate across the Internet, routing information must be shared; however, companies want to share only very limited routing information through EGPs. There are two common EGPs: EGP and the Border Gateway Protocol (BGP). In this chapter we will focus on one specific IGP: RIP. OSPF and BGP will be the focus of Chapter 7.

Distance Vector Protocols

Distance vector refers to an algorithm that routers use to propagate routing information. The idea of the distance vector is very simple. The router keeps a list of all known routes in a table. A router first initializes its routing table to contain an entry for each directly connected network. Each router sends a copy of its routing table to any other router it can reach directly. Each entry in the routing table identifies a destination network and gives the distance to that network, usually measured in metrics.

A distance vector means of route propagation is easy to implement, but has disadvantages. In a completely static environment where no workstations or computers change or move, this algorithm works best because it propagates routes to all destinations. Once routes change rapidly, the network may not stabilize. When routes change, the information propagates slowly from one router to another. Meanwhile, some routers may have incorrect routing information. The distance vector protocol is concerned only with how to get there and uses a next hop or tick count. This means that a distance vector protocol strictly measures how many routers must be crossed to reach the final destination. The fewer routers crossed, the better the hop or tick count, and the better the router.

RIP is a distance vector protocol that uses the Bellman-Ford algorithm. RIP makes its routing decision solely based on distance (hop count). It does not take into consideration congestion, line speed, or cost.

RIP Version 1

RIP is the most widely used IGP. This protocol was originally designed for small local networks and relies on physical network broadcast to make routing changes quickly. RIP was not designed to be used in large WAN networks, although today it is used in many large networks because of its ease in setting up and minimal hardware requirements for routers and switches.

RIP is a straightforward implementation of distance vector routing for local networks. Routers running RIP send out a User Datagram Protocol (UDP) broadcast message every 30 seconds onto the network to all IP subnets within the broadcasting range. The message contains information from a router's routing database. Each message consists of pairs of IP network addresses and an integer distance to that network (see Figure 6-3).

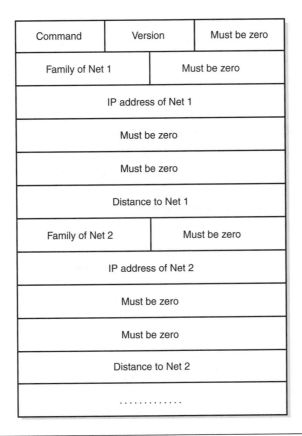

Command	Version	Must be zero
Family of Net 1		Must be zero
IP address of Net 1		
Must be zero		
Must be zero		
Distance to Net 1		
Family of Net 2		Must be zero
IP address of Net 2		
Must be zero		
Must be zero		
Distance to Net 2		
. . . .		

Figure 6-3   RIP message format

NOTE   Because RIP uses UDP, which is not guaranteed, routers broadcast updates every 30 seconds to ensure other RIP routers receive their updates.

The RIP message format consists of the following:

- **Command**   Specifies either a request for routing information (1) or a response (2). Responses contain the sender's routing table.

- **Version**   The protocol version number; a 1 represents RIPv1, and a 2 is used for RIPv2. This is important for the message to be read properly because the format for each version is different (see RIPv2 packets in Figure 6-8).

- **Family of Net 1**   Identifies the protocol family for the network addresses. IP addresses are assigned a value of 2. [RIP is also implemented with Internetwork Packet Exchange (IPX).]

- **IP address of Net 1**   IP address of the first network in the sender's routing table.

- **Must be zero**   RIPv2 uses this field, but RIPv1 cannot.

- **Distance to Net 1**   The number of gateway hops to the network. Values are limited to 1 through 15. Sixteen is considered unreachable.

> **NOTE**   A single 512-octet RIP announcement can contain a maximum of 25 networks.

Because RIP sends out the entire routing table every 30 seconds, a network with 200 routes sends out 8 of these 512-octet packets every 30 seconds.

RIP routers can behave in active mode and advertise their route tables. They also listen to updates from the network and fill their tables based on information they receive in advertisements from neighbors. A route to a destination is kept until an alternate route is found with a lower cost.

RIP has a list of routes currently known to the router, which it broadcasts unsolicited out of each interface every 30 seconds. This update contains known networks and the distances (hop count) associated with each one. No mask information is exchanged. Routing tables are also exchanged upon request by an initializing router entering the network and broadcasting for RIP routes. RIP routers also listen for updates every 30 seconds (because of a parameter known as broadcast timer, which can be changed).

Routers must time out what they learn via RIP. When a router installs a route in its table, it starts a timer for the route. The timer must be restarted whenever the router receives another RIP message advertising the route. After 90 seconds, if a router has not seen a network in the update messages, it is marked unreachable. After 90 more seconds, it is removed from the routing table. So the route becomes invalid if 180 seconds pass without the network being advertised again. When a route or router becomes unavailable, it can take several minutes for the changes to be propagated throughout the network. This is known as the slow convergence problem.

Once a router learns a path to a network from another router, it must keep the route until it learns a better one. Each router's routing table has a complete list of all of the network IDs and the possible ways to reach those networks (see Figure 6-4).

Destination	Metric	Next hop	Type	Protocol	Age	Index
27.30.1.0	0	27.30.1.90	Direct	Local	582	1
27.30.2.0	0	27.30.2.90	Direct	Local	582	2
27.30.3.0	2	27.30.1.91	Indirect	RIP	27	2
27.30.4.0	2	27.30.2.81	Indirect	RIP	15	1

Figure 6-4   Routing table on a Nortel Networks' router

The routing table consists of the following:

- **Destination**   The IP address of the destination network.

- **Metric**   The cost to the destination network. This is generally defined in hop counts, but can be ticks in IPX and other values in other RIP implementations.

- **Next hop**   The IP address of the next hop interface used to forward a packet through the network.

- **Type**   The type of route used. Direct means that this network is one of the router's directly connected interfaces, and the interface is identified. Indirect means that this network was learned from one of the routing protocols and identifies the router that the packet must be forwarded to for the destination network.

- **Protocol**   The routing protocol used to learn this route.

- **Age**   The number of seconds since this route was last updated. On a static or direct route, this number can become very large. It merely represents how long the circuit has been up. For an RIP route, by default, age should not be above 30 seconds. After 90 seconds, this route is advertised as unreachable (16 hops). After another 90 seconds, the route is flushed from the routing table.

- **Index**   The Nortel Networks-assigned number that identifies the circuit over which the next hop can be reached. It is numbered according to the way the administrator set up the interfaces and which circuit was created first.

This routing table can have hundreds and even thousands of entries in a large IP network with multiple paths. Since the maximum size of a single RIP packet is 512 bytes, large routing tables have to be sent as multiple RIP packets. Although RIP routers advertise the entire content of their routing tables, the router does not advertise a subnet or host out an interface that does not belong to that network. Instead, it advertises the natural network portion of the address only.

By default, RIP enables a maximum of 15 hops because of the time it takes all the routers to converge and stabilize the routing table. (Every packet has a default TTL of 30 seconds.) Sixteen hops is considered unreachable. Nortel Networks allows an implementation of extended RIP with 127 hops in the network topology. This is *not recommended*.

Although local interfaces have a cost of zero in the local routing table, a RIP update advertises that network at the configured interface cost (by default, one). In RIP metric, a router is defined as one hop away from directly connected networks, two hops away from networks that are reachable through one other router, three hops if two routers are crossed, and so on (see Figure 6-5). Nortel Networks defines directly connected routes as having a metric cost of zero.

When a RIP update is received, the router adds the cost configured for the incoming interface (usually one by default) to the advertised cost for the network. If the received advertisement is better (less hops) than anything already in the network, it is added to the routing table. If the cost is equal to what is already in the routing table, it is discarded *unless* it is received from the originating advertiser of this route. If the router that previously advertised this network is now advertising it with a higher cost, we assume the network moved and the router is informing us about it. This is the Bellman-Ford algorithm that RIP uses to build its routing tables.

Route Selection

Because the same route can come from many different sources, how does the router know which source is the best? A router first looks at route preference for the highest preference; in the case of a tie, the router analyzes route weight for the lowest choice. If both the preference and weight are the same (heard from the same protocol), the router uses whichever route it hears first. The route selected by the routing table manager as having won the tie is flagged and becomes part of the routing table. (See Table 6-1.)

Some implementations allow an Equal Cost Multi Path (ECMP), which maintains multiple equal cost routes to the same location. This takes additional memory in the routing table and can create a need for more routing update packets.

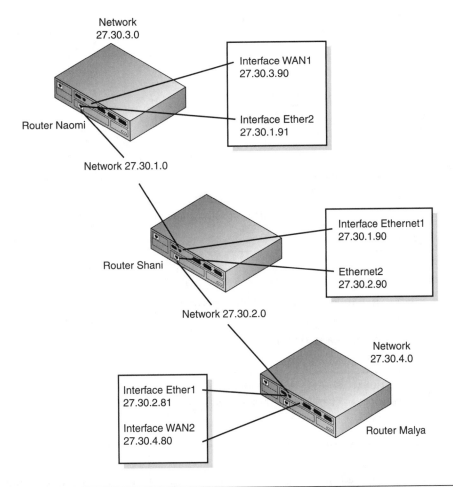

Figure 6-5   Building the routing table in Figure 6-4. The routing table in Figure 6-4 was taken off router Shani in this picture.

Issues Using RIP

RIP uses the number of hops (the hop count) to measure a route as the best route for the routing table. The hop count is actually the number of routers that a datagram encounters along the path from source to destination network. Obviously, using hop counts to calculate shortest paths does not always produce optimal results. For example, a path with a hop count of three that crosses three Ethernet LANs may be substantially faster than a path with a hop count of two that crosses two slow-speed serial links.

Table 6-1   How a Router Chooses the Best Route from the Routes Advertised

Routing Update Method	Preference	Weight
Directly connected networks	16	0
OSPF intra area routes	16	0
OSPF inter area routes	16	1
OSPF type 1 external routes	1	2
BGP routes	1	32
RIP routes	1	34
Static routes	16 by default can be set to 1.	36
OSPF type 2 external routes	1	No weight is indicated.

In a situation in which leaving RIP default parameters may create a nonoptimal network, an administrator may change parameters to create a more perfect network. An administrator can create a static route or add a cost to an interface.

CAUTION   Increasing the cost on an interface may mean that the maximum distance vector will be reached sooner.

As shown in Figure 6-6, administrators may choose not to use RIP or any routing protocol across a WAN link because of bandwidth issues. In this case static routes need to be created for all networks across the link so those networks still may be accessed. A static route can be assigned a preference from 1 to 16, with 16 being the most preferred. This preference is important if the IP router needs to select a route from the routing table and multiple routes exist to the same destination. Static routes with a preference higher than one take precedence over RIP routes that have a preference of one by default.

RIPv1 does not propagate network masks in its routing updates. Networks using RIPv1 therefore cannot contain variable length subnet masks (VLSMs).

Because RIPv1 contains no mask, it makes assumptions about received updates. If the update was received on an interface configured with the same network address, it applies the mask of that interface. If the host portion is zero, the natural mask is applied

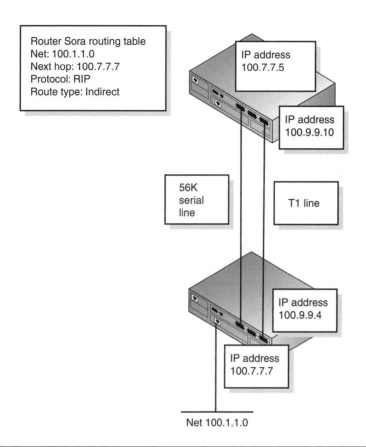

Router Sora routing table
Net: 100.1.1.0
Next hop: 100.7.7.7
Protocol: RIP
Route type: Indirect

IP address
100.7.7.5

IP address
100.9.9.10

56K
serial
line

T1 line

IP address
100.9.9.4

IP address
100.7.7.7

Net 100.1.1.0

Figure 6-6   Issues in an RIP network that is left to the default configuration with no administrative intervention. Here Router Sora has chosen the path to net 100.1.1.0 across the slower 56K serial instead of the much faster T1 line because of RIP.

to the address. In Figure 6-7, each router is configured with a 130.19.0.0 network with a different subnet mask. Router A's route table reflects the issue by using RIPv1 in this network. Since 130.19.0.0 is naturally a Class B network, it is summarized and advertised on the RIPv1 network, even though Routers B, C, and D have that network subnetted. Router A only accepts the first RIP announcement it hears for the network 130.19.0.0 (assuming cost is all the same) and forwards all packets to the router that announced the network. This will not enable the proper forwarding of packets destined for the 130.19.0.0 network off of Router C and the 130.19.21.0 network off of Router B.

Another problem can occur in RIPv1 networks that are misconfigured, as shown in Figure 6-7. If the host portion of the network is not advertised with a zero, (such as if

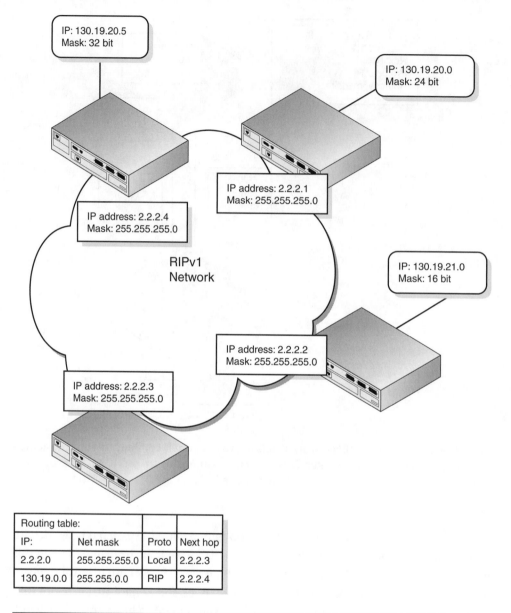

IP: 130.19.20.5
Mask: 32 bit

IP: 130.19.20.0
Mask: 24 bit

IP address: 2.2.2.1
Mask: 255.255.255.0

IP address: 2.2.2.4
Mask: 255.255.255.0

RIPv1
Network

IP: 130.19.21.0
Mask: 16 bit

IP address: 2.2.2.2
Mask: 255.255.255.0

IP address: 2.2.2.3
Mask: 255.255.255.0

Routing table:			
IP:	Net mask	Proto	Next hop
2.2.2.0	255.255.255.0	Local	2.2.2.3
130.19.0.0	255.255.0.0	RIP	2.2.2.4

Figure 6-7 Issues with RIPv1 in a network with VLSM

Router D were to advertise 130.19.20.4, which is the correct network address on a 30-bit mask), a 32-bit host mask (255.255.255.255) is applied to the address. This can be a real mess.

Additionally, RIP is not a secure protocol; it does not authenticate the source of any routing updates it receives. RIP cannot choose the best path based on link reliability or network load. It does not react to the dynamic environment of the network and continues to forward on paths that may be congested.

Although RIP is simple and well supported in the industry, it suffers from some problems because of its original LAN-based design. It really is a desirable solution only for small IP networks that have a small number of routers. RIP's use of broadcasting to propagate its update messages can create network issues. Broadcasting can create a broadcast storm that uses up all the bandwidth if too many hosts are running RIP on a single LAN segment. Large IP networks carry the broadcast overhead of large routing tables. This can be especially significant on WAN links where a significant portion of the bandwidth is devoted to carrying these RIP packets. As a result, RIP-based routing does not scale well for large networks or WANs.

RIP Version 2

RIPv2 was created to fix some of the elements of RIPv1. It supports several new features, including VLSMs, by including a subnet mask in the routing updates. Another improvement in RIPv2 is the use of authentication. RIPv2 uses the same simple password authentication provided in OSPF to prevent unauthorized routers from transmitting and receiving RIP updates from the network. Additionally, RIPv2 packets are transmitted using a multicast instead of a broadcast to save network bandwidth. The multicast address for all RIPv2 routers is 224.0.0.9.

The fields and format of a RIPv2 packet are identical to a RIPv1 packet (see Figure 6-3). Different values are entered into the fields to identify the packet for RIPv2 authentication and subnet masks:

- **Command** Specifies either a request for routing information (1) or a response (2). Responses contain the sender's routing table.

- **Version** The protocol version number, which is 1 for RIPv1 and 2 for RIPv2. This is important so that the message format is read properly.

- **Family of Net 1 (0xFFFF)** This field is identical to the field in RIPv1, but is set to 0xFFFF if authentication is used in this network. If this is set for identification, the next fields indicate authentication type and password.

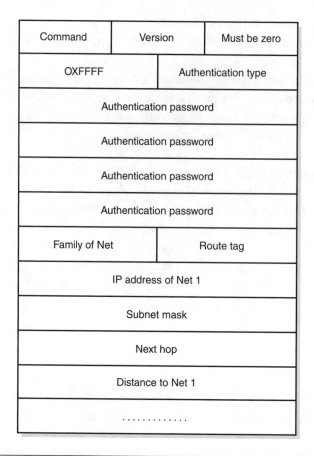

Command	Version	Must be zero
OXFFFF	Authentication type	
Authentication password		
Authentication password		
Authentication password		
Authentication password		
Family of Net	Route tag	
IP address of Net 1		
Subnet mask		
Next hop		
Distance to Net 1		
. . . .		

Figure 6-8   RIPv2 message format

- **Authentication type**   This field is set to 2 if there is authentication. That indicates a simple password to follow.

- **Authentication password**   A simple password that can be up to sixteen bytes (octets).

- **IP address of Net 1**   IP address of the first network in the sender's routing table.

- **Route tag**   A currently unsupported feature proposed for the future to allow originating routing protocols to mark packets entering the RIP network (BGP or OSPF).

- **Subnet mask**   RIPv2 enables a subnet mask to be sent with all RIP updates.

- **Next hop**   A currently unsupported feature that would enable a next hop address to be specified in a RIP update, instead of the router deriving the next hop address from the sending router.

- **Distance to Net 1**   The number of gateway hops to the network. Values are limited from 1 to 15. Sixteen is considered unreachable.

RIP Parameters

RIP, on Nortel Networks routers and switches, is a configurable parameter on a per-interface basis. This can help to control which networks are seen (for security purposes) and make RIP in the network more manageable. While enabling RIP is a global parameter and must be done before any interface can use RIP, some other parameters are on a per-interface basis. The following are some of the essential RIP interface parameters:

- **RIP supply and RIP listen**   These parameters determine if an interface sends out or listens to RIP updates. An interface can listen to RIP updates but not forward them, which would not allow any other router to use this interface as the next hop address (see Figure 6-9).

- **Default route supply and default route listen**   These parameters determine whether an interface supplies a default route of 0.0.0.0 into the network and whether the interface listens to a default route from the network. To supply a default route, one must be in the interface's routing table. An administrator can also choose this router to generate a default route into the network.

  Default route supply and RIP supply are separate parameters to enable an even stronger degree of administration abilities for the RIP network.

- **Broadcast/timeout/holddown timer**   Interfaces can change how often they send out RIP updates, how long a route stays valid in the routing table before it is marked unreachable, and how long a route stays unreachable before it is completely removed from the table. If an administrator wants to change these parameters for a very stable network, they must be changed all over the network so that routes do not time out waiting for updates.

- **Triggered updates**   If an administrator has chosen to extend the timers for RIP broadcasts, it will take longer for a network to converge or discover any network outages. Because the routers have to wait until the next broadcast cycle to advertise a downed network, it may take hours for network changes to be discovered. In this

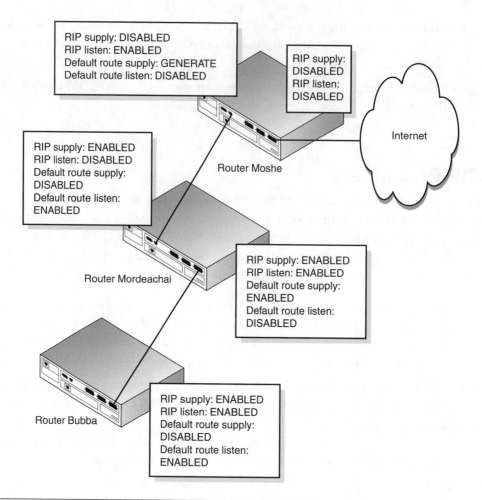

RIP supply: DISABLED
RIP listen: ENABLED
Default route supply: GENERATE
Default route listen: DISABLED

RIP supply:
DISABLED
RIP listen:
DISABLED

Internet

Router Moshe

RIP supply: ENABLED
RIP listen: DISABLED
Default route supply:
DISABLED
Default route listen:
ENABLED

Router Mordeachai

RIP supply: ENABLED
RIP listen: ENABLED
Default route supply:
ENABLED
Default route listen:
DISABLED

Router Bubba

RIP supply: ENABLED
RIP listen: ENABLED
Default route supply:
DISABLED
Default route listen:
ENABLED

Figure 6-9 Router Moshe is receiving RIP updates, but not forwarding them out other interfaces. This is because the router is a default router to the Internet and does not forward RIP routes to the global Internet.

case, it is essential to use the parameter triggered updates. In triggered updates, after the network goes down, the router advertises that network, even if 30 seconds have not passed and it is not time for a RIP update. All routers configured with triggered updates send out routing updates when a network outage or network change occurs, even if it is not time for a route update.

However, in the case of a network that is flapping up and down, RIP floods the network immediately, which can cause all sorts of other issues.

- **RIP mode**   This determines whether the interface sends out RIPv1, RIPv2, or RIPv2 aggregate updates. RIPv2 aggregate acts like RIPv1 to combine subnetworks into their natural class mask before sending them out. This saves bandwidth and allows for smaller routing tables; it may be very useful for summarizing in certain networks.

  As we discussed in the CIDR topic in Chapter 4, networks 176.1.0.0/24, 176.1.1.0/24, and 176.1.2.0/24, all the way up to network 176.1.255.0/24, could be combined into network 176.1.0.0/16.

- **Authentication type/authentication password**   In RIPv2 a network can use a simple password on RIP updates to ensure that only the proper routers receive the updates into their routing table. If passwords on the network do no match, routers are unable to include routes into their routing tables. This may cause network issues.

Routing Loops

Routing loops can occur in a RIP network when routers do not realize a network is down and continue to propagate false routing information out of their interfaces. A router can find out that a directly connected network is no longer available. Before this originating router can send out a routing update announcing the network is unavailable (hop count of 16), it receives an update from another router (which had originally received the update from him) stating that it knows how to get to this network. The originating router mistakenly believes this update, and puts this route in the routing table and adds one to the metric hop count of the route. The router that mistakenly sent out the update receives the route with the metric increased from the originating router. This router, believing that the network must have moved and the originating router is informing him of this, increases his metric hop count and resends the route. The originating router thinks this must be the new routing information and puts the route in his routing table with the new metric plus one. This goes on until the metric hop count reaches 16 and the network is finally deemed unreachable. This is called the hop count to infinity. In Figure 6-10, router Marc is updating the rest of the RIP routers about network 1.1.1.0.

In Figure 6-11, although router Marc realizes that network 1.1.1.0 is no longer reachable through him, he receives an update and believes that the network is available through router Phil. Router Phil knows only about network 1.1.1.0 through router Marc, but believes the network is still available and router Marc is informing him the

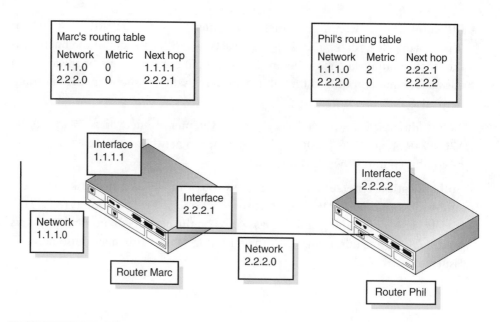

Figure 6-10 Routers connected to each other send standard RIP updates to fill their routing tables.

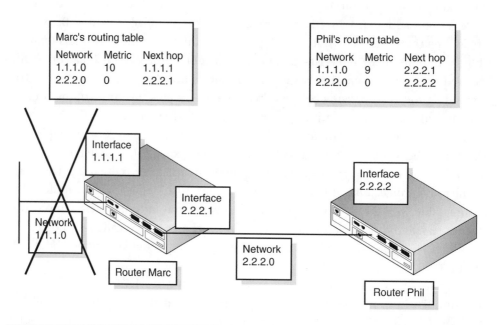

Figure 6-11 Routers on a route count to infinity because routers Marc and Phil do not realize that network 1.1.1.0 is down and are sending each other erroneous routing information.

network moved. Router Marc continues to propagate this network, adding a hop count, and so does router Phil until the hop count reaches 16 and the network is declared unreachable.

Two interface parameters can help to avoid routing loops and convergence issues: poison reverse and split horizon.

Poison Reverse

When using poison reverse, a router records the interface over which it received a particular route. Any routing information about that route is sent out the received interface with the cost of 16 or unreachable. This way, when a router advertises his route as unreachable, the routers that received his route do not advertise a better cost to that route back to him. In Figure 6-10, if router Marc advertises network 1.1.1.0 to router Phil, router Phil advertises the network back to him with a metric cost of 16.

Split Horizon

When using split horizon, a router records the interface over which it received a particular route and does not propagate its information about that route back over the same interface. In Figure 6-10, if router Phil receives a route from router Marc, it does not advertise its route back to router Marc. After just a few rounds of routing updates, all routers would agree that the network is unreachable.

Both poison reverse and split horizon can add to the problems of slow convergence on the network. Routes still take time to leave the routing table. For faster convergence time, it is essential to use triggered updates, which cause a RIP broadcast to be sent out immediately upon network changes without waiting for timers.

RIP Policies

RIP policies can be used to change RIP updates in the network. They may be used for security and in any case where a RIP parameter does not create the correct networking environment. RIP policies can be created for specific networks or a range of networks.

To specify a range of networks, aggregation is used resulting in a shorter subnet mask. Networks 176.1.0.0/24, 176.1.1.0/24, and 176.1.2.0/24, all the way up to network 176.1.255.0/24, could be specified individually or combined into a network range of 176.1.0.0/16. A RIP policy may also be used to change subnet masks on the network in the case of a RIPv1 routing update.

RIP Accept Policies

RIP accept policies are used to change portions of incoming RIP updates. Normally, updates are processed by the RTM as we explained before. RIP accept policies enables the administrator to select specific networks to ignore or include in the routing table. RIP accept policies can be used to listen to RIP updates only from certain routers or for specific networks. So even if an interface has RIP listen turned on, it can ignore specific networks and not allow them to be included in the routing table. Actions for an accept policy include accept or ignore. For actions of accept, a policy can additionally assign a specific mask to a network in the routing table or change the preference of a RIP route.

RIP Announce Policies

A RIP announce policy enables an administrator to include specific networks in a RIP update. It can also be used to limit the announcement of specific networks out of certain interfaces only. It can be used to conditionally generate a default route, or to announce only networks received from a specific router or routes received on a specific interface. It can also be used to aggregate networks into a single advertised route.

An announce policy can be created to conditionally generate a default route in the case of the network router receiving an announcement from the ISP router. A default route is created only when the Internet is available.

Summary

In this chapter we discussed the necessity of the routing protocols. We focused specifically on RIP. We mentioned many of the RIP features for both RIPv1 and RIPv2. We also mentioned the benefits of using RIP in a network and the issues with using RIP in a large network. In Chapter 8, we will discuss the OSPF routing protocol and the BGP protocol, and their benefits and limitations in a large and small network environment.

Review Questions

1. Why is RIP not the routing protocol of choice for large networks?
    A. It uses broadcasts to propagate update packets in the network.
    B. RIP can only store one route to each network.
    C. It cannot recover in case of a fault on a router.
    D. It has a parameter to trigger updates as soon as the network information changes.

2. Which two are contained in the routing table of a router? (Choose two.)
   A. Source networks
   B. Destination networks
   C. Age of the route
   D. Default routes

3. Which of the following is an interior gateway protocol?
   A. RIP
   B. EGP
   C. PPP
   D. BGP

4. An IP interface configured with RIP _____.
   A. Sends routing updates every 10 seconds
   B. Sends routing updates every 30 seconds
   C. Sends routing updates every 60 seconds
   D. Does not send any routing updates by default

5. What is the maximum number of hops allowed by default in an RIP network?
   A. 6
   B. 15
   C. 16
   D. 30
   E. 127

6. When an IP RIP interface configured with split horizon learns about a remote net-work, what does it do?
   A. It advertises the network out the received interface with a cost equal to the sum of the received hop metric and the interface's cost parameter.
   B. It advertises the network out the same interface with a cost of 16.
   C. It advertises the network out the same interface with a cost of 31.
   D. It does not advertise the network out the same interface.

7. A destination network of 0.0.0.0 in a routing table means _____.
   A. Any manager can manage the router
   B. All routes are unreachable
   C. All routes are reachable
   D. A default route

8. Which method does RIPv1 use to distribute its routing table?

   A. Unicast

   B. Multicast

   C. Broadcast

   D. Direct

9. How many networks is the maximum for a single RIP update?

   A. 10

   B. 25

   C. 50

   D. 512

10. What is the RIPv2 multicast address?

    A. 224.0.0.5

    B. 224.0.0.6

    C. 224.0.0.9

    D. 224.0.0.19

11. A RIP route is completely removed from the routing table after how many seconds?

    A. 120

    B. 180

    C. 270

    D. 360

12. Which of the following might appear in an IP routing table?

    A. RIP routes

    B. Static routes

    C. OSPF routes

    D. All of the above

13. A RIP announce policy can be used to _____.

    A. Generate a default route

    B. Change the weight of a route

    C. Change the next hop gateway of a route

    D. All of the above

14. How many IP routing tables are in the Nortel Networks' implementation of routing?

    A. One

    B. One per port

C. One per slot

D. One per interface

15. What type of protocol is RIP?
    A. Link state protocol
    B. Novell routing protocol
    C. Distance vector protocol
    D. Exterior gateway protocol

16. Which statement is true regarding RIPv2?
    A. It is a link state protocol and does not forward routing tables.
    B. It forwards only the subnet mask information when updating routing tables.
    C. It does not forward any subnet mask information when forwarding routing information.
    D. It passes along the subnet mask with address information when forwarding routing tables.

17. What is the purpose of a routing protocol?
    A. To segment different protocols into VLANs to enhance traffic flow
    B. To allow the segmentation of larger networks and maximize wide area traffic
    C. To allow for traffic to get from one network to another network with a different address
    D. To make the best use bandwidth by limiting the traffic that crosses it

18. What is a routing protocol?
    A. A control protocol that lets computers send each other e-mail
    B. A protocol that enables one computer to talk to another on a different network
    C. A set of rules that determines which data traffic travels when and where within a network
    D. A protocol that exchanges addresses and topology information within a network

19. Which statement best describes IP routing?
    A. It is dependent on TCP.
    B. It operates at layer 2 of the OSI model.
    C. It is a connection between two LANs where some path exists.
    D. It is an unintelligent connection between multiple LANs of the same type.

20. At which layer of the OSI model does routing occur?

    A. Physical layer

    B. Data Link layer

    C. Network layer

    D. Transport layer

21. What are the two main functions of a router? (Choose two.)

    A. To forward incoming packets based on routing table entries

    B. To make routing decisions based on the destination MAC address

    C. To make routing decisions based on the host portion of the destination IP address

    D. To determine if the destination host is locally attached by sending a multicast request

    E. To make routing decisions based on the network portion of the destination IP address

22. Which field within an IP packet is used to determine where a router will send packets?

    A. Router IP address

    B. Source IP address

    C. Destination IP address

    D. Default gateway IP address

23. What will a router do with a packet if there is no entry in the routing table for the destination network of the packet?

    A. Drop the packet.

    B. Send a broadcast out all interfaces.

    C. Forward the packet out all interfaces.

    D. Forward the packet to the next hop router.

24. What are two purposes of a router? (Choose two.)

    A. To create smaller broadcast domains

    B. To forward broadcast packets across a WAN

    C. To prevent local traffic from saturating WAN connections

    D. To minimize the configuration of gateways and subnet masks

Answer Key

1. **A.** RIP is not ideal for large networks because it uses broadcasts for updates that can cause issues with network bandwidth.

2. **B** and **D.** Routing tables contain destination networks and may also contain default routes.

3. **A.**

4. **B.** Interfaces configured with RIP send out routing updates by default every 30 seconds without any special configuration.

5. **B.** Fifteen is the maximum number of hops allowed and 16 is considered unreachable.

6. **D.** Using split horizon with RIP ensures that routes will not get readvertised out the interfaces they were received on.

7. **D.** 0.0.0.0 in the routing table represents a default route.

8. **C.** RIPv1 uses broadcasts packets to advertise its routing table; RIPv2 uses multicast packets.

9. **B.** A maximum of 25 networks can be advertised in a single RIP update.

10. **C.** 224.0.0.9 is the multicast address for all RIPv2 routers.

11. **B.** An RIP update will timeout by default after 90 seconds if not renewed and will be considered and advertised as unreachable. After another 90 seconds, it will be flushed out of the routing table for a total of 180 seconds before an RIP route leaves the routing table.

12. **D.** An IP routing table can have routes from many different sources, including RIP, OSPF, BGP, or static routes.

13. **A.**

14. **A.** There is only one routing table on a Nortel Networks router, and it is distributed to all slots and ports running IP.

15. **C.**

16. D. RIPv2 advertises both networks and their subnet mask by default.

17. C. The purpose of a routing protocol is to enable traffic from one network to reach another differently addressed network.

18. D. A routing protocol is responsible for exchanging routing and topology information (that is, the link is down) around the network.

19. C. IP routing is a connection between two LANs that have a way of connecting to each other.

20. C. Routers operate at layer 3, the network layer.

21. A and E. Routers forward packets based on the destination network (not the host) portion of the IP address (which they learn by doing the AND function with the subnet mask) and based on entries about the destination network in the routing table.

22. C. Routers look at destination IP addresses to forward packets.

23. A. If a router does not have a destination network in its routing table, it drops the packet and an Internet Control Message Protocol (ICMP) message is generated, stating the destination network is unreachable.

24. A and C. Routers do not enable broadcasts to pass through them and are therefore used in a network to create smaller broadcast domains and to prevent broadcasts and all local traffic from crossing into the WAN and saturating the WAN link.

TCP/IP Routing Part II

Introduction

In the last chapter, we discussed Internal Gateway Protocols (IGPs). The main focus was on RIP, a distance vector protocol. This chapter focuses on another IGP called *Open Shortest Path First* (OSPF.) OSPF is a link state protocol, and its implementations and benefits over RIP will be fully explored. We will also mention some of the issues that are associated with OSPF, because it is not just a plug and play protocol. Toward the end of this chapter, we will begin a discussion on an Exterior Gateway Protocol (EGP) called the Border Gateway Protocol or BGPv4. We will discuss how Internet Service Providers (ISPs) use BGPv4 and its requirements and issues as well. The technologies mentioned in this chapter will appear on the Data IP Fundamentals exam as well as product specific exams. In cases where there is a direct correlation between the exam objective and technologies mentioned here, we will refer back to this chapter.

Link State Protocols

There is a type of IGP routing protocol called a *link state protocol*. A link state protocol is one in which all participating routers advertise the state of local network links. These link state advertisements (LSAs) are then distributed to all other routers. The end result is that the routers all collect a database of the same information that together describes the network. Using this database, each router will then run some type of shortest path calculation (in this case, Dijkstra's algorithm) and produce the shortest path to each network and router. The shortest or best path will be the one with the lowest cost, which is equal to the sum of the cost of all links that make up the path.

Link state algorithms were designed to get around a lot of the issues that occur with distance vector algorithms. They take into account more than just the number of hops and are able to converge much faster. Link state algorithms, however, are more difficult to implement, and much care must be taken in designing this type of routed network. This will be apparent through the discussion of the details of an OSPF network.

Open Shortest Path First (OSPF)

OSPF is defined in RFC 1583/2178 and updated in RFC 2328. It was specifically designed for use in large IP networks of 50 or more routers. In larger networks, RIP may cause issues by using a lot of bandwidth or taking a long time to converge.

Routers using link state protocols, such as OSPF, do not exchange routing information. Instead, routers exchange link state information. Each router builds an advertisement describing its immediate surroundings. In the advertisement, only directly connected networks are included. This ensures only actual network topology information is exchanged and not hearsay information received from other routers.

Each router maintains a database describing the domain's topology. This database is called the link state database (LSDB). The LSDB of all routers contains information about the complete network. This information is pieced together from advertisements received from each of the other participating routers within the OSPF domain. Each router participating with OSPF (in a single area) has an identical database. The LSDB is made up of LSAs. Each advertisement in the LSDB was created by one of the routers in the OSPF domain and sent to every other OSPF router in a process called *flooding* in which LSAs are propagated throughout the OSPF domain.

Each LSA has a sequence number, which in addition to age, is used to determine which received LSA is newer. LSAs are aged in seconds. Self-originated LSAs are refreshed automatically every 1,800 seconds (half-hour), and the age is reset to zero seconds. An LSA that is older than 3,600 seconds is considered invalid.

LSAs are also sent out whenever there is a network topology change. These advertisements are immediately flooded to all routers in the OSPF domain. This prevents loop counts to infinity found in RIP. Using LSA information instead of exchanging whole networks for every change also enables OSPF to converge faster than RIP. Routers in an OSPF domain will also request link state updates from their neighbors when they notice that their database does not match that of their neighbors. (We will discuss this in further detail with the discussion of adjacencies later in this chapter.) This ensures that all the routers in the same area will have synchronized databases.

OSPF uses Dijkstra's algorithm to create a Shortest Path First (SPF) tree from which routes are created for inclusion in the routing table. Dijkstra's algorithm calculates the SPF tree based on the LSDB. Each router in the OSPF domain runs this algorithm in parallel. Each router creates a tree with itself as the root. Routers then step through the LSDB to build a SPF based on the best path. Each time this algorithm is run, all the known paths to a destination network or a router are mapped, and the lowest cost path is chosen as the new branch to the tree. This process is repeated until the best path to each destination is discovered. The result is a logical tree defining the best path to all points in the network.

NOTE   The LSDB does not contain the best route; only the SPF tree that is derived from the database contains the route for the routing table.

The best route is the path with the lowest overall cost to the destination, a network, or a router. OSPF is interested in the best outbound cost. In OSPF, the faster the link, the lower the cost associated with it. The larger the cost of the link, the less likely data will be routed over that link. An unreachable metric in OPSF is not likely. Routes can cross links with a cumulative cost of 65K or 65,535.

Dijkstra may recalculate based on LSAs received; however, OSPF recalculates routes quickly in the event of a topology change. Also, because only LSAs are flooded in the event of a change and not the entire LSDB, very little network bandwidth is used.

OSPF runs directly over IP, not relying on TCP or UDP. It uses its own Transport method protocol 89. This makes OSPF a very reliable protocol. It will not have to advertise its routing table every 30 seconds like RIP, which uses the unreliable UDP. OSPF uses multicast and unicast message types to advertise information rather than bandwidth intensive broadcasts. The multicast addresses of 224.0.0.5 and 224.0.0.6 are significant in OSPF. OSPF even enables the use of variable length subnet masks, because every OSPF packet contains subnet mask information.

OSPF Adjacencies

OSPF routers have identical LSDBs, which are maintained through a relationship called *adjacencies*. When two routers form an adjacency, they follow a process. First the two routers that are trying to form the adjacency exchange hello packets (see Figure 7-1).

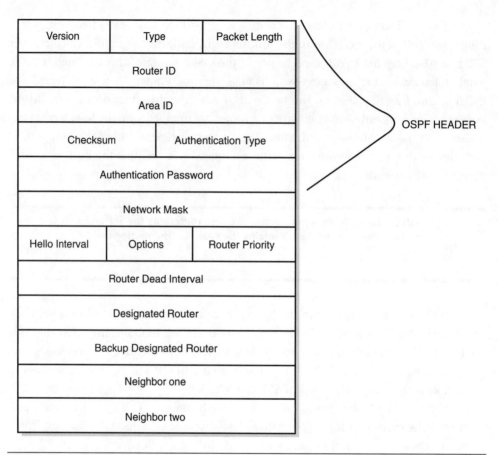

Figure 7-1 OSPF hello message

For two OSPF routers to form an adjacency, the area ID, authentication, network mask, hello interval, options, and router dead interval must match.

They decide whether or not to become adjacent to each other based on network type and information in the hello packet. Once the two routers have decided to become adjacent, one becomes the master, and the second router becomes the slave. The two routers send database descriptors to each other.

Database descriptors help each of the routers find out which LSAs are not in their database. The routers will then request the detailed information for LSAs not in their LSDB. Beginning with the master router, the routers will each send out link state requests for LSAs not in their database.

The slave router will be the first to send out link state update packets, which will be acknowledged with a LSA from the master upon receipt of the update.

When the master has completely updated his LSDB, he will assume the role of slave and fulfil the requests of the new master OSPF router. Once both routers have completely updated their databases, the adjacency is formed, and the router's LSDBs are synchronised. The two routers continue to exchange hello messages to maintain the adjacency (see Figure 7-1).

Routers also send out link state updates every 30 minutes for LSAs that have not changed. OSPF routers delete all LSAs in their LSDB every 30 minutes unless an update is received. This ensures that the LSDBs do not contain update messages from routers that are no longer communicating in the OSPF network.

When a new adjacency or a network topology change occurs in an OSPF network, the LSDB changes on all the routers in the Autonomous System (AS). This forces the OSPF routing table to become invalidated, for Dijkstra to be run against the new LSDB, and a new OSPF tree to be created, and finally, all the newly created routes to be submitted to the Routing Table Manager (RTM) for inclusion into the routing table.

OSPF Packet Types

1 – **Hello**   This packet type is used for discovering neighboring routers, deciding whether or not to form an adjacency, and maintaining adjacencies that are formed. The hello message is sent to the multicast address of 224.0.0.5 on point-to-point and broadcast networks and to a statically defined neighbor across an NBMA network (see Figure 7-2).

2 – **Database description**   This packet type is used to exchange databases between OSPF routers while forming adjacencies (see Figure 7-3).

3 – **Link State Request**   This packet is used for database synchronization between routers while they are forming adjacencies (see Figure 7-4).

4 – **Link State Update**   The packet that contains actual link state information. During the formation of an adjacency, a router requests a link state update if it notices information is missing in its LSDB (see Figure 7-5). It is also used in the flooding procedure to ensure all routers receive necessary updates.

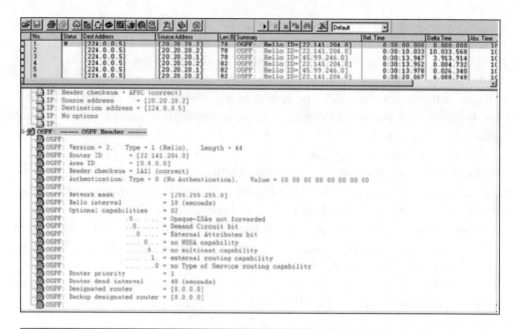

Figure 7-2 OSPF hello message as seen through a network analyzer

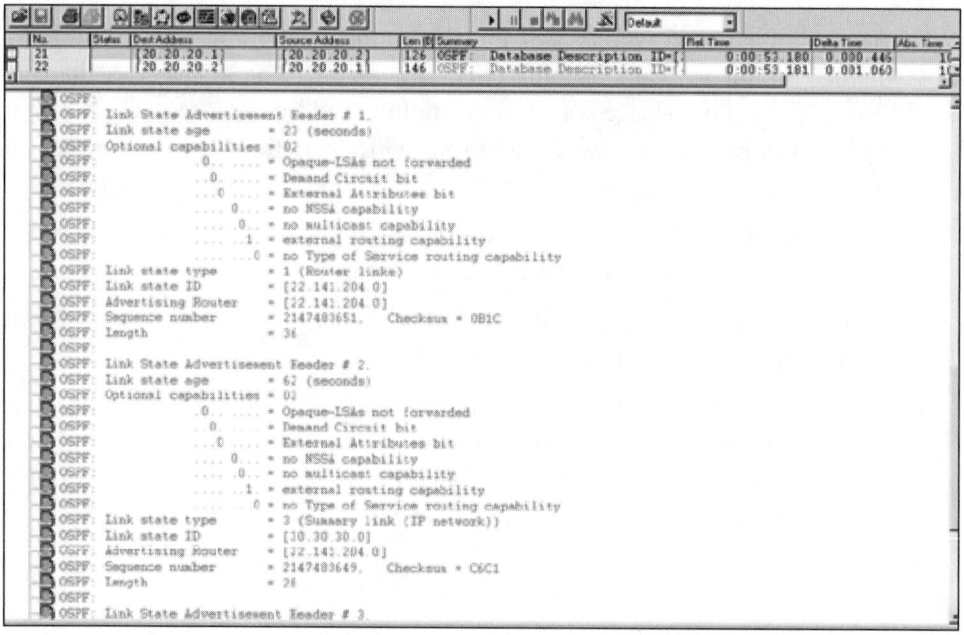

Figure 7-3 Database descriptor packets. These packets contain headers of all the LSA information in their LSDB without all the details.

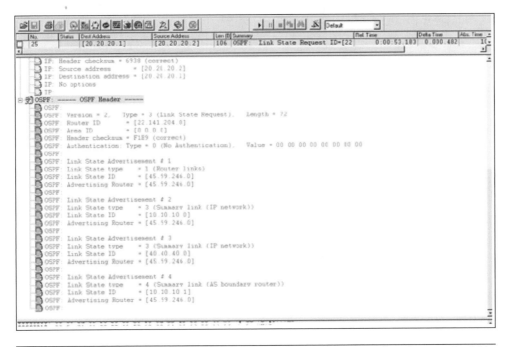

Figure 7-4   Link State Request packets are sent from each router in the adjacency for LSAs not currently in their LSDB.

5 – **Link State Acknowledgment**   Routers acknowledge the receipt of an LSA with an acknowledgement packet. This ensures a high level of network reliability and synchronous LSDBs (see Figure 7-6).

OSPF Network Types

OSPF forms adjacencies based on network types. The network type must be specified at the interface level when OSPF is added to a circuit. If the network is not properly defined, OSPF will not be able to form adjacencies correctly.

Point-to-point   A network of two directly connected routers. PPP, frame relay, and X.25 are types of point-to-point networks. Adjacencies in a point-to-point network are formed between the routers at both ends (see Figure 7-7). OSPF uses the multicast address of 224.0.0.5 for AllSPFRouters.

Figure 7-5 Link State Update packets contain the requested LSAs from the router that has those LSAs in its database.

Broadcast Any network with more than two routers that supports multicasts. Ethernet, Token Ring, and FDDI are all types of broadcast networks (see Figure 7-8). Adjacencies are formed with the Designated Router (DR) and the Backup Designated Router (BDR). (We will discuss those routers in the next section.)

Nonbroadcast multiaccess (NBMA) Used with a partially meshed network that does not support multicasting. OSPF must be directly sent to the address of each neighboring router. Frame relay and X.25 are non-broadcast multiaccess networks that must be statically configured with all IP addresses of neighboring routers in order for OSPF to function correctly (see Figure 7-9). Adjacencies are formed with the DR and the BDR.

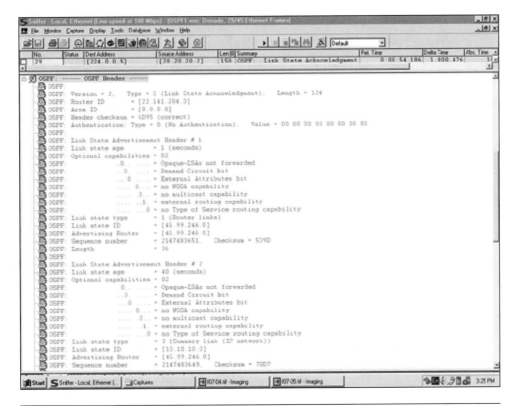

Figure 7-6   LSAs help to keep the OSPF network reliable.

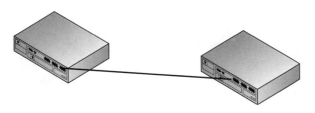

Figure 7-7   A point-to-point network is one link with a router on each side.

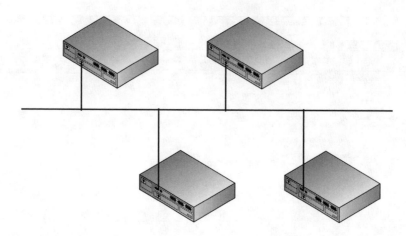

Figure 7-8   A broadcast Ethernet network with multiple OSPF routers that all have multi-casting abilities

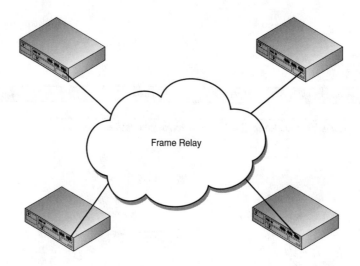

Figure 7-9   A frame relay network is often shown as a network with routers communicating through a cloud—the frame relay cloud.

Point to multipoint   Point to multipoint can be implemented in two ways. One is a proprietary network type that is used with a true hub and spoke topology. In this configuration, hub is always the DR. All routes traverse the hub and form adjacencies with the DR or the hub. The second implementation is commonly used in a nonfully meshed topology to overcome NBMA network issues. In this implementation of point to multi-point, an NBMA network is treated like a collection of point-to-point links. Neighbors do not need to be configured, and adjacencies are formed in the same way as a standard point-to-point network. This is the recommended implementation for point-to-multipoint hub and spoke type networks.

The Designated Router (DR) and the Backup Designated Router (BDR)

Forming adjacencies is a very resource- and bandwidth-intensive process. In an environment like a broadcast network or an NBMA network, having all the routers form adjacencies with each other is not necessary (see Figure 7-10).

Instead, all routers form an adjacency with a central router called the DR. Additionally, a BDR will be chosen for the network. This router exists for backup, in case the DR

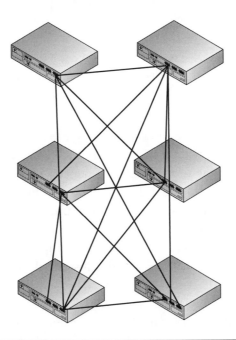

Figure 7-10   Forming adjacencies with all the routers in this broadcast network causes 15 adjacencies to be formed n + (n − 1) ÷ 2. The formula represents each router forming an adjacency with every other router in the broadcast network.

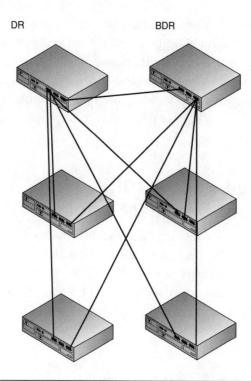

DR   BDR

Figure 7-11 Forming adjacencies with only the DR and BDR cause 11 adjacencies to be formed or 2n − 1. This formula represents all the routers forming adjacencies with only the DR and the BDR.

fails. All routers including the DR form adjacencies with the BDR (see Figure 7-11). This will ensure identical LSDBs without a lot of unnecessary bandwidth.

DRs are elected using the router priority parameter in the hello packets (see Figure 7-1). The router with the highest priority will become the DR. If router priorities are equal, then the router with the highest router ID becomes the DR. A router with the priority of zero can never become the DR. When a router is initialized, it checks for a DR. If no DR exists, this router can become the DR. If one exists, it will not attempt to become the DR regardless of its router priority. Instead, the router will check if a BDR is on the network. If no BDR exists, this router can become the BDR. If there is a DR and a BDR, the router will form adjacencies with both.

The DR maintains adjacencies with all the routers on the same physical network. It sends out Link State Updates using the multicast address of 224.0.0.5 for All-SPFRouters. Routers respond with updates to the DR at the multicast address of 224.0.0.6.

The Hello Message Process Revisited

Putting together all that was discussed about adjacencies, DRs, and hello messages, here is a detailed look at the hello process.

Router A receives a hello message (see Figure 7-1) from Router B. Router A will first check the area ID, hello interval, router dead timer interval, interface netmask, and options fields against its own parameters. If these values do not match, the hello message will be discarded; if the fields do match, then the router will process the message.

The next step for Router A is to find out if it is listed as a neighbor in the hello message. If Router B is already adjacent to Router A, then this hello message is considered a keep-alive, and Router A resets its timers. If Router A is not already adjacent with Router B, then the network type will be examined.

If the network type is point-to-point, Router A will attempt to complete the formation of the adjacency. If the network type is a multiaccess (NBMA or broadcast), Router A will only form an adjacency only if Router B is a DR or BDR.

OSPF Areas and the LSDB

In a very large network with many OSPF routers, the LSDB can become very large. The larger the LSDB, the more CPU it takes to make forwarding decisions and the more memory the LSDB consumes in the router or switch. An administrator may choose to divide the OSPF network into areas.

Networks that are grouped together in areas are grouped in a collection/range of network addresses. Each area is identified with a unique 32-bit area ID that is in the form of an IP address.

NOTE   **Nortel Networks does not recommend having more than 200 routers in a single area.**

The entire collection of areas and all the OSPF routers together are considered to be one AS. The individual topology for each area is hidden from other areas. A separate LSDB is maintained for each area. Routers internal to the area maintain only one LSDB for the area they are part of. The LSDBs are identical throughout an area. Routers that are part of multiple areas maintain an LSDB and run a copy of Dijkstra for each area they have an interface into. Networks outside the area can be summarized and are advertised into all other areas in the network.

All areas must be joined to a single area called the *Backbone area*. The Backbone area has an area ID of 0.0.0.0.

> **NOTE**   Although OSPF area IDs look like IP addresses, they are not actually addresses; they only use the same 32-bit dotted-decimal format.

It is used to connect all the areas together and to make sure the OSPF environment is contiguous. It is also used for interarea routing and can be extended through the use of virtual links.

Virtual Links

A *virtual link* is necessary to keep the Backbone contiguous. It is used when an ABR does not have a physical interface into the Backbone area 0.0.0.0. This link must be between two border routers that share interfaces into a common area called the *transit area*. A virtual link is created as a point-to-point link that originates from an ABR that is connected to the Backbone to an ABR that is not (see Figure 7-12).

A virtual link is not a physical point-to-point link. The path that packets will follow is actually the lowest cost physical path through the transit network. An adjacency must be formed across the virtual link so all necessary parameters must match. The virtual link will be advertised with the other router link advertisements using a router type 4 (virtual link) advertisement.

A virtual link can be used to eliminate the single point of failure created because all advertisements must traverse the Backbone network. If the virtual link provides the best path cost, then it will be used.

> **NOTE**   Nortel Networks does not recommend creating areas that are dependent on the use of virtual links. Rather, use a virtual link as a backup link.

The advantage of using areas is that routers that are internal to a single area have much less overhead and a smaller LSDB. Additionally, topology changes effect only the

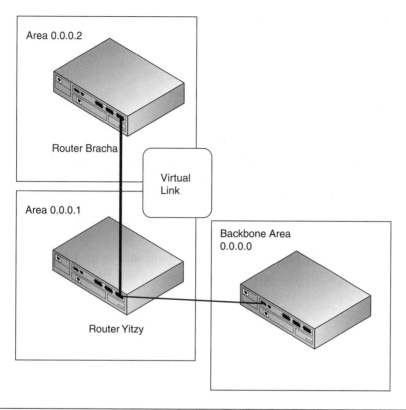

Figure 7-12 A virtual link can help to connect networks that are not contiguous to the Backbone area. In this figure, Area 0.0.0.2/Router Bracha is not connected to the Backbone area. It will use a virtual link through Area 0.0.0.1/Router Yitzy to connect to the Backbone.

area they occur in, and although changes are advertised outside the area through LSAs, the effect is much less processing-intensive. The most crucial benefit to areas is that in a well-designed OSPF network, networks can be summarized—sometimes into single routing statements. This can greatly reduce the amount of processing and size of the routing table.

OSPF Terminology

Intra-area routes Any routes that are within the router's area.

Interarea routes Routes that go between areas. All interarea routes must traverse the Backbone area.

AS external routes Routes that are learned via another protocol such as RIP or BGP.

Internal router   A router that is only connected to networks in a single area. Routers with only interfaces into the Backbone area can also be internal routers. These routers only maintain a single LSDB.

Area Border Router (ABR)   Any router that is attached to multiple areas. ABRs maintain multiple LSDBs, one for each area they have an interface in, and one for the Backbone area.

> **NOTE**   Nortel Networks recommends having no more than four to six areas maintained on a single router unless they are small. Smaller routers have more trouble maintaining multiple areas because of the memory and CPU requirements.

Backbone router   Any router that has at least one interface into the Backbone area 0.0.0.0. This router can also be an internal router or an ABR. All ABRs, are by definition, Backbone routers.

AS Boundary Router (ASBR)   A router that can exchange routing information with another router running a routing protocol that is not OSPF (that is, RIP or BGP). This router will advertise AS external routes into the OSPF domain. Every other router in the network will know the path to the ASBR.

Quick Quiz 1

Identify each router in the figure with its correct OSPF router type.

Answers

Routers A, B, and G are Internal routers.

Router F is an ASBR.

Routers H, C, D, and E are ABRs and Backbone routers.

A *Stub area* is a special type of area into which external routes are not flooded. Only a default route is sent into the Stub area. In general, Stub areas are nontransit areas (see Figure 7-14). They may even have only a default router into and out of the area (although Stub areas can have more than one router in them).

Nortel Networks enables a Stub area to be further optimized by having a parameter, which prevents summary links from being imported into the Stub area. Stub areas are

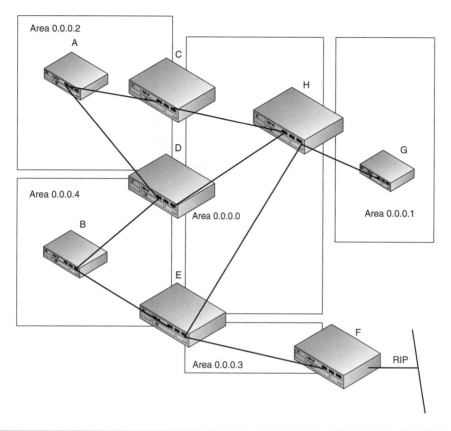

Figure 7-13 This figure shows an OSPF network with multiple areas.

beneficial because the LSDB on the routers in a Stub area is small, that ensures the routing tables are small, which means that fewer CPU cycles and less memory is needed for routers in this area.

OSPF Link State Types and Advertisements

0 – LS Stub They are derived from router links advertisements and are used to describe a point-to-point network without neighbors.

1 – Router link advertisement Generated by each OSPF router, they are sent to all other OSPF routers in the area. This advertisement describes the router's links in

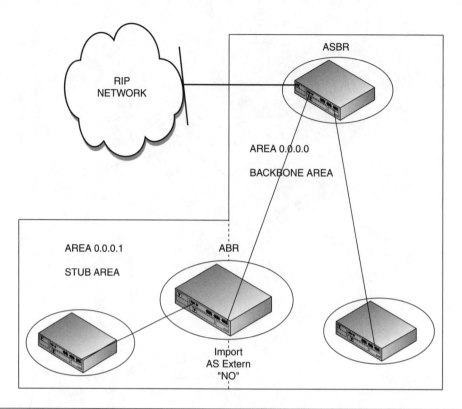

Figure 7-14 An example of a Stub area connected to the Backbone area, which is connected to a RIP network. RIP updates will be imported into the Stub area as a single default route.

the area. A router may have four types of network connections into an area, and they represent the four different types of OSFP networks that were discussed previously (see Figure 7-15).

- **Point-to-point (link type 1)**   Used for a network with only two directly connected routers

- **Transit (link type 2)**   Used for multiaccess networks with more than one router

- **Stub (link type 3)**   Used for multiaccess networks with no other routers

- **Virtual link (link type 4)**   Used to describe a virtual connection to the Backbone area

2 – Network link advertisement   Originated by the DR only on a transit network, this advertisement contains a list of all routers connected to the network

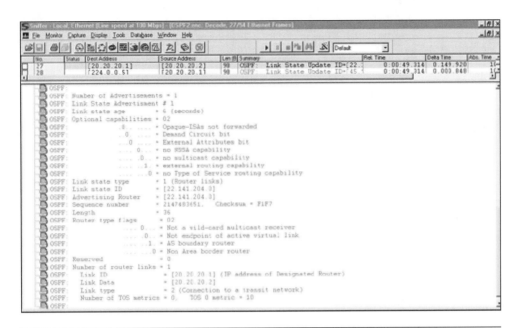

Figure 7-15 A sample router link advertisement that is advertising a transit network. Note the address of the DR is included in the advertisement.

and their router ID. It is passed from the DR within an area to all adjacent routers in the area (see Figure 7-16).

3 – Summary link advertisement Originated by ABRs, this advertisement describes networks within an area and is passed between areas. If ranges are not configured in the network, a summary link is generated for each network.

In a network that has more than one OSPF area, ABRs generate summary links. A summary link advertisement is created to advertise each network within the area to the Backbone and other areas. By default, there is one summary link advertisement for each network; however, with careful network planning, networks can be summarized into ranges and sent out as a single summary link advertisement to save network bandwidth. When summarizing a range of networks into a single advertisement, an aggregate subnet mask (like CIDR) is used. For example, an area containing the subnets 128.10.32.0—128.10.63.0 could be configured with the following range to generate a single summary link advertisement: Network—128.10.32.0, Subnet mask—255.255.224.0.

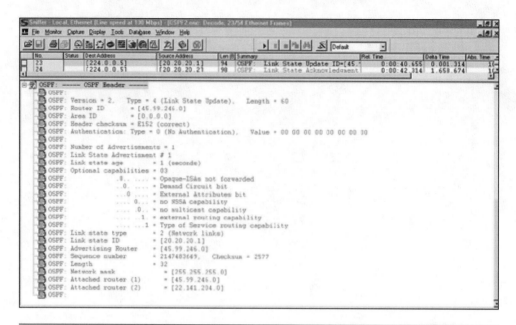

Figure 7-16 A network link advertisement is part of a Links State Update sent out by the DR of a transit network.

Summary link advertisements are sent from one area into the Backbone area and then from the Backbone area to all other areas. No summary links are ever sent directly to another area bypassing the Backbone area.

NOTE Networks can greatly benefit from summarization. The only way to be able to summarize networks is through careful planning when subnets are designed and assigned.

4 – AS summary link advertisement These describe a path to the AS ASBRs. This advertisement is passed between areas by the ABR.

Once a router is configured as an ASBR, it will announce this fact through a setting in the router link advertisement. This will cause ABRs to create and transmit a type 4 AS summary link advertisement to describe the router to the ASBR. Summary links contain the following important fields:

Link state ID The router ID of the ASBR

Advertising router The router ID of the ABR that originated this advertisement

Network mask   Set to zero and not used

Metric   The cost to the ASBR from the ABR sending the advertisement

AS summary links are flooded into all areas in the network with the exception of a Stub area that is configured with the parameter import summaries set to false.

5 – **AS external link advertisement**   Originated by AS BRs, they describe networks that are non-OSPF. By default, the ASBR creates one external advertisement for each network it learns and passes the advertisements between areas. These advertisements are not sent into a Stub area.

Type 1   Any route that is directly connected to the ASBR or is statically configured on the ASBR.

Type 2   Routes learned by the ASBR via external protocols like RIP or BGP.

OSPF External Routes

Networks use OSPF in conjunction with other routing protocols like RIP or BGP. In a scenario with multiple routing protocols, OSPF will consider itself to be the primary routing protocol in the AS. OSPF views all other protocols as external. This includes routes learned from RIP, static and default routes, and even directly connected networks running another routing protocol.

An ASBR is the router that has routing information from a non-OSPF protocol. The job of the ASBR is to send type 5 AS external link advertisements. An ASBR floods an AS external link advertisement for each external route it has learned all over the OSPF network. The exception, of course, is a Stub area, which does not import AS external links (see Figure 7-17).

Link state ID   Specifies the network number being advertised.

Advertising router   Specifies the router ID of the ASBR originating the LSA.

Network mask   The mask that is associated with the network.

E bit   Indicates whether the network is type 1 or type 2 external.

Metric   Specifies the cost to the external route from the ASBR.

Forwarding address   If set to 0.0.0.0, it indicates to send packets destined for the network to the ASBR; otherwise, it indicates another router to send the packets to.

Two types of external links in the OSPF network exist. A type 1 metric is for networks that are directly connected to the ASBR. The cost of this external network is configured

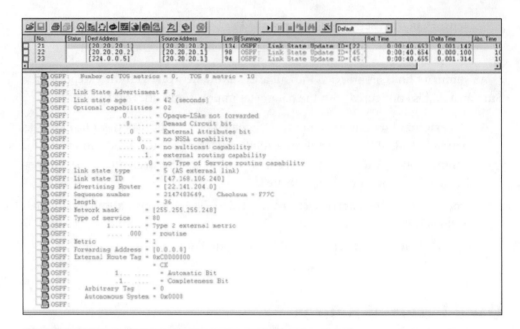

Figure 7-17 Details of an AS external link advertisement

as the sum of all internal and external costs for this route. A type 2 metric is for networks that are further away from the ASBR. They are networks that were learned via an external routing protocol and are advertised with the exact external cost they were received with. This is because OSPF does not add its OSPF cost to whatever the external routing protocol considers its cost because they are different.

> **NOTE** An OSPF router will always prefer a type 1 external route to a type 2 external route even if the type 2 has a lower cost because the cost was assigned by an external protocol.

Referring back to Table 6-1 in Chapter 6, it is possible to see that external type 2 routes have the lowest preference and are considered the worst route to take. OSPF routers will always prefer their own routes or at least an external type 1 route. Because an external type 2 route is one whose cost is unknown, it will only be chosen if no other route to the destination is available.

Issues Using OSPF

OSPF is very CPU-intensive, especially when OSPF is recalculating new routes. The LSDB and the SPF tree also consume additional memory. In a network with flapping routes, OSPF can consume much of the network resources if it is forced to run Dijkstra's algorithm as routes change frequently. To ease CPU utilization on a Nortel Networks router, the OSPF process will run as a soloist. Processing for the SPF will occur on only one slot of a multislotted router.

A major issue with OSPF is that it is not plug and play like RIP. If the network is not carefully planned, features like summarization and Stub networks will not be able to be used efficiently. These features are important for decreasing the size of the LSDB, which can grow very large in a network that is not using any summarization or areas.

OSPF Parameters

Critical information to configure in OSPF is

Router ID   Uniquely identifies the router in the OSPF domain. It is in the form of an IP address, but does not have to be a real IP address. By default, a Nortel Networks router will use the first configured IP interface's address for the OSPF router ID.

Metric cost   Enables the administrator to configure the path packets will take through the network. OSPF works with the least cost path. Obviously, the cost should be inversely proportional to the speed of the link.

OSPF slot   This parameter indicates on which slot the OSPF soloist can run together with Dijkstra's algorithm. Slots are represented with ones and zeros. Any slot that has a zero cannot run the OSPF soloist. On a Nortel Networks router, the OSPF soloist cannot run on the same slot as TI and the console connection (slot one for a BLN and slot seven for a BCN). The LSDB also exists on the slot that is running the OSPF soloist, but the routing table gets distributed to all slots running IP. If the slot running OSPF goes down, then an alternate slot will be chosen, which is also affected by this parameter.

Import AS extern   Setting this parameter to *no* will make an area a Stub area. All routers in the Stub area must have this parameter set to *no* or adjacencies will not be properly formed.

Import summaries   This parameter is set up on an ABR of a Stub area. If it is set to false, network summaries will not be flooded into this area; instead, a default route will be used. This can help to additionally reduce the size of the LSDB of the Stub area.

Some important parameters within an OSPF packet include

Hello interval   The frequency of Hello packet transmission, by default, is ten seconds.

Dead interval   The interval at which to declare the neighbor as down if no Hellos have been received, by default, 40 seconds. Once the dead interval has passed, the router will break the adjacency and flush all LSAs from this neighbor out of the LSDB.

Authentication type   This enables password authentication for OSPF. All routers within a single area must agree on the authentication type and password. No authentication is enabled by default.

Router priority   This field is used to elect the DR for a broadcast network. If the parameter is set to zero, then this router cannot be the DR.

Options   This field specifies if an area is a Stub area and does not allow external routes to be imported into the area.

OSPF Policies

OSPF policies only work on non-OSPF routes or AS external routes. Announce policies are created on ASBRs because they are the routers that deal with external routes from other protocols.

Accept Policies

OSPF accept policies apply to external type 1 and type 2 networks. They are used to enable or prevent routes from being inserted into the routing table, but not the LSDB or LSAs. This can mean that a router that receives updates from this router may have routes in the routing table that this router has chosen to ignore.

Announce policies can be configured on any OSPF router, except in a Stub area because no external routes are imported into the Stub area (see Figure 7-18).

NOTE   Accept policies affect routing tables, not LSAs, because nothing is allowed to prevent LSAs from being flooded around the OSPF network (because of the LSA.)

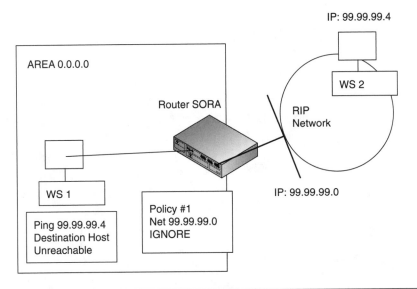

Figure 7-18 An OSPF accept policy that causes the external network 99.99.99.0 to be ignored on Router Sora. WS 1 will not be able to reach WS 2 because no packets can be forwarded to network 99.99.99.0 from Router Sora.

Announce Polices

OSPF announce policies operate on external route LSAs and control how they are advertised into the OSPF environment. OSPF announce policies are created on the ASBR because that is where the import of external routes into the OSPF network occurs. An announce policy can be used to manipulate or prevent inclusion of an external route into the LSDB.

Border Gateway Protocol Version 4 (BGPv4)

BGP is a distance vector External Gateway Protocol (EGP). As we discussed in the previous chapter, each company in the Internet is its own AS. Each AS that wants to become public is assigned a unique 16-bit AS number from the Internet authorities. Companies will use IGPs like OSPF for internal AS routing, but EGPs are used to route between ASs (see Figure 7-19).

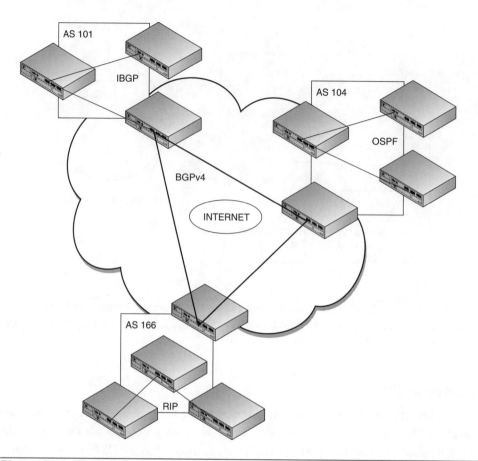

Figure 7-19 BGPv4 is an EGP that handles routing functionality between ASs. Within an AS, Interior Gateway Protocols, like OSPF and RIP, are responsible for routing functions.

The current Internet environment consists of large and small corporate networks, Backbone providers (large ISPs), and universities. It is a collection of diverse but interconnected ASs. EGP routing protocols used in this type of environment must be concerned with loop prevention, must be able to handle tens of thousands of routes, and must have flexibility in routing policies. EGPs are mainly concerned with network reachability as opposed to hop counts or metrics used in protocols like RIP or OSPF.

BGPv4 is the routing protocol that best handles all the diverse routing needs of the Internet community. BGPv4 uses TCP port number 179 for reliable transport, eliminating the need for frequent updates (like in RIP). Once the initial exchange of information is complete, only keep-alive messages and change messages are exchanged. BGPv4 includes information in routing updates to prevent loop detection. The information is called Network Layer Reachability Information (NLRI) and is actually a list of AS numbers that were traversed. This AS path information is updated by each BGP router with its local AS number and can be used to spot loops in cases where that AS number already exists in the NLRI. BGPv4 also has support for Classless Internet Domain Routing (CIDR) and supernetting. Furthermore, BGP is based completely on policies and offers many choices for forwarding decision-making. The Internet uses BGP between ISPs and between ASs.

BGP Peering and Route Policies

Routers that exchange BGP information with each other are called *BGP peers*. Routers can have an unlimited number of peers. BGP router's peers are configured instead of being learned dynamically. If a BGP peer is in another AS, the peer will be considered an external peer, and External BGP (EBGP) will be used to communicate between the peers. EBGP peers are generally part of the same IP network (on the same subnet). EBGP adds its AS number in all data that is being forwarded to its EBGP peers.

If the peers are in the same AS, the peer connection is considered an Internal BGP (IBGP) connection. IBGP peers do not need to be part of the same network. They do not have to be on the same subnet; however, all BGP routers that are part of the same AS must present the same view of the AS to all other external BGP routers. Because of this, all IBGP routers must share routing information. They may use an IGP (RIP, OSPF, or IBGP) to route information between each other. IBGP does not update path information when sending data between peers.

 NOTE In order for BGP routes to be propagated throughout an AS running OSPF, remember to configure the BGP/OSPF router as an ASBR so that it accepts external routes into the routing table.

BGP updates are sent to peers only and never sent via a broadcast or multicast. Therefore, when routers want to send BGP routing information, they must connect to a peer. When BGP attempts to establish a connection with its peers, it interacts in the following way. BGP first establishes a TCP connection with its peer using port 179. BGP sends a TCP open request to establish a connection, and the connection is established after the TCP has exchanged the traditional Syn, Syn Ack, and Ack messages. The next stage is for the BGP peers to establish a BGP connection using BGP open messages containing AS numbers and BGP identifiers (see Figure 7-20).

Figure 7-20   A sample BGP open message

If the router wants to share information with this peer, it will respond with a BGP open message of its own. Once the BGP connection is established, the routers then exchange information by transferring BGP update messages. The entire BGP routing table is sent using an update message. Each update message contains BGP path attributes. After the initial setup, only changes are exchanged. Whenever there are changes, updates are sent to reflect those changes only. If changes are infrequent, then BGP will send keep-alive messages to keep the BGP session established. (Keep-alive messages are also used when establishing BGP peer sessions to confirm the open messages.) Keep-alive messages are sent every 30 seconds, and if a peer misses three messages, the BGP peer connection is torn down. If a router wants to end the BGP session, it sends a BGP notification message. When a session with a peer is terminated, all information learned from a peer is deleted from the routing table.

BGP advertises NLRI and path attributes, not traditional whole routes. A route in BGP is considered a destination with attributes of a path to that destination. The complete AS path is advertised. BGP has two additional rules for routing. The first rule is that if a BGP router sees itself in the AS path, it will not accept the path. BGP will ignore all routes from peers that already contain their local AS number because that route represents a loop. The second rule of BGP is that routers only advertise the route they use even if they have multiple routes to a single location. This is to save on space in an already huge routing table necessary to host all the Internet routes.

The NLRI consists of an IP address and a prefix length, for example, 99.0.0.0/8. The prefix length is like a subnet mask, but it is not dependent on traditional class based networking. (Class B addresses can have a Class A mask.) This enables BGP to be a completely classless protocol and use CIDR and supernetting with ease. BGP is famous for doing aggregation. This is especially essential for an Internet routing protocol. Because the Internet has hundreds of thousands of routers, it is the job of administrators and ISPs to efficiently design networks so that multiple routes can be aggregated into single routes (see Figure 7-21).

Companies must make sure only to advertise networks that exist. Sometimes when aggregating networks, ISPs may include networks that are not presently assigned in the

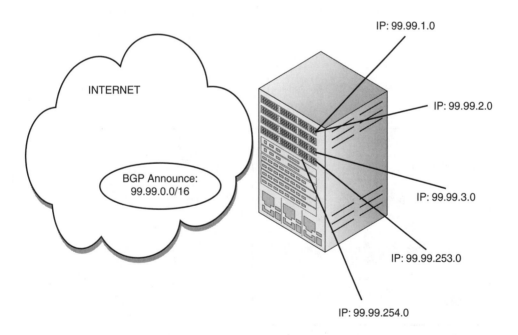

Figure 7-21 An ISP has a block of 99.99.0.0 networks. It can suballocate those networks to other smaller companies and then aggregate the networks back into a single Class B address in a BGP announcement.

aggregate advertisement. This can cause a black hole of networks that are listed in the Internet, but do not really exist.

BGP Parameters

To enable BGP, each BGP router must have these configurations (see Figure 7-22):

BGP identifier This uniquely identifies the BGP router in BGP update messages. This must be a valid IP address that is an interface on the router. A router running BGP and OSPF must use the same ID for both protocols.

Local AS This identifies the AS to which this BGP router belongs.

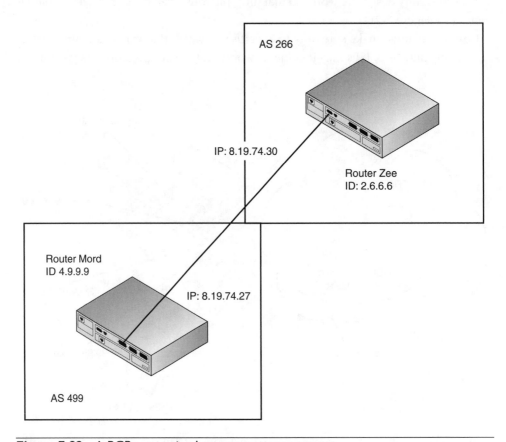

Figure 7-22 A BGP connection between two peer routers

Peer address   The IP address of the remote BGP router at the other end of this peer relationship.

Peer AS   The AS to which the remote BGP router involved in this peer relationship belongs.

Local address   The IP address of the local side of the BGP peer relationship.

Quick Quiz II

Identify each of the parameters listed (Local AS, and so on) from the perspective of Router Zee.

Answers

1. For Router Zee the Local AS = 266

2. Peer Address = 8.19.74.27

3. Peer AS = 499

4. Local Address = 8.19.74.30.

Quick Quiz III

Is this an IBGP peer connection or EBGP?

Answer

This is an EBGP peer connection.

BGP is a fully policy-based routing protocol. No BGP updates will be added to a routing table or advertised if BGP accept and announce policies are not correctly in place.

When a BGP network is set up, by default, no routes that are learned by BGP are accepted or injected into the routing table. No routes are advertised or announced to peers. Each network administrator must configure BGPv4 announce policies in order for BGPv4 to advertise routes and NLRI information to peers. Additionally, BGPv4 accept policies must be created so that BGP routes will be included into the routing table. ISPs have the ability to configure BGP announce policies that will aggregate all their networks into one announcement (see Figure 7-21). Small companies have the ability to configure BGP accept policies to accept routes from their ISP and insert only a default route into the routing table. This is especially useful if the company has only one Internet gateway router leading to the ISP. Otherwise, accept policies can be configured to add only necessary routes from the ISP into the routing table. This helps to limit the size of the routing table for ASs that are not involved in Internet routing.

NOTE ASs that are not involved in Internet routing are also called Stub ASs. ASs that have many connections to the Internet and enable traffic to pass through them destined for the Internet are called Transit ASs.

Summary

In this chapter, we discussed one IGP called OSPF and one EGP called BGPv4. An administrator that is attempting to create an efficient AS may use OSPF on internal routers to propagate routes around the network. OSPF uses LSDBs that are filled with LSAs to provide a method for routers to learn about all other networks and routers in the AS. An ISP would use BGPv4 for connecting routers to the Internet. BGPv4 provides an efficient means of communicating between ASs. BGPv4 works with policies to ensure that routing tables do not get too large, and routers only advertise and learn about routes that are necessary to provide routing in the Internet.

Review Questions

1. The OSPF protocol is a
   A. Link state protocol based on assigned costs.
   B. Distance vector protocol based on hop count.
   C. Link state protocol based on assigned costs and hop count.
   D. Routing protocol that can be configured to work based on hop count or assigned costs.

2. Which statement is true about OSPF?
   A. It is designed for use in large networks.
   B. It can be used to route IP and IPX packets.
   C. The same subnet mask must be used throughout a network running OSPF.
   D. It enables the use of the same network number in more than one place around the network.

3. Dijkstra's algorithm is used to:
   A. Build the LSDB.
   B. Send and receive LSAs.
   C. Build a shortest path first tree.
   D. Determine which routes are added to the IP routing table.

4. In an OSPF network, each router is defined by a unique:
   A. IP address
   B. AS number
   C. Link state ID
   D. OSPF router ID

5. Which statement is true about AS external link and AS summary link?
   A. AS external link advertises a single external network, and AS summary link advertises a range of networks.
   B. AS external link advertises the ASBR, and AS summary link advertises an external network.
   C. AS external link advertises the ASBR, and AS summary link advertises a range of external networks.
   D. AS external link advertises an external network, and AS summary link advertises an ASBR.

6. A type 1 external route in an OSPF network is a route that is:
   A. Learned by a non-OSPF protocol
   B. Statically configured on the ASBR
   C. Not directly connected to the ASBR
   D. Associated with a metric of one

7. How are ASs uniquely identified?
   A. By the IP address
   B. By the OSPF router ID
   C. By the BGP-4 router ID
   D. By the assigned AS number

8. In a BGP routing update, a network that is advertised as 100.0.0.0/16 represents which range of addresses?
   A. 100.0.0.0 to 100.255.255.255
   B. 100.0.0.0 to 100.0.255.255
   C. 100.0.0.0 to 100.0.0.255
   D. 100.0.0.0 to 100.0.0.0

9. A network administrator has configured BGP on all his router circuits. He is still not learning BGP routes. What could be the problem on this network?
   A. No BGP accept policies are configured.
   B. No BGP announce policies are configured.
   C. The BGP router must be configured to be an ASBR.
   D. A static route must first be configured to the BGP peer.

10. A network administrator is initializing BGP on a circuit of his router. What process will occur before BGP is initialized?

    A. IP comes up on the circuit.

    B. A BGP hello is sent out the circuit.

    C. A TCP connection must be established.

    D. A routing update is sent out the interface.

11. Which algorithm does OSPF utilize to calculate its routing database?

    A. Metcalf algorithm

    B. Dijkstra algorithm

    C. Shortest path first algorithm

    A. Distance vector routing algorithm

12. Which statement most accurately describes OSPF and routing updates?

    A. OSPF is a distance vector routing protocol not capable of passing the subnet mask information along with its routing updates.

    B. OSPF is a link state routing protocol that sends routing updates after a link state change, and the updates include the subnet mask information.

    C. OSPF is a link state routing protocol that sends routing updates after a link state change and does not include the subnet mask information.

    D. OSPF is a distance vector routing protocol and sends out regular routing updates that include subnet mask information at 30-second intervals.

13. Which element of an OSPF configuration would you change to create a preferred path?

    A. The interface area ID

    B. The path cost of the interface

    C. The IP address of the interface

    D. The subnet mask of the interface

    E. The holddown timer of the interface

14. Which address is the default Backbone area of an OSPF-routed environment?

    A. 0.0.0.0

    B. 10.0.0.0

    C. 127.0.0.0

    D. 255.255.255.255

15. When does the OSPF routing protocol send out routing updates?
    A. Every 30 seconds
    B. Every 60 seconds
    C. During nonpeak traffic periods
    D. When the status of a link changes

16. Which statement about the BGP4 is true?
    A. BGP4 routes cannot be summarized.
    B. BGP4 is a link state routing protocol that determines its routes based on shortest path first.
    C. BGP4 is a routing protocol used by major ISPs and determines best routes through a defined set of policies.
    D. BGP4 is a distance vector protocol used most commonly in enterprise data center networks.

17. BGP4 is used
    A. To bridge different protocols between disparate networks.
    B. To generate routes at the edge of the Internet for accessing Internet domains.
    C. On the edge of the Internet to receive and transmit Internet routes via policies.
    D. In cases where multiple paths are needed and the best gateway path should be used to enhance throughput.

18. From which routers does BGP learn networks?
    A. Distance vector routers
    B. Link state routers
    C. Other BGP routers
    D. All of the above

19. How are BGP routers associated together with each other?
    A. TCP connections
    B. Area numbers
    C. Router IDs
    D. AS numbers

20. BGP runs on which protocol?
    A. UDP, port 179
    B. TCP, port 179
    C. IP, port 89
    D. Its own transport method protocol, port 89

21. What are routers in BGP that communicate directly with each other and share routing information called?
    A. Neighbors
    B. Peers
    C. Adjacencies
    D. Speakers

22. What is another name for CIDR?
    A. Subnetting
    B. Supernetting
    C. VLSM
    D. BGP

23. Which of the following is a Stub area?
    A. A small area
    B. An area with only one router
    C. An area that has no connection to the Backbone area
    D. An area that does not allow import of external routes

24. Which situation would require a designated router?
    A. Every workgroup
    B. Every area
    C. Every Ethernet segment
    D. Every AS
    E. Every point-to-point link

25. How can an administrator reconnect an area that is cut off from the Backbone area?
    A. Using a link state router
    B. Using a virtual bridge
    C. Using a virtual link
    D. Having two Backbone areas
    E. Using an area link

26. Which method does OSPF use to advertise routing information?
    A. Broadcasts
    B. Anycasts
    C. Unicasts
    D. Multicasts

27. What are routers in OSPF that communicate directly with each other and share routing information called?
    A. Neighbors
    B. Peers
    C. Adjacencies
    D. Designated routers

28. If there are no network changes, how often does OSPF send out updates?
    A. Every 30 seconds
    B. Every 30 minutes
    C. Every 60 minutes
    D. Never

29. What is the default OSPF router dead interval?
    A. Ten seconds
    B. 60 minutes
    C. 40 seconds
    D. 30 minutes

30. Which priority will prevent the OSPF router from becoming the DR?
    A. Ten
    B. Zero
    C. One
    D. None of the above

31. Which is an OSPF internal router?
    A. A router that has all interfaces connected to area 0.0.0.0
    B. A router with interfaces in only two areas
    C. A router that does not import external routes
    D. A router that is not a DR or a BDR

31. Which is an OSPF ABR?
    A. A router that has all interfaces connected to area 0.0.0.0
    B. A router with interfaces in more than one area that maintains a database for each area
    C. A router that does not import external routes
    D. A router with all interfaces connected into the same area

33. Which two routing protocols allow for the use of a variable length subnet mask? (Choose two.)
    A. NRIP
    B. OSPF
    C. RIP Version 1
    D. RIP Version 2

Answer Key

1. **A.** OSPF is a link state protocol based on assigned costs. There are no hop counts in OSPF.

2. **A.** OSPF is for use in large networks. (Answer D makes no sense because a routed network can never have parts of the same network in different locations because routers will never know how to route packets.)

3. **C.** Dijkstra's algorithm is used to build the SPF tree.

4. **D.** OSPF uses OSPF router IDs for unique identification. Although the IDs appear to be IP addresses they do not have to be valid addresses at all.

5. **D.** External links advertise external networks, Summary links advertise ASBRs.

6. **B.** OSPF type-1 must be directly attached to the ASBR; all the other choices for this question were OSPF type-2 routes.

7. **D.** AS numbers are assigned from the Internet authorities.

8. **B.** Since 16 bits are significant, all the networks (10.0.0.0 to 10.0.255.255) are included.

9. **A.** BGP-4 is all policy based no routes will be learned without an accept policy.

10. **A.** IP must be initialized before BGP-4 or any other IP routing protocols can run.

11. **B.**

12. **B.** OSPF is a link state protocol and subnet mask information is included in updates. This is what enables VLSM in a network.

13. **B.** Interface cost is the most important factor in route determination in OSPF.

14. **A.** Backbone area is 0.0.0.0.

15. **D.** Updates are used to indicate topology changes in the network.

16. **C.** BGP4 is used by ISPs and is based on route policies.

17. **C.** BGP4 is used at the edge of the Internet between companies.

18. **C.** BGP routers can only learn network information from other BGP routers.

19. **A.**

20. **B.** BGP runs on TCP.

21. **B.** BGP routers that share information are called peers.

22. **B.** CIDR is also known as supernetting because it is the process of aggregating many networks into one announcement.

23. **D.** Stub areas do not import external routes.

24. **C.** Designated routers are necessary in broadcast networks. Ethernet segments are considered broadcast networks.

25. **C.** Virtual links are used to connect areas so they don't become cut off from the backbone area.

26. **D.** OSPF uses multicasting with the addresses of 224.0.0.5 and 224.0.0.6.

27. **A.** OSPF routers that share update information are called neighbors.

28. **B.** If there are no topology changes, updates occur every 30 minutes.

29. **C.** The default OSPF router Dead Interval is 40 seconds.

30. **B.** Routers with a priority of zero cannot be DRs.

31. **A.** An internal router is one with all interfaces in a single area in this case it happens to be the backbone area.

32. **B.** An ABR is an Area Border Router and is a router that is in multiple areas and maintains databases for each area.

33. **B, D.** OSPF and RIP2 allow for Variable Length Subnet Masks; the other protocols do not.

PNNI

In this chapter, you will

- Learn the basic function and purpose of PNNI
- Learn how to implement PNNI on a Centillion 100
- Learn how a Centillion 100 supports PNNI

When you want data to get from point A to point Z, it is important to have a well-defined method for determining the path to get it there. There may be many possible paths and some may be, for one reason or another, better than others. If a path that has been learned fails, a useful feature would build or learn a new path. Another consideration should be efficiency and scalability. Some additional points to consider are whether to make the method dynamic and the need to make it a standard for multi-vendor support. These are the highlights of PNNI. There is no exam in the certification track (either NNCSS or NNCSE) that is exclusively about PNNI. The Centillion exam (*Exam Name*: Centillion Switching (V4.0); Advanced Product Exam, *Exam Number*: 920-023), however, does require some knowledge about the subject as there is a section in the course material explaining a PNNI overview and there are labs in the class that make use of the feature. Therefore, a level of familiarity with the topic is required.

Private Network-to-Network Interface (PNNI)

What Is the Point?

Private Network to Network Interface (PNNI) is a standard composed of two categories of protocols. The first deals with the distribution of topology information, which is used for route computation. The second is for signaling, which is used to create the point-to-point and point-to-multipoint connections. These two categories fulfill the main purposes of PNNI including:

- Maintaining and distributing topology information so that each switch has an identical view of the network

- Maintaining a hierarchy that will make the protocol scaleable

- Creating Switched Virtual Circuits (SVCs) between nodes that support crankback, alternate path routing for call setup

- Supporting multivendor environment

Similarities and Differences to OSPF

If you are familiar with OSPF (discussed in Chapter 7), you are already familiar with the major concepts of PNNI. While many of the terms are different, the ideas the two protocols are based on are similar.

OSPF divides networks into manageable units referred to as "areas," while PNNI uses units called "Peer Groups." The Link State Database (LSDB) of the router within the OSPF Area is the same as the LSDB of every router within that Area. The same holds true for all switches in a PNNI Peer Group. Both OSPF and PNNI use Dijkstras algorithm to build a shortest path tree from which to derive routes.

Some differences between the two protocols should be noted. OSPF Areas are required to be adjacent to the Backbone Area; PNNI has no such restriction. OSPF has no hierarchical structure, making it less scaleable. OSPF does not summarize routes by default; PNNI does.

Basics

The ATM forum (www.atmforum.com) specification for PNNI 1.0 says, "PNNI routing applies to a network of lowest-level nodes. Data passes through lowest-level nodes to other lowest-level nodes and to end systems. End systems are points of origin and termination of connections."

Lowest-level nodes are switches, actual physical boxes that would hurt if you dropped them on your foot (as opposed to logical entities like Logical Group Nodes [LGNs], which we will discuss later). The term "lowest-level" implies that there are higher levels (if you inferred that, you are correct). PNNI has a hierarchical model in which nodes exist at multiple levels, which we will examine later in this chapter.

> **NOTE** An LGN is any node in the PNNI hierarchy. I mentioned lowest-level nodes earlier as an example of an actual physical device that exists in a Peer Group at its basic level. Each lowest-level node is also a LGN. However, LGNs also exist at higher levels in the PNNI hierarchy. They are the logical representations of entire Peer Groups. We will visit this idea in more detail later in the chapter.

Peer Groups

Each switch in a PNNI environment is a member of a Peer Group. A Peer Group is an organizational entity to logically group devices (similar to an OSPF Area). PNNI Peer Groups can be created to represent physical/geographical boundaries, organizational/management entities, or merely to manage the size of the PNNI database. Each Peer Group is identified by a Peer Group ID. The network administrator configures every switch in each Peer Group with the Peer Group ID of the Peer Group that the switch belongs to. As you can see from Figure 8-1 the Peer Group ID is manually configured by the network administrator when the switch is configured to take part in PNNI. When a switch initializes it sends HELLOs to its directly connected neighbors. In

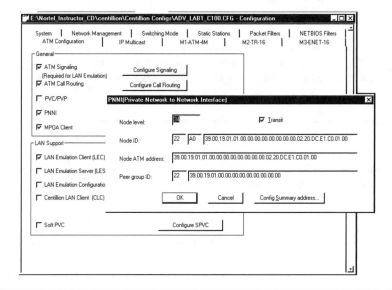

Figure 8-1   Peer Group ID configuration on a Centillion 100

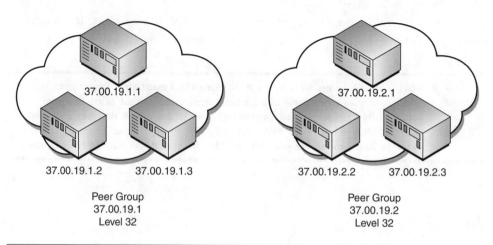

Figure 8-2 Peer Groups

this HELLO packet is the Peer Group ID. If the two directly connected switches have the same Peer Group ID, they belong to the same Peer Group (see figure 8-2). If the two directly connected switches have different Peer Group IDs, they are in different Peer Groups and become border nodes. The term border node reflects that the switches reside at the edges (border) of their Peer Groups and other Peer Groups. A border node has interfaces in more than one Peer Group. There is no added functionality or responsibility for border nodes. In Figure 8-3, switches 37.00.19.1.3 and 37.00.19.2.2 are border nodes.

NOTE Links between members of the same Peer Group are called Inside (or Horizontal) Links. Links between Border nodes are called Outside Links.

NOTE OSPF routers also need to determine the identity of their neighbors.

So, how are Peer Groups defined? Peer Groups are identified by an ATM switch's ATM address prefix. A portion of the prefix identifies the Peer Group. Bits 0 to 104 of

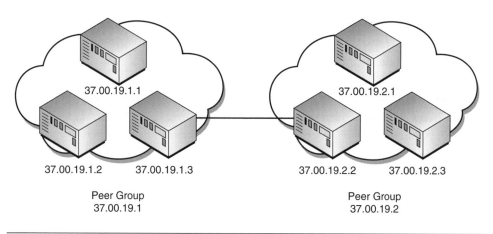

Figure 8-3 Border nodes

the ATM prefix are used to define the Peer Group. This number is called the Peer Group identifier. How much of the ATM prefix is used is indicated by the level indicator. In Figure 8-1, the uppermost value in the active window called the Node level is the Level Indicator. The level indicator is a one-byte field with a value between 0 and 104. All nodes in the same Peer Group also have the same level indicator.

Peer Groups also have leaders called the *Peer Group Leader* (PGL). The PGL is elected in a process called the PGL Election. Essentially the PGL is the Logical Group Node (LGN) with the highest PGL Priority (a value configured by the network administrator). The purpose of the PGL will be examined later.

HELLO

Let's assume that we have two switches sitting next to each other. These two switches are physically connected by a single link; they each have the same Peer Group ID and level indicator. How do these two switches find out that the other exists and is in the same Peer Group? The answer is the HELLO protocol. HELLOs are sent out over every physical link to aid in the discovery of neighbors. When a node receives a HELLO packet, the node examines the information and compares it with its own. The Peer Group ID is extracted and compared to that of the receiving node. If they match, the two switches belong to the same Peer Group and need to synchronize databases.

OSPF routers also perform similar tasks. When an OSPF router initializes, it sends HELLO packets out of its interfaces and uses the received HELLO packets to determine if and how to form adjacencies.

Just as OSPF routers in the same area synchronize databases, so do PNNI switches. All switches in the same PNNI Peer Group synchronize topology databases to reflect the same information (every node within a Peer Group knows everything about the Peer Group topology). Switches that are not in the same Peer Group do not synchronize databases. This helps to maintain the size of the databases as well as the amount of time necessary for convergence. We will discuss how connectivity between Peer Groups is maintained by the exchange of summaries later in this chapter.

For inside links (the links that join nodes belonging to the same Peer Group) there are three HELLO states:

- Down
- One-way inside
- Two-way inside

Down is self-explanatory. No HELLO packets have been received.

One-way inside occurs when a HELLO packet is received from a node whose Peer Group ID matches that of the receiving node, but the node that sent the HELLO is not yet aware of the receiving nodes Peer Group ID.

Two-way inside is achieved when a HELLO packet is received from a node and the HELLO includes the receiving node's own address in the Remote Node Identifier field. This tells the receiving node that the connected node (the one sending the HELLO) is aware of its existence.

HELLO packets are sent out of and received on a physical interface. Based on the information included in the HELLO messages, switches decide whether they belong to the same Peer Group. Their actions after this are based on the outcome of this decision. This, too, is similar to how OSPF functions.

Database Synchronization

Once HELLO packets have been exchanged and a relationship is established, it may be necessary to synchronize databases. In our previous assumption, the two nodes have determined they are in the same Peer Group, and they now need to synchronize their databases. This is what OSPF does when it exchanges LSUs to synchronize the LSDB.

PNNI neighbor nodes (nodes in the same Peer Group) send sequences of database summary packets. These packets identify (but do not include) all of the PNNI Topology State Elements (PTSEs) in a nodes topology database. These packets perform the same function as OSPF database descriptors). When these database summary packets are received, they are examined for any unknown elements. If unknown elements are found, the receiving node requests information about the unknown node from the sending node.

Nodes go through five states as they attempt to synchronize databases:

- NPDown
- Negotiating
- Exchanging
- Loading
- Full

Neighboring Peer Down (NPDown) is the initial state. No links have become active to indicate a neighbor needing to become synchronized.

Negotiating occurs when two neighboring peers decide to synchronize databases and that one peer should become the master (to decide sequence numbers).

Exchanging occurs when the node sends database summary packets to the neighbor.

Loading occurs when PNNI Topology State Packets (PTSPs) containing PTSEs (information about a specific link/node) are being sent from one node to another in response to a request to identify unknown elements.

Full is the final state in which all PTSEs have been received and processed. It is now possible to advertise links to the other peer.

For example, in Figure 8-4, switch B receives from switch A a database summary, which includes information about a PTSE that is not in switch B's database (exchanging). Switch B then requests the PTSE from the neighbor (loading) that originated the

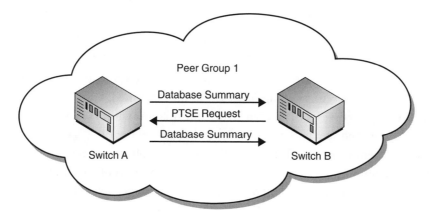

Figure 8-4   Synchronizing databases

description of the PTSE (switch A). Switch A responds with a PTSP that contains the requested PTSE. Once the PTSE is added to switch B's database (and if there were no other discrepancies), the databases are synchronized and the switches are in a Full state.

PTSPs and PTSEs

PTSPs contain one or more PTSEs. PTSEs contain the information in the database pertaining to a specific link/node.

Each PTSP (advertised in AAL type 5 packets) contains a header with the originating node ID and the originating node Peer Group ID.

Each PTSE header contains

- PTSE header checksum
- PTSE identifier (32 bits)
- PTSE sequence number (32 bits)
- PTSE checksum
- PTSE remaining lifetime
- PTSE type

Flooding

The flooding algorithm provides for reliable distribution of PTSEs throughout the Peer Group. It ensures that each node in the Peer Group has a synchronized topology database (that is, collection of PTSEs).

The flooding procedure is essentially as follows. PTSEs are encapsulated within PTSPs. When a PTSP is received, its component PTSEs are examined. Each PTSE is acknowledged by encapsulating its PTSE identifying information within an acknowledgment packet, which is then sent back to the neighboring peer. If the PTSE is more recent than the node's current copy, the PTSE is installed in the topology database and flooded to all other neighboring peers. The fact that the PTSEs were sent to these neighboring peers is remembered, and they will be retransmitted until acknowledged.

PNNI forum Specification PNNI 1.0 (5.8.3.1)

PNNI nodes send PTSPs under the following conditions:

- Expiration of a timer

- When a new (self-originated) PTSE occurs in the database

- When information pertaining to an old (self-originated) PTSE changes

- When a new (nonself-originated) PTSE occurs in the database

- In response to a PTSE request

This helps to ensure that all nodes in a Peer Group are kept up-to-date about the status and topology of the PNNI Peer Group.

Hierarchy

Now that we understand Peer Groups and their members, we need to discuss the hierarchy. The hierarchy is one of the features that make PNNI special and unique compared to other protocols like OSPF. OSPF has no defined hierarchy (one can be imposed upon OSPF, but it is not exactly the same). The hierarchy is part of what makes PNNI so efficient and scalable. In OSPF, addresses are advertised from one area into another with no attempt to summarize (there can be by default no attempt to summarize because nothing states that networks in an OSPF area share any common addressing scheme). Network administrators can impose their will on the design and make networks share common features that can be manually summarized, but those summaries are then advertised from area to area just like any other advertised route. PNNI strictly defines that all nodes in a Peer Group share the same Peer Group ID. Since the Peer Group ID is part of the ATM address, all nodes in a Peer Group have a common address. This common part of their addresses can serve as the summary for the entire Peer Group (since all nodes in the Peer Group have this in common).

If we have two Peer Groups (see Figure 8-5) 37.00.19.2 and 37.00.19.1 (each with a level indicator of 32 bits), we see that these unique Peer Groups have in common the first 24 bits (3 bytes) of their address. This becomes the address of the Peer Group at the next level in the hierarchy. We then get a logically created Peer Group with the Peer Group ID 37.00.19 (at level 24). Because no Peer Group is complete without members we have to have a few of those as well. The members of this Peer Group are the PGLs of the Peer Groups that formed this new level. If Peer Group 37.00.19.1 has a PGL 37.00.19.1.1, that PGL becomes a LGN of the Peer Group 37.00.19 and is identified as 37.00.19.1 (the

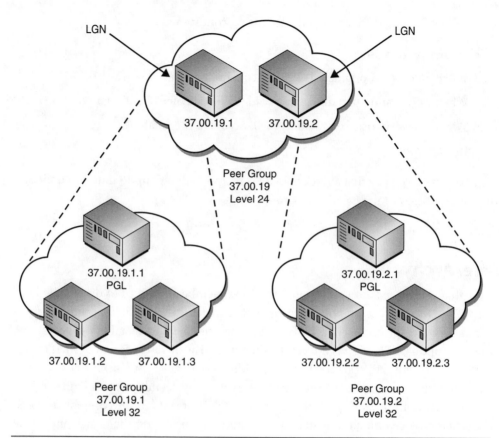

Figure 8-5 A hierarchy

same address as that of the Peer Group and the basis of the summarization). The same occurs for the Peer Group 37.00.19.2 and for all other Peer Groups combining at this level of the hierarchy.

The LGNs of the new Peer Group (which are really the PGLs of their lowest-level Peer Group) need to follow the same rules as all PNNI nodes. The LGNs send HELLOs to each other and flood PTSEs that describe the local Peer Groups topology. This is how PNNI summarizes external groups. The group 37.00.19.1 will learn about the group 37.00.19.2 when the LGNs of Peer Group 37.00.19 synchronize their databases by flooding PTSEs. The Peer Group 37.00.19.1 does not learn all of the details about Peer Group 37.00.19.2 topology, but it learns of its existence, that it is reachable, and how to get to it.

Getting There

When a device attached to a PNNI cloud needs to communicate with another, it issues a SETUP request. This request may include QoS parameters. It is the job of the ingress switch (the switch that receives the SETUP request) to find a path to the destination that meets any requirements that the source indicates. It does this by first locating the destination's prefix in its topology database and then checking resources along the paths that it is aware of to the destination.

PNNI uses Source Routing to select paths through the network and encloses the decision in the Designated Transit List (DTL), which is given to the source node (Token Ring fans will appreciate this!). Note that the DTL is not complete. If we examine a typical environment (see Figure 8-6), a DTL that could be generated by a SETUP request from switch 37.00.19.3.3 to switch 37.00.19.1.2 might look like this:

37.00.19.3.1----37.00.19.3.2----37.00.19.2----37.00.19.1

The DTL is specific only about its own Peer Group. Other Peer Groups are summarized. When the packet gets to a new Peer Group, that Peer Group's topology is scrutinized by the ingress switch of that Peer Group and builds a new DTL that accurately reflects the path to take through that Peer Group.

Crankback and Alternate Routing

Let's assume that the best path for a call from Peer Group 37.00.19.2 to Peer Group 37.00.19.1 is over the physical link from node 37.0.19.2.1 to physical node

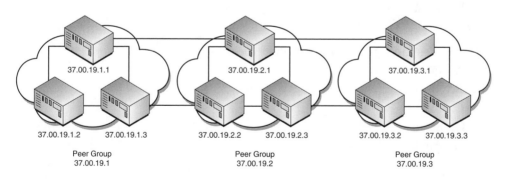

Figure 8-6 Multiple Peer Groups with multiple links

37.00.19.1.1 (refer to Figure 8-6). Everything is well and good as long as this link is fully functional. There is, however, the chance that this link will fail (just ask any network administrator with more than one day of on-the-job experience). If this occurs during a call SETUP when switch 37.00.19.2.1 intends to use that link, or if the request has already been sent down the link when the link breaks, no problem. Crankback and alternate routing allow us to recover by rerouting over alternate pathways (in this case the physical link from 37.00.19.2.2 to 37.00.19.1.3) without having to send the request all the way back to the originating node (37.00.19.3.3). In this case the egress (sending) switch (37.00.19.2.1) recognizes the failure and sends the request on to 37.00.19.2.2 for transport to the 37.00.19.1 Peer Group.

Signaling

PNNI signaling is the way in which calls are established and cleared over a PNNI network. PNNI signaling is based on UNI 4.0 signaling, supporting many, but not all, of its features. Some additional features, such as support for DTL and crankback, have been added to PNNI signaling, as they were not present in the UNI 4.0 standard.

Review Questions

1. PNNI is most similar to what layer 3 routing protocol?
   A. RIP II
   B. BGP
   C. OSPF
   D. Ethernet

2. PNNI supports the creation of what type of circuits?
   A. PVCs
   B. SVCs
   C. PVPs
   D. Serial
   E. Parallel

3. PNNI divides networks into manageable units called
   A. Borders
   B. Areas

C. BDs

D. Peer Groups

4. An LGN can be which of the following?

   A. A PNNI switch

   B. A logical member in a hierarchically raised PG

   C. A border node

   D. A PGL

5. Every switch in a PNNI environment is a member of a(n):

   A. Peer Group

   B. ELAN

   C. Area

   D. BD

6. Peer Groups are identified by an

   A. Area ID

   B. IP address

   C. Peer Group ID

   D. OUI

7. Fill in the blank. You may use one of the choices twice.

   Upon initialization, switches that are directly connected send _____ to each other. The purpose of this is to determine if the two switches are in the same _____. They determine this from examining the _____ present in the _____.

   A. Peer Group IDs

   B. HELLO Packets

   C. VPI/VCI

   D. RCC

   E. Peer Group

   F. LGN

8. Switches that are directly connected but are not in the same Peer Group are called:

   A. LGNs

   B. PGLs

   C. ASBRs

   D. Border nodes

9. Border nodes are responsible for
   A. Summarizing the PG topology to the other Peer Groups
   B. Securing the Peer Group from undesirable traffic
   C. Authenticating updates from other Peer Groups
   D. None of the above

10. How many bits make up an ATM switch's Peer Group ID?
    A. 20
    B. 0 to 104
    C. 6 to 12
    D. 20 to 120

11. The _____ tells us exactly how many bits are used to determine Peer Group membership.
    A. Level indicator
    B. PGL index
    C. LGN ID
    D. Depth code

12. What are the three HELLO states for switches sharing inside links?
    A. Down
    B. One-way inside
    C. Two-way inside
    D. Full

13. The five states that nodes go through while attempting to synchronize databases are
    A. Init
    B. Two-way
    C. NP Down
    D. Negotiating
    E. Exchanging
    F. Cold start
    G. Warm start
    H. Neighbor loss
    I. Loading
    J. Full

14. Database summary packets describe what to PNNI neighbor nodes?
    A. PTSPs
    B. PTSEs

C. HECs

D. LSUs

15. What provides for the reliable distribution of PTSEs throughout the Peer Group?
    A. Broadcasting
    B. Synchronizing
    C. Forwarding
    D. Flooding

16. Which of the following are circumstances under which PTSPs are sent?
    A. In response to a PTSE request
    B. With every RIP update
    C. When an SVC is established
    D. When information pertaining to an old (self-originated) PTSE changes

17. Why is it possible to summarize addresses so easily in PNNI, but not in OSPF?
    A. In OSPF, IP addresses of networks are not advertised from one area to another, just default routes.
    B. There is no need to summarize addresses in OSPF because the size of the OSPF routers' routing table is of no consequence due to highly efficient hardware and software.
    C. Addresses cannot be easily summarized in OSPF because no rule says addresses from noncontiguous ranges can not co-exist, making summarization a manual chore. PNNI addresses are subsets of their unique Peer Group ID so are easily summarized automatically.
    D. PNNI addresses cannot be summarized.

18. If a nodes ATM address is 37.00.19.2.A.2B.14.00.99.C4 and it has a level indicator of 48, what is its Peer Group ID?
    A. 37.00.19.2
    B. 37.00.19.2.A
    C. 37.00.19.2.A.2B
    D. We do not have enough information

19. The Peer Groups have members referred to as
    A. LECs
    B. LGNs
    C. ASBRs
    D. DTLs

20. If two Peer Groups exist (37.00.19.1 and 37.00.19.2), each with a level indicator of 32, how do they learn about each other and how to reach nodes in the other Peer Group?

   A. By directly exchanging summaries from one to another through border nodes

   B. By the PGL describing the local topology of the Peer Group 37.00.19 at level 24

   C. Through broadcasts

   D. Through multicasts

21. True/False

   SCVs are set up based on the transparent bridging method of determining device location.

   A. True

   B. False

22. True/False

   The DTL specifies every hop along every switch from the source to the destination.

   A. True

   B. False

23. What does the ingress node do when it receives a packet to transmit from another Peer Group?

   A. It drops the packet.

   B. It finds a path through its Peer Group to the destination and places the path in the DTL of the packet.

   C. None of the above

   D. All of the above

Answers

1. **C.** The Layer 3 routing protocol that PNNI is most similar to is OSPF. The two protocols share most of the major functions and algorithyms. They even use many similar names for abstract objects. They are both Link State algorithyms. RIP II is a distance-Vector algorithym and BGP is an Exterior Gateway Protocol (EGP) so there is no similarity there. Ethernet is a Layer 2 protocol.

2. **B.** PNNI supports the creation of Switched Virtual Circuits (SVCs).

3. D. PNNI divides networks into manageable units called Peer Groups. Peer Groups are defined by the network administrator and are typically implemented either organizationally, geographically, or some combination of the two. Attention can be paid to traffic patterns to maximize efficiency. Areas are a similar idea, but that is the tern used in OSPF.

4. A, B, C, D. A Logical Group Node (LGN) can be all of the above. For the LGN to even exist it must be a switch running PNNI, therefore A has to be correct. All switches running PNNI are LGNs therefore C and D are correct. Logical members of a peer group are what are most typically recognized as being LGNs. The most important thing to remember is that a LGN is a switch in a Peer Group. Nothing specifies that the switch must be a lowest level node, or that the Peer Group must be a logical group at a higher level of the hierarchy (although they may be).

5. A. The most basic unit of PNNI (after the LGN) is the Peer Group. Every switch participating in PNNI is a member of a Peer Group. B is a tempting answer but not necessarily correct. A switch participating in PNNI does not have to belong to an ELAN. C is a term associated with OSPF and is intended to confuse you. D is also incorrect.

6. C. Peer Group IDs are how Peer Groups are identified. They are a portion of the ATM address which is identified by the level indicator. A is an OSPF term intended to mislead you. B is incorrect because an ATM switch is not required to have an IP address (even though they usually do have them). D is how the manufacturers of devices maintaining a Media Access Control (MAC) address are identified.

7. B, E, A, B.

8. D. The correct answer is Border nodes. When switches connected by a point-to-point link initialize they send HELLO Packets. These packets incluse the Peer Group ID. Devices participating in PNNI need to determine if directly connected devices are in the same Peer Group or not because it determines how they will interact and share topology information. Devices that are directly attached, yet are in different Peer Groups are called Border nodes.

9. D. None of the above answers are correct. A Summarizing the PG topology to the other Peer Groups is the responsibility of the Peer Group Leader (PGL). B Securing the Peer Group from undesirable traffic is a function of network management. C Authenticating updates from other Peer Groups does not exist and is intended to mislead.

10. B.

11. A.

12. A., B., C.

13. C, D, E, I, J.

14. B.

15. D.

16. A.

17. C.

18. C.

19. B.

20. B.

21. False.

22. False.

23. B.

WAN Protocols

In this chapter, you will

- Learn the basics about PPP, Frame Relay, Welfleet Standard, ISDN, and other WAN solutions.

- Learn the minimum configuration necessary to configure each of these protocols.

- Learn which WAN protocols to implement in a given customer environment.

- Learn the necessary information to pass the WAN protocols portion of the Advanced IP/WAN protocols exam (920-015).

Wide area network (WAN) protocols differ from Local Area Network (LAN) protocols for a number of reasons. Traditionally, LAN protocols were capable of achieving very high bit rates (above 10 Meg), but over limited distances. This was fine for quite a while, until true enterprise networks began to emerge. WAN protocols are now able to transmit data over very long distances, but at low bit rates.

 NOTE We can now extend the range of our LAN protocols or increase the bit rates of some WAN protocols, but the cost of either of these choices is high. Depending on your business needs for bandwidth, these may be viable solutions, but for now these new technologies are mainly being employed by carriers and very large Enterprise networks. In this chapter, we will spend our time exploring the traditional WAN protocols that are most likely to be encountered in the real world (and certainly encountered on the Advanced IP/WAN Protocols Exam).

Exam Objectives

The topics that must be studied for the Advanced IP/WAN Protocols exam include the following:

- Describe the High-level Data Link Control (HDLC) frame format and channel operation.

- Explain the implementation and operation of a multiline circuit.

- Describe the use and operation of Breath of Life (BOFL) packets by a Nortel Networks router.

- List the HDLC-based WAN protocols.

- Identify the available log entries required to monitor the status of the WAN services.

- Describe the components, topologies, and characteristics of a Frame Relay (FR) network.

- Describe Frame Relay permanent virtual circuit (PVC) assignments.

- Identify link management options and line status sequences.

- Describe Nortel Networks service record functions, implementations, and management.

- Describe the different protocol and address resolution issues and options in a Frame Relay environment.

- Explain Frame Relay network operations over a fully meshed network using service records containing multiple PVCs.

- Explain Frame Relay network operations over a nonfully meshed network using service records containing multiple PVCs or single PVC.

- Explain the function and operation of Nortel Networks protocol prioritization.

- Identify the priority queuing and dequeuing algorithms used to prioritize traffic.

- Describe the use of protocol prioritization in the Frame Relay environment.

- Describe the components of the Point-to-Point Protocol (PPP).

- Explain the operation of the Link Control Protocol (LCP) and the Network Control Protocol.

- Identify the various phases of link operations for a PPP link.

- Explain the purpose of Link Quality Monitoring (LQM).

- Describe the various types of LCP messages.

- Identify the type of data compression and the supported protocols used in a Nortel Networks implementation.

- List the types of data compressed and the location of data within a packet.

- Describe the use of history tables in data compression.

- List and describe the functionality of the different compression modes

- Discuss the implementation of dial-on-demand, dial backup, and bandwidth-on-demand applications.

- Describe the implementation of the Integrated Services Digital Network (ISDN), Raise Data Terminal Multifrequency (DTR), V.25bis, and Hayes signaling applications.

- Identify event log messages, which can be used to troubleshoot dial services.

- Identify *Technician Interface* (TI) commands used to monitor the status of dial service connections.

WAN Protocol Support

BayRS supports a large number of WAN protocols including the following:

- Standard

- Pass Thru

- PPP

- Switched Multimegabit Data Service (SMDS)

- Frame Relay

- X.25

- Asynchronous Transfer Mode Data Exchange Interface (ATM DXI)

- Synchronous Data Link Control (SDLC)

- ASYNC

- BOT

- AOT

- Link Access Procedure Balanced (LAPB)

For a complete list of the protocols supported by any specific version of BayRS, please see the appropriate Release Notes for your version. The Release Notes can be obtained from support.nortelnetworks.com.

We will examine the HDLC frame, which is the basis for the four WAN protocols that we will be studying in this chapter. We will be examining Bay Standard (also referred to as Wellfleet Standard, or Standard), FR, PPP, Dial Services, and ISDN. Finally, we will look into some WAN protocol enhancements, such as compression and prioritization.

HDLC

The HDLC frame format is the basis for many WAN protocols, including the ones that we will be examining in this chapter (see Figure 9-1).

The frame begins and ends with a FLAG field (0x7E, 126 decimal, or 01111110 in binary) that is used to signal to the receiving station the beginning and end of a frame. Following the FLAG is the ADDRESS field. The size of this field varies depending on the protocol application being used. For example, Bay Standard uses an address of 0x07. The next field is CONTROL, which contains commands, responses, and sequence numbers. The value depends on the type of frame. The INFO field is where the user data is carried. The size of this field depends on the protocol. The next field is the *Frame Check Sequence* (FCS) that is used to verify the integrity of the frame from line errors. Finally, we encounter another FLAG that signifies the end of the frame.

HDLC uses three different station types (two distinct types and a third, which is a combination of the first two):

- Primary
- Secondary
- Combined

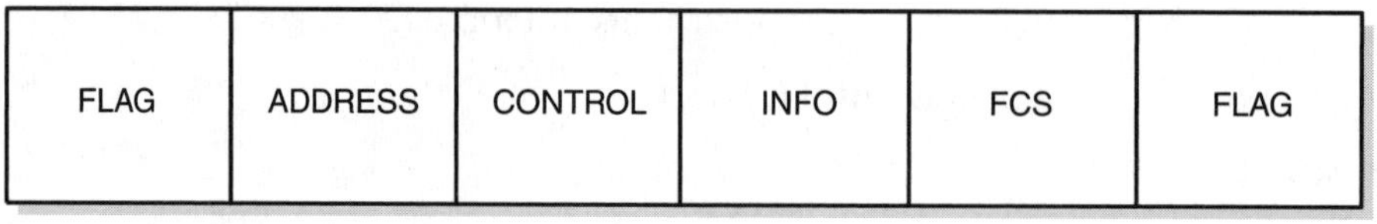

FLAG	ADDRESS	CONTROL	INFO	FCS	FLAG

Figure 9-1   HDLC frame

Primary stations control the data link operations. They send commands to which others respond. Primary stations communicate with secondary stations.

Secondary stations respond to commands from the primary stations. They cannot initiate communication until a primary polls them for data.

Combination stations can both send commands and respond to commands. Combination stations are peers.

HDLC also recognizes two channel types:

- Unbalanced

- Balanced

An example of an unbalanced channel would be a single primary station in a multipoint connection to numerous secondary stations.

A balanced channel has two combined stations on a point-to-point connection. Most WAN connections will use this configuration.

Bay (Wellfleet) Standard

Bay Standard (Standard) is the default WAN protocol selected when configuring WAN protocols via Site Manager (see Figure 9-2). It is a Nortel Networks proprietary protocol (did the name give it away?) and can only be used over dedicated point-to-point links between Nortel routers running BayRS.

> **NOTE** The Graphical User Interface (GUI) tool for managing Nortel Networks' routers is called Site Manager. For a detailed explanation on how to use Site Manager to configure a router, see Chapter 14.

Standard is easy to configure (no required parameters must be configured; just add Standard to a circuit and then add a layer 3 protocol). It can use multilane to add bandwidth and fault-tolerance. Standard uses an HDLC-like frame with the address field set to 0x07 (this address identifies the frame as a Standard frame) and the Control field set to 0x03 (Unnumbered Information).

Standard uses Ethernet encapsulation to encapsulate upper-layer protocols. The Ethertype field of the Ethernet header identifies the upper-layer protocols (IP, Internetwork Packet Exchange [IPX], AppleTalk). The Ethernet frame is then encapsulated in the HDLC-like Standard frame.

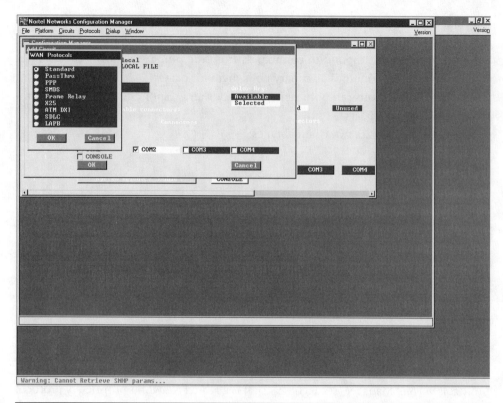

Figure 9-2 WAN protocol selection (standard)

The router tests the line periodically to verify that it is functioning. It does this by sending Breath of Life (BOFL) packets. By default, BOFLs are sent on lines configured to use BOFLs every five seconds. If a router misses five BOFLs (by having the BOFL timer expire five times without receiving a BOFL or data), then the router declares the link down. For a successful operation, both ends of the link must be configured identically in regards to BOFL enable and BOFL timeout for this to work. By the default settings, it takes BOFL 25 seconds (five missed BOFLs times fives seconds) to detect and declare a line down.

Bay Networks Multiline

Multiline enables a single logical circuit (the 172.10.20.4/30 network between two sites, as shown in Figure 9-3) to be made up of more than one physical line (see Figure 9-4). In this scenario, both Link A and Link B share the same network address and are used as one logical circuit with twice the amount of bandwidth. The two links are

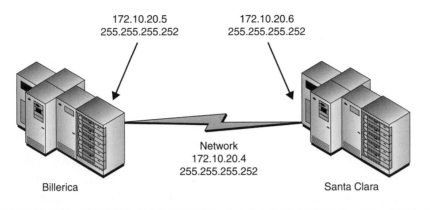

172.10.20.5
255.255.255.252

172.10.20.6
255.255.255.252

Network
172.10.20.4
255.255.255.252

Billerica

Santa Clara

Figure 9-3   Point-to-point network

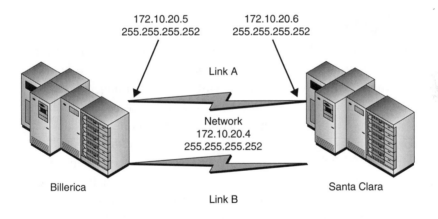

172.10.20.5
255.255.255.252

172.10.20.6
255.255.255.252

Link A

Network
172.10.20.4
255.255.255.252

Billerica

Santa Clara

Link B

Figure 9-4   Multiline network

also redundant to each other so that in the event that one fails (we can configure up to 16 physical lines in a single multiline), the remaining lines keep working.

Requirements

For lines to be part of a multiline circuit, the lines must all share the same characteristics:

- Bandwidth
- Maximum Transfer Unit (MTU)
- Encapsulation

When configuring multiline, consider the Data Path Chooser. The Data Path Chooser determines how data is distributed across the lines and can be used in two ways:

- Random
- Address-based (default)

Random is, obviously, random. Address-based performs a hash of the addresses in the packet and, based on the result, determines which line gets used. All conversations between specific stations will use the same lines. No attempt is made at load balancing. When a line fails or gets added, the equations change so that no pairs get disconnected or so that no lines go unused.

Frame Relay

Frame Relay is a standard that defines how network devices may communicate over Permanent Virtual Circuits, (PVCs) through a switched network (also, provisions exist for Switched Virtual Circuits [SVCs], which we will not be examining here as they are not a part of the certification process). Frame Relay is used (where available) when sites need connectivity for high speeds over short periods of time. Frame Relay does not require a private leased line from point A to point B (see Figure 9-5); the longer a leased line is, the more it costs. All that is necessary is that site A has a connection into a Frame Relay cloud (see Figure 9-6). The Frame Relay cloud (network) is usually a service provided by a carrier; the customer pays for the connection to the network (a leased line from the customer site to the edge of the Frame Relay network) and the amount of data that the carrier guarantees to carry.

Point A   Point B

Figure 9-5   Point-to-point over leased line

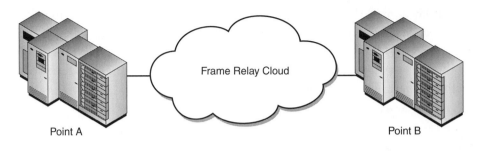

Figure 9-6   Connection to Frame Relay network

  NOTE   The different billing options available today are too numerous and confusing to cover here (not to mention that they have nothing to do with the certification track). It is enough at this point to know that if one is shopping for a Frame Relay service provider, to be sure to read the contract carefully and see if any competitors are in the area.

Let's examine the components that make up our Frame Relay network (see Figure 9-7). First, we have the Customer Premise Equipment (CPE); this is your stuff. This can be a router (what we will be focusing on), host, or Frame Relay Access Device (FRAD). The CPE acts as the Data Terminal Equipment (DTE).

Next, we have the Data Communications Equipment (DCE). The DCE will be the carrier's Frame Relay switch. It is the DCE that provides our connectivity into the Frame Relay cloud.

The connection between the DTE and the DCE is the access line. The access line includes everything from the physical port on the router to the physical port on the

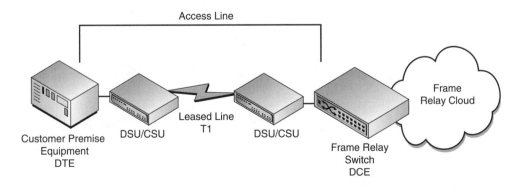

Figure 9-7   Frame Relay network components

Frame Relay switch. The physical ports on the Nortel Networks router can be SYNC, High-Speed Serial Interface (HSSI), or MCT1. The line can be T1, E1, Digital Data Service (DDS) via a Channel Service Unit/Data Service Unit (CSU/DSU), or T1/E1 directly into the router (with integrated CSU/DSU), or ISDN. The speed of the access line is usually between 56K and 45Meg.

PVC and DLCI

Here we will concern ourselves with how DTEs communicate across a Frame Relay network via PVCs. A PVC is a manually configured path through a switched network (see Figure 9-8).

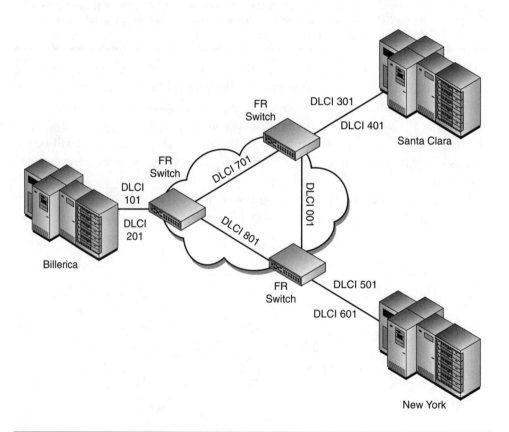

Figure 9-8 DLCIs and their local significance

NOTE Although SVCs are also supported in Frame Relay networks (see ITU-T Q.933, ANSI T1.617, FRF.4, and FRF.10), they will not be covered on the WAN/Advanced IP Configuration Exam that this chapter deals with.

The PVC is referenced by the DTE in the form of a Data Link Connection Identifier (DLCI). Just as in ATM where circuits through the network are assigned a VPI/VCI value (see Chapter 5), so too are circuits through a Frame Relay network assigned a numeric identifier (the DLCI). The DLCI can be a number from 0 to 1023, but of this range, a number of the values are reserved. DLCI values of 16 to 1007 are numbers that may be assigned to circuits that will carry user data. DLCI 0 is for signalling, 1023 is for Local Management Interface (LMI, covered later in this chapter), and 1 to -15 and 1008 to 1022 are reserved for uses yet to be determined.

Another similarity to ATM, a DLCI has local significance only (see Figure 9-8). Although a router in Billerica may see that DLCI 101 is associated with the network that leads to Santa Clara (end-to-end) the DLCI 101 only describes the link from the Billerica router to the DCE (point-to-point). The router in Santa Clara may use DLCI 301 for the connection to Billerica. The DLCIs used in the cloud have no bearing on this.

The ANSI T1.618 Frame

The frame to be used in Frame Relay networks is similar to the HDLC frame, but not exactly the same. Although the HDLC frame has six fields (FLAG, ADDRESS, CONTROL, INFO, FCS, FLAG), the ANSI T1.618 frame has only five fields (see Figure 9-9):

- **FLAG** 1 byte
- **ADDRESS** 2, 3, or 4 bytes
- **INFORMATION** The T1.618 recommended maximum at least 1,600 bytes
- **FCS** 2 bytes
- **FLAG** 1 byte

All of these fields are present in the HDLC frame and serve a similar purpose. You may have noticed that the CONTROL field is absent in the T1.618 frame. The role of the CONTROL field has been made a subdivision of the ADDRESS field. Since the only field to change appreciably is the ADDRESS field, it is this field that we will examine now.

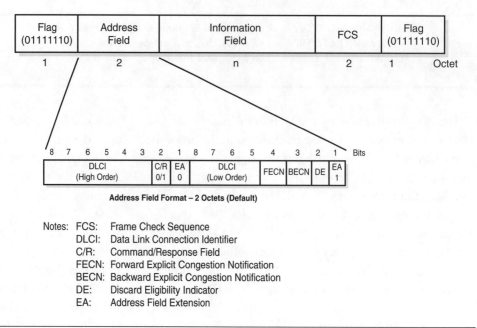

Figure 9-9 The T1.618 frame

As can be seen from Figure 9-9, the Address field has a number of subfields. I will discuss them out of order (I do this because I want to discuss the DLCI field last). The Command/Response field lets the receiving node know the purpose of the frame and it is used by the higher-layer protocols.

FECN stands for *Forward Explicit Congestion Notification* and BECN stands for *Backward Explicit Congestion Notification*. These bits are set in order to inform the receiving node of network congestion in the path.

Discard Eligibility (DE) tells a Frame Relay switch if the frame has high importance and should not be discarded in the event of congestion, or if the frame has a low importance and may be discarded. The user or the switch can set this bit.

We have now discussed all of the subfields, except for the DLCI and the *Address Extension* (EA). The DLCI identifies the value of the PVC. The EA is used to tell us how many bits in length the DLCI can be. Frame Relay enables 10-bit, 16-bit, and 25-bit DLCIs. The EA, when set to 0, tells us to expect more DLCI bits to follow. When the EA bit is set to 1, it tells the switch that no more DLCI bits will follow and the switch may compute the value of the DLCI.

Local Management Interface (LMI)

LMI messages define how the Frame Relay Access Device (FRAD/DTE) requests and receives information about the network (DCE). Through STATUS ENQUIRIES (which the FRAD sends to the network) and STATUS messages (which the network sends to the FRAD), information about the state of the network is exchanged. The DTE gets information on the following:

- Access line integrity
- New or deleted PVCs
- Status of the available PVCs

Three types of management interfaces are supported:

- LMI
- Annex D
- Annex A

The management types are not compatible with each other. LMI uses a DLCI of 1023, while Annex D and Annex A use DLCI 0 (Annex A/D have other differences that make them incompatible with each other). The roles of the DTE and the DCE differ in regards to management, so although the two ends of the connection need to be configured appropriately, they cannot both be configured the same. If two routers are set up in a lab for testing purposes, they must act as DTE/DCE (they cannot both be the same). In this case, set the management type to DLCMI NONE. This provides no management interface to the Frame Relay network.

During the polling process (every ten seconds by default), the router (DTE) learns about the access line integrity, new or deleted PVCs, and the status of existing PVCs. Every sixth polling cycle, a Full Status Enquiry is sent to the switch (DCE), which responds with a Full Status Response. The Full Status Response includes the complete status of all configured PVCs. The number of polling cycles between Full Status Enquiries is a configurable parameter and needs to match from DTE to DCE. The bits that follow the PVC number (DLCI) in the response make up the STATUS CODE, which include the following:

- **X0**   The channel is present and not active.
- **X2**   The channel is present and active.

- **X8**   The channel has been added and is not yet active.

- **XA**   The channel has been added and is active.

Topology Types

Two topologies must be considered in a Frame Relay network. They refer to the logical, not the physical topology:

- Full mesh

- Non-fully mesh

In a full mesh topology, a PVC is set up from every DTE to every other DTE (see Figure 9-10). In such an environment, every router (DTE) receives a routing update from

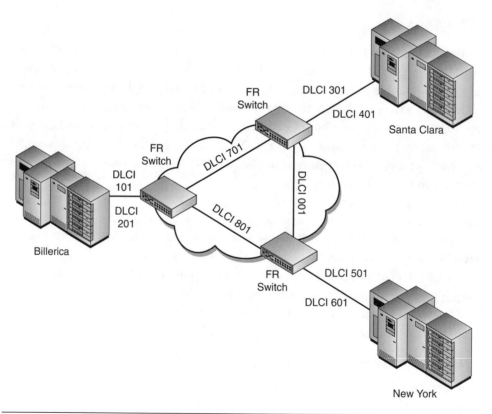

Figure 9-10   Full mesh topology

every other router. The key to understanding this environment is remembering that *no* route propagation issues exist for this type of topology because routing updates from separate routers are learned over unique DLCIs. Each DLCI acts here as a separate interface, so we will not run into any misdirected unicasts as we do in a hub and spoke nonfully mesh environment.

In the non-fully meshed topology, only PVCs are configured between DTEs that need to communicate with each other. Most common is the hub and spoke configuration where every DTE (spoke) has a PVC to a central (hub) DTE that all sites need to communicate with, but not to each other (see Figure 9-11). In this scenario, the spokes can communicate with the hub, but there will be issues for the spokes. When one spoke tries to communicate with another, it must direct all communication via the hub. If the spoke sends a unicast frame destined to another spoke, the hub drops it because the Media Access Control (MAC) address seems to be incorrect from a layer 2 point of view. In order to correct this, we add adjacent hosts to the spokes for the other spokes.

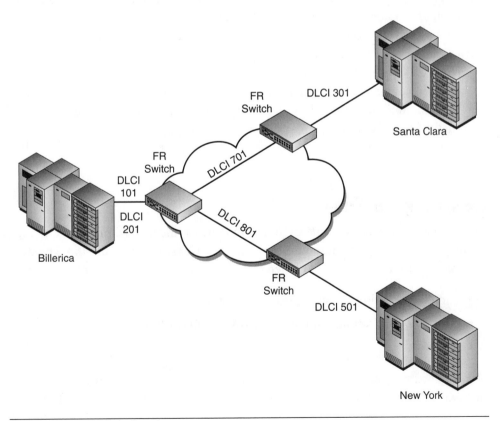

Figure 9-11   Hub and spoke

Route Propagation

Definite routing issues exist in a hub and spoke environment. When either poison reverse or split horizon (see Chapter 6) are configured, the hub receives all the routes to the remote locations, but either advertises them back at a cost of 16 (poison reverse) or suppresses the advertisement completely (split horizon). This makes it impossible for spokes to communicate with each other (even via the hub) because the spokes never learn about the networks on the other spokes.

We can deal with this issue in a number of ways. We can set the *Routing Information Protocol* (RIP) interface POISON REVERSE mode to ACTUAL. This will force the hub router to advertise all the routes back out to all the spokes. This will bring back the very issue that poison reverse and split horizon were meant to remove (count to infinity), but you win some, you lose some. It can also cause you to eat up a lot of bandwidth with the route updates.

Another method is to turn RIP Supply off on the hub, turn off RIP Listen on the spoke routers (on the interfaces that connect to the Frame Relay network), and configure default routes on the spoke routers. Use the hub router as the next hop address. A variation of this method is to generate a default route from the hub router and the spokes can learn it. RIP Supply still needs to be disabled on the HUB router interface that connects into the Frame Relay network.

You could configure static routes on all of the spokes to all the locations that they need to communicate with (if, in addition to having no life, you want to get no sleep). This method tends to become a management nightmare.

Finally, you could create a RIP Announce policy on the HUB router (also difficult to manage).

Address Resolution

After we have resolved any route propagation issues in the non-full meshed topology, we may still have address resolution issues. First, we will look at the three types of address resolution performed, and then we will examine the issues that can arise:

- Address Resolution Protocol (ARP) (RFC 1490)
- Inverse Address Resolution Protocol (INARP) (RFC 1293)
- ARPINARP

ARP functions just like it does for Ethernet, except that MAC addresses are replaced by DLCIs. This is used when the destination IP address is known, but not the DLCI that needs to be used to reach it. The ARP request is sent out all active DLCIs; when the destination replies, the source maps the DLCI it was received on to the IP address in the ARP cache.

INARP is used to discover the IP address at the end of the PVC. An INARP packet is sent out every new DLCI and the ARP cache is generated by the responses.

ARPINARP is the default method of address resolution. First, INARP is attempted when the DLCI is registered and if that fails then ARP is used when there is traffic to send.

Address Resolution Issues in Non-fully Meshed Networks

When we have a hub and spoke network, let's assume that router B wants to ping router C. If router A ARPs for the IP address of router B, that packet goes to router A (since that is the hub, all traffic goes to it). Router A sees the ARP request and realizes that it is not what it needs, so router A drops the packet, and the ping fails. To solve this problem, we create adjacent hosts (see Figure 9-12) on each spoke router for every other spoke

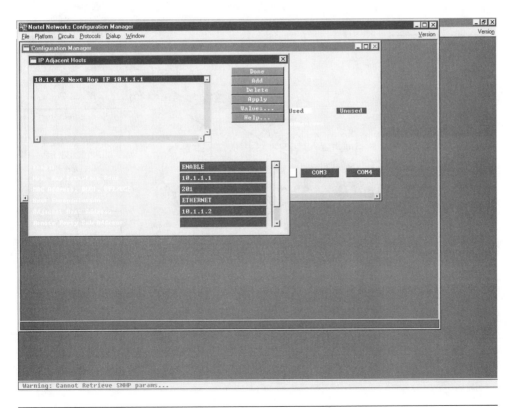

Figure 9-12 Adjacent hosts

router. When we have a configured adjacent host, there is no need to ARP. The frames are sent out as unicasts. The HUB forwards the unicasts normally.

Service Records

When adding Frame Relay to an interface on a router running BayRS, a default service record is created. A service record is a management entity for grouping PVCs and protocols. Each Frame Relay interface may have multiple service records and each service record may have multiple PVCs. Protocols are applied to service records just as they would be applied to an interface. If more than one PVC is issued to a service record, that protocol applies equally for each PVC. More than one protocol can be applied to a service record. For example, we may add both IP and IPX to a single service record, just as we could add both protocols to a physical interface (see Figure 9-13).

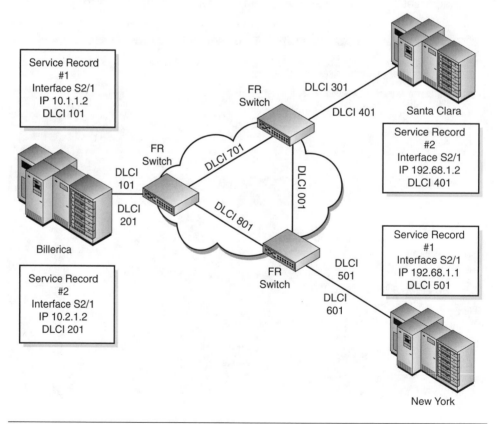

Figure 9-13   Service records and interfaces

CAUTION When a PVC is learned from a switch, if it is not already configured on a service record, it is added to the default service record. This could cause problems if the default service record is configured with protocols, and that configuration does not match the configuration of the PVC that has just been added to it. In order to keep this from causing havoc on the network, don't add any protocols to the default service record. Added PVCs just sit there going nowhere until you move them.

NOTE It is possible to move a DLCI from one service record to another. What happens if you delete a service record that contains DLCIs? The DLCIs are moved to the default service record. Consider the effect this could have on your network if you do this dynamically on a live network if protocols are configured on the default service record. It would be best to delete or move the DLCIs prior to deleting the service record.

When configuring service records on an interface, we use the following terms to describe them:

- Direct mode
- Group mode

Direct mode has a single PVC per each service record. This means that for our HUB router connected to two spoke routers (see Figure 9-14), there will be two service records with one PVC per service record. Each service record will have IP added to it and each one will represent a separate IP subnet. So, service record 1 has one PVC in it (101) and has an IP address of 10.1.1.1/16, while service record 2 has one PVC in it (201) and has an IP address of 192.168.10.1/24. Both of these service records can be configured on the same physical interface simultaneously.

Group mode has multiple PVCs per each service record (see Figure 9-15). If we add an IP address to the service record, all of the PVCs in the service record use the address equally. It means that the three routers in our hub and spoke environment are all on the same IP subnet (instead of being two separate subnets, as in Figure 9-14).

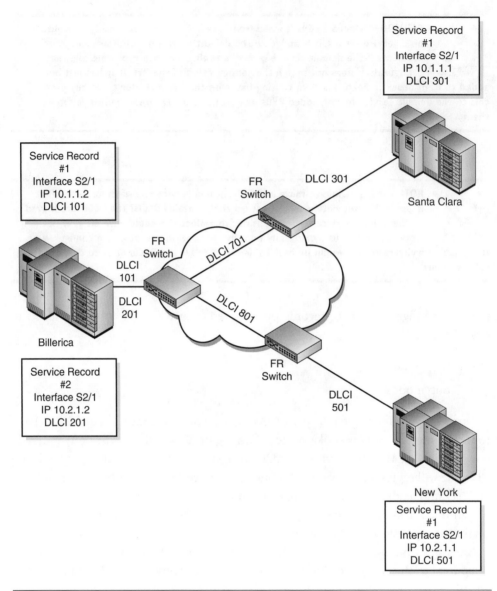

Figure 9-14 Direct mode

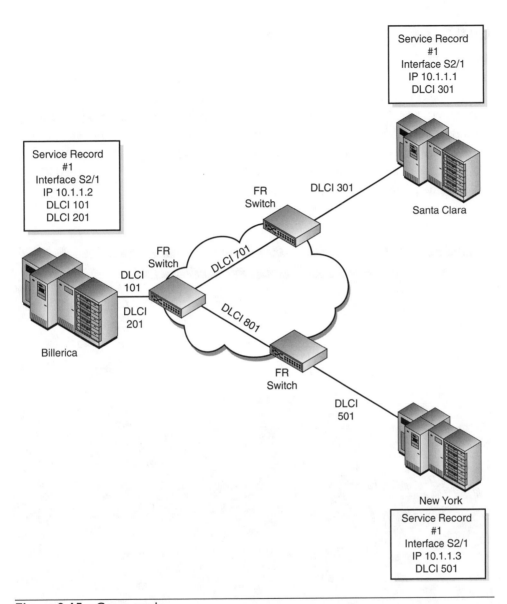

Figure 9-15 Group mode

Configuring Frame Relay

To configure Frame Relay using Site Manager first, we start by enabling a physical interface and adding Frame Relay as the WAN protocol. To do this, we go to the Configuration Manager in Site Manager and select an interface (see Figure 9-16).

After selecting the interface, the Add Circuit screen appears, confirming the interface we have selected, and it gives us the opportunity to rename the interface (see Figure 9-17). After naming the interface, we confirm our selection by clicking OK.

After confirming the circuit selection, the WAN Protocols screen appears and here we select Frame Relay (see Figure 9-18).

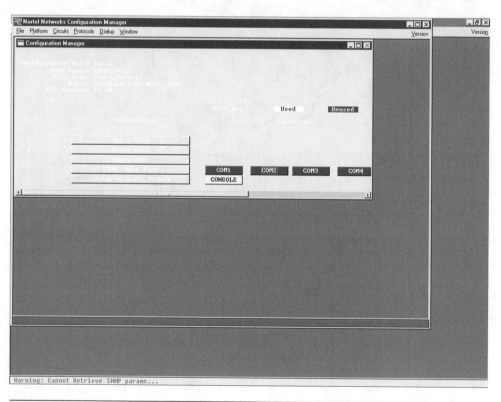

Figure 9-16 Configuration Manager

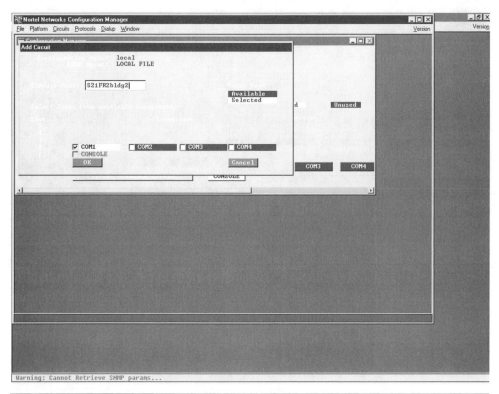

Figure 9-17 The Add Circuit screen

After confirming Frame Relay as the WAN protocol, the Select Protocols screen gives us the opportunity to add a protocol to the default service record (see Figure 9-19). A default service record is created automatically when you add Frame Relay to an interface. If you select a protocol at this point of the configuration, you will add that protocol to the default service record. We will *not* add any protocols at this point, so we will choose Cancel. At this point, we will be returned to the Configuration Manager screen.

We have now created and activated an interface with Frame Relay on it, but we have not configured it to do anything yet. To further work on the circuit, click the interface; when the Edit Connector window appears (see Figure 9-20), click Edit Circuit. Then the Frame Relay Circuit Definitions window pops up (see Figure 9-21). We will select

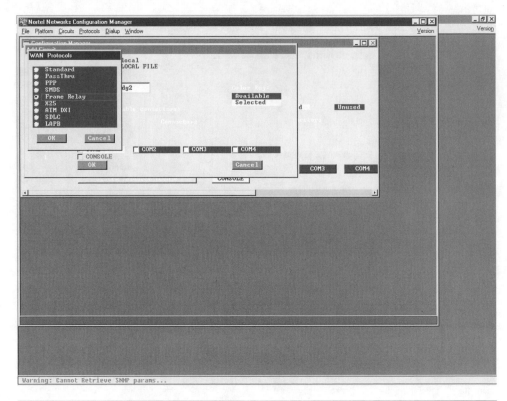

Figure 9-18   The WAN Protocols screen

Interfaces and the Frame Relay Interface List window appears (see Figure 9-22). From here, we can select the management type and configure the polling interval, address length, and other interface-level parameters. We will change the Mgmnt Type to REV 1 LMI. Click Apply and then click Done. This brings us back to the Frame Relay Circuit Definitions window. Now we will select Services. The Frame Relay Services List window now appears (see Figure 9-23).

The Frame Relay Services List window is where you will configure protocols for your service records and add or remove DLCIs to or from your service records. To add a service record from this window, click Add. This will bring you to the Frame Relay Service Add window (see Figure 9-24). If you need to add a DLCI to an existing Service Record,

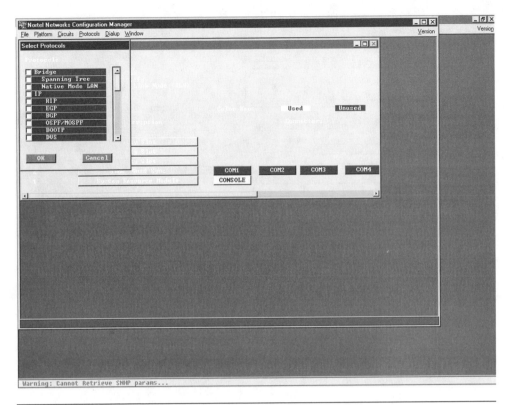

Figure 9-19 The Select Protocols screen

highlight the service record and click PVCs. This brings you to the FR PVC List (see Figure 9-25). From here, simply click Add and enter the DLCI for the new PVC.

Finally, you'll add a protocol to a service record. In the upper left-hand corner of the Frame Relay Service List window is a pull-down menu called protocols. Pull down the menu and click Add. Then you add and configure the protocol just as you would for any interface. Remember that protocols added to a service record apply only to that service record.

 NOTE For complete details on how to configure and customize Frame Relay, please refer to the Configuring Frame Relay Services document available from the Nortel Networks documentation web site.

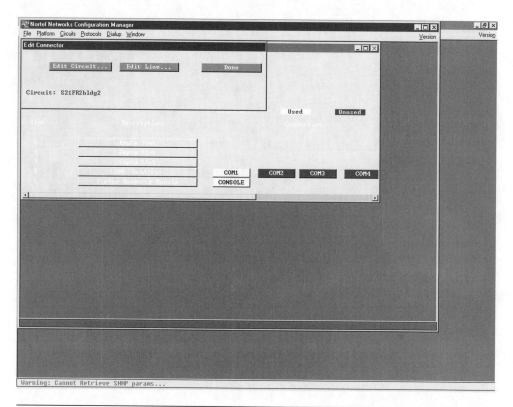

Figure 9-20 The Edit Connections window

PPP

The Point-to-Point Protocol (PPP) was created to overcome some of the deficiencies in HDLC and to be a standard for connecting equipment from separate vendors. PPP can be used to route or bridge frames over point-to-point (dedicated or switched) links.

PPP has three major functions:

- Link management
- Network-layer connection and management
- Multiprotocol encapsulation

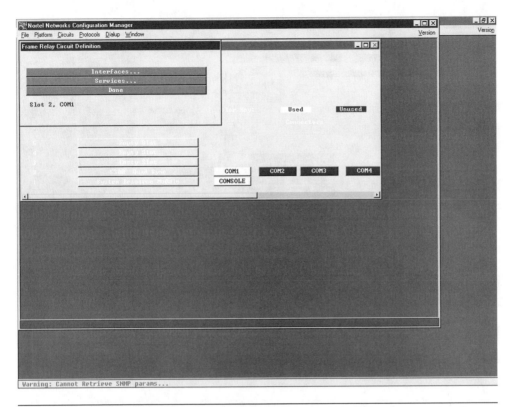

Figure 9-21   Frame Relay Circuit Definitions

PPP supports authentication through the Password Authentication Protocol (PAP) and Challenge Handshake Authentication Protocol (CHAP). It also supports multi-links and compression.

The following protocols can be enabled on a PPP interface:

- AppleTalk
- DecNet Phase IV
- IPX
- IP

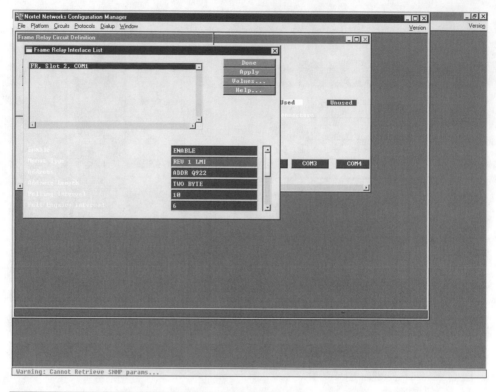

Figure 9-22 The Frame Relay Interface List window

- Open Standards Interface (OSI)
- Virtual Networking System (VINES)
- Xerox Network Systems (XNS)
- Transparent or translational bridging

PPP also has components. If you compare PPP to the OSI model, you will see that PPP includes both layer 1 and layer 2 functions. Two components are layered on top of each other (see Figure 9-26). The lower layer is the Link Control Protocol (LCP) and it must complete all of its functions before the higher layer can initialize. The higher layer is the Network Control Protocol (NCP).

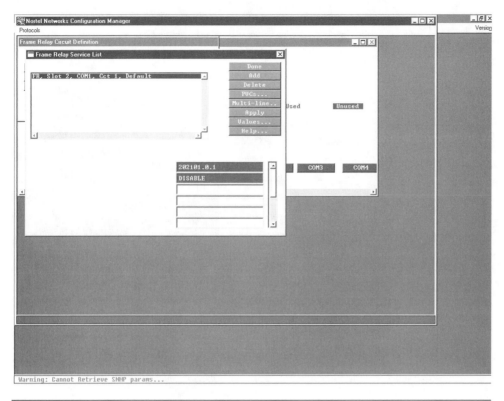

Figure 9-23   The Frame Relay Service List window

LCP

The LCP is responsible for opening the line, configuration parameters, authentication (PAP and CHAP), LQM, and terminating the line. If LCP is unable to complete any of its functions, we do not get to progress to the next level.

BayRS supports the following RFCs for LCP:

- RFC 1661 LCP

- RFC 1662 PPP in HDLC-like Framing

- RFC 1334 PPP Authentication Protocols—PAP and CHAP

- RFC 1989 PPP LQM

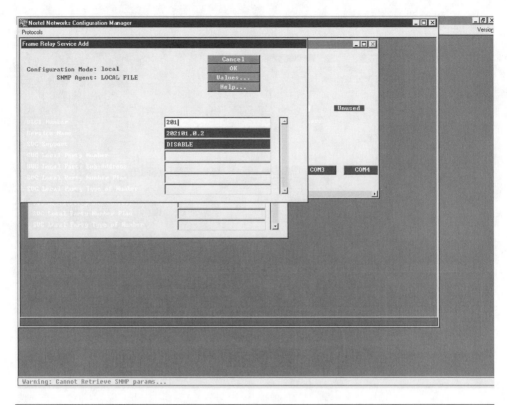

Figure 9-24   The Frame Relay Service Add window

Exam Objectives

The exam objectives for this section are as follows:

- Describe the components of PPP.
- Explain the operation of the Link Control Protocol (LCP) and the Network Control Protocol (NCP).
- Identify the various phases of link operations for a PPP link.
- Explain the purpose of Link Quality Monitoring (LQM).
- Describe the various types of LCP messages.

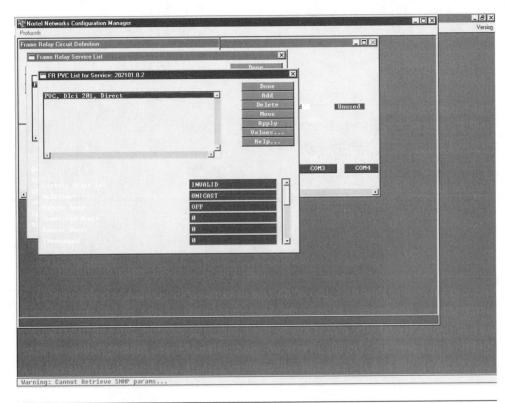

Figure 9-25 The FR PVC List

Three phases are involved in initializing a PPP interface (see Figure 9-27). Two of them are LCP functions and the third is an NCP function. They are as follows:

- Establishing the PPP link (LCP)
- Authenticating the link (LCP/optional)
- Negotiation of network-layer protocols (NCP)

Establishing the PPP Link

Before the transmission of data across the PPP link can occur, both ends of the connection (the point-to-point or switched circuits the router interfaces are connected to) must be aware of each other and negotiate configuration parameters. Each router

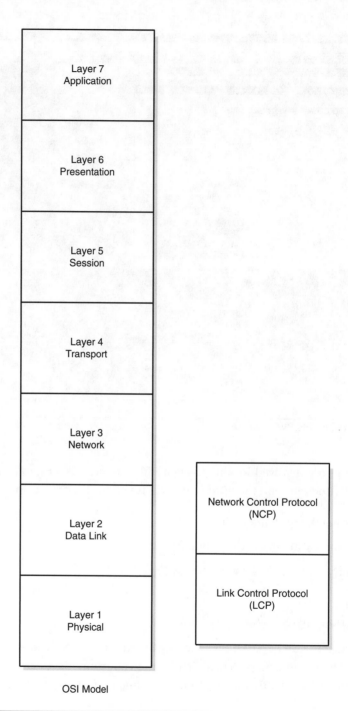

OSI Model

Figure 9-26 PPP and OSI

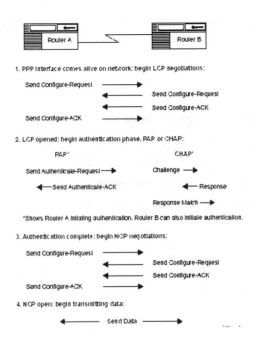

1. PPP interface comes alive on network: begin LCP negotiations:

Send Configure-Request ──────▶
                        ◀────── Send Configure-Request
                        ◀────── Send Configure-ACK
Send Configure-ACK ──────▶

2. LCP opened: begin authentication phase. PAP or CHAP:

   PAP*   CHAP*

Send Authenticate-Request ──▶   Challenge ──▶
   ◀── Send Authenticate-ACK   ◀── Response
                                Response Match ──▶

*Shows Router A initiating authentication. Router B can also initiate authentication.

3. Authentication complete: begin NCP negotiations:

Send Configure-Request ──────▶
                        ◀────── Send Configure-Request
                        ◀────── Send Configure-ACK
Send Configure-ACK ──────▶

4. NCP open: begin transmitting data:

   ◀────── Send Data ──────▶   .... .

Figure 9-27   PPP interface initialization

attempting to initialize a PPP interface will send a link configuration packet. A link configuration packet comes in four flavors:

- Config-Request
- Config-ACK
- Config-NAK
- Config-Reject

In Figure 9-28, you can see log entries from a router negotiating PPP LCP parameters.

NOTE   To see PPP events in the router log, use the command **log -ePPP**. For more information on the LOG feature of the router, see Chapter 14.

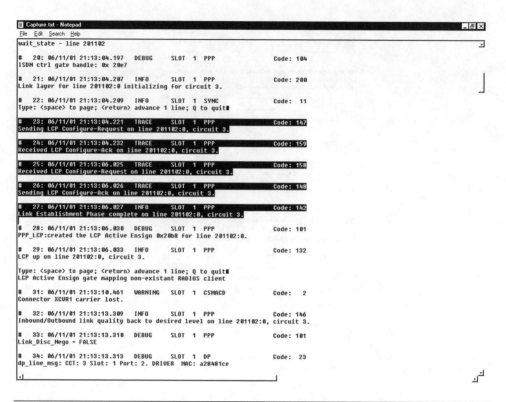

Figure 9-28 Log entries from a router negotiating PPP LCP parameters

The interface, upon first attempting to initialize, sends a Config-Request (log entry #23 and 25). The Config-Request packet includes LCP options such as the Maximum Receive Unit (MRU) size, authentication protocols (if any), the Link Quality Management (LQM) protocol, and others. If the router that receives the Config-Request can accept these options, it sends a Config-ACK (log entry #24 and 26) and we go to the next phase (authentication if it configured, NCP if not). If the router receiving the Config-Request cannot accept the options, it sends a Config-NAK, as shown in Figure 9-29.

The Config-NAK includes the offending parameter in the packet so that the routers can attempt to renegotiate the link by changing the problematic parameter. Following this, the routers try again, as shown in Figure 9-30.

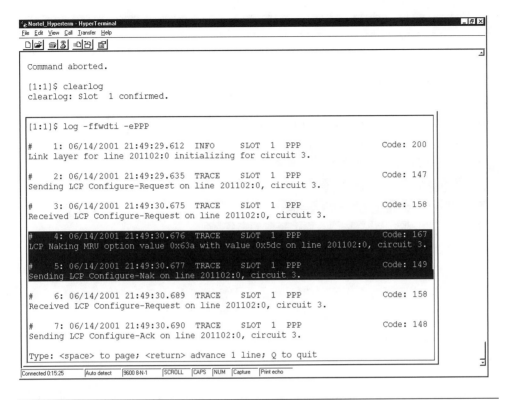

Figure 9-29   Config-NAK

Authentication

As mentioned earlier, BayRS supports two authentication protocols for PPP:

- Password Authentication Protocol (PAP)
- Challenge Handshake Authentication Protocol (CHAP)

Authentication occurs as part of the LCP initialization and can occur at user-defined intervals while the link is up.

PAP

PAP uses plaintext identifiers and passwords to authenticate two ends of the link. On both ends of the link, we enable PAP and configure the following:

- Local PAP ID
- Local PAP password

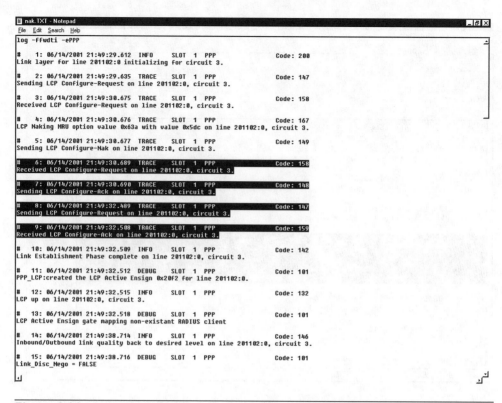

```
nak.TXT - Notepad
File  Edit  Search  Help

log -ffwdti -ePPP

#    1: 06/14/2001 21:49:29.612  INFO     SLOT  1  PPP          Code: 200
Link layer for line 201102:0 initializing for circuit 3.

#    2: 06/14/2001 21:49:29.635  TRACE    SLOT  1  PPP          Code: 147
Sending LCP Configure-Request on line 201102:0, circuit 3.

#    3: 06/14/2001 21:49:30.675  TRACE    SLOT  1  PPP          Code: 158
Received LCP Configure-Request on line 201102:0, circuit 3.

#    4: 06/14/2001 21:49:30.676  TRACE    SLOT  1  PPP          Code: 167
LCP Naking MRU option value 0x63a with value 0x5dc on line 201102:0, circuit 3.

#    5: 06/14/2001 21:49:30.677  TRACE    SLOT  1  PPP          Code: 149
Sending LCP Configure-Nak on line 201102:0, circuit 3.

#    6: 06/14/2001 21:49:30.689  TRACE    SLOT  1  PPP          Code: 158
Received LCP Configure-Request on line 201102:0, circuit 3.

#    7: 06/14/2001 21:49:30.690  TRACE    SLOT  1  PPP          Code: 148
Sending LCP Configure-Ack on line 201102:0, circuit 3.

#    8: 06/14/2001 21:49:32.489  TRACE    SLOT  1  PPP          Code: 147
Sending LCP Configure-Request on line 201102:0, circuit 3.

#    9: 06/14/2001 21:49:32.508  TRACE    SLOT  1  PPP          Code: 159
Received LCP Configure-Ack on line 201102:0, circuit 3.

#   10: 06/14/2001 21:49:32.509  INFO     SLOT  1  PPP          Code: 142
Link Establishment Phase complete on line 201102:0, circuit 3.

#   11: 06/14/2001 21:49:32.512  DEBUG    SLOT  1  PPP          Code: 101
PPP_LCP:created the LCP Active Ensign 0x20F2 for line 201102:0.

#   12: 06/14/2001 21:49:32.515  INFO     SLOT  1  PPP          Code: 132
LCP up on line 201102:0, circuit 3.

#   13: 06/14/2001 21:49:32.518  DEBUG    SLOT  1  PPP          Code: 101
LCP Active Ensign gate mapping non-existant RADIUS client

#   14: 06/14/2001 21:49:38.714  INFO     SLOT  1  PPP          Code: 146
Inbound/Outbound link quality back to desired level on line 201102:0, circuit 3.

#   15: 06/14/2001 21:49:38.716  DEBUG    SLOT  1  PPP          Code: 101
Link_Disc_Nego = FALSE
```

Figure 9-30   Log entries from a router negotiating NCP parameters

- Remote PAP ID
- Remote PAP password

Each end of the link gets configured with its own name (local ID) and gets told the local ID of the remote router (remote ID). The same goes for the local and remote passwords. All of the parameters are *case-sensitive* (this is for authentication after all). The routers exchange IDs and passwords and compare them to the locally stored values; if they match, authentication is successful. If authentication fails, check spelling and the accuracy of IDs and passwords. Figures 9-31 and 9-32 show the configurations for router A and router B.

Figure 9-33 shows what a successful authentication looks like in the router log.

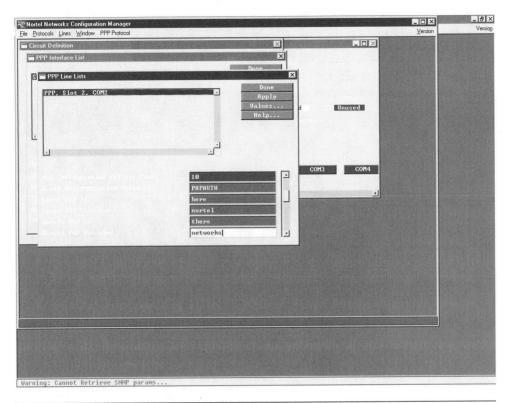

Figure 9-31 PAP configuration for Router A

CHAP

When CHAP is enabled on both ends of a link, each end is assigned the same CHAP secret and each end receives a unique local name (all is case-sensitive). The CHAP secret is not a password and it is never transmitted on the wire. The CHAP secret becomes part of the hashing algorithm, which generates a value that is transmitted from one router to the other. This value is compared to values generated by the remote router. If they match, the remote router hashes the value again and sends it back for a final test of the authentication. If this round passes, the router sends a success message and Authentication is complete.

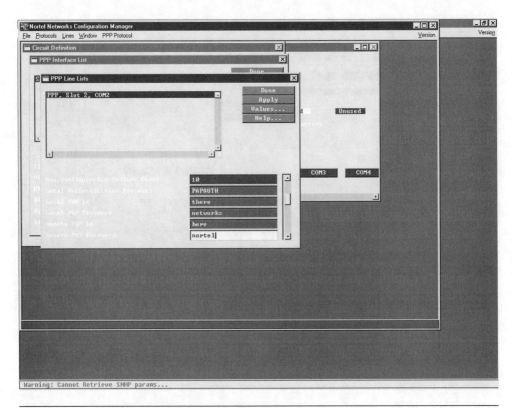

Figure 9-32   PAP configuration for Router B

 NOTE   Many good and detailed books on password encryption are available on the market; RFC 1334 has been written specifically for PAP and CHAP in PPP. Please read them for more detailed information on this subject.

 NOTE   For all dial services, you must use **PAP** or **CHAP**, either of which provides an identification mechanism that is essential to bringing up dial-on-demand, bandwidth-on-demand, and dial backup lines. Failure of either authentication protocol causes the connection to be dropped, without the network administrator's intervention.

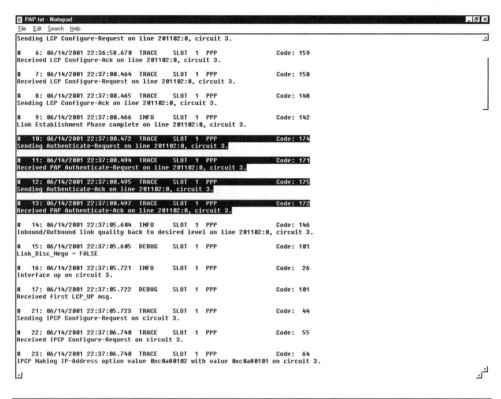

Figure 9-33   A successful authentication

Link Management

In order to verify the proper function of the line, the router can test the line periodically using three different methods:

- Link Quality Report (LQR)
- Echo requests
- BOFL

Link management is disabled by default. If you set the Link Quality Protocol of a PPP interface to LINKQR, you will enable LQR. The LQR report period needs to be the same on both routers, but they will negotiate the lowest configured value. LQR only needs to be configured on one side of the link. You configure inbound and outbound quality thresholds (as a percentage of the total number of packets sent in a report period). When LQR tests the link, it sends the remote router a packet containing counters that represent the total number of packets sent and received during the last report period. The remote router examines the numbers and compares them to the number of packets it sent and received. The difference is measured and a percentage is computed. After five periods, the percentages are examined, and if they fall below the user-defined threshold, the link is brought down. It then brings the link back up in an attempt to fix the problem dynamically.

NCP

The Network Control Protocol (NCP) is responsible for negotiating layer 3 protocols.

In order to enable a network-layer protocol, you must select it in the PPP Interface List window (see Figure 9-34). Available network-layer protocols include the following:

- RFC 1332 IP

- RFC 1377 OSI

- RFC 1762 DECnet Phase IV

- RFC 1552 IPX

- RFC 1763 Banyan VINES

- RFC 1378 AppleTalk

- RFC 1764 XNS

The NCP for IP is the Internet Protocol Control Protocol (IPCP). For IPX , it is the Internetwork Packet Exchange Control Protocol (IPXCP). For IPCP (or any other NCP) to initialize, all phases of LCP and authentication must complete successfully. If LCP does successfully initialize and multiple NCPs are configured (such as IPCP and IPXCP), one is not reliant on the other (IPCP may function even if IPXCP fails to initialize).

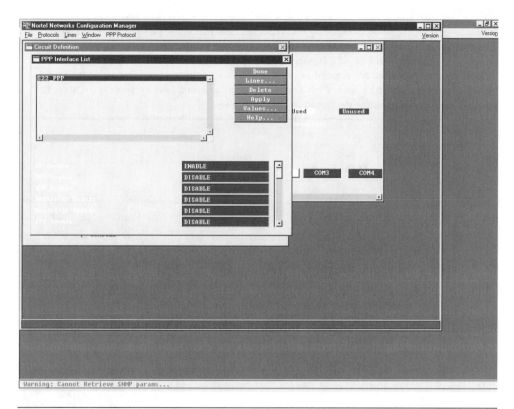

Figure 9-34 PPP Interface List

Negotiating Network-Layer Protocols

PPP uses various NCPs to determine the values of parameters during network-layer negotiations, the final phase of PPP initialization. Like the LCP, each NCP enables peer routers to negotiate various network options over the data link by transmitting configure-request, configure-ACK, configure-NAK, and configure-reject packets.

Network options include which network addresses to use and which media types to bridge. Once both peer routers agree upon network options, the network control protocol reaches the open state. The routers then begin transmitting user data packets for any upper-layer protocols over the link.

NOTE When configuring IPCP, it is necessary in older versions of code (pre-11.0) to manually create an adjacent host entry for the router at the far end of the link because ARP is not supported over PPP. With 11.0 of BayRS, adjacent host entries are created automatically over dedicated lines, but must be configured manually for switched lines. With BayRS 12.20, no adjacent host entries are created, nor are they necessary for either dedicated or switched lines.

Configuring PPP

To configure PPP on an interface, we go through the same steps in enabling the physical interface as we did for Frame Relay (refer to the "Configuring Frame Relay" section), but when we are asked to add a WAN protocol, we select PPP. Figure 9-35 shows a new pull-down menu option, PPP Protocol. This menu option appears as soon as we enable PPP on an interface on the router. Pull down the menu and select Interface. This brings

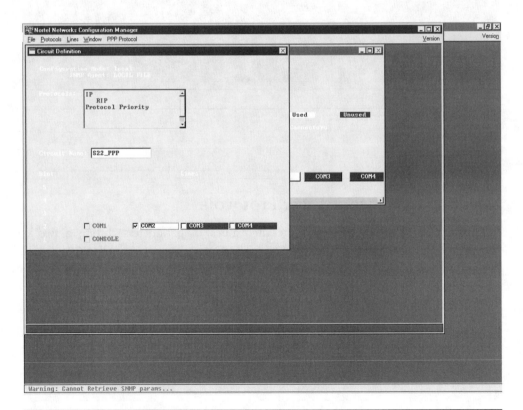

Figure 9-35 Circuit definition

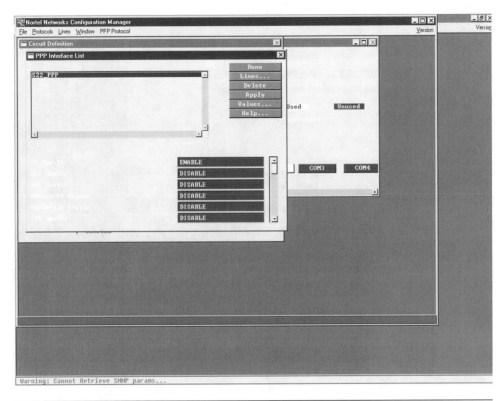

Figure 9-36   PPP Interface List

us to the PPP Interface List window (see Figure 9-36). This is where we enable and configure NCP-level parameters. If we click on Lines, we are brought to the PPP Lines List (see Figure 9-37) window where we can configure LCP-level parameters.

> **NOTE**   For complete details on how to configure and customize PPP, please refer to the Configuring PPP Services document available from the Nortel Networks documentation Web site.

ISDN and Dial Services

Integrated Services Digital Network (ISDN) is an internetworking technology that enables communication over switched digital lines. We will examine how ISDN is used

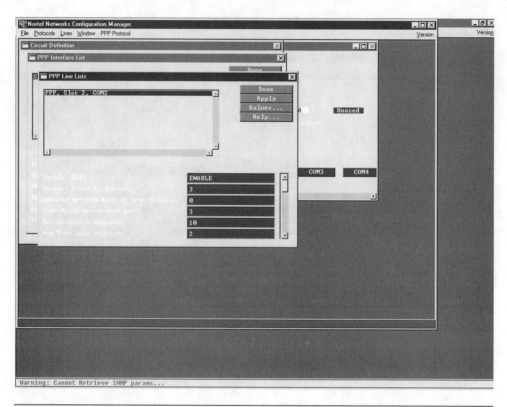

Figure 9-37 PPP Lines List

in connecting remote sites with low-bandwidth requirements or as a dial-backup, dial-on-demand, and bandwidth-on-demand solution.

Dial Services

Dial services connect remote users or sites to other sites through a switched network using dial-up lines (also referred to as switched lines). The difference between these lines and the leased lines (dedicated point-to-point connections between two locations) is that they are typically temporary connections at a relatively low bandwidth. Connections are made when needed and taken down when not. As such, their use causes the carrier less overhead and gives the carrier the capability to make use of its bandwidth when the customer is not using it, making it a cheaper alternative. Nortel Networks offers three types of dial services:

- Dial-on-demand
- Bandwidth-on-demand
- Dial backup

Exam Objectives

The exam objectives for this section are as follows:

- Discuss the implementation of dial-on-demand, dial backup, and bandwidth-on-demand applications.
- Describe the implementation of ISDN, Raise DTR, V.25bis, and Hayes signaling applications.
- Identify event log messages, which can be used to troubleshoot dial services.
- Identify Technician Interface (TI) commands used to monitor the status of dial service connections.

Dial-on-Demand

Dial-on-demand offers a low-cost solution for remote offices with very low or intermittent data transfer requirements. The router only initiates a dial circuit when it has data to send or at a time of day specified by the administrator. Also, a Force Dial parameter can be set to open a circuit regardless of whether there is data to send or not. For a remote site that only uses a WAN circuit a few times a day, this is an excellent configuration. The router terminates these circuits when an inactivity timer expires, at a time of day configured by the administrator, or when the Force Take Down parameter is set. For the router to be configured to accept incoming calls, it must be configured with PPP. Dial-on-demand services are supported on Async, Sync, and ISDN interfaces.

Demand Lines and Pools

A *demand line* is a physical interface for a demand circuit to use (interface is physical; circuit is logical). A *demand pool* is a grouping of one or more lines. You create a demand pool (all it requires is an ID) and then add interfaces (or lines) to it. All dial lines must belong to a pool.

Following are a few rules about pools:

- Pools must be configured before a dial service can be configured.

- Pools are identified by a pool ID.

- A router can have more than one pool.

- Lines go into pools.

- A single line cannot be in more than one pool *of a given type* (a single line cannot be in two dial backup pools at the same time).

- A single line can be in more than one pool of *different types* (a single line may be in both a dial backup pool and a dial-on-demand pool at the same time).

- Lines added to demand pools must be on the same slot.

- Lines added to backup pools can be on any slot.

Bandwidth-on-Demand

Bandwidth-on-demand enables us to configure dial lines to be connected when a line gets congested, allowing us to add the bandwidth of the new line to that of the congested line. This enables us to manage expenses by only paying for as much bandwidth as we use at a given time while still providing for additional performance needs. This is how the router supports RFC 1990 PPP Multilink Protocol.

Bandwidth-on-demand starts with an initial line. This can be a leased line or a switched line. When it becomes congested, a line is added from the bandwidth-on-demand pool. Congestion is determined by one of the routers configured to be the Congestion Monitor (see Figure 9-38). This router checks link utilization and compares it to the configured thresholds. If the link utilization is above the congestion threshold for more than ten exam periods (default 10), a new line is added to the bundle (bundle being the term for the lines currently functioning in the multilink, which does not include lines from the pool that have not been added to active service). When the congestion monitor sees that the utilization has fallen below the recovery threshold for ten consecutive recover periods (the default), it removes the link from the bundle.

Dial Backup

Dial backup services enable us to configure a line so that if a primary circuit fails (a dedicated point-to-point), a switched circuit will be established to take over. The primary circuit must be one of the following:

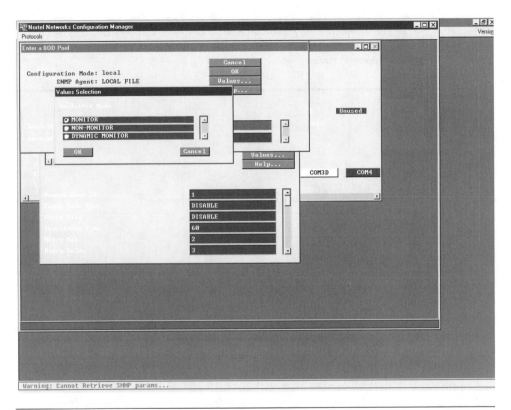

Figure 9-38   Bandwidth-on-demand monitor options

- A leased line running PPP
- A leased line running Bay Standard
- A direct mode Frame Relay PVC

Once a dedicated circuit is configured (on each router), a dial backup pool is configured (on each router). Lines are also added to the pool. The primary circuit is identified and tied to the pool. One end of the link will be configured as the master and the other the slave. The master is responsible for initiating the call. The master gets configured with CHAP local names and a CHAP secret. The slave gets configured with a WHOAMI table (a caller resolution table) that ties the incoming CHAP local name and secret to a primary circuit name.

NOTE For complete information on how to configure dial services, see the Configuring Dial Services document (part #308621-14.20), available from the Nortel Networks documentation web site.

ISDN

ISDN interfaces come in two types:

- Basic Rate Interface (BRI)
- Primary Rate Interface (PRI)

BRI provides for two bearer (B) channels and one signalling (D) channel. The B channels can provide data communication at a rate of 64 Kbps (or 56 Kbps). The two channels can be combined to provide 128 Kbps of user data. The D channel has 16 Kbps of bandwidth for signalling (call setup, teardown, and keepalive). This comes to a grand total of 144 Kbps. The BRI is sometimes referred to as 2B+D (because of its two bearer channels and its D channel).

PRI provides a total of 24 channels that are usually divided up into 23 B channels (64 Kbps) and one D channel (64 Kbps). The PRI is capable of operating at speeds of 1.544 Mbps (24 channels × 64 Kbps = 1.536 Mbps + 8 Kbps overhead = 1.544 Mbps). That is the speed of a T1. A PRI link is simply a T1 provisioned to provide ISDN operations.

NOTE See ITU-T spec Q.921 LAPD for frame format information and Q.931 for call control information.

ISDN Components

The International Telecommunication Union Standardization Sector (ITU-T) divides ISDN into functional groups and reference points (see Figure 9-39). The functional groups describe devices that provide ISDN functionality (like an ISDN modem or a terminal adapter). A single device may provide more than one function or multiple devices may be required. Reference points define the interface between two functions.

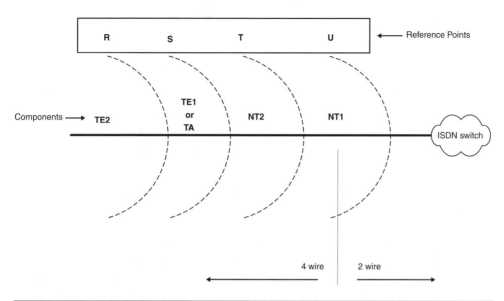

Figure 9-39 Reference points and functions

The following are defined functions:

- **Terminal Equipment 1 (TE1)** Consists of ISDN-compatible devices like a router with an ISDN interface.

- **Terminal Equipment 2 (TE2)** Consists of non-ISDN-compatible devices like PCs and analog telephones.

- **Network Terminator 1 (NT1)** The point where the phone company's wires end at your premises (the Demarc).

- **Network Terminator 2 (NT2)** Point where any switching services occur at your premises.

- **Line Terminator (LT)** Point where your network lines terminate at the phone company's Central Office (CO).

- **Exchange Terminator (ET)** Located at the phone company's CO. It performs the switching exchange functions.

- **Terminal Adapter (TA)** Provides ISDN connectivity to non-ISDN devices.

The following are the defined reference points:

- **R reference point** The point between the non-ISDN device and the TA. It is the boundary between your equipment and the ISDN network.

- **S reference point** The point between the terminal equipment and the switching device at your premises.

- **T reference point** The point between your switching device and the subscriber side of the local loop (that is, the wire between your phone and the phone company's CO).

- **U reference point** The point between the NT1 and the phone companies CO. It is where the subscriber side and the local loop meet.

A router in a BRI environment can act as either a TE1 if it has a BRI interface or a TE2 device connected to a TA from a sync port if it does not. The role of the router in this case is usually for remote office connectivity and/or dial backup over the ISDN BRI.

A router in a PRI environment (a router with an MCT1 interface) acts as a TE1 device. It does not need an NT1. This configuration is typically used at a large central location where many other routers will dial into it as part of an overall dial backup solution.

BRI Configuration

The following information is what you need to know when configuring a BRI interface:

- Which switch type to connect to:
  - National ISDN1
  - 5ESS
  - DMS 100
  - NET3
  - SWISSNET3
  - KDD
  - NTT
  - TS103
- Directory number for the ISDN interface
- Service Profile Identifiers (SPIDs)
- Bandwidth for the channel (64 or 56 Kbps)
- Support for caller ID

Your ISDN service provider provides all of the previous information for you.

If your router is connected via a sync port to a modem, ISDN TA, or DSU, you will need to tell the router how to communicate with it by defining a signalling method. One signalling method is V.25bis. It enables your router to access the modem by passing phone numbers from a configured list on the router to the modem. This is a software-based method of dialing. It works by sending command strings to the modem. This method enables flexibility because the router can support a list of multiple phone numbers to multiple destinations.

Another method of signaling is Raise Data Transmit Ready (DTR). This is almost the opposite of V.25bis. Using this method, phone numbers are stored on the modem. The router, when it wants to make a connection, simply sends a DTR signal to the modem, which, upon receipt of the DTR signal, dials the number it has configured. This is a hardware-based method of dialing and is less flexible than V.25bis because the modem cannot support the multiple phone numbers to multiple destinations that the router can. To call multiple locations, you need multiple modems. A special cable is required to connect to a Raise DTR device.

Additionally, Hayes signaling is another option that functions like V.25bis in that it also passes information stored on the router to the modem. The problem with Hayes signaling is that you need to configure the router with the AT command strings.

Using the LOG and the TI

To view the log entries for ISDN, two entities (-e) are helpful:

- -eSWSERV
- -eISDN

 NOTE for detailed information on the TI and the Log command, see Chapter 14.

Using the *show isdn local* command will enable you to view the status of the ISDN registration. Accepted means that registration is successful. Rejected means that registration was attempted but failed (usually a bad SPID), and a blank status usually indicates a bad line condition or an incompatible switch type has been set.

Compression

The purpose behind compression is to reduce the amount of traffic being transmitted in order to save bandwidth and money while increasing performance. It does this by removing redundant bit patterns from the data being transmitted and replacing them with code that replicates the bits in a more efficient manner. The WAN Compression Protocol (WCP) or Hi/fn LZS is how we accomplish this, and they come in both hardware and software forms, each with a choice of modes that we will examine.

NOTE Hi/fn LZS is licensed and distributed separately. It is also a standards-based protocol (RFC 1974) and can function with other vendor's hardware. WCP is Nortel Networks Proprietary.

Although hardware- and software-based compression will interoperate, WCP and Hi/fn LZS will not work together. WCP uses one algorithm, and Hi/fn LZS uses a different one. Software-based compression functions with PPP (WCP and Hi/fn LZS), Frame Relay (WCP), and X.25 (WCP). Hardware-based compression is available for the BN or ASN platform with the addition of a separate daughter card. This card removes the compression algorithm from the main processor and places it on the daughter card, increasing performance. It functions with PPP or Frame Relay and is used when high throughput is required.

CAUTION Regardless of which type of compression is chosen, it must be configured on both sides of the link. If not, the link will come up, but no traffic will be compressed.

Compression works by creating history tables. The tables keep track of the patterns in the data being sent (this is done on both sides of the link). If a match for a pattern is found, the length and offset are transmitted rather than transmitting the actual data. This reduces the traffic over the link. Two modes of operation are available:

- Continuous Packet Compression (CPC)
- Packet-by-Packet Compression (PPC)

In CPC (WCP and Hi/fn LZS), the tables are continuously maintained and modified. It is capable of error correction and the retransmission of lost frames (for WCP). This adds reliability to unreliable (connectionless) circuits. CPC generally has higher compression ratios than PPC, but it also uses more local memory on the slot of the router on which it runs.

In PPC (supported in WCP only), the table is reset with each packet transmission. This requires less memory but also removes the capability of error correction and retransmission.

Protocol Prioritization

Protocol prioritization is the capability to force the router into handling different types of traffic differently when it comes time to transmit them. It is implemented by configuring outbound filters to recognize different types of traffic and apply priorities to the different types. It is supported over Sync, MCT1, and MCE1 lines running the following:

- Frame Relay

- PPP

- Standard

- SMDS

Protocol prioritization is also available for HSSI running Frame Relay only. Protocol prioritization is automatically added to any circuit configured with PPP, Frame Relay, or SMDS. Outbound filtering is not available on the router until we add protocol prioritization. Once added, it creates queues. The traffic is moved to the queues before being transmitted. The router then uses an algorithm to feed the traffic from the different queues to the outbound buffer for transmission.

Four different queues are used:

- Interrupt

- High

- Medium

- Low

The difference between the types of queues is how you configure them, but common sense tells us that high is used for high-priority traffic, medium for normal traffic, and low for low-priority traffic. You can configure outbound filters to place traffic of a certain type into one of the queues. You cannot configure the Interrupt queue. It is used for management and no filter can be written to move traffic into it. The Interrupt queue has the highest priority.

 NOTE Queue size is configurable. When a queue is full, no more packets can be placed into it until some of the packets in the queue are removed (by transmission). Packets destined for a full queue are dropped (clipped).

The method in which packets are removed from the queue and transmitted is called dequeuing. Two dequeuing algorithms are available:

- Bandwidth allocation algorithm
- Strict dequeuing algorithm

In the bandwidth allocation algorithm, queues are serviced by transmitting their traffic until the traffic transmitted reaches a configured percentage of the available bandwidth. Once this percentage is reached, the router transmits traffic from the next queue until its percentage is reached. Then it continues to the last queue. Default percentage values are 70 percent for high priority, 20 percent for medium, and 10 percent for low.

In the strict dequeuing algorithm, queues are serviced from high to low for a period of time (referred to as latency) and then it starts over again. The router begins with the high-priority queue and transmits traffic from it until the queue is empty. Once empty (if any time is left in the latency period), the router transmits from the medium queue until it is empty or until the latency period is over. If the router empties the medium queue and time is left, it transmits data from the low queue. This method forces high-priority traffic out quickly, but it can cause medium- and low-priority traffic to wait a long time for transmission if a lot of high-priority traffic exists.

Review Questions

1. The binary equivalent of 0x7E is . . .
   A. 10000001
   B. 01111110
   C. 10101010
   D. 11110000

2. The purpose of the flag field is . . .

    A. To separate the fields within the HDLC frame.

    B. To pad the frame so it meets a 16-bit boundary.

    C. To separate one frame from another.

    D. None of the above.

3. What are the six fields of the HDLC frame?

    A. _____

    B. _____

    C. _____

    D. _____

    E. _____

    F. _____

4. Wellfleet Standard can be used to connect . . .

    A. Nortel Networks router to a Nortel Networks switch.

    B. Nortel Networks router to a Cisco switch.

    C. Nortel Networks router to a Nortel Networks router.

    D. Nortel Networks router to a Cisco router.

5. Which of the following protocols are not WAN protocols supported by BayRS?

    A. Standard

    B. PPP

    C. SMDS

    D. X.25

    E. T1

    F. SYNC

6. Which of the following are HDLC station types? (Choose two.)

    A. Combined

    B. Single

    C. Secondary

    D. Null

7. True/False

    Wellfleet/Bay Standard is not compatible with multiline.

8. BOFL stands for . . .

    A. Beginning of Line

    B. Be out of Link

    C. Best Offer Line

    D. Breath of Life

9. For lines to be part of a multiline circuit, they must all share the same . . . (Choose three.)
   A. Bandwidth
   B. MTU
   C. Slot
   D. Encapsulation

10. The DTE connects to the DCE in a Frame Relay network via the . . .
    A. Trunk
    B. Access line
    C. CIR
    D. Modem

11. The circuit that is manually configured on a Frame Relay device is called a . . .
    A. LMI
    B. LEC
    C. PVC
    D. SVC

12. The values given to circuits that are assigned manually in a Frame Relay network are called . . .
    A. VPI
    B. VCI
    C. FECN
    D. DLCI

13. The values used to identify circuits to a Frame Relay router have . . .
    A. Local significance only
    B. Global significance only
    C. Local and global significance only
    D. None of the above

14. Which field from an HDLC frame is not in the ANSI T1.618 frame?
    A. Flag
    B. Address
    C. Control
    D. Info
    E. FCS

15. _____ defines how a DTE requests and receives information about the network.

    A. ILMI

    B. LMI

    C. ICMP

    D. SNMP

16. What types of topologies are in a Frame Relay network? (Choose two.)

    A. Point-to-point

    B. Full mesh

    C. Ring

    D. Non-full mesh

    E. Bus

17. What is the default address resolution method for Frame Relay on a BayRS router?

    A. ARP

    B. INARP

    C. ARPINARP

    D. LE_ARP

18. Address resolution issues arise in _____ networks.

    A. Fully meshed networks

    B. Hub and spoke networks

    C. NBMA networks

    D. Point-to-point networks

19. A service record containing one DLCI for each network configured is referred to as . . .

    A. Direct mode

    B. Group mode

    C. Hybrid mode

    D. Passive mode

20. True/False

A service record may contain more than one DLCI.

21. True/False

A DLCI may exist in more than one service record.

22. True/False

More than one protocol may be applied to a service record.

23. Broadcast frames are handled by a group mode service record by . . .
   A. Dropping them
   B. Forwarding them to the first DLCI in the list
   C. Randomly forwarding the frame to a single DLCI
   D. Sending the frame out all DLCIs

24. What happens to DLCIs in a service record when the service record is deleted?
   A. The DLCIs are deleted.
   B. The DLCIs are randomly reassigned to the remaining service records.
   C. The DLCIs are re-assigned to the next service record in the list.
   D. The DLCIs are moved to the default service record.

25. Which of the following protocols can be enabled on a PPP interface? (Choose four.)
   A. IP
   B. OSI
   C. IPX
   D. AppleTalk
   E. NetBUI

26. PPP supports which authentication methods? (Choose two.)
   A. Token
   B. RADIUS
   C. PAP
   D. CHAP

27. The two components of PPP are . . .
   A. NCP
   B. SMTP
   C. PPTP
   D. LCP

28. Which component of PPP is responsible for IP addressing?
   A. LCP
   B. PPTP
   C. NCP
   D. SMTP

29. True/False
   Protocol prioritization is enabled by default on a PPP interface.

30. True/False:

Protocol prioritization is enabled by default on a standard interface.

31. What types of link management available for a PPP link? (Choose three.)

    A. LQR

    B. Echo requests

    C. SNMP

    D. BOFL

32. An ISDN BRI interface is capable of what bandwidth?

    A. 64K

    B. 128K

    C. 1.544 Mbps

    D. 2.021 Mbps

33. An ISDN PRI interface is capable of what bandwidth?

    A. 64K

    B. 128K

    C. 155 Mbps

    D. 1.544 Mbps

Answers

1. B. 01111110 (binary) is equal to 64 + 32 + 16 + 8 + 4 + 2, which equals 126 (decimal) which is equal to 7E (hex).

2. C. The Flag field defines the beginning and end of an HDLC frame. It is the first and last field of every frame transmitted.

3. FLAG, CONTROL, FCS, ADDRESS, INFO, FLAG

4. C. Wellfleet Standard is a proprietary protocol and can only be used to connect two Nortel Networks routers together across a point-to-point physical connection.

5. E, F. T1 and Sync are physical interface types and not WAN protocols.

6. A, C. Secondary stations can only respond to polls. Combined stations can send polls and respond to polls. Also, a third HDLC station type is known as the primary, which can only send polls.

7. False. Wellfleet Standard does support both multiline and multilink.

PART II

8. **D.** Breath of Life

9. **A, B, D.** Lines in a multiline circuit are not required to have their ports on the same slot. This adds to the flexibility and fault-tolerance because any available port of the proper type can be used without the need to purchase an entire new link module just to support this feature. Also, if one slot in the router were to fail, ports on a link module in another slot would be unaffected.

10. **B.**

11. **C.**

12. **D.** Data Link Connection Identifier.

13. **A.** The DLCIs that are used in a point-to-point connection between two Frame Relay routers are not transmitted across the network. A manually created, artificial, global significance can be imposed by the network administrator, but this would be merely a cosmetic change meant to make management easier for the network administrator.

14. **C.** The Control field does not exist in the T1.618 frame. Its functions have been transferred to subfields of the address field.

15. **B.**

16. **B, D.** These refer to the logical topologies and not the physical topologies.

17. **C.**

18. **B.** It is in a hub and spoke nonfully meshed network where address resolutions arise. Since the routers do not have a DLCI for each destination, they assume that the destinations are directly attached to the local interface. When the router is the hub router, there is no problem. When the router is a spoke router trying to communicate with another spoke router, the traffic must be transmitted to the hub, which may drop the traffic because it is improperly addressed.

19. **A.**

20. **True.** Placing more than one DLCI per service record is a group mode. This enables multiple point-to-point connections to be configured as a single network. It simplifies address management.

21. **False.** DLCIs must be unique to a single service record. It is the unique DLCI that enables a router to locate a resource. If a DLCI were to exist in more than one ser-

vice record, the router would not know which one actually leads to the intended destination.

22. **True.** A service record acts, in this case, like a physical interface. It can host more than one protocol.

23. **D.** Just as a switch forwards a broadcast frame out all ports (in a VLAN), except the port that the frame was received on, so does the Frame Relay router in group mode forward the broadcast frame out all DLCIs in a service record, except the one that the frame was received on.

24. **D.**

25. **A, B, C, D.** PPP does not support NetBUI.

26. **C, D.**

27. **A, D.** The LCP is responsible for negotiating layer 2 parameters. After the LCP is complete, the NCP can negotiate its layer 3 parameters. This should result in the successful configuration of a PPP link.

28. **C.** IP addressing is a layer 3 issue and is therefore a component of the NCP.

29. **True.**

30. **False.**

31. **A, B, D.**

32. **B.**

23. **D.**

PART III

Product Technologies

Hubs and Shared Media

At the most basic level, networks are designed to connect devices together. The most basic device used to connect computers (or other devices on a network) together is a *hub* or *shared media* segment. We will start our exploration of connectivity devices at this point. Although you may not find a place to install any hubs in new networks that you are designing, there may already be (and probably are) hubs existing in other parts of the network that you are adding on to or upgrading. I cannot think of anyone who manages a large Enterprise network that does not have some hubs somewhere in the mix. In this chapter, we hope to give you an introduction to the purpose of hubs, the network design of hubs, the features and functions of different types of Nortel Networks hubs, and the troubleshooting of hubs.

Exam Objectives

When taking the Hubs and Shared Media Core Technology Exam (920-013), you should expect to be asked questions on the following topics:

BayStack Ethernet Hubs

- Describe the features, functions, and components of BayStack Ethernet hubs.
- Identify management and configuration options for BayStack Ethernet hubs.

- Describe the functions of light-emitting diode (LED) indicators on BayStack Ethernet hubs.

- Install and configure an Ethernet network using BayStack Ethernet hubs.

Introduction to System 3000 Concentrators

- Describe the features, functions, and components of System 3000 concentrators.

- Describe the various modules available for the System 3000 chassis.

- Describe System 3000 backplane options.

Introduction to Fast Ethernet

- Identify the physical media that is supported by Fast Ethernet.

- Identify the repeater types and their operational characteristics.

- Identify the strategies involved in migrating from Ethernet to Fast Ethernet.

5000 Chassis

- Describe the features, functions, and components of the System 5000 concentrator.

- Describe functions of the LED indicators on the System 5000 concentrator.

- Identify System 5000 backplane options.

- List the various modules available for the System 5000 chassis.

- Describe the functionality of the supervisory module of the 5000 chassis.

- Install and configure an Ethernet network using System 5000 concentrators.

- Install and configure a Fast Ethernet network using System 5000 concentrators.

- Install and configure a Token Ring network using System 5000 concentrators.

Ethernet Connectivity for Distributed 5000 Hubs

- Differentiate between cascaded and local Ethernet segments.

- Describe the features, functions, and components of Distributed 5000 Ethernet hubs.

- Install and configure an Ethernet network using Distributed 5000 hubs.

Introduction to Hub Connectivity

- Describe the role of a hub in the network.

- Explain the numbering scheme for various Nortel Network hubs.

- Describe the network fit for BayStack System 3000, Distributed 5000, and System 5000 hubs and concentrators.

Introduction to Network Management

- Describe the basic functions of network management.

- Describe the capabilities of the Simple Network Management Protocol (SNMP).

- Associate network management levels with the features they support.

- Describe the BootP/Trivial File Transfer Protocol (TFTP) process.

- Configure network management modules (NMM) for basic operation.

- Identify various hardware management options.

5005 Chassis

- Describe the features, functions, and components of the System 5005 concentrator.

- Describe the functions of the LED indicators on the System 5005 concentrator.

- Differentiate System 5000 and System 5005 concentrator features, functions, and components.

- Describe the features, functions, and components of the System 5005 concentrator.

- Describe the functions of the LED indicators on the System 5005 concentrator.

- Differentiate System 5000 and System 5005 concentrator features, functions, and components.

Network Management Tools

- Identify the main tasks in each of the five areas of the Open Standards Interface (OSI) network management model.

- Describe how Optivity uses SNMP to provide network management functions.

- Identify the tasks that can be performed with Optivity Campus command.
- Identify Optivity views, applications, and utilities.
- Identify the Optivity views and applications that are used to perform different network management tasks.

Ethernet Network Design

- Distinguish between a collapsed backbone and a distributed backbone.
- Describe Ethernet network design guidelines.
- Compare and contrast characteristics of Ethernet physical media.

Ethernet Troubleshooting

- Define standard Ethernet troubleshooting procedures.
- Describe common Ethernet errors.
- Identify, isolate, and correct common problems in an Ethernet network.

BayStack 50x Token Ring Hub

- Describe the features, functions, and components of BayStack 50x hubs.
- Identify management and configuration options for BayStack 50x hubs.
- Describe the functions of LED indicators on BayStack 50x hubs.
- Install and configure a Token Ring network using BayStack 50x hubs.
- Describe features, functions, and components of BayStack 50x hubs.
- Identify management and configuration options for BayStack 50x hubs.
- Describe functions of LED indicators on BayStack 50x hubs.
- Install and configure a Token Ring network using BayStack 50x hubs.

Token Ring Network Design

- Describe Token Ring network design guidelines.
- Explain how cable layout affects trunk topology.
- Describe the use of distributed, sequential, and collapsed backbones.

- Design basic Token Ring networks with BayStack 50x, System 3000, and System 5000 solutions.

- Describe Token Ring network design guidelines.

Token Ring Troubleshooting

- Define standard Token Ring troubleshooting procedures.

- Describe common Token Ring errors.

- Identify, isolate, and correct common problems in a Token Ring network.

- Define standard Token Ring troubleshooting procedures.

- Describe common Token Ring errors.

- Identify, isolate, and correct common problems in a Token Ring network.

Connectivity

The primary purpose of a hub is to provide connectivity between two or more devices. It does this by providing the timing and repeater functions necessary for devices to communicate. The hub takes the data transmitted by one connected station and transmits it to all connected stations simultaneously. For our purposes, we will use an Ethernet hub as an example (see Figure 10-1). The common Ethernet standard is the 10BASE-T standard, which requires the use of two pairs of twisted-pair cable. One pair is used for transmission and is called the *transmit* (TX) pair. The other pair is used for reception and is called the *receive* (RX) pair. The hub takes the data from the TX pair of the transmitting station and puts it on the RX pair of all the other stations. The hub repeats the signal as it passes through the hub, thus increasing the effective signal strength.

Think of two devices as two people who are trying to communicate (see Figure 10-2). Their transmitters (TX) are their mouths and their receivers (RX) are their ears (see Figure 10-3). In order to communicate, the transmission from transmitter A needs to be

Figure 10-1 A hub

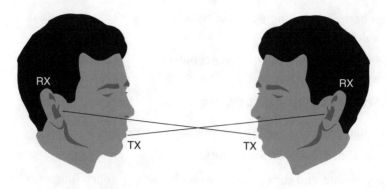

Figure 10-2   Communicating devices (talking heads)

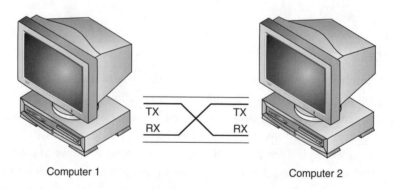

Figure 10-3   Communicating TX to RX (computers and an X)

received by receiver B. If the transmission from transmitter A goes to transmitter B, no communication occurs. By the same token, receiver A will never receive anything from receiver B because it is not sending anything to be received. There needs to be a mechanism that moves the transmitted data to the receiver. The hub provides this at the *port* (see Figure 10-4). Each port of a hub provides a crossover (X-over) function, placing transmitted data on the RX pair. A port that provides this function is referred to as an MDI-X port. Network interface cards (NIC) and router ports are MDI. For two devices to communicate, there must be an MDI-X and an MDI. If two MDI devices need to

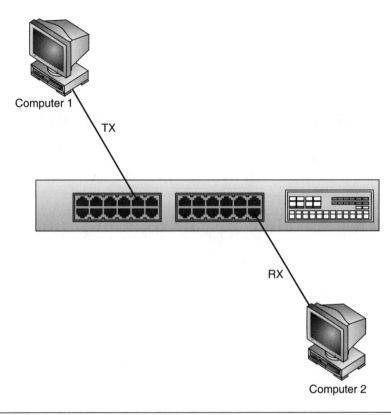

Figure 10-4   Communicating with a hub

communicate, there must be something to provide the MDI-X function between them (like a hub or a crossover cable).

All devices connecting to a hub (workstations, servers, printers, and so on) connect using a straight-through cable. This cable carries data from the TX pair of the device to the TX pair of the hub (the hub switches the data internally) and from the RX pair of the hub to the RX pair of the device. To connect to other communication devices such as another hub or a switch, you need to use a crossover cable. This must be done because the ports of the hubs are both MDI-X. There is nothing that is MDI along the path so no communication takes place. The crossover cable makes the transmitting hub look like an MDI device to the receiving hub, and vice versa (see Figure 10-5).

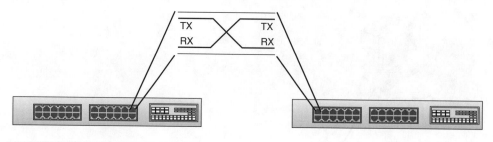

Figure 10-5   Two hubs

Different Types

There are, of course, different types of hubs to suit many different networking needs. For our purposes, the different types of hubs fall into two or more of the following categories:

- Stackable
- Modular
- Manageable
- Unmanageable

Stackable (Cascadable)

Stackable (cascadable) hubs are designed to be able to function on their own (a single unit) or together with others. When connected together with other hubs (stacked), the entire stack of hubs acts as a single large hub (see Figure 10-6). The advantage of such a device is that it enables you to purchase as few as one hub at first and then add another hub at a later date as your needs require. You don't need to purchase a hub that is way too large to suit your needs with features that you do not want to pay for. The BayStack 250 is an example of a stackable hub.

Modular

Modular hubs are designed to offer great flexibility and growth. The modular devices come with expansion slots (sometimes called *slots*) that enable you to install a wide variety of devices quickly and easily. These devices typically support more ports that can be added to the total number of connected devices or that provide connectivity to different types of media (such as fiber, coax, Unshielded Twisted Pair [UTP], or Attachment Unit Interface [AUI]). Modular hubs come in many different sizes. A System 5000 is an example of a modular hub (see Figure 10-07).

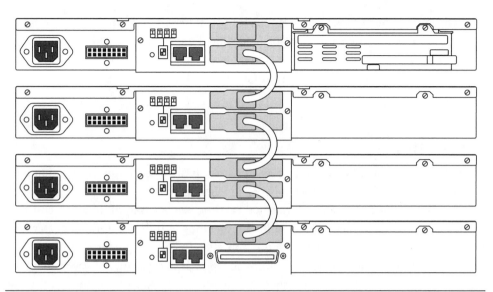

Figure 10-6 Stackable hubs

Manageable and Unmanageable

Hubs are either manageable or unmanageable. This refers to their capability to be managed remotely over the network. This is not a requirement for the hubs to function, but is a feature that can make network administration easier if used properly. Some hubs have management built in, some have management capabilities as an optional module that can be purchased separately, and others have no management capabilities at all. All of the hubs that we will cover in this chapter fall into the second group—hubs that have management capabilities as an optional module that can be purchased and installed separately.

NOTE A term that is often used when describing a hub is *port density*. Port density refers to the relative number of ports that a device supports. A hub with a high port density has a lot of ports, whereas a hub with a low port density has fewer ports.

Shared Media

A hub is a shared media device, but not all shared media are hubs. The term refers to the need for all devices attached to the media to compete, or share, the available

PART III

bandwidth. This means that only one device can transmit at a time. Both a hub and coax cable are shared media. The opposite of shared media is dedicated media. Devices attached to dedicated media do not have to share bandwidth so they can transmit simultaneously. A switch is an example of a dedicated media device.

Segments

While examining the different hubs, we will use the term *segment* often. A segment used to refer to a piece of cable to which devices attached. Segments can be attached to each other with repeaters. All segments attached via repeaters are part of the same collision domain. Now segment has a slightly different meaning. A hub is simply a repeater with multiple ports. Each cable attached to the hub, therefore, is a segment. A normal cable attached to a port that connects two hubs together is a segment. However, there are other types of segment. There are special segments that attach hubs together. These come in two types:

- Cascaded segments
- Backplane segments

Cascaded Segments

Cascade segments attach two or more cascaded hubs together via a cascade cable. The cascade cable is a special cable that comes with hubs that can be cascaded. Cascaded segments are not additional segments per se, but rather are a means of bringing segments closer together. When communicating from a device on port 1 of hub A to a device on port 3 on hub A, the data travels over two segments (see Figure 10-8). For a device on port 1 of hub A to communicate to a device on port 1 of hub B (if the two hubs are connected via a crossover cable), the data travels over three segments. If the hubs are connected via a cascaded segment, the data travels over only two segments, as if the two hubs were one (see Figure 10-9). Later when we examine network design, we will see how this can be a great advantage.

NOTE *Cascade* and *stack* mean the same thing. On the exam, expect to see both terms.

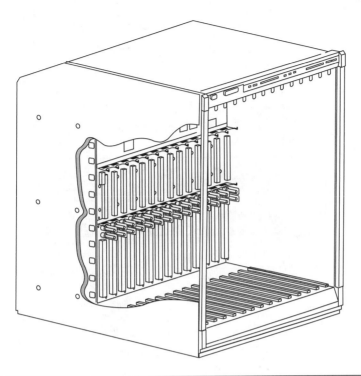

Figure 10-7 Modular hub

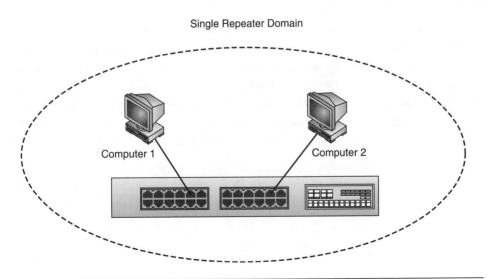

Figure 10-8 Devices attached to the same hub

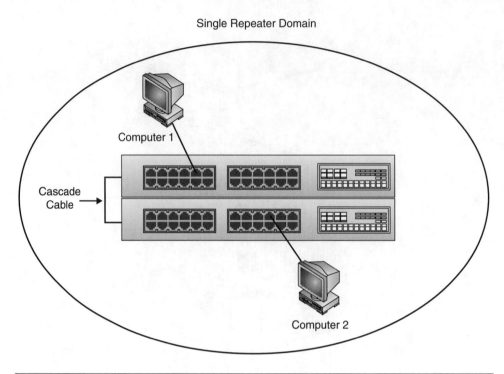

Figure 10-9   Devices connected to two hubs (cascaded segment)

Backplane Segments

Backplane segments exist in modular hubs like the System 3000 and System 5000 chassis. The *backplane* is the circuit board that the modules connect into that connects all the modules together. A backplane segment exists on the backplane and attaches modules together. Each module in a modular chassis acts like a hub. Two or more modules connected (attached) to the same backplane segment act as a single hub. Just like in the previous example on cascaded segments, when communicating between two devices that are on the same backplane segment, the data travels only over two segments (see Figure 10-10).

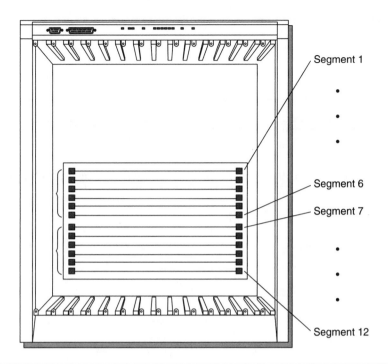

Figure 10-10   Backplane and segments

Model Numbers

Before discussing the actual devices themselves, we should take a little time here to learn the significance of model numbers. The model numbers of these devices (especially for the 3000 and 5000 systems) are actually very descriptive as to the devices' function and features. The model numbers are in a five-digit format (see Figure 10-11), where each digit describes a feature or function.

The first digit (V) tells us what device family we are dealing with. A 3 indicates a System 3000, whereas a 5 indicates a System 5000. 5DN is for the Distributed 5000 system.

The second digit (W) is for the topology. A 3 indicates Ethernet and a 4 indicates Fast Ethernet. A 5 represents a Token Ring. A 6 stands for a Taurus module (not part of the shared media course because it is a switching product). An 8 indicates a router and a 9 stands for a Fiber-Distributed Data Interface (FDDI).

The third digit (X) is the module type. A 0 is used for host modules and a 1 is used for network management modules. A 3 represents a retiming module and a 6 indicates a secure module.

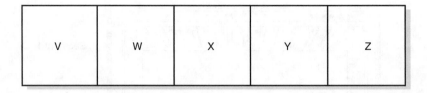

Figure 10-11   Model number positions

The fourth digit is for the media type. The following lists what each number stands for:

1   10BASE-2

2   Token Ring (STP) passive

3   AUI

4   Fiber

5   UTP (Token Ring active)

6   Remote device

7   25-pair telco

8   10BASE-T

Sometimes a fifth digit (Z) is used for device-specific options or revisions. So a 3308B indicates the following:

It is for a System 3000 (3308B).

It is Ethernet topology (3308B).

It is a host module device (3308B).

It is for 10BASE-T media (3308B).

It is a B revision (3308B).

 EXAM TIP   Know these numbers for the exam. You will be given a model number and be expected to identify the features from the number plan.

The 3000 Hub

The 3000 hub is really a chassis with 12 slots for modules. The chassis supports one power supply (a chassis can be purchased that supports redundant power supplies), a fan tray, and any module that is installed. The backplane determines which of the following technologies may be installed:

- Ethernet (Model 3000N)

- Ethernet and Token Ring (Model 3000NT)

- Ethernet and Token Ring with redundant power supply (Model 3000NTR)

- Ethernet, Token Ring, and Fast Ethernet (Model 3000C)

- Ethernet, Token Ring, and FDDI (Model 3000S)

- Ethernet, Token Ring, and FDDI with redundant power supply (Model 3000SR)

NOTE The chassis model numbers that end in the letter *R* do not have 12 slots for modules; they only have 9 slots. The additional power supply takes up 2 slots. The redundant power supply also requires the use of a summing module that controls the two power supplies. The summing module is installed between the two power supplies (it has to go in before the power supplies), and it takes up a full slot.

The chassis can support up to five backplane Ethernet segments, two backplane Token Rings, and either three FDDI paths or three Fast Ethernet segments.

The Backplane

When looking at the chassis backplane (see Figure 10-12), you will notice that it is divided into thirds. The lower third supports four of the five Ethernet segments (see the section "Backplane Ethernet Segments"). The middle third supports the fourth Ethernet segment and the two Token Rings. The upper third supports either Fast Ethernet or FDDI.

NOTE The Fast Ethernet backplane and the FDDI backplane are two separate backplanes that cannot coexist in the same chassis at the same time. They have different types of connectors for connecting to their appropriate modules. It is very important that you never try to install a FDDI module into a chassis that has a Fast Ethernet backplane. It will cause damage to the backplane and the module. The same holds true for installing Fast Ethernet modules into a chassis that has a FDDI backplane.

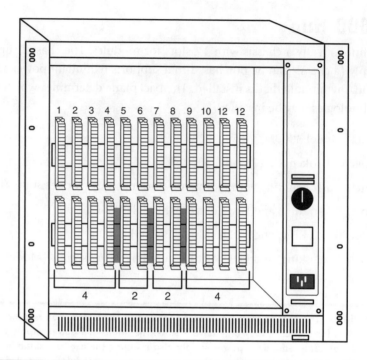

Figure 10-12   Backplane

The backplane provides connectivity for modules installed in the chassis and determines which modules may be installed. The backplane is also a conduit for power. The power supply (see Figure 10-13) is installed in a special slot (not one of the 12 for connectivity modules) at the far right side of the chassis. The power supply connects to the backplane, which distributes power to the installed modules and the fans. In a chassis in which redundant power supplies are to be installed, special backplanes are installed. These backplanes have extra connectors for the second power supply, which are located next to the connectors for the standard power supply at the right end of the backplane. This leaves us with fewer connectors for connectivity modules. With a redundant power supply installed, we may have a maximum of nine connectivity modules installed in a System 3000 chassis.

   NOTE   Backplanes can be replaced in the field. If you purchased a System 3000 chassis before the development of Fast Ethernet and want to add it to your chassis, all you have to do is install the Fast Ethernet backplane. This procedure requires you to power down the chassis and remove the rear cover (there are a lot of screws), but it is a relatively simple procedure.

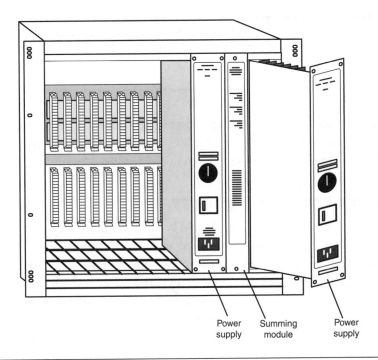

Power   Summing   Power
supply   module   supply

Figure 10-13   Power supplies

Installing and Removing Modules

In order to install a module into a 3000 chassis, line up the edge of the module (also referred to as a *card* or *blade*) with the guide rails on the top and bottom of the chassis and gently slide the module into the chassis until you meet resistance. At the bottom of each module (and at the top of some), there is a white plastic lever that should point towards you as you are inserting the module into the chassis. When you feel the resistance as the module rear meets the backplane, the bottom end of the lever will match up with the front edge of the chassis. At this point, you should lift the lever up. This causes the bottom end of the lever to push the module the rest of the way into the chassis. Once the lever is all the way up and the module is fully inserted into the chassis, the module can be secured with the screws that are at the top and bottom of all modules.

NOTE   Remember to always wear an antistatic wrist strap or other approved antistatic device when handling delicate electronic components.

NOTE Do not force modules into the chassis. You may inadvertently insert the module at an angle and bend the delicate pins in the backplane, damaging it beyond repair.

To remove a module from the chassis, first loosen the screws at the top and bottom of the module. Then lower the lever until the module pops out, disconnecting it from the backplane. Simply pull the module out the rest of the way.

Backplane Ethernet Segments

As I mentioned earlier, there are up to five backplane Ethernet segments in a System 3000 chassis. Four of these five segments reside on the bottom third of the backplane and are physically separated from each other by terminating resistors (see Figure 10-14) inserted into the backplane (see Figure 10-15). The fifth backplane Ethernet segment resides in the middle third of the backplane and is referred to as the *Ethernet B channel*. Each terminating resistor, when installed in one direction, separates two adjacent segments. When installed the other way, the terminating resistor unifies adjacent segments (making them one). Although the chassis may support as many as five backplane Eth-

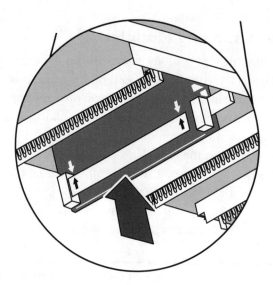

Figure 10-14 Terminating resistor

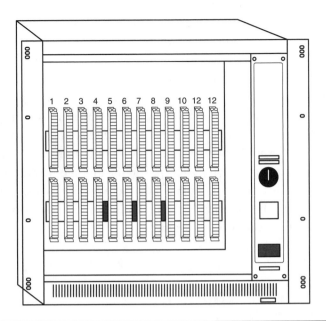

Figure 10-15   Terminating resistor location on the backplane

ernet segments, you may configure as few as two. You do not have to use all of the segments. The positions of the terminating resistors are as follows:

- Between slots 4 and 5

- Between slots 6 and 7

- Between slots 8 and 9

NOTE   A 3000 chassis with a redundant power supply has a maximum of four backplane Ethernet segments. The terminating resistor that would reside between slots 8 and 9 in the standard chassis backplane does not exist in the redundant power supply backplane. There are normally four backplane Ethernet segments on the A channel, but the fourth segment is four slots wide (slots 9–12). If we remove three of those slots for the extra power supply and summing module, it only leaves one slot for the segment. The technology in a System 3000 does not allow for a single-slot segment because a timing module is required for a segment to function and there are no host modules for Ethernet that provide timing; therefore, a single-slot segment is useless. For that reason, all chassis that support redundant power supplies have only three backplane Ethernet segments on the A channel; they are four, two, and three slots wide, respectively. All terminating resistors that belong in the chassis must be installed for proper Ethernet functions.

Therefore, there are a maximum of four backplane Ethernet segments on the bottom third of the backplane. Determining which of these segments a hub module belongs to depends on where it is placed in the chassis. In a System 3000 chassis (assuming that all the segments are configured to be separate), an Ethernet hub module placed in slot 2 cannot belong to backplane Ethernet segment 3. Backplane Ethernet segment 3 is only for modules installed in slots 7 and 8. Any hub modules in slot 2 are part of backplane segment 1. The only exception to this is for modules configured to use the Ethernet B channel. The Ethernet B channel is on the middle third of the backplane. A module can be configured (by moving a jumper on the module) to attach to the Ethernet B channel, which has a single backplane Ethernet segment that spans all 12 slots. When configured to use the Ethernet B channel, a hub module in slot 2 and a hub module in slot 11 are both on the same segment.

Ethernet Considerations in a System 3000 Chassis

There are three basic types of Ethernet modules for a System 3000 chassis:

- Host modules (hub modules)
- Network management modules (NMMs)
- Retiming modules

Host modules have the ports to which devices connect. They are the hub's port modules.

NMMs provide management (SNMP and console access) for the Ethernet segment and the chassis. An Ethernet NMM also provides the required timing for Ethernet segments. The use of an NMM is optional, but some timing must be provided on every Ethernet segment in the chassis that is populated with a host module.

Retiming modules provide no management, but they can be used to fulfill the timing requirement for populated Ethernet segments if no NMM is present.

 NOTE Do not place an NMM and a retiming module (or two NMMs or two retiming modules) on the same Ethernet segment. They will conflict with each other and provide no redundancy.

Types of Host Modules

There are many different host modules for Ethernet in a System 3000; we will examine the more popular (and useful) ones.

LEDs

All host modules have LEDs at their top portion that indicate the working status of the module. A brief description follows:

Status   When this light is green, the module is receiving DC power. In the case of an NMM, the status light indicates that the NMM is functioning properly.

Part (Partition)   When this light is amber, it indicates that the entire module has been portioned from the backplane by network management. This usually indicates that the module has been causing communication problems on the segment.

NM Cntrl (NMM Control)   When this light is amber, it indicates that one or more ports are under the control of network management. It usually indicates that a port has been portioned automatically because of excessive collisions or that the network administrator has used Optivity to shut off the port.

Port Status   When the green light is lit, it indicates the following:

- There is a device attached to the port.
- There is a good physical connection to the attached device.
- The device is powered on and connected to the network.

When the amber light is lit, it indicates that the port has been portioned. If no light is lit, it indicates the following:

- There is no device attached to the port.
- There is a bad physical connection to the attached device.
- The device is not powered on or connected to the network.

3308

The 3308 (see Figure 10-16) is one of the most popular host modules for a System 3000. It has 12 802.3I 10BASE-T-compatible RJ-45 Ethernet ports for unshielded twisted-pair (UTP) connections. There is also a channel select button (3308 B) on the

Figure 10-16 3308

front that enables the administrator to move the module from the A channel (bottom third of the backplane) to the B channel (middle third of the backplane) without removing the module from the chassis to move the jumper. The 3308A and 3308B are also hot swappable. Hot-swappable modules may be removed from the chassis while the chassis is powered on without causing any damage to either the module or the chassis. When populating a System 3000 chassis with 3308 modules and configuring a single backplane Ethernet segment, the chassis can provide a total of 132 Ethernet ports, 12 ports per module × 11 slots (one slot must be used for a timing module or NMM).

NOTE The letters following the 3308 model number indicate a revision. 3308 (no revision) only supports the Ethernet A channel. 3308A modules are hot swappable, but they provide no support for the Ethernet B channel (Ethernet A channel only). The 3308B is hot swappable and supports both the Ethernet A and B channels.

EXAM TIP Be able to do the math by yourself. You will probably have at least one question asking you to determine the maximum number of Ethernet ports you can have in a System 3000 chassis using type X modules. You will also have a similar question for the System 5000 and the BayStack.

3307HD

The 3307HD (see Figure 10-17) host module has two 50-pin telco connectors. Each telco connector provides 12 10BASE-T connections. Therefore, the 3307HD provides a total of 24 10BASE-T connections. The twenty-fourth port of the module can be switched to an RJ-45 port on the module by moving a jumper on the module (this port is often used for monitoring network activity and diagnosing problems). When populating a System 3000 chassis with 3307HD modules and configuring a single backplane Ethernet segment, the chassis can provide a total of 264 Ethernet ports, 24 ports per module × 11 slots (one slot must be used for a timing module or NMM). These modules are used mostly when a very high port density is required.

3301

These modules (see Figure 10-18) are popular in networks where legacy 10BASE-2 segments exist and there are no plans to replace them. The module has eight 10BASE-2 BNC ports. Each port can support up to 29 stations and each segment can be up to 185 meters long. Termination for the segment (each end of a 10BASE-2 segment must be terminated with a 50-ohm terminating resistor) is provided internally for each port, as is grounding (one end of a 10BASE-2 segment must be grounded).

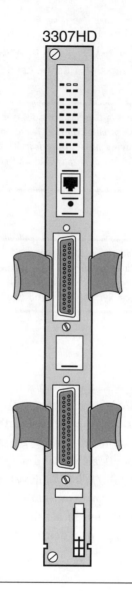

Figure 10-17 3307HD

3304A

The 3304A (see Figure 10-19) module provides eight 10BASE-FL ports and is typically used to tie remote segments into the network backbone. These ports are capable of functioning as redundant pairs. When configured to be redundant, the ports are both connected to the same device (such as a remote hub), but only one port will become

3301

Figure 10-18   3301

active. The second port goes into standby mode. When the active port senses a failure in the connection, it becomes inactive and activates the standby port. If the primary port senses that the primary link has become operational again, it does not transition automatically to active. This is to prevent an intermittently faulty link from bringing the network to a complete halt.

Figure 10-19   3304A

The ports may also be used in a nonredundant configuration. How the ports are configured is determined by jumper settings on the module. If you place the jumper in one position, it configures the ports to act redundantly. If you place the jumper in the other position, it configures the ports to act as normal hub ports (not redundant). The redundant pairs are predetermined. Ports 1 and 2 are redundant to each other, as are ports 3 with 4, 5 with 6, and 7 with 8. The pairs are configured independently of one another. It is acceptable for ports 1 and 2 to be configured to be redundant, while all the other ports are normal.

> **NOTE** There is the possibility of configuring ports other than the preconfigured pairs to be redundant if you use Optivity to configure the redundant pairs.

Management Modules

The ability to manage the hub is one of the more attractive features for a network administrator in a large network. It enables the network administrator to diagnose and fix problems in remote network devices without the need to involve the support staff at the remote location. This enables the administrator to fix problems in a more efficient and timely manner.

> **NOTE** This does not eliminate the need for a well-trained support staff at remote locations. No network management package, no matter how good, can replace hardware or insert even one cable. However, if you have ever tried to contact support personnel in a remote site at 6 A.M. to check the status of a port on a hub in a locked closet, you know that it can take valuable minutes or even hours just to find the person who knows where the equipment and the keys are. When time is of the essence, it is nice to be able to start working on a problem without having to wait for the other person to call you back.

The inclusion of an NMM on an Ethernet segment adds management to that segment. It provides the necessary timing for the segment and provides the SNMP engine and software that allows the monitoring and control from a network management station (NMS). For SNMP manageability, the NMM must (at minimum) be configured with the following:

- IP address
- Subnet mask
- Default gateway (if SNMP needs to be routed)

NOTE For details on network management and SNMP, see Chapter 15.

There are three types of NMM:

- Standard
- Advanced
- Advanced Analyzer

These are referred to as *agent levels* (see Chapter 15). They provide the following:

Standard

The Standard NMM includes support for

- Expanded views
- Configuration for all ports in chassis
- Port-level fault and performance stats
- MAU and repeater MIBs
- SNMP over IP/IPX

Advanced

The Advanced NMM includes support for all of the same features as the Standard NMM as well as support for

- System-level management
- Autotopology
- Port-level thresholds
- Allowed nodes security
- Port-to-MAC address associations
- Global show and find nodes
- The VLAN configuration of a specific chassis
- Out-of-band management
- Partial RMON 1 stats

Advanced Analyzer

The Advanced Analyzer NMM includes support for all of the same features as the Advanced NMM as well as support for

- Network-protocol-type distribution
- Port-level fault and performance analyzer correlation
- Packet capture
- Port-to-network address association
- Full RMON 1

The different agent levels are supported on two basic hardware platforms:

- 331xA
- 331xSA

331xA   This NMM comes in two forms: the 3313A and the 3314A (details to follow). The 331xA when purchased as a Standard agent level provides Standard management (see previous list). The really nice feature is that the Advanced agent is also present. For network administrators who want to purchase Standard agents today and want to upgrade at a later time, there is no new hardware to purchase or install to upgrade to an Advanced agent level. A license key code can be purchased separately. Once the license code (also called a *key code*) is entered into the NMM, it becomes an Advanced NMM. If you purchase an Advanced NMM from the beginning, you receive a Standard NMM and a key code together.

NOTE   It is very important not to lose the key code. It comes in the form of a certificate with the string of numbers and letters printed on it. The key code is specific to the NMM with which it was purchased. The key code purchased for one NMM will not work with another, even if they are the exact same type. There are circumstances (software upgrades) when the key may be erased from the NMM and will need to be reentered. If you lose your key code, it may be retrieved from Nortel Networks by calling 1-800-4nortel.

Both the 3313A and the 3314A have

- Support for the Ethernet A and B channel
- Flash EEPROM to store image code
- Hot-swappable features

PART III

- Support for modules with up to 24 host ports
- Service port menus
- Support for threshold settings

The 3313A (see Figure 10-20) also has an AUI port to attach other network devices to. The 3314A (see Figure 10-21) has a 10BASE-FL fiber port for the same purpose.

Figure 10-20   3313A

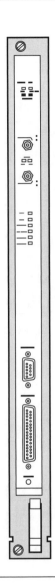

Figure 10-21 3314A

331xSA This NMM comes in two forms: the 3313SA (see Figure 10-22) and the 3314SA (see Figure 10-23) (details to follow). The SA stands for Advanced Analyzer. The 331xSA provides Advanced Analyzer management to the Ethernet segment on which it resides.

Figure 10-22 3313SA

Folklore told by employees of Bay Networks (and before that, Synoptics) claims that at one time, SA stood for "Super Agent" and that the name was changed to Advanced Analyzer, probably because Advanced Analyzer sounds more serious than Super Agent (which sounds like a TV show or a comic book). The SA probably stuck because it was already on most of the hardware.

Figure 10-23 3314SA

Both the 3313SA and the 3314SA have all the features of the 3313A and 3313SA as well as the following:

- Independent packet capture software
- SNMP communication over one backplane Ethernet channel
- BootP and TFTP configuration file downloading

Other Modules

There are many other modules available for the 3000 chassis that support Ethernet technology, but we will only discuss two more:

- 3333 (3334-ST) retiming module

- 3368 Lattisecure module

The 3333 provides no management functions at all. It merely provides the minimum retiming requirement for Ethernet segments. It supports only segments on the A channel. One module is necessary for every populated Ethernet segment that has no NMM. The model 3333 retiming module has an AUI port for connectivity to external devices. The 3334-ST is the same as a 3333, but it provides a 10BASE-FL fiber port.

The 3368 Lattisecure module looks just like a 3308 host module from the front. It has 12 10BASE-T RJ-45 Ethernet ports. If you look at it from the side, you will notice that there is quite a lot more hardware on the board. This is to support intrusion control and eavesdrop protection security.

Intrusion control inspects the MAC address of devices attached to the port as they attempt to transmit data. The board has a list of MAC addresses that are allowed to access the port. If there is a mismatch, the port is immediately partitioned. This keeps unauthorized devices from sniffing traffic as well as transmitting any.

Eavesdrop protection inspects the MAC address of stations attached to ports and compares it to the destination MAC address of the frame that is about to be transmitted out of a port to the attached device. If there is a match, the frame is transmitted normally. If there is a mismatch, it is obvious that the frame is not intended for the attached device. The frame is then altered by the board as it is transmitted. The entire data portion of the frame is filled with ones (11111 . . .) and the Cyclic Redundancy Check (CRC) is recalculated (so as not to trigger an error statistic). This means that devices will know that data is being sent, but they will never see the actual data.

NOTE When securing an Ethernet segment with either of these methods (eavesdrop protection or intrusion control), it is important to remember that all modules on the segment that are being secured need to support these features. If you put a single unsecured host module on the segment (like a 3308B), then no security applies to the devices attached to that module.

NOTE CRC is the same as the Frame Check Sequence (FCS) mentioned in Chapter 2. It is generated by the transmitting device based on the contents of the data carried in the frame and the length of the frame. The receiving device checks this number when it receives the frame. If the receiving device senses an error in the CRC, it discards the frame.

Backplane Token Rings

The middle third of the backplane supports two backplane Token Rings. Both of these rings span all 12 slots of the chassis. Token Ring hub modules in any slot can attach to either of the two rings. Moving a jumper on the module makes the ring selection (a Token Ring module can also be isolated from the backplane to create a ring on the module itself). The ring speed is also made by the use of jumpers on the modules.

Token Ring Considerations for System 3000 Chassis

There is no requirement for a Token Ring NMM or retiming module on any ring in a System 3000 chassis (populated or other) because Token Ring ports (by their nature) provide timing on a port-by-port basis. All modules on a Token Ring must be configured to use the same speed (4 or 16 Mbps), and all devices attached to these modules must attach at the same speed as the ring. The Token Ring NMM does provide some useful features besides management. It provides the service port menus for out-of-band management of the segment, and it provides the ring-in and ring-out ports for the ring.

Token Ring Host Modules

There are a number of Token Ring host modules that provide connectivity for Token Ring devices at 4 or 16 Mbps over different types of media. All Token Ring host modules support the following:

- 4 or 16 Mbps
- Per-port automatic ring wrap
- Hot-swappable features
- Connection to either of the two backplane Token Rings
- LEDs

LEDs

The LEDs on the front of a Token Ring host module are explained in the following sections:

Status   When this light is green, it indicates that all is functioning well. When it is off, it indicates that there is no power to the module.

Bypass   When this light is amber, it indicates that the entire module has been isolated from the ring by network management. When it is off, it indicates that the module is not isolated by network management.

NM Cntrl   When this light is amber, it indicates that one or more ports are being controlled by network management. When it is off, it indicates that no ports are under network management control.

Ring 1 and Ring 2   If one of these two lights is lit, it indicates the backplane Token Ring that the module is attached to.

4 and 16 Mbps   If one of these two lights is lit, it indicates the speed of the ring.

NM Wrap   When this light is amber, it indicates that the port is wrapped by network management. When this light is off, it indicates that the port is not wrapped by network management.

Phantom   When this light is lit, it indicates that there is a device attached to the port with a good physical connection, and it has loaded its Token Ring drivers and is providing a phantom current. This indicates that the device has entered the ring. When this light is off, it indicates that the device has not entered the ring (or that there is no device).

3502B

The 3502B (see Figure 10-24) Token Ring host module supports connections to hosts over either UTP or shielded twisted pair (STP), but not both at the same time. It is a passive module with 12 RJ-45 ports. It supports 4 Mbps over Cat 3 UTP cable and 4 or 16 Mbps over STP. The 3502B can support up to 250 stations on a single ring when populated with connections over STP or up to 132 when using UTP. Lobe lengths are as follows:

UTP Cat 3	100m@4 Mb/s	
UTP Cat 4	200m@4 Mb/s	100m@16 Mb/a

Figure 10-24   3502B

UTP Cat 5	200m@4 Mb/s	100m@16 Mb/s
STP Type 1, 1A, and 2	350@4 Mb/s	180@16 Mb/s
STP Type 6 and 9	200@4Mb/s	120@16 Mb/s
STP Type 8	150@ 4Mb/s	90@16 Mb/s

Jumpers on the board are used to set the ring to attach to and the speed of the ring. The module may function as an isolated ring. This means that the module is not connected to either of the backplane Token Rings. This creates a local ring on the module that has connectivity only to devices attached to any of the module's ports.

3504-ST

This module supports six fiber Token Ring ports (802.5J), which support connections of up to 2 km away. These ports may be used either as lobe ports (for stations) or as ring-in/ring-out ports. The module supports both backplane Token Rings and both 4 and 16 Mbps.

3505B

This module (see Figure 10-25) supports 12 connections (RJ-45) over either UTP or STP cable. In this module (as opposed to the 3502), both UTP and STP connections may be used at the same time. This is because this module is an active module. This means that each port on the module takes part in retiming. This also increases the maximum lobe cable distances, as shown in the following list:

UTP Cat 3	200m@4 Mb/s	100m@4 Mb/s
UTP Cat 4	300m@4 Mb/s	160m@16 Mb/s
UTP Cat 5	300m@4 Mb/s	180m@16 Mb/s
STP Type 1, 1A, and 2	600@4 Mb/s	300@16 Mb/s
STP Type 6 and 9	400@4 Mb/s	200@16 Mb/s
STP Type 8	300@4 Mb/s	150@16 Mb/s

There is one important thing to note about this module. It supports a maximum station count of 132 stations on a single ring regardless of cable type.

Management Modules

There are three different management modules (NMMs) for Token Ring in a System 3000 chassis. All NMMs provide Standard, Advanced, or Advanced Analyzer agent levels and service port menus. They also provide ring-in and ring-out ports for expanding a ring beyond the confines of the chassis. They also have status lights and an LED display to give diagnostic and fault information.

PART III

Figure 10-25   3505B

3513 and 3514

These NMMs (see Figure 10-26) provide either Standard or Advanced management (Advanced requires a license purchased separately as with the 3313 and 3314) to a backplane Token Ring. The 3513 provides STP ring-in and ring-out ports, whereas the 3514-ST has fiber ports.

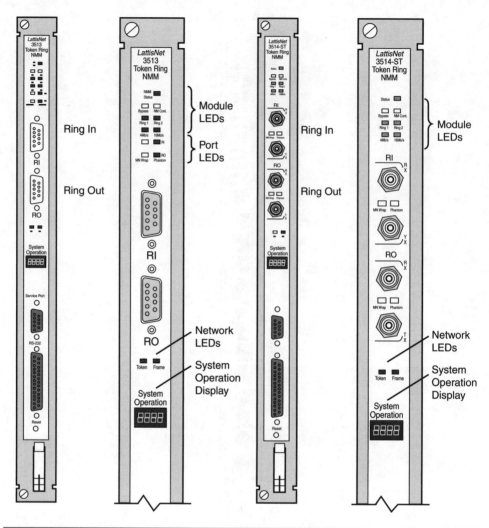

Figure 10-26 3513 and 3514

3517SA

The 3517SA provides Advanced Analyzer to a backplane Token Ring. It also provides both STP and fiber ring-in and ring-out ports. Although it is only possible to use a single ring-in port and a single ring-out port at any given time, it is possible to mix STP and fiber ports at the same time. (For example, a fiber ring-in and an STP ring-out port may be used at the same time.)

Other Modules

Repeaters

For networks that require extension via ring-in and ring-out ports but do not need management modules, there are Token Ring repeater modules that provide this function. The 3532 and 3534-ST modules provide ring-in and ring-out ports and no management (reducing the cost of the modules). The 3532 provides STP ports, while the 3534-ST has fiber.

Local Bridge

The 3522 local bridge can bridge two backplane Token Rings together or a backplane Token Ring with an external ring. The bridge supports transparent, source-route, and source-route transparent bridging modes. The ring speed of each ring being bridged is set independently of each other via jumper settings on the module.

The 5000 Chassis

The power and flexibility of the System 5000 chassis are simply amazing. It supports numerous technologies, sophisticated management, fault redundancy, and high port density all in a single box. The sheer number of devices available for the System 5000 makes it so flexible that it is difficult for a single person to master all of them. We will limit this section of the book to the modules and technologies that you are expected to know for the exam. We will first examine the System 5000 basics. Then we will examine the System 5005 chassis before we deal with the specifics about Ethernet or Token Ring and their associated modules. This is because the 5000 and the 5005 are both from the same product family and share most of the same features and almost all of the modules. The section on the 5005 chassis will basically just point out the few minor differences in the chassis and then we will move on.

The Basics

The System 5000 supports 12 backplane Ethernet segments, a maximum of 9 Token Rings, and up to 12 Fast Ethernet segments. There is also support for 2 FDDI networks (5 paths) and a total of 48 ATM ports (24 ports per switch × 2 switches; see Chapter 13.) Although we do not need to concern ourselves with FDDI or ATM at this time, the Ethernet, Token Ring, and Fast Ethernet are what we will be looking into, as well as the basics of the 5000 chassis.

The Backplane

The backplane of a System 5000 is really three separate backplanes (see Figure 10-27). There is a lower, middle, and upper third (as with the System 3000), but in a System 5000, the backplanes are physically separate and can be removed independently of each other.

The bottommost backplane is called the hub backplane. It distributes power to all 14 slots and provides the Common Management Bus (CMB) that allows out-of-band management with all slots in the chassis. The hub backplane also provides 12 backplane Ethernet segments and 9 Token Rings. The middle backplane provides the 12 backplane Fast Ethernet segments. We will look into the specifics later in the section dealing with the individual technologies.

When ordering a System 5000 chassis, the model number determines which backplanes you get. They are

- 5000N   Ethernet only

- 5000NT   Ethernet and Token Ring

- 5000F   Ethernet, Token Ring, and FDDI

- 5000BH   Ethernet, Token Ring, and ATM

- 5000BHC   Ethernet, Token Ring, ATM, and Fast Ethernet

- 5000C   Ethernet, Token Ring, and Fast Ethernet

- 5000CF   Ethernet, Token Ring, Fast Ethernet, and FDDI

- 5000S   Ethernet, Token Ring, and Taurus Fast Ethernet Switch

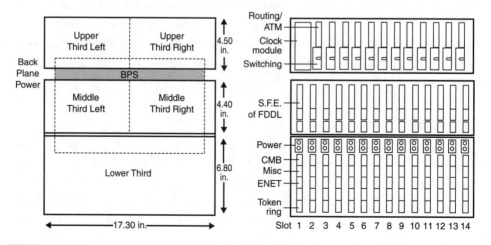

Figure 10-27 Backplanes

Remember, you can do a field upgrade on a 5000NT (for example) to make it a 5000BHC. The only limiting factor is the chassis model number that is inscribed on the chassis interior. If you remove the supervisory module from the chassis and gently lift the ribbon cable, you will wind the chassis model number. If this number ends in a C or greater letter, then the chassis is field upgradeable. Only very old chassis are not field upgradeable.

The Power

Power is provided to the chassis by means of up to three power supplies installed in the rear (see Figure 10-28). Each power supply can supply up to 950 watts of power (limited to 1,550 watts maximum not to overheat the chassis) and the power supplies are load balancing, redundant, and hot swappable.

Fans

Two fans are installed in the rear of the chassis below the power supplies and are hot swappable (see Figure 10-29). These fans provide cooling for the entire chassis. The chassis heat thresholds are 40 degrees centigrade (104 degrees Fahrenheit) and 60 degrees centigrade (140 degrees Fahrenheit). When the chassis reaches 40 degrees, it triggers a thermal warning; if the chassis reaches 60 degrees, it shuts down the -48 volts DC power to the front-installed modules (the chassis still maintains the 5 volts

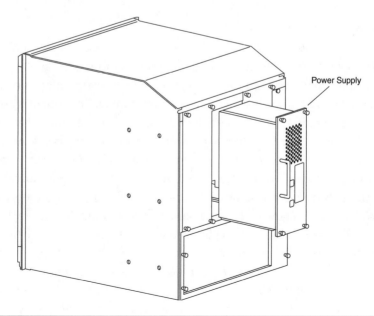

Figure 10-28 Power supply

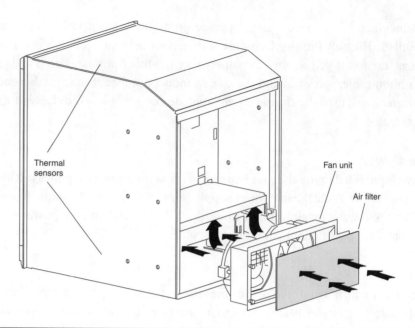

Figure 10-29 Fans

DC that is required for the sensors). The chassis also shuts down when reaching 0 degrees centigrade (32 degrees Fahrenheit).

The Supervisory Module

The 5110 supervisory module (see Figure 10-30) is one of the advanced features of the System 5000 chassis. The front-installed modules of the System 5000 are very flexible —so flexible that every port on a System 5000 may have a different configuration. The configurations for front-installed modules are stored in local memory on the modules. These configurations are also stored on the supervisory module. The supervisory module polls every slot in the chassis ten times per second and stores the configuration of the devices. The reason is that in the event that a module fails and needs to be replaced, the configuration will be restored automatically from the supervisory module. This can save the network administrator a lot of time trying to find the documentation that shows how to configure each of the ports on the module that was replaced.

The supervisory module also performs some other functions. The module also provides the access to the chassis management bus via the service port on the front of the chassis. Without the supervisory module, the service port will not function. There are LED indicators on the supervisory module that mimic the LED indicators on the front of the System 5000 chassis. Without the supervisory module, the LEDs on the front of

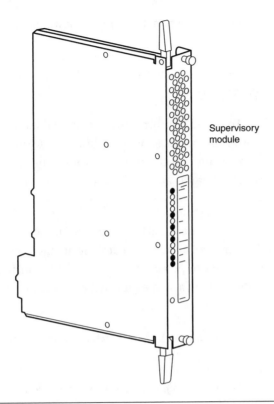
Supervisory
module

Figure 10-30 Supervisory module

the chassis will not function. The placement of another set of LEDs on the supervisory module is done so that while managing the chassis (from the rear), the technician will able to read the indicators without having to walk around the chassis. The supervisory module installs in the rear of the chassis to the right of the power supplies.

The LED indicators on the supervisory module are

- Power
- System
- PS1, PS2, and PS3
- Redundant
- Supv Mdl
- Thermal
- Fan

Power   The power LED is green when the chassis is powered on and off when it is not.

System   The system LEDs indicate the operational status of the chassis. When the green LED is lit, the system is completely operational. When the amber LED is lit, there is a fault somewhere in the chassis.

PS1, PS2, and PS3   These LEDs indicate the operational status of the power supplies (PS). If the LED is green, the power supply is present and functioning. If the LED is amber, the power supply is present but not functioning (or has been disabled by the supervisory module). If both lights are out, then there is no power supply for the indicated number.

Redundant   When the redundant LED is lit (green), it indicates that the power supplies are in a redundant mode. This means that there are more power supplies than are necessary to meet the minimum power requirements of the installed modules. Therefore, we are in a condition where a single (at least) power supply may fail without having any impact on the function of the network.

Supv Mdl   If this light is lit (amber), then there is a failure of some component of the supervisory module.

Thermal   If this light is lit (amber), the chassis has exceeded the temperature threshold.

Fan   When this light is lit (amber), one or both of the fans has failed. If both of the fans have failed, the chassis will stop operating.

Clock Modules

A difference in the System 5000 chassis (compared to the 3000 chassis) is the clocking. All technologies require some sort of clocking for the signal being transmitted. In the System 3000 chassis, this clocking was provided by either an NMM or retiming module for Ethernet. In a System 5000, the clocking is provided by dual, redundant clock modules installed in the chassis directly on the hub backplane. They are replaceable, but they are not hot swappable. In order to find them, you must remove the fan unit from the rear of the chassis and then remove a metal cover that protects the modules. The module closest to the supervisory module is the primary.

The 5005 Chassis

The first difference between the 5000 and the 5005 is the number of slots. The 5005 chassis has only eight slots (see Figure 10-31). Even though it has six less slots, both chassis are the same width. This is because the power supplies and the fans in the 5005 have been moved from the rear (in the 5000) to the front of the chassis on the right-hand side where the other six slots belong. This greatly reduces the depth of the chassis. The reason for all of this is that the 5005 is meant to be a wiring closet solution for high-capacity wiring closets. The reduced depth of the unit (along with the fact that there are no components that can be serviced from the rear) make it easy to place this unit in almost any wiring closet, whereas the System 5000 chassis would be very difficult (and in some cases, impossible) to work on in some environments.

There are still 12 backplane Ethernet segments and 2 FDDI networks (5 paths), but there is a maximum of 5 backplane Token Rings. There are also (optionally) 12 Fast Ethernet segments, 1 ATM switch, or the Taurus (5005S) switch backplane.

There is a supervisory module in the slot farthest to the right (next to the power supplies). It is usually hidden from view by the power supply cover. The service port for the 5005 chassis is actually part of the supervisory module. The supervisory module in the 5005 has the same function as the supervisory module in the 5000 chassis, but they are not interchangeable. The supervisory module in the 5005 also maintains the backup clocking module.

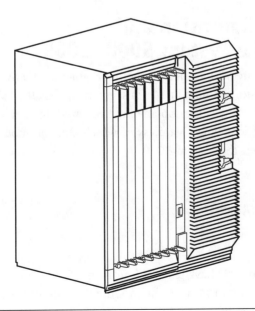

Figure 10-31   5005 chassis

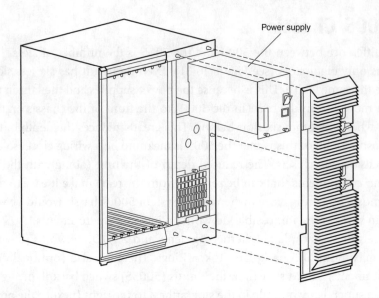

Figure 10-32   5005 power supplies

There are only two power supplies (see Figure 10-32) for the 5005 chassis, and they are load balancing and redundant when both are installed.

Ethernet Configuration and Devices for the System 5000 (5005)

As noted earlier, there are 12 backplane Ethernet segments in a System 5000 (5005). Each segment is a collision domain and each segment spans all 14 slots of the chassis. Any Ethernet module (or any cluster on any Ethernet module) can attach to any of the 14 backplane Ethernet segments regardless of which slot the module is in. This is a great improvement from the System 3000 in which physical module placement was very important.

Ethernet Host Modules

Common Features

All modules in a System 500x have LED indicators to tell the network administrator or technician who is standing in front of the module the current status. These LEDs are located at the extreme top of the module. There is a 1 inch by 2.5 inch (more or less) window where they are all displayed. At the top of this window is a rectangle that contains the model number of the module. This is the first LED. It is called the *annunciator*. The annunciator tells the basic status of the module. An amber annunciator indicates that the module is performing diagnostics, boot up, or has failed. A green LED indicates that the module is functioning correctly. The rest of the LEDs are as follows:

Segment Connection   These LEDs (S1, S2, S3 . . . S12) indicate which backplane Ethernet segment the module is connected to. This is a important troubleshooting indicator because it can clear up any number of misconceptions as to how you thought you set it up. ISOL means that the module is isolated from the backplane. Data flashes on when there is activity (traffic) on the segment.

Interconnect Status   This is for the fiber port (if any) or another type of interconnect port (AUI). For fiber ports, there is a REM LED and a Rdn LED. REM is green when the port is connected to a device that supports remote signaling and the port is not receiving a remote fault signal. If the REM is amber, it indicates that there is a fault in the path between the two ends. The Rdn LED lights up green if the port is in redundant mode and there is no fault. If this LED is amber, the redundant connection has failed. If the LED is off, the port is not configured as a redundant port.

Port Status   These LEDs indicate the state of the individual connections to the hosts. When they are green, there is link; when they are amber, the port has been partitioned; when they are off, there is no link.

Options

Some of the modules available for the System 5000 (5005) have different options available. Some of these options are module specific and some of them can apply to a number of modules. We are going to take a closer look at two of the options/ideas that are common to a number of modules: clusters and security.

Clusters   A cluster is the smallest unit that can be assigned to a segment. The entire cluster functions as a whole. In some modules (like a 5308), all of the ports on the module are part of one big cluster. This type of module is called a *module-level* cluster. If the cluster on a module like the 5308 is placed on backplane segment 1, all of the ports are on backplane segment 1 and have connectivity to all of the ports (in any slot regardless of the cluster or module type) that have connectivity to backplane segment 1.

Some modules (like the 5378) have multiple clusters, with each cluster being made up of numerous (in this case, five) ports. This is called a *multi-* or *multiple-port* cluster. Each cluster can be assigned individually, so cluster A may be on backplane segment 1, while cluster B is on backplane segment 2. All of the ports in cluster A have connectivity to all the other ports in cluster A and all of the other ports on backplane segment 1, but have no connectivity to the ports of cluster B or backplane segment 2.

There is also a per-port-level cluster (also called a *single-port* cluster). A 5308PS module has per-port-level clusters (the *P* in the model number indicates the per-port or single-port cluster). Each of the 24 ports on the module is a separate cluster and can be assigned individually. Therefore, this type of module lends the most flexibility.

Security Some modules offer the same type of security as the 3368 Lattisecure module. These modules are referred to as *S* modules, or *secure* modules. They are identifiable by the *S* at the end of their model number.

The Modules

We will start off by examining six different Ethernet host modules. They are

- 5308-AF
- 5304P
- 5307
- 5308PS
- 5378-F
- 5300PS

5308-AF

The 5308-AF (see Figure 10-33) is a popular, multipurpose module. To begin with, it has 18 ports. Ports 3 through 18 are RJ-45 10BASE-T ports. Port 2 is an AUI port for connecting to external devices. Port 1 is a fiber port. This module is often used because it allows for diverse connectivity options while still guaranteeing normal (10BASE-T) host connectivity. There is a rotary switch (dial) on the module that can be used to physically select the backplane Ethernet segment to attach to. This is not the preferred method. It is usually preferred to use the service port menus to select the segment attachment or use network management (Optivity) to do it. The reason for this is simply that if you rely on the rotary switch, you have to remove the module from the chassis in order to view or change it. You may have set it to segment 4, but the module is connected to segment 2 because someone changed it via the service port menus (changes made via the service port or network management override the switch setting). It is therefore much less confusing to leave the switch setting at the factory default

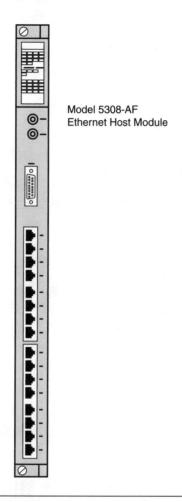

Model 5308-AF
Ethernet Host Module

Figure 10-33   5308-AF

setting and use network management to manage. When you make changes using the service port or network management, the changes happen immediately without having to power down or reboot the module.

There is one limiting factor in this module. It is only able to choose from any 6 of the 12 backplane segments at a time. This is a limitation of the old design. When the segment bank selector is in one position, the module can see and therefore connect to one of the first six backplane segments (1–6). When the segment bank selector is in the second position, the module is able to see and therefore connect to any one of the last six backplane segments (7–12).

5304P

This module (see Figure 10-34) has ten 10BASE-FL ports. Because this module is a *P* module, any of the ports may be configured independently of the others to connect to any of the 12 backplane Ethernet segments or any of 3 local segments. The local segments have no connectivity to the backplane segments. The ports can operate as individual ports or as redundant pairs.

5307xx

This module (see Figure 10-35) has either 2 (5307) 50-pin telco connectors, each connector supporting 12 10BASE-T connections, or 3 (5307HD) 50-pin telco connectors.

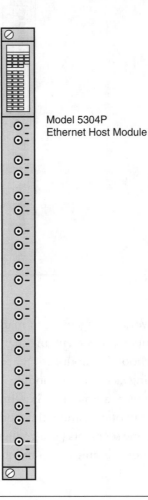

Model 5304P
Ethernet Host Module

Figure 10-34   5304P

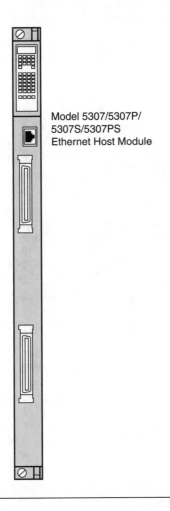

Model 5307/5307P/
5307S/5307PS
Ethernet Host Module

Figure 10-35 5307

Therefore, this module supports either 24 (5307) or 36 (5307HD) 10BASE-T connections. There is also an RJ-45 port (MDI/MDI-X) that can be used instead of one of the connections of the telco connector. The 5307P module can connect ports simultaneously to each of the 12 backplane Ethernet segments as well as up to 3 local segments.

5308PS

The 5308PS (see Figure 10-36) is a very popular module. It supports 24 10BASE-T connections (RJ-45 ports) and supports port-level clusters as well as security. Each of the 24 ports may attach independently to any of the 12 backplane Ethernet segments or any of the three local segments. This module is often used for workstation connectivity. The

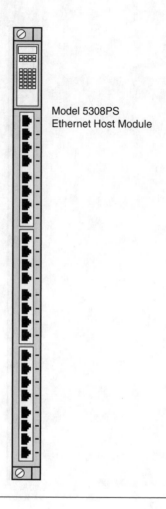

Model 5308PS
Ethernet Host Module

Figure 10-36   5308PS

extreme flexibility of the port-level clustering combined with the ease of use of the RJ-45 port makes this module useful. The System 5000 chassis populated with 14 of these modules can support 336 Ethernet ports.

5378-F

The 5378-F (see Figure 10-37) module is often referred to as a *multiport cluster module* (or simply a cluster module). There are a total of 20 Ethernet ports on this module. Sixteen of these ports are RJ-45 and the remaining four are 10BASE-F ports. The ports are grouped into clusters of five. Each cluster has one 10BASE-F port and four RJ-45 ports. The clusters are labeled cluster A, B, C, and D. Each cluster is treated as a whole. That

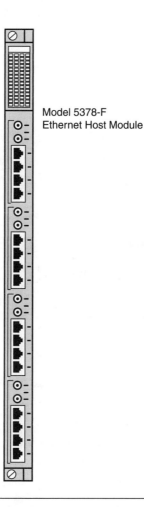

Model 5378-F
Ethernet Host Module

Figure 10-37 5378-F

means that if cluster A is on backplane segment 3, then all 5 ports in the cluster are on backplane segment 3. A module like this is typically used in collapsed backbones to tie remote devices into a data center via the fiber ports. The RJ-45 ports are typically connected to workstations or servers closer to the data center.

5300PS

This module is in itself modular (see Figure 10-38). Consisting of 8 fixed RJ-45 ports (acting as a single cluster), there are also 4 Media Dependent Adapter (MDA) slots in which different media adapters can be installed to add even greater flexibility to your network design. MDAs include the following:

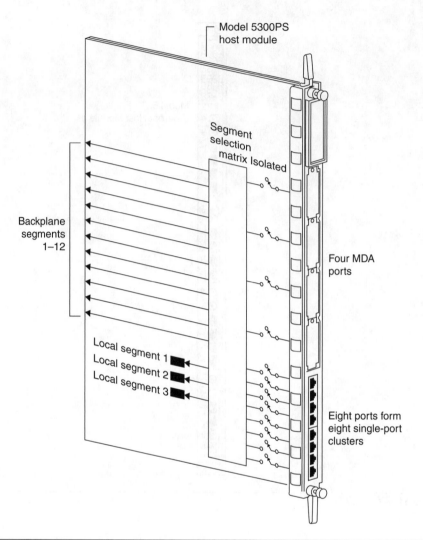

Figure 10-38 5300PS

- **5300-T** This MDA is a single RJ-45 10BASE-T port.

- **5300-F** This MDA has a single 10BASE-F (multimode fiber) fiber port.

- **5300-2** This MDA has a single 10BASE-2 BNC port. This port is internally grounded and terminated.

- **5300-SM** This MDA has a single-fiber (single-mode) port.

- **5300-A** This MDA is a single AUI port (female).

- **5300-D** This MDA is a single reverse AUI port (male).

The ports that are on the MDA are treated as single-port clusters that can be assigned independently of the others to any of the 12 backplane Ethernet segments or any of the 3 local segments.

The Management Modules

There is really only one NMM available for Ethernet management in a System 5000 (5005) chassis, but it does come in two different configurations. The 5310A/SA NMM is both an Advanced (A) agent and an Advanced Analyzer (SA) in the same piece of hardware. When you purchase an Advanced agent, the 5310A/SA comes with a daughter card called a Management Communication Engine (MCE) installed on board. The MCE provides Advanced-level management to one backplane segment. When purchased as an Advanced Analyzer (SA) agent, the module comes with a Data Collection Engine (DCE) in place of an MCE. The DCE provides Advanced Analyzer functions. The 5310A/SA supports up to three DCEs.

The NMM in a System 5000 (5005) functions slightly differently than in a System 3000. In a 3000, the NMM is assigned an IP address. In a 5000, the DCE (or MCE) is assigned an address. The DCE is then assigned to a backplane segment (the IP address of the DCE must be on the same subnet as the segment that it is assigned to) where it acts as a host on the segment and collects data directly from the segment.

The LEDs for the NMM are slightly different than those for the host modules. The first set of LEDs tells which backplane segments are being utilized (not which segments are being managed). The next set of LEDs indicates whether an MCE or a DCE is installed in position A and which segment it is assigned to. The last two sets of LEDs are for MCE/DCE B and C.

On the face of the NMM, there are three windows that each have a display for one of the DCE/MCEs. Above each window is a six-digit hexadecimal number. This number is the MAC address (the last 3 bytes) of the DCE installed in that position. All the DCEs have the same first 3 bytes of their MAC address (000081).

Token Ring Configuration and Devices for the System 5000 (5005)

There is a difference between the 5000 chassis and the 5005 chassis for backplane Token Rings. In a 5000 chassis, there are a maximum of nine Token Rings on the backplane, but they all stem from five larger rings. There are five Token Rings on the backplane of the System 5000 that reside on the hub backplane. Each Token Ring spans all 14 slots in the chassis. From top to bottom, they are numbered Ring 1, 2, 3, 4, and 5.

Any of the backplane Token Rings may be attached to any of the 14 slots in the chassis when the hub is in this configuration. This is called *through* mode.

It is also possible to have nine Token Rings on the backplane. This is called *split* mode. When in split mode, the first four rings (Rings 1, 2, 3, and 4) are split down the middle between slots 7 and 8. When the rings are split, they are wrapped to form eight smaller rings that span slots 1 through 7 for Rings 1, 2, 3, and 4, and slots 8 through 14 for Rings 6, 7, 8, and 9. Ring 5, which is never split, continues to span all 14 slots of the chassis. In order to attach to Ring 1 when the chassis is in split mode, the card must be one of the slots on the left side of the chassis (slots 1 through 7). In order to attach to Ring 7 when the chassis is in split mode, the card must be one of the slots on the right side of the chassis (slots 8 through 14).

To split the backplane Token Rings of a 5000 chassis, use the service port menus or Optivity.

In the 5005 chassis, this possibility does not exist. There are five backplane Token Rings and no possibility of splitting them. All five Token Rings span all eight slots of a 5005 chassis.

Token Ring Host Modules

Common Features

All Token Ring host modules for a System 5000 (5005) have common LEDs. The first set of LEDs indicates the backplane ring that the module is attached to (R1, R2, and so on). After that comes the ring speed indicator (or 16MB). Finally, there are the port status LEDs. In the case of Token Ring, green means inserted into the ring, amber means wrapped, and off means no connection.

The Modules

We are now going to look at five different Token Ring host modules for the System 5000 (5005):

- 5502
- 5505S
- 5505PS
- 5575A-F
- 5575A-C

5502/5505S

The 5502 module has 24 RJ-45 ports that support either UTP or STP connections at either 4 or 16 Mbps. The board is considered a module-level cluster, meaning that all ports attach to the same ring as the others. The module may be isolated from the backplane to form a single local ring with no connectivity to any of the backplane Token Rings. The module supports an automatic ring wrap if a device attempts to attach at the wrong speed.

The 5505S module supports all of these features, but it has active per-port retiming, giving extra distance to its lobe cables. It also supports security.

5505PS

The 5505PS has 20 RJ-45 ports, which are port-level clusters. Each port may be attached to any of the backplane Token Rings independently of the others. There is also a local ring, which has no connectivity to any backplane Token Rings. It also supports security on each port.

5575A-C/5575A-F

These modules are cluster modules with a total of six RJ-45 ports and two sets of ring-in/ring-out ports (unlike the System 3000, where the ring-in/ring-out ports are located on the NMM). The ports are divided into two clusters that are configurable independently of each other. The A-C has DB-9 connectors for STP ring in/ring out and the A-F has fiber ports for extended distances. There is also an RJ-45 port that is a separate cluster from the rest. It is used as a monitor port for diagnostic equipment. There is a button below the port that is used to select the ring to which the port attaches.

Other Modules

As an addition to the host modules, there is a module known as the 559 Embedded Management Tool (EMT). This is a small card that attaches to other host modules. It expands on the manageability and functionality of older host modules. Newer modules have the feature built in. The EMT adds to the statistics that can be gathered, adds security, and reduces jitter, which enables the network ring population to be increased.

Network Management Modules (NMM)

There is a single NMM available for Token Ring in a System 5000 (5005): the 5510 NMM. It has a single DCE built in so it provides Advanced Analyzer management. An additional DCE may be added on expanding the Advanced Analyzer management to up to two rings with a single 5510 NMM.

Other Considerations

With Token Ring, you must remember that network design is largely dependent of the support of the network's devices. The following shows a matrix of the capabilities of the modules discussed previously (see Figures 10-39 and 10-40).

Cable	Type	Speed	Maximum lobe length in meters		
			5502	5505S/ 505PS	5575A-C/ 5575A-F
STP	1, 2, 1A	4	350	600	600
		16	180	300	300
	6, 9	4	200	400	400
		16	120	200	200
	8	4	150	300	300
		16	90	150	150
UTP	CAT 3	4	100	200	200
		16	NA	100	100
	CAT 4, 5	4	200	300	300
		16	100	160	160
Fiber		NA	NA	NA	2,000

Figure 10-39   Maximum lobe cable distances

Cable	Type	Speed	Maximum lobe length in meters		
			5502	5505S/ 505PS	5575A-C/ 5575A-F
STP	1, 2, 6, 8, 9	4,16	250	132	132
UTP	CAT 3	4	132	132	132
		16	132	132	132
	CAT 4,5	4	132	132	132
		16	132	132	132

Figure 10-40   Maximum number of stations on a ring

The Distributed 5000 Concentrator

The Distributed 5000 (referred to as the D5000) is a modular, stackable hub that supports configuration switching like in a System 5000 chassis. There is full management support, which is optional. Up to eight hubs can be stacked together to form a unit that is managed as a single device that can support up to 288 ports over up to 27 segments (3 cascaded and 24 local). It supports an optional Redundant Power Supply Unit (RPSU) and a wide variety of modules.

 NOTE The D5000 is sometimes referred to as a *switching hub*. Do not be confused—the *switching hub* refers to the fact that the hub supports configuration switching. This is not an Ethernet switch or a router. The D5000 is a hub only. It has no support for any technology other than 10Mb Ethernet.

The Chassis

There are two different types of chassis for the D5000 (see Figure 10-41). There is a three-slot chassis (5DN003), which has three slots for host modules and a slot for an optional NMM. There is also a two-slot chassis (5DN002), which has two slots for host modules and no slot for an NMM. The 5DN002 is managed only while in a stack with a 5DN003 with an NMM installed. The 5DN002 and the 5DN003 both support the optional RPSU. Each chassis has its own power supply and fans, as well as LEDs for status.

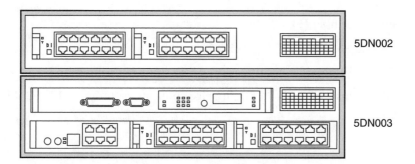

5DN002

5DN003

Figure 10-41 D5000

Segments

The D5000 has three segments that are cascade segments. The cascade segments are accessible to every unit in the stack. Ports from different host modules in different chassis may all be assigned to the same cascaded segment. When this is done, a cascaded segment functions just like a backplane segment in a System 5000 chassis. The ports act as if they were in the same hub; they form a single repeater domain. Each chassis also supports three local segments. Ports from different host modules in the same chassis may be assigned to any of the three local segments. There is no connectivity between the local segment and any other segment (local or cascaded). A stack that is fully populated with eight D5000 chassis can support three cascaded segments plus three local segments per chassis (eight), or 8×3, which is 24 local segments for a grand total of 27 segments.

Host Modules

We will look at four different modules that have many of the same features (and similar model numbers) as the System 5000. Each of these modules is available both as a *P* module (port-level cluster) or a *PS* module (port-level cluster with security).

- **5DN308**   This module has 12 RJ-45 10BASE-T ports and supports either STP or UTP cable. The first port is configurable as MDI/MDI-X via a button on the face of the module.

- **5DN378**   This module has six MDI-X 10BASE-T RJ-45 ports, one MDI 10BASE-T RJ-45 port, and one of the following:
    - AUI (A)
    - Multimode fiber (F)
    - Single-mode fiber (SM)

- **5DN304**   This module has three 10BASE-FL ports (ST connectors).

- **5DN307**   This module has 1 50-pin telco connector supporting 12 10BASE-T connections.

LEDs

The difference between D5000 and other devices we have examined so far is that the D5000 host modules have no LEDs (with the exception of the fiber modules). All the LEDs are on the chassis itself. The window has LEDs for the following:

- Power (Pwr)

- Fan status (Fan)

- Redundant Power Supply Unit (RPS)

- Isolated (ISOL)

- Cascaded segment attachment (Seg1, Seg2, Seg3 . . .)

- Local segment attachment (Lcl1, Lcl2, Lcl3 . . .)

- A row of numbers to indicate the units number within the stack (1–8)

- Port status (1–12)

NOTE   The 5DN003 concentrator has three rows of LEDs to indicate port status. The 5DN002 concentrator has two rows of LEDs to indicate port status.

5DN310/SA NMM

The NMM is optional for the operation of the stack. When installed, it connects to any of the three cascaded segments. The NMM supports up to three DCMs (similar to a DCE), which also connect to any of the three cascaded segments. Unlike a System 5000 NMM, the NMM in the D5000 gets a single IP address. Addresses are not assigned to the DCMs. The NMM provides either an Advanced or Advanced Analyzer agent, as well as the service port for out-of-band access. The NMM also provides similar functions to a supervisory module in the System 5000 in that it stores device configurations.

Stacking

D5000s are stacked by means of a cascade cable (provided with the chassis) that goes from the cascade down port of one chassis to the cascade up port of the next. The unit numbers are determined when the stack is powered up and the topmost unit is unit 1. In order to remove a unit from a working stack, first disconnect the power. Then detach the cascade cables. Connect the free ends of the disconnected cables together. Then remove the unit from the rack.

PART III

BayStack Hubs

We have looked at large enterprise class hubs up until now. You should expect to find them in data centers and densely populated wiring closets. The BayStack product line offers another type of solution. The BayStack product line is a stackable, manageable, and flexible solution that can grow as your needs grow and enable you to get started without making a huge monetary commitment. The BayStack product line offers numerous products that fall into four basic classes:

- BayStack 100
- BayStack 150
- BayStack 200
- BayStack 250

NOTE We will discuss the BayStack 100 and 150 here. We will save BayStack 200 and 250 for the section "Fast Ethernet."

BayStack 100

The BayStack 100 (see Figure 10-42) comes in four basic forms: 12- and 24-port RJ-45, and 2 50-pin telco and 6-port fiber (ST). On the RJ-45 models, one port is MDI/MDI-X configurable. All have an expansion slot for an NMM (optional) and can function alone or in a stack of up to ten units. All units have 2 slots for media adapters (10BASE-T, 10BASE-2, fiber, and AUI), making the total number of ports available per unit 26. Ten units in a stack bring a grand total of 260 ports maximum per stack. Each hub in a stack may be isolated or may attach to any of three cascaded segments. The BayStack 100 hub is a module-level cluster so all ports on the hub attach to the same segment as the rest of the hub. The hubs also support the use of an RPSU. This is an entry-level 10BASE-T hub with the capability to grow. You can even use the NMM in a single unit

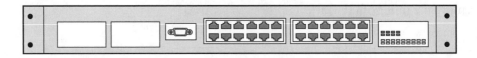

Figure 10-42 BayStack 100

in the stack to manage a unit that is not part of the stack. There is a management extension port on the back of the hub that can be connected (standard Cat 3 or higher Ethernet cable) to the management extension port of a remote hub (a hub not part of the cascade, sometimes referred to as a *remote cascade*) that does not have an NMM. You will able to manage it through the NMM in the other hub. Only management information flows through this cable. If you plan for the hubs to be connected and pass user traffic, you will need to connect via a cable from one of the ports on the front of the hub.

Hubs are cascaded together with cascade cables (supplied with the hubs) from cascade down port to cascade up port. There are three different NMMs available: Standard, Advanced, and Advanced Analyzer. There is no need to have an NMM in every hub just to manage the stack as long as you have one per stack (you do not even need one per stack if you do not want to manage the stack). The cascaded segment that a hub attaches to can be set in one of three ways:

- Service port menus

- Optivity

- Dip switches on the rear of the hub

The NMM in a hub does not have to be attached to the same segment at the hub. Because all three cascaded segments flow through each hub, every hub has access to all the segments and therefore so does the NMM. The NMM can be configured to follow the hub it is installed in (default) or it can be moved independently by moving the jumper on the NMM board.

 NOTE Even though you have installed an Advanced Analyzer in a stack, you only have Advanced Analyzer management on the segment to which it is attached. The remaining segments have Standard management only. That is usually enough, but if you need more, you can install one NMM for each segment that you need Advanced (or better) management on.

BayStack 150

The BayStack 150 (see Figure 10-43) also comes in two basic models with a few options available. There is a 12-port (152 and 153) and a 24-port (150 and 151) model. Both models have an AUI port on the rear of the hub. Two of the hubs (150 and 152) support the optional NMM, which can be installed in the rear of the hub. These hubs are

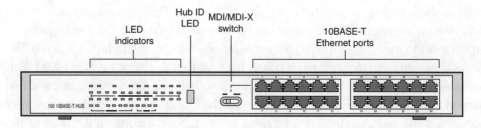

Figure 10-43 BayStack 150

stackable (up to eight hubs in a stack). A fully populated stack will have 200 ports (24 ports × 8 hubs = 192 + 8 AUI ports = 200). A typical configuration is to cascade a single 150 with an NMM together with seven 151s (no NMM). Then the entire stack can be managed by the NMM in the 150. The hubs can be managed via the comm. port (150 and 152 only), Telnet, Optivity, or via a web management interface.

A major feature of the BayStack 150 is that the cascade cable is no longer a proprietary cable; however, it is not a standard Cat 3 (or higher) cable with RJ-45 connectors. Now units in a stack may be up to 100 meters apart (from first hub to last).

Ethernet Network Design and Troubleshooting

Until now, we have discussed a number of hubs that provide Ethernet connectivity. It is now time to discuss some network design guidelines that will aid in designing new networks and troubleshooting problems in existing networks.

There are two basic network designs for Ethernet:

- Distributed backbone
- Collapsed backbone

Distributed Backbone

This type of network is one that was very popular until recently (in the last five years or so). This type of network places routers and even servers in wiring closets and away from the network center (see Figure 10-44). Workgroups are segmented by routers, and

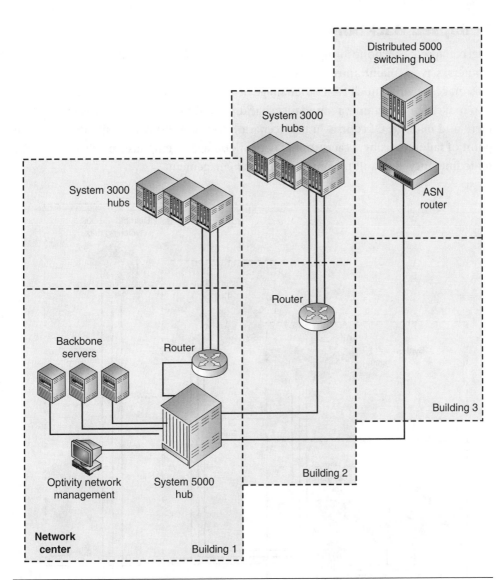

Figure 10-44   Distributed backbone

their traffic is routed back to the data center. This scenario was a good one before the age of true high-capacity routers and switches that were capable of very high port density and throughput. The processing was off-loaded onto multiple smaller routers. This scenario worked to a point, but management, security, and backups were issues because the devices were remote to the network core and there were many of them.

Collapsed Backbone

The collapsed backbone brings all of the routing functions and backbone devices (routers, servers, mainframes, and so on) back into the data center (see Figure 10-45). This makes security much easier to manage because everything is located in one area. It also makes fault tolerance, redundancy, backups, and troubleshooting easier to implement and manage. Of course, in this scenario, there is a distinct possibility of a single point of failure causing a catastrophic network outage so emphasis needs to be placed on redundancy and fault tolerance as well as management.

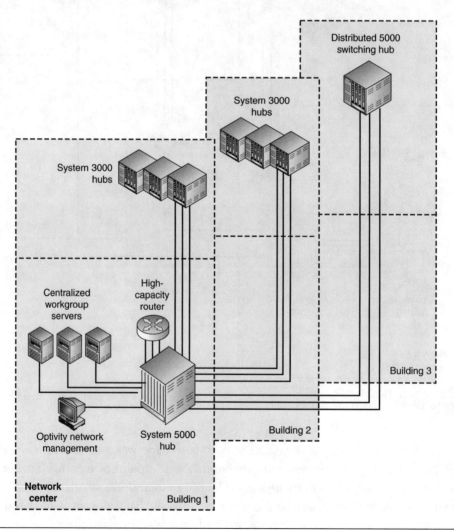

Figure 10-45   Collapsed backbone

Physical Media

There are four basic types of physical media that you may use in your network. Of course, the type of physical media in use will be determined by network needs as well as projected network growth. The types of media are the following:

- 10BASE-5 thick coax (legacy)

- 10BASE-2 thin coax (legacy)

- 10BASE-T UTP

- 10BASE-F fiber optic

The coax cable will be left over (legacy) from prior networking projects and may need to be maintained. Its limitations are that it is difficult to manage, difficult to reconfigure once it has been laid out, and difficult to locate faults because of the bus topology. Faults also affect the entire segment. On the brighter side, it has a high resistance to Electro-Magnetic Interference (EMI) and relatively long cable segments (10BASE-5 has 500-meter segments and 10BASE-2 has 185-meter segments).

10BASE-T will be used in current networking environments. Even though 100BASE-T (discussed later) is the technology being purchased today for desktops and even servers, both technologies are capable of using the same cable (Cat 5) so migrations are not necessarily a problem if all you need to do is go from 10 to 100. The UTP cable is characterized as easy to work with, inexpensive, and easily migrated from 10 to 100. Also, the star topology is easy to maintain and troubleshoot, and it limits the size of the fault domain in effect. On the downside, it has a relatively low resistance to EMI and shorter cable distances (100 meters) than coax or fiber.

10BASE-F fiber is used almost exclusively in environments where there are high levels of EMI, great distances to be traversed, or high security restraints. The fiber-optic cable has an incredibly high resistance to EMI. The cable has very low attenuation so cable distances can go from 2 km (multimode fiber) to 20 km (single-mode fiber). The fiber is also very delicate so tapping the cable to steal data is very difficult. The downside to fiber is that it is expensive and difficult to work with, requiring highly skilled and trained professionals to install and troubleshoot (making it even more expensive).

Repeaters

A repeater is a device that retransmits a signal so it can travel further. It is a physical-layer device. If you have ever played operator, you should be able to see quickly what problems can occur. The process of simple repetition can be repeated only so many times before the content is damaged beyond recognition. There is also the matter of delay. Each of these devices in a collision domain increases the delay of the signal as well as decreases the interpacket gap (the space between packets on the wire necessary to determine when a device is transmitting and when it has stopped), which can cause all traffic on the network to grind to a halt. Therefore, there are rules as to how many such devices may be used on a segment before a device that performs some throttling and verification gets involved.

5-4-3

There is a rule known as the 5-4-3 rule (see Figure 10-46). It stands for the following:

- **Five segments** Between any two devices attempting to communicate, there can be a maximum of five segments. This must be a worst-case scenario for the segment.

- **Four repeaters** Connecting the five segments together can be no more than four repeaters.

- **Three populated segments** Only three of the segments along the path can be populated (including the source and destination).

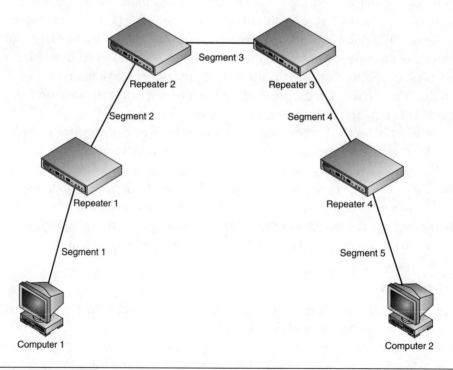

Figure 10-46 5-4-3 rule

This is the rule that applies to 10BASE-5 and 10BASE-2 networks. For 10BASE-T networks, the rule is slightly modified. Because of the technology involved in creating the star topology, there is no need to limit the number of populated segments along the path; therefore, the rule becomes the 5-4 rule.

On the hub exam, you may be asked questions about what type of hub to suggest to a customer who needs to connect x amount of devices of type y together. Remember that we do not need to sell a dentist a fully loaded System 5000 with all the bells and whistles to support his or her three-node LAN, and no data center that needs to add connectivity for 200 high-end servers will be happy with a bunch of BayStacks. Use common sense.

Troubleshooting

The ability to troubleshoot network problems quickly and effectively is probably the most important skill a network administrator can have. The problems that can crop up on a healthy network range from an unplugged cable to bad application programming, and the network administrator needs to be able to recognize the difference. That does not mean that the network administrator needs to be a programmer, but he or she needs to be able to recognize the source of the problem as coming either from the network (hub, switch, router, and so on) or from the workstation/server application. Every minute that the application or network is down costs money so you need to be prepared to fix the problems before they occur.

The most important thing that can be done is to prepare for trouble before it actually occurs. Try and determine likely sources of trouble (new apps, new hardware, heavily utilized segments, old equipment, and so on) and consider methods of correcting the errors. Have a list of contacts and phone numbers for the tech support staff at remote locations and off hours, vendor support, and consultants. Keep documentation handy and updated. I find that most networks are sorely lacking in this area. Keep the training of networking techs up-to-date.

Once a problem has occurred, try to define the symptoms accurately. "It don't work" may be the point of view of the user on the other end of the telephone, but that is not a helpful piece of information to the person trying to fix the problem. See how many users are affected. Does this problem cover a specific area or pattern? Is the problem constant or does it come and go? Consider the possible causes. Attempt to prove or disprove the possible causes. Do not attempt to make multiple changes simultaneously to fix your problem. You could end up fixing your problem and causing a more catastrophic one at the same time. When you happen to fix the problem, attempt to determine the potential for reoccurrence either at the same place or other places in the network. Document the fix. This way you (or someone else) will not spend hours or days reinventing the wheel if and when it happens again.

An accurate and up-to-date network baseline can be a very useful tool when determining the cause of a problem on the network (see Chapter 15 for more information on network baselining).

Remember that not all problems come from the network (even though the users and application-support folks will tell you otherwise). Even so, it will be up to you to determine the true cause. Therefore, consider the following when troubleshooting possible (emphasis on possible) hub-related issues:

- Cables and physical-layer problems

- Design issues (layer 1 and 2)

- Configuration issues (layer 2)

- Server and application problems

- Network protocol (layer 3) problems

Eighty percent of all network issues are at the physical layer (the cable is too long, the cable is too loose, the cable is the wrong type, the cable is missing, and so on). Design issues can cause segments to be completely isolated or create loops that bring the segment down. The configuration of the devices may lead to the loss of management or communication. Bridges may be filtering traffic or not using the proper bridging mode. The network may be delivering the traffic perfectly, but the server app does not respond (application or server malfunction). There may be routing issues or other layer 3 issues to consider.

Fast Ethernet

The Basics

You should already have an understanding of how Ethernet works (Chapter 2) so Fast Ethernet should be fairly easy. Fast Ethernet (IEEE 802.3U) uses the same CSMA/CD MAC layer protocol as regular 10BASE-T Ethernet with one minor difference. The bit time (the length of a bit) has been reduced by a factor of ten. In other words, we can now transmit 10 bits in the same amount of time that we used to transmit 1 or transmit 100 bits in the same amount of time that we used to transmit 10.

> **NOTE** Please note the distinction—we are not making the bits travel faster. The rate at which a single bit travels from point **A** to point **B** is still the same. The difference is that now we can put more bits on the path at the same time. Try imagining a highway—we have not increased the speed limit, but we have made the roads wider to handle more cars.

The rest of the protocol still works the same way. The transmitting device is required to listen (carrier sense) before transmitting to detect if another device is transmitting (we will discuss modifications to this scheme soon). There is still a back-off algorithm to eliminate additional collisions once collisions do occur. The major changes are in the physical-layer standards. The following physical-layer standards are in use:

- **100BASE-TX** This is compatible with the two-pair Cat5 UTP cable that has been installed in most locations. It is also compatible with two-pair STP type 1 cable and two-pair 100-ohm STP cable.

- **100BASE-FX** This is the standard for 100Mb transmission over fiber.

- **100BASE-T4** This is the standard for 100Mb transmission over four-pair Cat3 cable.

There are two key differences to note about these three standards (other than those already noted):

- 100BASE-TC and 100BASE-FX both use the same encoding scheme (125 MHz with 4B/5B encoding), whereas 100BASE-T4 uses a different encoding scheme (25 MHz with 8B/6T encoding).

- 100BASE-TC and 100BASE-FX are both capable of operating in full duplex, whereas 100BASE-T4 is not. This is because 100BASE-T4 uses two of its four pairs bidirectionally.

Full-Duplex

Full-duplex operation enables a device to both transmit and receive at the same time. This idea is incompatible with the original 10BASE-T standard where a collision is defined as sensing traffic over the RX pair while transmitting (CSMA/CD). In order to operate in full-duplex, we need to first guarantee that there are no other devices competing for the bandwidth between the transmitting station and the receiving station. This is accomplished by connecting both devices to dedicated media, such as a switch port. Once this has been accomplished, we can make the devices operate in full-duplex by merely forcing the devices to stop detecting collisions, that is, to turn off the collision detection. Because we know that the dedicated media guarantees that there will be no collision, traffic that is received while transmitting no longer needs to be regarded as a collision so we do not need to detect it as such.

There can be full-duplex transmission between the following:

- A workstation and a switch port

- A workstation and another workstation connected via a crossover cable

- A switch and another switch

- A switch and a router

- A router and a workstation connected via a crossover cable

The only case in which full-duplex cannot be implemented is between any device and a hub. A hub is, by definition, shared media. Because full duplex requires dedicated media, the hub is disqualified.

Repeater Types

There are two classes, or types, of repeaters defined for Fast Ethernet: the Class I (translational) repeater and the Class II (transparent) repeater. The translational (Class I) repeater supports both 100BASE-TX/100BASE-FX signaling and 100BASE-T4 signaling. Because 100BASE-TX and 100BASE-FX use the same signaling method (125 MHz with 4B/5B encoding), it is easy to implement both physical standards into one repeater. However, 100BASE-T4 uses a different signaling. It uses 25 MHz with 8B/6T encoding. Therefore, there needs to be a translation (hence, the term "translational repeater") from the signaling used by 100BASE-TX/100BASE-FX and 100BASE-T4 if they are both to be supported in the same repeater at the same time. All Nortel Networks Fast Ethernet hubs (repeaters) are of this type.

The transparent repeater supports only one signaling system, either 125 MHz with 4B/5B encoding or 25 MHz with 8B/6T. This type of repeater is not supported by Nortel Networks.

There is a side effect created by the existence of two types of repeaters. The translational repeaters because of the translation being provided are capable of supporting a single repeater hop only in a collision domain. The transparent repeaters (because they do not translate) are capable of supporting two repeater hops per collision domain (see Figure 10-47). This limitation of Class I repeaters is mitigated by the capability to stack hubs (making them a single repeater hop) and connect hubs via switches (creating multiple collision domains).

Figure 10-47   Repeater hops and Class I/Class II repeaters

Fast Ethernet Devices

There is Fast Ethernet support in all of the devices that we have previously seen in this chapter (except for the D5000). We will now look at Fast Ethernet support in the following:

- System 3000
- System 5000 (5005)
- BayStack

Fast Ethernet in the System 3000

When the Fast Ethernet backplane is installed in a System 3000 chassis (upper third of the backplane), the chassis supports three Fast Ethernet segments. These segments span all 12 slots of the chassis. Jumpers on the host module (or Optivity network management) select segment attachment. There are two Fast Ethernet host modules available for the System 3000 chassis:

- 3405
- 3475-FX

The 3405 has 12 RJ-45 ports with port 1 MDI/MDI-X configurable. The 3475-FX has 11 RJ-45 ports and a 100BASE-FX fiber port.

There is also a Fast Ethernet NMM for the System 3000 (completely optional). It provides advanced agent support.

Fast Ethernet Support for the System 5000 (5005)

There is Fast Ethernet support for the System 5000 (5005) chassis when the Fast Ethernet backplane is installed in the middle third of the backplane. This backplane supports 12 Fast Ethernet segments. The number of Fast Ethernet segments available depends on the modules being used. The 56xx host modules support 12 Fast Ethernet segments, but the 54xx hub modules only support 3 Fast Ethernet segments. There are two 54xx host modules:

- 5405
- 5475-FX

The 5405 host module has 16 RJ-45 ports with port 1 being MDI/MDI-X configurable. The 5474-FX host module has 14 RJ-45 ports and 2 100BASE-FX fiber ports. Both modules are single port clusters. These host modules are unique in that they are given IP addresses. This allows for images to be downloaded from a BootP-TFTP server. There is no Fast Ethernet NMM for the 54xx line; the host modules are managed through a 5310A/SA Ethernet NMM.

There are two 56xx host modules:

- 5605P
- 5675P-FX

The 5605P has 24 RJ-45 10/100 autonegotiating Ethernet ports. The 5674P-FX has 20 RJ-45 10/100 ports and 2 10BASE-FX ports that perform store-and-forward bridging for use as uplink ports. The modules are port-level clusters and can attach ports to any of the 12 backplane Fast Ethernet segments or 12 Ethernet segments independently of each other. These modules also both support three 10Mb local Ethernet segments and five 100Mb local Fast Ethernet segments.

There is an NMM for the 66xx product line: the 5616A/SA. It provides either Advanced or Advanced Analyzer management for the Fast Ethernet modules and segments as well as the Ethernet modules and segments. Up to three DCMs (similar to a DCE but more advanced) can independently monitor both an Ethernet and a Fast Ethernet segment.

Fast Ethernet Support in BayStack Hubs

The Fast Ethernet BayStack hubs have much in common with the other products in the BayStack product line:

- They can work alone or in a stack.
- They are manageable or unmanageable.
- They come in a variety of port densities.

- There are two basic Fast Ethernet BayStack hubs:

  - 200

  - 250

Each of these is actually a miniature product line in itself. There are four different 200 series hubs and four different 250 series hubs.

200 Series Fast Ethernet BayStack

This series of hubs is made up of the 202, 203, 204, and 205 BayStack hubs. The 202 and the 203 both have built-in NMMs to provide network management through SNMP via the built-in DB-9 serial port or Telnet. The 202 has 12 100BASE-TX RJ-45 ports, and the 203 has 12 100BASE-TX RJ-45 ports and an 100BASE-FX uplink port. These hubs are meant to be used as stand-alone devices or operate in a stack with other 204 and 205 hubs. The 204 has 24 RJ-45 100BASE-TX ports and the 205 has 12 RJ-45 100BASE-TX ports. There is a single Fast Ethernet segment that the hubs connect to when cascaded together. Up to 8 hubs can be cascaded together for a total of 192 unmanaged ports or 180 managed ports.

250 Series Fast Ethernet BayStack

This series of hubs is made up of the 250, 251, 252, and 253 BayStack hubs. Each of these hubs contains two segments: one 10 Mbps and one 100 Mbps. The 250 and 253 are considered the *master* hubs and have internal NMMs. They also have an internal bridge to provide bridging from a 10 Mbps segment to a 100 Mbps segment. Without a 250 or 253 in the stack, there is no connectivity from the 10 Mbps segment to the 100 Mbps segment. With a 250 or 253 in the stack, there is complete connectivity for all the hubs in the stack for both cascaded segments. All of the hubs have 10/100 autosensing ports and a full stack can support 125 managed ports. The 250 and 251 hubs each have 12 RJ-45 ports and the 252 and 253 each have 24 ports. The 253 has an additional fiber uplink port. You can have multiple 250 or 253 hubs in the same stack to provide master hub redundancy. Port redundancy is also configurable via Optivity.

The 50x BayStack Token Ring Hub

The 50x BayStack Token Ring hub provides high port density, flexibility, and manageability to Token Ring users and administrators who need new Token Ring equipment. The 50x has 24 ports on an optional MDA module for ring-in/ring-out ports that can be installed in the MDA slot, support for both STP and UTP cabling, support for an external RPSU, and an optional management and multiring expansion module.

There are four types of hub in the 50x series:

- 501
- 502—Standard NMM
- 503—Advanced NMM
- 504—Advanced Analyzer NMM

The 501, 502, and 503 are upgradeable by removing the cover of the hub and placing a new NMM inside.

Up to seven hubs can be cascaded together to create a single ring with 156 users, or if multiring expansion modules are used, up to 12 hubs can be configured to support 288 users across up to 48 rings. The multiring expansion module provides cascade up and down ports (just like on the Ethernet BayStack product line) and adds port-level clustering to the hub. The module also creates four hub-level rings and four cascaded rings. A hub with a management module can use its first six RJ-45 ports to cascade to remote hubs (by connecting to one of the remote hub's first six ports) that are not managed via a straight-through cable of up to 100 meters. You cannot connect two managed hubs or two cascade hubs together using front ports. The modular ring-in/ring-out ports can be used to attach to older equipment (like an IBM 8228) to extend the ring.

Token Ring Network Design and Troubleshooting

Token Ring networks need to be very carefully designed. There are a number of things you should pay attention to:

- Type of cable used
- Trunk cable distances
- Lobe cable distances
- Choice of modules
- Data rate requirements

- Station counts

- Multivendor products and support in a mixed environment

Factors Affecting Cable Types and Distance

Cable length and cable type can be affected by a number of different factors. Jitter is one problem that affects regenerated signals. Each time the signal is regenerated, its timing in relation to that of the original signal is thrown slightly off, to the point that it can become unrecognizable after enough regenerations. To compensate for this jitter, we limit the number of stations on the ring. The active monitor also has the capability to remove some of the effects of jitter. Also, the EMT can be used to filter out this effect in older System 5000 modules.

Attenuation is the weakening of a signal over distance. The longer the cable, the greater the attenuation. The effects of attenuation are greater on UTP than on STP, and fiber suffers from attenuation the least of all.

Crosstalk is the leaking of the electromagnetic signal from one cable to another causing errors. This is affected by signal strength and the length of the cables. The effects of crosstalk can be reduced by twisting the cables around each other. This is where twisted-pair cables come from. The more the cable is twisted, the less it suffers from crosstalk.

Passive host modules require the use of shorter lobe cables (the cable connecting the workstation to the hub) because they do not regenerate their signals. Active host modules regenerate signals so they allow for longer lobe cables. Also, the use of 16 Mbps reduces the maximum length of a cable compared to 4 Mbps because the higher data rate is more susceptible to factors that would corrupt the signal over distance.

UTP is the least favorable cable for use in Token Ring networks because it suffers the most from crosstalk, attenuation, and other factors. STP is the standard cable for use in Token Ring networks. Fiber is least affected by any of these problems and offers great distances even over high data rates. Each networking device has its own specifications for cable length that should be followed.

Factors Affecting Trunk Cable Distances

Trunk cables (the cables used to interconnect Token Ring hubs) are also affected by network conditions and device types. Figure 10-48 is an example of maximum trunk cable length for ring-in/ring-out ports on different System 3000 modules:

Model	Cable Type	Distance
3513	STP	335.5 Meters
3532	STP	335.5 Meters
3517SA	STP	335.5 Meters
3514-ST	Fiber	2,000 Meters
3534	Fiber	2,000 Meters
351717-SA	Fiber	2,000 Meters

Figure 10-48   Trunk cable maximum length

Factors Affected by the Choice of Module

It is important to not exceed the maximum number of allowed stations on a Token Ring. You may forget to consider that not only workstations and servers count as stations on a Token Ring. Other networking components (router ports, bridge ports, and so on) also need to be counted as stations on the ring. Figure 10-49 is a chart of Nortel Networks Token Ring hub devices that are equivalent to stations on a ring.

It is also important to note the manufacturer's stated maximum stations per ring for the particular networking device. Refer to the documentation that comes with each device to see what it supports.

Backbones

There are three backbone configurations that are used in Token Ring networks:

- Distributed
- Sequential
- Collapsed

The distributed backbone (see Figure 10-50) features internetworking devices located in wiring closets (just like in the Ethernet distributed backbone) and resources (like servers) are located close to the users. The idea is to keep the users close to the servers that they access most of the time (70 percent) and let them connect to servers that they use less (30 percent) often via internetworking devices such as bridges and routers. This was known as the *70-30 rule*. In this design, the backbone is added to as the network grows. The advantage of such a design is that there is no single point of fail-

Model	Description	Station Equivalent	
5575A-x	Host module	1 per trunk connection	
5511	DCE		1
5510	NMM		1
5505P	Host module	1 per ring	
5505PS	Host module	1 per ring	
3513	NMM		5
3514-ST	NMM		5
3517SA	NMM		4
3522, 2722	Local bridge		1
3532	Repeater module		4
3534-ST	Fiber optic repeater module		4
354-ST	Fiber optic extender		1
3504-ST	Fiber optic host module		1

Figure 10-49   Station equivalents

ure. When an internetworking device goes down, only one segment is affected. The greatest disadvantage is that it is more difficult to administer because resources are scattered around the network.

The sequential backbone still has servers and resources and internetworking devices located close to the users (like the distributed backbone), but there is a true backbone laid out that is accessible to each floor (see Figure 10-51). The backbone is attached to via a backbone ring in the chassis. The users are kept on a separate user ring in the chassis and the two rings are bridged together. The main advantages are the ready accessibility of the backbone, a lack of a single point of failure, and enhanced manageability. The main disadvantage is the cost because this model requires additional internetworking devices and NMMs.

The collapsed backbone houses all the resources in the data center (just like in the Ethernet collapsed backbone) along with all of the internetworking devices (Figure 10-52). The entire backbone is located in the data center and the user rings are bridged onto it via the bridges located in the data center. The advantages of such a design are that management is greatly simplified because all of the resources are now located in a single location. The disadvantages are that physical limitations may prevent a pure collapsed backbone from being developed at given locations and that a single point of failure exists in the data center if reliability and redundancy are not planned into the design.

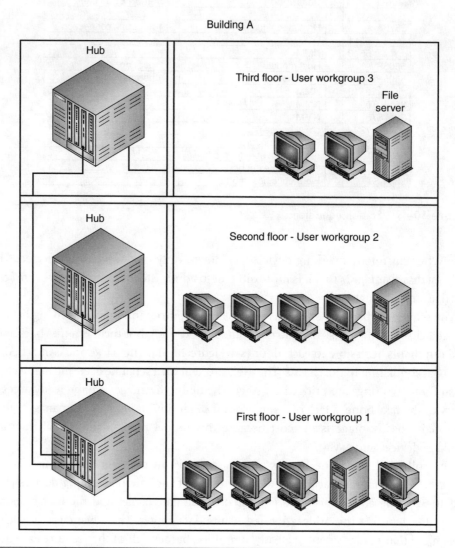

Figure 10-50   Distributed backbone

Building A

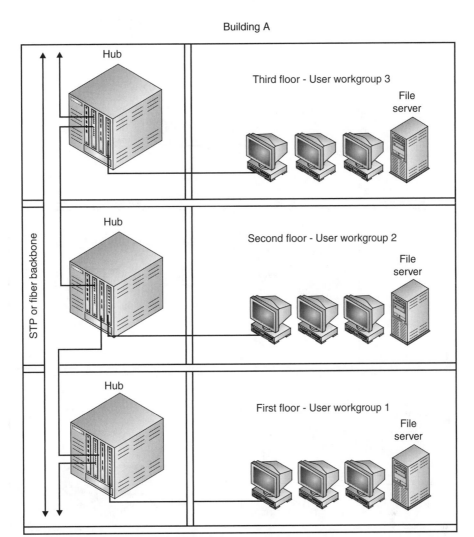

Figure 10-51 Sequential backbone

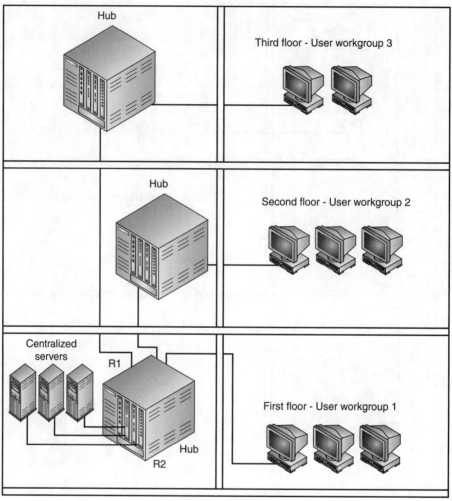

Figure 10-52   Collapsed backbone

Questions

1. The primary purpose of a hub is to _____.
   A. Route traffic between two or more networks
   B. Provide translation between different MAC layer protocols
   C. Provide connectivity between two or more devices on the same network
   D. Manage network devices

2. For communication to occur between two devices, we need to ensure that _____.
   A. TX traffic from device A is sent to the TX pair of device B
   B. TX traffic from device A is sent to the RX pair of device B
   C. RX traffic from device A is sent to the RX pair of device B
   D. None of the above

3. A port that moves TX traffic to the RX pair of the receiver is referred to as a _____.
   A. MDI-X port
   B. MIDI port
   C. MDI port
   D. DCE port

4. Which of the following are types of hubs? (Choose all that apply.)
   A. Stackable
   B. Divisible
   C. Modular
   D. Manageable
   E. Bridge

5. Which of the following are examples of stackable hubs? (Choose all that apply.)
   A. 5000BHC
   B. D5000
   C. BayStack 250
   D. 3000F

6. Backplane segments are _____.
   A. Shared among multiple devices by means of an external cable
   B. Switched connections that limit the extent of the collision domain
   C. Inflexible and not implemented in modern hardware
   D. On the circuit board that joins the modules together in the chassis

7. A module with the model number 5308P would best be described as
   _____.
   A. A System 5000 Ethernet host module for 10BASE-T networks with port-level clusters
   B. A System 5000 Token Ring host module for UTP with port-level clusters
   C. A System 5000 Ethernet NMM for 10BASE-T networks
   D. A System 5000 Ethernet host module for 10BASE-T networks with module-level clustering

8. The System 3000 chassis is capable of supporting which technologies? (Choose all that apply.)
   A. Ethernet
   B. Token Ring
   C. ATM
   D. FDDI
   E. Fast Ethernet

9. How many power supplies can be installed in a System 3000 chassis with the model number 3000NTR?
   A. One
   B. Two
   C. Three
   D. Four

10. How many slots are in a System 3000 chassis?
    A. 8
    B. 10
    C. 12
    D. 14

11. What is the maximum number of Ethernet host modules that can function in a System 3000 chassis?
    A. 11
    B. 12
    C. 7
    D. 14

12. The method for dividing the A channel backplane Ethernet segments in a System 3000 chassis is _____.
    A. Terminating resistors
    B. Optivity

    C. DIP switches

    D. The A channel is a single continuous segment and cannot be divideds

13. How many Ethernet backplane segments are there in a System 3000 chassis with a redundant power supply?

    A. Three

    B. Four

    C. Five

    D. Six

14. A System 3000 chassis with 1 3310A/SA NMM and 11 3307HD modules can support how many 10BASE-T connections?

    A. 132

    B. 182

    C. 172

    D. 264

15. What is the minimum information that is necessary to configure for an NMM to provide SNMP management across a routed network? (Choose all that apply.)

    A. IP address

    B. Subnet mask

    C. Encryption

    D. Default gateway

16. There are a total of how many backplane Token Rings on a System 3000 backplane?

    A. One

    B. Two

    C. Five

    D. Nine

17. How many NMMs are required for two Token Rings to function as a System 3000 chassis?

    A. One

    B. Two

    C. Three

    D. None of the above

18. How many redundant power supplies are supported in a System 5000 chassis?

    A. One

    B. Two

C. Three

D. Four

19. How many backplane Ethernet segments can be utilized in a System 5000 chassis at the same time if only two 5308P modules are installed and there are no NMMs?

    A. 0

    B. 2

    C. 12

    D. None of the above

20. True/False

    The supervisory module is necessary for the System 5000 chassis to function.

21. The 5005 chassis supports how many power supplies?

    A. One

    B. Two

    C. Three

    D. Four

22. How many Token Rings are supported in a single stack of D5000s?

    A. One

    B. Two

    C. One per chassis

    D. None

23. How many Ethernet segments total are in a fully populated stack of D5000s?

    A. 27

    B. 3

    C. 12

    D. 11

24. True/False

    The best place to install a BayStack 100 or 150 would be in a data center.

25. Which is a drawback of the collapsed backbone network design?

    A. Management issues in an environment where all the resources are located in a single space

    B. Security issues arising from the location of all resources in a single area

    C. A single point of failure possibly causing a catastrophic network breakdown

    D. All of the above

26. The 5-4-3 rule dictates that _____.

    A. Five repeaters may be used to connect four segments together, three of which may be populated

    B. Five segments may be connected by four repeaters and three of the segments may be populated

    C. Five users may be on each of four segments, three of which are connected to repeaters

    D. None of the above

27. The difference between Ethernet (10 Mbps) and Fast Ethernet (100 Mbps) is what?

    A. Fast Ethernet uses very fast media to move each bit faster.

    B. Fast Ethernet uses multiple lines to move more data.

    C. Fast Ethernet makes each bit smaller so that more of them may be transported in the same amount of time.

    D. Fast Ethernet is compatible with 802.5 and therefore causes no collisions that would slow down transmission.

28. Full-duplex communication can occur between which devices?

    A. A switch and a hub

    B. A hub and another hub

    C. A hub and a router

    D. A switch and a router

Answers

1. C. The primary purpose of a hub is to provide connectivity between two or more devices on the same network using the same MAC layer protocols. The routing of traffic between different networks is the primary purpose of a router (a layer 3 device). Providing translation between different MAC layer protocols is done by a router (a layer 3 device) or a translational bridge (a layer 2 device). The management of network devices may or may not be a feature of any given hub, but that is not the hub's primary purpose.

2. B. Transmitted traffic (TX) from device A needs to be sent to the RX pair of device B for communication to occur. Just as when you talk (transmit), your voice needs to reach the ears (receive) of the person that you with which want to communicate. TX traffic from device A sent to the TX pair of device B is the equivalent of talking into someone else's mouth (we will not discuss that here). RX traffic from device A sent to the RX pair of device B is the equivalent of sitting with your ear next to someone else's ear waiting for his or her ear to send something to you (we will not discuss that here either).

3. **A.** The MDI-X function is the crossing over of data from one pair (the TX pair) over to another pair (the RX pair). This is a standard function of all hub ports and is required for communication to occur. A MDI port is a port that does not provide this feature and is used only when connecting to another hub (MDI-X) port.

4. **A, C, and D.** Hubs may be stackable, modular, manageable, or unmanageable. They may be combinations of these. A bridge is not a hub by definition. A bridge is used to separate collision domains within a broadcast domain. All devices (Ethernet) attached to a hub (single segment) are within the same collision domain because they are connected to the same shared media.

5. **B and C.** The D5000 is an example of a stackable/modular hub. The BayStack 250 is an example of a stackable hub. They both can be either managed or unmanaged, and can be connected to cascaded segments (stacked). The 5000BHC and 3000F are both examples of modular hubs that are not stackable.

6. **D.** The backplane is the circuit board in the chassis to which all modules attach and it provides connectivity between the modules in the chassis. A backplane segment is an Ethernet segment that all the Ethernet modules can connect to as if they were all one big hub. All Ethernet devices on the same segment are part of the same collision domain and a single repeater hop. Segments that are shared among multiple devices by means of an external cable are cascaded segments like those in a stack of BayStack 250s. Switched connections are in bridged or switched environments and not in hubs.

7. **A.** The breakdown of the numbering method for modules with the 5308P model number is the following.

   5 = System 5000

   3 = Ethernet

   0 = Host module

   8 = 10BASE-T

   P = Port-level clusters

8. **A, B, D, and E.** There is no ATM support for the System 3000.

9. **B.** The *R* stands for redundant power supply. A chassis with a backplane that supports redundant power supplies can support a maximum of two power supplies.

10. **C.**

11. **A.** The number of slots in a System 3000 chassis is 12. If these 12 slots are configured to be a single Ethernet segment, then a maximum of 11 Ethernet host modules may be installed in the chassis because 1 module per segment must be a module that provides timing. There are two types of Ethernet modules that provide timing: the NMM and the retiming module. Neither of the two modules that provide timing are host modules. Therefore, the formula for determining the maximum number of Ethernet host modules that can function on a segment in a System 3000 chassis is

    $X - 1$ = Max number of host modules on the segment

    X = The number of slots on the segment

12. **A.** Three terminating resistors on the backplane are used to divide the A channel Ethernet segment into four separate segments. The B channel is a single continuous segment and cannot be divided. Optivity cannot change the segmentation of the A channel because that is dependent on the physical positioning of the terminating resistors, which cannot be moved via Optivity.

13. **B.** When the redundant power supply is installed in a System 3000 chassis, it fills up 3 of the 12 available slots (2 slots for the power supply and 1 more slot for the summing module), leaving a total of 9 slots. There are normally four backplane Ethernet segments on the A channel, but the fourth segment is four slots wide (slots 9–12). If we remove three of those slots for the extra power supply and summing module, it only leaves one slot for the segment. The technology in a System 3000 does not allow for a single-slot segment because a timing module is required for a segment to function and there are no host modules for Ethernet that provide timing; therefore, a single-slot segment is useless. For that reason, all chassis that support redundant power supplies have only three backplane Ethernet segments on the A channel and they are four, two, and three slots wide, respectively.

14. **D.** Each 3307HD module supports 24 10BASE-T connections over 50-pin telco connectors: $24 \times 11 = 264$ connections.

15. **A, B, and D.** The IP address, subnet mask, and default gateway must be configured on an NMM for it to be able to provide SNMP-based management on an IP

routed network. The community strings that are necessary for SNMP-based management have default values that will function perfectly well, but are a security liability because they are well known.

16. **B.**

17. **D.** No Token Ring NMMs are required for Token Ring to function in a System 300 chassis regardless of the number of rings being utilized.

18. **C.**

19. **C.** There is no limitation on the number of segments that are utilized at one time and no requirement to use even a single NMM in the chassis at all. Timing is provided from the system clock modules installed in the chassis backplane. Because a 5308P module has port-level clusters, we have a total of 48 ports that can be divided among as many of the backplane segments as we choose.

20. **False.**

21. **B.**

22. **D.** The D5000 is an Ethernet-only device. There is no support for Token Ring or any other technology.

23. **A.** There are a total of three local Ethernet segments per chassis. There may be a total of eight chassis per stack: $8 \times 3 = 24$ local Ethernet segments. There are an additional three cascaded Ethernet segments: $24 + 3 = 27$.

24. **False.** The BayStack 100 and 150 are designed as cost-effective solutions that are designed to grow with your needs and give a small initial investment. Although the BayStack product line does offer a fairly high port density, it does not offer the wide range of technologies and flexibility of a System 5000 solution, which is the preferred hub for a data center solution.

25. **C.** The problem with the collapsed backbone is that if not enough attention is paid to reliability and redundancy, then a problem with a single piece of equipment could cause a network-wide failure. The security and management problems are normally associated with distributed backbones.

26. **B.** The 5-4-3 rule states that five segments may be connected together by four repeaters and that only three of the segments may be populated.

27. **C.** The main difference between Ethernet and Fast Ethernet is that the bit time in Fast Ethernet has been reduced by a factor of ten. Stated differently, the length of

a Fast Ethernet is one-tenth of that of an Ethernet bit. Because the bits are smaller, more of them can move along the same cable in the same amount of time.

28. **D.** Full-duplex communication is only able to occur across dedicated media. This is because the key to full-duplex communication is the disabling of the Ethernet collision detection function. If we disable collision detection on a dedicated channel, then full-duplex communication is possible. If we disable collision detection on a shared channel, we will cause so many collisions as to render communication impossible. Therefore, anytime that shared media such as a hub is involved, full-duplex communication becomes impossible. The switch and the router are capable of using full-duplex communication because they can have dedicated media between them.

## CHAPTER 11

BayStack Switches

When you go to take your Switching Core Technology Exam (Exam Number 920-016), you will be required to show your familiarity with a number of switching products and ideas. Among these products is, primarily, the BayStack switch line. It is this product line that we will be examining in this chapter (the other switching products such as the Accellar and the Centillion, which have their own exams, as well as the technology involved, will be treated in their own chapters). It is important to note that although you may currently work in an environment that has a large number of hubs, current trends and needs for high bandwidth and other services (such as virtual local area networks [VLANs]or quality of service [QoS]) dictate that new network implementations will rely almost exclusively on switches both in the data center and the wiring closet. The BayStack line of switches is very versatile and popular today, and it is constantly being improved.

 NOTE Please forgive the repetitive nature of much of the material in this chapter. The devices being described here are all of the same product line and therefore have many features or services in common.

Exam Objectives

On the exam, you will be expected to show your knowledge of the following topics:

- Identify the differences between bridging and routing.
- Match the various components of an 802.3 Ethernet frame with its function.

- Identify the correct definition of a collision domain.

- Identify the correct definition of a broadcast domain.

- Match the definitions that correspond to the first three layers of the Open Standards Interface (OSI) model.

- Match the following terms with their definitions: repeater, bridge, router, and transceiver.

- Identify the correct definition for Carrier Sense Multiple Access with Collision Detection (CSMA/CD).

- List the various speeds at which a standards-based implementation of Ethernet operates.

- Match the following terms with their definitions: twisted pair, fiber optics, and coax.

(All of the previous topics have been dealt with in Chapter 2.)

- Identify the features and functions of the Spanning Tree Protocol.

- List the characteristics of a learning bridge.

- Identify the flooding, forwarding, and learning process of transparent bridges.

- Identify the characteristics of Transparent Bridging.

- Identify the characteristics of Source Route Bridging.

- Identify the function of a routing table on a network bridge.

- Match the definitions to the various types of VLANs.

- Identify the function and application of the proposed 801.1Q specification.

- List the steps for VLAN formation in both cell- and frame-switched environments.

- Identify differences between cut-through and store-and-forward switching.

- Identify the characteristics of frame- and cell-switching technologies.

(All of the previous topics have been dealt with in Chapter 3.)

- Identify the difference between a Permanent Virtual Circuit (PVC) and a Switched Virtual Circuit (SVC).

- Match the LECS, LAN Emulation Client (LEC), LAN Emulation Server (LES), and Broadcast Unknown Server (BUS) with the appropriate definition.

- Identify a Permanent Virtual Path (PVP).

- Match the terms PVC and PVP.

- Identify various types (ATM Adaptation Layers [AALs]) and their uses.

- Identify user-to-network interface (UNI) and network-to-network interface (NNI) differences.

- List the functions of each LAN Emulation (LANE) component.

- List how LANE services Virtual Channel Connections (VCCs) are established.

- Identify the functions of Interim Link Management Interface (ILMI).

(All of the previous topics have been dealt with in Chapter 8.)

- Identify instances where BayStack 350/350T-FHD would be used.

- List the hardware features of the BayStack 350/350T-FHD switches.

- List the software features of the BayStack 350/350T-FHD.

- Identify the configuration parameters and requirements of the BayStack 350/350T-FHD switches.

- List, in order, the steps required to implement VLANs on BayStack 350/350T-FHD switches.

- Identify the upgrade process for the BayStack 350/350T-FHD switches.

- List, in order, the steps to configure MultiLink Trunking (MLT) on a BayStack 350.

- Identify instances where BayStack 303/304 switches would be used.

- List the hardware features of the 303/304 switches.

- Identify the configuration parameters and requirements of the BayStack 303/04 switches.

- List the advanced features of the BayStack 303/304 switches.

- Identify instances where BayStack 450 switches would be used.

- List the hardware features of the BayStack 450 switches.

- List the software features of the 450 switches.

- Identify the configuration parameters and requirements for the BayStack 450 switches.

- List, in order, the steps required to implement VLANs on the BayStack 450 switches.

- Identify the upgrade process for the BayStack 450 switches.

All of the remaining material (that material not specified as being covered in another chapter) will be covered here.

The BayStack 303/304

The BayStack 303/304 are a pair of Ethernet/Fast Ethernet switches designed to be user-friendly and cost-effective. Ready to run right out of the box, they require little if any configuration, while also being fully manageable switches with a number of supported features to answer many connectivity needs. They come in two basic configurations and have an optional expansion module slot for added connectivity. The BayStack 303/304 are the entry-level switches for solutions that require flexibility and growth, but not all the bells and whistles (as well as costs) of a higher-end product.

The BayStack 303

The BayStack 303 has 24 10BASE-T ports. Its twenty-fifth port is 10/100 BASE-TX and the expansion module slot accommodates either one additional 10/100 BASE-TX port (10/100 BASE-TX MDA) or a 100BASE-FX port (100BASE-FX MDA).

 NOTE The Media-Dependant Adapter (MDA) enables a modular switch to be configured with a port(s) that matches the desired cable type. This adds flexibility and functionality to the switch.

The BayStack 304

The BayStack 304 has 12 10BASE-T ports. Its thirteenth port is 10/100BASE-TX and the expansion module slot accommodates either one additional 10/100BASE-TX port (10/100 BASE-TX MDA) or a 100BASE-FX port (100BASE-FX MDA).

Both the 303 and the 304 have a serial port for management and light-emitting diodes (LEDs) showing port and switch status located on the front of the switch.

Features

The BayStack 303/304 both have the following features:

- Full-duplex line rate for the aggregate throughput for 64-byte packet sizes:
  - 387206 pps for the 304
  - 476192 pps for the 303

- Address database size of 1,023 addresses without flooding

- Spanning Tree Protocol

- Simple Network Management Protocol (SNMP) support

- Expansion module

- Console/comm port

- Management via

  - Console port menus

  - Telnet menus

  - Web interface (Netscape 3 or Internet Explorer 4 or higher)

  - SNMP

- Store-and-forward switching

- Eight VLANs

- Two address-learning modes on high-speed ports

- Support for Optivity

  - Expanded View

  - Omni View

  - Multisegment Autotopology

- Telnet (up to two simultaneous inbound sessions)

- 802.3U-compliant autonegotiation (each port supports 10 half/full and 100 half/full)

- Port mirroring

- Four Remote Network Monitoring (RMON) groups

- Limited destination address filtering

- LEDs

- Upgradeable firmware via the Trivial File Transfer Protocol (TFTP)

Media-Dependant Adapters (MDAs)

The BayStack 303/304 comes with an Expansion Module slot that supports one of two different MDAs. The 100BASE-FX MDA is used to attach to a 100BASE-FX fiber connection on a switch, hub, or router (probably located in a data center). The SC type connector supports multimode fiber only.

The 10/100BASETX MDA has a single RJ-45 port, which is capable of running in either 10 Mbps or 100 Mbps at either half or full duplex over Category 5 Unshielded Twisted Pair (UTP) cable.

When installing an MDA, remember that the switch must be turned off. The MDAs are not hot swappable.

Console Port

The Console Port (located on the front panel) is the initial point of management for the BayStack 303/304. By connecting the appropriate management cable (standard db-9F to db-9F straight-through serial cable) to the Console Port, you can open a terminal emulation into the Console Interface (CI) of the switch. The settings for the Console Port are

- Baud: 9,600
- Data bits: 8
- Stop bit: 1
- Parity: no
- Flow control: Xon/Xoff

VLANs

The BayStack 303/304 supports eight port-based VLANs. VLAN support enables us to reduce broadcast traffic on network segments by separating devices by function rather than just by physical location. For a review on VLANs, refer to Chapter 3.

Telnet

The BayStack 303/304 supports up to two inbound Telnet sessions. Telnet functionality enables the switch to be managed remotely by any user who has TCP/IP configured on their workstation. Support for multiple inbound sessions enables more than one person to have access to the switch at any one time. In order for Telnet to function, the switch must be configured with an IP address, subnet mask, and a default gateway (if it is to be accessed across a routed network).

Conversation Steering

The BayStack 303/304 support conversation steering for diagnosing network problems and monitoring network usage. Conversation steering enables the network administrator to copy all traffic to and from one port (the monitored port) to another port (the monitoring port) where a network management device such as a Sniffer or other device is located. Only one port on a BayStack 303/304 can be monitored at a time.

Security

Security on a BayStack 303/304 revolves around SNMP community strings, passwords, and destination address filtering. SNMP community strings help identify SNMP requests from authorized users. The SNMP community string is a simple security method for identifying managers. Two types of community strings are used:

- Read-only
- Read-write

Users whose SNMP community strings match the read-only string may view switch parameters through an SNMP management station, but they will not be able to change any values. Users whose SNMP community strings match the read-write community string will be able to read and write to the switch's configuration. Read-write access gives the user the ability to change the operating parameters of the switch.

Passwords determine management via Telnet, a web interface, or the console. When a user attempts to use one of these interfaces, he or she is prompted for a password. Supplying the correct password will give the user access to manage the switch.

Destination address filtering enables a network administrator to enter up to eight Media Access Control (MAC) addresses into the switch's filtering database. This causes the switch to drop all packets addressed to one of these addresses, eliminating communication to that address via the switch. If the switch's address is entered, this causes the switch to drop all packets destined for the switch's MAC address. This has the effect of disabling all forms of remote management, forcing the administrator to use the console interface to manage the switch.

Configurations

The flexibility of the BayStack 303/304 lends itself to a wide variety of uses (such as network configurations or applications). The most commonly used applications are as follows:

- Desktop switch application
- Segment switch application
- High-density switched workgroup application

Desktop Switch Application

This configuration places the switch in the wiring closet, replacing the hub. This application has the user workstations connecting directly to the switch with a dedicated 100-Mbps connection to the data center. With the hub, all the users contend for the same bandwidth, yet here we have all the users receiving their own dedicated connection (causing a great increase in bandwidth available to the users).

Segment Switch Application

This configuration places the switch either in a large wiring closet or in the data center. We use BayStack 303/304 as the backbone and connect the other hubs/switches on that floor into individual ports on the 303/304. Again, we have a dedicated high-speed connection to the data center. This greatly reduces the number of users competing for the same shared media bandwidth.

High-Density Switched Workgroup Application

In this case, the users require an even greater increase in performance to the data center. We still connect users and servers to the BayStack 303/304s, but then we collapse the 303/304s back into a BayStack 350 or 450. We then use a dedicated Gigabit Ethernet port from the 350/450 to connect to other workgroups and the data center via an Accellar (Passport) 1xxx/86xx.

The BayStack 350

The BayStack 350 is a versatile yet cost-effective solution to many networking needs. Two different models and an array of MDAs give the BayStack 350 Ethernet, Fast Ethernet, Gigabit Ethernet, Asynchronous Transfer Mode (ATM) functionality, as well as a wide array of uses. This device is a midlevel solution, providing more functionality and flexibility than the BayStack 303/304 while still being not too heavy a solution to put in a wiring closet.

Physical Description

The BayStack 350 comes in two models:

- 350-24T
- 350-12T

The 350-24T has 24 RJ-45 connectors on the front panel for user/server and inter-switch connectivity. They support standard 10BASE-T/100BASETX connections with CAT 5 UTP cable. All these ports are MDI-X. A modular uplink/expansion module slot is available as well for expandability (we will visit the various options in this section).

The 350-12T has 12 RJ-45 connectors on the front panel for user/server and inter-switch connectivity.

All BayStack 350 switches support a modular uplink/expansion module slot for expandability, LEDs for port and operating status, and a comm port for switch management. On the rear panel of all BayStack 350s is the AC power receptacle.

Features

All BayStack 350s support the following features:

- A high-speed forwarding rate at up to 3 million pps
- A store-and-forward switch with a 2.56-Gbps switch fabric
- A learning rate of 3 million addresses per second
- An address database size of 32,000 addresses without flooding
- Spanning Tree Protocol
- IEEE 802.1Q port-based VLANs
- SNMP support
- High-speed uplink/expansion module
- Rate/limiting
- Console/comm port
- Internet Group Management Protocol (IGMP) snooping
- IEEE 802.1P prioritizing
- VLANs (802.1Q and protocol)
- Telnet (up to four simultaneous inbound sessions)
- 802.3U-compliant autonegotiation (each port supports 10 half/full and 100 half/full)
- MLT
- Port mirroring
- Four groups of RMON
- Security

PART III

- LEDs

- Configuration file download/upload support

- Upgradeable firmware via TFTP

Some, but not all, of the previous features are defined here. In the interest of space and simplicity, I have tried to limit the information here to what is necessary for managing the device and what will be required for the exam. For more information on all of these features, please refer to the "Using the BayStack 350" document available from Nortel Networks Documentation web site.

High-Speed Uplink/Expansion Module

The high-speed uplink/expansion module (or MDA) gives the BayStack 350 the capability to support a higher port density or added functionality (depending on the MDA chosen). The available MDAs are as follows:

- 10BASE-T/100BASE-TX

- 100BASE-FX

- 1000BASE-SX

- 1000BASE-LX

- ATM

The 10BASE-T/100BASE-TX MDA (400 4TX MDA) adds four RJ-45 ports that can be configured individually. This module is for adding port density without going to the extreme of adding a new switch.

The 100BASE-FX adds either two SC fiber connectors (400-2FX MDA) or four MT-RJ connectors (400-4FX MDA). In both cases, the fiber is multimode only. These modules are typically used to support uplinks to data centers (because they are capable of going distances of up to 2 km). They can be used to connect to servers, workstations, or other switches that support fiber interfaces.

The 1000BASE-SX (S stands for short-wave) is used almost exclusively for high-speed uplinks to data centers. The supported cable type is multimode. This MDA comes in two versions:

- 450-1SX

- 450-1SR

The 1SX has a single-fiber (SC) connector and supports a maximum distance of 550 meters. The 1SR has two physical connectors, but only one can be active at any time. The second connector is for redundancy. When the first port fails, the second port will become active.

The 1000BASE-LX (*L* stands for long-wave) is used almost exclusively for high-speed uplinks to data centers also, but it supports connections over single-mode fiber at a distance of up to 5 km (it also supports multimode fiber for connections of up to 550 meters). Two versions of this MDA are available:

- 450-1LX

- 450-1LR

The 1LX has a single-fiber (SC) connector and is similar to the 450-1SX in function. The 1LR has two physical connectors, but only one can be active at any time. The second connector is for redundancy. When the first port fails, the second port becomes active (similar to the 450-1SR).

The ATM MDA is truly a great addition to the 350 BayStack. It enables up to four ATM forum LANE LECs to be configured on the BayStack 350. Ports on the 350 are assigned to the LEC, which is assigned to an ELAN, and the 350 is connected into an ATM network via the SC fiber connector. The ports operate at OC-3 speed (155 Mbps). ATM MDAs come in two versions:

- 450-2M3

- 450-2S3

Both modules feature two ports that are redundant to each other. These ports can both be active at the same time. If one port fails, traffic is rerouted to the second port. The "M" MDA supports multimode fiber and the "S" MDA supports single-mode fiber.

NOTE   Remember, for ATM theory and LANE configuration, refer to Chapter 5.

Console Port

The Console Port (located on the front panel) is the initial point of management for the BayStack 350. By connecting the appropriate management cable (a standard db-9F to db-9F straight-through serial cable) to the Console Port, you can open a terminal emulation into the Console Interface (CI) of the switch. The settings for the Console Port are as follows:

- Baud: 9,600
- Data bits: 8
- Stop bit: 1
- Parity: No
- Flow control: Xon/Xoff

VLANs

The BayStack 350 supports up to 64 VLANs. Both port-based and protocol VLANs are supported. 802.1Q tagged ports are also configurable. For a review on VLANs, refer to Chapter 3.

Telnet

Telnet functionality supports up to four inbound sessions. Password protection is optional (but highly recommended). Telnet offers a login timeout as well as a failed login guard. An inactivity timeout and an allowed source address also are supported.

MultiLink Trunking (MLT)

MLT gives us the ability to increase throughput and add physical-layer redundancy. MLT is when two or more ports (up to four ports per MLT group and up to six MLT groups per BayStack 350 switch) are configured to act as a single port. They all connect to the same destination (another switch or server), and their bandwidth is added together to form a single large pipe.

For example, if we connect four 100BASE-T ports from one switch to another switch, we can take 100 Mbps × 4 ports = 400 Mbps (multiply that number times 2 if running full duplex). An added bonus is if one of the physical links fails, the remaining links continue to function, thus giving us a measure of fault tolerance and redundancy. You can configure two Gigabit ports in full duplex for a total of 4,000-Mbps throughput. MLT ports in the same MLT group can be distributed. This means that the port members of the MLT group do not need to be next to each other (ports 1, 2, 3, 4).

Port Mirroring

Port mirroring (sometimes referred to as port spanning, port copying, or conversation steering) is used with diagnostic tools (such as an RMON probe or a Sniffer) to view traffic on the network to gauge network activity or troubleshoot a problem. Because, in a switch, traffic is only forwarded to the port it is intended for (the port where the destination device is physically located), ports where a Sniffer is plugged into only receive broadcast frames. Port mirroring tells the switch that all traffic destined for port X is also sent to port Y in addition to port X (where X is the port that has the destination device and Y is the location of the Sniffer). This ensures that our *monitoring* device sees all the traffic that the *monitored* device sees.

Nortel supports two types of port mirroring:

- Port-based mirroring
- Address-based mirroring

Port-based Mirroring   Port-based mirroring simply copies traffic from port X to port Y, as described previously, but a few enhancements have been added as well. The BayStack 350 supports port-based mirroring of all traffic that is

- Received by port X
- Transmitted by port X
- Transmitted and received by port X
- All traffic between port W and port X
- And all combinations of these

Address-based Mirroring   Address-based mirroring supports all of the various combinations that port-based mirroring supports but is based on MAC addresses. This comes in handy when you need to monitor traffic between two devices that are not directly connected to the switch (they are connected to hubs that are connected to the switch). If you used port-based mirroring, you would capture all of the traffic from (and to) all of the devices attached indirectly to those ports. If you use address-based mirroring, you will capture only the traffic with the specified MAC addresses.

Security

The BayStack 350 offers three levels of security. Between them, they enable an administrator to configure who is allowed to access the switch (connect to the switch and pass or receive data) and who can manage the switch. The four types of security offered are as follows:

- MAC address-based security
- Remote Access Dial-In User Service (RADIUS)-based security
- SNMP-based security

MAC Address-based Security   MAC address-based security enables the network administrator to configure a list of MAC addresses (up to 448) that are allowed to connect to the switch. You can also configure specific ports to allow or disallow any MAC address, all of them, or a specific one. The ports can also be configured to send traps, filter, or disable, should a violation occur (or any combination of the three). This is all part of the BaySecure feature available on many Bay/Nortel Network products. To learn more about BaySecure, refer to the Bay Network's Guide to Implementing BaySecure LAN Access For Ethernet (Part number 345-11061).

RADIUS-based Security   RADIUS-based security provides the capability of determining the level of administrative access (read-write or read-only) that a user can have to the switch. This is done through your (separate) RADIUS server (refer to its documentation).

SNMP-based Security   SNMP-based security uses IP filtering to impose administrative access to the switch.

Configurations

The flexibility of the BayStack 350 lends itself to a wide variety of uses (network configurations or applications). The applications most often used are as follows:

- Desktop switch application
- Segment switch application
- High-density switched workgroup application
- ATM application

Desktop Switch Application

This configuration places the switch in the wiring closet, replacing the hub. This application has the user workstations connecting directly to the switch with a dedicated

100-Mbps connection to the data center (the Gig connection is not typically needed in this scenario). With the hub, all the users are contending for the same bandwidth, yet here we have all the users receiving their own dedicated connection (causing a great increase in the bandwidth available to the users).

Segment Switch Application

This configuration places the switch either in a large wiring closet or in the data center. We use a BayStack 350 as the backbone and connect the other hubs/switches on that floor into individual ports on the 350. Again, we have a dedicated high-speed connection to the data center. This greatly reduces the number of users competing for the same shared media bandwidth.

High-Density Switched
Workgroup Application

In this case, the users require an even greater increase in performance to the data center. We still collapse the other hubs/switches into the 350, but then we take a Gig port to connect to an Accellar (Passport) 1000/8600 back in the data center. The advantage here is the greatly increased bandwidth to the data center, giving the users extra performance from the network.

ATM Application

For a long time, in order to connect to an ATM network, you had to connect to an Ethernet or Token Ring port on a Centillion. Now we have the ATM MDA for the BayStack 350 that enables direct connections to an OC-3 interface on an ATMSpeed module in a Centillion switch. The ATM MDA gives us up to four LECs to which any number of ports on the switch can be added.

The BayStack 450

The BayStack 450 is one of the most versatile stackable switch solutions available. It supports a huge number of features as well as high port density, manageability, fault tolerance, and redundancy. It is manageable through the Console Interface (CI), Telnet, Optivity, and Device Manager.

Physical Description

The BayStack 450 comes in three models:

- 450-24T
- 450-12T
- 450-12F

The 450-24T has 24 RJ-45 connectors on the front panel for user/server and inter-switch connectivity. They support standard 10BASE-T/100BASETX connections with CAT 5 UTP cable. All these ports are MDI-X. A modular uplink/expansion module slot is available as well for expandability (we will visit the various options later).

The 450-12T has 12 RJ-45 connectors on the front panel for user/server and inter-switch connectivity.

The 450-12F has 12 MT-RJ port connectors for high-density, fiber-based 100BASE-FX (IEEE 802.3U) connections. They support connections of up to two kilometers over multimode fiber. Single-mode fiber is *not* supported.

All BayStack 450 switches support a modular uplink/expansion module slot for expandability, LEDs for port and operating status, and a comm port for switch management. On the rear panel of all BayStack 450s is the AC power receptacle, the Redundant Power Supply Unit (RPSU), and the Cascade Module Slot. The Cascade Module is part of what makes the BayStack such a flexible and expandable solution and will be discussed later in this chapter.

Features

All BayStack 450s support the following features:

- A high-speed forwarding rate of up to 3 million pps
- A store-and-forward switch with a 2.56-Gbps switch fabric
- A learning rate of 3 million addresses per second
- An address database size of 32,000 addresses without flooding
- Fail-safe stacking
- Spanning Tree Protocol
- SNMP support
- A high-speed uplink/expansion module

- Rate/limiting

- Console/comm port

- IGMP snooping

- IEEE 802.1P prioritizing

- VLANs (802.1Q and protocol)

- Telnet (up to four simultaneous inbound sessions)

- 802.3U-compliant autonegotiation

- MultiLink Trunking (MLT)

- Port mirroring

- Four groups of RMON

- Security

- LEDs

- Configuration file download/upload support

- Upgradeable firmware via TFTP

Some of the previously mentioned features are defined here. For more information on all of these features, please refer to the "Using the Baystack 450" document available from the Nortel Networks Documentation web site.

Fail-Safe Stacking

Fail-safe stacking refers to the capability to connect up to eight BayStack 450s together using a BayStack 400-ST1 cascade module. The module is inserted in the cascade slot in the rear of the chassis and is connected to another cascade module in another BayStack 450, 410, or Business Policy Switch (BPS) (using the cascade cables provided with the module). Each connector in a cascade module is labeled "Cascade A out" (the left connector) or "Cascade A in" (the right connector). The devices are connected by attaching the out connector on one switch to the in connector on another switch. The fail-safe feature is the capability to configure a loop by connecting the topmost and bottommost switches in the stack by using another (longer) cascade cable. This cable provides a redundant path should one of the cables or units in the path fail. The interswitch connections will loop at the point of the failure and the additional cascade cable will maintain the connectivity.

High-Speed Uplink/Expansion Module

The high-speed uplink/expansion module (or MDA) gives the BayStack 450 the capability to support a higher port density or added functionality (depending on the MDA chosen). The available MDAs are as follows:

- 10BASE-T/100BASE-TX
- 100BASE-FX
- 1000BASE-SX
- 1000BASE-LX
- ATM
- Gigabit Interface Converter (GBIC)

The 10BASE-T/100BASE-TX MDA adds four RJ-45 ports that can be configured individually. This module is used for adding port density without going to the extreme of adding a new switch.

The 100BASE-FX adds either two SC fiber connectors or four MT-RJ connectors. In both cases, the fiber is multimode only. These modules are typically used to support uplinks to data centers (because they are capable of going distances of up to 2 km). They can be used to connect to servers, workstations, or other switches that support fiber interfaces.

The 1000BASE-SX (*S* stands for short-wave) is used almost exclusively for high-speed uplinks to data centers. The supported cable type is multimode. Two versions of this MDA are available:

- 450-1SX
- 450-1SR

The 1SX has a single-fiber (SC) connector and supports a maximum distance of 550 meters. The 1SR has two physical connectors, but only one can be active at any time. The second connector is for redundancy. When the first port fails, the second port will become active.

The 1000BASE-LX (*L* stands for long-wave) is used almost exclusively for high-speed uplinks to data centers also, but it supports connections over single-mode fiber at a distance of up to 5 km (it also supports multimode fiber for connections of up to 550 meters). Two versions of this MDA exist:

- 450-1LX
- 450-1LR

The 1LX has a single-fiber (SC) connector and is similar to the 450-1SX in function. The 1LR has two physical connectors, but only one can be active at any time. The second connector is for redundancy. When the first port fails, the second port will become active (similar to the 450-1SR).

The ATM MDA is truly a great addition to the 450 BayStack. It enables up to four ATM forum LANE LECs to be configured on the BayStack 450. Ports on the 450 are assigned to the LEC, which is assigned to an ELAN, and the 450 is connected into an ATM network via the SC fiber connector. The ports operate at OC-3 speed (155 Mbps). Two types of ATM MDAs are available:

- 450-2M3

- 450-2S3

Both modules feature two ports that are redundant to each other. These ports can both be active at the same time. If one port fails, traffic is rerouted to the second port. The "M" MDA supports multimode fiber and the "S" MDA supports single-mode fiber.

NOTE   Remember, for ATM theory and LANE configuration, refer to Chapter 8.

The GBIC module provides a single, hot-swappable port for use with various supported GBICs, which are hot swappable.

NOTE   The MDAs are not hot swappable. The switch should be powered down before installing or replacing an MDA.

Console Port

The Console Port (located on the front panel) is the initial point of management for the BayStack 450. By connecting the appropriate management cable (standard db-9F to db-9F straight-through serial cable) to the Console Port, you can open a terminal emulation into the Console Interface (CI) of the switch. The settings for the Console Port are as follows:

- Baud: 9,600

- Data bits: 8

- Stop bit: 1
- Parity: No
- Flow control: Xon/Xoff

VLANs

The BayStack 450 supports up to 64 VLANs. Both port-based and protocol VLANs are supported. 802.1Q tagged ports are also configurable.

Telnet

Telnet functionality supports up to four inbound sessions. Password protection is optional (but highly recommended). A login timeout is offered as well as a failed login guard. Inactivity timeouts and allowed source addresses also are supported.

MultiLink Trunking (MLT)

MultiLink Trunking (MLT) gives us the ability to increase throughput and add physical-layer redundancy. MLT is when two or more ports (up to four ports per MLT group and up to six MLT groups per switch or stack) are configured to act as a single port. They all connect to the same destination (another switch or server), and their bandwidth is added together to form a single large pipe.

For example, if we connect four 100BASE-T ports from one switch to another, we can take 100 Mbps × 4 ports = 400 Mbps (multiply that number times two if running full duplex). An added bonus is if one of the physical links fails, the remaining links continue to function, thus giving us a measure of fault tolerance and redundancy. We can configure four Gigabit ports in full duplex for a total of 8,000-Mbps throughput. MLT ports in the same MLT group can also be distributed. This means that the port members of the MLY group don't need to be next to each other (ports 1, 2, 3, 4), and they don't even need to be on the same switch. Port 1 on switch 2 can be in a MLT group with port 17 on switch 5 (in a stack configuration). This is a very powerful feature.

Port Mirroring

Port mirroring (sometimes referred to as port spanning, port copying, or conversation steering) is used with diagnostic tools (such as an RMON probe or a Sniffer) to view traffic on the network to gauge network activity or troubleshoot a problem. Because, in a switch, traffic is only forwarded to the port that it is intended for (the port where the destination device is physically located), ports where a Sniffer is plugged into only receive broadcast frames. Port mirroring tells the switch that all traffic destined for port X is also sent to port Y in addition to port X (where X is the port that has the destination device and Y is the location of the Sniffer). This ensures that our *monitoring* device sees all the traffic that the *monitored* device sees.

Nortel supports two types of port mirroring:

- Port-based mirroring
- Address-based mirroring

Port-based Mirroring   Port-based mirroring simply copies traffic from port X to port Y, as described previously, but a few enhancements have been added. The BayStack 450 supports port-based mirroring of all traffic that is

- Received by port X
- Transmitted by port X
- Transmitted and received by port X
- All traffic between port W and port X
- And all combinations of these

Address-based Mirroring   Address-based mirroring supports all of the various combinations that port-based mirroring does but is based on MAC addresses. This comes in handy when you need to monitor traffic between two devices that are not directly connected to the switch (they are connected to hubs that are connected to the switch). If you use port-based mirroring, you would capture all of the traffic from (and to) all of the devices attached indirectly to those ports. If you use address-based mirroring, you will capture only the traffic with the specified MAC addresses.

Security

The BayStack 450 offers four levels of security. Between them, they enable an administrator to configure who is allowed to access the switch (who can connect to the switch and pass/receive data) and who can manage the switch. The four types of security offered are as follows:

- MAC address-based security
- EAPOL-based security
- RADIUS-based security
- SNMP-based security

MAC Address-based Security   MAC address-based security enables the network administrator to configure a list of MAC addresses (up to 448) that are allowed to connect to the switch (or stack). You can also configure specific ports to allow or disallow any MAC address, all of them, or a specific one. The ports can also be configured to send traps, filter, or disable, should a violation occur (or any combination of the three). This is all part of the BaySecure feature available on many Bay/Nortel Network products. To learn more about BaySecure, refer to the Bay Network's Guide to Implementing BaySecure LAN Access For Ethernet (Part number 345-11061).

EAPOL-based Security   EAPOL-based security gives the network administrator the ability to use Extensible Authentication Protocol (EAP) to determine how a device connects to a switch. It can (in conjunction with a RADIUS server) enable or disable users from accessing a switch and even dynamically assign ports to VLANs based on authentication credentials.

RADIUS-based Security   RADIUS-based security gives you the ability to determine the level of administrative access (read-write or read-only) that a user can have to the switch. This is done through your (separate) RADIUS server (refer to its documentation).

SNMP-based Security   SNMP-based security uses IP filtering to impose administrative access to the switch.

Configurations

The flexibility of the BayStack 450 lends itself to a wide variety of uses (such as for network configurations or applications). The applications most commonly used are as follows:

- Desktop switch application
- Segment switch application
- High-density switched workgroup application
- ATM application
- Fail-safe stack application

Desktop Switch Application

This configuration places the switch in the wiring closet, replacing the hub. This application has the user workstations connecting directly to the switch with a dedicated 100-Mbps connection to the data center (the Gig connection is not typically needed in this scenario). With the hub, all the users are contending for the same bandwidth, yet here we have all the users receiving their own dedicated connection (causing a great increase in bandwidth available to the users).

Segment Switch Application

This configuration places the switch either in a large wiring closet or in the data center. We use a BayStack 450 as the backbone and connect the other hubs/switches on that floor into individual ports on the 450. Again, we have a dedicated high-speed connection to the data center. This greatly reduces the number of users competing for the same shared media bandwidth.

High-Density Switched Workgroup Application

In this case, the users require an even greater increase in performance to the data center. We still collapse the other hubs/switches into the 450, but then we take a Gig port to connect to an Accellar (Passport) 1000/8600 back in the data center. The advantage here is the greatly increased bandwidth to the data center, giving the users extra performance from the network.

ATM Application

For a long time, in order to connect to an ATM network, connecting to an Ethernet or Token Ring port had to be done on a Centillion. Now the ATM MDA for the BayStack 450 enables us to connect directly to an OC-3 interface on an ATMSpeed module in a Centillion switch. The ATM MDA gives us up to four LECs to which any number of ports on the switch can be added. This can be done with a stand-alone switch or a stacked configuration.

Fail-Safe Stack Application

When we have a stacked configuration of 450s (using the cascade modules), we can make use of the extra cascade cable going from the last unit in the stack back to the first unit in the stack to ensure that if any single unit in the stack fails, data will always have a path to any of the remaining switches. If we combine this with the MLT feature for connectivity back into the data center, we can see that a complete loss of connectivity is going to be a rare occurrence (if ever).

Review Questions

1. Which of the following is not a feature of the BayStack 350?
   A. Spanning Tree Protocol
   B. 802.1Q support

    C. 802.1P support

    D. Cascade module support

2. How many VLANs does the BayStack 350 support?

    A. 8

    B. 16

    C. 32

    D. 64

    E. None of the above

3. True/False

The BayStack 350 is a cut-through switch.

4. Which MDA is not supported on the BayStack 350? (Choose two.)

    A. 10BASE-T/1-BASE-TX MDA

    B. 100BASE-FX MDA

    C. 1000BASE-SX

    D. 1000BASE-PX

    E. ATM

    F. FDDI

5. Which MDA supports connections over single-mode fiber?

    A. 1000BASE-SX

    B. 100BASE-FX

    C. 100BASE-TX

    D. 1000BASE-LX

6. MultiLink Trunking (MLT) supports up to _____ ports per MLT group and up to _____ MLT groups per switch.

    A. Two, four

    B. Four, six

    C. Four, two

    D. Four, four

7. Which of the following ports can be in an MLT group together?

    A. 1, 2, 3, 4

    B. 1, 3, 5, 6

    C. None of the above

    D. A and B

8. Port mirroring is supported on the BayStack 350 in order to . . .
   A. Copy traffic to a network-monitoring device.
   B. Keep broadcast traffic off specified segments.
   C. Increase security.
   D. Increase throughput.

9. True/False
   Port mirroring can be configured on a BayStack 350 to copy all traffic in a conversation between MAC address A and MAC address B.

10. True/False
    MAC-based security enables a network administrator to configure a list of MAC addresses that are allowed to manage a switch.

11. The BayStack 350 supports which of the following security systems? (Choose three.)
    A. SNMP
    B. RADIUS
    C. TACACS
    D. MAC address-based
    E. Secure ID

12. Which of the following network configurations does the BayStack 350 not support?
    A. Desktop switch application
    B. Segment switch application
    C. High-density switch application
    D. ATM application
    E. Fail-safe switch application

13. The BayStack 450 comes in which three configurations?
    A. 24-port fiber
    B. 24-port RJ-45
    C. 12-port RJ-45
    D. 12-port fiber

14. Which of the following is not a feature of the BayStack 450?
    A. 802.1Q support
    B. 802.1P support
    C. Cascade
    D. 802.5 support

15. The BayStack 450 is manageable through . . .
   A. CI, Telnet, Optivity, Device Manager
   B. CI, Telnet, Optivity, Switch Manager
   C. CI, Telnet, Optivity, Site Manager
   D. CI, Telnet, Optivity, SpeedView

16. How many BayStack 450s are the maximum that can be in a single stack?
   A. Six
   B. Eight
   C. Ten
   D. One per NMM

17. A BayStack 450 can exist in a stack with which of the following switches? (Choose all that apply.)
   A. Other 450s
   B. 410
   C. BPS
   D. 350

18. A BayStack 450 can have a maximum of _____ 100BASE-TX ports.
   A. 12
   B. 24
   C. 26
   D. 28

19. The BayStack 303 switch can . . .
   A. Support up to two 1000BASE-SX ports.
   B. Support up to 24 MT-RJ ports.
   C. Support up to 25 RJ-45 ports.
   D. Support up to 24 100BASE-2 ports.

20. Which of the following is not a feature of the BayStack 304?
   A. Store-and-forward switching
   B. 802.1Q
   C. 802.1D
   D. 802.3U

21. When connecting to the console port of a BayStack 303/304 , the terminal should not be configured . . .
   A. With 14.4K baud
   B. Without parity.

C. With eight bits

D. With one stop bit

22. The switch needs which of the following to be configured for proper switching to occur before it can be placed in a live network? (Choose all that apply.)

A. IP address

B. Subnet mask

C. SNMP community strings

D. VLANs

E. None of the above

Answers

1. **D.** A physical examination of the BayStack 350 will reveal that no location for a Cascade module needs to be inserted. This feature is available only on BayStack 410s, 450s, and 460s (business policy switch).

2. **D.** Both the BayStack 350 and 450 support 64 VLANs. The BayStack 303/304 only support eight.

3. **False.** All BayStack switches are store-and-forward switches. This means that the switch buffers the entire frame and performs an Frame Check Sequence (FCS) before forwarding.

4. **D and F.** These modules do not exist. The BayStack product line doesn't offer support for FDDI and there is no 1000BASE-PX module.

5. **D.** The 1000BASE-LX MDA supports single-mode fiber.

6. **B.**

7. **D.** Any combination of ports can be in an MTL group. No limitations exist concerning the physical location of any port members of an MLT group.

8. **A.** Port mirroring copies traffic from one location on a switch to another place on a switch that is dependant on defined criteria (port, source address, or conversation) that the switch supports. This is necessary in a switched environment because unicast traffic is not transmitted to all ports as in a shared media (hub) environment. This makes network-monitoring devices like a Sniffer useless unless some method of copying traffic to a desired location is used.

9. **True.** This feature is supported on the BayStack 350 and 450.

10. **False.** MAC address-based security enables a list of MAC addresses to be configured that are allowed to connect to the switch to send and receive traffic. It has nothing to do (directly) with the capability to manage a switch.

11. **A, B,** and **D.** TACACS is the property of Cisco, and SecureID is not supported.

12. **E.** The BayStack 350 has no support for the stacking feature. Only the 4xx models support that feature.

13. **B, C,** and **D.**

14. **D.** 802.5 is Token Ring and is not supported by the BayStack 450.

15. **A.** Switch Manager, Site Manager, and SpeedView are not supported for the BayStack product line.

16. **B.** Eight switches are supported in a stack.

17. **A, B,** and **C.** All switches in the 4xx line (450, 410, and the 460) support the cascade feature and can coexist in one stack.

18. **D.** These are 24 fixed ports plus four ports from the 10/100 BASE-TX MDA.

19. **C.**

20. **B.** The BayStack 304 does not support 802.1Q.

21. **A.** The supported speed of the connection is 9600 bps.

22. **E.** None of the BayStack switches needs to be configured in order to support network connectivity. All of the configurable parameters add flexibility and manageability to the network design but are not necessary to support connectivity in a single VLAN.

Passport 1000 and 8000 Series Switches

In this chapter we will discuss the Nortel Networks Passport 1000 and 8000 series of products. It is important to note that this product was originally known as the Accelar series. This chapter directly relates to the Using the Accelar 1000 (V2.0) exam, which is being discontinued at this time. A replacement exam is under development that will cover later versions of the Passport software and hardware as well as the 8000 product line. This chapter can be useful to administrators who do not want to take the Passport exam, but do need a better knowledge of their layer 3 switch.

Note to Reader

In this chapter there will be commands to execute in order to complete certain tasks. The syntax for the CLI commands is case sensitive. The format for commands used in this chapter is to display the commands as mono font for ease of reading and to italicize those parameters that require user input. Some examples are given for commands, and in these, too, the user input is italicized for comparison to the original command. (There is no actual italicization done when entering commands in the CLI.) When there is a command given under the title GUI, it is a series of steps for a command that can be followed in Device Manager.

Layer 3 Routing Switches

The idea behind a routing switch is to be able to perform standard routing functionality (layer 3), but use switching techniques for speed (layer 2). A routing switch is generally highly optimized for IP-only traffic. It works by moving the routing function of IP into the hardware of the switch and out of the software implementation, because software is slower. This provides fully integrated, high-performance, wire-speed layer 3 switching as well as IP routing at every port. The routing switch can switch and route packets at the same speed with no performance loss. A layer 3 switch, also called *cut-through switching*, uses the route once to switch many architectures. The idea is to make tables of known packets above layer 2 (for layer 3 and even layer 4), similar to the Media Access Control (MAC) tables of traditional switches. This helps to make packet-forwarding decisions at very high speeds. The first time an address is seen in the layer 3 switch, it may have to be routed if it belongs to another network. Once it becomes a known address, all traffic to that address will be switched at the speed of layer 2 switching.

Layer 3 switches have the capacity to aggregate large switched networks; they can handle large amounts of traffic from multiple virtual local area networks (VLANs) at Gigabit Ethernet speeds. They can also be used to offload IP routing from the current software routers. It is important to note that just as a traditional router cannot provide the IP performance of routing switches, routing switches do not route every protocol. Rather, routing switches are high-performance, high-feature switches that enable switching or IP routing with complete flexibility.

 NOTE The current version of the Nortel Network's Passport routing switch can also route Internet Packet Exchange (IPX). We will discuss this a little bit later in the chapter.

Older routers were created to support multiple protocols and wide are network (WAN) connectivity. We will be discussing routers in Chapter 14. Because not many networks run legacy protocols, the need for multiprotocol routers is not the same. IP is the protocol of choice and not just for data, but for emerging multimedia applications as well (such as voice over IP, webcasting, and netmeetings just to name a few). Because of the explosion of Internet use, companies need to do a lot to manage, control, and provide bandwidth for their IP applications.

NOTE   We are still required to use a real software-based router implementation when looking to route non-IP traffic.

Passport 1000 Series Fundamentals

The Passport series switches are Nortel Network's premier layer 3 routing switches. They can switch at layer 2, route at layer 3, and are blazing fast. The Passport switch combines routing and switching functionality in a single box, sometimes even on the same port. Unlike a traditional software-based router, the Passport moved routing into the hardware, gaining wire speed for its layer 3 functionality. Every port on a Nortel Networks Passport routing switch can be configured to route, switch, and/or to establish filtering (VLAN) criteria. Passport switches can be used in different configurations, depending on where they are deployed in a the network; perhaps wiring closet Passport boxes are only serving as layer 2 switches, whereas data center Passport boxes are actually routing IP. In another scenario, some Passport boxes are implementing VLANs to switch non-IP protocols, whereas others are routing among IP subnet-based VLANs.

The Passport series routing switches support Gigabit Ethernet technology, as well as conventional 10-Mbps Ethernet and 100-Mbps Fast Ethernet. Heavy-duty servers, connections to other switches, and power users might require gig links. Other users could be confined to 100MB ports. Slower users on older equipment could have ports assigned to 10MB. Because of the technology of auto-negotiation, the switch could set ports to 10MB or 100MB and to half or full duplex, depending on a highest common denominator with other equipment that share the wire.

The Passport 1000 Series

The Passport 1000 series consists of the Passport 1050, 1100, 1150, 1200, and 1250. These are Ethernet-only LAN switches. They can run Fiber, Gigabit, or Fast Ethernet, and traditional Cat5 cabling with speeds of 10MB, 100MB, or 1GB, in a half- or full-duplex configuration.

- **Passport 1050/1051**   12-port 10/100 BASE TX stand-alone, fixed-configuration unit with a single 1000BASE-SX Gigabit Ethernet port

Figure 12-1 Passport 1051 with 12 10/100 Ethernet ports and a single Gigabit Ethernet SR port. (It appears to be two Gigabit Ethernet ports, but it is actually one port with a LinkSafe partner.)

The Passport 1050 comes with a fixed configuration of 12 autosensing 10/100 BASE TX ports for server and workstation attachment. A single 1000BASE-SX Gigabit Ethernet port can be used for server connectivity or connection to a corporate backbone. The Passport 1051 has a single 1000BASE-SR Gigabit Ethernet port for LinkSafe configurations (see Figure 12-1). The Passport 1050 routing switch is well suited for aggregation of 10/100 desktop switches into a single Gigabit Ethernet for further network connections.

- **Passport 1100**   16-port 10/100 BASE-TX stand-alone configuration with two expansion module slots

Supporting Gigabit Ethernet, 100BASE-FX, or additional 10/100-Mbps Ethernet ports, the Passport 1100 base unit includes 16 autosensing 10/100-Mbps Ethernet ports with two built-in expansion slots for field-installable modules (see Figure 12-2). The expansion slots can contain one each of any of the modules in Table 12-1. The 1100 can be equipped with redundant power and LinkSafe. With the redundant power supply, the model is called the 1100R. All modules are hot swappable. The Passport 1100 is ideal for the wiring closets, power workgroups, and server farms.

- **Passport 1150**   Four-port 1000BASE-SX Gigabit Ethernet stand-alone configuration with two expansion module slots

Supporting 10/100-Mbps Ethernet, 100BASE-FX, or Gigabit Ethernet additional ports, the Passport 1150 base unit includes four Gigabit Ethernet ports with two built-in expansion slots for field-installable modules (see Figure 12-3). The I/O modules are shown in Table 12-1, which are the same ones that are used in the 1100. The 1150 can be equipped with redundant power and LinkSafe. With the redundant power supply, the model is called the 1100R. All modules are hot swappable. The Passport 1150 is ideal for the backbone switch of small-size businesses and server farms.

- **Passport 1200**   Eight-slot modular chassis, two slots reserved for redundant CPU/switch fabrics, and six slots available for I/O ports

Figure 12-2 Passport 1100 with 16 10/100 Ethernet ports and two expansion modules. The modules in this Passport are actually the 1102 SR, two Gigabit ports with LinkSafe.

Table 12-1 I/O Modules for the Two Expansion Slots in the Passport 1100 and 1150 Series Switch

1102SX	Two-port 1000BASE-SX Gigabit Ethernet module
1102SR	Two-port 1000BASE-SX Gigabit Ethernet module with LinkSafe
1102LX	Two-port 1000BASE-LX Gigabit Ethernet module
1102LR	Two-port 1000BASE-LX Gigabit Ethernet module with LinkSafe
1102XD	Two-port long-distance Gigabit module, SC single mode fiber connectors
1108TX	Eight-port autosensing 10/100 BASE-TX Ethernet module
1104FX	Four-port 100BASE-FX Ethernet module
1108FX	Eight-port 100BASE-FX with MT-RJ connectors

Figure 12-3 Passport 1150 with four Gigabit Ethernet ports and two expansion slots. The expansion modules in the 1150 are the same as the ones in the 1100 in Figure 12-2.

The Passport 1200 and 1250 are a cabinet-like configuration with space to slide in shelves that contain the boards necessary for a network's configuration. In the Passport 1200, the cabinet itself is called the *chassis*. It comes with two power supplies and eight slots for boards. These slots can hold six I/O boards and two boards for system processing. These boards are also called *blades*. The configuration is as follows: Slots one, two, and three can contain I/O boards. Slots four and five contain the system processor called the Silicon Switch Fabric (SSF). Only one SSF is absolutely necessary; a second SSF is used for backup and failover should the primary SSF go down. Slots six, seven, and eight can contain three more I/O boards for a total of two processors and six I/O boards.

The Passport 1200 can be configured with up to 12 Gigabit Ethernet ports, up to 96 autosensing 10/100 BASE-TX Ethernet ports, 96 100BASE-FX ports for fiber connectivity, or with a combination of the three technologies (see Figure 12-4). Table 12-2 shows all the possible I/O modules for the 1200 switch. For enhanced reliability, the Passport 1200 switch can be equipped with redundant power, redundant gigabit links (LinkSafe), and redundant switch fabric modules. All modules are hot swappable. The Passport 1200 is ideal for high-density backbone and network center applications as well as high-performance servers or workstations.

- **Passport 1250** Four-slot modular chassis, one slot reserved for CPU/switch fabric, and three slots available for I/O ports

The 1250, literally half of a 1200, has four slots. Slots one through three can contain I/O blades, while slot four is reserved for the SSF processor board (see Figure 12-5). No backup processor is available. It can be configured with up to six Gigabit Ethernet ports, up to 48 10/100 BASE-TX or FX ports or any other I/O modules from Table 12-2. It has only one power supply and one switch fabric module. All modules are hot swappable.

Figure 12-4 Passport 1200 with a 1202 SR I/O blade two Gigabit ports with LinkSafe in slot one. Slot two contains a 1208FX, eight-port 100MB Fiber. Slots three, six, seven, and eight contain 1216TX with 16 10/100 Ethernet ports. Slot four and five contain the SSF modules. The SSF in slot four contains a flash card.

Figure 12-5 A Passport 1250 with a 1202 SR blade, two Gigabit ports with LinkSafe in slot one, and two 1216 blades with 16 10/100 Ethernet ports in slots three and four. Slot four contains the SSF module.

Table 12-2 I/O Modules for the Passport 1200 and 1250 Series Switches

1202SX	2-port 1000BASE-SX Gigabit Ethernet module
1202SR	2-port 1000BASE-SX Gigabit Ethernet module with LinkSafe
1202LX	2-port 1000BASE-LX Gigabit Ethernet module
1202LR	2-port 1000BASE-LX Gigabit Ethernet module with LinkSafe
1202XD	2-port long-distance Gigabit module, SC single mode fiber connectors
1216TX	16-port autosensing 10/100 BASE-TX Ethernet module
1208FX	8-port 100BASE-FX Ethernet module
1216FX	16-port 100BASE-FX module, MT-RJ connectors
1216TF	14-port 10/100 BASE-TX with RJ-45 and 2-port 100BASE-FX with MT-RJ connectors
1208FL	8-port 10BASE-FL Ethernet module

Passport 8000 Series Fundamentals

The Passport 8000 series has two major switches within the product line: the Passport 8100, which is a layer 2 only switch, and the Passport 8600, which is a layer 2 and 3 switch (see Figure 12-6). We are not going to discuss the Passport 8100 switch in this chapter.

The Passport 8600 routing switch is designed for use in the campus and building backbones where higher performance, routing, and MAN/WAN integration are required. The Passport 8600 comes in a six- and ten-slot chassis. System components are common to both six- and ten-slot chassis. The 8010 chassis features eight I/O slots and two processor slots. The CPU/SSF processor module, known as the 8690, will be located in slots five and six. The Passport 8000 switch supports redundant switch

Figure 12-6   Passport 8600. Slots one to four have 8148TX blades with 48 10/100 Ethernet ports. Slots four and five contain the SSFs, one primary and one backup. Slots seven to ten contain 8108GBIC blades that can support eight Gigabit ports of SX, LX, or XD. (These flavors of Gigabit Ethernet can be mixed on a single GBIC card.)

fabric/CPU modules, eliminating single points of failure and providing total system resilience. The 8010 also features two fan trays and three power supplies. In the 8006 chassis, there are only four I/O slots, the processors are the same, and there is only one fan (basically, the top half of the 8010). The I/O slots can include any of the I/O modules from Table 12-3, as well as some new ones that are currently under development.

The 8600 can be equipped with up to three load-sharing and load-balancing power supplies. A fully loaded chassis would be able to operate with any two power supplies present, providing power redundancy. All power supplies can be hot swapped.

Table 12-3   I/O Modules Available for the Passport 8600 Routing Switch

8624FX	24-port 100BASE-FX Fast Ethernet routing switch module (MT-RJ)
8632TX	32-port mixed-media module for 10Base-T/100Base-TX with two slots for GBICs
8648TX	48-port 10/100 Ethernet routing switch module (RJ45)
8608SX	8-port 1000BASE-SX Gigabit Ethernet routing switch module (SC)
8608 GBIC	8-port Gigabit Ethernet routing switch module

NOTE The 8608 GBIC module requires GBICs. They come in four flavors: 1000BASE-SX GBIC (SC) for MultiMode fiber, 1000BASE-LX GBIC (SC) for Multi-Mode and SingleMode fiber, 1000BASE-XD GBIC (SC) for SingleMode fiber up to 50 km, and 1000BASE-ZX GBIC (SC) for SingleMode fiber up to 70 km.

NOTE I/O modules that are under development include one- and two-port 10-Gigabit Ethernet routing switch modules. Two-slot MDA baseboard supports up to eight OC-3 or two OC-12 ports for Asynchronous Transfer Mode (ATM) interface applications, and a three-slot MDA baseboard supports up to six OC-3 or three OC-12 ports for Synchronous Optical Network (SONET) interface applications.

Software features include everything supported in the Passport 1000 and more. VLAN support, 802.1Q trunking, IP/IPX routing, RIP/OSPF, to name just a few features, and all support is RFC standard. There is also Quality of Service (QoS) with eight queues per port as well as other filtering features new to the LAN environment and very efficient for a WAN router. The Passport 8600 also supports ATM and Packet over SONET in the latest release.

Passport 8000 provides scalable switching bandwidth from 50 to 256 Gbps, together with system and interfaces modules for edge switching, core routing switching, and multiservice MAN/WAN integration.

Passport 1000 and 8000 routing switches contain two main hardware components: the Silicon Switch Fabrics (SSF) CPU module, and the I/O modules (see Figure 12-7). The SSF is the core of the switch; learning is done on the SSF. Forwarding is done on the I/O modules.

Silicon Switch Fabric (SSF)

The heart of the Passport routing switch is the SSF module. The SSF is the core of the switch and is where the actual packet forwarding occurs. The SSF is integrated into the motherboard of the fixed configuration Passports, namely the 1050 and 1100/1150 series. It is a separate unit in the Passport 1200/1250 and Passport 8100/8600.

The SSF module contains two primary components: a CPU subsystem and the central shared memory switch fabric (see Figure 12-8).

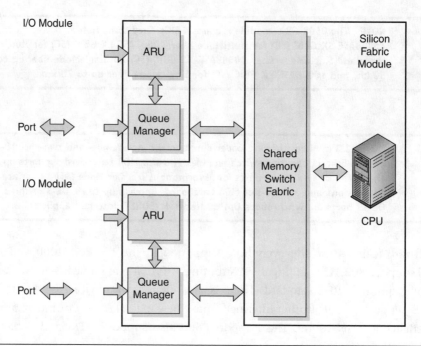

Figure 12-7 This figure shows the Passport system as a block diagram. There are two primary modules as shown in the figure: the SSF module and the I/O modules.

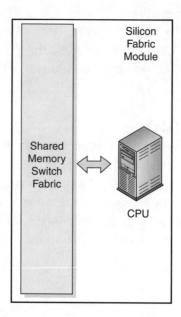

Figure 12-8 Logical view of the SSF in the Passport series

CPU

The CPU module performs all necessary functions for all protocols and uses the information received to build routing and bridging tables. The CPU runs the algorithms and learns information from layer 2 protocols like Spanning Tree, bridging algorithms, and also works with layer 3 routing protocols like Routing Information Protocol (RIP), RIPv2, Open Shortest Path First (OSPF), IPX RIP, and Service Advertising Protocol (SAP). Routing and bridging tables computed by the CPU are stored in 32MB (16MB for the old 1297 SSF) of main memory. These tables are then distributed automatically to each I/O card's individual forwarding table. The Address Resolution Unit (ARU) on the I/O cards will be responsible for using these tables for the address lookup of ingress packets. (ARUs will be discussed in the next section with the I/O modules.) The CPU is responsible for updating the forwarding table on each I/O module's ARU in response to routing and bridging topology changes. The CPU is not involved with the main switching data path; that is the job of the switch fabric.

NOTE The ARU has been renamed the RaptAru for the Passport 8600 series.

Switch Fabric

For all of the Passport layer 3 switches, the central switch fabric is responsible for switching all data flowing through the switch. The fabric is implemented as a shared memory fabric. The Passport 1000 series routing switches has a 15-Gbps switching fabric, while the Passport 8600 series routing switch modules supports a switch capacity of 128 Gbps, easily upgradeable to 256 Gbps. All data traffic between ports in the routing switch must traverse the shared memory switch fabric located on the SSF.

Both the Passports 1200 and 1250 share a common SSF board, which comes in two hardware revisions: the 1297 and 1298. The older SSF boards, such as the 1297, were only equipped with 16MB of RAM on the board. They do not have a system-clocking device and therefore cannot keep system time or date stamp the log file. Using the date command from the Runtime CLI will yield an error of *no on board system clock*. That tells the administrator that this is a 1297. This card cannot be used to run software code level 2.0 or above unless it has been upgraded to 32MB of RAM. The Passport 1297 is easily recognizable as it does not have a debug Ethernet port on the front panel. The port is used for diagnostics on the card itself and can be difficult to access when the card is inside the Passport. Because the Debug Ethernet port is used only in extreme situations, when all I/O ports have failed, engineering felt that it would be okay to hide the port. To access the port, the I/O card above the SSF would have to be removed to fit an Ethernet cable inside the Passport. The SSF 1298 is then easily recognized by its diagnostic port on the front of the card. It has 32MB of RAM and an internal clocking feature. Log files will now have the accurate time and date stamped on the log entry.

The 8690, the CPU/Switch fabric for the 8600 series, is the heart of the routing switch (see Figure 12-9).

As shown in the Figure 12-9, the SSF in the 8600 series is made up of two separate boards joined into one module to make upgrading easier. It is the combination of the components: a PowerPC-based processing engine and a high-speed bandwidth shared memory switch fabric. Just like the 1000 series, there is a switch fabric and all switching is done on that module; there is no local switching. The Passport 8600 also uses ARUs on its I/O modules to handle forwarding into the switch fabric only these have been renamed to RaptARU for this product.

I/O Modules

The I/O modules provide the interface to the network and packet buffering. A wide range of I/O interconnect modules are available for the Passport series of routing switches. Some I/O modules are built in the box, as with the 1050/1100 series. The Passport 1200 and 8600, on the other hand, have interchangeable I/O modules that can be increased as the network demands grow. I/O boards come in several flavors depending on port needs. Each I/O module contains a number of different interface types, includ-

Figure 12-9   The physical view of the Passport 8600's SF/CPU module

ing 10/100 BASE-TX, 100BASE-FX, and 1000BASE-SX or LX. Although the port counts and speeds may change, each I/O module operates similarly.

Each I/O module consists of two components: the front-end board used for physical media connections and a backplane that contains the ARU and output queues. In the 8600, the I/O modules are actually two logical halves combined into one card (similar to the SSF card of the 8600) that makes it easier to distinguish the two functions. The front half is the physical Ethernet ports and their Queue Managers while the back, called the Backplane Forwarding Module (BFM), is where the RaptARU resides.

The I/O modules contain two processors involved in packet forwarding: the Queue Manager and the ARU.

Queue Managers

The Queue Manager is responsible for receiving packets from the network ports and the SSF module and coordinating the flow of data on the I/O module. A Queue Manager, called a *GID* for gigabit interfaces or *QUID* for all other Ethernet ports, is the interface between the data ports and the shared memory switch fabric. Each I/O module has one or more Queue Managers. If there is more traffic on a port than the Queue Manager can switch, there will be contention. In this case, buffering will occur, and some packets will be stored in memory until they can be processed. Because receiving packets take priority over transmitting packets, queuing occurs on the outbound side or on transmit and not on the receive side.

Figure 12-10 A physical view of the eight-port Gigabit card for the Passport 8600, named the GBIC

ARUs

Packet-forwarding information is derived from distributed routing tables created by the CPU and forwarded to the ARUs on the I/O modules. Table information is distributed across a 400MB bus between the CPU and the ARU. The ARU accepts forwarding records from the CPU and forwards unknown packets to the CPU for learning or handling. When the CPU flushes its tables, all ARUs flush theirs.

The ARU acts from the forwarding table contents and processes packets according to the information there. Packet forwarding decisions are made locally on the I/O module when the ARU uses the tables to resolve local routing and switching addresses and forward packets through the switch fabric, independent of the CPU. The ARUs on each I/O blade maintain their own address table for both routed and switched traffic. Each I/O has its own ARU for quick table lookups, but all ARU tables have common data in them even layer 2 only ports that don't need routing tables. The ARU is responsible for address lookups, packet segmentation, and reassembly and switch fabric access. The ARU consults the forwarding table, a table of routing, switching, VLAN, QoS, and policy information, to make all of its forwarding decisions. The forwarding engine also checks each packet for current network policies.

ARU tables for the Passport 1000 can contain up to 24,000 entries per switch to provide capacity for large network configurations. The RaptARU for the Passport 8600 supports up to 32,000 MAC addresses or routing entries in its table, per switch.

The forwarding entries stay in Passport's tables for approximately 5 minutes (300 seconds). If the address is not accessed in 5 minutes/300 seconds, the address is dropped, and the memory location is ready for another entry.

Redundant SSFs

In mission-critical environments, the Passport 1200 and 8600 offer features designed to provide high levels of reliability. To protect against switch or processor faults, users can install two SSF CPU modules: one active and one standby CPU with fast failover in the event of a loss of one CPU. This feature enables the Passport to continue operation in the event of a primary CPU failure. Only one CPU is active at any time so if the primary CPU fails, the other will have to relearn routing and switching tables. There is a 100MB connection through which the CPUs communicate with each other.

For the 8600, there is an additional benefit to having two SSF modules. The two switch figures can do load sharing, which increases the total switch fabric bandwidth from 64GB to 128GB across the backplane. If there is only one CPU/SF module, all data is switched through it. If there are two, then half the I/O ports will be taken care of by CPU 0, while the other half will be sent to CPU 1. This enables a network engineer to take full advantage of the eight gigabit I/O cards without oversubscribing the ports and causing packets to be buffered and possibly dropped.

For both the Passports 1000 and 8600, the CPU on the first active SSF becomes the master. With the 8600 however, an administrator can use a parameter to force the SSF to wait before attempting to become master. This enables the administrator to set a specific CPU to become the master.

Command `config bootconfig master <cpu-slot>`

Example `config bootconfig master 5` Running this command from the Runtime CLI will force the CPU in slot five to become the active (primary) CPU, unless it is unavailable.

In a network configured with redundant SSFs, it is essential that both SSFs have the same source image, bootstrap image, runtime configuration, and boot configuration. The Boot Monitor only allows the live SSF to be accessed. CLI enables telnet, console, or rlogin access to the secondary SSF. The address to access the secondary SSF is 127.0.0.*x*, where *x* is the secondary SSF slot numbers.

To ensure proper backup of the SSFs, save the configuration file to the standby SSF. Or use the

Command `copy flash:<filename> tftp <dest ip of secondary SSF>`

Example `copy flash:acc2.0.7 tftp 127.0.0.6` In this example, the filename is acc2.0.7, and the destination redundant SSF is located at 127.0.0.6.

LinkSafe

To guard against cable faults, optional LinkSafe redundant gigabit link modules can be installed in the Passport 1200, 1100, and 1150 products. LinkSafe provides physical layer redundancy and automatic switchover on Gigabit Ethernet ports. The technology enables two Gigabit ports that share circuitry to have separate cabling but to be seen by the switch as a single port. Because each of the ports have separate cabling if there is a fiber failure, the second Gigabit port will take over and pass traffic. The failover process is almost instantaneous, and no traffic is dropped.

There is no configuration necessary for LinkSafe because it is a hardware-based failover solution. With Device Manager, it is possible to force ports to be active (primary) or redundant.

NOTE   When we discuss configurations of the Passport, it is crucial to understand that there are different hardware and software revisions. Not all configurations are supported on older revisions of hardware or older code. The current Passport 1000 version of hardware is ARU3/B modules, and the level of software support is at 2.07 with release 2.1 being released as this book is being written. The Passport 8000 series runs on 3.0 software. To run IPX, User Datagram Protocol (UDP) forwarding, and Brouter interfaces, the Passport must be configured with the 2.0 or greater level of code revision and have the latest hardware. Features like Virtual Router Redundancy Protocol (VRRP), Multilink Trunking (MLT), and IP subnet VLANs have been available since the 1.3.1 code revision and run safely with the ARU2/A hardware revision.

Command   show sys sw   The CLI command to check the software version of the Passport 1000 or 8000

Command   show system info   The CLI command to check hardware revisions

Passport Boot Process

The Passport 1000 boot process differs slightly from the boot process of the Passport 8600. The Passport 1000 series first loads the Boot Monitor from flash, then the Boot Monitor loads the runtime image, and the runtime image loads the user configuration from Nonvolatile Random Access Memory (NVRAM).

The Passport 8600 also loads the Boot Monitor from flash, which in turn loads **boot.cfg**, which contains the boot flags, runtime image, and the **config** file locations. Next the runtime image is loaded and in turn loads **config.cfg**, the switch configuration, which contains the custom settings for the network. **Boot.cfg** and **config.cfg** are ASCII files that are stored on the system flash.

Boot Monitor Interface

The Boot Monitor Interface is used to configure and display boot options, manage the nonvolatile file system, configure boot flags, reset or boot system with defaults, and Trivial File Transfer Protocol (TFTP) to and from the switch. It is accessible before the runtime image has been loaded. When booting a Passport switch, if the autoboot flag is enabled, the boot process will automatically stop at the Boot Monitor stage. If autoboot is disabled, the user will still be able to get into the Boot Monitor prompt by pressing any key when they see the prompt "Press any key to stop autoboot."

The autoboot prompt says monitor on the Passport series. In the Boot Monitor mode, no user configuration is available.

The Boot Monitor Interface is also available on the Passport 8000 series from the Runtime CLI from the **config bootconfig** prompt.

CAUTION   Do not to use the Boot Monitor mode unless the switch is inaccessible any other way. No ports can forward traffic, no VLANs exist, and no IP addresses are associated with ports while the Passport switch is in the Boot Monitor Mode because the user configuration has not been loaded.

It is preferable to make all system changes while in runtime configuration mode from the CLI, which we will be discussing next. There are some commands that are important and accessible through the Boot Monitor.

NOTE   It is sometimes possible to access a command without typing out each word fully. Sometimes three letters can be recognized in place of the full word of a command.

Boot Flags for Configuring Startup

Flags determine some of the system boot up configurations. If an administrator wants to manage this information within the Boot Monitor, the following is involved:

Command flags This command enables the administrator to see and make changes to the flags that determine how the boot process proceeds. Typing in the flags command on a Passport 1000 series switch brings up four flags:

- **autoboot** Enabled by default, this parameter has the Passport booting up into the runtime configuration mode unless stopped by the user pressing any key. Disabling autoboot stops the Passport boot process in the Boot Monitor mode.

- **factory default** Disabled by default, this flag enables the Passport to load the normal user configuration after loading the runtime image. Enabling this parameter causes the default configuration to be loaded and all user configurations and changes to the switch to be ignored.

Command `config sys set flags factorydefault true` This command can also be used in the Passport 1000 series to reset the switch to factory default configuration. It is run from the Runtime CLI.

- **ports in isolated mode** Disabled by default, this parameter puts all new ports as members in the default VLAN. Enabling this parameter causes all new ports to be viewed by the switch as isolated router ports.

- **debug mode** Disabled by default, this parameter causes switches to automatically reboot after a fatal error.

For the Passport 8600, the flags are accessed with the command `config boot-config flags info` (see Figure 12-11).

Some of the accessible flags that we can see from Figure 12-11 are

- **accelar-8100-mode** True by default, this parameter causes the switch to act as a layer 2 switch only. For the Passport 8600, this flag should be set to false.

- **Autoboot, factorydefaults, debugmode** These flags are the same concept as the ones in the Passport 1000 discussed previously.

- **ftpd** False by default, setting this parameter to true enables an FTP server on the switch.

- **telnetd** False by default, setting this parameter to true enables a Telnet server on the switch for users that require remote access and management abilities through IP.

- **tftpd** True by default, this parameter enables a TFTP server on the switch.

```
Passport-8610:5/config# bootconfig
Passport-8610:5/config/bootconfig# flags
Passport-8610:5/config/bootconfig/flags# info
flags 8100-mode false
flags autoboot true
flags daylight-saving-time false
flags debugmode false
flags debug-config false
flags egress-mirror true

flags factorydefaults false
flags ftpd false
flags machine-check false
flags logging true
flags reboot true
flags rlogind false
flags telnetd false
flags tftpd false
flags trace-logging false
flags verify-config true
flags wdt true
```

Figure 12-11 This figure shows the results of a `config/bootconfig/flag/info` command.

> **NOTE** Enabling the FTP server and the Telnet server will have no effect until the Passport switch is rebooted.

Commands that Control Boot Order

Command choices *<primary, secondary>* *<config-file, image-file, info>* This command sets the order for booting and specifies file location for the config and image files.

Other Useful Boot Monitor Commands

Command ip   Passport 1000

Command net ip   Passport 8000

It is possible to use the ip or net ip command in the Boot Monitor and create an IP address to access the Passport switch through the Diagnostic Ethernet Port. This option should only be used if it is impossible to access the switch through the CLI or any other ports.

> **CAUTION** Be careful when assigning an IP address to the Diagnostic Ethernet Port. It will not show up in CLI, but can cause conflicts when attempting to create VLANs or ports with the same address or even a different address on the same network. (Because the Passport is a layer 3 switch and acts like a router, it cannot have two IP addresses on the same network.)

Command ping   Once an IP address has been set up in the Boot Monitor, an administrator can use the ping command to check the IP address. (Because the switch is not forwarding from any ports in Boot Monitor, this command cannot be used to reach remote devices.)

It is unnecessary to save with Boot Monitor because all configurations are saved as soon as they are made.

Command boot   This command boots the Passport switch with the user configuration and brings the switch to the Runtime CLI.

Runtime CLI

The CLI enables users to access and configure a Passport switch through a serial port, Telnet session, or a modem. CLI access through the serial port is usually accomplished with a hyperterminal type of program. Settings for the serial (Com) port for the hyper-terminal session should be 9600 bps, 8 data bits, no parity, and 1 stop bit.

Logging into the Passport Switch

There are several usernames and passwords that exist by default on the Passport switch. Each username and password combination is responsible for a different level of access into the Passport switch:

- Read-only access enables users to view configurations and statistics without being able to make any changes. This default login is **ro** for the username and **ro** for the password.

- For access to view and edit setting dealing with layer 2 (switching) functionality only, the username is **L2** and the password is **L2**. OSPF, Dynamic Host Configuration Protocol (DHCP), and all other layer 3 settings will not be visible with this login.

- Read-write access enables users to change and update all Passport functionality except security and password settings. The default login is username **rw** and password **rw**.

- Layer 3 access is no different than read-write access, but a separate username of **L3** and password of **L3** have been provided for this access.

- The superuser who has all rights to change all settings including passwords and security is the default login of **rwa** with the password of **rwa**.

CAUTION For security purposes, companies should never leave the default username and passwords in effect.

Command `config cli password <ro, 12, 13, rw, rwa>` This command enables an administrator to change usernames and passwords.

The CLI is a tree-like system. To navigate the tree, one can enter a partial command hit enter and get into the correct context and enter the command there *or* enter the full command on one line. To navigate the CLI, it is good to know some basic commands:

Command `back`   Takes the user back one level in the CLI tree.

Command `box, top`   Takes the user back to the top of the CLI tree.

Command `ctrl + p`   This command can be used to repeat a previous command.

CLI, by default, gives 25 lines of a command result and then waits for user input to move on to the next page. Sometimes it is beneficial to have the CLI scroll without prompting for user information so one can get to the end of a command where the information a user is looking for might be located.

Command `config cli more <true, false>`   Setting CLI more to false causes the CLI to continuously output information without pausing after one screen and waiting for a user prompt.

File System

There are three different file systems in the Passport 1000 series: the BOOTEEPROM, the flash, and the Personal Computer Memory Card International Association (PCMCIA). The BOOTEEPROM is 512KB and is where the Boot Monitor and runtime configuration are stored. The BOOTEEPROM is sometimes called NVRAM. The flash is 4.5MB of onboard memory and is the storage location for the runtime image and other backup configurations or image files that the user chooses to store. The PCMCIA is an additional memory card that is purchased and installed in the slot in the front of the Passport SSF for the Passport 1200 and 1250 series only.

The Passport 8000 series has only the onboard flash and PCMCIA memory. The flash is divided into the boot section of 2MB, and this is where the Boot Monitor image resides. The rest of the flash is 16MB in size and is used for runtime images, configuration files, the system log, and storage for any other files. The PCMCIA is an additional memory card that is purchased and installed in the slot in the front of the Passport SSF.

In the Passport 1000 series the file system is a linked list (non-FAT) with each file having a name and a number. Files can be accessed by using their name or position on the flash.

Command `dir (or dir flash)`   Shows a directory of the files on the flash of the switch

> **Command** `dir pcmcia` Shows a directory of the files on the PCMCIA card of the switch

File Types

The Passport 1000 series marks files with a flag that indicates their types.

Deleting files in this system merely marks the file as deleted (with a D flag) and does not create free space on the drive. To recover the disk space from deleted files, a squeeze will be necessary. This actually copies the files and then reorganizes them back to the flash or PCMCIA card in order leaving free space that is reusable for other files.

> **Command** `delete <flash,pcmcia>:<filename, #>` This command marks a file for deletion, but does not actually remove the file from the media.

> **Command** `recover <flash,pcmcia>:<filename, #>` A file that has been deleted can be brought back with the `recover` command.

> **Command** `squeeze <flash,pcmcia>` This command actually brings back the free space by completely deleting all files marked deleted and re-creating the file structure.

> **Command** `format <flash,pcmcia>` The `format` command formats the media and removes all files completely (just like the `format` command used in any other OS).

CAUTION Once the `squeeze` or `format` command is used, all files involved are permanently deleted. The `recover` command will no longer be useful for retrieving files.

Table 12-4 Flags and File Types for the Passport 1000 Flash and PCMCIA File Systems

C	Configuration file
X	Executable file
Z	Compressed file
D	File slated for deletion
L	Log file
T	Trace file

The Passport 8000 series has a true file system. Files are accessed by their pathnames, and no number is associated with files. Squeezing the flash or PCMCIA card is not necessary. It is possible to use the PCMCIA card from a Passport 8000 in a standard laptop to access files from the Passport 8000.

 NOTE The PCMCIA card is not compatible between the Passport 1000 and 8000 series. Additionally, these PCMCIA cards are not compatible with the router flash card.

Command `remove flash c2` This command is used instead of the `delete` command for the Passport 8000 series.

Saving the Configuration

In order to ensure that user configuration remains with the Passport switch after a reboot, it is essential to save the configuration. This will then become the user configuration that is loading after the runtime image is loaded during the boot process.

Command `save` Saves the configuration file to NVRAM on a Passport 1000 series switch

Command `save flash:config1` Saves the configuration to flash on a Passport 1000 series and names the file config1

Quick Quiz 1

How would one save the configuration to the PCMCIA card and name it config2?

Answer

save pcmcia:config2

Command `save config file flash:c2` Saves the configuration file for a Passport 8600 onto a flash card and names it c2

Command `save config standby \flash\c2` Saves the configuration to the standby SSF on a Passport 8600 to a flash card and names it c2

To save the configuration to the secondary SSF of a Passport 1000 series, Telnet to the secondary SSF with the following commands:

Command `Telnet 127.0.0.<5,6>` Depending on which slot the secondary SSF is in, execute the following copy command.

Command `copy config tftp <primary ssf 127.0.0.x>` To copy the file using TFTP, use this command. Make sure to give the source of the config file as the primary SSF 127.0.0.<5,6>.

Command `show sys config` This is a particularly useful command to see the configuration file, especially for a Passport 1000 where configuration files are binary and can only be viewed with a proper editor. A Passport 8000 configuration is actually saved as an ASCII file and can be viewed and changed offline or online with any editor program.

Command `source <filename>` To run a configuration file that was edited or created offline for a Passport 8000 series, use this command.

The System Log and the Syslog Utility

The Passport 1000 series has a log file that is 256 bytes long. It is saved on the flash. The Passport 8600 does not save the system log as a file in the onboard flash. Logs are lost during reboot unless they have been saved to the PCMCIA card. The log file is essential for troubleshooting the Passport switch. It saves events that occurred on the switch (like a port going up or down or a reboot of the switch) so that an administrator can analyze them:

Command `config log <clear, info, level, screen>` This command enables an administrator to make changes to the log file.

Command `show log file <tail>` This command displays the content of the log file (see Figure 12-12). Using the tail switch displays the content of the log file with the most recent event (last entry) displayed first.

There is also a Syslog utility that enables log messages to be sent to a Unix host with specific severity levels. The Syslog must first be enabled, and then an administrator can configure a host to send the Syslog information:

Command `config sys syslog state <enable disable>` This command globally enables the Syslog utility.

Command `config sys syslog host <hid> address <IP address> host <enable disable>` This command enables sending Syslog messages to a host configured here with its IP address.

Accelar-1200> show log file tail
285: [10/23/2001 08:38:03] WARNING Code=0x1ff0009 Task=tShell Blocked unauthori
zed cli access
284: [10/23/2001 08:11:32] WARNING Code=0x1ff0009 Task=tShell Blocked unauthori
zed cli access
283: [10/23/2001 07:59:26] Save to selected device ... done.
282: [10/22/2001 21:58:36] WARNING Task=tCppRxTask Frame buffer utilization has
 exceeded 90% threshold
281: [10/22/2001 16:35:37] Save to selected device ... done.
280: [10/22/2001 15:10:11] INFO: Code=0x0 Task=tTrapd: Link Down(7/8)
279: [10/22/2001 15:09:48] INFO: Code=0x0 Task=tTrapd: Spanning Tree Topology Ch
ange(StgId=1, PortNum=7/8)
278: [10/22/2001 15:09:44] INFO: Code=0x0 Task=tTrapd: Link Up(7/8)
277: [10/22/2001 15:07:29] INFO: Code=0x0 Task=tTrapd: Link Down(7/8)
276: [10/22/2001 15:07:06] INFO: Code=0x0 Task=tTrapd: Spanning Tree Topology Ch
ange(StgId=1, PortNum=7/8)
231: [10/19/2001 01:06:17] INFO: Code=0x0 Task=tTrapd: Link Up(8/10)
230: [10/19/2001 01:06:14] INFO: Code=0x0 Task=tTrapd: Link Down(8/10)
229: [10/19/2001 01:06:12] INFO: Code=0x0 Task=tTrapd: Link Up(8/10)
228: [10/19/2001 01:06:09] INFO: Code=0x0 Task=tTrapd: Link Down(8/10)
227: [10/19/2001 01:05:46] INFO: Code=0x0 Task=tTrapd: Spanning Tree Topology Ch
ange(StgId=1, PortNum=8/9)
203: [10/19/2001 00:31:14] INFO: Code=0x0 Task=tTrapd: Spanning Tree Topology Ch
ange(StgId=1, PortNum=7/11)
185: [10/18/2001 22:30:12] WARNING Task=tRclpTask The RtrId in the packet and m
y RtrId=10.228.0.242 are identical - ifIndex=302 inPort=7/12 srclp=10.228.15.1 d
stlp=224.0.0.5 msgTyp=1
184: [10/18/2001 22:30:02] WARNING Task=tRclpTask The RtrId in the packet and m
y RtrId=10.228.0.242 are identical - ifIndex=302 inPort=7/12 srclp=10.228.15.1 d
stlp=224.0.0.5 msgTyp=1

Figure 12-12   This figure shows a log file from a Passport 1200 switch.

NOTE This log file shows that someone tried to access the CLI with the wrong user information, with ports in the Passport going down, and causing Spanning Tree to reconverge and send out topology change messages and also OSPF issues.

Show Versus Monitor Command

The show command is used to give a snapshot of the information at the time that the command is executed. The monitor command will refresh the screen with updated information. To set the monitor interval for self-updating, use the following command:

Command   config cli monitor interval <1..600>

The monitor command can be used in most commands instead of the show command. (In this book, examples given use the show command, but note that the monitor command may be useful in one's own environment.)

Trace Commands

There is a trace facility that is used to see detailed information on the status of the switch for a specific polling period. It can be used for advanced troubleshooting, with the aid of a Nortel Network technical support person. It is only available to users with rwa access:

Command show trace level

Command trace level <mode> <level>

Table 12-5 shows some of the trace modes that an administrator may use in his or her network to gain troubleshooting information on the Passport switch. There are additional less commonly used trace modes.

Table 12-5 Common Trace Modes Used for Troubleshooting a Passport Switch

Mode	Description
0	Common—All inclusive
I	SNMP—Info from Device Manager
2	RMON
5	STG Manager—Spanning Tree packets
9	CP port—Packets to and from CPU
II	VLAN Manager—IGMP L2 packets
14	IP+RIP—IP functions on the network
15	Additional IP information

NOTE There are additional less commonly used trace modes as well.

Table 12-6   Trace Levels and Their Explanations

0	Disabled
I	Very terse
2	Terse
3	Verbose
4	Very verbose

NOTE   In most cases, a level 3 trace will be the most useful.

Command `trace off`   Turns off the trace.

Command `trace info`   Displays the results of the trace. It actually shows a file created from the trace buffer. (The `show trace file` command can also be used.)

Command `trace info tail`   Shows the trace buffer from the end to the beginning.

Command `trace clear`   Clears the buffer. It is important to clear the buffer before rerunning the trace command; otherwise, data in the buffer will not be useful or current.

CAUTION   This command is very CPU intensive. Don't leave this trace running for a long time because it will slow down processing on the Passport. Additionally, the memory buffer can fill up very fast especially if one is doing a verbose level trace.

Command `show sys perf`   This command can be used to analyze CPU utilization and is not a resource-intensive command.

Upgrading the Passport Switch

When upgrading the Passport, both the image file and the Boot Monitor files must be updated. Updating the image file is a matter of downloading the new image onto the flash and using that image for booting (see Figure 12-13). Updating the Boot Monitor files requires a boot from a new monitor file that actually goes out and burns the new boot information into the prom of the Passport switch.

```
Accelar-1100/show# dir

Device: flash

FN Name                   Flags   Length

-- ----                    -----   ------

1 ac1a2070.img                XZN   1888132

2 syslog                   LN   131072

--                          ------

2  files            bytes used= 2031616 free=2162512


Accelar-1100/show# copy tftp:ac10b205.img flash:ac10b205.img

Enter source tftp server address [99.99.99.199]:

[09/23/2001 08:10:15]  Start tftp cli timer

tftp starting ... Press any key to abort the operation.

tftp result: success

Accelar-1100/show# dir

Device: flash

FN Name                   Flags   Length

-- ----                    -----   ------

1 ac1a2070.img                XZN   1888132

2 syslog                   LN   131072

3 ac10b205.img                XZN    88928

--                          ------

3  files            bytes used= 2162688 free=2031440
```

Figure 12-13   This figure shows the Passport 1200 flash directory containing two files. The user then performed a copy command to transfer the file ac10b205.img from the TFTP server 99.99.99.199 to the Passport flash. The final directory command shows the Passport 1200 flash now contains three files with the new file ac10b205.img in position three.

When updating the switch, it is essential that there be no redundant SSF in the Passport (1200 or 8600) chassis. If there is a redundant SSF, remove it and make sure to do the upgrade twice, once for each SSF.

 CAUTION Failure to remove the redundant SSF will cause issues with the upgrade.

The next step in the process is to copy the correct version of the runtime image onto the flash. This can be done with a TFTP copy command:

Command `copy tftp:<srcfilename> flash:<destfilename>`

Example `copy tftp:ac10b205.img flash:ac10b205.img`

The Passport will prompt for the address of the TFTP server and then attempt to retrieve the file.

If it is possible, the best-case scenario is to have the new image as the first file on the flash. Doing this may be difficult because the image files are now large. It may be necessary to copy files to new locations (even a remote TFTP server), delete files, and squeeze the flash:

Command `copy flash:<srcfilename> tftp`

If no TFTP server address or destination filename is specified, then the Passport will prompt the user for the information.

If it is not possible to move the image to the first position in the flash, it is important to set the primary boot choice to the new image location. (In our example, that was position three.)

For the Passport 1000,

Command `config sys set boot <primary, secondary, tertiary>`
`<flash, pcmcia, net, skip, nvram, config>:<filename, file-`
`position>`

Example `config sys set boot primary flash:3`

For the Passport 8000,

Command `config bootconfig choice <primary, secondary, ter-`
`tiary> image-file <filename>`

Example `config bootconfig choice` *primary* `image-file` `acc301.img`

It is also necessary to update the Boot Monitor. One can either copy the Boot Monitor to the flash card and then boot from that file *or* do a remote network boot using that file as the boot file. This will automatically update the boot prom:

Command `boot tftp ip <tftp server address> file <bootfile name>`

Example `boot tftp ip <10.10.10.10> file <accboot2.0.7>`

CAUTION Be very careful when updating the boot prom not to turn off the switch because this process actually deletes all the information in the boot prom and resets the information.

Creating the Initial IP Address for Access to the Passport Switch

To create the initial IP address on the Passport, the user must have local com port CLI access. Once the first address is created, the user can use Device Manager or Telnet to access the Passport switch remotely. First check to see the IP status of the switch (see Figure 12-14):

Command `show ip interface`

Command `config vlan <vid> ip create <IP address/mask>` This command is used to add an IP address to a VLAN. (We will discuss later in the chapter VLAN types and which VLANs can have an IP address.)

Example `config vlan 1 ip create 10.10.10.1/255 .255.255.0`

Command `config ethernet <port number> ip create <IP address/mask>` This command is used to add an IP address to an Ethernet port. Only isolated router ports and Brouter ports can have an IP address.

Example `config ethernet 1/16 ip create 10.10.10.10/24`

Command `config ethernet <port number> ip delete <IP address/mask>`

Example `config ethernet 1/16 ip delete 10.10.10.10/255 .255.255.0`

```
Passport-8610:5# show ip interface


=================================================================
                                  Ip Interface
=================================================================
INTERFACE IP              NET          BCASTADDR  REASM    VLAN  BROUTER
          ADDRESS         MASK         FORMAT     MAXSIZE  ID    PORT
-----------------------------------------------------------------
Vlan1     10.10.10.1      255.255.255.0  ones       1500     --    false
Vlan3     10.10.12.1      255.255.255.0  ones       1500     --    false

Passport-8610:5#
```

Figure 12-14 This figure shows the result of the show ip interface command. There are two addresses configured on this Passport. One is associated with VLAN1 and the second is associated with VLAN3.

Quick Quiz 2

What is the command to delete the IP address from VLAN 1 that we created previously?

Answer

```
config vlan 1 ip delete 10.10.10.1/24
```

NOTE As one can see when using CLI, it is necessary to use a mask when creating an IP address. It is okay to use either the full 32-bit address of the mask or its Classless Interdomain Routing (CIDR) notation.

Device Manager

Device Manager is a GUI application that runs on the Windows-based operating system as well as some flavors of UNIX. Installing Device Manager on a PC creates a new program group called *Nortel Networks Frame Switch Manager*. (Older versions of the software will create a program group called the *Bay Networks Frame Switch Manager*.) Device Manager is used for managing Passport (and 450) switches across a network through Simple Network Management Protocol (SNMP) polling and GET and SET commands (see Figures 12-15 and 12-16). The Passport switches must have an IP address that is accessible to the management station.

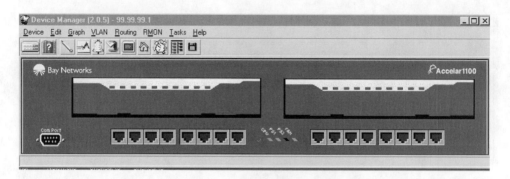

Figure 12-15   A view of the Passport 1100 using Device Manager

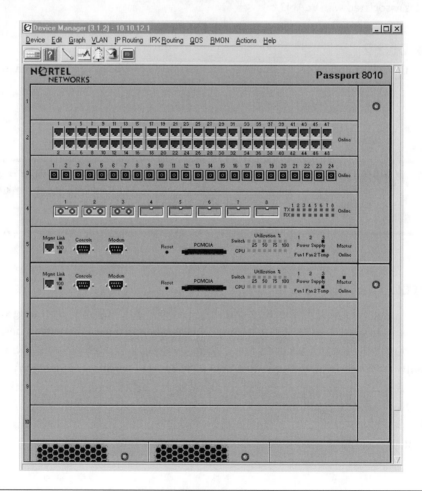

Figure 12-16   A view of the Passport 8000 using Device Manager

> **NOTE** It is necessary to use a version of Device Manager that is compatible to the level of software that is on the devices. Device Manager is generally only backward compatible for about two or three versions. This is because `GET` and `SET` commands may change in versions of software as Management Information Bases (MIBs) get updated and added for new features.

In addition to a username and password, Device Manager also requires community strings for access (see Table 12-7).

Command `config sys set snmp info` This enables SNMP information to be viewed.

Command `config sys set snmp community <ro, rw, 12, 13, rwa> <communitystring>` This command enables a user to change SNMP community strings.

Using Device Manager, an administrator can view a single Passport switch. Viewing options include the entire chassis, a single or multiple slots, or a single or multiple port. Device Manager can be used to set parameters for the system, the chassis, boot up, and routing, as well as TFTP, SNMP, and Spanning Tree Groups (STGs) (see Figure 12-17). As we continue along this chapter, we will see in more detail how to configure switches using Device Manager.

> **NOTE** An administrator that has a powerful machine can run multiple instances of Device Manager each looking at a different Passport switch.

Table 12-7   Default Community Strings for SNMP Access

Read-only	Public
Layer 2	Private
Layer 3	Private
Read-write	Private
Read-write-all	Secret

PART III

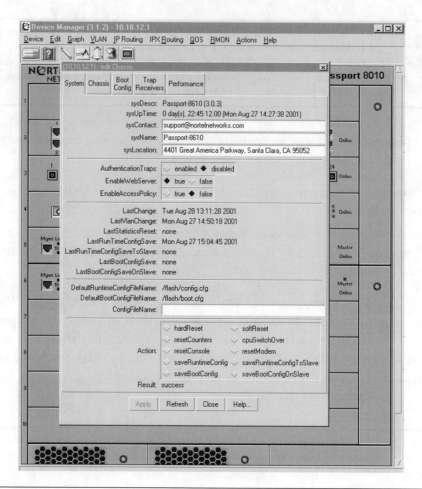

Figure 12-17   A view of the system parameters using Device Manager on a Passport 8000

Device Manager has a feature called *VLAN Manager*. We will discuss this software after discussing the features of VLANs.

Web-Based Management

The Passport routing switch has a Hypertext Transfer Protocol (HTTP) server that supports limited web-based management of a single device using a standard browser (Internet Explorer or Netscape). This server is enabled by default and can use the same usernames and passwords of the other management utilities (see Figure 12-18).

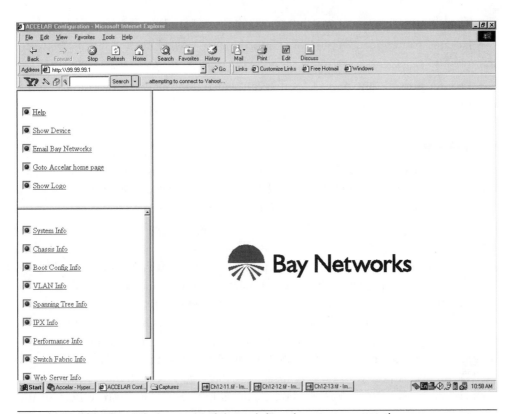

Figure 12-18 The default screen of the web-based management tool

CAUTION The Code Red virus that has been affecting web servers can affect the Passport if this web-based management tool is enabled. It may be best to disable this feature: Command `config web-server <enable, disable>`

Port Configurations

We discussed in the beginning of this chapter the different physical port configurations that can exist for the multitude of Passport switches like 10/100 MB-Ethernet, Gigabit Ethernet LX, SX, and XD. We are now going to discuss software configurations of Passport ports and how they can be configured to route, switch, or do both. There are three distinct configurations available for ports on the Passport routing switch:

- **VLAN port**   A port that switches packets according to layer 2 information only

- **Isolated router port**   A port that performs layer 3 switching and routing between VLANs

- **Brouter port**   A one-port VLAN that can switch nonroutable protocols and route IP and IPX

VLAN Ports

A VLAN port is a classical switch port that examines packets based on layer 2 information. This is the most common type of Passport port that can belong to different VLANs. VLAN ports can be access ports or tagged ports.

Access Ports

An access port is the standard port type. A port on the Passport that is an access port carries traffic that is untagged. Traffic that is untagged is traffic that is from a VLAN on a single switch with destinations to a workstation or possibly another VLAN on the same switch. An untagged port can belong to only one like type VLAN like one port-based VLAN. It can also belong to some policy-based VLANs at the same time; however, it can only belong to one policy-based VLAN for any given protocol (that is, only one IPX VLAN). An access port with tagging disabled expects to receive frames without tags. Because no tag is present, VLAN membership is implied from the type field of the packet itself and the receiving port. These untagged frames are called *implicitly tagged frames*, and the concept of them is very crucial to understand. This concept will be explained in great detail further in the chapter.

A port with tagging set to false may erroneously receive tagged frames. For this possibility, the access port can be configured to discard tagged frames or to associate them with the default VLAN.

 NOTE   To gain a better understanding of access ports, it is important to understand tagged ports and the contrasts between them.

Tagged Port

A tagged port (formerly known as a trunk port, but because of the confusion with MLT, it is not known that way anymore) is a Passport port with tagging enabled. Any port on the switch can be used as a tagged port, and all frames from the port will be sent out tagged. A tagged port can be a member of any and all VLANs and all STGs. Traffic is tagged with an 802.1Q tag to define where the traffic originated and is destined. When traffic leaves one switch and enters another, it is only with the tagged 802.1Q information that it will be defined as belonging to a VLAN that is common to both switches. Tagged ports are used mostly to extend VLANs between switches. By coordinating VLAN IDs (VIDs) across multiple switches, VLANs can be extended to multiple switches.

Figure 12-19 shows the details of an 802.1Q protocol tag. In the specification for 802.1Q tagging, an addition 4-byte (octet) header is inserted in a frame after the source address and before the frame type. The tag contains the VID with which the frame is associated. If a frame is received on a trunk port, it is considered to be an explicitly tagged frame. VLAN association is derived from the tag.

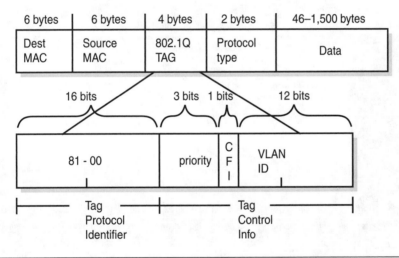

Figure 12-19   A packet constructed with the 802.1Q protocol standard

Whether or not tagged frames are sent or received is configured at the port level. Tagging is set as true or false for the port and applied to all VLANs on the port. Tagged ports will trunk any number of port-based VLAN traffic to another switch. A Passport tagged port can be configured to discard untagged frames or to associate them with a VLAN. In the latter case, when an untagged frame is received on a tagged port, it is sent to the user-specified default VLAN:

Command `config ethernet <ports> perform-tagging <enable, disable>`

Example `config ethernet 2/2 perform-tagging enable`

GUI Click on the port. Right-click and choose edit port > vlan tab > perform tagging set to true (see Figure 12-20).

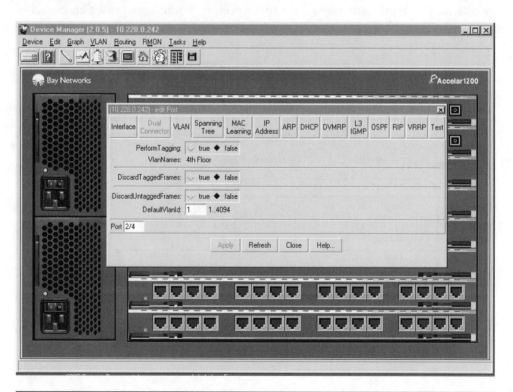

Figure 12-20 This figure shows the Device Manager screen for creating tagged ports.

VLANs Revisited

VLANs were discussed in Chapter 3, but now we will go into a more detailed explanation including how VLANs are used in the Passport switch.

VLAN Definitions

As we mentioned in Chapter 3, a VLAN is a collection of switch ports that make up a single broadcast domain. A VLAN can be defined for a single switch, or it can span multiple switches. VLANs are logical entities created in the software configuration to control traffic flow. Membership in workgroup segments can be determined logically instead of by user location, and adds, moves, and changes can be easily configured as the network evolves.

The Passport 1000 series enables network managers to create up to 123 port-based or policy-based VLANs. VLANs can be based on switch port or by protocol. Protocols supported include IP, IP-subnet, IPX, NetBIOS, DECnet, SNA, and others. VIDs fall in the range of 1 to 4094. The VLANs that can be created are not an actual maximum because if an organization has multiple STG, Internet Group Management Protocol (IGMP) snoop groups, and MLT groups, then some VLANs will not be able to be created. VLANs actually use a multicast group ID or MID, unfortunately, so do multicast groups, STGs, and so on, and there are only 124 available.

Types of VLANs

There are two major types of VLANs used to segment users based on different administrative needs:

- Port-based VLAN
- Policy-based VLAN

Port-based VLAN

As we mentioned in Chapter 3, a port-based VLAN is a VLAN in which ports are explicitly added to the VLAN. When creating a port-based VLAN, it gets assigned a VID, which is what is used to coordinate VLANs across multiple switches.

Typically, an access port can only be a member of a single port-based VLAN. Port members of a port-based VLAN can be configured as always or never. If an administrator tries to use management software to put an access port that is already a member of a port-based VLAN into another port-based VLAN, he or she will be successful. However, the last port-based VLAN will be the new VLAN for that port:

Command `config vlan <vid> create byport <sid>`

Optionally, it is possible to name the VLAN by adding to the end of the command name `<name>`.

Example `config vlan 2 create byport 1 name PortVlanA`

Command `config vlan <vid> ports add <ports>`

Example `config vlan 2 ports add 4/1 4/7`

Command `config vlan <vid> ports remove <ports>`

Example `config vlan 2 ports remove 4/1 4/7`

Policy-based VLAN

A policy-based VLAN is one in which ports are dynamically added to the VLAN based on traffic coming into the port. Port members of a policy-based VLAN may be configured as always, never, or potential. When a port is designated as a potential member of the VLAN, incoming traffic is monitored. When the incoming traffic matches the policy, the port is dynamically added to the VLAN. Potential member ports that have joined the VLAN are removed from the VLAN if no traffic matching the policy is received within the aging time. A port that is a potential member of a policy-based VLAN becomes a participating member of the VLAN when the port receives a data frame that matches the policy type defined for that potential VLAN port. Until that time, the port will not transmit any data frames from that VLAN. Participation will continue until the aging time expires (default of 600 seconds). A port's membership in a VLAN is determined by traffic coming into the port.

 CAUTION **A port that is attached to a server or routers should be designated as an always member of the VLAN. If a server is connected to a port that is only a potential member of the policy VLAN and the server sends out very little traffic, a client may not be able to reach the server if the server port has timed out of the VLAN.**

A policy-based VLAN is a VLAN in which ports are dynamically added to the VLAN based on traffic coming into the port. Frames are analyzed based on frame content with three criteria that will determine port membership. They are the three subtypes of the policy-based VLANs:

- Protocol-based VLANs
- MAC VLANs
- IP subnet VLANs

Protocol VLANs   Protocol VLANs enable the localization of protocol traffic onto specific ports. This is very useful for ensuring that only ports with users of that protocol will have to see that protocol's traffic:

Command `config   vlan   <vid>   create   byprotocol   <sid>`
`<protocol>`

Example `config vlan 3 create byprotocol 1ipx name byprotocol3`

MAC VLANs   Passport products support MAC-based VLANs with the software revision of 2.0 or higher. Frames are associated with a MAC VLAN based on source MAC address. Creating a source MAC VLAN requires a static list of MAC addresses that will be members of the VLAN:

Command `config vlan <vid> bysrcmac <sid>`

Example `config vlan 10 bysrcmac 1`

NOTE   **Remember, a name can also be included with the command** `name`
`<value>.`

NOTE   **Routing is not supported on a MAC-based VLAN.**

IP Subnet VLANs   Membership in an IP subnet VLAN is based on the IP source address and mask inside the frame. Access ports can be members of multiple IP subnet VLANs. These VLANs are routable. By permitting multiple subnets on a single Passport port, subnet-based VLANs enables multinetting support. *Multinetting* is having more than one IP address, each from a different subnet, which is associated with the one physical port on a router or end station (see Figure 12-21). Multinetting and IP subnet-based VLANs enable the number of host addresses to be expanded beyond the subnet limitation by enabling the assignment of two or more IP addresses to a single port. Each IP subnet VLAN enables a port to forward traffic to an IP segment that is configured for that port. One port may, therefore, be forwarded traffic for multiple networks and for more workstations than traditional subnet masks might allow.

Class C masks normally enable only 255 workstations, but because there are two different networks on a single port, there can be 512 workstations in the network shown in Figure 12-21.

 NOTE In the scenario of multinetting, the router will know to forward all packets received from both the 201.99.10.0 network and 201.99.11.0 back to the same port. Workstations need to be statically configured not to forward packets from the partner subnet to the router, but rather to place them on the LAN:

Command `config vlan <vid> create byipsubnet <sid> <IP address/mask>`

Example `config vlan 4 create byipsubnet 1 10.10.10.0/24`

An administrator may want to view the forwarding database of a VLAN on the network and see which MAC addresses have been learned for that specific VLAN. This may help the administrator find possible network loops or workstations that may have Network Interface Cards (NICs) that are causing issues:

Command `show vlan info fdb-entry <vid>`

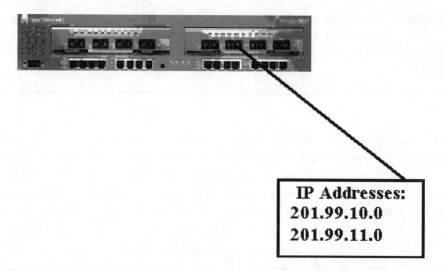

IP Addresses:
201.99.10.0
201.99.11.0

Figure 12-21 As seen in this figure of a Passport switch, one port has two IP addresses, each with a Class C mask.

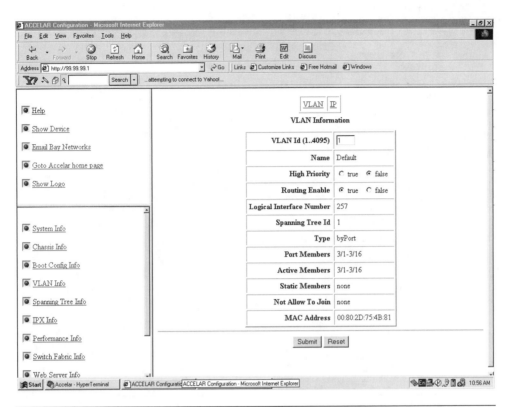

Figure 12-22 Viewing VLAN information with the web-based management tool

To see and change VLAN information in Device Manager, the context is

GUI `vlan>vlans` In this context, it is possible to create VLANs, modify port membership, change or add IP/IPX addresses, and view the forwarding database.

VLAN Manager

VLAN Manager is a GUI-based tool that comes with Device Manager. It is used to manage VLANs across multiple switches. To use VLAN Manager, the administrator must specify a domain or group of switches that will be managed (see Figure 12-23).

VLAN Manager can be used to observe ports in multiple VLANs across all switches defined in the domain (see Figure 12-24).

If VLAN Manager is used to create a protocol-based VLAN, all ports on the switch become potential members of the VLAN. This can cause issues because potential ports

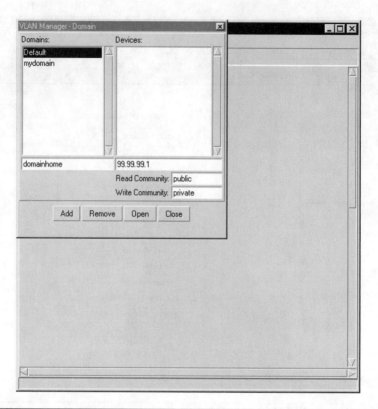

Figure 12-23 Opening a domain in VLAN Manager

become full-fledged VLAN members if protocol traffic is detected on the port. Thus, ports on the switch might end up in a VLAN without the administrator noticing! An administrator can only use VLAN Manager to move ports into a port-based VLAN. VLAN Manager can also be used to create trunk ports. By merely dragging a port to the trunk port line, the port becomes a trunk port and can be added to multiple VLANs.

Unassigned VLAN

One more important VLAN that should be mentioned is the unassigned VLAN. VLANs that do not belong to a port-based VLAN are members of the unassigned VLAN—VID zero. If a port belongs to a policy VLAN and frames that have entered this port do not belong to that policy (that is, an IPX VLAN port see IP frames entering) and the port is a member of the unassigned VLAN (that is, not a member of any port-based VLANs),

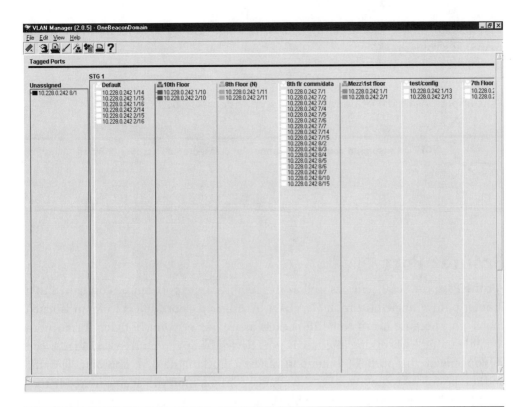

Figure 12-24   Viewing VLANs with VLAN Manager

the frame will be dropped. Ports only in the unassigned VLAN have no Spanning Tree associations and do not participate in the Spanning Tree Protocol (STP) negotiations. Isolated router ports are an example of a port in the unassigned VLAN. This VLAN cannot be deleted, as it is system created.

Isolated Router Ports

For the Passport 1000 series, any port can be configured as an isolated router port. Ports that are in isolated router mode behave like a traditional router port, only routing IP packets and not performing any bridging functions. The IP address for the isolated router port is associated with the physical port. Isolated router ports participate in RIP, OSPF, and all other layer 3 functions and do not participate in the STP. An isolated router port can never be in blocking mode because Spanning Tree does not affect the port; however, no VLANs can exist on this port. To create an isolated router port, an administrator merely assigns an IP address to a port. A port that has an IP address is viewed as a router port:

Command `config ethernet <port> ip create <ip address/mask>`

Example `config ethernet 1/1  ip create 10.10.10.10/24`

> **NOTE** An isolated router port cannot be created on a Passport 8600.

Brouter Port

For the Passport 8600 series as well as the 1000 series, a port can be configured as a Brouter port, a single-port routable VLAN. This Brouter port differs from an isolated router port because it can route IP packets as well as perform bridging for all nonroutable traffic. The routing interface is not affected by Spanning Tree, and VLANs can still operate on this port. A Brouter port can be a blocking state for nonroutable traffic and still be able to route IP traffic. This strange configuration will enable routed IP traffic to pass through a port that is in a blocking state for other VLANs. Brouter ports represent the Passport routing switch support for simultaneous routing of IP and bridging of other protocols on a single interface, preventing OSPF and RIP convergence from being dependent upon Spanning Tree convergence.

Command `config ip <port> ip create-brouter <IP address/mask> <vid>`

> **NOTE** The difference between a Brouter port and an IP VLAN configured to do routing is that the interface of the Brouter port is not subject to the Spanning Tree state of the port.

NOTE Brouter ports utilize VIDs. They will not show up with a `show VLAN info all` command, but if an administrator tries to use the VID that is dedicated to the Brouter port, he or she will get an error message stating that VID is in use. This can be a bit confusing.

Switches X, Y, and Z are connected together and pass IP, IPX, and AppleTalk traffic (see Figure 12-25). Spanning Tree will force one of the links in this looped configuration into a blocked status. This figure shows the link between X and Z in a blocked state. This prevents some of the links configured from being able to pass traffic, even routed traffic, which should not be subjected to Spanning Tree convergence times, but should rely on only the convergence of layer 3 protocols like OSPF or RIP. This is not a sensible configuration because routed traffic normally avoids loops through routing protocols and defined paths not through the layer 2 configuration limitations of Spanning Tree configurations.

Brouter ports enable simultaneous bridging and routing. Switches X, Y, and Z could be configured to simultaneously route IP and bridge the other protocols. This enables links to remain active for routing, removing the convergence time of Spanning Tree for IP traffic and speeding the reaction to network failures. IP traffic is routed around failures according to OSPF or RIP. Non-IP traffic would still be subject to the longer convergence times of Spanning Tree.

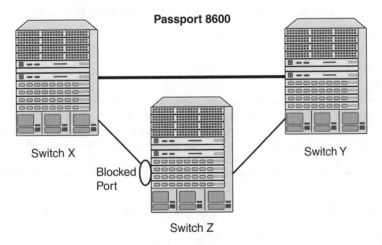

Figure 12-25 This figure shows three Passport 8600s configured with STP. The port between switches X and Z has been blocked by Spanning Tree to prevent network loops.

STGs

As defined in Chapter 3 and the IEEE 802.1D protocol, STP detects and eliminates logical loops in a bridged/switched network. When physical path redundancy exists, the Spanning Tree algorithm configures the network so the switch/bridge uses only one most efficient path. If that path fails, the protocol automatically reconfigures the network to make another path active but never enables redundant paths to be active at the same time; that would cause a loop.

A network may have multiple instances of STP. The collection of ports in one Spanning Tree instance is called a Spanning Tree Group (STG). Each STG has its own root and bridge parameters. The Passport supports up to 25 instances of Spanning Tree. The STG Protocol is not VLAN aware, so the ports associated with a VLAN must be wholly contained within a single STG. A VLAN is considered a subset of ports in a single STG.

Many networks do have multiple STGs. There are a few reasons to do so, although it does make the network more complex. One of the main reasons for the need for multiple Spanning Tree instances is because the STP is not VLAN aware, and this can cause issues of connectivity (see Figure 12-26).

Figure 12-26 shows three Passport 8600s configured with a loop between them. A Spanning Tree has blocked the port between switch one and switch two. Those two switches share VLAN IP1. The problem that will occur in this figure is that IP VLAN1 traffic will not be able to go from switch one to switch two because of the blocked port. Because IP VLAN1 does not exist on switch three, the traffic from switch one to switch two will not go over the alternate path provided by spanning tree. If an administrator would make three instances of Spanning Tree—one for each switch—no ports would be blocked, and no loop would exist because each of the switches has traffic for different VLANs.

 NOTE For Figure 12-26, an administrator can also create each IP VLAN on every switch and use tagged ports between the switches. This way IP VLAN1 traffic can reach switch two from switch one by going through switch three. With that configuration, only a single instance of Spanning Tree would be necessary:

Command `config stg <sid> <create, delete> add ports <port>`

A VLAN exists in only one STG, as does an access port. Trunk ports may be a member of every STG. Bridge Protocol Data Units (BPDUs) (see Chapter 3) from STG one (the default STG, STG1) are not tagged, but use the standard 802.1D frame format. All other BPDUs from STG 2-25 are tagged with an 802.1Q tag.

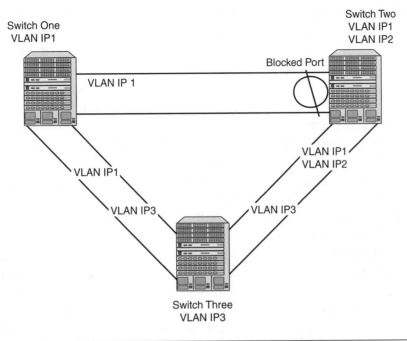

Switch One
VLAN IP1

Switch Two
VLAN IP1
VLAN IP2

Blocked Port

VLAN IP 1

VLAN IP1
VLAN IP2

VLAN IP1

VLAN IP3

VLAN IP3

Switch Three
VLAN IP3

Figure 12-26   This figure demonstrates the issues that Spanning Tree can cause for VLANs.

The Passport Forwarding Process (Layer 2)

Packets with a destination MAC address that does not belong to the Passport routing switch are packets that are handled at layer 2. The passport forwarding process for a layer 2 frame involves switching the frame to the correct VLAN.

When a Passport receives a frame, the forwarding decision for the frame will be based on the port options and VLAN configuration of the port on which the frame is received. VLAN membership for any inbound data frame is determined by examining characteristics of the frame. The frame is associated with a VLAN through explicit or implicit tagging. Once VLAN membership is determined, the frame is forwarded to its destination. A data frame may be a member of one VLAN only.

A frame is explicitly tagged if it is received on a tagged port and has an 802.1Q tag. When a packet arrives at a routing switch on a trunk port, we can immediately tell which VLAN it belongs to by the 802.1Q tag. The tag control information (TCI) has the VID. (Refer to Figure 12-19 for clarification.) In this instance, the frame is already associated with a VLAN in its tag; no forwarding decision is required. The frame is merely sent to the VLAN marked in the tag. If an untagged frame is received on a tagged port, that is an error. An administrator can choose to discard or forward the frames to a management VLAN. If the administrator chooses not to discard untagged frames on a tagged port, a default port-based VLAN on STG1 should be specified to accept the dropped frames.

A frame is implicitly tagged if the frame is received without a tag. Because no VLAN tag is present, VLAN membership is implied from the content of the frame itself and the port on which the frame is received. Passport routing switches try to associate a frame with the source MAC address (MAC-based VLAN), source IP address (IP subnet VLAN), protocol-based VLAN, and then port-based VLAN. Untagged frames are associated with a VLAN according to the following criteria.

If the frame arrives on an access port, the Passport will go through a decision-making process to determine the destination VLAN of the frame. The first check is for the MAC address of the packet. If there is a match to an existing MAC-based VLAN, the packet will be sent off to the MAC VLAN identified. If there is no MAC-based VLAN, there will be an examination for IP subnet information. If the IP subnet VLAN is defined on the port and the source network matches, the data frame becomes a member. There may be more than one IP subnet VLAN defined on a port. Next, the switch will decide if the inbound frame belongs to a policy VLAN by examining the protocol type field of the packet. If the frame's protocol type field matches a defined policy VLAN on the ingress port, then its VLAN membership is established. If the packet's type field does not match a defined policy VLAN configured on the ingress port or no policy VLAN is configured on the port, the packet is member of the port-based VLAN assigned to the ingress port. If there is no port-based VLAN defined on this port, then the frame will be dropped. The layer 2 frame decision process can be summarized as follows:

- Does the frame belong to a source MAC-based VLAN?

- Does the frame belong to a source IP subnet VLAN?

- Does the frame belong to a protocol-based VLAN?

- What is the port-based VLAN of the receiving port?

 CAUTION Port-based VLANs are on the bottom of the decision tree. If a port is a member of a port-based VLAN and a policy VLAN and traffic comes in that is of that protocol, the data frames will be seen as part of the protocol VLAN. This could be used for filtering but can also be confusing, so watch out.

Configuration and Troubleshooting

Many utilities are available to configure and troubleshoot the Passport network and switch. Before configuring the switch, it is essential to understand what configuration the switch has when it is removed from its box.

Factory Default Configuration

Passports are factory configured with all ports in a port-based VLAN called the *default VLAN*. With all ports in the default VLAN, the switch behaves like a layer 2 switch. The VID of the default VLAN is always one, and it is always a port-based VLAN. The default VLAN cannot be deleted or changed. When a user-defined port-based VLAN is deleted, all ports are moved back into the default VLAN to help maintain connectivity.

Additionally, there is only one single STG, STG one, and it is 802.1D compliant. Spanning Tree FastStart is disabled, and there are no IP addresses by default on the switch. Traffic priority for all ports is set to normal, and all ports are configured as access ports.

Displaying the ARP Cache

The Address Resolution Protocol (ARP) commands enable users to add or delete static entries in the ARP table (which maps IP addresses to MAC addresses):

Command `config ip arp add ports <port> ip <ip address> mac <mac address>`

Additionally, for troubleshooting purposes, an administrator may want to view the ARP cache to see if a MAC address mapping to an IP address appears in the cache was learned properly and on which port the address was learned. This can help administrators find duplicate IP addresses on the network:

Command `show ip arp info`

IP Routing (Layer 3)

If a packet comes into the Passport with a destination MAC address of the port or VLAN that has routing enabled, the destination IP address is examined. The packet may be a management packet destined for the port or VLAN, or the packet may be a packet that needs routing.

There are three types of router interfaces for the Passport switch: isolated router ports, virtual router interfaces for routing between VLANs, and Brouter ports. Isolated routing ports have IP addresses associated with physical ports. VLAN routing (port-based or IP policy VLAN) has IP addresses assigned to the VLAN and not associated with any physical ports. Brouter ports fall into the VLAN routing category.

The difference between isolated router ports and VLAN virtual router ports is when routing is configured on a VLAN, an IP address is assigned to the VLAN. That IP address acts like a virtual router interface and does not require any physical ports to be connected to that address. Instead, the IP address can be reached through all of the ports in the VLAN and becomes the IP address through which frames are forwarded out of the VLAN.

Because a given port can belong to multiple VLANs (some of which may be configured to route others not), there is no longer a one-to-one correspondence between the physical port and the router interface. Virtual router interface addresses can also be used for management like SNMP or Telnet.

Routed traffic can be forwarded to another VLAN within the routing switch or to an isolated router port. Using virtual VLAN router ports has another advantage. When setting up two VLANs to route between, no front panel connection is required! No external router is required, not even an extra port on the Passport is consumed. All that is necessary for full routing between all VLANs is to configure the VLANs with IP addresses and to set up the VLANs to route. Remember from Chapter 6 that routing requires the use of a routing protocol (RIP or OSPF) or static routes to enable sharing of IP addresses between VLANs or networks.

NOTE The Passport supports routing on the following types of VLANs only: Port-based VLAN, IP subnet-based VLAN, and IP protocol-based VLAN. It is not supported on MAC-based VLANs or VLANs based on other protocols, even IP version 6. IP addresses can be configured on a port-based VLAN, an IP VLAN, and must be configured for an IP subnet VLAN.

Prior to version 2.0 code, a created VLAN was automatically considered up on the switch. Whether there were ports in use on the VLAN or not, this VLAN would begin to advertise itself into the routing table if it was configured to do RIP or OSPF. With 2.0 code of software, a VLAN is only considered available if there is a port in the VLAN that has network connectivity and is active. IP addresses do not advertise for isolated router ports or VLANs that are not considered up. An administrator can force ports to remain in the up state and advertise availability even if nothing is plugged into the ports.

To verify IP addresses for the Passport, it is a good idea to use the ping utility to test connectivity:

Command `ping <ip address> <16..4076> <1..9999> <-I #> <-t #>` `<-d>` This command can optionally specify the size of a ping packet, the number of times to run the command, the interval between transmissions, no answer time out value, and debug mode.

Example `ping 10.10.10.10 256 99 -I 5 -t 40 -d` In this example, a ping packet of 256 bytes will be sent out 99 times, with 5 seconds between each packet, will wait 40 seconds for a response, and will bring back the results in a debug reporting fashion.

The Passport supports IP routing with static routes, RIP, and OSPF (see Figure 12-27).

Static Routes

Static routes and their necessity were discussed in Chapter 6. The following are the commands used to create static routes on a Passport switch.

Command `config ip static-route create <IP address/mask>` `next-hop <value> cost <value>` This command is used to create a static route.

Example `config ip static-route create <10.10.10.0/24 > next-hop <3.3.3.3> cost <2>`

Command `config ip static-route delete <IP address/mask>` This command is used to delete a previously created static route.

RIPv1 and RIPv2

RIPv1 and RIPv2 were discussed extensively in Chapter 6. The following are the commands to configure RIP for the Passport switches.

Command `config ip rip <enable, disable>` This command globally enables RIP on the Passport switch.

```
Accelar-1200> show ip route info
```

```
===============================================================================
                                   Ip Route
===============================================================================
```

OWNER	DST	MASK	NEXT	COST	VLAN	PORT	CACHE
OSPF	0.0.0.0	0.0.0.0	11.229.0.241	2	50	8/16	TRUE
OSPF	11.248.0.4	255.255.255.252	11.248.0.241	2	50	8/16	TRUE
OSPF	11.248.0.12	255.255.255.252	11.248.18.2	2	12	7/14	TRUE
OSPF	11.229.0.80	255.255.255.252	11.229.15.254	2	17	8/14	TRUE
OSPF	12.229.0.192	255.255.255.224	12.229.18.2	2	12	7/14	TRUE
LOCAL	12.229.0.240	255.255.255.240	12.229.0.242	1	50	-/-	TRUE
TRUE LOCAL	100.228.10.0	255.255.255.0	100.228.10.1	1	13	-/-	
TRUE LOCAL	00.228.22.0	255.255.255.0	100.228.22.1	1	2	-/-	
TRUE LOCAL	100.228.33.0	255.255.255.0	100.228.33.1	1	3	-/-	
TRUE LOCAL	100.228.44.0	255.255.255.0	100.228.44.1	1	4	-/-	

Total 10

Figure 12-27 This figure shows the routing table of a Passport 1200 switch. There are routes that are locally configured on the Passport as well as routes learned via OSPF.

CAUTION If RIP is not enabled globally, ports and VLANs cannot run RIP no matter how they are configured.

Command `config ip rip updatetime <seconds>` This command is used to change the number of seconds between RIP updates, which is 30 seconds by default.

Command `config ip rip holddown time<seconds>` This command is used to change the number of seconds before a route is marked down. It is usually three times the update time or 90 seconds by default.

Command `config vlan <vid> ip rip <enable, disable>` This command enables RIP on a VLAN.

Command `config ethernet <ports> ip rip enable` This command enables RIP on a port.

Command `config ip rip <send, receive> <IP address>` mode `<notsend, rip1, rip1comp, rip2>` This command enables the sending or receiving of RIP on an interface and the RIP version that interface will use; the choices are: RIPv1, RIPv1 compatible, and RIPv2. We discussed RIPv1 and RIPv2 in Chapter 6. RIP compatible is a mode where the interface generally acts like RIPv2 but sends out RIPv1 packets from interfaces that are in RIPv1 networks.

Command `config ip rip send 10.1.1.1 mode rip2`

GUI routing > ip > rip > interface config > send version dropdown

Command `config <vid> ip rip <default listen, default supply> <enable, disable>` This command enables or disables default route listen or supply. (For more details, see RIP information in Chapter 6.)

The following commands are used to create RIP policies. (For more information on RIP announce policies, see Chapter 6).

Command `config ip rip announce <policyID>` All commands are executed in this context, so the user must either enter this context in CLI or type this command before all the rest of the policy commands that follow.

Command `create`

Command `action announce` Used to create an announce policy.

Command `add-route-source <static, rip, ospf, direct>` Adds routes to announce.

Command `remove-route-source <static, rip, ospf, direct>` Removes routes that should not be included in the RIP announcement.

Command `rip metric <#>` Assigns a metric cost to advertised routes.

OSPF

OSPF was discussed extensively in Chapter 6. The following are the commands that are used to set up OSPF for the Passport switches.

As with RIP, OSPF first must be globally enabled before it can be added to a port or a VLAN. These commands enable OSPF globally from the CLI or from Device Manager:

Command `config ip ospf router-id <routerid>`

Command `config ip ospf enable`

GUI global > routing > ospf > enabled

After OSPF is enabled globally, it can be added to a port or VLAN:

Command `config ethernet <port> ip ospf enable`

GUI edit port > ospf

Command `config vlan <vid> ip ospf enable`

GUI edit vlan > ospf

Command `show ip route info` (see Figure 12-27)

IP Forwarding

The Passport routing switch is very versatile. In a network it can act as a layer 2 switch, perform layer 3 routing, or act as both a layer 2 switch and a layer 3 router. In a scenario where the Passport may be doing layer 2 switching, only an administrator can globally disable the routing function of the Passport. By setting the IP forwarding parameter to Not Forwarding, the Passport will no longer forward at layer 3. In the Passport when IP forwarding is disabled, there will be no routing between VLANs. Hosts can no longer use their Passport as the default gateway. IP addresses that are assigned to VLANs will be used for management purposes only but will still be reachable using the `ping` command:

Command `config ip forwarding <enable, disable>`

Virtual Router Redundancy Protocol (VRRP)

The router on a specific network can be the single point of failure to a client that is dependent on this router for connectivity to remote networks. If the default gateway assigned to the workstation (in the workstation IP configuration parameters) becomes unavailable, even if there are other routers in the intranet, this client will not be able to leave his or her broadcast domain. VRRP is designed to eliminate the single point of failure that exists because a single static default gateway router is assigned to an end station, and that router can go down. It introduces the concept of a virtual IP address (transparent to users) shared between two or more routers connecting the workstation's subnet to the enterprise network. With the virtual IP address as the default gateway on end hosts, VRRP provides a dynamic default gateway redundancy in the event of a failure. By having multiple Passports associate themselves with the same virtual IP address, another Passport can respond to a request for the default gateway at this IP address if the primary or master gateway is unavailable. The technology works without having to make changes to the workstation that is still given a single IP address for its default gateway (see Figure 12-28). The difference now is that a backup Passport can respond to requests for the default gateway should the primary gateway Passport be unavailable.

Figure 12-28 shows two groups of workstations on a single LAN. Each of these workstations has a default gateway configured that is actually a virtual router address. In this configuration there are two routers that share the virtual address. The workstations do not need to be aware of the underlying configuration and are only concerned with the IP address that is assigned to them. If one router with the virtual IP address becomes unavailable, the other VRRP router on the network can forward traffic on behalf of these workstations. Both the Passport 1000 and 8600 support up to 256 VRRP groups with 8 ports enabled in each VRRP group.

The VRRP Process

VRRP dynamically chooses a virtual router from one of the VRRP routers on the LAN to become the master VRRP router. The master is the VRRP router that is assuming the responsibility of forwarding packets sent to the IP address associated with the virtual router and answering ARP requests for these IP addresses. The master forwards packets sent to the virtual IP address. While in the master state, the router functions as the forwarding router for the IP address associated with the virtual router. The master also responds to ARP requests for the IP address associated with the virtual router and forwards packets with a destination MAC address equal to the virtual router MAC address.

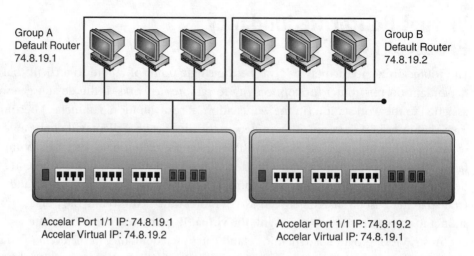

Group A
Default Router
74.8.19.1

Group B
Default Router
74.8.19.2

Accelar Port 1/1 IP: 74.8.19.1
Accelar Virtual IP: 74.8.19.2

Accelar Port 1/1 IP: 74.8.19.2
Accelar Virtual IP: 74.8.19.1

Figure 12-28   This figure shows workstations on a single LAN using two different default gateway addresses that are actually virtual router addresses.

NOTE   The MAC address for the VRRP interface is a virtual MAC beginning with 00-00-5e-00-01.

When a VRRP router is initialized, if it is the IP address owner, it will have a priority of 255 and will become the master. The IP address owner is the VRRP router that has virtual router IP addresses as real IP addresses. An IP address owner exists only if the VRRP address is also a primary address, an address selected from real addresses and used as the VRRP address. It can respond to pings, Internet Control Message Protocol (ICMP), Transmission Control Protocol (TCP) connections, and can be used for management like SNMP.

The master must not accept packets addressed to the IP address associated with the virtual router if it is not the IP owner. This is essential to understand because when using VRRP and management (SNMP and so on), the VRRP interface will not accept frames that are addressed to it unless the VRRP interface is the owner of that IP address (priority = 255.)

CAUTION This can cause management problems if the address used by the management station is the VRRP interface IP address. This is because (and this is a mistake many administrators make for lack of understanding) only the real owner of the IP address can respond to management requests sent to that address. Do not mix up the VRRP addresses and the IP address that actually belongs to the Passport switch, which may or may not be part of a VRRP setup.

When a router boots up, if it is the IP address owner, it will become the master; otherwise, the router with the highest priority becomes the master, and it becomes the backup router.

The virtual backup is the router that is available to assume forwarding responsibility should the current master fail. In a backup state, a VRRP router monitors the availability and state of the master router. It does not respond to ARP requests and must discard packets with a MAC address equal to the virtual router MAC address. It does not accept packets addressed to IP addresses associated with the virtual router.

The master router must also send out hello packets to all backup routers to let them know that the master is up. The backup routers expect to receive hello messages within specified intervals. If a backup router does not receive a hello message from the master router within four hello intervals, it may need to transition to become the master router.

The election process provides a dynamic failover of forwarding responsibility if the master becomes unavailable. If the master router goes down, the backup router chosen as master sends the VRRP advertisement and the ARP request with the virtual router MAC for each IP address associated with the virtual router and transitions to the master state.

To create VRRP on the Passport switch, configure ports on multiple switches (at least two up to eight) to use the same Virtual Router ID (VRID) and the same virtual IP address:

Command `config ethernet <port> ip vrrp <vrid> address <IP address>`

Example `config ethernet <2/3> ip vrrp <4> address <4.4.4.4>`

GUI port > vrrp > insert

VRRP can also be created on virtual router ports of VLANs that have IP addresses and routing enabled:

Command `config vlan <vid> ip vrrp <vrid> address <IP address>`

GUI vlan > ip > vrrp > insert

Critical IP Interface

The VRRP support on the Passport also has an enhanced feature called *critical IP interface*. The purpose of this setting is to prevent a VRRP interface from becoming a master if an IP interface configured on the Passport is not active. Additionally, if the critical IP interface becomes unavailable on the Passport serving as the VRRP master, it will transition to the backup state and another router will become the master instead (see Figure 12-29).

In Figure 12-29, the servers are not virtual router interfaces, but if the LAN connecting the workstations to the mail server B7K go down, all traffic from the workstation via

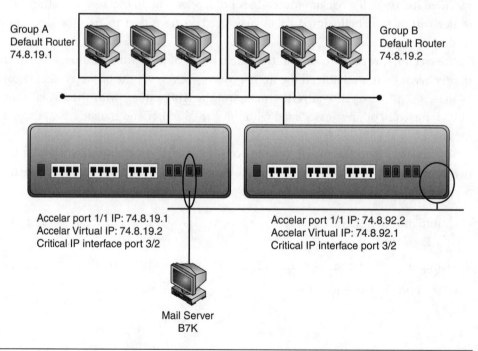

Figure 12-29 This figure depicts a network with a mail server B7K on a network with two Passports that are running in a VRRP configuration.

the network is still available. Therefore, the administrator should configure the LAN with B7K as a critical IP interface, and then if that LAN becomes unavailable to the Passport, the VRRP router goes into the backup state and stops forwarding traffic. The other VRRP router becomes master and forwards traffic for both groups of workstations. This effectively forces all traffic to continue to be forwarded to the mail server B7K via the LAN ports that are up:

Command `config ethernet <port> ip vrrp <vrid> critical-ip <IP address>` This command is used to create a critical IP address for an Ethernet port.

Equal Cost Multi-Path (ECMP)

ECMP routing provides load balancing and fast recovery from router or trunk failures (see Figure 12-30). Normally, in a RIP or OSPF network, routers will receive and send out routing updates to determine the best path to all networks. The routing table will then contain one route to each and every network. With ECMP, multiple paths will be maintained in the routing table to the same network as long as the paths are of equal cost. In fact ECMP enables up to four different equal cost paths to any single network. This enables traffic to be load balanced across more than one physical pipe if dual paths to other networks exist. In case of logical or physical route failure, traffic will continue to flow normally across the other routes available to that network. ECMP requires more memory for the routing tables and is more processor intensive because it requires the switch to maintain multiple routes to all destination networks whenever possible.

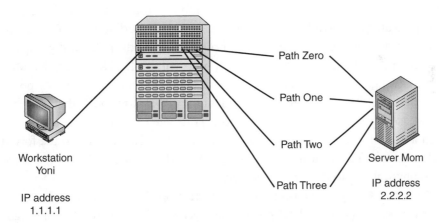

Figure 12-30 This figure shows an example of a network with ECMP enabled. All traffic from the source workstation Yoni to the destination server Mom will use path three.

If there are multiple possible routes to a single network, the switch will then need to decide which route to use. ECMP uses a hash of source/destination IP addresses of packets to determine via which path to send packets. The hash works with doing an XOR on the six least significant bits of the source and destination and then doing a MOD function with the number of paths available. The answer will determine which path to use.

NOTE The last six bits (see Figure 12-30) of the IP address of Yoni (1.1.1.1)=000001, of Mom (2.2.2.2)=000010. The exclusive OR (XOR) function equals 000011 or 3. Four MOD 3=3 MLT.

MuliLink Trunking (MLT)

MLT is a point-to-point connection that enables configuration of multiple physical ports to logically act like a single port with the aggregated bandwidth of the ports. Grouping multiple ports into a logical link is one way of achieving higher aggregate throughput on a switch-to-switch or server-to-switch connection. MLT also provides media and module redundancy, which is highly useful for preventing failure of essential applications.

The Passport 1000 supports up to eight MLT groups and up to four links per MLT group. Four Gigabit Ethernet ports can be combined into a single MLT group with a total aggregated bandwidth of four gigabits! For the Passport 8600, MLT supports eight ports per group, with up to 32 groups. In both cases all ports in the MLT group must be the same speed, duplex, and hardware (all ports will be TX, LX, SX, or FX). MLT may span slots for greater redundancy. MLT is also compatible with the STP. The ports must be in the same STG, and they transmit identical BPDUs as though they were a single port. MLT ports can be tagged ports or access ports, but cannot be isolated router ports. When a new MAC address is learned on a MLT port, it is entered into the forwarding database and marked as learned on the MLT port. The Passport will need to determine which physical link to forward packets across.

MLT ports use a similar hash to that of ECMP to decide over which path traffic is to be forwarded. Traffic that is bridged, namely layer 2 traffic, will use a hashing algorithm that is based on source and destination MAC address. Routed traffic, layer 3, uses an algorithm based on source and destination IP address. Just like with ECMP, the six least significant bits of the address will be XORed and a MOD function will be performed to determine the path to use. All traffic from one source destined to one destination will always travel over one specific port (the hash and the MOD function will always return the same numerical value). This is to ensure that packets arrive in order and properly (see Figure 12-31).

MLT helps to improve network performance and resilience by having multiple physical ports acting like one link. If any of the ports (or even slots in an MLT configuration

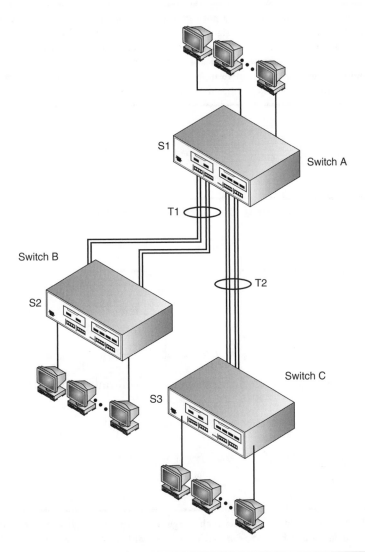

Figure 12-31 This figure shows three Passport 1100s with two MLT groups between them. Switch A has an MLT group to Switch B and Switch C.

with ports on different slots) were to become unavailable, the other ports would continue to forward traffic, and the change would be completely unnoticed by the user. The configuration in Figure 12-31 gives the network a high level of redundancy as well as bandwidth aggregation. Even greater network resilience can be achieved by using ports on different modules/slots to be included in the MLT group.

 CAUTION STP will block any path in a looped configuration that is not the least cost. Port costs are assigned from the Passport by default. Gigabit links in the Passport have the lowest cost, a cost of one. That means that multiple Gig links will have the same cost of one and may not be realized as the lowest cost path. As an administrator, it is essential to manually assign port costs and to make the MLT link the lowest cost so that it does not become blocked because of STP:

Command `config mlt <mid> <create,delete>`

 NOTE MID represents the MLT ID that the administrator assigns this trunk:

Command `config mlt <mid> <add, remove> ports <ports>` This command can be used to add or remove ports from an MLT.

Example `config mlt 12 add ports 3/1 3/3`

If this MLT is supposed to perform tagging or stop performing tagging, the command is

Command `config mlt <mid> perform-tagging <enable,disable>`

Command `show mlt info <mid>` This command shows the MLT information.

NOTE MLT replaces LinkSafe technology by providing a higher level of physical redundancy and backup while giving additional bandwidth to the user.

Port Mirroring

For traffic analysis using a network analyzer, the Passport supports port mirroring. In a simple, shared media network, a network analyzer (also known as a *sniffer*) can be plugged into a port on the common media and used to view all traffic coming into and being sent out of every port on the network. However, the Passport ports are all part of a separate collision domain, and therefore, no port can see traffic from any other ports unless the traffic is directed there. For security, this is very beneficial, but traffic monitoring becomes impossible in this scenario. If an administrator wants to see the types of frames/traffic that is being sent on the port, simply plugging in a sniffer will not work. Port mirroring enables any port in the Passport to be monitored for its ingress traffic. Simply specify a destination port on which to see mirrored traffic, and specify the source ports from which traffic is mirrored. Any packets ingressing the specified port will be forwarded normally, but a copy will also be sent out to the mirroring port. This enables a network engineer to plug a sniffer or probe into the second port (the mirroring port) to review all traffic on the port needing monitoring. Administrators can then analyze all frames/packets flowing into the Passport port to determine if a problem has occurred. Packet traffic is uninterrupted on the mirrored port and packets flow normally to their destination ports. A more sophisticated network analyst can monitor traffic based on specific MAC addresses. By setting up appropriate filters, only specific packets with a certain source or destination MAC address are copied to the mirror port.

NOTE So as not to see unintended traffic, remove the port being used for the mirroring (destination traffic) from all VLANs. That will assign the port into the unassigned VLAN. Additionally, disable Spanning Tree for the port:

Command `config diag mirror-by-port <id>` All the commands that follow are in this context so the administrator either should go to this context in CLI or type out this string before the rest of the commands.

Command `create in-port <value> out-port <value>` This command is used to create a mirrored port that is being monitored (in port) and a mirroring port that traffic is being sent to (out port).

Command `enable <true, false>`

Command `delete`

Command `mirrored-port <ports>` This command changes the in port.

Command `mirroring-ports <ports>` This command changes the out port.

> **NOTE** It is better not to rely on mirroring for troubleshooting. It is preferable to use a hub whenever possible.

Dynamic Host Configuration Protocol (DHCP) and BootP Relay

DHCP and BootP, as we discussed in Chapter 4, are features of the IP addressing protocol. They enable an administrator to assign addresses at a central server and have users and workstations dynamically acquire IP addresses anywhere on the network. Network managers can configure or decide to configure only a small number of DHCP servers in one central location for ease of management. DHCP and BootP have one issue that is essential to understand. As we mentioned before, the DHCP/BootP process consists of workstations that send out a request packet for an IP address. Because these workstations have no address the destination of these packets are to the broadcast address, (IP address 255.255.255.255. MAC address of FF-FF-FF-FF) and the source address contains all zeros. Responses from the server giving out the IP address will be a broadcast as well. If the DHCP client is on a subnet that does not include a DHCP server, the broadcasts are by default not forwarded to the server on a different subnet.

Routers do not normally forward broadcasts. The Passport, however, can be configured to relay these DHCP broadcast packets to all networks that have a BootP/DHCP server configured (see Figure 12-32). Alternatively, the Passport can take this broadcast packet and convert it to a unicast to forward directly to a DHCP/BootP server at a known address. This will save on the amount of broadcast traffic that is seen on the LAN. (We all know that broadcast traffic must be processed by each and every NIC to make sure the data is not for the local workstation.)

The Passport can be configured to forward the broadcasts to a server through an isolated or virtual router port. The router interface can be configured to forward DHCP broadcasts to other locally connected network segments or directly to the server's IP address. DHCP must be enabled on a per routable interface basis:

Command `config vlan <vid> dhcp-relay <enable, disable>` This command enables DHCP relay for a VLAN.

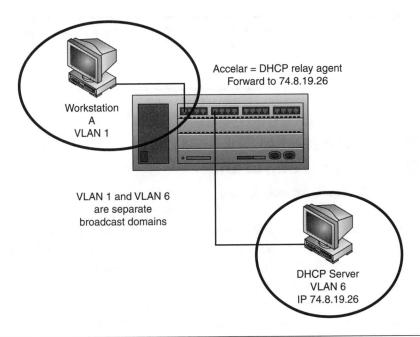

Accelar = DHCP relay agent
Forward to 74.8.19.26

Workstation
A
VLAN 1

VLAN 1 and VLAN 6
are separate
broadcast domains

DHCP Server
VLAN 6
IP 74.8.19.26

PART III

Figure 12-32 This figure shows workstation A in VLAN 1 trying to reach the DHCP server in VLAN 6. Because each VLAN is a separate broadcast domain, the Passport will have to relay the DHCP information to the server on VLAN 6.

Command `config ethernet <ports> dhcp-relay <enable, dis-able>` This command enables DHCP relay for a port.

Command `config ip dhcp-relay create-fwd-path agent <IP address> server <IP address> mode <bootp, dhcp, bootp_dhcp> state <enable, disable>` This command is used to create the relay agent on a specific interface.

Most enterprise networks use multiple DHCP/BootP servers for fault tolerance. The Passport can support single or multiple DHCP/BootP servers for network redundancy and load sharing. The Passport forwards copies of the DHCP/BootP client request to up to ten servers. The Passport can also enable clients to have a preferred server with a backup should the primary fail. In this instance the Passport will hold DHCP/BootP requests and not send them out to the LAN with the backup DHCP/BootP server unless it becomes clear that the primary is not responding with an IP address for the client's requests.

NOTE The Passport is not a DHCP or BootP server. They can help the process of DHCP and BootP by forwarding client and server packets across local or remote networks.

Uniform Datagram Protocol (UDP Forwarding)

UDP is one of the means that workstations use to communicate with servers for services like time synchronization, file transfers, and terminal access. Some network applications rely on UDP to request a service or locate a server for an application. Microsoft workstations, especially Windows 95 stations that do not have WINS support, use UDP to register names. The issue with UDP is identical to that of DHCP: UDP relies on broadcasts, which cannot cross a router. If a host is on a network or VLAN that does not have UDP services available, the workstation will not get serviced from another VLAN because UDP broadcasts are not forwarded to other segments or VLANs. Passport routing switch can support UDP forwarding. To use UDP forwarding on the Passport, an administrator will need to set up filters/policies to enable UDP broadcasts to be forwarded through specific ports where certain workstations are connected:

Command `config ip udpfwd protocol <UDP port>create <Protocol name>`

Example `config ip udpfwd protocol <53>create <DNS>`

QoS

Today's network can consist of voice, video, and specialized data traffic all using the same bandwidth. IP telephony and voice, videoconferencing, and other applications that are high-bandwidth, real-time, and mission-critical applications are driving the need for better services in the campus network. They require specialized attention beyond the traditional best-effort services provided in the Ethernet networks. The prioritization of business-critical is now a real necessity because of the diversity of today's business applications. Business-critical applications, such as voice traffic, should not contend for bandwidth with the casual web surfer or file transfer. Instead, policies that guarantee QoS for particular applications may be created to ensure that critical applications have higher-priority access to network resources.

QoS is the classification of traffic according to different levels of services. Because different types of traffic have different susceptibilities towards delay, latency, jitter, and bandwidth, they need different levels of service. Classification is using a set of criteria to select frames and group them into different classes for preferential treatment of one class relative to another. The criteria used to classify frames can be the source or destination layer 2 or 3 addresses, source or destination TCP/UDP ports, network protocol, or even any combination of field values within a frame that meets user-specified rules. Network resources need to be reserved to achieve the desired QoS for the higher classes.

Means of Achieving QoS

There are several ways to achieve QoS in the network. An administrator should choose whichever method is most suited to his or her environment.

IP Filters

A key component of providing QoS is a switch's capability to control IP traffic. The Passport routing switch supports IP filters that can be used to control traffic and provide levels of security (see Figure 12-33). For any given port, a list of filters may be specified to apply to frames entering that port. Each filter consists of a set of values to be matched and the actions to be taken if a match is found.

The Passport switch supports source/destination filters that look to match a specific IP source or destination address with a specific mask. Additionally, there is support for global filters that can look at the protocol type, TCP/UDP source, or destination port number. These fields actually represent applications, users, and departments that exist within the network traffic. The Passport routing switch can then make intelligent decisions based on the action that the filter specifies. A filter can specify actions to be taken on a matching frame, including forwarding the packet to the appropriate egress port, or discarding a packet that is unrecognized, or mirroring the frame to a defined port.

All Passport switches currently support eight global filters per port or group of four ports. A Passport 1000 also supports 1024 source and destination filters, whereas a Passport 8000 switch supports the definition of 4096 filters of these filters for each port on the switch.

Priority Settings Using IEEE 802.1P

The IEEE 802.1P provides a standards-based way to set the priority bits in a frame's header and to map these settings to traffic classes, with each class corresponding one-to-one to a different queue. Standards-based priority queuing enables prioritization of traffic, so important network traffic always get through.

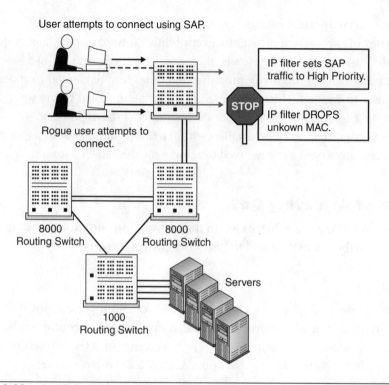

User attempts to connect using SAP.

IP filter sets SAP
traffic to High Priority.

STOP

Rogue user attempts to
connect.

IP filter DROPS
unkown MAC.

8000
Routing Switch

8000
Routing Switch

Servers

1000
Routing Switch

Figure 12-33 An IP flow filter can be used to deliver high-priority queuing for essential applications as well as security in the network.

Queues, however, require memory hardware in the switch for storing frames awaiting transmission. If a switch provides eight queues per port for the eight priority settings, each queue will store frames with a specific priority setting to provide complete differentiated services. To minimize costs, however, fewer queues may be provided per port than the eight priority settings; in such switches, frames from several priority settings may be lumped together in one queue. If a switch has only one queue, then all frames irrespective of priority settings are mapped to traffic class zero. With only one queue, all traffic is treated the same and is acted upon first come first serve. There is no QoS in this situation.

If a switch has two queues, then if an IP frame is received with an IP Precedence/TOS bit setting priority setting of four or higher, the frame will be assigned to the higher-priority traffic queue one. A frame with a bit setting of three or less is assigned to the lower-priority traffic queue zero and is treated as normal priority or best effort.

Passports also enable priority setting through 802.1Q tagging. If an IEEE 802.1Q-tagged frame is received with the user priority bits set to greater than zero, then the frame is treated as a high-priority frame and assigned to the high-priority queue. When a high-priority frame is sent out of a trunk port, the user priority bits are set to seven.

Passport Queuing and Prioritization

With Passport routing switches, an administrator can set traffic prioritization to assign a packet or data stream in a high-priority queue so that it goes through the network with minimal latency. Bandwidth and queues are assigned to give mission- and time-critical frames the higher-priority service needed.

The Passport 1000 switches supports queuing and prioritization for traffic using two queues, enabling the switch to operate in either of two priority modes: best effort or priority. The routing switches prioritize traffic using queues and headers. As each packet forwards through the ARU, a header is attached. Each time a packet is forwarded within the switch, it is placed in either a high- or low-priority queue, depending on the information in the internal packet header. At each stage within the Passport 1000 switch, packets designated as high priority are sent before packets tagged as low priority.

In best effort mode, the factory default setting, all traffic is treated with the same priority. Frames are queued for transmission on a first-in first-out (FIFO) basis. In priority mode, high-priority traffic flows through the switch fabric using a high-priority data path, with output buffers reserved for high-priority traffic.

An administrator can implement priority queuing in four ways in the Passport 1000:

- **By port**   Specifying that any traffic from a particular port should be classified as high (or low) priority.

Command   `config ethernet <ports> high-priority <true, false>` This command is used for the Passport 1000 series to set a port to high or low priority.

- **By MAC address**   Specifying that a learned or a static forwarding entry should have a high or low priority.

Command   `config vlan <vid> fdb-entry monitor <mac> status <value> <true, false>`

- **By VLAN**   Specifying any VLAN to be a high- (or low-) priority VLAN, and have all traffic passing through this VLAN treated as high- (or low-) priority traffic.

Command   `config vlan <vid> high-priority <true, false>`

- **By IP flows**   Specifying IP flows to identify a particular stream of traffic at the IP layer and at the TCP/UDP layer for high (or low priority). Setting IP flows as a priority method enables the use of source and destination IP address and source and destination IP port (the port used for Telnet, FTP, and Network File System [NFS]) to identify IP traffic flows.

Command `config ip ipflow create src-ip <value> src-port <value> dst-ip <value> dst-port <value> protocol <value>`

When a port is configured for high priority, all frames received on that port are assigned to the high-priority queue. For a MAC address that is configured high priority, all frames originating from that MAC address are assigned to the high-priority queue. With a VLAN configured for high priority, all frames received on any of the active ports of that VLAN are assigned to the high-priority queue. Finally, if an IP frame meets an IP filter specification, the filter action can be set to assign the frame to a high-priority queue.

The Passport 8000 routing switch provides eight output queues per port to utilize all eight types of traffic. Each queue may have up to 32 time slots assigned. In each time slot, the queues are serviced in a round-robin sequence, starting with the highest-priority queue seven and going down through to the lowest-priority queue zero. Each time slot assigned to a queue is an opportunity to transmit a packet. The priority setting zero (the default) does not map to traffic class zero; it maps to traffic class two and is used as the default priority to ensure interoperability with switches and traffic that have no priority setting.

The IEEE provides the following descriptions of traffic types for the cases where multiple queues are available in a switch:

Network control traffic Traffic that is necessary to keep the network operational and must get through the network with the highest priority. It is assigned to queue seven.

Voice traffic Requires less than 10-ms delay and jitter (one-way transmission through the LAN infrastructure of a single campus). It is assigned to queue six.

Video traffic Requires less than 100-ms delay and is assigned to queue five.

Controlled load traffic Important business applications that will receive bandwidth preallocation through some form of reservation that begins with the flow of traffic from the application. This traffic is assigned to queue four.

Excellent effort traffic Traffic that is treated with the best best-effort service that a network can provide. It is assigned to queue three.

Best effort traffic Traffic flowing on most networks, especially LANs, today. This traffic is assigned to queue zero.

Background traffic   Traffic that can flow on the network without impacting other users and applications, such as huge downloads of files. It is assigned to queue one.

The traffic class for queue two is reserved for future use.

Command `config ethernet <port> qos-level <0..7>` This command sets the priority for a port to use one of the eight queues listed previously.

IP Multicast Support

The idea behind multicast support is to reduce the overall network load caused by applications that need to be viewed by many people at one time. This can be accomplished by multicasting the data across the network instead of forwarding the traffic to all segments and users. Instead, the data is only sent to end users that have a need for the data and have requested membership in the group of users getting the data (also called the *multicast group*).

Multicast traffic is traffic that may be sent from one workstation to many users, or many workstations to one workstation, or many-to-many workstations. Multicasting is more efficient than broadcasting for reaching multiple workstations at once and only workstations that request an application or service. As discussed in Chapter 4, the addresses for multicast traffic lies in the range of Class D IP addresses, from 224.0.0.0 through 239.255.255.255. Multicast traffic is sent from one workstation (or a group of workstations) to a specific group of workstations in the multicast group. All workstations in the multicast group share a common IP address and even share in some cases a common MAC address (mapped to that IP address). An example of a multicast group is all routers using RIPv2. All RIPv2 routers share a multicast IP address of 224.0.0.9. A router sending out RIPv2 updates will send updates to that address. Only RIPv2 routers will process those updates, and all other workstations will drop the frame when it is received in the NIC.

IP multicasting is actually the preferred method for delivering desktop videoconferencing and distance learning within the IP network. Networks that do not support multicasting are forced to broadcast these applications throughout the entire network, (possibly multiple times, perhaps even out of every switched port) wasting network bandwidth.

The Passport routing switch provides very efficient native IP multicast services to address, route, and deliver information to multiple destinations with a single transmission without wasting bandwidth. Passport routing switches optimize IP multicast in switched VLAN environments by forwarding IP multicast traffic only to ports with group members. The Passport 1000 product supports up to 1024 separate IP multicast streams within a network, whereas the Passport 8600 has support for up to 16,000 separate IP source subnet/multicast groups.

To discover group membership and optimize multicast traffic, the Nortel Networks layer 3 routing switch provides support for two standard protocols that can be used to interoperate with multicast routers in the network:

- IGMP, both versions 1 and 2

- Distance Vector Multicast Routing Protocol (DVMRP)

Internet Group Management Protocol (IGMP)

Network devices use IGMP to join and leave multicast groups. Passport switches generate IGMP queries on all ports and subnets to discover membership in multicast groups. IP hosts use IGMP to report their multicast group memberships in response to the Passport's query. Additionally, Passport layer 3 switches can listen to IGMP report messages to determine on which VLAN, or switch port, a multicast group member is connected. These group members may belong to a VLAN that has ports that may contain members and ports with nonmembers or members of other groups. The Passport will only forward the multicast traffic to the ports with group members even within the single VLAN. If necessary, the Passports can also forward the multicast traffic to other group members located in other parts of the network (see Figure 12-34).

IGMP also enables a host to report joining or leaving a multicast group without waiting for a query from the local router. Users may join or leave the group at will:

Command   `config ethernet <ports> ip 13-igmp`   This is the context for all IGMP commands for an Ethernet port. (IGMP can also be configured on an interface or VLAN.)

Distance Vector Multicast Routing Protocol (DVMRP)

Routers themselves use DVMRP to construct an optimum distribution tree for efficient forwarding of multicast traffic from a source to all active destinations in a group. Basically, this is like a loop-free shortest-path route that traffic will flow over. This tree is constructed on demand from a multicast source, which serves as the root of the tree, to destination multicast group members that act as the leaves of the tree. Once this tree is

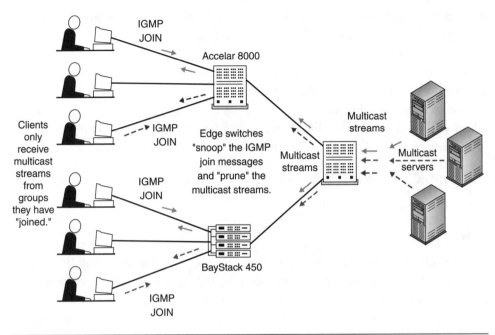

Figure 12-34 This picture shows the Passport switch allowing ports with multicast users to join the multicast group while pruning ports that contain no users out of the multicast stream.

created, DVMRP enables it to change dynamically if hosts leave the multicast group or if the multicast source application changes locations.

> **Command** `config ethernet <port> ip dvmrp <enable, disable, info>` This command is used for setting up DVMRP on an Ethernet port. Just like with IGMP, DVMRP can be applied to an interface or a VLAN.

Additional Support in IP Multicast Optimization at Layer 2

There are two features that enable the Passport to maximize support for multicast clients.

IGMP Snooping

The Passport routing switch listens to the group reports from each port in a VLAN and builds a database of multicast group members per port. Multicast frames received for a group are forwarded only to those ports that have members in the group addressed. VLAN ports without group members are pruned (excluded) from the multicast distribution and will not receive unnecessary traffic. By using this feature known as *IGMP snooping*, the Passport routing switch enhances multicast performance, greatly reducing nuisance traffic to noninterested workstations.

To keep the forwarding database current, the switches force active members to periodically report their membership, forward IGMP queries from other multicast routers to all ports on a VLAN, and relay membership reports to other multicast routers:

Command `config vlan <vid> igmp-snoop state <enable, disable>`

IGMP Proxy

In a shared-media LAN if a host were to report its group membership in an IP multicast group to a querying local router, all hosts on the LAN including other members of the group receive the report. If one host reports membership in a group, no other hosts do because as long as one there is even one member in a multicast group on the network, the router will forward multicast frames to the LAN. In a switched virtual LAN, the Passport switch simulates this with a feature called the *IGMP proxy*. Here even if the Passport routing switches receives multiple reports for the same multicast group, it will only forward the first report to a multicast router. If a new group is reported, the Passport routing switch will forward this new information to the upstream router. It also relays queries from the multicast router to all ports of the VLAN. By acting as an intelligent IGMP Proxy and not forwarding all reports to the upstream router, the Passport routing switch greatly reduces unnecessary traffic that can consume bandwidth, buffers, and processing power:

Command `config vlan <vid> igmp-snoop report-proxy <enable, disable>`

Management Access Policies

Management access policies are used to secure a Passport system by creating access lists for specific services. Only the IP addresses specified in the access list can do any type of management to the system. The services specified in these lists can include HTTP, rlogin, SNMP, and Telnet. When creating access policies, a filter is created that will be matched to IP addresses for allowing or refusing management access. The filter with the highest precedence will be used unless there are two filters with the same precedence, in which case the filter with the lowest filter ID will take precedence (the last filter created).

Command `config sys access-policy policy <pid>` This is the context for the commands that are used to create an access policy from CLI.

 CAUTION When creating an access policy, SNMP management could become denied. This will cause issues with using Device Manager (see Figure 12-35). Be sure to specify in CLI and/or Device Manager when creating policies that SNMP is enabled.

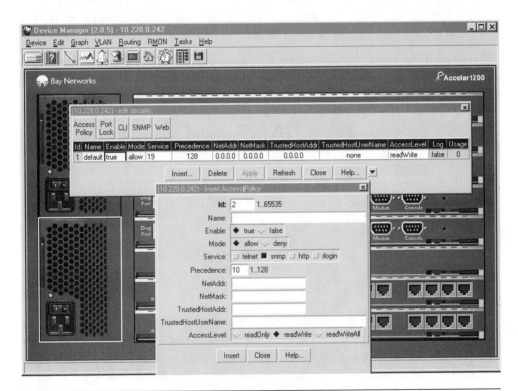

Figure 12-35 This figure shows the creation of a management filter using Device Manager. It is also possible to see the default filter that exists on the Passport.

Internetwork Packet Exchange (IPX) and IPX Routing

IPX is a connectionless layer 3 protocol that is involved in routing, addressing, and switching in a Novell environment. The Passport has support for IPX with

- Dynamic IPX RIP routing.

- Support for Service Advertising Protocol (SAP) used by clients to find services in an IPX network.

- Static and default route support.

- Four IPX network addresses are supported per interface.

Command `config ipx forwarding enable` This command is used to globally enable IPX for the Passport switch. After the global enabling of IPX, the protocol can be added to ports or VLANs.

Command `config vlan <vid> ipx create <IPX network #> <encapsulation type>`

Encapsulation type is optional in the previous command. There are four Ethernet encapsulation types available: Ethernet II, 802.2 (LLC), 802.3 (RAW), and 802.3 (SNAP). Novell commonly uses 802.2 in its newer operation systems.

Example `config vlan 9 ipx create 0x00000009 ethernet-ii`

Command `show ipx route` Shows the IPX routing table

Command `show ipx sap` Shows the current services learned by the Passport

Command `config ipx static-route create <IPX network #> <next hop> <hop-count> <tick-count>` Creates a static IPX network route

Spanning Tree may cause timeouts for Novell clients attempting to boot up and log in. As explained previously in Chapter 3, the STP may cause a port to remain down for up to one minute. This can cause issues with Novell clients. It is essential to have ports, with Novell clients attached, to utilize FastStart. The command to enable (or disable) FastStart on a port is

Command `config ethernet <port> stg <sid> faststart <enable, disable>`

Additionally, there are many IPX show commands that are accessible from the CLI. They can be used to help the administrator troubleshoot and configure an IPX network.

Locked Ports

Once a port is configured properly, a manager may decide to lock the port. This prevents others from making changes to the port without unlocking the port first. The hope is that a user that will have to first unlock the port may think twice about why the port was locked in the first place and resist making unknown changes. To lock a port, the administrator first enables port locking and then configures a specific port to be locked:

Command `config sys set portlock on` This command globally enables port locking.

Command `config ethernet <port> lock true` This command is used to lock a specific port.

GUI Go to the edit > security > port lock > and select ports to lock and set lock value to true.

Port Errors and Port Statistics

It is important for an administrator to pay attention to port errors. These can indicate if a port is failing. Port statistics can help an administrator determine if a port is receiving and transmitting packets properly (see Figure 12-36):

Command `show ports error <main, extended> <port#>`

Command `show ports stats interface <extended, main>`

Command `clear ports stats`

Passport-8610:5/show/ports/stats# interface

Passport-8610:5/show/ports/stats/interface# extended

==

Port Stats Interface Extended

==

PORT_NUM	IN_UNICST	OUT_UNICST	IN_MULTICST	OUT_MULTICST	IN_BRDCST	OUT_BRDCST
2/1	0	0	0	0	0	0
2/2	277	256	0	1424	83	10
2/3	0	0	0	0	0	0

Passport-8610:5/show/ports/stats/interface# main

==

Port Stats Interface

==

PORT_NUM	IN_OCTETS	OUT_OCTETS	IN_PACKET	OUT_PACKET	IN_FLOWCTRL	OUT_FLOWCTRL
2/1	0	0	0	0	0	0
2/2	52173	135078	360	1690	0	0
2/3	0	0	0	0	0	0

Figure 12-36 This figure shows the port statistics using both the extended and the main context for a few ports on a Passport 8600.

Summary

In this chapter we discussed in great detail the Nortel Networks Passport 1000 and 8000 series of products. We focused on the versatility of the Passport layer 3 switches and their different roles in the network. We covered how to use CLI to perform various tasks on the Passport for layer 2 and layer 3 functionality. We introduced Device Manager and VLAN Manager, two other configuration tools that are GUI based. We also examined in great detail many possible different port configurations for the Passport switch for its many different functions in the network.

Questions

1. How many packets per second can the Passport switch route/switch?
   A. 500,000 packets per second
   B. 1,000,000 packets per second
   C. 5,000,000 packets per second
   D. 7,000,000 packets per second

2. Which Passport model is ideal for desktop switching?
   A. 1050
   B. 1100
   C. 1200
   D. 8100
   E. 8600

3. Which Passport model can be configured with redundant SSF modules?
   A. 1100
   B. 1150
   C. 1200
   D. 1250

4. LinkSafe provides which type of protection?
   A. I/O module failure
   B. Cable breaks
   C. SSF failure
   D. Chassis failure

5. Which statement is true about tagged ports?
   A. All tagged ports reject untagged packets.
   B. A tagged port may be a member of multiple port-based VLANs.
   C. A tagged port may be a member of only port-based VLANs.
   D. BPDUs from the default STG are tagged when sent out a tagged port.

6. Which value is stored in the boot options configuration?
   A. The system MAC address
   B. The IP address of the default VLAN
   C. The console username and password
   D. The flags used during system startup

7. Which CLI user password combination has layer 2 access?
   A. Public, read only
   B. l2, l2
   C. rw, rw
   D. L2, L2
   E. ro, ro

8. Which statement is true about MLT?
   A. MLT can be configured on isolated router ports.
   B. MLT groups can be configured as access or trunk ports.
   C. A single MLT group can contain mixed speeds and media ports.
   D. MLT is supported on all revisions of hardware and software.

9. When a Passport switch receives a RIPv2 announcement on a RIPv1 port it will
   _____.
   A. Accept the routes that are being advertised with their masks.
   B. Accept the routes that are being advertised, but reject the masks and use natural masks.
   C. Ignore the announcement.
   D. Accept the routes that are being advertised, and use masks that are configured on the switch.

10. Which statement is true about an isolated router port on a Passport switch?
    A. It is based on a port-based VLAN.
    B. It can be part of an MLT.
    C. It is a VLAN with only one port.
    D. It may not be blocked by Spanning Tree.

11. Which statement is true about VRRP?
    A. VRRP requires the administrator to change the addresses of all the hosts on the network.
    B. VRRP master cannot be forced into backup state by another router.
    C. The virtual router MAC is the MAC address of the real interface.
    D. A VRRP router configured with the priority of 255 owns the VRRP IP address.

12. What is the purpose of the critical IP interface?
    A. To force a VRRP interface to a master state if an interface is up
    B. To force a VRRP interface to the backup state if an interface is down
    C. To provide a redundancy for hosts with a fixed configuration
    D. To force a VRRP backup on another router to become master if an interface is up

13. Which is true about IP subnet VLANs?

    A. VLAN membership is based on a frame's destination IP address.

    B. VLAN membership is based on a frame's source IP address.

    C. IP subnet VLANs are the same as multinetting.

    D. IP subnet VLANs cannot be configured on a port that has an IP policy VLAN.

14. Which statement is true about UDP forwarding?

    A. UDP forwarding acts on TCP and UDP packets.

    B. This features supports forwarding BootP packets as well as other UDP packets.

    C. UDP broadcasts use multicast MAC addresses.

    D. Ports can be added to forward UDP.

15. What is the syntax of the command used to add ports 3/2 3/8 to a port-based VID 312?

    A. `vlan 312 add ports 3/2-3/8`

    B. `config vlan 312 ports add 3/2-3/8`

    C. `config vlan add ports 3/2-3/8   312`

    D. `config ports 3/2-3/8   add vlan 312`

16. A port is configured to be in an IP protocol-based VLAN and a port-based VLAN. What happens to an IPX packet that comes into this port?

    A. The packet is flooded to all ports of the IP protocol-based VLAN only.

    B. The packet is dropped.

    C. The packet is flooded to all ports of both the IP protocol-based VLAN and the port-based VLAN.

    D. The packet is flooded to all ports of the port-based VLAN only.

17. What is the order used to enable IP RIP to a new VLAN?

    A. Create VLAN, enable routing, add ports, and enable RIP.

    B. Create VLAN, add ports, enable RIP, and enable routing.

    C. Create VLAN, add ports, enable routing, and enable RIP.

    D. Enable RIP, create VLAN, add ports, and enable routing.

18. Why would an administrator create multiple STGs?

    A. To make the network more complex

    B. To make the network simpler

    C. To prevent loops

    D. To load balance

PART III

19. What command is used to see the files on a PCMCIA card?
    A. dir
    B. dir flash
    C. dir pcmcia
    D. show dir

20. In what order is a packet that is ingressing a port examined?
    A. Tag, port, protocol, and drop
    B. Protocol, tag, port, and drop
    C. Tag, protocol, port, and drop
    D. Port, protocol, tag, and drop

21. What is the default state of the ports in a policy-based VLAN that was created using VLAN Manager?
    A. Always
    B. Never
    C. Unassigned
    D. Potential

22. Which two of the Passport layer 2 series switches utilize PCMCIA cards? (Choose two.)
    A. 1200
    B. 1051
    C. 1150
    D. 8600

23. Which is not active in Boot Monitor mode?
    A. Console port
    B. Diagnostic Ethernet Port
    C. PCMCIA slot
    D. I/O ports

24. During the boot process, which flag determines whether or not to add new ports into the default VLAN?
    A. Autoboot
    B. Factory default
    C. Ports in isolated mode
    D. Ports in default VLAN mode

25. Which does not have to be identical on both SSFs in a redundant SSF configuration?

    A. Source image

    B. Boot configuration

    C. Runtime configuration

    D. Source image file position on the flash

26. Which file type is not valid on the Passport routing switch?

    A. Log

    B. Trace

    C. Debug

    D. Executable

    E. Compressed

27. Which statement about VLANs is not true?

    A. VLANs are associated with layer 3 traffic.

    B. VLANs are associated with layer 2 traffic.

    C. VLANs confine broadcast traffic within software-defined boundaries.

    D. VLANs are physical networks divided into logically independent broadcast domains.

28. Which of the following does not contribute to updating the CPU's routing table?

    A. 802.1D table updates

    B. RIPv1 or RIPv2 updates

    C. OSPF link state database updates

    D. Modification from a management interface

29. Which statement about Passport access ports is false?

    A. Can only connect to end stations

    B. Can only be in one STG

    C. Can only be in one VLAN of the same type

    D. Can be in one IPX, one IP, one MAC-based, and one port-based VLAN at the same time

30. Which statement is true about FastStart?

    A. Goes into learning mode first

    B. Goes into forwarding mode first

    C. Sends ARP requests to all stations attached to it

    D. Uses the normal Spanning Tree process at startup

PART III

31. Which statement is true about prioritization on the Passport switch?
    A. Passport does not recognize prioritization.
    B. Priorities are only examined at egress of the packet.
    C. A low-priority VLAN that receives a high-priority packet will demote the packet to low priority.
    D. A low-priority VLAN that receives a high-priority packet will not demote the packet to low priority.

32. Which device within the Passport is responsible for sending out ARP requests?
    A. ARU
    B. CPU
    C. SSF
    D. Queue Manager

33. What is the definition of a domain under VLAN Manager?
    A. A collection of switches
    B. All Passport switches in the network
    C. Passport switches on defined subnets only
    D. A collection of switches defined by their STG

34. Which statement about the validation process of VLAN Manager is true?
    A. Trunk ports are validated for connectivity.
    B. VLAN colors are validated across switches.
    C. Ports are validated for the VLANs that they belong to.
    D. VLANs are validated for compatibility across switches.

35. How many STGs may a VLAN be part of?
    A. One
    B. Two
    C. None
    D. As many as the administrator configures

36. Which statement is true about the default VLAN?
    A. The default VLAN can be deleted.
    B. The default VLAN has a VID of one.
    C. The default VLAN has a VID of zero.
    D. The default VLAN can be reconfigured as a policy-based VLAN.

Answers

1. **D.** 7,000,000 pps for layer 2 or layer 3 traffic.

2. **A.** 1050 is a 10/100 desktop switch designed to aggregate bandwidth to a single Gigabit Ethernet uplink.

3. **C.** 1200 has redundant SSF modules in positions four and five.

4. **B.** LinkSafe only protects from cable breaks; every other type of failure will affect both ports and cause the loss of redundancy provided by LinkSafe.

5. **B.** Tagged ports can be a member of multiple like VLANs, even multiple port-based VLANs.

6. **D.** The flags that are used during startup is the only thing that is configured in the boot options; the rest of configuration is stored in the user configuration.

7. **D.** L2, L2 is the combination username and password for layer 2 only permissions.

8. **B.** MLTs can be configured as access ports or trunk ports. (All the ports must be configured the same.)

9. **B.** RIPv1 accepts the advertisement, but ignores the masks and uses the natural mask *unless* that network is configured on the port receiving the RIPv1 update. In that case, it will use the port's subnet mask for that network.

10. **D.** An isolated router port is *not* affected by Spanning Tree.

11. **D.** A VRRP router is automatically assigned a 255 priority for all IP addresses that actually exist on the router.

12. **B.** The critical IP interface parameter in VRRP is used to force a router that is master into the backup state if a critical interface is down.

13. **A.** Packets are added to specific IP subnet VLANs based on destination IP address. It is important to remember that a port can be a member of both an IP VLAN and an IP subnet VLAN.

14. **D.** Ports must be added to forward UDP traffic to the correct network that has the UDP services.

15. B.

16. D. The packet is flooded to all ports of the port-based VLAN because it is an IPX packet, and only an IP protocol VLAN and a port-based VLAN exist on the port.

17. C. Create the VLAN first, then add ports, then enable routing, and only then can one have RIP running.

18. D. Multiple STGs would be created for load balancing. Without multiple STGs, trunk ports carrying VLAN traffic between switches could get blocked, and VLANs would not be able to communicate between switches.

19. C.

20. C. Any packet ingressing the switch is checked for an explicit tag first. If no tag is available, the packet is examined for a policy VLAN matching the ingress port. If no policy VLAN is available, the switch checks for a port VLAN. If no port-based VLAN exists on the port, then the packet is dropped.

21. D. When using VLAN Manager to create policy-based VLANs, all ports on the switch become potential members of this policy-based VLAN.

22. A and D. The Passport 1200, 1250, 8000, and 8600 can all utilize PCMCIA cards. The other Passport switches cannot.

23. D. I/O ports are not active in monitor mode and therefore the switch does no traffic forwarding while in monitor mode.

24. C. The parameter of ports in isolated mode, when set to true, makes all new ports into isolated router ports; if it is set to false, all new ports will be added to the default VLAN.

25. D. The file position may be different for the SSFs as long as the boot options are configured properly to point to the correct location for the system image.

26. C.

27. A. VLANs are layer 2 broadcast domains and are not involved in layer 3 routing decisions.

28. A. 802.1D is the Spanning Tree standard for transparent bridging and has nothing to do with layer 3 routing tables.

29. A. An access port can connect to other Passport switches, hubs, or end stations and is not restricted in that manner.

30. B. FastStart goes into the forwarding mode immediately and does not go through the Spanning Tree phases unless it recognizes a potential loop in the network configuration.

31. D. The Passport switch can recognize and respect prioritization. A packet that is prioritized at the edge of the network will maintain its prioritization throughout the network. A VLAN with a low priority will not cause the packet to receive a low-priority marking.

32. B. The CPU is responsible for all table maintenance and updates. Unknown addresses are sent to the CPU to do the necessary ARP requests.

33. A. In VLAN Manager, a domain is a collection of switches defined by the administrator.

34. B.

35. A. Because STGs are not VLAN aware, VLANs can only be a member of a single STG.

36. B. The default VLAN has a VID of one. It cannot be deleted or changed.

Centillion ATM Switches

The Centillion ATM switch is a highly competent edge device that offers exceptional Token Ring switching as well as Ethernet, Fast Ethernet, and ATM services. It is positioned as a device that provides end users access into an ATM-switched network. The product offers redundant hardware and software services and wide support for standard and proprietary software services. The purpose of this chapter is to help prepare you for the Centillion Switching (V4.0) Advanced Product Exam (920-023), which is part of the NNCSE track.

Exam Objectives

The following is a list of items that you may be tested on. Please note that many of the topics, like Source Route Bridging (SRB), frame switching, ATM, LAN Emulation (LANE), and Private Network-to-Network Interface (PNNI), have already been covered in Chapters 2, 3, 5, and 8.

- Describe the flooding, forwarding, and learning process of transparent bridges.
- Explain the Spanning Tree Protocol to block looping.
- Describe the RIF information process of source route bridges.
- Describe the basics of frame- and cell-switching technology.
- Explain how frame- and cell-switching technologies create VLANs.
- List and describe the general features of the Centillion switch.

- Describe the C50, C100, and 5000BH chassis and placement of modules.

- Describe the functions of the Master Control Processor (MCP) and list the available modules.

- Explain the hardware redundancy features of the Centillion switch.

- Describe the features and role of SpeedView and the Command Line Interface (CLI).

- Explain bridge groups and the types of ports that compose a bridge group.

- Describe Virtual Ports (VPORTs), list the VPORT types, and compare and contrast the types.

- Describe the features of the TokenSpeed, EtherSpeed, and ATMSpeed modules.

- Describe the Virtual Token Ring feature.

- Explain how Source Route RIF Proxy works.

- Give an overview of frame processing and forwarding within a Centillion switch.

- Explain the Redundant MCP feature of the Centillion switch.

- Use the CLI in command mode to view switch parameters and statistics.

- Use the CLI in config mode to configure default and IP parameters.

- Install the SpeedView for Windows application on a PC with the proper system requirements.

- Use a variety of methods to connect the management workstation to the Centillion switch and upload and download configurations.

- Register multiple switches using the Simple Network Management Protocol (SNMP).

- View a switch, enable and disable ports, and reset the switch.

- Download the proper system image file for both the Centillion 100 switch and the Model 5000BH chassis.

- Perform basic switch configurations using the system, network management, switching mode, and static station windows.

- Explain the function of TokenSpeed, EtherSpeed, and ATMSpeed module configuration parameters.

- Explain how the ATM model is used to pass cells from end system to end system.

- Identify ATM address format fields.

- Differentiate between a user-to-network interface (UNI) and a network-to-network interface (NNI).

- Differentiate a Centillion Circuit Saver network from a GIGArray network and explain how each network type processes frames.

- Plan and configure a switch for both load balancing and redundancy.

- Plan and assign Permanent Virtual Paths (PVPs) and Permanent Virtual Circuits (PVCs) for Centillion LAN Clients (CLCs) and pass-through connections using SpeedView for Windows.

- Configure CLCs in circuit saver and turbo modes using SpeedView for Windows.

- Describe how VPORT bridging operates through combining VPORT types.

- Assign logical ATM addresses to Centillion switches in a network.

- Plan Interim Interswitch Signaling Protocol (IISP) link use in a network.

- Configure logical IISP link groups.

- Given an ATM network topology, select the appropriate signaling configuration.

- Configure port signaling parameters for ATMSpeed modules.

- Plan and configure an ATM call routing table for IISP links.

- Define the purpose and use of LANE.

- Describe the function of each component of LANE.

- Explain how LANE moves information in the network.

- List and explain how the LANE services VCCs are established.

- Explain how Centillion-based LANE applications work.

- Configure the LAN Emulation Server and Broadcast and Unknown Server (LES/BUS) pairs.

- Configure the LAN Emulation Configuration Server (LECS).

- Configure a LANE VPORT (LAN Emulation Clienet [LEC]) on a Centillion switch.

- Configure redundant LANE services.

- Configure the Centillion network to use redundant LES/BUS pairs.

- Use the show vport and show LES commands to identify the LES/BUS pair that a LEC is using.

- Describe the PNNI hierarchical model.

- Describe the roles of PNNI nodes, Peer Group Leaders, and border nodes.

- Differentiate between inside links and outside links.

- Explain how the Hello Protocol is used on the Routing Control Channel.

- Summarize how PNNI topology information is exchanged within and between peer groups.

- Explain the relationship between Level Indicators, Node Identifiers, and Peer Group Identifiers.

- Explain the use of Source Routing, Crankback, and Alternate Path Selection with call establishment.

- List the PNNI functions that are supported on the Centillion 100 and 5000BH switches.

- Identify scenarios in which Centillion switches may be deployed using PNNI.

- Configure PNNI on Centillion 100 and 5000BH switches.

- Describe the NetBIOS filter and proxy features.

- Describe the capabilities and applications of packet filtering.

- Explain the functions of packet filter parameters.

Centillion Switch Overview

Here we will examine the basics of the Centillion 100 switch family.

General Features

The Centillion 100, 50, and 5000BHC platforms support a wide variety of hardware and software features. Some of these features follow:

- UNI 3.0, 3.1, and 4.0 signaling

- IISP

- VLANS (port- and protocol-based)

- Multiple Spanning Tree groups

- Packet filtering

- Management through CLI and SpeedView for Windows (GUI)

- Service port for out-of-band management

- Redundant power supplies

- Ethernet

- Fast Ethernet

- Token Ring

- ATM (OC-3, OC-12)

- PNNI

- Quality of service (QoS)

- Multiprotocol over ATM (MPOA)

- Soft Permanent Virtual Circuits (SPVCs)

- Internet Group Management Protocol (IGMP)

- Event logging

- Redundant Master Control Processor (MCP)

- Token Ring full-duplex operation

- Full LANE services

- Redundant LES/BUS pairs

- MultiLink Trunking (MLT)

- 802.1Q support (version 4.1 and above)

Platforms

The Centillion comes in three basic hardware platforms:

- The Centillion 100

- The Centillion 50

- The 5000BH

The Centillion 100

The Centillion 100 is a six-slot chassis that supports up to two power supplies for redundancy and redundant MCP. The MCP module provides initialization, topology updates, and network management features. The chassis is capable of supporting a wide variety of Ethernet switch modules (EtherSpeed), Fast Ethernet switch modules (FastEtherSpeed), Token Ring switch modules (TokenSpeed), and ATM switch modules (ATMSpeed). The modules are available with a variety of options, such as port type, port density, memory, speed, and others. Any combination of modules can be placed in the chassis; the only requirement is that one module must be an MCP module. The various modules are interchangeable from either a Centillion 100 or a Centillion 50.

The backplane of the Centillion switch is a 3.2 Gbps ATM backplane and a 400 Mbps control bus. Switching is distributed and parallel. Each switch module independently manages the transfer of cells to and from the backplane.

The Centillion 50

The Centillion 50 is a three-slot chassis that can be configured in a number of ways. One version is merely an empty three-slot chassis that can support any of the modules that the Centillion 100 supports. Another Centillion 50 supports a fixed ATM MCP and EtherSpeed module with one empty slot remaining for any Centillion 100 module of your choice. Another Centillion 50 supports a fixed ATM MCP and TokenSpeed module with one empty slot remaining for any Centillion 100 module of your choice.

The Centillion 50 supports up to two power supplies for redundancy and an MCP. The MCP module provides initialization, topology updates, and network management features.

The backplane of the Centillion switch is a 3.2 Gbps ATM backplane and a 400 Mbps control bus. Switching is distributed and parallel. Each switch module independently manages the transfer of cells to and from the backplane.

The 5000BH

The 5000BH is a standard Nortel Networks 5000 chassis with an additional backplane in the upper-third backplane position. This backplane supports both a Parallel Packet Express (PPX) for routing modules and two separate Centillion 3.2 Gbps Centillion backplanes. These two backplanes are referred to as the Centillion Left and the Centillion Right. There is no connectivity between the two halves. If you imagine two Centillion 100s, one on top of the other, and you rotate them as a unit 90 degrees, that is essentially what you get in a 5000BH. Since the 5000 chassis is much larger than a Centillion 100, the switch modules are not interchangeable, but there is an equivalent 5000BH module for every Centillion 100 module.

The Master Control Processor (MCP)

The MCP is the brains behind the switch and you must have at least one per switch or your switch will not work. The switch image is stored on and runs on the MCP, so it won't boot without it. The MCP is responsible for switch initialization, topology updates, and management. The MCP is also responsible for address resolution in a LANE environment. The MCP comes integrated on a switching module so you do not lose a slot in the box that could otherwise support hosts or switch connections. There were at one time three different types of MCP modules: EtherSpeed MCP, TokenSpeed MCP, and ATMSpeed MCP.

The EtherSpeed and TokenSpeed MCPs are no longer supported and their last images (2.x) do not support full LANE services. The only MCP currently being produced is the ATMSpeed MCP. Luckily for us there is more than one type of ATMSpeed MCP module. The good thing is that their functionality is the same, differing only in port speed, type, and density.

The different types of MCP modules are

- TokenSpeed module (no longer supported)

- EtherSpeed module (no longer supported)

- ATMSpeed with four 155 Mbps multimode fiber (MMF) ports

- ATMSpeed with one 622 Mbps MMF port

- ATMSpeed Media Dependent Adapter (MDA) with two MDA slots supporting two ports per slot (supports both MMF and single-mode fiber [SMF])

The different MCP modules are available for both the Centillion 100/50 chassis and the 5000BH chassis. An MCP module is recognizable from the extra connector on the module face. In the case of a Centillion 100/50 MCP module, the connector is a mini-DIN-8 connector (it resembles a PS2 mouse or keyboard connector). In the case of a 5000BH MCP module, the connector is a DB-25. These connectors are for console connections for out-of-band management.

Older MCPs for the Centillion 100 used to come in two different styles, the wiring closet MCP and the network center MCP. The wiring closet MCP contained less memory and buffers than the network center MCP. Currently, all MCPs now have the same amount of buffers and memory. Older MCPs contained 2MB of flash memory for images and configurations. As of version 4.1 a minimum of 4MB flash is required.

Hardware Redundancy

The Centillion 100 supports hardware redundancy in two ways:

- Redundant power supplies

- Redundant MCPs

A Centillion 100 can be configured with two hot swappable power supplies that will function redundantly when installed together. There are no situations where a fully populated chassis requires more than one power supply for functionality.

A Centillion 100 also supports redundant MCPs. If one MCP fails, the other one will take over. The fail-over is not transparent. The switch will reboot as part of the fail-over process. For redundant MCP functionality to work properly, the MCPs should

- Be the same type
- Have the same amount of memory
- Have the same image

For redundant MCP functionality to work, the MCPs *must*

- Be in slots 1 and 2 (in 500 BH slots 2,3, and/or 8,9)
- Be ATM MCPs
- Be running at least version 3.0 software (image)

When we have a configuration with a Primary and Standby MCP, only the Primary MCP is accessible. The Standby MCP will function as a switching module only (no MCP functionality while in Standby state). You will not even be able to make a serial connection to the Standby MCP.

The factors that determine which MCP becomes the Primary (active) MCP and which becomes the Standby are as follows:

Priority (configurable parameter)	Highest wins
Memory	Highest wins
Image	Highest wins
Slot	Slot 1 wins

The MCP with the highest MCP priority becomes the Primary. In the event of a tie, the MCP with the most memory becomes the Primary. If we still have a tie, then the MCP with the most recent Image wins. If all are tied, then whichever MCP is in slot 1 becomes the Primary (this should be the rule rather than the exception).

Switch Management

The switch is managed in one of two methods:

- CLI
- SpeedView for Windows

Command Line Interface (CLI)

The CLI is the primary point of viewing switch functions and troubleshooting. The CLI has many commands with rich and useful output to view network health and help find the cause of a problem. Configuration of the switch through the CLI is not allowed except for the initial configuration of an IP address and associated parameters.

> **NOTE** There are a few other parameters that you may change from the CLI, but they are not part of the typical switch configuration. VLANS, VPORTs, LANE, and the other major functions of the switch are not configured from the CLI.

The CLI has two modes: command mode and config mode.

Command mode is the access granted initially when you make a connection to the switch through the console port. It has a limited subset of commands available for viewing switch parameters. From the command mode the switch cannot be reset, nor can a configuration file (config) be saved.

Config mode has the complete list of commands available to it. From config mode, the IP address can be set, SNMP community strings, files can be saved, and the switch can be rebooted. To move from command mode to config mode, enter the config command. You will be prompted for a password. When you successfully enter the password, you will be in config mode. To leave config mode, type **exit**.

Commands entered through the CLI can be shortened. For example,

```
show fdb mcp
```

can be expressed as

```
sho f mc
```

> **NOTE** If you are in the CLI in config mode, you must exit from config mode before trying to access the switch from SpeedView (you will get an error message otherwise). Also, if you are configuring the switch in SpeedView and you need to access the switch through the CLI, you must close your SpeedView session. There is a five-minute inactivity timer associated with the CLI after which the session is closed.

In order to give the switch an IP address, subnet mask, and default gateway, you would use the command

```
ip address 141.251.10.1 gw 141.251.10.255 mask 255.255.255.0
```

where ip address is the command to specify the IP address, gw means the default gateway, and mask stands for the subnet mask. This must be done from config mode. The config must then be saved and the switch must be rebooted. To view IP address information from the CLI, type **IP INFO**.

NOTE   It is important to remember that while the ATMSpeed MCP has two interfaces that can be assigned an IP address (the MCP function and the Ethernet port), a default gateway can be assigned to only one of them.

Changes made in the CLI do not take effect until the switch is rebooted. Changes are lost during a reboot if the command

```
save config config
```

is not entered first. The command save tells the switch to save some information. The config tells the switch to take all operating parameters (the switch's configuration) to be saved. The second config tells the switch to place those parameters in the area of nvram memory (flash) reserved for these parameters. Please note that the Centillion does not allow you to name the config file, nor does it have a file system that can be managed as a BayRS router does. The configuration file is called config and cannot be changed. There can be only one instance of a config on a Centillion at any one time. Alternate configurations can be stored on the TFTP server that the SpeedView management station has.

The event log is a useful feature used from the CLI that allows us to see what has occurred in the switch and is useful for troubleshooting. The log can be viewed in one of three places:

- The CLI window
- SYSLOGD server
- TFTP server

The CLI window allows events to be viewed and is subject to pre- and postfiltering.

The SYSLOGD server is a UNIX server running the SYSLOGD daemon. The log events can be exported to the SYSLOGD server to be written to a file. The event log is subject to pre- and postfiltering.

The TFTP server is any workstation running TFTP server software. Events are exported to the tftp server and are written to a file, subject to prefiltering only.

Prefiltering refers to the level and type of events that are saved to the event log database as they occur. Postfiltering refers to which events that are in the event log database we wish to view. Events can be filtered based on the following criteria:

- Severity

- Entity

- Module

- Port

NOTE To configure logging, you must be in config mode.

Logging is disabled by default and must be enabled. Use the following command to enable logging:

```
log enable
```

You must specify where the log should be sent, so your complete command may look like this:

```
log enable cli
```

This would send log messages to the CLI. Other options are TFTPSAVE and SYSLOGD.

After enabling logging, you can specify severity, entity, slot, and port to log. Then logging must actually be started. You use the following command to start logging:

```
log start ddhhmmss
```

This tells logging to start and continue for the amount of time specified. The format is DD=days, HH=hours, MM=minutes, SS=seconds. If no time is specified, the default is 1,000 days. Once log events have been saved to a buffer, they can be viewed using the following command:

```
log dump
```

SpeedView

SpeedView is the graphical user interface (GUI) tool provided for managing Centillion 100, 50, and 5000BH switched networks. Some of its features include

- Online and offline configuration
- Statistics
- Per-port enable/disable
- Switch reboot
- TFTP upload/download of configurations
- TFTP download of switch image
- Flush forwarding database
- In-band and out-of-band access to a switch

System Requirements   The system requirements for using SpeedView are

- Windows NT 4.0 or Windows 95/98*
- 32MB or RAM*
- Minimum 20MB hard drive space*
- 9,600 bps serial port
- TCP/IP stack
- NIC card and IP address

 NOTE   *Please refer to the Release Notes for your specific version of SpeedView.

The three methods of installing SpeedView are Typical, Compact, and Custom.

Typical installs all three components included with SpeedView—SpeedView, BootP/TFTP server, and switch image. Compact installs only the SpeedView. Custom installs those components that you choose.

 TIP   You may not want to choose the Typical option. When Typical looks for the switch image, it can't locate it and the installation fails. Choose Custom and de-select the switch image. After the installation is complete, you can copy the switch image manually.

Connecting to the Switch   When you launch SpeedView for the first time, you get the Preferences screen that asks how you want to connect to the switch (Figure 13-1).

The option to choose the connection type is in the upper left-hand corner. For an in-band connection, choose SNMP. This requires that the switch be configured with an IP address and a connection to the network. If you wish to connect via a serial port, simply choose the correct one from the list. If you choose to communicate with the switch via SNMP, you then need to add the switch to the MAP window (Figure 13-2).

To add a switch to the map from the Node pull-down menu, choose Node > New > Switch.

To make management of large networks easier, SpeedView gives you the option of arranging switches in groups. To add a group, choose Node > New > Group. To add a switch to a group, first highlight the group that you want to put the switch into, and then follow the same steps to add a new switch.

When you select the switch to add, you get the Switch Information screen (Figure 13-3). In the Switch Information screen, you are asked to provide the switch IP address or host ID and community strings. You may optionally select the switch box type. If you are unsure, you may select Unknown and the SpeedView station will determine the switch type automatically. After discovering the new switch on the network, the switch

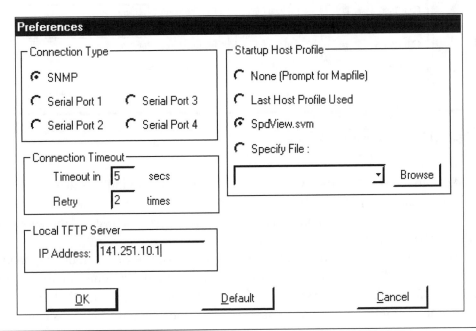

Figure 13-1   Preferences

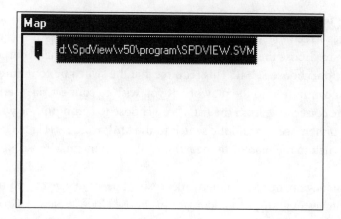

Figure 13-2 Map

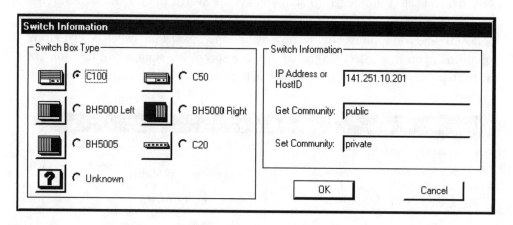

Figure 13-3 Switch Information

is added to the selected group with a green circle next to it to indicate that it is functioning (Figure 13-4). If it is not found, it is added with a red circle next to it.

If you right-click a switch and select Configure, you get the Switch Configuration window (Figure 13-5).

We will get into the specific details of exactly how to use some of the more important features of SpeedView later, but for now we'll have a quick look at some of the different options. If you examine the Switch Configuration window (Figure 13-5) closely, you will notice a number of tabs lined up in two rows along the top. These tabs represent the major configuration features of SpeedView. We will examine some of them briefly here.

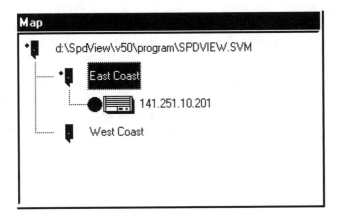

Figure 13-4   Map with new switch

E:\Nortel_Instructor_CD\centillion\Centillion Configs\ADV_LAB1_C100.CFG - Configuration

ATM Configuration	IP Multicast	M1-ATM-4M	M2-TR-16	M3-ENET-16
System	Network Management	Switching Mode	Static Stations	Packet Filters	NETBIOS Filters

Switch name: Boston_C100

Description: Centillion 100 MCP version 4.0.2 Advanced Image (9904300)

Contact: Eric Renkoff

Location: Boston, MA

Password:

Confirm password:

Admin Mac address: 000500043B87   Reset Mac addr on config download

Token Ring Max frame size: 4472

Station table aging timer: 300   secs

NetBIOS Name table aging timer: 300   secs

NetBIOS query interval: 5   x 100 millisecs

Source Route Unknown Frame Flood

Figure 13-5   Switch Configuration window

EXAM TIP You will be asked on the exam which tab you would go to in order to configure a certain feature. This is intended to test your familiarity with the interface. Here is a tip: Even if you do not have a copy of the book handy (perish the thought) but you want to refresh your memory of what items are on what tab, you do not even need a real switch. You can install SpeedView and open a config file offline. This also comes in handy if you want to practice making changes to a switch's configuration, but you don't happen to have a switch available.

Getting Acquainted The tabs that we will look at now are the following:

- System
- Network Management
- Switching Mode
- Static Stations
- Packet Filters
- NetBios Filters
- ATM Configuration

The System tab is the tab you see in Figure 13-5 and it is the first tab that is displayed when you open a Switch Configuration window. From here you can set the following items:

- Switch name
- Contact
- Location
- Password
- Admin MAC address
- Token Ring max frame size

The Network Management tab is next in line (Figure 13-6). From here you can configure the following items:

- Primary IP address
- Secondary IP address
- Management VLANs

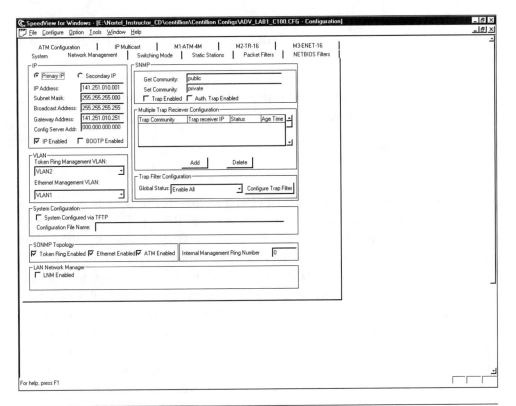

Figure 13-6 Network Management tab

- SNMP community strings
- Trap receivers
- SONMP topology

The Primary IP address is that of the MCP itself. The Secondary IP address is that of the Ethernet port located on ATM MCP modules. It can be used as an alternate method to access the switch in the event of an emergency. Please remember when configuring this port address that only one default gateway can be configured, either for the Primary or the Secondary IP address but not both.

The Management VLANs options serve to remind us that the Centillion switch is a layer 2 device. VLANs are broadcast domains and as such are part of a single IP subnet. To go from one IP subnet to another, you need a layer 3 device. Since this is the case, we have to assign the MCP to a VLAN (the MCP has an IP address making it a part of some IP subnet). Only other hosts in the same VLAN will be able to ping or manage the MCP without the use of a layer 3 device (router) to route packets to it. The MCP can belong to two management VLANS simultaneously—one Ethernet VLAN and one Token Ring VLAN.

SNMP community strings are the simple passwords like text strings that are included in an SNMP request to identify the level of privilege that the user or device making the request has. The default strings are

- Read only = public
- Read/write = private

Please do not leave these strings at their default settings. These are well-known industry standards and many companies (not just Nortel) use them as their defaults as well.

The SynOptics Network Management Protocol (SONMP) topology determines whether or not the switch generates SONMP hello packets on the specified topology (such as Ethernet, Token Ring, or ATM). These hellos enable optivity maps to accurately determine the physical connectivity between devices on segments and subnetworks.

The Switching Mode tab is where we configure Spanning Tree groups, bridging, and VLANs. To discuss these topics we need to examine a few new ideas. In a normal switch Spanning Tree, Bridge Protocol Data Units (BPDUs) are sent out every port regardless of what VLAN that port belongs to. The reason for this is simple. The 802.1D Spanning Tree protocol was created long before the idea of VLANs existed; therefore, there was no VLAN capability built in to the 802.1D protocol. Two ports in different VLANs send out the same BPDU because they are in the same Spanning Tree domain (there is only one instance of Spanning Tree running on the switch). In order to overcome the problem, the Centillion (and other switches like the Accellar) implement the idea of Spanning Tree groups. A Spanning Tree group is an instance of Spanning tree (a Spanning Tree domain). BPDUs from one Spanning Tree group do not cross over to other Spanning Tree groups. We then add VLANs to the Spanning Tree group (Figure 13-7) and we are ready to connect. One or more VLANs can belong to the same Spanning Tree group. All the other rules of Spanning Tree apply.

On the lower-right side of this window (Figure 13-7) is where you create new Spanning Tree groups. Once you create a Spanning Tree group, you can add a VLAN to it by clicking the Add VLAN button (Figure 13-8). You can name, number, and choose the VLAN type (port- or protocol-based). Then you can specify ports by either selecting them from the Cards/Ports section of the window (lower-left corner) or by going to the appropriate modules tab and altering the ports properties there. Spanning Tree and Bridging mode are configured for the entire Spanning Tree group.

The next three tabs mostly explain themselves. The Static Stations tab is where you can add a MAC address statically to a port. This means that even when the aging timer

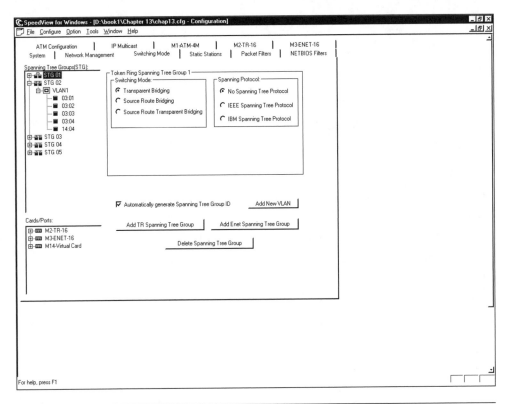

Figure 13-7 Switching Mode

of the port expires due to a lack of activity, the MAC address will not be flushed from the table. This can help reduce broadcast traffic. The Packet Filters tab will be discussed later, but it is where packet filters are created (you guessed that one didn't you).

The NETBIOS Filters tab allows us to configure NETBIOS filters and create a NET-BIOS name proxy to increase security and reduce broadcast traffic through the switch.

The ATM Configuration tab (Figure 13-9) is very important to us. It is where we configure all of our ATM services. The first button on this tab is the Configure Signaling button (Figure 13-10). It is where we assign the switch the ATM prefix and specify what level of ATM services we are going to allow the switch to provide. There are three levels:

- Full LANE services
- LEC only—no IISP
- ATM switch only

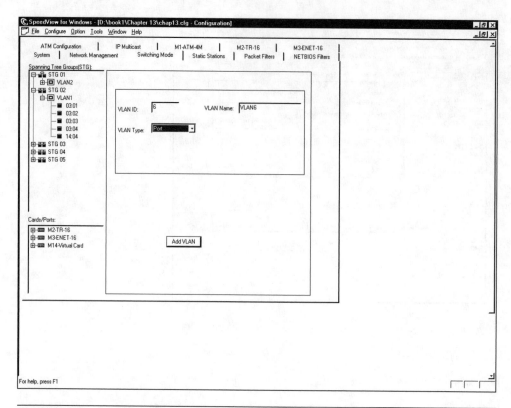

Figure 13-8   Add VLAN

Full LANE services enables the switch to become any entity in a LANE environment (such as LEC, LECS, or LES/BUS). The *LEC only—no IISP* level loads none of the components necessary for a switch to become a LES/BUS or a LECS. *ATM switch only* enables the switch to be a switch in the path of an SVC but not to be any other LANE component.

The ATM Configuration window is where we create a LES/BUS for an ELAN (configure LES/BUS), where we make the LECS for the ELAN (configure LECS), and where we make the LEC (configure LEC) (Figure 13-9). We will go into more detail later when we go over all the steps. Know also that the Configure CLC button is where we go to set up Centillion Mode PVCs.

Sending Stuff to the Switch   What could you possible want to send to the switch? How about new configuration files and new switching software (switch images)? For this reason SpeedView comes with its own TFTP server, but you can use other TFTP

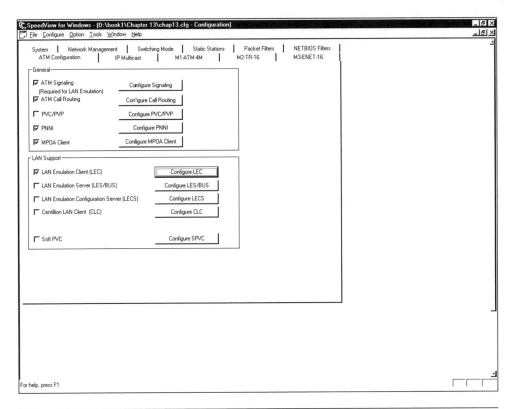

Figure 13-9 ATM Configuration

servers if you wish. If you are in the MAP window and you right-click the switch (or select the Switch pull-down menu), two choices stand out:

- TFTP Download Configuration
- TFTP Download Software

TFTP Download Configuration allows you to select a configuration file to send to the switch. The file may be browsed if you are using the local TFTP server, or typed in if not. In most cases, online changes are dynamic and the switch does not need to be rebooted for the changes to take effect. The following is a list of changes that do require a switch reset for the changes to take effect:

- IP address
- Subnet mask
- Broadcast address

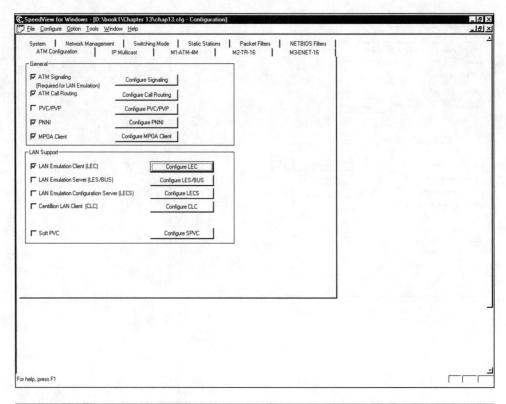

Figure 13-10   Configure Signaling

- Gateway address
- Admin MAC address
- Token Ring max frame size
- ATM signaling
- ATM port designation
- ATM prefix
- All fields in the MPOA client
- SONMP

After downloading a config to the switch and rebooting (if necessary), save the configuration to flash. If you fail to do so and the switch reboots, you will revert back to the previous configuration. This is a nice safety net. If you misconfigure something that causes you to lose contact with the switch, all you have to do is power the switch off and on to recover.

TFTP Download Software allows you to upgrade your switch image.

CAUTION   Sending the wrong image type or interrupting the transfer by powering down the switch can cause a fault so disastrous that you may not be able to recover. In these cases, you must return the MCP module to the factory.

Virtual Ports (VPORTs)

A Virtual Port (VPORT) is the logical entity that we create on a Centillion switch to give legacy clients access to ATM services. A VPORT ties a VLAN and one or more ATM interfaces together. There are two types of VPORTS:

- Centillion mode VPORT

- LANE VPORT

A Centillion mode VPORT combines a VLAN and one or more ATM interfaces together with either a VPI-based (in turbo mode) or a VCI-based (in circuit saver mode) PVC. Centillion VPORTs (CLC or Centillion LAN Client) are configured by clicking the Configure CLC button (Figure 13-9) and using the Centillion LAN Client Configuration window to add the appropriate VPORT type and values (Figure 13-11). This is a proprietary method of creating PVCs and is considered to be simple to set up and reliable. A drawback to this method is that it does not scale well to large networks.

A LANE VPORT is an ATM Forum standard LAN Emulation Client (LEC) in either turbo mode or circuit saver mode. The LEC VPORT is created by using the Configure LEC button and adding the LEC VPORT (Figure 13-12). You are required to add a VLAN to the LEC but not an ATM port or VPI/VCI values. This is because LANE supports SVCs and the signaling necessary to dynamically create and tear down circuits as necessary.

Virtual Token Ring

The Virtual Token Ring feature was added to help overcome Source Route Bridging hop count limitations. In a Centillion switch, Token Ring ports that are assigned the same ring number belong to the same Vring (Virtual ring). When bridging a frame from two ports that are in the same Vring, the frame is transparently bridged. This means that the ring/bridge numbers are not added to the Routing Information Field (RIF) of the Token Ring header and therefore we eliminate one hop from the maximum allowed.

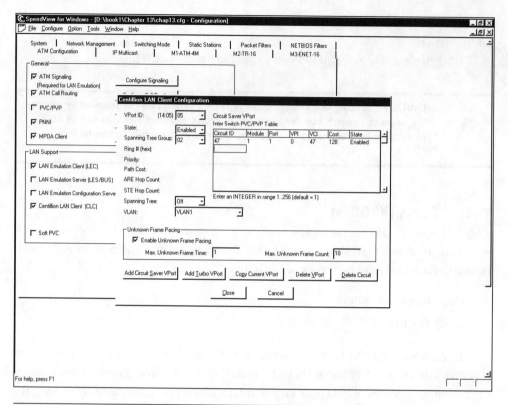

Figure 13-11   Centillion LAN Client Configuration

Frame Processing

We need to note that there is a difference in the way that frames are processed when using circuit saver or turbo mode VPORTs.

Frame Processing with Circuit Saver Mode VPORTs   When switches are connected together with circuit saver mode VPORTs, there is a single Virtual Channel between the switches that is shared by all of the modules. The module that has a frame to forward must forward the frame to the MCP for processing before it can be sent because the MCP is the terminating point of the channel.

Frame Processing with Turbo Mode VPORTs   When switches are connected together with turbo mode VPORTs, there is a channel for every module installed in the switch. Since each module is the terminating point of a channel, there is no need to forward the frame to the MCP for processing. Each module is capable of forwarding the frame directly over its own channel.

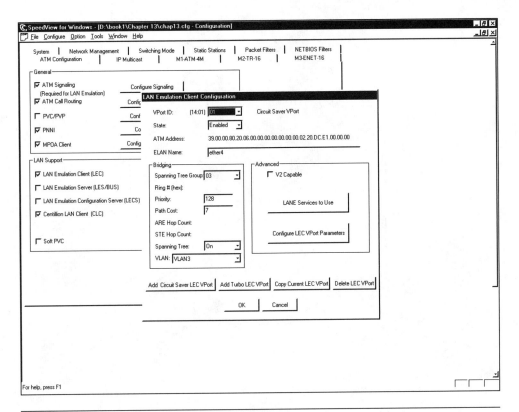

Figure 13-12   LAN Emulation Client Configuration

LANE Configuration

Let's go through a step-by-step implementation of a simple LANE environment with three Centillion switches. Examining Figure 13-13 you will see that our lab is made up of three Centillion 100 switches connected in a full mesh and multiple legacy workstations. For our lab we will create

- One LES/BUS on switch C
- One LECS on switch B
- Three LECs (one LEC per switch)

The three switches will be identified as follows:

Switch A: ATM address 39.00.00.80.20.01.00.00.00.00.00.00.00

IP address   141.251.10.1

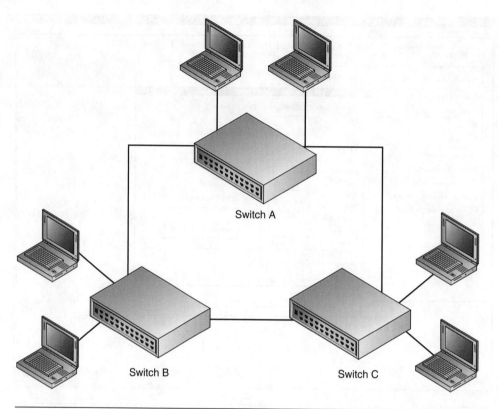

Figure 13-13 LANE Lab

Mask	255.255.255.0
Switch B:	ATM address 39.00.00.80.20.02.00.00.00.00.00.00.00
IP address	141.251.10.2
Mask	255.255.255.0
Switch C:	ATM address 39.00.00.80.20.03.00.00.00.00.00.00.00
IP address	141.251.10.3
Mask	255.255.255.0

Creating the LES/BUS

We start with the LES/BUS because it is this entity that defines the ELAN. Start by configuring signaling and an ATM address (Figure 13-13).

NOTE   **This will be done on all three switches as well as IP addresses so I will not mention this step again.**

Apply the appropriate address (see previous information) and select FULL ATM Services. Then click OK.

Next click the Configure LES/BUS button and select Add LES/BUS (Figure 13-14). The information required here is the ELAN NAME (for this lab called the ELAN LAB1, it is case sensitive) and LAN TYPE (Ethernet or Token Ring). Notice that the ATM address is supplied automatically (the prefix that we configured in the previous step and the six bytes of the MAC address of the switch followed by the one-byte selector). You do not need to provide any additional information to create the LES/BUS.

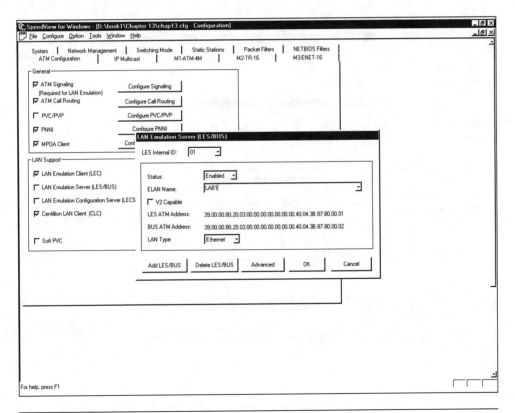

Figure 13-14   Add LES/BUS

Creating the LECS

The LECS is the component that helps a LEC locate a LES/BUS. To configure this component (on switch B), go to the ATM Configuration window and click Configure LECS. Select the Add ELAN button and type in the name of our ELAN (LAB1 from the previous step) (Figure 13-15). Remember that the name of an ELAN is case sensitive; lab1, Lab1, LAB1, and LAB 1 are four separate ELAN names as far as LANE is concerned. One of the most common mistakes is mistyping the ELAN name at some point of the LANE configuration.

In the upper portion of the LECS configuration screen, we have the ATM address of the LECS. You have a choice of a user-defined address or the ATM well-known addresses for the LECS. Choose the well-known ATM Forum address (Figure 13-16).

In the bottom portion of the screen we have the LES address portion. This is where the LECS is configured with the address of the LES/BUS. You add the entire ATM address of the LES (including the selector) here and click Add LES.

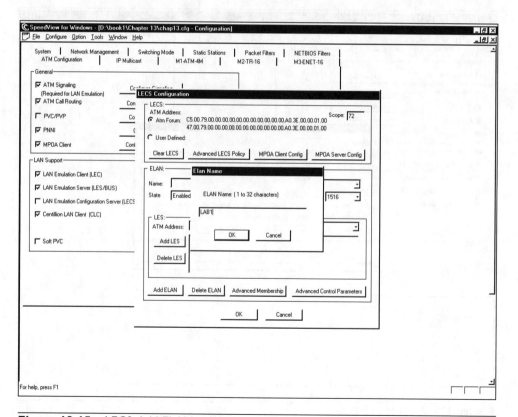

Figure 13-15 LECS Add ELAN name

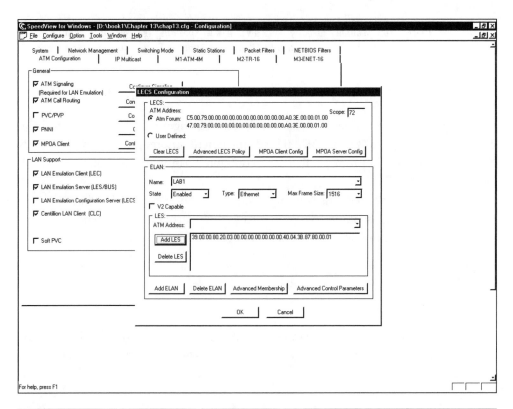

Figure 13-16   LECS ATM address configuration

TIP **If you pull down on the arrow to the right of the LES ATM address box, you will see the ATM address of the switch that you are currently configuring. If you are configuring the LECS and the LES/BUS on the same switch, this saves you a bit of typing.**

When you are finished, click OK.

Creating the LEC

The final stage in setting up the ELAN is creating the LEC. Before we create the LEC itself, we want to have a VLAN to add to the LEC. Go to the switching mode screen and in Spanning Tree group 2 create a VLAN 1. Make sure that you do all of the following steps on all three switches.

> **NOTE** You probably already have a **VLAN 1** in Spanning Tree group 2. That is fine. Use that one, or make any **VLAN** in any Spanning Tree group that you want.

Go to the ATM Configuration window and click Configure LEC. Next click Add Circuit Saver LEC VPORT. The VPORT ID will increment automatically. Type the ELAN Name (LAB1) in the appropriate field and configure Spanning Tree group 2, VLAN 1. Click OK.

At this point all that remains is to make sure that you have completed all the steps for all of the switches, sent the configurations to the switches, and rebooted them.

The LANE CLI commands that you need to become familiar with are

```
show vport status all
show les
show lecs
show rlec
```

The show vport status all command shows the status of a LEC on the switch you use the command on. If there is more than one LEC, you will see them all. You can specify which LEC to view if you only want to see a specific LEC. Among other things, it may show you the following:

- The name of the ELAN

- The address of the LECS

- The address of the LES (and its connection state)

- The address of the BUS (and its connection state)

This is excellent information to use when troubleshooting why the LEC cannot connect to the ELAN. If the LES address is missing, you know that there is a problem getting it from the LECS. If the LES address is present but not connected, you know that the address may be wrong or there may be a physical problem with the LES or your connection to the LES. Always check the name first.

The show les command is issued on a LES/BUS to see the following:

- The name of the VLAN

- The address of the LES

- The address of the bus

- The address of connected clients (LECs)

- The address of any redundant LES/BUS pairs

This can help you further troubleshoot issues involving client connectivity or just simply to verify ELAN health.

The show lecs command is issued on the LECs and it shows the name and LES address for all ELANs that it provides LES information for.

Configuring IISP

For situations that require it, you can configure IISP links. IISP links are static routes from one switch to another. This can be of great help for connectivity between PNNI Peer Groups that do not have Peer Group Leaders. A Centillion 100 is incapable of functioning as a Peer Group Leader for PNNI. This means that while PNNI Peer Groups can be configured and SVCs will be created within them, summarization between the Peer Groups will not occur. IISP allows us to create static routes between the Peer Groups and manually summarize the addresses. We are even able to configure redundant and/or load-balancing links between the groups.

In Figure 13-17, we have two Peer Groups (39.00.19.1 and 39.00.19.2) and no Peer Group Leader in either of the Peer Groups. Although PNNI will run between the switches inside of a group, we need to configure IISP to connect the two groups together. We will configure a port on the 39.00.19.1.3 switch for IISP (Figure 13-18). When we choose IISP as the UNI or NNI, we then need to choose either UNI 3.0 or 3.1 (the important thing is that both sides of the link be the same UNI signaling type). We then need to define the port as either the User side or the Network side (the important thing here is that both sides of the link must be different because it is the Network side of the link that determines the VPI/VCI value for a call). This summarizes the entire Peer Group 39.00.19.2 to the Peer Group 39.00.19.1. Then you go to the other side and do the opposite.

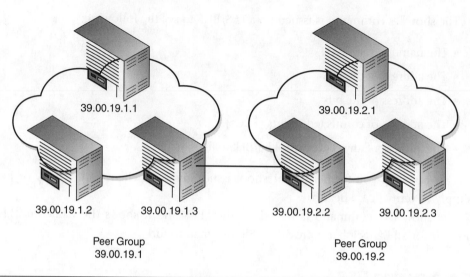

Figure 13-17 Peer Groups with IISP

After creating the port signaling, we need to make the call route table. This is where we configure the static routes and summarization of the groups. Click the Configure IISP button on the ATM Configuration window and type the Peer Group ID in the ATM Address field (see Figure 13-19). You then click the Partial Prefix button (this tells the switch that you are leaving all the remaining bytes of the address blank), specify the module and port that you just added IISP signaling to, and click Add. This tells the switch (in our case) that all switches that begin with the address 39.00.19.2 can be found off module 1, port 2.

Configuring PNNI

Configuring the switch to run PNNI is actually much easier than configuring IISP. Click the Configure PNNI button from the ATM Configuration window and set the node level and the Peer Group ID. (Refer to Chapter 8 for how to design your PNNI network.) The number in gray to the left of the Peer Group ID (Figure 13-20) is the node level represented in hex. After this you need to configure a port to use PNNI signaling.

Go to the ATM Module tab (Figure 13-22) and highlight a port that you want to use PNNI signaling. Click the Edit button. This will bring you to the signaling parameters for the port (Figure 13-21). Click Add Logical Link and enter a VPI value. Selecting PNNI in the UNI or NNI window (Figure 12-23) is all you need to do here. All of the other values are set by default. This is all you need to do to configure PNNI.

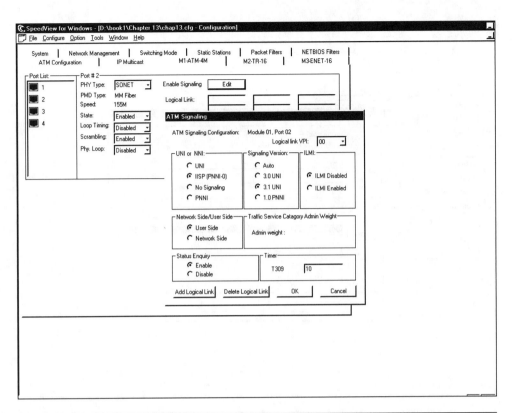

Figure 13-18 ATM signaling/IISP

Configuring SpeedView Filters

SpeedView filters enable you to implement powerful packet filters on the Centillion switch. Packet filters enable you to

- Provide network security
- Reduce traffic
- Analyze network performance by copying traffic to a network probe
- Monitor and control traffic flow

Filters may be applied only to legacy network ports (Ethernet or Token Ring). The switch supports up to a total of 64 filters (32 inbound and 32 outbound). A filter may be predefined, such as the filter that is used to copy traffic to a monitor port, or a filter

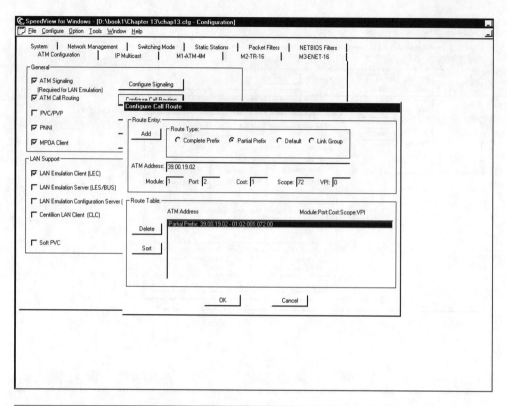

Figure 13-19   Call route table

may be created to examine any field (the maximum size is 12 bytes) in the first 255 bytes of the frame.

Filters are defined in the following manner. A starting point or point of reference must be defined. The SpeedView utility refers to this as the *type* (Figure 13-24). The filter logic uses one of two points of reference for Token Ring or a single point of reference in the case of Ethernet frames.

For a Token Ring frame (Figure 13-25), the starting point can be either the beginning of the MAC header or the beginning of the LLC header.

For an Ethernet frame the starting point is the beginning of the MAC header.

Once the starting point has been determined then the offset must be specified. The offset tells the filtering logic to count X (the offset value) bytes from the starting point into the frame before examining the contents of the frame. In this manner we locate the field within the frame to be scrutinized.

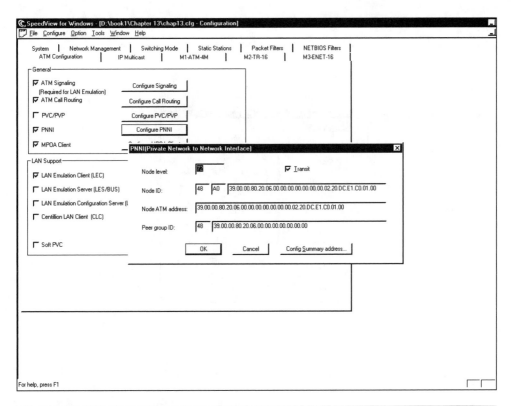

Figure 13-20 PNNI configuration

Then a value (in hex format) needs to be specified. This is the identifying factor of the filter. If the value were to be the IP address 141.251.10.1, then we would enter 8d.f6.0a.01 in the value field of the filter. 8d.f6.0a.01 is the hex equivalent of 141.251.10.1.

Next, a condition must be expressed. A condition can be any of the following:

- EQ (equal)

- NE (not equal)

- LT (less than)

- LE (less than or equal to)

- GT (greater than)

- GE (greater than or equal to)

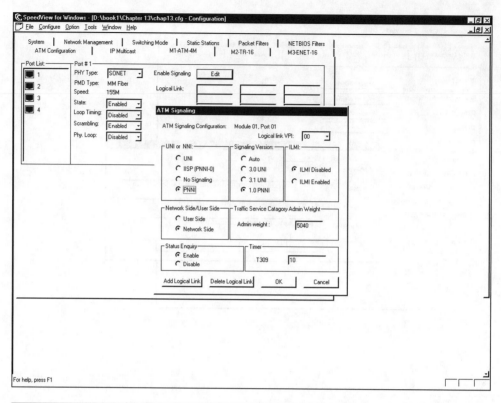

Figure 13-21 ATM signaling

The default value is EQ. The condition determines if the frame being scrutinized meets the criteria of the filter or not.

Following the condition, we decide what to do when a frame matches the condition and what to do when the frame fails the condition. Enter a number that corresponds to a filter sequence here. This means that if this happens (match or fail), go to this sequence number. If no other sequences are to be applied, insert the number 0 here.

In addition, we have the forwarding (FWD) mode. This determines what to do with the frame meeting or failing the criteria. There are three forwarding modes: Normal, Drop, and Alt. Normal (the default) treats the frame as if there were no filter in place and forwards it. Drop causes the frame to be discarded. Alt causes the frame to be forwarded, but to an alternate port.

Finally, we have two additional columns (fields) that are only used under special circumstances. The first one is Mon Dest, which stands for Monitor Destination. When using a network-monitoring device such as a Sniffer, Fluke, or other type of protocol/

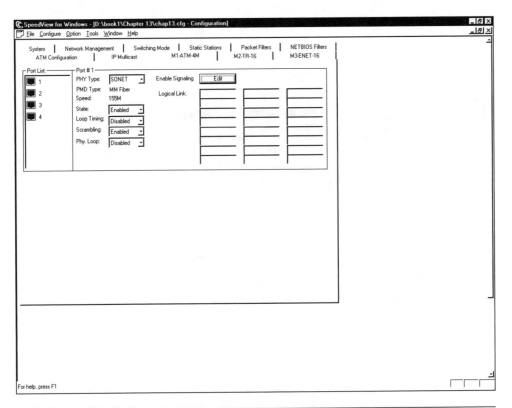

Figure 13-22 ATM Module Configuration window

traffic analyzer, the Mon Dest represents the port on the switch where the monitoring device is located. You enter the location of the monitoring device SLOT:PORT—for example, 3:2 would mean slot 3, port 2. This field is used in conjunction with a filter that is designed to look for specific types of traffic (which is defined by specifying the offset, length, and value). When traffic of the specified type is seen, it is copied to the Mon Dest port. It is also forwarded normally to its intended destination. This helps you work around the basic management problem inherent in all switches. Although switches are more efficient than hubs, they are difficult to manage because the traffic that passes through them is mostly invisible to management devices.

The second one is the Addl Dests, which stands for Additional Destinations. This field is used when you intend to send traffic to more than one destination.

For an example of a working filter, refer to Figure 13-24. FLTR_002 is a single sequence filter. It is the second filter on the switch. The type is MAC. This means that the starting point is the first bit of the source address at the MAC header. The Offset is

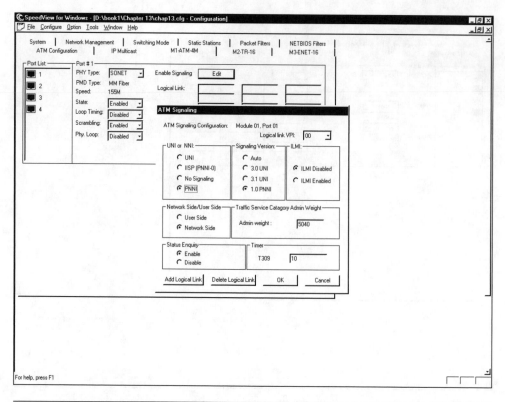

Figure 13-23   Configured for PNNI

30 (bytes). In the case of this filter, we are looking for the source address of the IP header (found 30 bytes into an Ethernet frame). The value is C0.20.0A.05. This is hex for 192.32.10.5. This is the address we have set our filter to look for. The condition is EQ (EQual to). This means that we are looking for values that are the same as this one (not greater or less). Match is equal to 0. This means that if we have a match for the filter (30 bytes in from the start of the MAC header we find the value C0.20.0A.05), then we have found what we are looking for and are done, and we apply the event specified for FWD. The zero means do not apply any further sequences or filters.

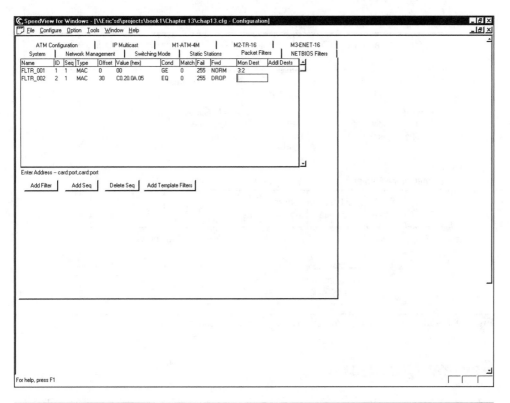

Figure 13-24 SpeedView packet filters

If the number 2 had appeared, the switch would have gone to the second sequence in the filter. If there were no second sequence in the filter, the switch would have gone on to the next filter.

Fail is equal to 255. This means that if we fail to meet the criteria of the filter, go on to the next filter. Since there are no more filters, we forward the packet normally in the event of a failure. FWD is set to DROP. This means that if we meet the criteria (match or fail) that apply to this filter, then this is what is done to the frame. In this case, a frame meeting the criteria specified previously will be dropped.

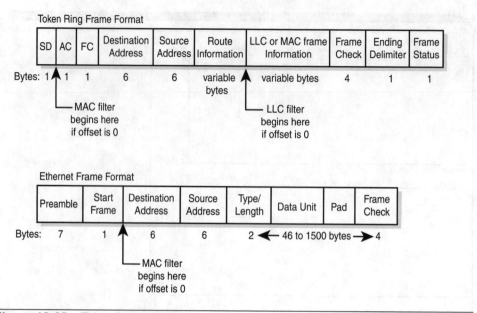

Figure 13-25   Token Ring and Ethernet reference points

Review Questions

1. Which of the following is not a supported feature of the Centillion 100 switch?
   A. PNNI
   B. FDDI
   C. Token Ring
   D. Spanning Tree
   E. 802.1Q

2. How many slots are available in a Centillion 100?

3. How many power supplies can go in a Centillion 100?

4. Which modules from a Centillion 100 can be shared with a Centillion 50?
   A. 4-port ATM MCP
   B. 8-port TokenSpeed
   C. 16-port EtherSpeed
   D. All of the above

5. How many MCP modules must a Centillion switch have in order to function properly?

6. Can a TokenSpeed MCP run version 4.x of the switching software?

7. When attempting to attach a console cable to an ATM MCP in a 5000BH chassis, which type of connector is required?
   A. mini-DIN-8
   B. db-9
   C. db-25
   D. V.35

8. What types of redundancy does the Centillion 100 offer? (Choose two.)
   A. Power supply
   B. Fail-safe
   C. MCP
   D. PPP multilink

9. Which of the following is not required for redundant MCPs to function?
   A. Minimum software version 3.x
   B. Two or more MCPs
   C. MCPs in slots 5 and 6 of the chassis
   D. ATM MCPs

10. When determining which of the MCPs will become the Primary one, which of the following is considered first?
   A. Memory
   B. Image
   C. Slot
   D. Priority

11. What are the two methods of managing the Centillion switch?
   A. Tivoli
   B. SpeedView
   C. CLI
   D. Site Manager
   E. Quick2Config

12. When you have selected a switch to configure, which of the following tabs in SpeedView will allow you to view/set a switch's IP address?
    A. System
    B. Network Management
    C. Switching Mode
    D. Static Stations

13. When you have selected a switch to configure, which of the following tabs in SpeedView will allow you to view/set a switch's call route table?
    A. ATM Configuration
    B. IP Multicast
    C. Switching Mode
    D. Static Stations

14. When you have selected a switch to configure, which of the following tabs in SpeedView will allow you to view/set a switch's Spanning Tree groups?
    A. ATM Configuration
    B. IP Multicast
    C. Switching Mode
    D. Static Stations

15. When creating a LECS on a Centillion 100, which of the following pieces of information do you have to provide? (Select all that apply.)
    A. ELAN name
    B. ELAN type
    C. ELAN location
    D. LES address
    E. LECS address
    F. VLAN members

16. Which of the following are VPORT types supported on the Centillion?
    A. Centillion mode VPORT
    B. LEC VPORT
    C. MPOA VPORT
    D. LANE VPORT

17. Which of the following are components in a LANE environment? (Choose all that apply.)
    A. LECS
    B. LEC
    C. LES

D. BUS

E. MPOA

F. PNNI

G. SVCs

18. Which standard protocol is used to configure static routes between switches that do not support the creation of SVCs or address summarization?

A. IP

B. ILMI

C. ANSI

D. IISP

19. Which side of the IIPS link determines the VPI/VCI values for the call?

A. The Network side

B. The User side

C. The Internal side

D. The Interim side

Answers

1. **B.** The correct answer is FDDI. There is no FDDI support on the Centillion 100 switch. PNNI is a method for generating SVCs in ATM networks and is fully supported in the Centillion 100. Token Ring modules exist for the Centillion 100 and are in fact the original supported topology. Spanning Tree is the standard (IEEE 802.1D) that prevents layer 2 loops from bringing down a network segment while providing for redundancy. 802.1Q is the standard that specifies how inter-VLAN communication occurs and is supported on software version 4.1 and above.

2. **Six.** There are six slots in a Centillion 100. The Centillion 50 has three slots. The 5000BH sometimes causes confusion. A 5000 chassis has a total of 14 slots, but the 5000 chassis is *not* a Centillion 100. The 5000BH contains two Centillion 100 busses in its backplane, which gives us two Centillion 100 switches (we refer to them as the Centillion Left and the Centillion Right). The busses are separated from each other between slots 7 and 8. Some people mistakenly believe that this gives them a seventh slot switch, but slots 1 and 14 are not part of the Centillion bus; therefore, even in a 5000BH, a single Centillion 100 switch has only six slots.

3. **Two.**

4. **D.** All modules are interchangeable from a Centillion 100 to a Centillion 50.

5. **One.** A single Centillion must have at least one MCP module to function properly. Under the proper circumstances a second MCP may be added for redundancy.

6. **No.** The TokenSpeed MCP and the EtherSpeed MCP are not supported after switch software version 2.x. This means that their functionality is limited when compared with an ATM MCP running the most recent version of the software.

7. **C.** The db-25 connector is required to connect a console cable to the ATM MCP in the 5000BH chassis. It is important to remember that the db-25 for the Centillion is not the same as the db-25 for the BN router platform (or any other product).

8. **A, C.** The Centillion supports two hot-swappable, load-balancing, redundant power supplies. The switch also supports (under the correct circumstances) redundant MCPs. The redundant MCPs mean that the failure of one will not cripple the network because the fail-over happens automatically. Fail-safe is a feature of the Accellar for port-level redundancy and PPP multilink is supported in the router platforms.

9. **C.** For MCPs to be redundant they must be in slots 1 and 2 of the switch chassis. Additional MCPs may be placed in any other slot(s), but they will not be redundant.

10. **D.** The priority, a configurable parameter, is considered first when determining which of the two MCPs will become the Primary.

11. **B, C.** SpeedView is the GUI management application for managing Centillion switches. It provides the capability to manage the switch both in-band and out-of-band. With it you can configure all operating parameters and upgrade the switch software. The CLI is another method of managing the switch both in-band (Telnet) and out-of-band (console cable), but the configuration possibilities are extremely limited. The CLI is primarily used for the initial assignment of an IP address (so the switch can then be managed in-band with SpeedView) or for troubleshooting. There are an extensive number of show commands that can be used to view the operation of the switch as well as logging facilities.

12. **B.** The Network Management tab enables you to set system configuration settings such as the following:

- IP address
- Subnet mask

- Default gateway
- Management VLAN

13. **A.** The ATM Configuration tab enables you to set system configuration settings such as the following:

- Call routing
- Signaling
- ATM address
- PNNI
- MPOA
- LANE

14. **C.** The Switching Mode tab enables you to

- Create Spanning Tree groups.
- Configure Spanning Tree.
- Select the bridging/switching mode.
- Create VLANS.
- Assign VLANS to Spanning Tree groups.
- Assign ports to VLANS.

15. **A, B, D, E.** An ELAN name, ELAN type, LES address, and LECS address must all be supplied to create a LECS on a Centillion 100 switch.

16. **A, D.** Centillion mode VPORTs are the proprietary type of VPORT that uses Permanent Virtual Circuits (PVCs) and Permanent Virtual Paths (PVPs) to tie VLANs together across ATM ports. LANE VPORTs are LECs that are an ATM forum standard supporting Switched Virtual Circuits (SVCs). Both are supported on the Centillion.

17. **A, B, C, D.** The LECS, LEC, LES, and BUS are all parts of the LANE environment. The LECS provides services to the LEC to locate the LES. The LEC provides access to the ELAN. The LES provides services to the LEC. The BUS helps locate unknown devices and handles broadcasts for the LEC. MPOA, PNNI, and SVCs are all ATM technologies and ideas that are not specific components of LANE.

18. D. The Interim Interswitch Signaling Protocol (IISP) is used to generate standards-based circuits between switches that do not support signaling to create SVCs or that cannot perform address summarization.

19. A. The Network side determines the VPI/VCI values for calls.

## CHAPTER 14

BayRS Routers

This chapter will cover the Nortel Networks router products. We will be examining routers in details, their functions, commands to perform various tasks with the routers, and their roles in a network. In this chapter we will cover how to configure the routers using the Technicians Interface (TI) as well as Site Manager. This chapter can be used to prepare for the Nortel Networks Support Specialist Certification for the Enterprise Track. It correlates to the Router Exam (920-014), which is a 90-minute proctored exam with 60 questions. A 60 percent or higher is required to pass this exam. For the exam preparation, the objectives that this chapter will attempt to cover are listed in the following sections.

NOTE In this chapter there will be commands to execute in order to complete certain tasks. The syntax for the TI commands is case sensitive. The format for commands used in this chapter will be displayed in mono font for ease of reading and those parameters that require user input will be italicized. Some examples are given for commands, and in these too, the user input is italicized for comparison to the original command. (There is no actual italicization done when entering commands in the TI.) When there is a command given under the title **GUI**, it shows steps for a command that can be followed in Site Manager.

Exam Objectives

These are the specific objectives for the router exam that will be covered in this chapter.

Router Hardware

- Differentiate between Nortel Networks field replaceable units (for example, link modules, net modules, expansion modules, and so on).

- Differentiate between port-to-port and slot-to-slot data flow.

- Differentiate between the Fast Routing Engine (FRE), FRE-2, and ATM Routing Engine (ARE) routing engines.

- Differentiate between various Nortel Networks router models.

- Interpret various router status indicators.

Router Software

- Describe local boot processes on various Nortel Networks routers.

- Describe the major differences between EZ Install, Net Boot, and Directed Net Boot.

- Differentiate between various image files for Nortel Networks routers.

Technician Interface (TI)

- Be able to use TI scripts.

- Be able to use various operating commands to manage the router.

- Describe the different types of TI connections to the various types of Nortel Networks routers.

- Describe various ways to log into and out of the Nortel Networks router.

- Use TI to perform system administration functions such as boot, run diagnostics, display software version, set passwords, and so on.

- Use TI to view and save event logs.

Site Manager Basics

- Define the router configuration functions: local, remote, and dynamic.

- Describe how the Image Builder tool is used to modify a boot image.

- Describe how the Report Generator tool can be used to document contents of a configuration file.

- Describe the function of the Statistics Manager and how it can be used to verify proper operation of any circuits configured.
- Describe the purpose of using Site Manager.

IP Addressing

- Define the addressing standard used for IP communications.
- Define the appropriate IP network address to be assigned to each physical network in a given IP addressing scheme.
- Identify the appropriate subnet mask for a given IP addressing scheme.

Source Route Bridging

- Be able to interpret Source Route Bridge parameters on a Nortel Networks router operating in a source route environment.
- Explain how the Token Ring End Station parameter can be used on Nortel Networks routers operating as a source route bridge.
- Explain the basic principles of source route bridging.
- Explain the function of the Routing Information Field (RIF) of a source route frame.
- Explain the route discovery process in a Nortel Networks router operating in a source route environment.

Transparent Spanning Tree Bridging

- Define the global and interface parameters that manage transparent bridge operation on a Nortel Networks router operating as a transparent bridge.
- Define the parameters that govern the operation of the spanning tree algorithm.
- Describe the difference between forwarding and flooding a frame.
- Describe the operating principles of a translational bridge and transparent bridge.
- Describe ways to ensure a loop-free bridge topology.

Management Information Base (MIB)

- Describe the architecture of the Management Information Base (MIB).
- Identify the TI commands used to display and modify the Nortel Networks MIBs.

IP Services

- Define the primary and secondary functions of IP.

- Describe the purpose and function of commonly used IP services such as Address Resolution Protocol (ARP), Routing Information Protocol (RIP), static routes, Circuitless IP, Proxy ARP, Reverse ARP (RARP), and so on.

- Describe what can be contained in the IP header and the function of the various components.

- Differentiate between various types of IP traffic filters, such as inbound and outbound, and explain the basic structure of an IP traffic filter template.

- Identify the predetermined criteria for IP traffic filters and their functions.

Router Management

- Configure a Nortel Networks router to send traps to any remote IP station.

- Configure a Nortel Networks router and Site Manager workstation for proper Simple Network Management Protocol (SNMP) community name access.

- Describe filter options within the Events Manager.

- Describe the architecture of SNMP.

- Understand features and functions of Events Manager, Router Files Manager, Statistics Manager, and Trap Monitor.

Router Fundamentals

Routers are used to interconnect networks locally and from all over the globe. Routers use a variety of protocols to connect networks. Nortel Networks routers support layer three LAN protocols like Appletalk, DECnet, Open Standards Interface (OSI), Transmission Control Protocol/Internet Protocol (TCP/IP), RIP, Open Shortest Path First (OSPF), and others on supported local area network (LAN) interfaces of Ethernet, Fiber Distributed Data Interface (FDDI), and Token Ring. Nortel routers also support wide area network (WAN) protocols, such as Switched Multimegabit Data Service (SMDS), Asynchronous Transfer Mode (ATM), Frame Relay, and Point-to-Point Protocol (PPP), as well as others. WAN interfaces include TI/FTI on a synchronous interface, high-speed serial interface (HSSI), Multichannel TI (MCT1), and Integrated Services Digital Network (ISDN). The routers we will discuss in this chapter also support bridging algorithms like Source Route Bridging, Translational Bridging, Transparent Bridging, and Spanning Tree Algorithm.

Product features include

- Complete SNMP network management support
- Dynamically configurable, giving the administrator the ability to make system changes on-the-fly without having to reboot the router
- Hot swap of field-replaceable modules
- Redundancy and fault management capabilities, including dual power supplies, logging, and trap messages
- Ability to partially boot some slots of the router without rebooting the complete router

Router Platforms

Nortel Networks produces routers for networks of all sizes. The administrator should understand each router and its capability when choosing a router that fits with his or her environment.

The Access Nodes (ANs): Small- to Midsize Remote Office Routers

There are several AN routers that are specifically designed for smaller remote offices.

The AN/Access Node Hub (ANH) Router

The AN is a small router used for connecting small, remote offices with a minimal cost. It is a fixed configuration router with a single Ethernet, a single Token Ring, or both. It also contains two synchronous interfaces with an expansion slot available for a third synchronous interface, a second Ethernet adapter, or an ISDN Basic Rate Interface (BRI). Ethernet support includes both an 802.3 (XCVR) port and a 10BASE-T UTP port, although only one is operable at any time. Synchronous interfaces can operate simultaneously and support X.25, V.35 with internal or external clocking. The AN also has one console/modem port (for TI and xmodem access) and a slot in the front for a flash card (see Figure 14-1). The AN can boot off a flash card locally or boot from the network with a centrally configured boot server. (The boot options will be discussed later in the chapter.)

Figure 14-1   An AN router with a slot in the front for a flash card

Figure 14-2   An ANH router—with an 8-port hub

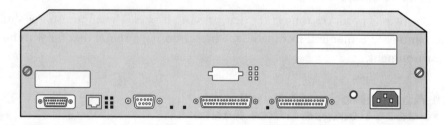

Figure 14-3   The rear view of an AN router

The ANH router is an AN router with an 8- or 12-port hub (see Figure 14-2). Both ANH models (ANH-8 and ANH-12) are equipped with two synchronous ports. Port 8 on the ANH-8 and port 12 on the ANH-12 can be crossover ports. From the router's perspective, the hub is seen as a single Ethernet network segment. The ANH uses the same configuration and boot image as the AN as no configuration is available for the hub (see Figure 14-3). The hub can be monitored through SNMP GETs and SETs to see statistics and operational status.

The Passport Advanced Remote Node (ARN)

The ARN is an AN router that has modularity built in, providing a flexible router solution for a small or remote office (see Figure 14-4). The ARN is designed to integrate the

Figure 14-4 An ARN router front view

functions of multiple devices into a single manageable router. The LAN—Ethernet, 10/100 BASE-TX, 100BASE-FX, and Token Ring interfaces of the ARN—offers flexible connectivity. Its two WAN adapter module slots provide an array of options for integrating devices (ISDN BRI, Data Service Unit/Channel Service Unit [DSU/CSU], and V.34 modem) for primary and backup WAN connectivity.

The ARN has a single LAN connection, either Ethernet or Token Ring, and two WAN ports. WAN ports can accommodate serial links, CSU/DSU, ISDN BRI, or V.34 modems. Expansion modules can be used to add up to three additional WAN ports and/or an additional LAN port (see Table 14-1).

The ARN comes equipped with 4-, 8-, 16-, or 32MB of memory and supports a flash card in the rear (see Figure 14-6). There is a V.34 console module for modem access and an optional redundant power supply unit (RPSU).

Table 14-1 I/O Modules for the Expansion Slots of the ARN Router

Modules
Tri Serial
Ethernet
Ethernet + Tri Serial
Token Ring
Token Ring + Tri Serial

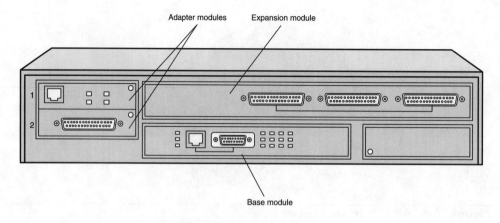

Figure 14-5 ARN router pictorial front view

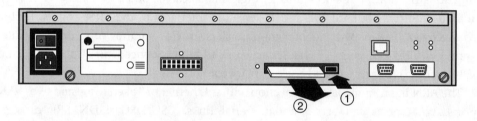

Figure 14-6 An ARN router rear view. Notice that the flash card is in the rear of the ARN.

The Access Stack Node (ASN) Router

The Nortel Networks ASN router (also an AN router) is a stackable router useful for growing and evolving remote offices and network centers (see Figure 14-7). A single ASN unit provides performance of up to 50,000 pps with 12 network connections. A fully configured stack of four ASN units can reach up to 200,000 pps with 48 network connections. The ASN-2, an updated model of the ASN, also includes support for an external redundant power supply.

The ASN architecture is designed to grow with the network, enabling solutions that can be expanded with ease because the ASN router is a stackable router. Up to four ASNs can be stacked, which can be configured with up to 48 LAN interfaces to be managed as a single router (see Figure 14-8).

Figure 14-8 shows each ASN can support four net modules. Choices of modules are listed in Table 14-2. Stacking four ASNs enables 12 modules to be populated with

Figure 14-7 A frontal view of the ASN

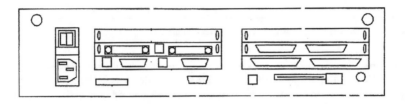

Figure 14-8 A rear view of the ASN with four net modules

ports, while four modules will be reserved for the stacking module (one for each ASN located in position four).

Multiple ASNs are stacked together through a Stack Packet Exchange High-Speed (SPEX-HS) net module and cable. The SPEX-HS cable provides a 256-Mbps interconnect.

Table 14-2 ASN Net Modules

Net Modules
10 Base-T Dual Ethernet
100 Base-T Ethernet
Dual synchronous
Quad synchronous
ISDN BRI/Dual Synchronous*
Quad BRI
FDDI
Dual Token Ring

*Indicates the module can only be placed in positions one and three on the ASN because the net module is tall.

(continued)

Table 14-2   ASN Net Modules *(continued)*

Net Modules
MCE1
Dual port MCT1
Hardware Compression**
HSSI
SPEX-HS

**For use with the Dual Sync or Dual Sync/ISDN BRI net modules.

 NOTE   The original ASNs used a SPEX cable with a 160-Mbps uplink (see Figure 14-9). This cable had to be terminated for all unused connections and used both ports of the SPEX net module.

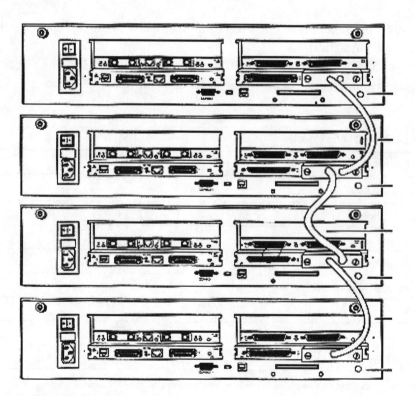

Figure 14-9   A stacked ASN with a SPEX cable

There must be a SPEX net module in position four for each of the ASNs in the stack. An additional SPEX-HS cable can be installed for additional bandwidth and to provide fault tolerance in the same net module as the primary SPEX-HS. When stacking ASNs, each ASN must have a unique slot ID. It is preferable to give the ASN on the bottom the slot ID of one and work upward from the bottom. Site Manager displays the stack in ascending order.

If an ASN in the stack fails, the SPEX-HS cable can route around that ASN and continue to forward traffic between the remaining units. The failed ASN can be hot swapped and a new ASN can be put back into the stack. The SPEX-HS cable must be connected prior to powering up the ASN or the router will fail diagnostics.

The Backbone Node (BN) Series Routers: Large-Size Enterprise Routers

The BN router family features a layered system software architecture and extensive fault management capabilities that minimize downtime by isolating malfunctions so other router components are not affected. High availability is made possible by symmetric multiprocessor architecture, along with hardware redundancy options, fully distributed system software, and comprehensive fault management capabilities. Dynamic reconfiguration and nondisruptive operational servicing (hot swap) enable online changes in hardware and software configuration. Support for redundant AC line cords, power supplies, network interfaces, and routers seamlessly yield the highest levels of network availability. All BN products can be configured with multiple processors, each with its own connection to the backplane bus. This provides redundancy in processing, software image storage, and fault resistance.

Utilizing Nortel Networks Routing Services (BayRS) (called BayRS because it was created and written by Bay Network engineers well before Nortel and Bay Networks merged) multiprotocol routing software, the BN routers facilitate interoperability in and support for major network and bridging protocols and wide area services. The BN routers also support the latest technologies, like Fast Ethernet, Gigabit Ethernet, and ATM. LAN connectivity includes Ethernet/802.3, 4- and 16-Mbps Token Ring/802.5, FDDI, and 100/1000 BASE-T. Wide area connections are provided through synchronous lines operating from 1200 bps to 52 Mbps, including Fractional T1, T1/E1, HSSI, and DS0A support. ATM networks can operate at up to 155 Mbps when connected using a SONET/SDH STS-3/STM-1 interface.

BN routers scale to meet the throughput and connectivity requirements of the largest networks by providing an extensive choice of LAN and WAN interfaces. Table 14-3 shows some of the supported link modules for the BN routers. There are many more

Table 14-3 Link Modules for the BN Product Line

Link Modules
Dual 100Base-T Ethernet with 64MB FRE processor
Dual Ethernet Dual Sync with 64MB FRE processor
Quad Ethernet with 64MB FRE processor
Quad Token Ring with 64MB FRE processor
Single Token Ring Dual Sync with 64MB FRE processor
FDDI—single-mode, multimode, or hybrid 64MB FRE processor
SONET/SDH multimode and single-mode fiber with 32MB DRAM 6MB SRAM
DS3 with 32MB DRAM and 6MB ARE processor
Octal Synchronous with 64MB FRE processor
Quad Synchronous with 64MB FRE processor
HSSI with 64MB FRE processor
Single, Dual, and Quad Multichannel TI with 64MB FRE processor
Single and Dual Multichannel TI with 64MB FRE processor

networks interfaces available, and the ones listed are also available in most cases with 32MB processors or below.

The BN series has two major routers within the product line: the BLN and the BCN.

The Backbone Link Node (BLN) and BLN-2 Routers

The BLN router offers a forwarding rate of up to 1.4 million pps to provide an ideal backbone routing solution for mid-sized network centers and large regional offices. The BLN offers 32 WAN interfaces and a comprehensive set of LAN interfaces with complete fault resilience to support all networks completely and reliably.

The BLN is a modular router with five slots (see Figure 14-10.) The BLN comes standard with an SRM-L in slot one, leaving four slots that can be configured with four processor cards and link modules (refer to Table 14-3). Additionally, the BLN comes with a single flash card and a single power supply. Figure 14-11 shows a BLN rear view.

The BLN-2 offers a redundant power supply that provides load sharing and fault tolerance. The power supply is hot swappable, and the BLN-2 can operate fully loaded with only one power supply if necessary (see Figure 14-12).

Figure 14-10   A BLN front view

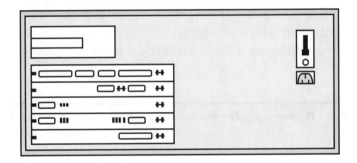

Figure 14-11   A BLN rear view

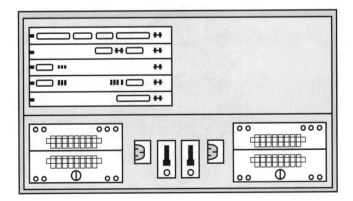

Figure 14-12   A rear view of a BLN-2. Note the second power supply available.

> **NOTE** When using two power supplies, it is a good idea to plug the supplies into different outlets and different circuits for total redundancy.

The Backbone Concentrator Node (BCN) Router

The BCN router has forwarding rates of up to 5 million pps and offers 104 WAN interfaces, 52 LAN, and 13 ATM, or FDDI interfaces (see Figures 14-13 and 14-14). The BCN is a powerhouse designed to meet the needs of the largest networks and most critical applications, with the capability to route traffic regardless of data protocol or network topology.

The BCN has 14 slots with an SRM-L standard in slot seven. An additional 13 slots are available for adding link modules and system processors (refer to Table 14-3). There is room for four power supplies with only one being the absolute minimum number of power supplies necessary if there are only four or less slots in use. Three power supplies are necessary for a fully loaded BCN, and four power supplies provide redundancy and fault tolerance.

> **NOTE** The power supplies are interchangeable between the BCN and the BLN.

Figure 14-13 A front view of a BCN

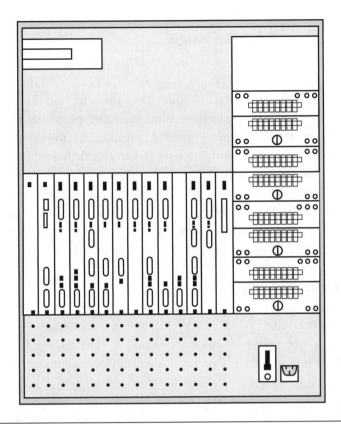

Figure 14-14   A rear view of the BCN

NOTE   The Gate Access Management Entity (GAME) or the OS of the router will send generate error messages if a power supply fails. Failure of a power supply can also be seen by the LED on the power supply itself.

Additional Hardware Features of the Nortel Networks Routers

Nortel Networks routers have hardware features that enable them to provide excellent services for all types of networks.

Symmetric Multiprocessor Architecture

Nortel Networks BN routers achieve the industry's highest performance and availability through an innovative symmetric multiprocessor architecture that distributes processing power to each network interface module. The symmetric multiprocessor architecture is based on three major elements: link modules, processor modules, and a processor interconnect (which will be expanded on shortly). Link modules provide the physical network interfaces and are directly attached to a dedicated processor module —either a Fast Routing Engine (FRE) or an ATM Routing Engine (ARE)—to form an Intelligent Link Interface (ILI). The system performance of the BN routers actually increases as the number of LAN, WAN, or ATM interfaces increases because each interface has its own processor. If a processor or link module fails in any system with multiple ILIs, the remainder of the system continues to operate unaffected.

Fast Routing Engine (FRE)

FRE processors are packet-processing engines that work with a variety of LAN and WAN interfaces for the BN routers (see Figure 14-15). Each network interface, or link module, on a BN router is supported by its own dedicated FRE card that resides in the front of the BN router. Each FRE card has dynamic RAM (DRAM) containing the operating sys-

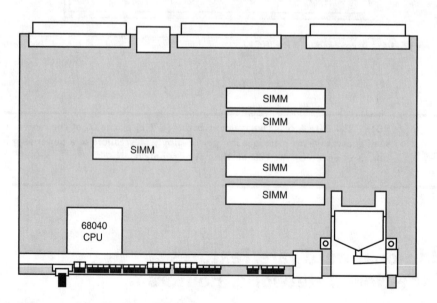

Figure 14-15 The FRE processor of a BN router

tem, routing tables, and configuration information. This helps to guarantee network availability and prevents the failure of one processor or network interface, causing the whole router to fail. Additionally, each FRE card connects to four Parallel Packet Express (PPX) rails and a link module. The FRE card provides a high-speed packet buffer cache for the routing processor. The FRE card has two PPX connections that connect the FRE card with the link modules and one Parallel Processor Interconnect (PPXI).

The PPXI has one transmitter that has one connection to each of the four PPX rails, but can only transmit from one connection at a time. The PPXI also has four receiver rails that connect to all four PPX rails and can accept packets from all rails at once.

 NOTE Every FRE card also has a slot that can contain a system flash card.

The newest processor, the FRE4-PPC, achieves forwarding rates exceeding 400,000 pps (64-byte packets) and is available with 32-, 64-, or 128MB (older FRE card had 8MB or 16MB of memory) of configurable local and global memory (DRAM). This memory can be used for buffering, storing and forwarding of packets, storing code for the processor, routing tables, MIB data, configuration, and event logs.

Memory for the FRE card is actually broken up into the two sections of global and local memory. By default, 25 percent of all memory is allocated to global memory, while 75 percent is used for local memory. Global memory is used for packet buffering. Local memory holds the operating system load and the configuration file and is used by the bridging and routing protocols. The more protocols an administrator has running in his or her environment, the more local memory will be required.

ATM Routing Engine (ARE)

The ARE is the ATM routing engine. It runs with 10.0 or higher version of the BayRS router software. It is used with ARE link modules for an ATM interface. This processor module works with Nortel Networks single-port SONET/SDH Multimode (155-Mbps) fiber, single-port SONET/SDH single-mode (155-Mbps) fiber, and single-port DS3/E3 interface (45/34-Mbps) high-performance ARE link modules. Full support for Token Ring and Ethernet LANE is also provided.

AREs are available with 8-, 16-, or 32MB of DRAM for local memory. Additionally, the ARE supports up to 6MB of virtual buffer memory (VBM), a memory management mechanism for cell/packet buffering that enables the BN routers to handle the processing of up to 2,000 simultaneously active virtual channels.

System Resource Modules (SRMs)

Each SRM provides arbitration and termination for two 256-Mbps PPX processor data paths. One SRM is included with each BN router and provides a 25-pin D-connector for a terminal or modem to access the Technician Interface (TI) for diagnostic and maintenance operations. The BN routers also support an optional SRM for 1-Gbps total bandwidth and PPX processor redundancy. With two SRMs installed, each FRE and ARE processor can access all of the four PPX processor paths. Each SRM operates independently, providing for complete fault resiliency.

SRM-L   The SRM-L is required for the BN series and resides in the rear (link side) of slot one of a BLN or slot seven of a BCN. This SRM-L provides system interconnect and arbitration of two data paths in the backplane. Each data path provides 256 Mbps of available bandwidth, so the SRM-L enables 512 Mbps of total backplane bandwidth. The SRM-L also supplies the TI connection and an RS232 interface for an external modem connection.

SRM-F   The SRM-F is an optional second SRM that resides in the front (FRE side) of slot one of a BLN or slot seven of a BCN. It provides connection to two additional rails in the backplane or an additional 512 Mbps of total backplane bandwidth. With both the SRM-L and SRM-F in place, a BN router can support 1 Gbps of total bandwidth to the backplane. The SRM-F also provides redundancy and backup in case the SRM-L fails. If either of the SRMs fail, they can be hot swapped with a new SRM, while two other data paths continue to operate at 512-Mbps aggregate. The BN router can continue to forward traffic with only one SRM module; however, without the SRM-L, there are no external connections for direct TI access.

Parallel Packet Express (PPX)

PPX provides fast processor to processor (FRE card to FRE card) transport of data packets. It consists of four redundant data paths called *rails* that make up the main part of the backplane interconnection of a BN router. Each rail has eight data lines to enable data to move an octet at a time in parallel on each rail. (Arbitration of the rails is provided by the SRM.) Each FRE and ARE processor has access to all four paths simultaneously and can transmit over one path as it is receiving data from all four paths. All processors are peers on the PPX; none has priority. The FRE card uses a random path selection algorithm to decide which rail to use, thereby providing for load balancing across the PPX. The FRE card maintains knowledge of the integrity of the rails by sending out Breath of Life packets (BOFLs) to each rail. Upon hearing an answer from the rail, the FRE knows that rail is available and randomly chooses a rail to send data from those that are available. If a single PPX processor data path becomes unavailable, the load is automatically distributed across the remaining paths, providing for continuous operation. The PPX cannot perform fragmentation if a data packet is too large.

Link Modules

The link modules provide the interface to the network for local and wide area networking as well as packet buffering. A wide range of I/O interconnect modules are available for the BN routers. Each link module is connected to a FRE module, and the combination of module processor is called Intelligent Link Interface (ILI). Multiple ILIs are like having multiple high-speed routers connected via high-speed backbone.

> **NOTE** FRE card + Link Module = ILI.

Link modules have ports to provide the physical interface to each type of network, drivers dependent on the port types and the PPXI, which connects the link modules with the FRE card. Link modules are located in the back of the BN routers.

Flash Memory Module

System software and configuration parameters are stored in the flash Personal Computer Memory Card International Association (PCMCIA) memory module more commonly known as the *flash card*. The flash card is nonvolatile and can be read and written to many times.

> **NOTE** Although the flash card is a PCMCIA card, it is not compatible with any of the Passport switch product flash cards.

The flash memory PCMCIA card may be anywhere from 2MB to 100MB in size, depending on the manufacturer. Flash cards may be used in all the router platforms;

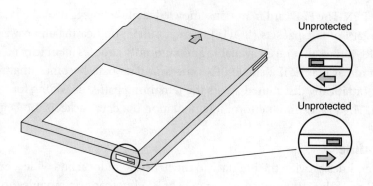

Figure 14-16 A router flash card

however, there must be at least one flash card per BN or stacked ASN router (see Figure 14-16). Any or all of the FRE cards or stacked ASNs can contain additional flash cards for redundancy. Each flash card contains file system storage for software images, configuration files, event logs, and scripts. The format of the flash card is specifically for GAME and is not DOS compatible. Names for files on the flash card can be up to 15 characters with extensions, but the extensions are not recognized by the GAME operating system. (.log does not mean anything to the GAME, and a log file can be named with any extension.) A flash card is identified by a volume ID that is the same number as the slot that the flash card is in.

NOTE A flash card in the FRE of slot six would be identified as 6:.

Port-to-Port Data Flow

Direct attachment of the processor module and link modules means that only data traveling between different link modules (slot-to-slot) must utilize the processor interconnect. For port-to-port data flow, data enters the link module, and the packet is buffered on the link module in global memory. Software runs on the CPU associated with the link module and inspects the frame for the routing protocol type. If the CPU does not have the protocol loaded in local memory, the CPU will attempt to bridge the packet. If no bridge protocols are loaded, the packet will be dropped. If the packet was determined to be routable, the CPU compares addressing information in the packet to address tables in the local memory. The CPU modifies the packet for the appropriate port of the same link module by changing any necessary information in the frame's header. The CPU directs the link module to move the frame from memory to the appropriate port on the same link module.

NOTE No PPX rails are needed to transfer packets from one port to another on the same slot.

Slot-to-Slot Data Flow

Data enters the link modules and is buffered on the link module in global memory. Software on the CPU inspects the frame for a routing protocol. If that routing protocol is not loaded in local memory, the packet may be bridged and sent back onto the rails if a bridging protocol is loaded. If no bridging protocols are loaded into local memory, the packet will be dropped. If the packet is routable then the CPU will compare the address in the frame to the address in the CPU's tables in local memory. The CPU then modifies the packet for the appropriate port of a link module in another slot. The CPU directs the PPXI to move the packet on an available rail from memory of this slot to another slot. The PPXI asks the SRM for permission to use the rail chosen, and the packet is then transferred to the remote buffer.

Hardware Data Compression

Hardware-based compression is supported for Frame Relay, ISDN Primary Rate Interface (PRI), and Point-to-Point Protocol (PPP) with Nortel Networks' Advanced Compression Coprocessor, a daughter-card mounted on an FRE processor. Nortel Networks' hardware compression enables WAN connections to send twice the amount of data over existing WAN interfaces. Performance achieved for aggregate compressed throughput reaches 60 Mbps, the equivalent of 2 Mbps full duplex (4 Mbps aggregate) over eight 2.048-Mbps links. The Advanced Compression Coprocessor is available in configurations supporting 128 and 256 contexts, where contexts can be divided into 8KB or 32KB histories.

Soloist Processes

Normally, processing for each network interface is done by the directly attached processor module, each running its own copy of routing and bridging code and having its own copy of the forwarding tables. Management and routing updates are automatically done on the processor module that receives them and then forwarded to other processor modules. Routing protocols that are CPU intensive, however, are activated on only one processor module. These processes are called *soloists*. TI, Circuitless IP, and OSPF are all soloist processes. All modules receive routing updates from the protocols, but do not need to run the algorithms or maintain the tables for these protocols.

NOTE Protocols that are not CPU and resource intensive, like TCP/IP and RIP, can run on all processors simultaneously.

In the case of a CPU failure on the slot running the soloist process, any other processor that is configured to run the process may do so. Configuring which slots can run the soloist process can be done with a slot mask. Any position in the mask that is set to binary one can run the soloist process, while slots that are set to zero cannot run the process. Soloist processes cannot run on the SRM slot (slots one in the BLN and seven in the BCN).

Router Boot Process

Each router has its own boot image file that contains a compressed executable version of the operating system and protocols the router will run (see Table 14-4). Different software packages are available that comprise different LAN/WAN suites and contain protocols that are needed for specific companies. The boot images appear as one file, but actually contain multiple executable files including the system kernel. It is because of the uniqueness of the system kernel on each of the router products that each router has its own boot image file.

Table 14-4 Router Products and Their Respective Boot Image Filenames and Default Locations

Product	Filename	Boot Image Location
AN, ANH-8, ANH-12	An.exe	Flash card rear panel
ARN	Arn.exe	Flash card rear panel
ASN	Asn.exe	Flash card rear panel
BLN, BLN-2, BCN	Bcn.exe	Flash card in FRE

CAUTION: Changing the name of the boot file will cause the router to fail in a default boot attempt because the boot file image name is burnt into the electrically erasable programmable read-only memory (EEPROM) memory of each router.

In addition to a *boot* image file, each router will look to load a configuration file named *config* by default. An administrator can make many configuration changes to the router, but must always be sure to name the changed configuration file *config* so that when the router boots up it will use this file. If an administrator ever wants a clean copy of the default configuration before any changes were made, there is a file *ti.cfg* that is a copy of the *config* file for a new router with no configuration. On an ASN, this file is called *ti_asn.cfg*, and on an ARN it is called *ti_arn.cfg*.

NOTE The default config file (and ti_asn.cfg) on an ASN are larger.

Command `boot` This command warm starts the entire router, causing a new load of the image file and configuration file. Log files are not erased during a warm boot. It is the same as pressing the reset button in the front panel of a BN router for less than three seconds.

NOTE Holding down the reset button on the front panel of a BN router for more than three seconds causes a cold boot of the router.

Specifying a filename with the `boot` command enables the system to boot with that boot image or configuration file:

Example `boot 2:- 2:myconfig.cfg` This command boots the system using the default image file in volume 2 and the configuration file called myconfig.cfg also stored in volume 2.

Command `reset <slot#>` This command can be used to reset a specific slot. Resetting the slot that is currently running the TI process causes the process to run on the next available slot.

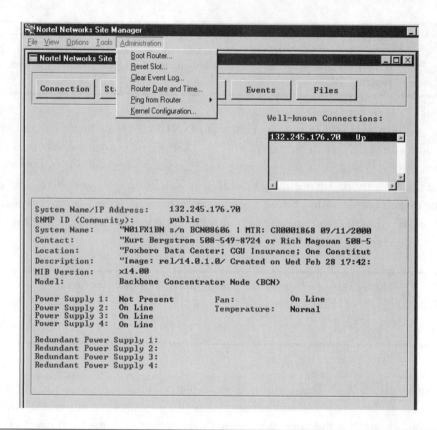

Figure 14-17   The Site Manager Administration menu with various useful tools for managing a router

Site Manager can also be used to boot a router with a named configuration and image file or reset a specific slot (see Figure 14-17).

GUI   *<slot #>* Administration > Boot Router > Choose volume and filename for image and configuration files

GUI   Administration > Reset Slot > Choose slot to reset

Command   diags   *<slot #>* This command cold starts the router. This consists of a CPU, backbone, link diagnostic, and reboot process that reloads the image and configuration file, clears all the logs, and resets the system's statistics. An administrator can specify one or more processor modules to perform diagnostics or force diagnostics to occur on the whole router.

Example   diags   *4,5* This command cold boots slots four and five of the router.

> **NOTE** All types of reboots will cause a flushing of the routing tables.

The default router boot process differs on the different router platforms because of the router's probable function. The default boot process for the BN and ASN is designed for a local boot from a flash card. This is because the BN and ASN are generally the backbone of the network. The AN and ARN look to boot remotely by default. This is because these routers are generally used for smaller remote offices that may not even have their own administrator. Usually, these routers are managed from a central location.

The Default BN and ASN Boot Process

Each FRE card or ASN unit loads diagnostics and boot programs from onboard EPROM memory. The diagnostics run independently on each module and verify memory, access to the PPX (SPEX for the ASN), and communication with its link module. Each FRE card or ASN unit then sends out up to five broadcast requests every half a second for a boot image file from the backplane (or SPEX). If there is no answer from the backplane, then the FRE card or ASN will see if there is a local flash card available with the boot image file. At least one of the FRE cards or ASNs must have a local boot image available and loads the image into RAM. This module can then service other FRE cards or ASNs that do not have a local flash with the boot. After the boot image is loaded, each FRE card or ASN then transmits up to five broadcast requests for a configuration file from the backplane. If there is no response, the FRE card or ASN will then look again for a config file on its local flash. A router without a config file can still boot, but the process will take much longer, and the TI prompt will be a $ without any volume mounted.

> **CAUTION** In a system with multiple flash cards, all cards must have the same boot image and config file otherwise different modules can boot with different software code and different configurations.

The Default AN and ARN Boot Process

The AN or ARN routers run an internal diagnostics test to verify the integrity of the hardware. The routers then sends a BootP request for an IP address across the network five times out of their synchronous (COM) ports. If there is no answer, the routers will attempt to boot locally.

Additionally, the AN, ASN, and ARN routers have the option of loading their configuration file from the network as well. This remote load option is available on the Ethernet and Frame Relay interfaces. It is important to note how the router is currently configured to boot. By default, AN and ARN routers are configured to use the EZ Install option.

Command `getcfg` This TI command is used to verify the boot options for a router.

By default, the ASN boots an image and configuration file locally, while the AN and ARN boot an image file from the network and a configuration file locally. For centralized administration purposes, there are three types of remote boot options available for the AN, ARN, and ASN routers.

EZ Install

The EZ Install process starts with a router sending a proprietary BootP request for an IP address from an upstream Nortel Networks router. The upstream router assigns the router an IP address that is its address + 1. After obtaining this IP address from the upstream router, the router sends a second BootP request for the pathnames of a configuration and/or boot image. A BootP server responds with the IP address and directory path for the configuration and/or boot image. The requesting router processes the BootP response and sends a Trivial File Transfer Protocol (TFTP) request for the configuration and/or boot file (see Figure 14-8).

Command `bconfig image network` This TI command sets up the router to use BootP to request an image file from a remote server whose address is unknown.

Command `bconfig config network` This TI command sets up the router to use BootP to request a configuration file from a remote server whose address is unknown.

Net Boot

A router that already has an IP address configured can send out a BootP request for the address of the configuration and/or boot image file only. Once this router receives the

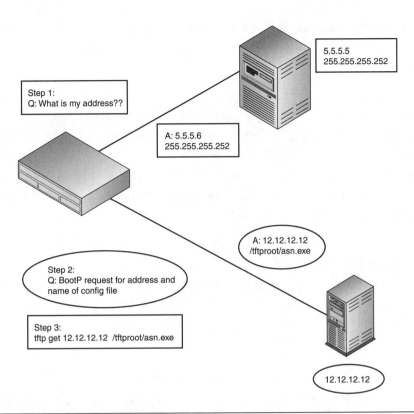

Step 1:
Q: What is my address??

5.5.5.5
255.255.255.252

A: 5.5.5.6
255.255.255.252

A: 12.12.12.12
/tftproot/asn.exe

Step 2:
Q: BootP request for address and name of config file

Step 3:
tftp get 12.12.12.12 /tftproot/asn.exe

12.12.12.12

Figure 14-18   The EZ Install process for a Nortel Networks ASN router

IP address of the configuration file server, it can do a TFTP get request to receive the configuration and/or boot image file:

Command `ifconfig -s<slot#> <xcvr1, COM1, COM2> <ipaddress> <subnet mask>`   This command defines an IP address and subnet mask for an Ethernet or COM port on the router. This address will be stored in the EPROM of the router and will be available even before the router boots up.

Example `ifconfig -s1 xcvr21 10.10.10.45 255.255.0.0`   This command configures the IP address of 10.10.10.45 with a 16-bit mask onto the second Ethernet port of slot one.

Directed Net Boot

A router can be configured with an IP address as well as the IP address and pathname for the configuration and/or boot image file. This information will be stored in the

Prom of the router and will not be erased through a cold or warm reboot. In this case the router will only have to send out a TFTP request to the configuration file server to request the configuration and/or boot image file:

Command `bconfig image network <ipaddress> <pathname>` This TI command is used to set up a directed net boot by providing an IP address and pathname for the image file across the network. The router should already have an IP address stored in EPROM that was created with the `ifconfig` command.

Example `bconfig image network 10.10.10.97 /tftpboot/asn.exe` This command gets an image file named asn.exe from the tftpboot folder of a network server located at 10.10.10.97.

Quick Quiz 1

How would an administrator set up a directed net boot for a router with the address of 99.9.9.1 (default mask) on slot 3/com1 whose configuration file was located at a server 99.9.9.14 in the temp directory?

Answer

First the administrator will have to do an `ifconfig` command to set up the router with the proper IP address: `ifconfig -s3 COM1 99.9.9.1 255.0.0.0`. Afterwards, the command to set up the router with the address of the server is `bconfig config network 99.9.9.14 /temp/config`.

Technician Interface (TI)

The TI enables users to access and configure a router through a serial port, Telnet session, or a modem. TI, through the local console port, is the only way to configure a router until an IP address is set up because modem access is disabled by default. TI access through the console port (called *out of band access*) is usually accomplished with a hyperterminal type of program. Settings for the serial (COM) port for the hyperterminal session should be VT-100, 9600 bps, 8 data bits, no parity, and 1 stop bit.

To connect a console cable to a BN router, a 25-pin connector is attached to the SRM-L in the back of the BN router. The Access product routers use a nine-pin connector attached to the rear of the router. The exception is the ANH-8 that has the connector in the front.

NOTE   The cables used by the BN and the Access products are different as are the cables used in the Access products themselves. The newer ASNs use female connectors, while the older ASNs use male connectors.

TI is a soloist process that runs automatically on all routers but will only run on a single processor module (FRE card) in a multislotted system (BN). It will become active in the first slot to boot with an operating system and configuration. If the slot running TI is reset, the process will move to the next available processor on a multislot system (or as configured in the slot mask) or restart after the router completes the boot sequence for a single-slot system (ARN or AN).

 NOTE   A stacked ASN could have four active TI sessions because each ASN is a single slot system and runs TI.

Logging into the Router

There are two usernames and passwords that exist by default on the router. Each username and password combination provides a different level of access into the router:

- Read-only access enables users to view configurations and statistics without being able to make any changes. The default read-only user is User.

- The superuser that has all rights to change all settings, including passwords and security and uses the default login of Manager.

 CAUTION   For security purposes, companies should never leave the default password in effect.

To enter into a router the administrator uses the login command, which is entered for him or her at the default start up screen. TI does not log out users or have a time out by default. An administrator should never leave a computer with the Manager login active. For safety, it is best for an administrator to use the User login for all router management unless changes will have to be made to the router. To log out of the router, the administrator should use the `logout` command:

Command `logout`

To change the password for the Manager or User, use the `password` command. This command must be executed with a manager's access level so the `system` command can be entered to change from user access to manager's access:

Command `system` This command enables the administrator to change from the User access to Management access.

Command `password <Manager, User>` This command enables an administrator to change usernames and passwords.

NOTE Once a password is entered into the system, it should not be forgotten. Systems with lost passwords can only be recovered through Nortel technical support.

The TI soloist runs on a single processor module in the BN routers. When assigning a new password, the GAME distributes the new password to nonvolatile RAM (NVRAM) in all processor modules. This is what ensures that the system retains the passwords and running TI on a different slot would not leave a backdoor open for users to get in and make trouble. The exception is in the case where a new processor module is inserted in the BN router. It is necessary to reassign the password to the new slot; otherwise, TI will not require a password when run from that slot.

NOTE If an administrator forgot the password on a BN router, it is possible to insert a new FRE card into the router (or one with a known password), force TI to run from that processor, and reassign the password from that new FRE card.

Accessing TI brings up a default prompt that indicates the console port or slot TI was loaded on. The prompt is in the form of [x:y] where x is the slot number or ASN stack number on which TI is active, and y is the port number for the TI connection. y will always be one except for an ASN, which will have x and y both the ASN stack number.

Quick Quiz 2

What will the default prompt of an AN router be?

Answer

1:1 because there is only one slot for an AN and one console port.

File System

The file system for the flash card of the router is a type of a linked list and is not based on FAT. In this type of file system, each file has an end of file (EOF) that is linked to the beginning of the next file (BOF). Files cannot be renamed; they can only be copied with a new name. Additionally, deleting files does not create free space on the drive, but deleted files remain in the linked list unable be accessed. Deleted files cannot be recovered either. To recover the disk space from deleted files, a compact of the flash card is necessary. This actually copies the files and then reorganizes them back to the flash card in order , leaving free space at the end of the flash card that is reusable for other files (called *contiguous free space*).

The `dinfo` command displays the slot numbers where flash cards are installed, the state of the flash card (corrupted or formatted), the total number of bytes used, free space, and contiguous free space (see Figure 14-19):

Command `dinfo` Shows the status of the flash cards in the router

```
[13:N99PA1] $dinfo

VOL    STATE       TOTAL SIZE    FREE SPACE    CONTIG FREE SPACE
-----------------------------------------------------------------
  5:   FORMATTED   16777216        814760          700748
  9:   FORMATTED   33554432      14962165        14962165
 10:   FORMATTED   33554432      15078657        15078657
```

Figure 14-19 The results of a `dinfo` command

Filenames can have up to 15 characters or digits. The first character of a filename must be a letter. Extensions are not recognized but can be used, and periods are viewed by the system merely as an additional character:

Command `dir <parameter>` The directory command displays a list of files on a volume. The administrator can enter different parameters to see specific files or volumes.

Example `dir *.cfg` Displays all the files with a .cfg extension that are on the current volume.

Example `dir 4:????` Displays all files that are on volume 4 that have four characters in the filename.

Quick Quiz 3

Is there a difference between the command `dir *.*` and `dir *` ? Which file will not be displayed with the `dir *.*` command?

Answer

Yes, the `dir *.*` displays only files that contain extensions and have a period in them. The file *config* will not be displayed because it does not contain a period, and the flash card does not recognize and understand the concept of extensions.

Command `cd <volume#>` This command is used to display or change the active directory. This command does not change the TI prompt, which represents the slot that is running the TI soloist and not the active volume.

Command `copy <parameters>` This command copies a file with the parameters named. This command also can rename a file by copying the file with a new name and deleting the file with the old name.

Example `copy config alt.cfg` Copies the config file on the active volume to a file named alt.cfg on the same volume.

Example `copy * 3:` Copies all the files on the active volume to volume 3.

Command `delete <volume #:>:<filename>` This command marks a file for deletion, but does not actually remove the file from the media.

Example `delete *` Deletes all the files on the current volume.

NOTE Even files with extensions will be deleted because as we said before, the file system views the period as a character and extensions are meaningless.

Command `partition` This command partitions a flash card into two equal volumes that can then be accessed as a: or b:.

NOTE This command is used less often than the other commands mentioned but can be used for backing up files to a partition that users do not know about and cannot accidentally delete.

Because only contiguous free space is usable by the file system, the `compact` command is necessary to enable the free space to become contiguous free space.

Command `compact <volume #:>` This command actually brings back the free space to contiguous and usable free space by completely deleting all files marked deleted and re-creating the file structure. After the command is executed, free space and contiguous free space should be the same number.

NOTE If power fails during a `compact` command, all the files will be lost, and the flash card may become corrupt.

NOTE The `compact` command is very processor intensive and takes priority over every other router activity. It is best to run the `compact` command during low usage times for the router.

Command `format <flash,pcmcia>` The `format` command formats the media and removes all files completely (just like the `format` command used in any other OS).

NOTE Once the `format` command is used, all files involved are permanently deleted.

Saving the Configuration

In order to ensure that user configuration remains with the router after a reboot, it is essential to save the configuration. This will then become the user configuration that is loading after the Runtime Image is loaded during the boot process.

Command `save config` Saves the configuration file to the flash memory on the router

The System Log

Events on a router are stored by the system in each processor module in 64KB buffer of memory. Approximately 4,000 entries are stored on a first-in first-out (FIFO) basis, and the oldest events will get overwritten when new events occur. Event logs are saved during a warm boot, but a cold start, removing a module, or running diagnostics on a slot will cause the log to be deleted.

To display the log file the administrator uses the `log` command (see Figure 14-20). Because the log is stored in a binary format, using a type command will not be of use for viewing logs:

Command `log`

There are many options for viewing the log in a filtered form so the administrator can see only the events that pertain to a specific issue. The `-d<date>` is used to view a log file starting from a particular date. The `-t<time>` is used to view a log file from a specific time. The `-e<entity>` command is used to view specific entities in the log file. Entities are entered in all capitals, and they are things like OSPF, TFTP, and ARP. The `-s<slot#>` option is used to view events from a particular slot only (of a stacked ASN or BN product). The `-p<rate>` option is used to poll the log and bring up new log events as they appear. The default polling rate is five seconds, but can be changed in accordance with the needs of the administrator. The `-f<severity>` is used to view certain severity levels of the log. These include i for information, f for fault, w for warning, t for trace, and d for debug.

```
$ log

#   1: 09/06/2001 04:47:45.003  INFO    SLOT  2  GAME           Code:  11
Starting image rev/14.00/1D11 Wed Oct 18 21:33:11 EDT 2000

#   2: 09/06/2001 04:47:46.023  INFO    SLOT  2  GAME           Code:   9
BackBone 2 became re-connected
BackBone 3 became re-connected

#   3: 09/06/2001 04:47:46.742  INFO    SLOT  2  GAME           Code:  10
slot  5 became re-connected

#   4: 09/06/2001 04:47:46.796  INFO    SLOT  2  GAME           Code:  10
slot  3 became re-connected

#   5: 09/06/2001 04:47:54.222  INFO    SLOT  2  NVFS           Code:  42
Volume 2: Service initializing.

#   6: 09/06/2001 04:47:58.339  INFO    SLOT  2  MIB            Code:   4
Using configuration file '2:config'

#   7: 09/06/2001 04:47:58.468  INFO    SLOT  2  MIB            Code:   3
Service initializing.

#   8: 09/06/2001 04:48:01.539  INFO    SLOT  2  TI             Code:  41
TI Port Manager initialized on slot 2.

#  10: 09/06/2001 04:48:01.546  INFO    SLOT  2  TI             Code:  43
TI session for port 1 initialized on slot 2.

#  11: 09/06/2001 04:48:04.015  INFO    SLOT  3  GAME           Code:  11
Starting image rev/14.00/1D11 Wed Oct 18 21:33:11 EDT 2000

#  12: 09/06/2001 04:48:13.734  INFO    SLOT  2  IP             Code:   4
Protocol initializing

#  13: 10/30/2001 14:59:10.008  WARNING SLOT  3  TI             Code:  39
Invalid login attempt by Manager on port 0.
```

Figure 14-20   The log file. Take a close look; there are many interesting entries displayed in this log file.

Example   `log -s2 -eOSPF -fftdw`   This command displays the log file from slot two filtered for the OSPF events of fault, trace, debug, and warning.

NOTE   Because the trace and debug views of the router log are very resource intensive, the only way to see these severity levels is to use the `-f` option when using the `log` command. They are not displayed by default with the plain `log` command.

Filtering the log with TI enables the router to filter all events from the requested slots before bringing down the log file to the screen.

NOTE   Site Manager can also be used to display the log file. Any filtering of the log with Site Manager occurs only after the log has been pulled down from the slots.

To save the log file unfiltered, the administrator has to just type the location of where the log should be saved:

Command `save log <volume:destination file>`

Example `save log 3:log1.log` This saves the log file as log1.log to the third volume on the router.

The `save` command can also be used to save a filtered copy of the log using the same parameters that were mentioned previously for viewing a filtered log file:

Example `save log 2:tftp.log 10/26/01 9:03:00 TFTP tf`

Quick Quiz 4

Which log entities will an administrator save using this command and what will be the filename and location of the saved log?

Answer

The administrator will save only TFTP trace and fault events that have occurred after October 26, 2001 at 9:03. The file will be called tftp.log and will exist on the third volume of the router.

The `log` command can also be used to view a previously saved log file. The administrator must specify the location of the saved log file and can use any of the parameters to filter the view of the saved log file:

Command `log <slot:filename>`

Example `log 3:log1.log -tOSPF -ffw`

It is possible to clear the log from all slots or from specified slots. The reason for clearing a log may be to see if a fault reoccurs or for other troubleshooting purposes.

Command `clearlog` The command used to clear the log can also use the `-s<slot#>` parameter.

It is also possible to clear the event log from Site Manager.

GUI   Administration > Clear Event Log

TI Scripts

TI scripts are precreated programs that an administrator can use to manage the router and information stored in the MIBs. Information about protocols, services, and circuits can all be seen with different TI scripts. In addition to TI scripts that are available as embedded programs or batch files, users can create TI scripts that are useful to their needs and networks.

Show Commands

Show commands display system configuration information, state information of circuits and protocols, and statistical information. The show command is used to give a snapshot of the information at the time that the command is executed. Show commands can be used to find out which circuits are available, which routes are being propagated and learned from which routing protocol, and other information that will be discussed in the rest of this chapter.

Monitor Commands

Monitor commands display the same information as the show commands except the monitor command refreshes the screen periodically. Any new information will be revealed on the screen as the router is continuously polled for updated information.

Menu Commands

The menu command provides a menu to other scripts. All menu files end with a .mnu extension. Users can also create custom menus and delete menus for protocols that are not being used on the system.

 NOTE   For smaller flash cards, it may make sense to delete unused script commands from unused protocols or move them to a backup server to free up space on the flash card.

Aliases

An administrator can create aliases, or small batch files, to run multiple tasks. For example, if an administrator wants to save certain log events every morning and then clear the log, he or she can write a small alias to do the commands, save it with one filename, and run that alias every morning (see the following example).

Command `alias <name>` This command is used to create aliases or to see commands in the alias specified. When creating an alias, the name of the alias will be followed by double quotes with a string of commands separated by commas.

Example `alias morninglog "save log 2:todaylog.log -eOSPF ffw; clearlog; tftp put 10.10.10.10 2:todaylog.log"` This command creates an alias called morninglog that saves the OSPF events in the log to a file called todaylog.log and then TFTPs the file onto a remote server located at 10.10.10.10.

Aliases are stored in RAM until the router is rebooted. To permanently save the aliases that have been created, use the `save` command and specify a filename:

Command `alias` Shows which aliases are currently in memory

Command `save aliases <filename>` Saves all aliases currently in RAM to the file specified

The debug.al file contains 100 useful aliases created by Nortel Networks. To use aliases that are not currently in memory (either from the debug.al file or from aliases that the administrator has created him or herself), they must be loaded into memory.

Command `source aliases` This command loads all aliases into memory.

Command `run <aliasname>` This command loads and runs the specific alias named.

To delete aliases, use the `unalias` command:

Command `unalias <aliasname>` Deletes the named alias

Other TI Commands

Some other useful TI commands include the following:

Command `run setpath <volume #>` This ensures that the volume that the script commands are located on is in the search path much like the DOS path command.

Command `Ctrl + c` This is used to stop a command that was just issued.

Command `! <# of times to repeat>` This command (called the `bang` command) repeats the last command executed, and optionally, it repeats it the number of times asked for in the repetition count.

The `history` command can be used to view TI commands most recently entered during the current console session. By default, 20 commands are saved in a history list, but up to 40 commands can be saved.

Command `history <number>` This command lists all the current commands stored in the history list. Adding an optional parameter of a number executes that command from the history list (see Figure 14-21).

Command `help` This command alone gives a list of available commands, but can be used together with a command to get a specific command syntax for that command.

Example `help ping` Use this command to find out the syntax for a `ping` command.

```
$ history
     8  dinfo
     9  dinfo 3
    10  dinfo 3:
    11  menu
    12  show
    13  ip
    14  dir
    15  tftp put config 47.102.193.48
    16  system
    17  system
    18  tftp put config 47.102.193.48
    19  system
    20  system
    21  getcfg
    22  bconifg
    23  bconfig
    24  log
    25  date
    26  loadmap
    27  sho ip circ

$ history 25
date
Oct 30, 2001 15:10:12 [GMT]
```

Figure 14-21 The `history` command and the execution of command 25 from the list

Command `more <on,off>` This command enables an administrator to view output before it scrolls off the screen. When the `more` command is on (which it is by default), the system forwards a number of lines to the screen and waits for the user prompt for the next page of information (24 is the default). Turning more off enables the output of a command to scroll when one screen is finished to the next screen.

 NOTE It may be useful to turn more off when attempting to read the end of a long log file.

Command `stamp` This command is used to display the current software version and the date and time it was created.

 NOTE The `stamp` command shows the version of software on the FRE running the TI soloists. Make sure all FRE cards are running the same software.

Command `show hardware image` This command displays the version of software running on all FRE cards.

Command `show hardware config` This command displays the configuration file the FRE card is running as well as the volume that the configuration file was loaded from.

 NOTE If there are multiple volumes that the FRE cards will be booting from, it is essential to ensure that the configuration information is identical on all of them.

Command `date` This command enables the administrator to display date, time, and offset from Greenwich Mean Time (GMT). Time is based on a 24-hour clock. To change the values held for the date, time, or offset, the `date` command is used alone with the parameter that needs changing.

Example `date 12/28/01 19:45 -5` This command changes the date, time, and the GMT offset. Leaving out one of the parameters causes the system to use the currently set value.

> **NOTE** Changing the date, time, or GMT sets the new date and time for all the slots of the ASN and BNs. The new date and time will not change the events that are already in the log file, but the GMT will change even for the older entries.

It is also possible to change the routers date, time, and GMT from Site Manager (see Figure 14-22).

GUI Administration > Router Date and Time

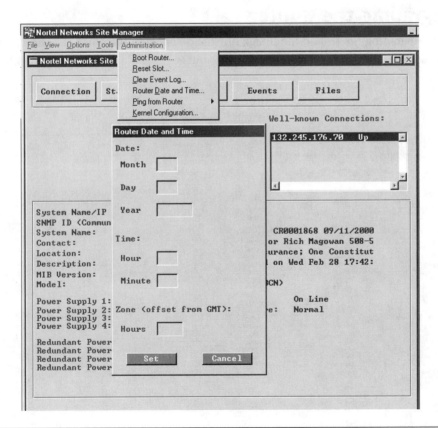

Figure 14-22 Changing the router's date, time, and GMT from Site Manager

BCC

The BCC is a Command Line Interface (CLI) that offers more configuration capability than TI. BCC is a tree-like system starting with the box content. To navigate the tree, one can enter a partial command hit enter and get into the correct context and enter the command there or enter the full command on one line (see Figure 14-23). BCC runs as a soloist.

To configure the router using BCC, the administrator enters the `config` context. Changes made with the BCC to the router configuration are dynamic and take place immediately. The changes will not be made to the saved configuration file and will not be available the next time the router is rebooted unless the `save config` command is used.

Upgrading the Router

When upgrading the router, the image file, the diagnostics information, and the boot monitor files must be updated. Updating the image file is a matter of downloading the

```
[1:N01FX1]$bcc

    Welcome to the Bay Command Console!

    * To enter configuration mode, type config

    * To list all system commands, type ?

    * To exit the BCC, type exit

bcc> ?
System Commands:
    ?                  exit                pktdump
    back               format              prom
    bccExit            getcfg              pwc
    bconfig            help                readexe
    boot               help-file-version   record
    cd                 history             reset
    check              ifconfig            restart
    clear              info                rm
    clearlog           loadmap             save
    commit             log                 securelogin
    compact            logout              show
    config             lso                 snmpserver
    cp                 mbulk               stamp
    cwc                mdump               stop
    date               mget                system
    delete             mlist               telnet
    diags              mnext               tftp
    dinfo              more                type
    dir                mset                unmount
    disable            partition           xmodem
    display            password
    enable             ping

bcc> config
Reading configuration information, please wait . . . done.
Port Config: Invalid Slot-Conn Combination for  "atm/11/1"
Port Config: Invalid Slot-Conn Combination for  "atm/13/1"
```

Figure 14-23 BCC options and help

Table 14-5 Boot Image Upgrade and Diagnostic Upgrade Files for the Various Router Products

Product	Boot Upgrade File	Diagnostic Upgrade File
AN, ANH-8, ANH-12	anboot.exe	andiag.exe
ARN	arnboot.exe	arndiag.exe
ASN	asnboot.exe	asndiag.exe
BLN, BLN-2, BCN	freboot.exe	frediag.exe

new image onto the flash and using that image for booting. Updating the diagnostic information and boot monitor files requires a boot from a new diagnostic or monitor file that actually goes out and burns the new boot information into the prom of the router. The files that contain the boot and diagnostic information for the router are different for each of the router platforms (see Table 14-5).

Command `prom -v <vol:filename>` This command is used to compare a file in the volume listed with the information in the EPROM. The administrator uses this command to compare both the boot upgrade file and the diagnostic upgrade file with the EPROM to find out if a PROM update is necessary.

NOTE Some code upgrades require new **PROM** information and some do not.

Command `prom -w <vol:filename> <slot#>` This command erases the current EPROM information for the slot listed and copies the content of the file named into the EPROM. It is used to upgrade the boot and diagnostic information if it is necessary.

NOTE Although it is possible to upgrade multiple slots at once, it is not recommended. If there is a power outage during an **EPROM** update, the **EPROM** can get corrupted or will have no information at all, and that slot's **FRE** card would have to be replaced.

PART III

Before burning a file to the EPROM, it may be a good idea to verify the integrity of the file:

Command `readexe <vol:filename>` This command is used to validate a file by examining the file header and comparing it to the checksum data in the file.

Creating the Initial IP Address for Access to the Router

To create the initial IP address on the router, the user must have local COM port TI access. Once the first address is created, the user can use Site Manager or Telnet to access the router remotely. It is a good idea to first check the IP status of the router (see Figure 14-24):

Command `show ip circuits`

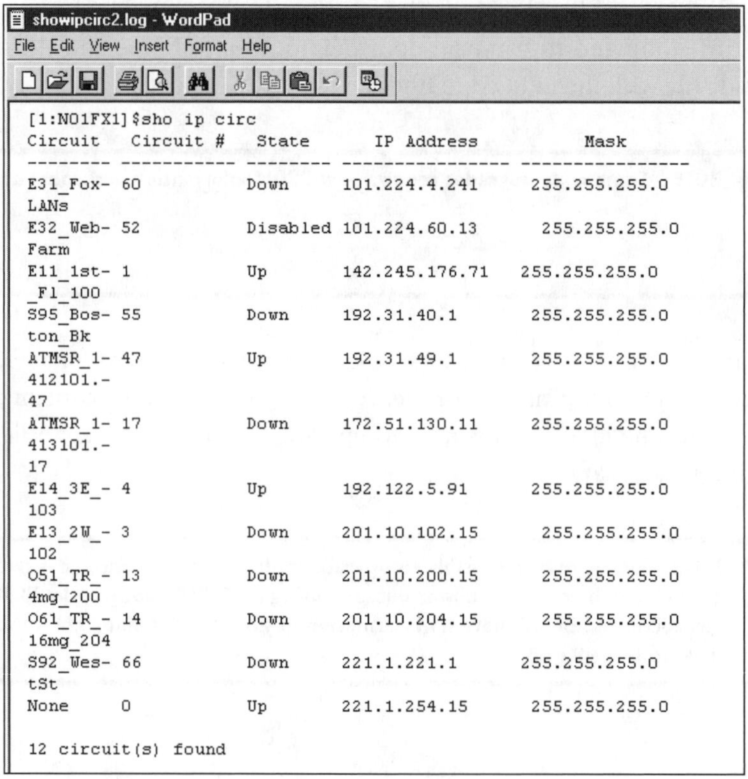

```
showipcirc2.log - WordPad
File  Edit  View  Insert  Format  Help

[1:NO1FX1]$sho ip circ
Circuit    Circuit #   State      IP Address        Mask
--------   ---------   --------   --------------    ----------------
E31_Fox-   60          Down       101.224.4.241     255.255.255.0
LANs
E32_Web-   52          Disabled   101.224.60.13     255.255.255.0
Farm
E11_1st-   1           Up         142.245.176.71    255.255.255.0
_F1_100
S95_Bos-   55          Down       192.31.40.1       255.255.255.0
ton_Bk
ATMSR_1-   47          Up         192.31.49.1       255.255.255.0
412101.-
47
ATMSR_1-   17          Down       172.51.130.11     255.255.255.0
413101.-
17
E14_3E_-   4           Up         192.122.5.91      255.255.255.0
103
E13_2W_-   3           Down       201.10.102.15     255.255.255.0
102
O51_TR_-   13          Down       201.10.200.15     255.255.255.0
4mg_200
O61_TR_-   14          Down       201.10.204.15     255.255.255.0
16mg_204
S92_Wes-   66          Down       221.1.221.1       255.255.255.0
tSt
None       0           Up         221.1.254.15      255.255.255.0

12 circuit(s) found
```

Figure 14-24 This figure shows the result of the `show ip circuits` command.

If there is no IP address configured, the administrator must configure the initial IP address. First the administrator should boot the router with ti.cfg, the default configuration, to make sure nothing is configured for the router. Next, the administrator can run a batch file called install.bat that walks him or her through a series of setup options to create an initial IP address for the router.

Command `install.bat` This command runs the installation batch file to set up an initial IP address on a router. It does so by first finding out which link modules are available, querying the administrator to choose a link module, asking for an IP address, subnet mask, routing protocol, and SNMP information. The `install.bat` also enables the administrator to change the TFTP default volume, enable Telnet and FTP, and then displays a summary of the configuration information. An administrator can also choose to save the information to a configuration file:

Command `install_arn.bat` This command runs the installation batch file to set up an initial IP address on an ARN router specifically.

NOTE The install.bat file makes all configuration changes dynamically, and no reboot of the router is necessary. If a mistake was made during the running of the file, don't just rerun install.bat—reboot the router with ti.cfg or a default configuration first.

Once an IP address is created, the `ping` command can be used to test network reachability. The IP address will be used for connectivity to Site Manager:

Command `ping <parameters>` This command is used to test network reachability of a remote device using the Internet Control Message Protocol (ICMP) utility.

Parameters of the `ping` command include `-<protocol>`, where protocol can be ipx, at, or osi. The most common type of ping is an IP ping: `<ip address>` — when using an IP ping, a destination address must be specified, `-t <timeout>` shows the number of seconds each ping times out. `-r <repeat count>` shows the number of pings to send out. `-s<size>` shows the size in bytes of the ping packets (by default 16 bytes). Like a `trace route` command, `-p <path>` shows the hops to the destination address. `-v <verbose>` shows statistical information that is useful for troubleshooting like round-trip time and success rate. `-a <address>` specifies a source address for the ping packet to use to verify connectivity from a specific router interface.

Quick Quiz 5

What does the command `ping 12.12.12.12 -p -r12 -s56` do?

Answer

Sends 12 ICMP echo requests with traceroute enabled to the address 12.12.12.12. Each ICMP packet is 56 bytes.

It is also possible to ping from Site Manager with all protocols using various parameters (see Figure 14-25):

GUI   Administration > Ping from Router > Choose protocol to ping with.

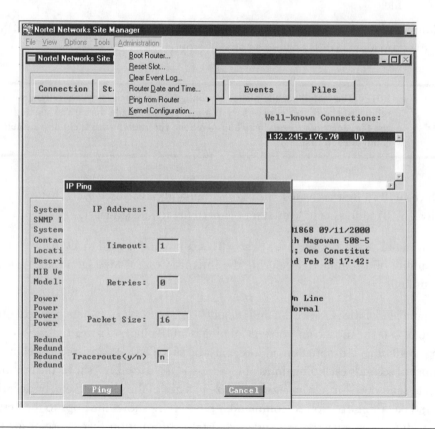

Figure 14-25   Performing an IP ping with Site Manager

Site Manager

Site Manager is a GUI application that runs on the Windows-based operating system as well as some flavors of UNIX. Site Manager was designed as a tool to configure all network routers from a single workstation (one at a time). Site Manager works with SNMP polling and the GET and SET commands, using the User Datagram Protocol (UDP) of a WinSock-compliant IP stack. To manage a router using Site Manager, the router must have an IP address that is accessible to the management station that may be local or across the network (see Figures 14-26 and 14-27).

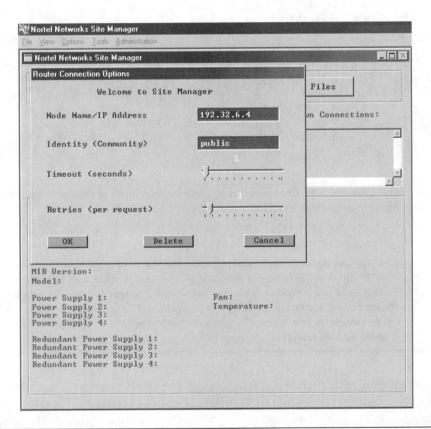

Figure 14-26 The default window for Site Manager uses a bogus Nortel-assigned IP address. The administrator must change this address to the address of the router that is being managed.

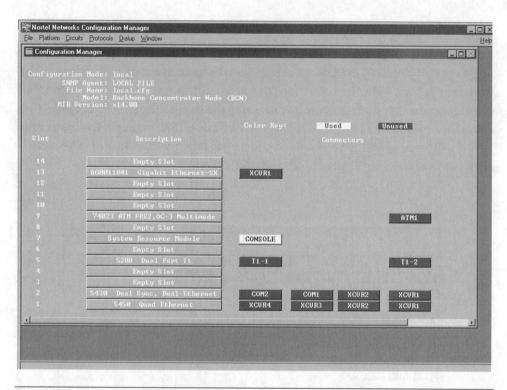

Figure 14-27 A view of a BCN router using Site Manager. Some of the slots are populated and some are not. Various link modules are being used.

 NOTE It is necessary to use a version of Site Manager that is compatible to the level of software that is on the devices. Site Manager is generally only backward compatible for about two or three versions. This is because the GET and SET commands may change in versions of software as MIBs get updated and added for new features.

When installing Site Manager, a folder called *WF* will be created. It contains three subfolders: CONFIG, MIBS, and LIB. Each of these folders will be discussed later in this chapter together with their functions in the discussion of different Site Manager tools.

Site Manager requires community strings for access because it is an SNMP-based program (see Table 14-6).

Table 14-6   Default Community Strings for SNMP Access

Access Type	Default Community Name
Read-only	Public
Layer 2	Private
Layer 3	Private
Read-write	Private
Read-write-all	Secret

Site Manager enables the configuration of routers through a tool called *Configuration Manager*. There are four modes for accessing and configuring routers:

- Local

- Remote

- Dynamic

- Cache

Local mode allows the administrator to open a file stored on the Site Manager workstation, make changes to the file, and TFTP the file back to the router. The configuration changes will only take effect after a reboot of the router with the newly configured file. Local mode also allows the administrator to create a new router configuration from scratch by creating a new empty file in the CONFIG folder in the WF directory on the Site Manager workstation. Site Manager will prompt the administrator to choose the hardware platform and link modules for the configuration to be created.

Remote mode allows the administrator to make changes to a configuration file that is stored on a remote router. The process will TFTP the remote file from the router, enable the administrator to make changes, save the file, and TFTP the file back to the remote router. Changes will take effect with the next boot of the router using the configuration file created.

Dynamic mode allows the administrator to make dynamic changes to the router that take place immediately and do not require a reboot. It is important to save the dynamic changes to a configuration file to ensure that changes will be available even once the router is rebooted. Dynamic changes cannot be made to the port that has the IP addresses that is being used for the Site Manager connection because that will cause Site Manager to fail.

Cache mode allows administrator to make dynamic changes to the router, but instead of making the changes in real time (like Dynamic mode), a copy of the configuration file is downloaded to the Site Manager workstation, and changes are made locally. This is a very good option for administrators to avoid lock up issues and configuration corruption that occurs with Dynamic mode.

NOTE Remember, Site Manager performs SETs and associated GETS using SNMP and UDP. Packets can get lost, and that will corrupt the configuration file. With UDP, there is no method for preventing that from occurring.

SNMP Security for Site Manager

For security purposes, community names and access type for SNMP can be changed in Site Manager:

GUI Protocols > IP > SNMP > Communities   This will bring up a new menu bar with only File and Community click on Community again > Add Community > Name the community and choose the level of access (read only or read/write) (see Figure 14-28).

Once a community name is enabled on the router, use can be restricted to specific IP addresses or managers. By default the address 0.0.0.0 is configured, which means all managers are accessible. To specify a specific manager that will be a member of the community, add the IP address of the Site Manager workstation (see Figure 14-29):

GUI Protocols > IP > SNMP > Communities >   Click on the community name > Community menu again > Manager menu will appear > Add Manager > Add the IP address for the manager.

SNMP management enables any workstation with the proper IP address to manage the router. It is possible for a hacker to use the proper IP address and masquerade as a manager and make unauthorized changes to the router. To prevent this, an administrator can take additional security measures by putting the router in secure mode and creating a password that must be entered for any SNMP set request to take effect:

Command wfsnmp mode <1, 3>   This command enables (3) or disables (1) SNMP secure mode. A value of three sets the wfsnmp mode to enabled and a value of one sets wfsnmp security to disabled.

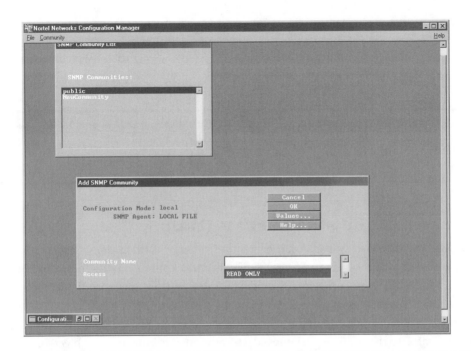

Figure 14-28   Creating a new SNMP community in Site Manager

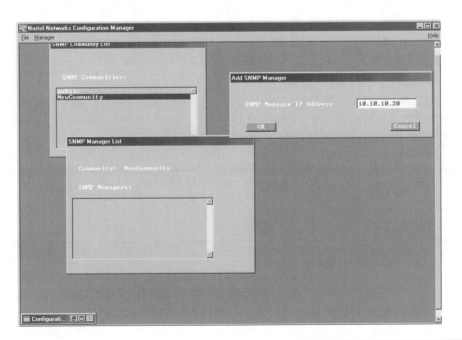

Figure 14-29   Adding a manager to the community

Once the router is in secure mode, the next step is to create a password:

Command wfsnmpkey <*password of six letters*> This command sets the password for SNMP set commands.

NOTE Secure mode does not work with the manager address of 0.0.0.0. A specific manager address must be created (refer to Figure 14-29).

Management Information Base (MIB)

The MIB is a database that sits on the agent or router. It is often drawn as a tree structure with a root and objects with leaves. The Internet community defines some of the tree as a standard, and other parts contain vendor and product specific information. The MIBs define all the manageable variables on a Nortel Networks router (and other products). When a client issues an SNMP GET request to the router, a MIB variable is queried and retrieved. The variable is typically an attribute of an object or router resource. For example, a circuit is an object, and the IP address of the circuit is an attribute of the object. All Nortel Networks MIB variables begin with a prefix of 1.3.6.1.4.1., as defined by the Internet community. Nortel MIBs that reference 7.x and above router software end in an 18.3, representing Bay Networks/Wellfleet (the name of the company before the merger of Nortel and Bay Networks as we mentioned in the beginning of this chapter). MIBs are usually referenced in ASN.1 notation using either numbers (as partially seen previously) or names. The structure of accessing a MIB is to use the object, attribute, and instance. A wildcard (*) can be used in place of either the attribute or the instance to specify all attributes or all instances of a particular object.

NOTE There are files located in the MIB folder of the WF directory on the Site Manager workstation that can be helpful in finding specific MIBs and their syntax.

MIBs are accessible through TI using the list, SET, and GET commands. The list command is used to display a description of the MIB object. The GET command is used to provide the administrator with the value of an attribute. The SET command is used to dynamically change MIB attribute values. If changes are made to a variable dynamically, the administrator must use the commit command to cause the changes to take effect:

Command `list` This command lists all the MIB objects by name and identifying number.

 NOTE If part of the MIB name is known, inputting part of the MIB name with a star can narrow down the list of MIBs to only MIBs with that string in the name.

Command `list <object>` This command lists all the attributes for a specific object.

Example `list wfIpAddrEntry` Shows all the attributes for IP addresses on the router. See Figure 14-30 for the result of this command.

Command `list instances <object>` This command lists all the instances of a specific object.

Example `list instances wfIpAddrEntry` Shows all the instances of IP addresses on the router. See Figure 14-30 with a router that has four IP addresses.

Once all the parameters are known, the administrator can perform a GET command:

Command `get <object.attribute.instance>` This command asks the router to give the value of a specific MIB object.

Example `get wfIpAddrEntry.3.172.17.185.2` This command gets the third attribute (the subnetmask) of the IP address instance 172.17.185.2 of the object IP address entry.

Example `get wfIpAddrEntry.wfIpAdEntNetMask.172.17.185.2` This command does the same thing as the previous command; it just uses the name of the attribute (wfIpAdEntNetMask) instead of the ASN.1 numerical value (3). For results of these commands, see Figure 14-30.

Example `get wfIpAddrEntry.*.172.17.185.2` This command asks the router for all attributes of the IP address object instance 172.17.185.2. For results of this command, see Figure 14-30.

Command `set <object.attribute.instance> <value>` This command is used to change a MIB's value. Only an administrator can use this command.

Command `commit` This command is used after all the SET commands to make sure that they take effect immediately.

```
$ list wfIp*
wfIpBase = 1.3.6.1.4.1.18.3.5.3.2.1.1
wfIpBaseRtEntry = 1.3.6.1.4.1.18.3.5.3.2.1.2.1
wfIpBaseHostEntry = 1.3.6.1.4.1.18.3.5.3.2.1.3.1
wfIpInterfaceEntry = 1.3.6.1.4.1.18.3.5.3.2.1.4.1
wfIpStaticRouteEntry = 1.3.6.1.4.1.18.3.5.3.2.1.5.1
wfIpAdjacentHostEntry = 1.3.6.1.4.1.18.3.5.3.2.1.6.1
wfIpTrafficFilterEntry = 1.3.6.1.4.1.18.3.5.3.2.1.7.1
wfIpForwardEntry = 1.3.6.1.4.1.18.3.5.3.2.1.16.1
wfIpNetToMediaEntry = 1.3.6.1.4.1.18.3.5.3.2.1.18.1
wfIpAccCtrlFilterEntry = 1.3.6.1.4.1.18.3.5.3.2.1.19.1
wfIpAccCtrlNetworkEntry = 1.3.6.1.4.1.18.3.5.3.2.1.20.1
wfIpAccCtrlUserHostEntry = 1.3.6.1.4.1.18.3.5.3.2.1.21.1
wfIpAddrEntry = 1.3.6.1.4.1.18.3.5.3.2.1.22.1
wfIpInternalHostEntry = 1.3.6.1.4.1.18.3.5.3.2.1.23.1
wfIpIntfCfgEntry = 1.3.6.1.4.1.18.3.5.3.2.1.24.1
wfIpIntfStatsEntry = 1.3.6.1.4.1.18.3.5.3.2.1.25.1
wfIpIntfStatsIcmpEntry = 1.3.6.1.4.1.18.3.5.3.2.1.26.1
wfIpGreTnlEntry = 1.3.6.1.4.1.18.3.5.3.2.1.27.1
wfIpGreConnEntry = 1.3.6.1.4.1.18.3.5.3.2.1.28.1
wfIpFilterRuleEntry = 1.3.6.1.4.1.18.3.5.3.2.1.29.1
wfIpFilterConfigEntry = 1.3.6.1.4.1.18.3.5.3.2.1.30.1
wfIpFilterStatsEntry = 1.3.6.1.4.1.18.3.5.3.2.1.31.1

Command aborted.

$ list wfIpAddrEntry
wfIpAdEntAddr = 1
wfIpAdEntIfIndex = 2
wfIpAdEntNetMask = 3
wfIpAdEntBcastAddr = 4
wfIpAdEntReasmMaxSize = 5

$ list instances wfIpAddrEntry
inst_ids  = 172.17.7.2
            172.17.60.1
            172.17.150.1
            172.17.185.2

$ get wfIpAddrEntry.3.172.17.185.2
wfIpAddrEntry.wfIpAdEntNetMask.172.17.185.2 = 255.255.255.0

$ get wfIpAddrEntry.wfIpAdEntNetMask.172.17.185.2
wfIpAddrEntry.wfIpAdEntNetMask.172.17.185.2 = 255.255.255.0

$ get wfIpAddrEntry.*.172.17.185.2
wfIpAddrEntry.wfIpAdEntAddr.172.17.185.2 = 172.17.185.2
wfIpAddrEntry.wfIpAdEntIfIndex.172.17.185.2 = 4
wfIpAddrEntry.wfIpAdEntNetMask.172.17.185.2 = 255.255.255.0
wfIpAddrEntry.wfIpAdEntBcastAddr.172.17.185.2 = 1
wfIpAddrEntry.wfIpAdEntReasmMaxSize.172.17.185.2 = 4622
```

Figure 14-30 This figure displays the TI MIB commands of `list` and `GET` and how they are used.

Managing Statistics with Statistics Manager

Statistics Manager is a tool that is useful for troubleshooting the router. It has many utilities that can enable the viewing of MIBs, displaying of statistic screens, building custom screens, and adding screens to a list for viewing. The Statistics Manager works with polling a router looking for specific SNMP GET requests. It then can be used to display the information stored in the variables of the GET requests. Only one router can be polled at a time as with all other Site Manager functions:

GUI   Statistics hot button, or

GUI   Tools > Statistics Manager

Quick Get

MIBs are also available through a Site Manager MIB browsing utility called *Quick Get*. This utility enables a user to see if a MIB is read only or read write, see the data type of the MIB (string, integer, and counter), and see the syntax and valid values for the MIB (see Figure 14-31). Quick Get also provides a description of each MIB but does not show the MIB in ASN.1 format:

GUI   Statistics hot button > Tools > Quick Get

Screen Builder

Screen Builder enables a user to build a customized statistic screen:

GUI   Tools > Statistics Manager > Tools > Screen Builder

To create a customized screen, a user will choose MIB variables to be included in the screen (see Figure 14-32). Each MIB variable should be given a column with the appropriate name and width. Once the MIB, column name, and width are defined, the column must be saved with the Save Column option (Saved columns have an asterisk). A user can create several columns including a Totals column (using the Total button), which will total any other columns together and give a value. Finally, the user must save the screen and name it and choose a mode for the screen. Screens created in circuit mode poll the router every five seconds for updates of the statistics and MIB values

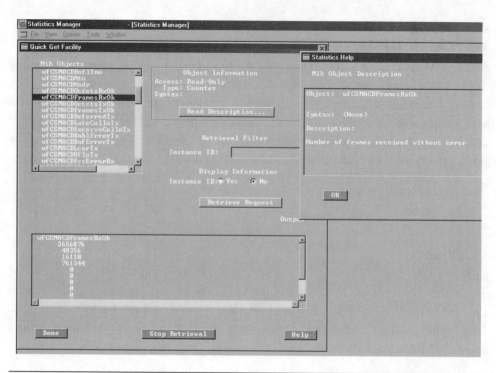

Figure 14-31 Quick Get displaying the value and description of the MIB for CSMA/CD frames received without an error

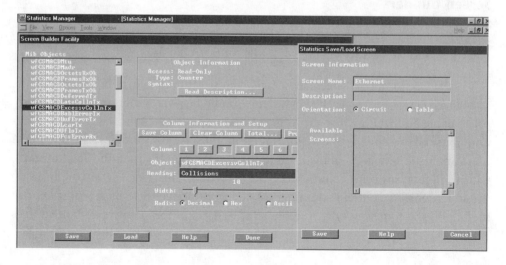

Figure 14-32 Creating a custom screen with Screen Builder

defined in the screen. Table mode polls the router initially to create the data in the screen that remains static.

Screen Manager

Site Manager comes with default screens created by Nortel Networks engineers for ease of administration and viewing statistics. These screens are saved in the WF\LIB\ WFSCRNS directory on the Site Manager workstation. Users can also create or modify default screens with Screen Builder, and those are saved in the WF\WFSCRNS folder. In order to view default screens or user created screens, the screens must be placed in the list of Current Screens in Screen Manager (see Figure 14-33):

GUI Statistics hot button > Tools > Screen Manager

Launch Facility

The Launch Facility enables the user to choose from a list of screens from the Current Screen List in Screen Manager and display or launch the screen. This starts the polling

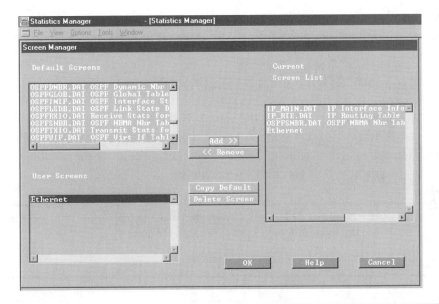

Figure 14-33 Screen Manager has three windows: one for the default screens, one for user screens, and the Current Screen List, which has screens that can be launched.

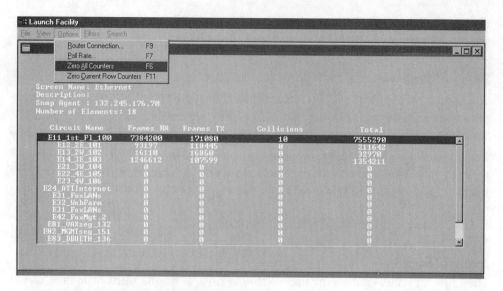

Figure 14-34 The screen Ethernet that was created with Screen Builder shows statistics for CSMA\CD transmits, receives, and collisions.

of the router for the MIB objects defined in the screen and displays the information in columns:

GUI   Statistics hot button > Tools > Launch Facility

Figure 14-34 shows an option in the Launch Facility for zeroing counters. This will enable the administrator to see the difference in the MIB variable from the time the counter was zeroed. (For example, the administrator wants to see the number of collisions for the time that he is watching the counters.)

NOTE   Zeroing the counters will not affect the information stored in the MIB. To see the actual MIB values again, relaunch the screen.

Creating Circuits Using Site Manager

Site Manager enables the creation of circuits that will be used in the network as different interfaces with different protocols. To configure circuits, simply choose the port that the circuit will be associated with. This brings up a list of available circuits with the one selected highlighted. A default name is associated with the circuit. The first part of the name is a letter that identifies which type of circuit this is:

E   Ethernet

E1   E1

F   FDDI

H   HSSI

MCTI   Multichannel TI

O   Token Ring

S   Synchronous

T1   T1

After the letter representing the circuit type, there are two or three numbers. The numbers represent the router slot and the port on the slot. On a BCN, the first number can be between 1 to 14, but on an AN, the first number is always one. An ASN has three numbers: the first representing the number of the ASN in the stack, the second representing the net module, and the third representing the port number.

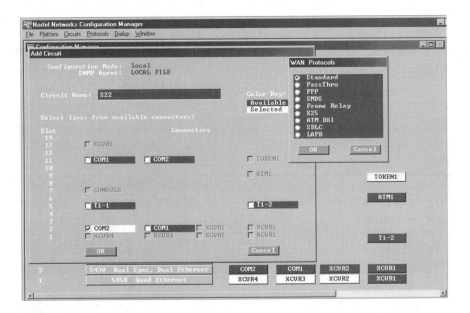

Figure 14-35   Creating a WAN circuit that uses COM2 in slot two of a BCN. The name of this circuit is S22.

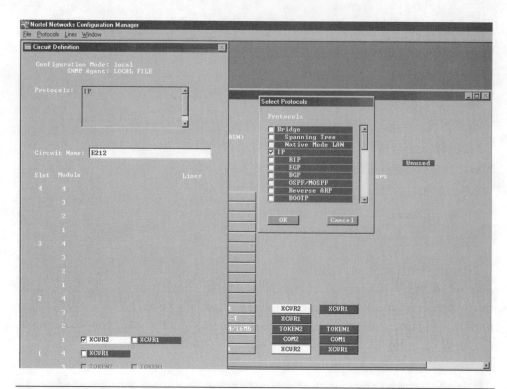

Figure 14-36 Adding protocols to an Ethernet circuit on an ASN. Notice this Ethernet port is on the second of a stack of ASNs, located in net module one, port two and is named E212.

NOTE It is a good troubleshooting tool to name circuits with the networks they are associated with (see Figure 14-35).

GUI Tools > Configuration Manager > Choose configuration file type > Choose port to configure

When creating a WAN port (like the one created in Figure 14-24), a menu with WAN protocols automatically pops up. WAN circuits also require a clocking method (internal or external) to work.

The next step to creating the circuit is to add the necessary routing and bridging protocols. If the user wants to add protocols to the circuit, he can do so later as well (see Figure 14-36):

GUI Tools > Configuration Manager > Choose file type > Click on circuit > Edit Circuit > Protocols > Add/Remove Protocols

IP Services

The primary function of IP (as we mentioned before in Chapter 4) on a host or router is to accept data from the higher-layer protocols (TCP or UDP), create a datagram, and route the datagram through the network to its destination. Secondary functions of IP include fragmenting and reassembling packets as necessary and packet lifetime control with the Time to Live (TTL) field.

 NOTE Remember that the source and destination IP addresses of a datagram will never change, but the MAC addresses on the packet will change to reflect next hop routers that forward the packet to its ultimate IP destination.

IP Addressing

We discussed IP addressing in detail in Chapter 4. It is essential to understand these concepts for the router exam and to completely understand what a router does. We are

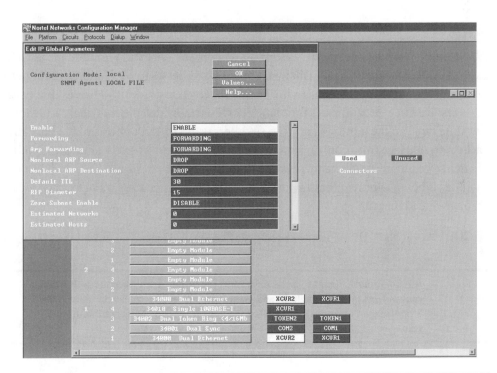

Figure 14-37 Some global IP parameters for the IP network

not going to review those concepts here again; this is just a reminder note that questions about IP addressing, subnetting, and supernetting can appear on this exam.

Some global IP parameters that were mentioned in Chapter 4 can be configured using Site Manager (see Figure 14-37):

GUI Configuration Manager > Protocols > IP > Global

The parameters that are important to pay attention to include Default TTL (how long a packet will remain in the network before it is timed out [default 30 hops]), RIP Diameter (how many routers a packet may pass through before RIP declares the destination unreachable [default 15], Zero Subnet Enabled, (whether this network will allow zero subnets or not [no zero subnets by default]), and Estimated Networks (how much contiguous space is preallocated for networks in the routing table [default of zero is 500]).

> **NOTE** The Estimated Hosts parameter is discussed next in the ARP section.

ARP

All Nortel Networks router products support ARP for the LAN and WAN circuits as well as ATM. ARP, as we discussed in Chapter 4, maps IP addresses to MAC addresses for network connectivity. The router has a host cache in which it stores IP addresses that have been resolved to MAC addresses through ARP requests. By default, this host cache does not time out, but the administrator can set intervals up to 1,200 seconds and have the cache refresh itself. This is only necessary in an environment where IP addresses will be changing frequently or where there is not enough memory in the router and too much memory is being allocated for the host cache. ARP is an interface parameter is enabled through Site Manager:

GUI Protocols > IP > Interfaces (refer to Figure 14-37).

> **NOTE** To flush the ARP cache on a router, it is necessary to bounce IP from the router. That means disable IP and then reenable it. This cannot be done from Site Manager, as once IP is disabled the router will not be accessible from Site Manager.

IP Forwarding

The router is very versatile. In a network it can act as a layer 2 bridge or perform layer 3 routing. In a scenario where the router may be acting like a layer 2 bridge, an administrator can globally disable the routing functions. By setting the IP Forwarding parameter to Not Forwarding, the router will no longer forward at layer three. There is a parameter for ARP Forwarding that should be set to Not Forwarding as well.

GUI   Protocols > IP > Interfaces (refer to Figure 14-37).

> **NOTE**   In the router when IP and ARP Forwarding are disabled, there will be no routing.

Proxy ARP

Proxy ARP, as we mentioned in Chapter 4, is used when nodes on a network are not aware of subnet masking. The router in this situation can respond to ARP requests received on one interface (network) destined for another network. The router supplies its own MAC address in the ARP reply and makes the network appear as one physical segment to hosts that are not subnet aware. Proxy ARP is an interface parameter and is enabled in the same location as ARP.

Reverse ARP (RARP)

RARP, as we mentioned in Chapter 4, is used to obtain an IP address from a MAC address. It is most often used by a diskless workstation to request an IP address from a server so that it can then receive an operating system and configuration. When enabling RARP on a router, a static MAC address to IP address table must be created. RARP is enabled on the router through Site Manager. It must be added as a protocol when creating or editing a circuit. It is available only for LAN interfaces (Ethernet, Token Ring, and FDDI). Once RARP is enabled on a circuit, a static RARP table should be created (see Figure 14-38):

GUI   Protocols > IP > Reverse ARP > Map Table   Add an entry by clicking on the Add button and specifying an IP address and a MAC address.

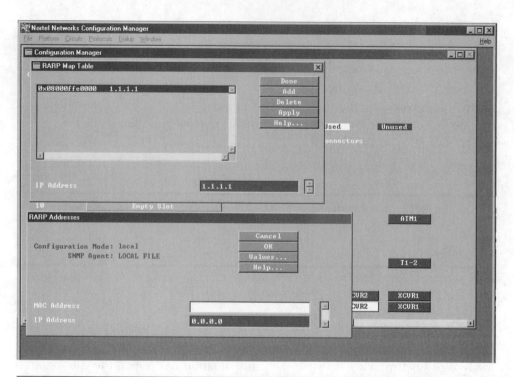

Figure 14-38   Adding a static mapping to the RARP Map Table

Dynamic Host Configuration Protocol (DHCP) and BootP Relay

DHCP and BootP, as we discussed in Chapter 4, are features that enable dynamic IP addressing. DHCP and BootP work with broadcast packets, and although routers do not normally forward broadcasts, they can be configured to forward these broadcasts to a DHCP and a BootP server. This can be especially essential in a network with routers that are using a remote boot option (EZ Install and so on) and depend on BootP to receive configuration information. If there are no local BootP servers, routers may need to forward BootP requests to remote subnets that have BootP servers configured.

To configure BootP and DHCP on the router, the BootP protocol must be added to the circuits that will forward BootP/DHCP traffic (see Figure 14-39).

   GUI   IP > BootP > Relay Agent Interface Table

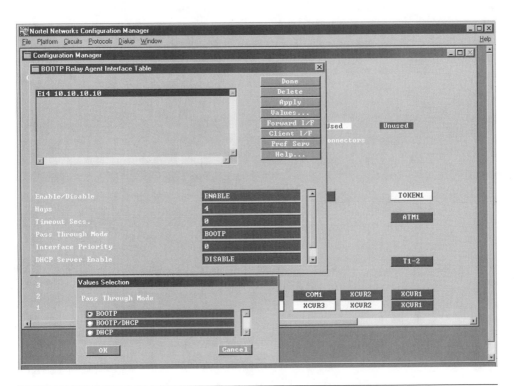

Figure 14-39 An interface in Site Manager configured with BootP can forward BootP/DHCP or both. This is configured in the pass-through mode parameter.

Once the circuit is configured with BootP, a Relay Agent Interface Table must be configured to define which circuits can receive BootP/DHCP requests and which circuit will forward out the requests. One inbound circuit can forward requests out of multiple outbound circuits or multiple inbound circuits can forward requests to only one outbound circuit if that is where the BootP/DHCP server resides (see Figure 14-40).

GUI   IP > BootP > Relay Agent Interface Table > Forward I/F

A preferred server can also be configured so that BootP/DHCP packets are forwarded as unicast packets instead of multicast packets.

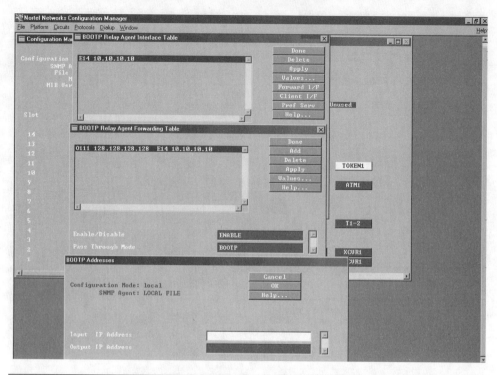

Figure 14-40   Configuring an Interface table to forward BootP/DHCP requests

Circuitless IP

Circuitless IP enables an administrator to assign an IP address to the router that is not mapped to a specific interface (see Figure 14-41). This enables one or more interfaces of the router to become disabled without the administrator losing connectivity to the router. As long as one physical interface of the router is available, the circuitless IP will be available and will use that interface.

There can only be one circuitless IP address created per router, and it must follow all the rules for creating interfaces on routers. This interface cannot be on the same network as any other interfaces in the router and certainly cannot have the same node address as any other interfaces. A circuitless IP address cannot be configured in the non-forwarding mode. The circuitless IP is considered a soloist process.

    NOTE   Because the circuitless IP address must be a unique subnet and will have no other routers on its network, it makes sense to use the 30 bit subnet mask of 255.255.255.252, which has only two nodes on that network.

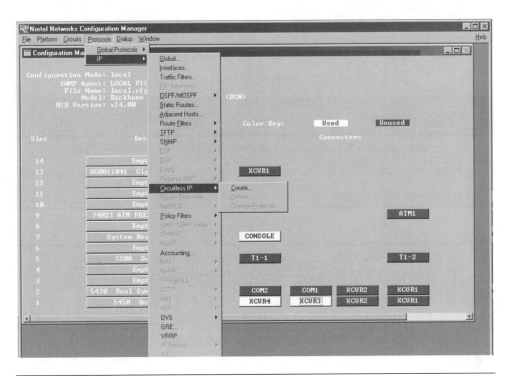

Figure 14-41 The menu to create a circuitless IP circuit

GUI From the configuration manager window > Protocols > IP > Circuitless IP > Create

To configure the circuitless IP, the administrator must input an IP address and subnet mask. An administrator may choose to optionally configure a slot mask to force the circuitless IP process to run only on specific FRE cards.

Telnet

Any PC with a network connection can run a Telnet terminal emulation program to establish a remote TI session on a router. The PC would act as a Telnet client, while the router acts as a Telnet server.

To enable Telnet on the router for remote TI connections, a TCP socket must first be created from configuration manager:

GUI Protocols > Global Protocols > TCP > Create TCP

Next, the Telnet server services should be enabled for inbound Telnet access from a client to the router:

GUI   Protocols > Global Protocols > Telnet Server > Create Telnet Server

The router can also be set up as a Telnet client that enables outbound Telnet access from the router to another router or Telnet server.

GUI   Protocols > Global Protocols > Telnet Client > Create Telnet Client

NOTE   Once a Telnet session is established, all TI commands are available.

NOTE   Unlike TI, Telnet sessions will timeout if there is no activity. This is because it is based on TCP and is connection oriented.

TFTP

TFTP (as we mentioned in Chapter 4) provides a simple file transfer service that depends on UDP. The router will be able to, by default, act as a TFTP server or client and can respond to get and put commands to retrieve or save files to the router. The remote host must have similar TFTP capabilities:

Command tftp <get, put> <remote ip address> <filename> <filename>   A TFTP get from the router transfers a remote file from the IP address mentioned in the command with the filename mentioned and places it on the router with the new filename specified. (Leaving the second filename off would just give the file the same name on the router as it had on the remote host.) A TFTP put from the router will put a file whose name is specified in the command onto a remote host whose IP address is specified:

Example tftp put 10.10.10.10 3:log1.log   This command specifies taking the file log1.log from the third volume of the router and sends it to a remote host at IP address 10.10.10.10.

Quick Quiz 6

What will the name of the file be on the remote host in the previous example?

Answer

log1.log because no other filename is specified.

Site Manager can be used to change other TFTP parameters like default TFTP volume, retry timeouts, close timeouts, and retransmits.

FTP

As we mentioned in Chapter 4, FTP is another method for transferring files to and from a remote IP host. FTP differs from TFTP, however, because it uses the TCP connection-oriented protocol, establishes a control connection as well as a data connection before transferring data, and enables a client to examine directory listings and delete files on the server. A Nortel Networks router can support FTP server functionality, but cannot initiate an FTP session. To set up FTP on a router, a TCP socket must first be created (like with Telnet):

GUI   Protocols > Global Protocols > TCP > Create TCP

Once the TCP socket is opened, the FTP server can be set up:

GUI   Protocols > Global Protocols > FTP > Create FTP

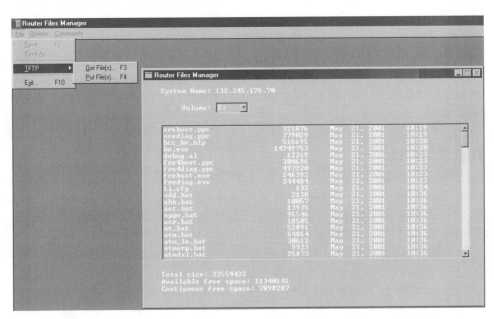

Figure 14-42   Router File Manager TFTP commands menu and the contents of volume two of a router

Site Manager can be used to change other FTP parameters like default volume, login retries, idle timeout, and max sessions.

Router Files Manager

Router Files Manager is a graphical tool in Site Manager that enables the management of the flash card and files as well as TFTP functionality (see Figure 14-42). It is possible to look at a directory of all the volumes, compact the flash card, delete files, and format the flash. It is also possible to see the used, free and contiguous memory of a flash card:

GUI   Tools > Router Files Manager > Commands

It is additionally possible to perform TFTP get and put commands from this utility:

GUI   Tools > Router Files Manager > Files > TFTP

NOTE   Performing TFTP get and put commands are from the perspective of the Site Manager workstations. So a put command will place a file from the workstation onto the router, and a get command will do the reverse.

Layer 3 Routing

The Nortel Networks routers support all types of routing protocols, including RIP, OSPF, BGP, and static routes. Only static routes, RIP, and default routes are mentioned here because they are exam objectives, while OSPF and BGP were covered in Chapter 7.

Static Routes

Static routes are useful in a network to reach destination networks that may not be using routing protocols and therefore are not being advertised. Creating a static route enables packets to be forwarded to that network from a known network on the router (see Figure 14-43).

To configure a static route in Site Manager, it is important to note the route information of IP address and subnet mask as well as the next-hop address (which *must* be an interface configured on the router):

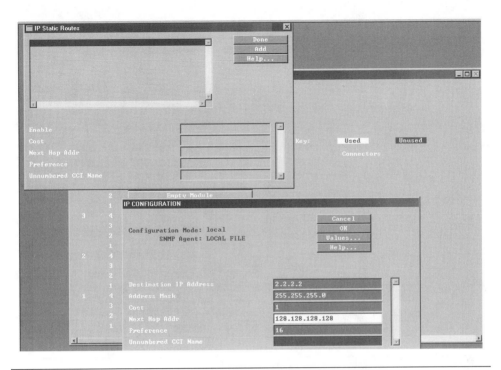

Figure 14-43 Adding a static route to the network

GUI Tools > Configuration Manager > Choose file type > Protocols > IP > Static Routes > Add

RIPv1 and RIPv2

RIP, as we mentioned extensively in Chapter 6, is a routing protocol that enables dynamic propagation of routes via UDP. RIP can be configured via Site Manager on all interfaces that will be participating in RIP routing updates (see Figure 14-44):

GUI Configuration Manager > IP > RIP Interfaces

There are many important parameters with RIP, as shown in Figure 14-44. RIP Enable, RIP Supply, and RIP Listen are all separate parameters that can be enabled or disabled, depending on the network and interface needs. Additionally, Default Route Supply and Listen are separate from RIP Supply and Listen so an interface may just be listening for default routes and not be participating in RIP updates. The parameter Poison Reverse can be set for Poisoned, Split, and Actual (as shown in Figure 14-44).

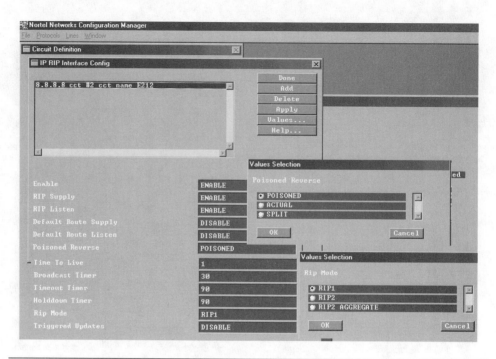

Figure 14-44 IP RIP interface parameters

Poisoned causes networks in advertisements to be sent out with a value 16 (unreachable) from the interface the network was received on. Split is Split Horizon, which does not readvertise networks out the interface on which it was received. Actual does not change the RIP default, which is to advertise networks even out the interface received with the value received plus one. Actual can cause routing loops to occur. The TTL is set to one by default, but can be changed to two for networks that have other vendor routers that may discard packets with the Time To Live field set to one. The RIP Broadcast, Timeout, and Holddown Timers decide how often routers broadcast RIP updates, how long a route will remain active in the route table if not renewed in an announcement, and how long an inactive route is advertised as unavailable. The parameter RIP mode is very important (and it is shown in Figure 14-44); depending on the type of RIP used in the network, it will be RIPv1, RIPv2, or RIPv2 aggregate, which acts as RIPv1 and aggregates certain networks back to their default mask. The Triggered Update parameter, if enabled, causes RIP to send out an update anytime the network changes, even if the RIP Broadcast Timer has not expired.

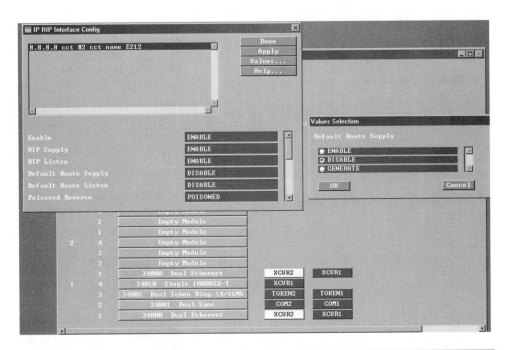

Figure 14-45 The parameters for the Default Route Supply are Enable, Disable, and Generate.

Default Routes

Default routes are created to give a router an interface out which to forward all unknown networks. This is very useful in scenarios where there is an Internet connection via a default gateway router, and not all Internet routes are known to all routers in the network. Default routes are advertised as 0.0.0.0 and are forwarded to the router that generated or supplied the default route. Default route parameters are modified with the RIP interface configuration parameters (see Figure 14-45):

GUI   Configuration Manager > IP > RIP Interfaces > Default Route Supply

A router that is the Internet router will generate the default route. Any router that has the capability to forward routes to the Internet router can supply a default route by enabling this parameter. Notice that Default Route Supply and Default Route Listen are separate parameters, so a router that is not supplying a default route may still listen for one.

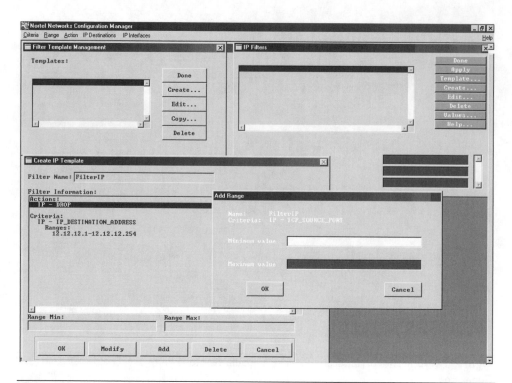

Figure 14-46   Creating a filter template

IP Traffic Filters

Traffic filters enable a router to examine a packet and based on configured parameters log, drop, or relay the packet. Inbound filters apply to packets coming into circuits while outbound filters apply to packets leaving the circuit and are implemented through protocol priority and traffic shaping.

Creating a filter is done by creating a filter rule that uses a created filter template that is applied to a circuit. Each filter is associated with a specific protocol and router circuit, and up to 127 filters per circuit and supported protocol are possible. The order that the filter is added to the circuit is very important because it determines the precedence for the filter and the order in which the filter will apply. The filter with the highest precedence will be compared to information in the packets and will act first.

A traffic filter is created through a filter template, using Site Manager and clicking a circuit (see Figure 14-46).

GUI   Tools > Configuration Manager > Click a circuit > Edit Circuit > Protocol > Edit IP > Traffic Filters > Template > Create

This template is reusable and predefined for specific traffic but is not associated with a circuit. Templates are stored on the Site Manager workstation in the file called template.flt. Templates have three components:

- Criteria
- Ranges
- Action

Criteria are the parts of the frame header that will be examined on every frame. These fields are protocol specific because the information will be different for each protocol. One example of filter criteria is an IP source address. Criteria can also be user-defined created by specifying the exact number of bits from the header start or header end of the frame and number of the bits to examine. Figure 14-46 shows a template filter with two criteria. The criteria IP destination address has been defined, and the administrator is adding a criterion for TCP source port.

NOTE Creating a user-defined filter requires a high degree of packet knowledge as the administrator must know the offset in the packet for the bits that need to be compared to a value and acted upon.

Ranges are numeric minimum and maximum values for the criteria. In the example of an IP source address, the range could be 10.10.10.1 to 10.10.10.10, encompassing ten workstations. Ranges must also be specified for user-defined criteria. In Figure 14-46, the criterion IP destination address has a range of 12.12.12.1 to 12.12.12.12.254, encompassing all the workstations in the 12.12.12.0 network.

Action defines what should happen to frames that match the criteria and range. Actions can include accepting the frame, dropping the frame, and logging an event to the event log as well as some other protocol-specific actions. An administrator can log accepted or dropped frames. Figure 14-46 shows the action of drop has been chosen for all packets that match the criteria.

Once the template filter is created, it can be used to create a template rule (see Figure 14-47):

GUI Tools > Configuration Manager > Click a circuit >Edit Circuit > Protocol > Edit IP > Traffic Filters > Create

The template rule will be given a name a precedence and be associated with a circuit. Finally, the IP traffic filter will be created (see Figure 14-48).

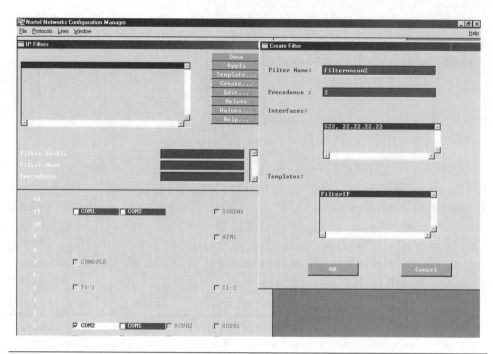

Figure 14-47 Creating a filter rule to be applied to a circuit to create a filter

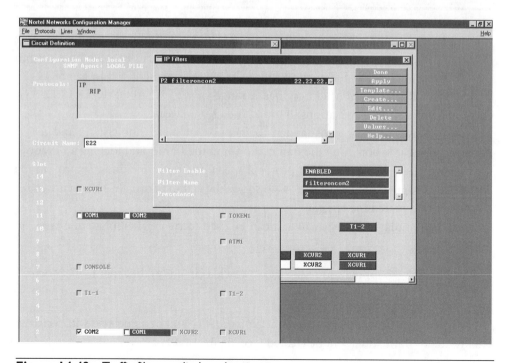

Figure 14-48 Traffic filter applied to the circuit

NOTE Changing the IP traffic filter template *does not* change the filter. The filter must be removed from the circuit; the template rule must be re-created and then reapplied to the circuit.

Router Management and Troubleshooting

Once a router is configured in the network, it must be managed and maintained. If there are issues with the router, troubleshooting utilities will need to be used to determine the cause of the problems and their solutions.

Router Management

The Site Manager software comes with tools that give an administrator some aid in managing and troubleshooting the routers in the network. These utilities are useful, and every administrator should become familiar with how they can be of help in different situations.

Image Builder

Image Builder is a utility in Site Manager used to customize (add or remove protocols) the system image file (an.exe, bn.exe, and so on). Each router comes with an image file that contains the operating system kernel, IP modules, bridging, PPP, and some other files. Additional components like OSPF, ATM, BGP, and Novell IPX routing are part of the Corporate Suite package. The Image Builder is useful for adding protocols to the existing boot image or possibly removing protocols to create a smaller image for saving room on the flash card. Image Builder also shows how large the image file is in compressed and uncompressed forms (see Figure 14-49). To use the Image Builder utility, the image software should be located on the Site Manager workstation:

    GUI   Tools > Image Builder

Launching Image Builder from Site Manager creates a BUILDER.DIR directory with a subdirectory for the software release that has a subdirectory for the router model of the software image that was opened. All of the files that make up the software image are copied into this newly created directory. The administrator can then make changes to the image file, save the new image to the hard drive, and use TFTP to send the image to the router flash card to be used the next time the router boots.

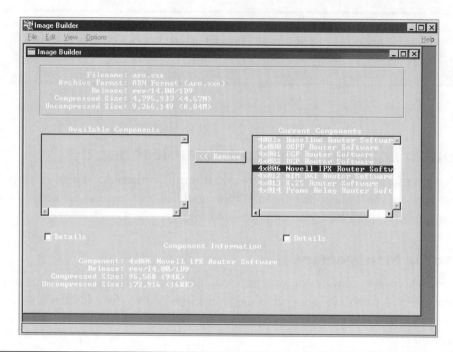

Figure 14-49   Image Builder is used to remove or add protocols to a software image file.

Report Generator

Report Generator is a very critical utility used for viewing and verifying a configuration file. Configuration files are stored in binary forms and cannot be viewed; however, Report Generator is a Site Manager utility that converts the configuration file into an ASCII format to be viewed. Additionally, Report Generator helps in comparing configuration files and to enable an administrator to have a hard copy of all router settings (see Figure 14-50):

GUI   Tools > Report Generator

Figure 14-50 shows some of the levels of detail available when generating a text file from a configuration file. The utility can show all the MIBs that have defaults but were not changed specifically, the MIB names for all the attributes of the router, and raw hexadecimal configuration data. The generated report can also contain warnings for unrecognized attributes and a warning for any MIB variable that does not have a default value and was not specified in the configuration either.

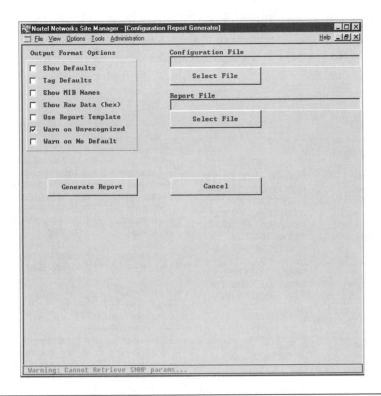

Figure 14-50   Report Generator enables the creation of a text file from any router configuration file.

   CAUTION   None of the additional options mentioned are a requirement for the generated report and can actually make the output very difficult to read.

Router Troubleshooting

At times, it may be useful to find out which applications are loaded on each slot as well as the address location and the size of the applications loaded. This can be especially useful in situations where a router crashes in trying to troubleshoot which application may have caused the crash.

Command `loadmap` This command displays all of the load addresses and sizes for all applications on all slots onto the screen. A slot number can be specified if an administrator only wants to view one slot worth of information. Specifying a filename dumps the information to a file on the flash card (see Figure 14-51).

```
$ loadmap
----------------------
Loadmap from SLOT 3:
----------------------
   --> http.exe            0x3037d3f0  0265312
   --> arp.exe             0x303dced0  0100824
   --> ftp.exe             0x30408ea0  0046112
   --> tcp.exe             0x30453500  0076632
   --> tftp.exe            0x303f58c0  0020936
   --> snmp.exe            0x30466070  0041352
   --> tn.exe              0x30470210  0044324
   --> ip.exe              0x3047af50  0456224
   --> hdlc.exe            0x303bf980  0083948
   --> ilacc.exe           0x303d4180  0036156
   --> dsde2.exe           0x303be060  0006416
----------------------
Loadmap from SLOT 5:
----------------------
   --> http.exe            0x30375e00  0265312
   --> arp.exe             0x303b6a70  0100824
   --> ftp.exe             0x303e97f0  0046112

   --> tcp.exe             0x303cf460  0076632
   --> tftp.exe            0x30421a50  0020936
   --> snmp.exe            0x30413350  0041352
   --> tn.exe              0x30476080  0044324
   --> ip.exe              0x30480dc0  0456224
   --> tms380.exe          0x303f4c20  0124696
   --> dtok.exe            0x3041d4f0  0005860
----------------------
Loadmap from SLOT 4:
----------------------
   --> http.exe            0x3039a710  0265312
   --> arp.exe             0x3042a550  0100824
   --> ftp.exe             0x30442f40  0046112
   --> tcp.exe             0x3044e370  0076632
   --> tftp.exe            0x30460ee0  0020936
   --> snmp.exe            0x304660c0  0041352
   --> tn.exe              0x30470260  0044324
   --> ip.exe              0x3047cfb0  0456224
```

```
----------------------
Loadmap from SLOT 2:
----------------------
   --> http.exe            0x3036a060  0265312
   --> arp.exe             0x303aacd0  0100824
   --> ftp.exe             0x303c88a0  0046112
   --> tcp.exe             0x303fc000  0076632
   --> tftp.exe            0x303c36c0  0020936
   --> snmp.exe            0x3040eb70  0041352
   --> tn.exe              0x30422df0  0044324
   --> ip.exe              0x304764b0  0456224
   --> fsi.exe             0x303d9d80  0139888
   --> fddi.exe            0x3041fa40  0005000

$ loadmap 2
----------------------
Loadmap from SLOT 2:
----------------------
   --> http.exe            0x3036a060  0265312
   --> arp.exe             0x303aacd0  0100824
   --> ftp.exe             0x303c88a0  0046112
   --> tcp.exe             0x303fc000  0076632
   --> tftp.exe            0x303c36c0  0020936
   --> snmp.exe            0x3040eb70  0041352
   --> tn.exe              0x30422df0  0044324
   --> ip.exe              0x304764b0  0456224
   --> fsi.exe             0x303d9d80  0139888
   --> fddi.exe            0x3041fa40  0005000
```

Figure 14-51 The results of a `loadmap` command and a `loadmap 2` command

Events Manager

Events Manager is one of the utilities included in Site Manager, and it is used to view router log files. There are four options when reviewing log files:

- Get Current Log File
- Get Remote Log File
- Load Local Log File
- Save Output to Disk

Getting a current log file option polls the router and displays the log file that was active in the router at the time of the command. In order to display the log file, Site Manager transfers the entire file to the local Site Manager drive in a file called wellflt.log. Once the file is transferred locally and displayed, a user can sort the log file by ascending or descending order (to see the newest events first) and also filter the log.

NOTE   In TI all filtering of the log is done while the events are being downloaded from the active log file. In Events Manager, the filtering is done after the log file is retrieved from the router.

Getting a remote log file displays an event log that was saved previously on a flash card using the TI save log command.

Loading a local log file retrieves a saved log from the Site Manager workstation. This option is available even if the user is not connected to an active router. This file must be a log file that was saved with the TI save log command in binary format.

Saving output to disk actually saves the log file in an ASCII format to be displayed at another time. The system will ask for a path and filename when saving the log file.

NOTE   ASCII log files cannot be reopened with Events Manager, but can be displayed with a text editor (see Figure 14-52).

GUI   Tools > Events Manager

Figure 14-52   Viewing a log file with Events Manager

Each log event has an event number, a date and time the event occurred, the severity of the event (fault, warning, info, debug, and trace), the slot the event occurred on, the entity that generated the event, a code assigned to the event, and text describing the event. Logs can be filtered in the Events Manager by severity, slot, and entity (see Figure 14-53).

 NOTE   When a log file is saved with the Save Output to Disk option, it is saved with the filters active in Events Manager at the time of the save.

The system can also generate custom events when a threshold for a particular variable defined by a user is reached. The router can monitor itself for a user-defined condition, and when that condition occurs, it will create an event in the event log. Any MIB variable that has an integer variable can be monitored for specific levels. The level can be an absolute value or a percentage that is reached during a specific polling interval. The condition is reported to the event log each time the threshold is reached continu-

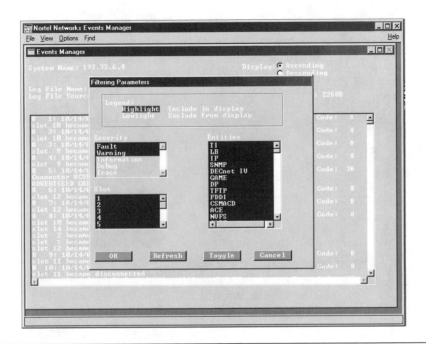

Figure 14-53 Events Manager filter options

ously, or throttled, and only reported as many times as the user defines. Thresholds are defined in Site Manager (see Figure 14-54):

GUI Global Protocols > Thresholds > Choosing values enables the administrator to see every MIB and choose the appropriate one for the configuration needed.

It is possible to see from this figure that thresholds can be defined as info, warning, or debug log events.

Trap Monitor

Trap Monitor is a tool that comes with Site Manager that is used to display traps that have been sent from routers to the SNMP client (manager).

SNMP generic traps are sent automatically from an agent to the management station if one is configured. There are seven generic traps: coldStart, warmStart, linkUp, linkDown, authenticationFailure, egpNeighborless, and enterpriseSpecific. The first six traps are self-explanatory, but the enterpriseSpecific trap will differ for each company. Nortel Networks uses the enterpriseSpecific trap to allow any event in the event log to be sent as a trap.

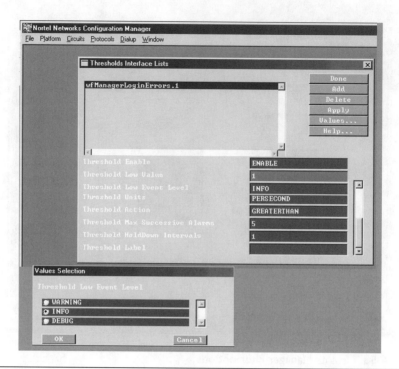

Figure 14-54   Defining a threshold for manager login errors

Routers can send SNMP standard traps or events from the log file based on severity, slot, or entity. Trap messages are sent via UDP port 162 (all other SNMP messages are sent UDP port 161) but go to only one network management station at once. Routers are configured to send a trap to a specific management station based on SNMP community names. Traps are always sent to IP addresses that are configured as managers of a community. To configure a router to send traps, the administrator will need to add managers to the default community or more preferably create a community for trap receivers. Managers are added to a community by adding the IP address of the Site Manager station that will be receiving the traps (refer to Figures 14-28 and 14-29).Finally, it is necessary to specify which level of traps the router should send to the defined manager (see Figure 14-55). The manager can receive no traps (none), the six SNMP generic traps (Generic), Enterprise Specific traps (Specific), or both Generic and Specific traps (All).

GUI   Protocols > IP > SNMP > Communities > Click the community name > Community menu again > Manager menu will appear > Add Manager > Add the IP address for the manager

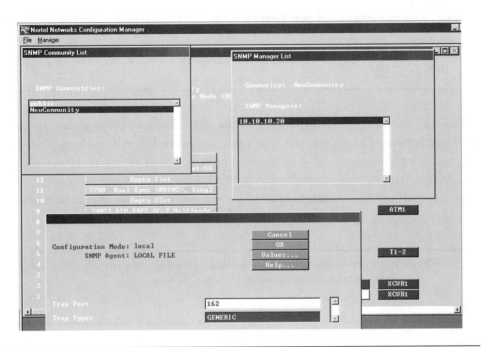

Figure 14-55 Using Site Manager to specify the port a manager will receive traps on as well as the trap types the manager will receive

To cause Enterprise Specific traps (from the event log) to be sent as a trap message, it is necessary to configure traps on a per interface level:

GUI Protocols > IP > SNMP > Trap Configuration > Interfaces

Traps can be sent based on slot, entity, and severity levels. Exceptions can be created so that specific entity codes will not be sent as a trap.

After the router has been configured to send traps they can be viewed in Trap Monitor. The router must be online and using the community name specified for the trap receiver. The Trap Monitor dynamically displays all incoming trap messages:

GUI Click Traps

Under the File menu in Trap Monitor an administrator can choose to load a history file that will show all the new traps created since the last time the history file was cleared. Additionally, the administrator can clear the history file or save the trap messages to an ASCII file.

> **NOTE** Saved ASCII files cannot be loaded back into Trap Monitor.

The Filter menu in Trap Monitor enables the filtering of an incoming trap. The messages can be filtered by severity (fault, warning, and so on) or by IP address of sending trap agent. An address of 0.0.0.0 in the IP addresses displays all trap messages from all routers that send messages. An IP address of 255.255.255.255 refuses trap messages from all agents on the network. Specific IP addresses of agents that should be displayed must appear before the 255.255.255.255 address, or they will be ignored.

> **NOTE** Filtering does not change which trap messages the agent sends; it only displays the traps the administrator chooses to view.

Layer 2 Bridging

Nortel Networks routers can act as bridges in a LAN environment. We discussed bridges extensively in Chapter 3, and we are now going to look at the specific bridging capability of the routers and how to configure them in Site Manager.

Transparent Bridge Parameters

A Nortel Networks router can function as a transparent bridge to separate and connect LANs into collision domains. To enable bridging on a router, first add the necessary bridging protocols to the interfaces that will be performing bridging functions. Then make sure to enable bridging globally and change the parameters as necessary for the interfaces as well (see Figure 14-56):

    GUI   Protocols > Bridge > Global

There are two additional important parameters in Figure 14-56 to examine when enabling transparent bridging: Bridge Table Size and Enable Forwarding DB.

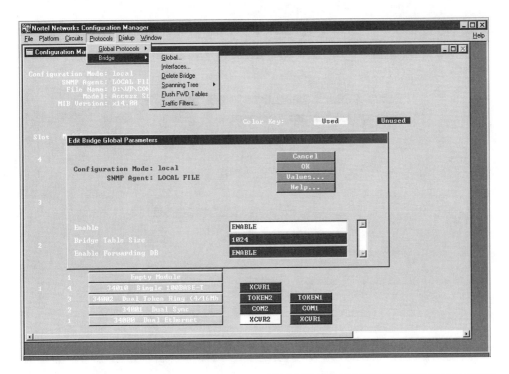

Figure 14-56   Globally enabling bridging for the router. This bridge menu will not appear if none of the circuits have been configured with bridging protocols.

Bridge Table Size specifies the number of MAC addresses that will fit in the forwarding table. The options are between 1024 to 131072. If only 1024 entries are allowed into the forwarding table, but there are more hosts on the network, some hosts will never be learned by the bridge, and packets destined for these hosts will always be flooded. On the other hand, making the forwarding table too large wastes memory.

Enable Forwarding DB is an important parameter for troubleshooting. When this feature is enabled, a copy of the forwarding table is created (a mirror image of the MAC addresses and associated ports), which enables the administrator to view the forwarding table in Statistics Manager.

To enable interfaces to perform Transparent Bridging, change the parameters for the interface in Site Manager (see Figure 14-57):

GUI   Bridge > Interfaces

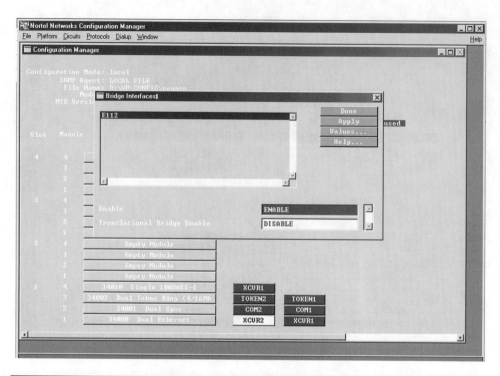

Figure 14-57   Interface parameters for Transparent Bridging

Figure 14-57 shows an additional interface parameter for transparent bridging called *Translational Bridge Enable*. This parameter specifies whether or not this interface will translate source route Token Ring packets (with a RIF field) into ethernet transparent packets.

Spanning Tree Parameters

As we mentioned before, it is not wise to have transparent bridging in a network without Spanning Tree because loops can occur that will bring down the network.

To enable Spanning Tree, it must be configured as a protocol on at least one circuit in the network. In Site Manager, it is important to change the global parameters for Spanning Tree and then the interface parameters as necessary (see Figure 14-58):

GUI   Bridge > Spanning Tree > Global

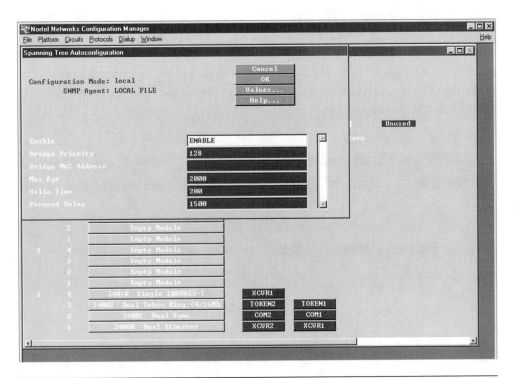

Figure 14-58 The global parameters for Spanning Tree

Among the parameters in Figure 14-58, it is important to remember Bridge Priority will be the most critical factor in determining the Root Bridge. The lower the value, the more likely this bridge will be chosen as root. Notice also that an administrator can change the MAC address of the bridge, which may also be a factor in determining the Root Bridge. The Max Age, Hello Time, and Forward Delay parameters should be the same for all bridges in the Spanning Tree group, but if they do not match, then the Root Bridge's parameter will be the one in effect.

Interface parameters can also be configured for Spanning Tree (see Figure 14-59).

GUI   Bridge > Spanning Tree > Interfaces

Figure 14-59 shows the important interface parameters for Spanning Tree: Priority and Path Cost. Priority will determine whether or not a port becomes the root or designated port. (Lowest priority wins.) Path cost influences how this bridge will determine its Root Bridge and forward traffic. Path cost should be inversely proportional to the speed of the link. The higher the link speed, the lower the path cost so that data will more likely use faster-speed links.

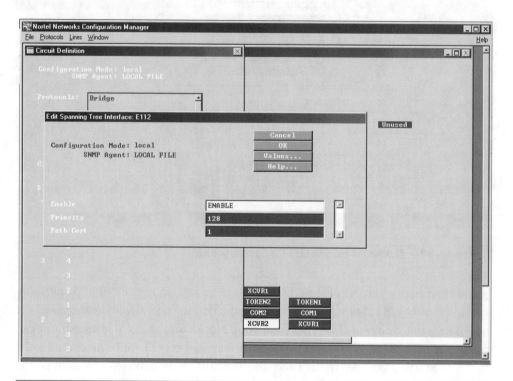

Figure 14-59   Interface parameters for Spanning Tree

Source Route Bridge Parameters

A Nortel Networks router that has Token Ring interfaces can perform source route bridging. To enable source router bridging globally for the router, the protocol must first be added to a Token Ring Interface (see Figure 14-60):

GUI   Protocols > Source Routing > Global

There are two important parameters that must be configured for source route bridging to work. Each source route bridge must have a unique Internal LAN ID (which is used to extend the bridge ring number limitation to seven) and a Source Route Bridge ID (which can be the same for all bridges in the Token Ring environment).

PART III

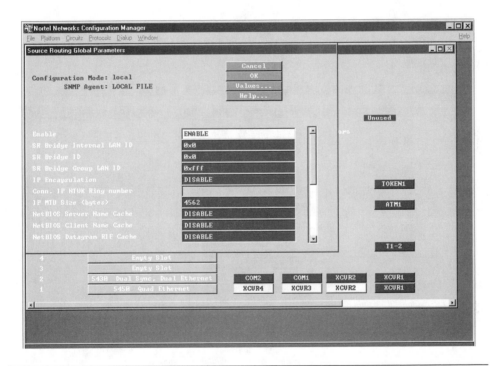

Figure 14-60   Source Route Bridge global parameters

It is necessary to change interface parameters for the interfaces that will be running source route bridging (see Figure 14-61):

GUI   Source Routing > Interfaces

It is important to make sure that the interface has the correct Source Route Ring number. Interfaces can also be configured to provide end station support to Ethernet workstations in a Token Ring environment. As discussed in Chapter 3, source route bridges do not maintain routing tables—that is the task of the end station. Ethernet end stations that cannot send RIF broadcast packets to find paths to destination servers require Token Ring bridges to do this for them. This feature can be configured on an interface in Site Manager (see Figure 14-62):

GUI   Protocols > Source Routing > Interfaces > Click the interface and scroll down to find the Token Ring End Station parameter and set it to enable.

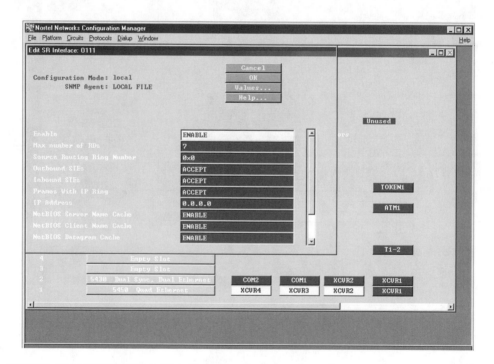

Figure 14-61   Source Route Bridge interface parameters

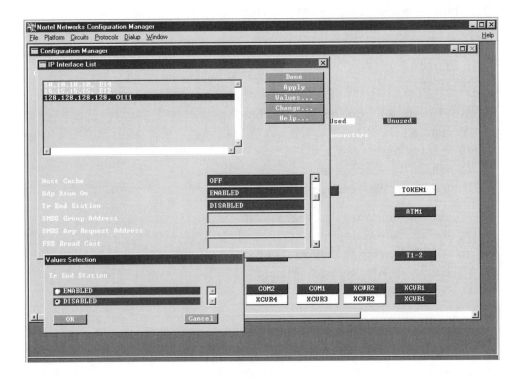

Figure 14-62 Token Ring end station support

Summary

This chapter covered the Nortel Networks Router products. We examined the AN, ASN, ARN, and BN routers in detail including their functions, commands to perform various tasks with the routers, and their roles in a network. In this chapter we also covered the configuration of the routers using the TI. We discussed extensively the different utilities available with Site Manager. We also discussed the layer 2 and layer 3 capabilities of the router and learned how to set up the routers to act in various network scenarios.

Questions

1. Which of the following is a WAN protocol?
   A. PPP
   B. HSSI
   C. Ethernet
   D. Token Ring

2. Which of the following is a LAN interface?
   A. PPP
   B. ATM
   C. FDDI
   D. HSSI

3. Which of the following describes the BLN?
   A. It has a hub.
   B. It is a backbone device.
   C. It has a fixed configuration.
   D. It supports WAN connections only.

4. Which of the following describes an AN?
   A. It is a backbone device.
   B. It has a fixed configuration.
   C. It supports WAN connections only.
   D. None of the above.

5. Which router is stackable in design?
   A. AN
   B. AFN
   C. ANH
   D. ARN
   E. ASN
   F. BLN
   G. BCN

6. Which router is a router and a repeater combined?
   A. AN
   B. AFM
   C. ANH
   D. ARN
   E. ASN
   F. BCN
   G. BLN

7. Which router uses the SRM-L and the SRM-F?

   A. ANH

   B. ASN

   C. Backbone Node devices

   D. Fixed configuration routers

8. Which component is required in the router and provides the TI?

   A. ILI

   B. PPX

   C. SRM-F

   D. SRM-L

9. Which is the role of the link module?

   A. Arbitrates the bus

   B. Provides the connection to TI

   C. Runs the main CPU processes

   D. Provides the network connections

10. The SPEX-HS provides what total bandwidth of processor interconnects between the ASN units?

    A. 100 Mbps

    B. 160 Mbps

    C. 256 Mbps

    D. 512 Mbps

    E. 1 Gbps

11. Which protocol is used to retrieve the location of an ASN configuration file?

    A. FTP

    B. RARP

    C. TFTP

    D. BootP

    E. Telnet

12. Which protocol is used to retrieve an ASN configuration file?

    A. FTP

    B. RARP

    C. TFTP

    D. BootP

    E. Telnet

13. Which protocol provides for the dynamic assignment of client IP addresses?
    A. UDP
    B. ARP
    C. DHCP
    D. RARP
    E. Telnet

14. Which protocol provides TI access through an IP network?
    A. UDP
    B. FTP
    C. RARP
    D. DHCP
    E. BootP
    F. Telnet

15. What is the purpose of RARP?
    A. It's used to obtain an IP address.
    B. It's used to obtain a MAC address.
    C. It's used to obtain a DLCI number.
    D. It's used to obtain an AppleTalk address.

16. Where is the connection for the TI console access on the BCN?
    A. SRM-L
    B. SRM-F
    C. Rear panel
    D. Front panel

17. Where is the connection for the TI console access on the AN?
    A. SRM-L
    B. SRM-F
    C. Rear panel
    D. Front panel

18. Where is the connection for the TI console access on the ANH-8?
    A. SRM-L
    B. SRM-F
    C. Rear panel
    D. Front panel

19. Which is a secondary function of the IP protocol on a router?

    A. Packet lifetime control

    B. Advertising known networks

    C. Routing diagrams through the network

    D. Discovering the MAC address associated with an IP address

20. Which Site Manager tools enables the creation of a text file that contains the router's configuration?

    A. Image Builder

    B. Screen Builder

    C. Report Generator

    D. Configuration Manager

21. Which Site Manager tool enables the addition of ipx.exe to bn.exe?

    A. Image Builder

    B. Screen Builder

    C. Report Generator

    D. Configuration Manager

22. Which two are part of the Baseline router software? Choose two.

    A. IP

    B. IPX

    C. OSPF

    D. ATM routing software

    E. Operating system kernel

23. The Events Manager gives the user the ability to view _____.

    A. Global memory

    B. Events that have been tracked

    C. Routing table updates with a polling option

    D. A file that was saved to the flash using the TI `save log` command

24. Events in the Event Manager can be filtered by which three options?

    A. Slot

    B. Date

    C. Time

    D. Entity

    E. Severity

    F. Router model

25. In which format is the log file saved if a user uses the Save Output to Disk option in Events Manager?
    A. EBCDIC
    B. PostScript
    C. ASCII text
    D. Raw binary form

26. In which format is the log file saved when a user does the TI command `save log`?
    A. EBCDIC
    B. PostScript
    C. ASCII text
    D. Raw binary form

Answers

1. A.

2. C.

3. B. BLNs are Backbone Node Devices.

4. B. ANs are fixed configuration devices.

5. E. ASNs are stackable.

6. C. ANH is an AN router and a repeater.

7. C. SRM-L and SRM-F are found in the Backbone Node Devices (BLN and BCN).

8. D. SRM-L has the console port that enables TI access.

9. D. Link modules provide the network connections.

10. C. SPEX-HS provides a 256MB interconnect.

11. D. BootP provides the *location* of the ASN configuration file.

12. C. TFTP is used to retrieve the ASN configuration file once the location is known.

13. C. DHCP provides for dynamic assignment of IP addresses.

14. F. Telnet enables TI over the networks.

15. A. RARP is used mostly by diskless workstations to get an IP address.

16. **A.** TI connection for the BCN is provided by the SRM-L.

17. **D.** The TI console on the AN is on the front panel.

18. **C.** The ANH-8 is the only one of the AN products with the TI console in the rear.

19. **A.** Packet lifetime control through TTL is a secondary function of IP.

20. **C.** Report Generator creates a text-based configuration file.

21. **A.** To change the image file bn.exe, use the Image Builder tool.

22. **A and E.** IP and OS kernel are part of the Baseline software.

23. **D.** Events Manager can be used to view a file saved using the TI `save` command.

24. **A, D, and E.** Logs can be filtered by slot, entity, and severity level.

25. **C.** The Save Output to Disk saves the log file to an ASCII file.

26. **D.** The `save log` command in TI saves the log file as a binary log file.

## CHAPTER 15

Network Management

One of the most difficult tasks in the world (in my humble opinion) is the management of Enterprise networks. When the profession of network management was in its infancy (10 or more years ago) it was impossible to manage an entire Enterprise network from a single location. Today it merely seems impossible. With an understanding of how Simple Network Management Protocol (SNMP) and Remote Monitoring (RMON) work, we will be able to understand how network management suites like Optivity work to make the lives of overburdened network administrators around the world a little simpler. Over the years there have been a number of different network management packages from Nortel Networks and many versions. We will examine briefly Optivity Enterprise 8.X and Optivity NMS 9.X here.

Exam Objectives

On the exam you may be tested on the following topics:

- Differentiate essential network management elements.
- Summarize the OSI Network Management areas.
- Categorize the OSI model for networking.
- Differentiate SNMP manager/agent components.
- Identify the Optivity Enterprise suite of applications.

- Identify the hardware and software requirements for the Optivity Enterprise suite of applications.

- Summarize Nortel Networks agent features.

- Identify Nortel Networks NNM and probe hardware.

- Describe the network topology processes for Nortel Networks devices.

- Describe the steps necessary for network discovery.

- Summarize Enterprise Command Center documentation functions.

- Summarize Routerman documentation features.

- Summarize NetAtlas documentation features.

- Summarize NodalView's documentation features.

- Summarize Expanded View documentation features.

- Summarize agent manager documentation features.

- Define the measurement points of baselining a network.

- Summarize performance statistics.

- Summarize Optivity Performance Tools.

- Configure Optivity Performance Tools.

- Summarize the four levels in which Optivity Tools collect performance statistics.

- Describe configuration switching.

- Describe LANarchitect modes.

- Demonstrate the ability to use the LANarchitect application to balance traffic across System 5000 hub segments.

- Manage redundant links.

- Summarize the usage of the three NETarchitect applications.

- Distinguish the File Manager device file system components.

- Categorize the steps to retrieve device configurations.

- Summarize the Revision Control database (RCD) stored configuration files.

- Describe device configurations.

- Describe components of the Optivity Fault Management system.

- Categorize the levels of Fault Management Tools.

- Utilize fault management tools at the Enterprise, Network, Data Link, and Physical levels.

- Summarize Optivity processes.

- Summarize Optivity application command line equivalents.

- Summarize Optivity configuration file.

Simple Network Management Protocol

Before we can begin to discuss the various applications and tools available to manage a network, we should first examine the mechanisms that enable the applications to function. In order to have a better understanding of network management applications we have to understand the protocols that they use. Simple Network Management Protocol (SNMP) is the protocol used by Optivity and most other network management suites to help us manage our Enterprise networks.

What It Does

SNMP is part of the TCP/IP protocol. So in order for a device to be managed through SNMP, it must be reachable via IP. SNMP uses User Datagram Protocol (UDP) as a transport protocol because it is connectionless; so it has low overhead, but it is also unreliable. Many users with experience using network management applications are familiar with the fact that sometimes requesting data once is not enough to get the desired response. This is largely due to the use of UDP as the transport. Most important to remember is that SNMP only supports three types of operations. They are

- GET

- SET

- TRAP

The GET operation is used to request a piece of stored information and to reply to that request. The SET operation is used to change a piece of stored information. The TRAP operation is used to send an alert when a defined event has occurred.

All of the preceding is interesting information, but what good does it do us? Who is doing the requesting, and what is doing the responding? For this to be clear we need to realize that the SNMP model is a client/server application, and that the network administrator (or at least his workstation) is the client (not the server that his ego would have him believe).

SNMP works because an intelligent component on a network device maintains a database of information about the network device. This is called the agent in SNMP terminology. The agent is the server component of our client/server model, and it responds to requests from the client. The agent stores information in the database and makes updates to that information regularly. Some of the information may be viewed and changed (read/write), some only viewed (read only). The information can be as trivial as the name of the room that the network device is stored in or as vital as the state of a specific port on a router (up or down). Both of the previously mentioned pieces of information would be good to know (from the network administrator's point of view) and can be retrieved by the network administrator by using the proper client to issue a GET REQUEST to the agent for the desired information. The agent (in a perfect world) will respond to the GET REQUEST with a GET RESPONSE that includes the desired information.

NOTE When referring to network devices here, we typically mean routers, switches, bridges, and hubs. It should be noted that some people refer to Novell file servers as network devices, and they are also correct. From an SNMP perspective, any computer can be a network device if it has a processor and the correct software (see the following "Secret Agent" section). Routers, switches, bridges, and even hubs are also computers (highly specialized) that run software and can process instructions. Part of the software that these devices process can be the SNMP agent that stores the information and responds to commands.

The client in this configuration is our SNMP management program. For our purposes, we will assume that the SNMP management program will be Optivity, even though there are others. We will use Optivity for two reasons, firstly because it is specifically designed to enable the network manager to get the most management out of his Nortel Networks equipment and secondly because it is the Optivity exam that we are preparing for in this chapter. The management program runs on a workstation, which we will refer to as the Network Management Station (NMS) because it hosts our management client. Many people call the NMS a server because it provides a service for the network administrator. From one point of view this is correct, but from a strictly SNMP perspective (and on the exam), the server is the network device running the SNMP agent. The NMS merely retrieves the data collected by the agent. The agent is really doing the work on behalf of the NMS (the client).

Secret Agent

The agent of an SNMP manageable device is a computer. A computer is a combination of a processor and software (also RAM, I/O, and so on). For the purposes of an SNMP agent, the computer is a highly specialized and dedicated one. At first glance it does not even look much like a computer. On devices like system 3000 and 5000 hub products, the management agent resides on the Network Management Module (NMM), which is a modular (and in some cases optional) component. It is added to the chassis to provide management capabilities to the hub. The module has a processor, and it has flash storage (SIMMs) to hold the software component. It can communicate either in-band or out-of-band (or both). In the switch line the agent can be either modular or integrated (depending on the model switch). In the router product line management is integrated into the system. For the purposes of traffic and RMON analysis, the agent may reside on an external RMON probe.

The software component contains all of the manageable information about the device. When new capabilities are added, the software typically needs to be updated. When the device is booted, the software is loaded into RAM, and the configuration is applied. The agent keeps track of events and changes to the device's state (health) and configuration by noting these items in the database now in RAM. This database is referred to as the Management Information Base (MIB). The MIB is a tree-like structure, which is capable of storing all aspects of a system's operational state and configuration. The MIB can be queried in order to obtain information. When the NMS sends an SNMP GET REQUEST, the MIB is being queried for information. The request specifies which object and instance are required from the MIB. The agent looks the information up in the MIB and responds.

NOTE The Object of my Instance: Some evening when you are having trouble sleeping, try reading about ASN.1 notation. It specifies a syntax, or naming convention, that is used for storing information in the tree structure. We will not go into detail here, but I do want to discuss objects and instances. Every aspect about the network device is an object. For example, on a BayRS router, sync ports and all things associated with sync ports (to a certain degree) are objects referred to as *wfSyncEntry*. The state of a port (up, down, or disabled) is an object wfSyncEntry.3 where 3 is the third object under the group wfSyncEntry. We have now defined the object, but not the instance. In other words, which port will we now examine? The syntax states that the instance follows the object. So if we wanted to look at port 1 in slot 3, the syntax for the instance would be .3.1. All together the object and instance are expressed as wfSyncEntry.3.3.1.

Get Ready

The NMS (the client) uses the GET REQUEST (UDP port 161) to retrieve information from the agent. The agent responds to the GET REQUEST with a GET RESPONSE. In this manner a NMS can retrieve specific information at any time at the administrator's request, or polling can be initiated during which the NMS periodically makes the same GET REQUESTS in order to continually update the status of a given piece of information. This is typically how a device's health (operational status) is determined. At every user-defined interval (30 seconds, 5 minutes, 24 hours, and so on), a GET REQUEST is sent to the agent by the NMS. The response can determine the health of the device. This can be used by the NMS to determine what color to display next to the device in a map or list. In this manner, at a glance (without any other user intervention), the NMS can give a quick status update on the health of our network.

NOTE In many networks, the NMS is a dedicated workstation with lots of resources (RAM, hard drive space, fast processor, and so on) at which no other work is performed. When located in a perfect universe, the NMS is also secured in a room with limited access and requires you to log in to use it.

Get SET

Getting information that is stored in the database (the agent) is very important, but we can also alter that information. On a switch port, for example, a read/write variable in the database refers to the operational mode of the port (enabled or disabled). The administrator can use the NMS to issue a SET REQUEST (UDP port 161) to change the status of the mode from enabled to disabled or vice-versa. Because SNMP runs over IP, we do not need to have direct physical access to the console port of the switch to make this change. SNMP is an application unto itself, so we do not have to invoke a separate Telnet session to make this change.

Trapped at Last

There is also the potential for the agent to send (actually initiate the transmission of) data to the management station. This is called a *trap*. Traps are sent (UDP port 162) when predefined conditions (such as loss of link) are met. The purpose of the trap is to alert the network manager to the presence of a condition that was defined as interesting either by being a standard trap (there are seven) or by being user defined. The seven standard (RFC 1215) traps are

- Link Up

- Link Down

- Cold Start

- Warm Start

- Authentication Failure

- EGP Neighbor Loss

- Enterprise Specific

All of the first six traps are self explanatory and obvious as to their meaning. The seventh, Enterprise Specific, enables for the creation and inclusion of proprietary trap types specific to a hardware or software platform.

The purpose of the traps is to help monitor unusual network conditions. It is important that we emphasize the word *unusual*. We should hope that the events that occur normally are the ones that we want to occur. If traps are sent for events that occur normally, the network would be inundated with traps; the processors of our network devices would be spending most of their cycles processing management traffic rather than business-related traffic. The unusual events are the ones that we need to look out for. Router links going down are unusual and probably undesirable (unless as part of a planned maintenance window). The same goes for warm/cold starts. It is these events that TRAPS were designed to bring to our attention.

The agents have a list of trap receivers. The network administrator, when configuring the device, creates this list on the agent. The trap receiver is usually the NMS and/or another station running some management application. Traps are sent only to stations in the trap receiver list. It is not unusual to run more than one SNMP management platform. The station receiving the traps displays them for the network administrator to see.

NOTE Obviously, there are events that occur normally that are not necessarily helpful. Collisions and ring purges are absolutely normal and detrimental to our throughput. However, if we sent a trap for every collision or ring purge, then we wouldn't get any work done. We need to strike a happy medium between what we do need to be alerted to, and what we can look for if and when we are interested in knowing.

Confidentially Speaking

Something to ask yourself at this point might be how does the protocol protect against outside intrusions? Each agent will only accept requests from a device that is in its community. A community (or community string) is defined on the agent and assigned a name and an access level, such as a name of Private and an access level of Read/Write. A NMS wanting to manage this device will need to know the correct community, Private, to use in order to manage this device through SNMP. All requests coming to the device are checked for correct community strings, and requests without the correct community strings are dropped and logged.

 NOTE Community strings are case sensitive. Also, manageable devices are sent from the factory with default community strings. These defaults provide a false sense of security because the default settings are well known. Many common defaults are public, private, security, secret, and null or blank.

There is something to note at this point. SNMP version I does not use any form of encryption. Community strings are transmitted in clear text. This means that any device capable of sniffing data from the network will be able to uncover the community strings with very little hard work. To compensate for this, some devices enable you to define management stations to accept SNMP requests from. In addition to having the correct strings, the stations must have the correct IP address or the agent will drop the packets. This is some additional protection.

The OSI Model

5 Layers? Don't be confused. The OSI has more than one model. The OSI model for network management has five concentric circles (See Figure 15-1). The circles represent the five different management areas. They are

- Fault
- Security
- Performance
- Accounting
- Configuration

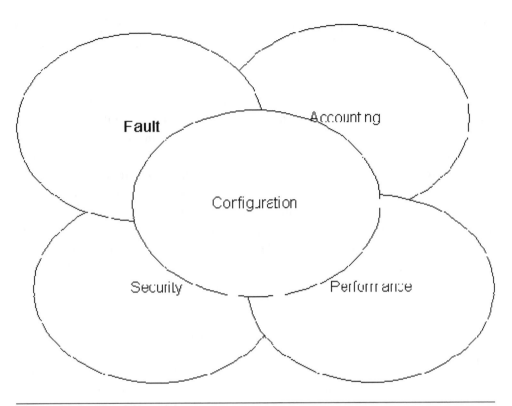

Figure 15-1   The OSI model

 NOTE This model is an important theory of how to manage a network, any
network. The smallest and the largest networks all need, to some extent, the
ideas that we are about to discuss. Some of them are beyond the realm of any
software package, and some of them are not a part of Optivity specifically.
These ideas are necessary to know in order to have an understanding of how network
management is to be implemented and how a NMS may be of use.

Your Fault

Fault management deals with the identification of a fault domain and the isolation of
specific problems. It includes the sending of traps that alert of fault conditions, and it
includes the procedures and methods to resolve problems and return the network to a
prefault condition. Fault management is often referred to as *fire fighting*. Putting out the
network fires is only a part of fault management. An all-encompassing fault management

strategy includes the mechanisms that alert the administrator of the fault condition (hopefully before the user picks up the telephone to complain), the methodology used to pinpoint the location of the fault (one that may include the use of the NMS), and the strategy for resolving the issue.

Remember that resolving the issue does not necessarily mean restoring the original environment as it was prior to the fault (although that is what we would do in a perfect world). It is always desirable to restore the network to the normal condition, but that is not always possible. In cases where hardware fails and replacements are not readily available, the network may have to be re-engineered on the spot with the equipment on hand (that is a business decision). In more extreme cases, for instance when a catastrophe removes an entire business location, much more drastic measures are necessary. This requires the use of an integrated disaster recovery plan. The plan is a list of what to do in the event of . . . (don't manage a network without one). All of this falls under the heading of fault management.

Maximum Security

In today's world it is more important than ever to have a complete network security plan in place. Viruses are being discovered at an astounding rate, and the damage that they inflict costs huge amounts in lost work, overtime, lost data, and more. Data can be altered, copied, and stolen. We need to remember that in a business scenario, data is money. The methods that are used to compromise network security are too numerous to be told here in a single chapter (and this chapter isn't even devoted to the topic), and even good books on network security don't cover all the bases. We will mention a few of the basics here and move on.

Physical Security

It all starts at the physical level. Keep your network resources (file servers, workstations, hubs, switches, and so on) in a secure environment. Even company employees have no business being near most of the network assets with the exception of his or her own workstation and a couple of printers. Keep it all locked up. Servers and routers should be kept in a highly secure data center with severely limited access. Video monitoring and security guards are absolutely necessary. No one goes in without an absolute need, and all vendors and consultants should be escorted at all times. All assets should be marked (tags that cannot be removed) and inventoried regularly. Laptops are stolen all the time, and stolen laptops are treasure troves for anyone trying to breach your security procedures. Have a strict policy on what data may be stored on laptops and what to do in the event that one is stolen.

Data Security

There are many levels of data security. There is data security at the operating system level, which dictates who has access to what local and remote files. There is data security at the backup level, which dictates who has access to the backup tapes and accounts. There is data security at the network monitoring level and many more. Strict policies need to be implemented and published about what is allowed and what is not.

 NOTE It is very important to remember that it is absolutely necessary to consider the ramifications of what can be done on a network, and decisions must be made as to what is permitted and what is not. These decisions will not be of much use if the employees are not made fully aware of them. Without published documents about data security procedures, how can we possibly expect the employees to know what jeopardizes network security and what does not? Employees are not, for the most part, technical. Even though the readers of this paragraph may have an excellent grasp of the possible pitfalls, you need to remember that the customer that you support is a lawyer, banker, doctor, intern, salesman, and so on, who does not know (until you tell them) about data security.

Password Security

What is the most import policy regarding passwords? Many people will say that it is choosing a password that is made up of letters and symbols/numbers, no repetitive letters, at least one capital letter, no dictionary words, change it every month, use different passwords for different systems, don't tape passwords to the monitor, and so on.

All of these are good. All of these are also useless if you tell some joker on the phone, pretending to be from tech support and trying to help you with a problem, your username and password. The process is called *social engineering*, and it goes something like this: The hacker (that is what he is) calls the switchboard claiming to be an important customer and asks to be connected to some random (or specific person). The call is transferred, and the call now appears to be from an internal source (and therefore less suspicious). When the user picks up the phone, the hacker now switches gears and says that he is from tech support and is calling about the trouble reported last week (who remembers what trouble was reported last week) and claims to have fixed the problem, but needs the users' username and password to test the system. The users, grateful that tech support fixed the problem without bothering them with questions like what did you do to break it, readily tells the techie/hacker what he wants to know, effectively handing over the whole cookie jar.

Educate your users about proper password security procedures; don't just yell at them. Make the policy part of that published document that I mentioned in the section on data security.

Performance

Analyze and optimize network response. Performance monitoring deals with how many seconds (or parts thereof) a user has to look at his/her screen waiting for something to happen after they click their mouse. That is what it comes down to. You can count bits/second and dropped packets till you are blue in the face and prove to the user that only .00000001 percent of the available bandwidth is being used, but when they (users) have to wait, your phone will start to ring. (They will complain about how much time they waited for you to pick the phone up as well.) Making sure that your data is flowing as well as can be will be a gauge for you as a network administrator to see where the problems are occurring, and for this you will need a baseline.

Baseline

A baseline is a sample of the status of the network on a given segment over a period of time during normal and heavy work periods. It will include statistics for

- Packets/second
- Bytes/second
- Average packet size
- Errors/second
- Dropped packets
- Retransmissions/second
- Top N talkers (if available)
- Anything else useful in your environment

There can be a separate baseline for specific devices like

- Routers
- Servers
- Switches
- Terminal servers
- VPN servers

These numbers will provide you with an example of how the network runs when it is healthy (or at least normal) so that you can determine if anything has changed when the user calls to complain. If you are really good, you will notice performance issues before the users do.

You need to remember that baselines need to be updated. The time to update the baseline is whenever something changes. Depending on the network environment, protocols in use, network operating system, applications in use, and so on, just adding (or removing) one workstation/protocol/application to the mix is enough to take a fully functioning network and turn it into a high-tech (and very expensive) bottleneck. You need to know what the baseline was like just before the changes were made and how they look just after the change. Try and predict the effect that the changes will have on the baseline before implementing them.

Accounting

Just like it sounds, accounting is how to assign costs to the use of network resources for the purposes of billing. The administrator determines the cost of printing one sheet on a printer and keeps track of how many sheets you print per month so that your department can be billed accordingly. How much does 1 Gigabyte of information stored on a server's hard drive cost? How much do 100 Megabytes of bandwidth cost? There are systems that can keep track of who uses and owes what after the administrator assigns costs. The costs are recorded and reports are generated.

> **NOTE** I realize that many of you are not interested in this aspect of network management, but let's focus on the word management for a minute. Your position is a managerial one. You are responsible for, among other things, a budget. You need to cost justify upgrades, and you need to be able to bill a department when its needs force you to purchase and upgrade equipment.

Configuration

Configuration management overlaps all the other circles because they are all dependent on proper system configuration. How is configuration done? How are remote devices configured? Who is allowed to configure devices? What tools and protocols are used? How are configuration changes tracked? What is the approval procedure to follow prior to making changes to the device's configuration? When are network changes made? These are just a few of the questions that need to be addressed when devising a configuration management strategy for an enterprise network.

The slightest change in the configuration of a network device can have extreme effects (either positive or negative), so it should be the end of a long process that involves impact studies and the generation of a recovery plan if the change negatively impacts the network. Everyone wants to get their hands on a router or a switch and add an interface or a routing protocol (because, let's face it, it's fun), but there can be extreme consequences if done blindly.

Optivity Enterprise 8.X

Optivity Enterprise 8.X is a Unix-only version of the network management software suite. It contains many applications and tools necessary in order to maintain an enterprise network.

Supported Platforms

For Optivity Enterprise 8.X, the supported platforms and requirements for the NMS are as follows:

Hardware:	RS/6000 and Power PC
	700 Seriers
	800 Series
	SUN SparcStation 10 or 20
	ULTRA SPARCStations
OS:	AIX 4.1, 4.2
	HP-UX 10.0, 10.10, 10.2
	Solaris 2.5, 2.5.1, 2.6
Network Management Platform:	Netview 4.1, 5.0
	Network Node Manager 4.1, 4.1.1, 5.0, 5.0.1
	Domain Manager 2.3
Window Environment:	AIX Motiff
	CDE
	OpenWindows

> **NOTE** A quick word about network management platforms. The Optivity Enterprise suite of applications (prior to 9.X) does not include a management platform. The management platform is the application that binds the UDP ports (161, 162) and actually makes the SNMP GET REQUESTS and the SET REQUESTS. The Optivity applications ride on top of the management platform and make use of its facilities.

You will require a minimum of 98 MB RAM (128 recommended). Hard drive space will vary, depending on the platform and which components are installed, but if all components are installed, then at least 1 Gigabyte of hard drive space will be needed.

Agent Features

There are three levels of management features (typically) available for Nortel Networks devices. The three agent types are

- Standard
- Advanced
- Advanced Analyzer

Standard

The standard agent includes support for

- Expanded view
- Configuration for all ports in chassis
- Port-level fault and performance stats
- MAU and repeater MIBs
- SNMP over IP/IPX

Advanced

The advanced agent includes support for all of the same features as the standard agent as well as support for

- System-level management
- Autotopology

- Port-level thresholds
- Allowed nodes security
- Port-to-MAC address associations
- Global Show and Find nodes
- VLAN configuration of a specific chassis
- Out-of-band management
- Partial RMON I stats

Advanced Analyzer

The advanced analyzer agent includes support for all of the same features as the advanced agent as well as support for

- Network protocol type distribution
- Port-level fault and performance analyzer correlation
- Packet capture
- Port-to-network address association
- Full RMON II

Topology Process

In order for any graphic representation (dynamically generated) of the network to be possible, there needs to be a process by which devices discover their proximity to other devices. This is the topology process. Network devices (which support the autotopology feature) generate hello packets and exchange them. These hello packets describe the device, and the other devices learn about the connectivity to the device by examining these packets. There are two types of hello packets: Flatnet Hellos and Subnet Hellos.

Flatnet Hello

The Flatnet Hello packets follow the boundaries of a collision domain. They will pass through a hub, but they will not pass a switch, bridge, or router. This means that any device that receives a Flatnet Hello is on the same Flatnet (collision domain) as the sending device.

Subnet Hello

The Subnet Hello packets follow the boundaries of a broadcast domain. They will pass through a hub, bridge, and a switch. They will not pass through a router. This means that any device that receives a Subnet Hello is on the same Subnet as the sending device but not necessarily on the same Flatnet as the device. That will be determined if and when a Flatnet Hello is received.

NOTE In some cases you may need to alter the filtering tables of older bridges or switches for the autotopology process to work. A bridge or switch should be configured to discard packets from the address 0x010081000101 (Flatnet Hello) and forward packets from the address 0x010081000100 (Subnet Hello).

Discovering the Network

In order to populate the Optivity database with devices, we need to either discover them or add them manually. The steps necessary to discover devices depend on the platform (Domain Manager, Network Node Manager, or Netview), but the process is similar. The platform is given the address of a seed device (usually a router). The seed device is a device that can provide (via the ARP cache) the addresses of devices that should be added to the network database. Included in these addresses are the addresses of other routers whose ARP caches can be read to enable the discovery process to discover every device on the network. Limits can be placed on how many and which subnets are discovered.

The Enterprise Command Center

The Enterprise Command Center's (ECC) function is to be a place to organize network devices and a starting point from which to launch other applications. The ECC divides the network up into campuses and regions and displays them in the Domain window. All devices are subdivided in their campus or region by their device type (switch, hub, bridge, router, and so on) in the resource window. Specific devices in these subfolders are then displayed as contents in the contents window. From the ECC you can:

- Obtain a view of your enterprise network.
- Launch an Optivity application or view to perform configuration, performance, fault, and security management tasks.

- Launch Optivity RMON tools.

- Navigate through your network to a particular object.

- Find a specific device.

- Create, delete, and modify devices and domains.

NOTE   There is no facility in Optivity to perform accounting management.

NOTE   If you are familiar with any of the versions of Optivity Campus, you are familiar with the Campus Command Center (CCC). The CCC and the ECC are similar in their function if not in their appearance.

Baselining

We baseline a network in order to understand the current average operating performance of the network. It is important to note that the baseline process is an ongoing one. The baseline of the network changes with every user, protocol, application, server, or workstation added, removed, or just moved. By comparing current data to the baseline, we can determine the impact of changes made to the efficiency of the network. We can also determine if unexpected changes have occurred. For all this to be of any use, the baseline stats must be current and meaningful.

Baseline samples need to be taken at meaningful points on the network as well. Do not expect a baseline of the LAN segment that connects the conference rooms together to be indicative of the overall health of the network. Backbones and highly utilized segments (server farms and data centers) are prime baseline points. Switches are good points to monitor from because they typically are used to segment a network into separate collision domains (and even broadcast domains) and are capable of delivering both per port and Backplane statistics. (In the case of layer 3 switches, they can even provide layer 3 stats as well.) Routers make excellent points to monitor from as they can give a breakdown of the layer 3 traffic. Hubs show us the performance of a specific shared media area of the network. There are also layers of statistics to gather. Layer 3 statistics will show us the relative health of the internetwork and requires a probe at each location to be monitored. Layer 2 statistics will show us the health of individual segments and therefore will require a probe on each segment to be monitored. Layer 1 statistics will give us the health of specific links. Thankfully, the routers and hubs/switches can monitor the status and statistics of their individual links.

Configuration Switching

Configuration switching is a term meant to describe the System 5000's (and to some extent the BayStack line as well) extreme flexibility. The typical System 5000 chassis supports up to 9 Token Rings and 12 Ethernet segments on the Backplane alone. This does not include the local rings or segments that any given module may support. Configuration switching is how devices are assigned to any of these segments/rings. Let's examine a bit of terminology here.

Segments

A segment is a collision domain. The Backplane of a System 5000 has 12 Ethernet segments that span all 14 slots of the chassis (see Chapter 10). Individual modules may also have a number of local segments that do not attach to the Backplane segments.

Clusters

A cluster is the smallest unit that can be assigned to a segment. The entire cluster functions as a whole. In some modules (like a 5308), all of the ports on the module are part of one big cluster. This type of module is called a *module-level cluster*. If the cluster on a module like the 5308 is placed on Backplane segment 1, all of the ports are on Backplane segment 1 and have connectivity to all of the ports (in any slot regardless of cluster or module type) that have connectivity to Backplane segment 1.

Some modules (like the 5378) have multiple clusters, with each cluster being made up of numerous (in this case five) ports. This is called a *multi* or *multiple port-cluster*. Each cluster can be assigned individually, so cluster A may be on Backplane segment 1 while cluster B is on Backplane segment 2. All of the ports in cluster A have connectivity to all the other ports in cluster A and all of the other ports on Backplane segment 1, but no connectivity to the ports of cluster B or Backplane segment 2.

There is also a per-port level cluster (also called a *single-port cluster*). A 5308-PS module has per-port level clusters. Each of the 24 ports on the module is a separate cluster and can be assigned individually. This type of module therefore lends the most flexibility. Configuration switching is about how we move clusters to segments.

LANarchitect

LANarchitect is the application used to move clusters from one segment to another. When LANarchitect is launched against a specific system 5000 chassis, all of the segments are displayed along with all of the clusters assigned to that segment. The simple process of dragging and dropping a cluster from one segment to another is all it takes to move a cluster from one network to another.

 NOTE Extreme caution should be exercised here. These changes are dynamic, so you had better make certain that you are about to move the port that you intend on moving and not the one next to it. If you move a port form one segment to another, it is gone. This may not mean much until you consider that the segment that the port now belongs to is on another IP network than the segment from where it originated. If the IP address of the device attached to that port was not changed prior to the move, it has now lost all contact with the network. This is not always such a big deal, you can always drag the port back, but it may prove to be an embarrassment (or a practical joke, but I am not suggesting that you do that). If you should happen to move a DCE (you can do that in LANarchitect), it is going to be lost if you do not take the proper precautions. To get it back you will have to physically access the chassis and re-assign it through the serial port.

Aside from the obvious ease of setting up initial workgroups, this feature can be used to generate high-performance workgroups or to change traffic patterns to support times of heavy traffic loads. LANarchitect functions in two modes:

- System mode
- Device mode

In system mode, LANarchitect uses the Optivity database to identify physical connections. You can use LANarchitect to configure VLANs across two or more of the devices within the same VLAN configuration domain.

In device mode, LANarchitect shows all of the switches in the community and enables you to configure VLANs within a community of LattisSwitch hubs that can consist of one or more hubs, or a single system 5000 hub.

NETarchitect

NETarchitect is a tool that greatly simplifies configuration management. This tool enables you to create and modify, up/down-load configurations and images to devices in your network. It makes the process of keeping track of different versions of images and configurations simple. It can be used to validate a configuration before sending the configuration to a device. It provides security for access to configuration files and provides for multiple users to work simultaneously without interfering with each other's work.

This tool is especially useful in an Enterprise network where the number and types of network devices being managed are great. Configurations and images can be stored for a large number of devices as a central repository, for emergency restoration, or simply as the remote boot destination for network devices that support this feature.

NETarchitect is a GUI tool that stores device information in a tree-like structure. Underneath the tree root, there are folders. Folders can contain other folders or objects. Objects represent actual network devices. Furthermore, the NETarchitect database can be limited to include only devices that the administrator wants, and multiple databases can be managed from a single location. The database is referred to as a *domain*, and the domain is the entire list of objects being managed. In this manner, security can be managed at the domain level by placing devices in domains and limiting who has access rights to a given domain.

Domains are created using the Domain Administration tool found under the Tool menu. From here, clicking on the Create Domain button will start the process. You provide a name for the domain and a path (location on the workstation's hard drive) to store the database.

NOTE This tool can eat up a lot of hard drive space. Remember that domains are databases, which do take up room on a hard drive. Image and configuration files do take up room on a hard drive. Be careful to manage the amount of space you have available to use.

Domains can also be copied and deleted from this tool. Also, from here passwords can be assigned to domains for security.

NETarchitect enables you to create objects based on templates. It supports drag-and-drop. NETarchitect has a tool that verifies changes that you make to a device's configuration before you implement them. It does this by maintaining a database of configuration mistakes commonly made and searches for matches. This is not a perfect system as it is only as perfect as the database of errors, but it can keep you from making some common blunders. NETarchitect will not enable you to save a file until the changes have been verified. If errors are detected, they are displayed for you, and they must be fixed before you will be allowed to save the file.

Reset Changes is also a very useful tool that causes the configuration to be restored to its status when it was last verified, if you need to start over.

Optivity NMS 9.X

In many ways, Optivity NMS 9.X is merely the next revision of the Enterprise version of Optivity. In other ways, it is the merger of two management packages (Optivity Enterprise and Optivity Campus) using the unique advantages of each version to create a more powerful, flexible, and useful tool. Optivity NMS 9.X combines the raw power of a Unix operating system with a client/server model that allows for multiple client types and the simplicity and user-friendly NT operating system for clients. The best features of the tools from both predecessors have been combined and improved upon to make a truly flexible and powerful management system.

 NOTE   We mentioned earlier that SNMP is a client/server application by its nature and that the NMS is the client. That is the SNMP model. Optivity NMS 9.X is also a client server application in its own right. The NMS software is installed on a single machine, and this machine is the client that makes requests of the server (the agent). It (the NMS station) is also a server that makes requests on behalf of Optivity NMS client workstations. This enables the server to be maintained in a single location and have a large investment in resources while still enabling multiple users to interact with the system simultaneously from less expensive systems.

Today's Optivity

Optivity today is a true suite of software products with each product having its own tools. All of these products are designed to function together:

- **Optivity NMS**   Optivity NMS gives the network administrator the tools necessary to manage the various network components. It also gives a single launching point for all the other applications.

- **Optivity service level management**   Optivity service level management gives the administrator the ability to better view application performance.

- **Optivity policy services**

- **Optivity NetID**   Optivity NetID gives the administrator a tool that offers DNS and DHCP services to an enterprise network with a unified management interface.

- **Optivity NetConfigurator**   Optivity NetConfigurator gives the administrator revision control over configuration changes as well as auditing of those changes.

- **Optivity VPN manager**   Optivity VPN manager gives the administrator a tool for managing Contivity VPN devices. VPN manager runs as a component of NetConfigurator.

Support

Optivity NMS 9.X supports a range of server and client platforms.

Servers

Optivity NMS 9.X supported server platforms are

- Solaris

- HP-UX

- AIX

- Windows NT

Clients

Optivity clients can be installed on the same platforms as the server. There are two additional client types; the client software can be installed on a Windows 95/98 workstation and a Java enabled web browser can also be a client to the Optivity NMS 9.X server.

NOTE   Although an Optivity NMS client running on a Windows NT platform can be a client of an Optivity NMS server running on a Unix platform, an Optivity client running on a Unix platform cannot be a client of an Optivity NMS server running on a Windows NT platform.

Optivity NMS Applications

Some of the applications that Optivity NMS includes are

- InfoCenter
- Expanded view
- OmniView
- Fault summary
- LANarchitect
- Path trace
- OIT manager

InfoCenter

InfoCenter is the central application from where all other Optivity tools and applications can be launched. It replaces the ECC and the CCC from earlier versions of Optivity. The InfoCenter maintains folders, which helps organize the devices into logical and ordered groupings.

Expanded View

Expanded view gives the user a graphical representation of the physical device. From here you can view LED status, VLAN configuration (or configuration switching for system 500), attached devices, statistics, and diagnostics information. Ports can be enabled and disabled from here. Modules or ports can be reset. There are three views for Expanded views:

- **Front view**   This view shows the front of the device.
- **Rear view**   This view shows the rear of the device as well as the status of temperature and fans. In a System 5000, it will also show installed backplanes.
- **Logical view**   This view displays VLAN and configuration switching (System 5000) configuration of the device.

OmniView

OmniView is an excellent tool for viewing the performance of your network devices. OmniView replaces older versions of OmniView as well as LAN summary, WAN summary, Nodal view, and RouterMan. OmniView can be used to get performance statistics from

- Hubs
- Switches
- Routers
- WANs
- Segments
- Subnets
- VLANs
- ELANs

OmniView enables you to monitor network performance and traffic at layers 1, 2, and 3. OmniView enables you to launch against multiple devices simultaneously. Once a particular arrangement of devices or graphs has been created, it can be saved as a workspace. Once a workspace has been saved, it can be opened again and again, providing a consistent view of a particular device or segment.

NOTE Workspaces are saved locally on the workstation on which they are created. They do not follow you from client to client.

Fault Summary

Fault summary enables you to see a list of fault messages for network devices. Fault messages tell about events that occurred on the device in question that are of significance. Fault messages are made up of traps that are reported. Faults for a device can be displayed all at once or filtered by type or severity. Fault summary can even be configured to stop monitoring specific faults for a time. Faults can be removed from fault summary after their cause has been fixed.

LANarchitect

Is the tool that is used to manage workgroups on System 5000, Distributed 5000, and 28K (LattisSwitch) switches. It displays graphically the VLANs, Backplane segments,

Cascaded segments, and local segments available (depending on the device). It can be used to drag and drop clusters (see the LANArchitect section of the previous section on Optivity Enterprise 8.X) from one segment or VLAN to another. This change happens in real time, so extreme caution must be used while making these changes. If you make a change to a device that severs the connectivity between the device and your Optivity NMS, then you loose all contact to that device (not a good career move).

Path Trace

The Path Trace utility is used to determine the network path between two devices. This is an incredibly useful tool for troubleshooting or documenting networks. By default, the Path Trace utility performs a real-time trace between the two devices. Path Trace can also be configured to trace the path based on the Optivity database.

OIT Manager

Optivity Integrated Toolkit (OIT) manager provides the means for installing modular support for new devices and device support. Occasionally, new devices with cool new features come out. The NMS needs to be made aware of these devices or features. In the past, entire new versions of the NMS needed to be installed or complicated patches needed to be applied. Now with the OIT manager, the support is added as a module to the NMS. Running OITInstall will integrate the application with the NMS.

Review Questions

1. SNMP stands for
   A. Smart Network Management Protocol
   B. Secure Network Management Protocol
   C. Simple Network Management Protocol
   D. Simple Network Management Procedure

2. There are three types of SNMP operations. Which of the following is not an SNMP operation?
   A. Trap
   B. List
   C. Set
   D. Get

3. SNMP uses which of the following transport protocols?
   A. UDP
   B. TCP
   C. IP
   D. RIP

4. SNMP uses which port numbers?
   A. TCP 161
   B. TCP 162
   C. UDP 161
   D. UDP 162

5. An SNMP agent is
   A. A dedicated workstation running NMS software and binding UDP port 162
   B. A man wearing a trench coat and hat who talks in whispers and walks in the shadows
   C. Specialized hardware and software that resides in a network device
   D. All of the above

6. What network devices can maintain an SNMP agent? (Choose all that apply.)
   A. Router
   B. Hubs
   C. Switches
   D. Novell file servers
   E. Source route bridges

7. The SNMP client
   A. Pays for services either in cash or with a credit card, but never with a check.
   B. Is usually a dedicated workstation running NMS software.
   C. Is integrated into most pieces of network hardware.
   D. Sends SNMP TRAPs on TCP port 162.

8. True/False
   NMP agents regularly send unsolicited updates to the NMS to let the network administrator know the state of the network devices.

9. An SNMP Community string is
   A. The name of a business unit
   B. Like a password
   C. A network connection
   D. None of the above

10. True/False

SNMP community strings are an excellent security measure.

11. Which of the following are not parts of the OSI network management model?

A. Fault

B. Security

C. Physical

D. Accounting

E. Performance

F. Configuration

12. Which of the following deals with the ability to keep track of and manage network problems, including notification of and isolation of the area of the problem?

A. Disaster recovery

B. Fault management

C. Trap receiving

D. Fault monitor

13. Which of the following would be a system that keeps track of the integrity of the network's privacy?

A. Privacy management

B. Secrecy management

C. Password security

D. Security management

14. Which management system analyzes the efficiency of the network?

A. Performance management

B. Network trends management

C. RMON2 management

D. Configuration management

15. In order to understand the current state of the network, we must compare it to the

A. Baseboard

B. Basement

C. Baseball

D. Baseline

16. True/False

    Once a well-developed baseline has been created for a network, it should be kept for the life of the network or until there is a request from upper management to create a new baseline.

17. Which of the following are included in configuration management? (Choose all that apply.)

    A. Security management

    B. Fault management

    C. Performance management

    D. Accounting management

18. Which of the following agent levels is the minimum required on a network device to be able to use the Expanded view feature?

    A. Standard

    B. Advanced

    C. Advanced Analyzer

    D. None of the above

19. Which of the following agent levels is the minimum required on a network device to be able to use the Packet Capture feature?

    A. Standard

    B. Advanced

    C. Advanced Analyzer

    D. None of the above

20. Which device(s) will a Flatnet Hello not pass? (Choose all that apply.)

    A. Hub

    B. Switch

    C. Bridge

    D. Router

21. Which device(s) will a Subnet Hello not pass? (Choose all that apply.)

    A. Hub

    B. Switch

    C. Bridge

    D. Router

22. For the purposes of configuration switching, a cluster is which of the following?
    A. A port
    B. A module
    C. A chassis
    D. The smallest unit that can be assigned to a segment

23. Which of the following tools is used to assign clusters to segments?
    A. Routerman
    B. Quick2config
    C. LANarchitect
    D. NETarchitect

24. InfoCenter on Optivity NMS 9.X replaces which tools from earlier versions of Optivity? (Choose all that apply.)
    A. CCC
    B. ECC
    C. BCC
    D. BBC

25. Which tool would you use to get performance statistics from network devices?
    A. Expanded view
    B. Front view
    C. OmniView
    D. Performance view

Answers

1. C. SNMP stands for Simple Network Management Protocol.

2. B. There is no List operation in SNMP. There is a List command in the operation on the BayRS router software that is used for browsing the MIB, but that is not an SNMP operation. A trap is an automated response to a predefined condition. A Set is used to change a read/write MIB variable to a desired state. A Get is used to view a Desired MIB variable's current state.

3. A. SNMP uses UPD as a transport (layer 4) protocol. This was done in part to give SNMP very low overhead. Because UDP is a connectionless protocol there are no connections to establish and keep track of. This has the unfortunate disadvantage of making SNMP unreliable.

PART III

4. **C, D.** SNMP uses UDP ports 161 and 162. GETs and SETs are sent over UDP port 161 while the NMS listens for TRAPs on UDP port 162.

5. **C.** An SNMP agent is a combination of hardware, software, and a network device. The hardware consists of memory, a processor, and storage. The processor to do the work, the memory to hold the MIB objects and their values, and the storage to keep the software locally in the event that the device looses power. These items are all together in a network device.

6. **A, B, C, D, E.** All of these devices are capable of maintaining an SNMP agent. In the case of the router, the processor, memory, and storage are integrated into the system and the software is part of the router image. In the hubs, switches, and bridges, the hardware and software may be integrated (like a Passport 8600 or a Centillion 100) or they may be modular (like a System 5000 Ethernet hub). Novell file servers are capable of using their processor, memory, and storage as an SNMP agent while providing other network services, providing that the SNMP software is loaded.

7. **B.** The SNMP client is the NMS running a suite of software applications used to manage the network devices. From this workstation, the network administrator can manage many aspects of the network. Many people confuse this SNMP client workstation with the SNMP server. They mistakenly assume that the NMS provides management services. It is, in fact, the SNMP agents that provide network management services and they are the servers in this client/server application. The NMS workstation provides a means of accessing the services provided by the agents.

8. **False.** An SNMP agent only sends unsolicited information (TRAPs) in unusual circumstances. The NMS may regularly poll the agents in the network (at user defined intervals) for a status update.

9. **B.** The SNMP community string is a password-like identifier that authenticates SNMP requests to the SNMP agent. When a request is received with an invalid community string, the request is denied and the event is logged. When a request is received with a correct community string, the request is processed.

10. **False.** SNMP community strings are only as secure as the physical network. Community strings are not encrypted or protected in any fashion from protocol analyzers, so anyone who can view network traffic can view the community strings. Also, the default, community strings of network devices are well known. As with any password, it must be changed from its default value or it is worthless.

11. **C.** The Physical layer is part of the OSI model for network protocols, but not for the network management model.

12. **B.** Fault management deals with the identification of a fault domain and the isolation of specific problems. It includes the sending of traps that alert of the fault conditions existence as well as the procedures for repairing the condition or removing the condition's negative impact on the network.

13. **D.** Security management is the system that keeps track of the integrity of the network's privacy from intrusion. Security management is a very large responsibility in today's networks and it is multifaceted.

14. **A.** Performance management keeps track of the statistics that help us discover the throughput, latency, utilization, and error rate of the network.

15. **D.** The baseline is a sample of the network performance over a given period of time. The baseline statistics should include packets/second, bytes/second, average packet size, errors/second, dropped packets, retransmissions/second, top N talkers, and other statistics that are of concern to you.

16. **False.** A baseline's validity is temporary at best. The baseline data is only valid as long as the network stays in the current status. As soon as an application, protocol, server, OS, printer, or other device is added/removed from the network, the baseline needs to be invalidated and a new one must be made.

17. **A, B, C, D.** All of these management types are included in configuration management. The management of any of these aspects of the network requires changes to the configuration of network devices and therefore falls under the blanket of configuration management.

18. **A.** Standard is the minimum level of agent that supports Expanded view.

19. **C.** Only the Advanced Analyzer agent is capable of supporting Packet Capture.

20. **B, C, D.** Flatnet Hellos follow the boundaries of a collision domain. This means that a Flatnet Hello remains in the collision domain that it originated in. Because bridges, switches, and routers separate collision domains from one another, a Flatnet Hello will not pass through them.

21. **D.** A Subnet Hello follows the boundaries of a broadcast domain. That means that a Subnet Hello will remain within the same broadcast domain that it originated in. Because a router separates broadcast domains from each other, a Subnet Hello will not pass through it.

22. D. A cluster is either a port, group of ports, or an entire module (depending on the module type). It is the smallest unit that can be assigned to a segment.

23. C. LANarchitect is the tool used to assign clusters to segments.

24. A, B. CCC and ECC have been replaced by the InfoCenter tool in Optivity NMS 9.X.

25. C. OmniView is the tool most suited to the task of gathering performance statistics from a wide variety of network devices at many levels.

Contivity Extranet Switches

Introduction

This chapter will cover the Nortel Networks Contivity Extranet Switching (CES) products. Each Contivity Virtual Private Networking (VPN) switch is a single hardware device that provides routing, firewall, bandwidth management, encryption, authentication, and data integrity for secure tunneling across managed IP networks and the Internet. Contivity VPN switches can be used to connect remote users, branch offices, suppliers, and customers with the security and control expected from private networks. We will be examining the CES in detail, looking at its functions and the commands that perform various tasks with the CES. In this chapter we will cover how to configure the CES using the Command Line Interface (CLI) as well as the web-based management tool. This chapter can be used to prepare for the Nortel Networks Support Specialist Certification for the Intelligent Internet track (formerly known as *Carrier*).

NOTE In this chapter there will be commands to execute in order to complete certain tasks. When there is a command given under the title GUI, it is a set of steps that can be performed in the web-based management tool.

Exam Objectives

Certification is based on the knowledge and skills necessary to install, support, troubleshoot, and maintain the Contivity portfolio (4X00, 2X00, 1X00, 600, 400, and 100). The test is based on release 2.60–3.50 for the Contivity 600 through 4600, and 7.00.x–7.11.1 for the II 100 and 400 (renamed the Contivity 100 and 400 switches).

NOTE Although the II 100 and 400 products have been renamed for reasons of standardization with Nortel Networks, we will continue to refer to them as II in this chapter for ease of distinction between those switches and the mainline Contivity 1600, 2600, and 4600 products.

In order to prepare for the exam a user should know the objectives that are posted on the Certification web site for this exam. These objectives are as follows:

- Features and functions of the Contivity product portfolio
- Fundamentals of VPN technology
- Functional knowledge of related technologies
- Integrating Contivity systems into an existing network infrastructure
- Provisioning a Contivity system
- Administration
- Problem identification and troubleshooting
- Contivity VPN Client (various Windows operating systems)
- IP networking
- VPN (IP Security [IPSec], Layer 2 Tunneling Protocol [L2TP], and Point-to-Point Tunneling Protocol [PPTP])
- Security (firewall, Remote Authentication Dial-In User Services [RADIUS], and so on)

Fundamentals of VPN Technology

VPN technology is the capability to create a private data network that uses the public network for connecting data centers, remote offices, and business partners. VPNs are concerned with several security issues because there are machines along the connection path that are not in control of the enterprise (for example, the routers within the Internet). Additionally, the Internet carries traffic from many different source locations, some from the internal network, some not. To protect the internal network segment, that is, the hosts and routers that are part of the enterprise, there must be a firewall or router that resides between the internal and external network. The idea behind a VPN is to extend an enterprise's private network across the Internet through a private tunnel. VPN architecture can be deployed for three different scenarios:

- Branch office connections
- Extranet VPN
- Remote access VPN

In the scenario of a branch office, remote internal networks must connect to each other securely. VPN technology that is used for connecting remote branch offices of a corporation with each other is primarily concerned with protecting company data as it flows across the public Internet (see Figure 16-1). Also a concern is securing the internal network from the rest of the world.

The Extranet VPN scenario serves to connect corporations through secure tunnels to their business partners, vendors, and subsidiaries (see Figure 16-2). Business partners can authenticate to a firewall and router or directly to a company's server, depending on a company's security policies. A tunnel can then be established to encrypt packets from the client through the Internet to the server. This configuration brings with it concerns of manageability because of different policies that must be maintained for each business partner. These policies must include appropriate security, IP addressing schemes, and encryption of data while being easy to maintain and manage.

The final VPN model is for remote access VPNs. These are created to enable connections from the home-based or travelling corporate users to the internal corporate networks for access to all types of services (see Figure 16-3). In this scenario the concerns will be to secure the internal network from intruders and to ensure that others cannot read any data sent over the Internet. The access for remote users in this scenario will be to have clients use local Internet providers with local numbers. The clients will dial up or use a DSL/cable modem to access the Internet service provider (ISP) and then establish an authenticated and encrypted tunnel to the corporate intranet afterwards. Authentication prevents unauthorized users, while encapsulation ensures that no one over the Internet can read the client's data.

The remote access VPN traffic will have three basic segments: the client connection to the local ISP, the Internet, and the intranet. To use Extranet access for security into a private network, a user would first dial up to a local ISP. Once validated by the ISP, the

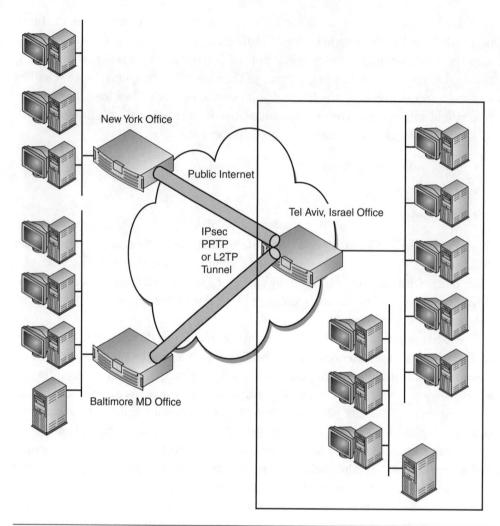

Figure 16-1 Branch office VPN connections

client would then initiate a secure VPN tunnel to the enterprise network using a secure tunneling protocol (PPTP or IPSec, which will be discussed further on in the chapter in detail). To connect to the enterprise the user must provide a user ID and password, which is validated by the Extranet switch to a local or remote Lightweight Directory Access Protocol (LDAP) database. Subsequent authentication of the user will include a profile with the user's information, such as the type of access, hours of access, and IP address for the local intranet. Once the tunnel is established and the user is authenticated, the user can now access network resources from the corporate network.

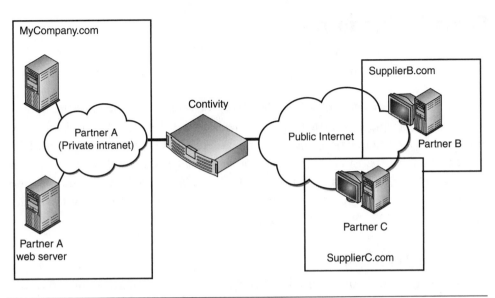

Figure 16-2 An Extranet VPN created to secure connections between MyCompany.com and two of their suppliers, SupplierB.com and SupplierC.com

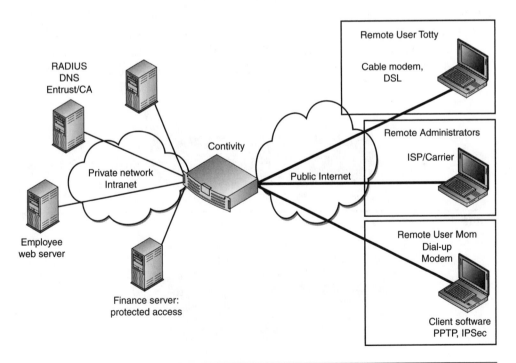

Figure 16-3 A remote access VPN with users dialing into the corporate intranet

Contivity Platforms

II (Contivity) 100, designed for the branch/home office, is a fixed configuration switch that features a stateful firewall requiring NAT. It only supports up to five users/branch office tunnels.

The II 100 features a Pentium-class, 300 MHz processor with 16MB RAM and 8MB of Flash memory (replaceable, expandable). There are two 10/100 Ethernet LAN ports; one is a standard internal port, and one can be used for all Ethernet networking. There is one additional expansion port that can support a v.90 analog modem, ISDN with or without NT1, or XDSL on a 1MB modem. There is also a serial port for out-of-band management or PPP as well as single and dual analog ports. The Contivity 100 comes with VPN Switch 100 software, a CD, and online HTML documentation.

II (Contivity) 400

It supports up to 30 branch office tunnels. Designed for the branch/home office is a fixed configuration switch that features a Stateful firewall requiring NAT.

The II 400 features 64MB memory with interfaces that include two 10/100 Ethernet LAN ports and one 10/100 Ethernet expansion port that is a 7-port 10/100 Ethernet auto-sensing switch. Additionally, there are two expansion ports that can hold T1 with CSU/DSU or E1, V.35, or X.21. The expansion ports can also be used for V.90 dual analog modems, ISDN with and without NT1 network termination, or XDSL on a 1MB modem. It additionally features a built-in web cache for fast internal access and comes

Figure 16-4   Contivity 100

Figure 16-5   Contivity 400

standard with Contivity 400 software. The Contivity VPN Client software comes along with an unlimited distribution license, a CD, and online HTML documentation.

Contivity 600

Designed for the small corporate offices, it has one open PCI slot and runs Stateful firewall. It supports up to 30 simultaneous users/branch office tunnels.

The Contivity 600 features a 300 MHz Celeron processor with 64MB memory, one private 10/100 Ethernet, one standard 10/100 Ethernet, and one PCI expansion slot that supports V.35, X.21, and T1. It comes standard with Contivity 600 software, a CD, and online HTML documentation (Figure 16-6).

NOTE   This Contivity switch does not support the 3.5 software code.

Contivity 1600

Designed for the small corporate office, it has one open PCI slot and runs Stateful firewall. It supports up to 200 remote/branch tunnels.

The Contivity 1600 replaces the former Contivity 1500 (Figure 16-7). The 1600 features a 433 MHz Celeron processor with up to 128MB and a floppy disk drive. The available interfaces include one private 10/100 Ethernet, one standard 10/100 Ethernet, and one PCI expansion slot. The expansion slot can house a V.35, 10/100 Ethernet, and

Figure 16-6   Contivity 600

Figure 16-7   The older Contivity 1500

Figure 16-8   The newer Contivity 1600

T1 with integrated CSU/DSU. The switch also comes standard with Contivity 1600 software, the Contivity VPN Client software with an unlimited distribution license, a CD, and online HTML documentation (Figure 16-8).

Contivity 2600

Designed for the medium corporate office with three open PCI slots and the Stateful firewall software, it supports up to 1,000 simultaneous users/tunnels.

The Contivity 2600 features a 733 MHz Pentium II processor with 128MB memory and a dual 10/100 Ethernet with three PCI expansion slots. Optional interfaces include a 10/100 Ethernet LAN card, a T1 with integrated CSU/DSU, an encryption card, a single-and-dual port V.35 WAN card, or a high-speed serial interface (HSSI) card. It comes with a 125W power supply. It includes the Contivity 2600 software and Contivity VPN Access IPSec Client software with unlimited distribution license, a CD, and online HTML documentation (Figure 16-9).

Contivity 4600

Designed for the large corporate office with five open PCI slots and Stateful firewall support, it supports up to 5,000 simultaneous users/tunnels.

The Contivity 4600 replaces the 4500 and features a dual 800 MHz Intel Pentium processor with a 256MB memory standard. It allows for a maximum 1GB of memory

Figure 16-9   Contivity 2600

Figure 16-10   Contivity 4600

through expansion. There are five PCI expansion slots that can include dual 10/100 Ethernet LAN ports, a dual-port V.35 WAN card (that supports speeds up to T1/E1 line rates of 1.544/2.048 Mbps), or a single-port HSSI WAN card (that supports speeds up to T3/E3 line rates of 45/34 Mbps). There are dual, redundant, and auto-switching power supply systems with dual-line cords and even a dual, redundant storage system. The product comes standard with the Contivity VPN Switch 4600 software and Contivity VPN Access IPSec Client software with an unlimited distribution license as well as printed and online HTML documentation (Figure 16-10).

Cryptography

Cryptography is the science of keeping data and communications secure. Secure communications is the most essential component of VPN communications. There are many technologies used to ensure security.

Encryption and Decryption

Encryption is the process of hiding a message by transforming it into something that is not readable. Decryption is returning the message to its original clear text form.

The most commonly used form of encryption for data communications works with keys that are essentially just large random numbers. Cryptographic security relies on keys and random number generation. The strength (that is, its capability to withstand unauthorized decryption) of an encryption algorithm (the formula that is used to encrypt and decrypt) is related to the key size and how difficult it is to computationally break the algorithm. Currently used keys are chosen from a huge set of possible values. Secure key exchange is the most important factor in secure communications. All exchanges of key information must be encrypted and authenticated to ensure that key information does not get compromised. If the key is compromised, then no authentication exists. There are two types of key algorithms: symmetric keys and asymmetric keys.

Symmetric keys are also known as *secret-key algorithms*. The decryption and encryption key are the same, and they are agreed on by the sender and receiver before any communication takes place. Data Encryption Standard (DES) is an algorithm that is used for generating 56-bit secret keys. A stronger version of this is the triple-DES (3DES), which uses 168-bit keys. A weaker 40-bit version exists for export purposes. Symmetric keys are used in the Encapsulation Security Protocol (ESP) for IPSec.

Asymmetric keys are also called *public-key algorithms*. They use two different keys: a public key, which is known to everyone, and a private key, which belongs to a specific owner. The private key cannot be determined from the public key. A message gets encrypted with a public key of the recipient and can only be decrypted with the private key of the same recipient. Additionally, a message encrypted with a private key can only be decrypted with the sender's public key. This can help to verify the sender of the message who is the only one with the private key. RSA is the most popular public-key algorithm.

Data Integrity Options

Data integrity is used to verify that a message has not been changed along the path. Hashing is the function that is used to check the validity of a message. It works with the sender calculating a mathematical hash (the total number obtained by applying a formula) and appending it to each message sent. The recipient calculates the same mathematical hash on received messages and compares the result with the hash in the packet. If the hashes match, then the message was not changed from sender to receiver. Hashing algorithms include Message Digest 5 (MD5), which is available in IPSec and uses a 128-bit hash and Secure Hash Algorithm-1 (SHA-1) that uses a 160-bit hash and is even more resistant to attacks because of the larger hash value. The output of the hash value is placed in the authentication data field of the Authentication Header (AH).

Encrypting the hash with the private key creates digital signatures.

Public Key Infrastructure (PKI)

PKI is a set of algorithms for public and private key generation and distribution used in encryption and digital signing. PKI standards define the management protocols needed to support registration, initialization, certification, key pair recovery, key pair updates, revocation requests, and cross-certification. It is a framework of protocols and services for certificates (documents tied to specific public keys, individuals, or organizations), Certification Authority (CA, the central location for registering certificates and providing assurance of the validity of the certificate), and administrative tools (for distributing, revoking, and storing certificates).

Certificates are used because people on the Internet do not know where data is coming from. The idea behind digital certificates is to bind a file to the public key. This file is validated through a third-party CA that uses the international standard X.509 certificate protocol and verifies each applicant before validating certificates. Digital certificates, available through Entrust and Verisign, enable the integrity of signed documents because they are signed with the private key of the CA and therefore can be authenticated. It is more trustworthy than a simple public key encryption because the public key here is certified by a third-party trusted entity. Public key and digital certification provide strong authentication needed for VPN.

Tunnel Certificates

X.509 certificates are used to authenticate IPSec-based tunnel connections. The switch supports RSA digital signature authentication in the IPSec ISAKMP key management protocol. Remote users can authenticate themselves to the switch using a public key pair and a certificate as credentials. In addition, the switch uses its own key pair and certificate to authenticate the switch to the user.

X.509 certificate usage begins with a client initiating a tunnel connection. The client signs the request and sends the user's X.509 certificate. CES verifies the user's certificate through the CA, making sure the certificate has not been revoked. CES verifies the signature on the tunnel request using the public key. If the client is valid, the CES signs a response and sends its server X.509 certificate. The client verifies the certificate using the CA and then verifies the signatures using the public key. Each time a tunnel is initiated certification maintenance is performed.

Smart Cards

Smart Cards are beginning to play a role in private key authentication because digital certificates are available to anyone with access to the private key, and that might not be secure. The technology offers a secure way to authenticate users for access to information and applications on the Internet. The private key never leaves the Smart Card that provides secure storage for the key. All cryptographic functions requiring the use of a private key take place on the Smart Card itself. The card is pin protected and becomes unusable after a number of failed pin number attempts.

Contivity Features

The Contivity switch offers many features for creating powerful VPN networks. In addition, the CES supports all the technologies mentioned previously as well as other protocols to ensure the security of communications and protection of data.

Reliability

The CES offers powerful Intel processor architecture, multilevel authentication servers, and automatic backups of all system data. In addition, some CES switches offer redundant components for greater reliability.

Client Software

Contivity offers the Contivity Extranet client that runs on Windows 95, 98, 2000, or Windows NT 4.0. Windows 2000 is supported with this Nortel client (Contivity Extranet) or its own client that uses other tunnel protocols such as PPTP and L2TP.

Public and Private Interfaces

The CES uses different interfaces for the private-side LAN and the public network to provide inherent security for the network. Private interfaces are those that connect only to trusted networks—the LAN within the corporation (the internal network). The private interface can accept management traffic (HTTP, SNMP, Telnet, and FTP) as well as pings. The private interface also accepts tunneled protocols (such as IPSec, PPTP, L2TP, and L2F) that can be used for secure management access to the switch. There is a management IP address on the private network and an IP address that represents the LAN and is an end point for tunnel traffic. The LAN interface on the system board of the Contivity switch is always a private interface. All other interfaces can be public or private.

Public in the title *public interface* refers to the public data networks. Public interfaces connect to the public Internet. Because public interfaces are not trusted, they can only accept tunnel connections like IPSec, PPTP, L2TP, and L2F, in contrast to the private interface that accepts both regular (nontunneled) and tunneled protocols. Additional interfaces that are inserted into the expansion slots are set to public by default.

Tunneling Protocols Support

Tunneling is actually the process of wrapping a packet inside another packet by adding a new header to an old packet. The entire old packet becomes the data portion of the new packet (as we have seen with IP headers that have Ethernet frames inside).

NOTE Previously, tunneling was used to carry traffic of a nonsupported protocol across the network by disguising it as another type of protocol traffic. The II boxes (Contivity 100 and 400) mainly created tunnels to carry IPX traffic in a wholly IP network.

The switch uses tunneling through the Internet to create secure extranets. Remote connectivity through the public network requires a protocol for safe transport, and a connection from the remote user's PC to the Internet tunneling created for VPN access is created to provide protection of the data inside the packet. The Contivity supports PPTP, L2TP, and IPSec tunneling for security.

To form a tunnel, the remote user first establishes a connection with the public data network's point-of-presence (POP), typically through an ISP. After the Internet connection is up, the remote user launches a second dial-up connection, and this specifies a connection to a switch. Instead of a telephone number to establish the link, the second connection uses an IP address (or a name if the IP address has been entered into a domain name service server).

This second connection could use either PPTP or the IPSec tunneling protocol. Tunnels built using L2TP or L2F are slightly different. The tunnel begins at a piece of networking equipment (the network access server or NAS) located at the ISP instead of the remote user's PC. The user simply dials into the ISP with a telephone number that causes an L2TP or L2F tunnel to connect directly to a specific corporation.

Point-to-Point Tunneling Protocol (PPTP)   Microsoft Windows workstations can use the native dial-up networking client for creating VPN tunnels with the Contivity switch instead of installing the Contivity client software (see Figure 16-11). Dial-up networking uses PPTP that can include compression and encryption. This PPTP client is available for the most common Microsoft client operating systems.

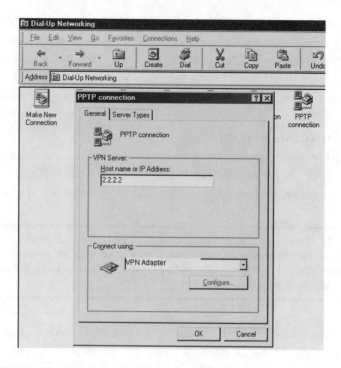

Figure 16-11 Using the Microsoft dial-up networking utility to create a VPN connection

 NOTE Microsoft clients should configure the VPN connection to log on to a remote domain and disable the NetBEUI protocol (see Figure 16-12).

PPTP supports the use of Password Authentication Protocol (PAP), which does not encrypt usernames or passwords, and Challenge Handshake Authentication Protocol (CHAP), which encrypts only passwords. Neither PAP nor CHAP provides data encryption. PPTP clients can also use Microsoft Challenge Handshake Authentication Protocol (MS-CHAPv2) to provide both the authentication and encryption of passwords and data (see Figure 16-13). The encryption types available for PPTP is either not encrypted or an encryption based on RC4. This is a secret-key encryption that can be used with various key lengths, including RC4-40 or RC4-128. PPTP also supports IPX tunneling.

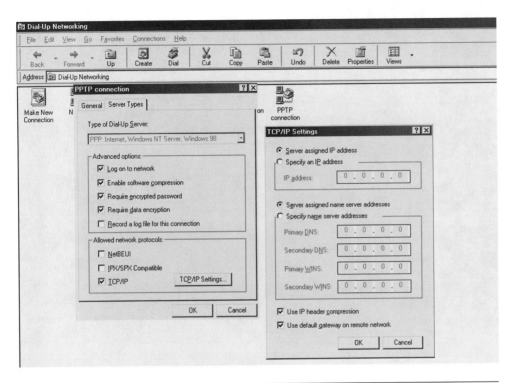

Figure 16-12 Properties of a VPN connection for Microsoft clients using the dial-up networking client

GUI > Services > PPTP

Because of laws regulating encryption technologies in other countries, CES must sometimes negotiate downwards to a lower level of encryption to be able to communicate with other switches.

Layer 2 Forwarding (L2F)   Nortel Networks, Cisco, Shiva, and other vendors support the L2F tunneling protocol. L2F tunnels are generally established between the NAS at the ISP and the switch. There is no direct client software required for L2F beyond the PPP dialer software, such as the dial-up networking utility provided with Windows 95 and Windows 98. L2F provides IP address translation using encapsulation and support for IPX tunneling, but it does not perform encryption. L2F tunnels are actually made from the ISP to the corporate switch on behalf of the user; therefore, ISPs must offer services that are based on L2F. Currently, L2F is available only on a limited basis.

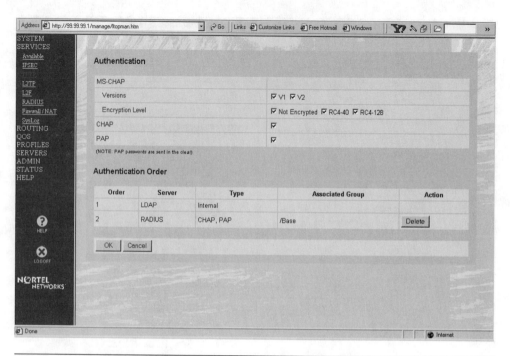

Figure 16-13   PPTP authentication types available on the CES

Layer 2 Tunneling Protocol (L2TP)   Nortel Networks, Cisco Systems, Microsoft, and other vendors support L2TP. L2TP enables PAP, CHAP, or MS-CHAP authentication and compression, as well as the capability to assign DNS and WINS servers to the tunnel. It combines the best features of the L2F and PPTP tunneling protocols. It works by creating the tunnel from the NAS at the ISP all the way to the corporate network. This type of tunneling is called *transport mode* as it enables encryption all the way through. The host to ISP provider connection is no longer insecure, and now the client appears as though it was on the same subnet as the rest of the corporate intranet.

L2TP does have some disadvantages because authentication is provided only at tunnel end points and not for each individual packet in the tunnel. This leaves an exposure to enable hackers to break into the tunnel session and mount attacks because there is no encryption of user data packets. Additionally, there is no refreshing of keys so if a key is broken, the security of the packets will be compromised.

IPSec   The Extranet client software provided with the CES uses IPSec to create tunnels. IPSec is the most secure and works with other security methods to provide the best overall tunneling. It is designed to operate in every network and not to interfere in a network where it is not supported. IPSec enables key exchange through the Internet

Security Association and Key Management Protocol (ISAKMP)/Oakley and Internet Key Exchange (IKE). ISAKMP is an automatic method for setting up security associations and managing keys. The ISAKMP standard requires that all communication of keys must be authenticated, and encrypted hackers cannot gain access to key information. Additionally, key information should only pass among authenticated users in a session.

Oakley is actually the key management protocol itself. IKE uses ISAKMP and Oakley to manage keys for the IPSec, AH, and ESP protocols. IKE uses preshared keys, digital signatures, and public key encryption for key management. IKE is based on UDP and uses port 500 for both the source and destination.

IPSec uses AH protocol number 51 and ESP protocol number 50 to provide authentication to the origination of data, data integrity, and replay protection. Data integrity is ensured through the checksum hashing, and authentication of the originating data is done through a secret shared key. Encryption options available through IPSec include DES and Triple or no data encryption at all (see Figure 16-14). Usernames and passwords are never transmitted clear; they are encrypted using SHA-1.

GUI > Services > IPSec

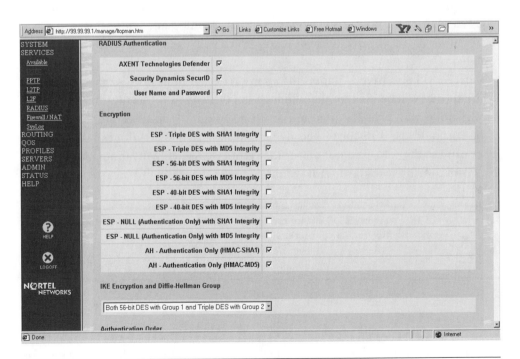

Figure 16-14 Services IPSec encryption possibilities

NOTE Nortel Networks provides two versions of the IPSec client due to export restrictions. The standard version supports DES (56-bit key) encryption, and the enhanced version supports Triple DES (3DES, 168-bit key).

L2TP over IPSEC IPSec transport mode can be used to provide additional security for L2TP traffic for both remote access traffic and branch office tunnel traffic. Windows 2000 can act as a peer in a branch office connection using L2TP/IPSec or IPSec tunnel mode. Also, Windows 2000 can act as a client using L2TP/IPSec. Authentication for L2TP/IPSEC tunnels can be either a shared, secret, or digital certificate.

To configure a Windows 2000 client using the dial-up-networking utility with L2TP over IPSec, the Windows 2000 client will have to have a CA and server certificate installed. Creating a Windows 2000 certificate server that is able to issue IPSec certificates can provide the client with necessary certificates. Windows 2000 clients will have to configure the dial-up-networking client to use a VPN with L2TP that has the IP address of the Contivity switch. Additionally, the client will need to dial in with the user ID and password created on the CES. L2TP must use the minimum data protection required with IPSec but no encryption, as well as automatic addressing and DNS. Encryption will be provided through IPSec, which will also use the certificate that was installed.

The CES will also have to import the appropriate certificate and assign it to the tunnel traffic that will be used for the Windows 2000 client. Additionally, the CES should have a group with an L2TP user and an IPSec account. The IPSec properties of the account should use a distinguished name and have digital certificates. Alternatively, IPSec can use the Allow All option for the certificate, which will automatically assign Windows 2000 users to the default group.

NOTE Windows 2000 clients can also be configured as an end point in a branch office tunnel connection.

Authentication

Authentication is one of the most important functions that the switch provides because it identifies users. The remote user attempting to dial in to the switch must be authenticated before gaining access to the corporate. The switch supports several authentications that work with group profiles. When a user attempts to get into the network, the switch references his group profile to determine encryption strength, filtering profile, quality of service (QoS) attributes, and other information for that user. Using both user and group profiles enables users to be grouped together for common attributes but still supports certain exceptions for individual users. System and resource access is provided through the user ID and not a source IP address to support mobile users and users coming from other organizations.

The CES was designed to be used in networks with an existing remote access system; therefore, it can take advantage of an existing authentication infrastructure that is used for traditional remote access. An external database can be used for centralized storage of usernames and passwords, thereby easing administration. This database can be accessed via an intermediary protocol, such as LDAP or RADIUS.

There are three authentication methods utilized by the CES: internal LDAP, external LDAP, and RADIUS.

Internal and External LDAP   LDAP is based on x.500 directory services and is defined in the RFC 1777. It is designed for directory management and serves to enable the operating system to create an authentication database. LDAP is gaining fast acceptance as the directory model for the Internet with Microsoft, Netscape, and Novell all supporting LDAP in their directory service strategies. A directory service is a central repository of user information. LDAP is used because it is standardized, optimized for lookups, uses TCP/IP, and can access many types of data. LDAP is based on directory entries that consist of entities that are a collection of attributes. Each attribute has a distinguished name (DN) that is used to refer to the attribute. An attribute also has a type and a value. Some attributes are required, and some are allowed. This is noted in an attribute called *object class*, which also determines the rules that the entry must obey. The directory is hierarchical, reflecting the organizational structure of the company employing it.

In the Contivity, the LDAP directory is the central location for user information, including groups, users, filters, hours, networks, and domains, as well as branch office configurations. LDAP is used for authorizing connections to the CES; for example, the CES uses LDAP to create groups with different attributes such as hours, idle timeouts, and authorization. A group can be one or many users that have common attributes. When a user provides authentication information to establish a tunnel, that information is checked against the LDAP database.

When more than one Contivity switch is being used, a company may choose to use an external LDAP database for centralized management. In this case the internal LDAP server will be disabled. The external LDAP database used in the network must be populated by one of the Contivity switches or it will not be able to be used directly (see Figure 16-15).

NOTE LDAP databases that are populated without using Contivity can only be used with a **RADIUS** server that supports LDAP Proxy.

GUI > Servers > LDAP

RADIUS RADIUS is a distributed security system that uses an authentication server to verify dial-up connection attributes and authenticate connections. RADIUS is commonly used for remote access authentication; in fact, it is the most commonly used

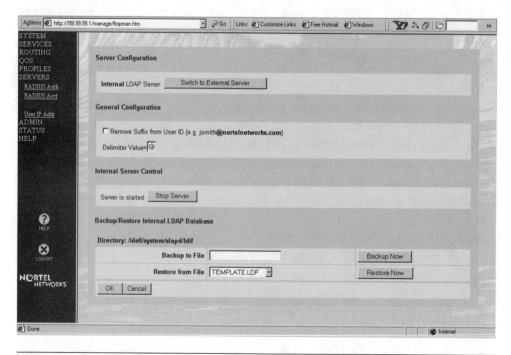

Figure 16-15 An administrator can choose to use internal or external LDAP. Note this GUI is also the location for backing up and restoring the LDAP database.

authentication method for ISPs and has wide-range vendor support as well. RADIUS is also useful in companies that already have an existing RADIUS database. RADIUS authentication lets an administrator identify remote users before giving them access to the central network.

The RADIUS application has a server and client component. The server has server software located in a central office. It has authentication access information and can also provide accounting. RADIUS accounting enables the server to collect data during a remote user's dial-in session that can later be used to determine billing charges for the client. The RADIUS client can be a router or Remote Access (RAS) server that has client software. A RADIUS client can use a username and password information that is not in the LDAP database but is forwarded to the RADIUS server for authentication. The RADIUS server will return the class attribute of the user if it is found in the RADIUS database (see Figures 16-16 and 16-17). The return list of supported LDAP attributes for the CES versions 3.5 and before are five: Class (group name of user), Framed-IP-Address (a static IP address for user in tunnel), Framed-IP-Netmask (the subnet mask to be used with static IP address assigned), Filter-ID (a filter to be applied for the tunnel session), and MS-MPPE-Keys. There are three additional attributes recognized with

PART III

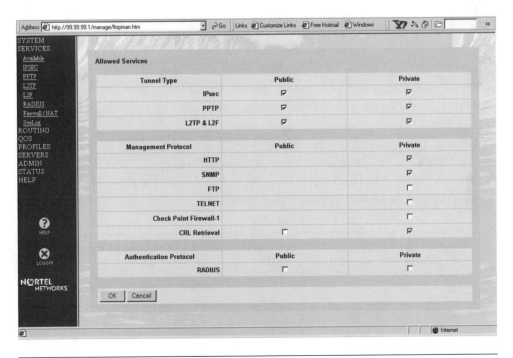

Figure 16-16   Enabling the RADIUS server

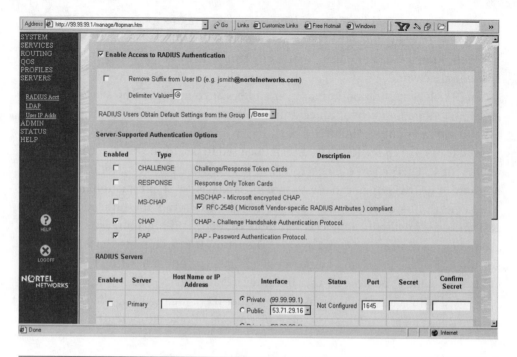

Figure 16-17 Servers > Radius Authentication

CES version 3.6 and above: DNS (domain server IP address), WINS (WINS server IP address), and NBNS (NetBIOS domain name). The CES will then take this data and apply it to the attributes of the corresponding group in the local LDAP database.

GUI > Services > Available > and then enable RADIUS on the public or private interface

GUI > Services > RADIUS Authentication > Enable the RADIUS server to be used for authentication (up to three servers)

NOTE RADIUS is provided on the private side, the public side, or through Proxy. (CES authenticates using LDAP.)

To use RADIUS, specify the RADIUS servers by supplying a host name or IP address, interface type, port number, and password. Then specify whether the RADIUS server will be accessed through the private or public interface. If the RADIUS server will be accessed through the private interface, the management IP address will be used; through the public interface an IP address must be defined.

CES can utilize RADIUS for groups using PPTP, where the user will end up being associated with the default group. RADIUS can also be used with IPSec support, in which the user gets bound to a group based on the Group ID and password. For both PPTP and IPSec, the RADIUS server may pass back a class attribute that takes precedence in determining the group to bind.

NOTE IP addresses and access hours are attributes that are extracted from the local LDAP database for the users.

RADIUS Proxy is using the Contivity as a RADIUS server. The client's section of configuration is used to specify the names of the remote public hosts that are permitted to forward requests to the switch for authentication. By entering the IP address of the remote RADIUS client, this enables the switch to receive authentication from that client. Each client can have its own unique secret for additional security. The default client is used to enable any client with the matching secret key to be able to send authentication requests to the RADIUS server.

CAUTION It is less secure and therefore less preferred to use the default client.

CES can use the LDAP and RADIUS services in conjunction with each other. By default the user ID is first checked against the LDAP database. If the user is found in the LDAP database, the user is assigned to a group and acquires that group's attributes. Next, the password is checked, and if it is correct, the switch allows a tunnel to be formed. If the user ID is not in the LDAP database, then the user and password are checked against the RADIUS database. If the user and password are correct, the switch checks to see if the RADIUS server returned a Class Attribute. The RADIUS Class Attribute is treated as an LDAP group name. If the LDAP group exists, the switch applies the attributes of this group to this user's session and forms a tunnel. If the group name does not exist, the user is given the RADIUS default group's attributes. If the user ID and password are incorrect, the switch rejects the user request.

Contivity Placement

The Contivity is designed to be set into an existing network with only a minimal amount of reconfiguration to the network. It can use existing services like RADIUS or provide its own authentication. The CES can be placed behind the router or firewall or provide a single box solution. In fact, there are many ways to set up CES access for users.

The first configuration (see Figure 16-18) is when the Contivity switch is connected to the public network in parallel with the router and firewall that provides Internet access. This is the simplest configuration and doesn't require any additional router configuration. Internet traffic will flow through the router and firewall as before, and secure tunnel traffic will travel through the CES. This configuration also provides a redundant connection to the Internet should the router go down and provides the best possible performance for CES connections that do not have any additional latency because of the router or firewall. This configuration is also secure as long as the CES is configured to properly enable and disable access to the appropriate network sites.

A second configuration (see Figure 16-19) has the CES placed behind the router that provides the Internet access for the company. This is used in situations where companies need to maintain public access networks. This configuration does not require reconfiguration of the router either, but it does add on latency for tunnel traffic by forcing it to go through the router to reach the CES. This setup also has CES traffic bypassing the firewall, making it especially critical to ensure that the CES is set up with the proper security and filters.

In the third configuration (see Figure 16-20), the CES is placed behind both the router and the firewall. This solves the issue of CES traffic bypassing the firewall but

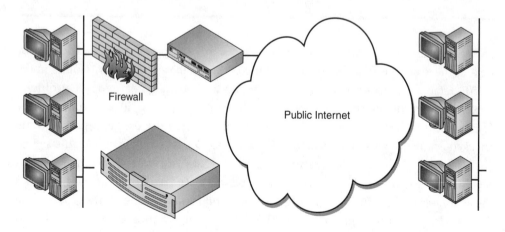

Figure 16-18   Placing the Contivity switch in parallel with the router

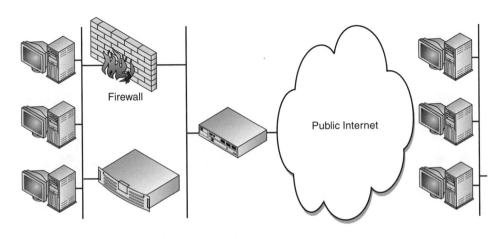

Figure 16-19 Placing the Contivity switch behind the router

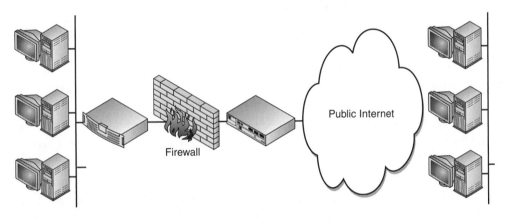

Figure 16-20 Placing the Contivity switch behind the router and the firewall

now adds the firewall as another latency issue and possible bottleneck. Additionally, the firewall will need to be reconfigured for this to work.

NOTE Firewalls must enable UDP source/destination port 500 for ISAKMP/IPSec key management messages to pass through and protocols 50 (ESP) and 51 (AH) for user data to pass through.

The final configuration (see Figure 16-21) shows the CES being used as an all-in-one solution without the need for an additional firewall to exist in the network.

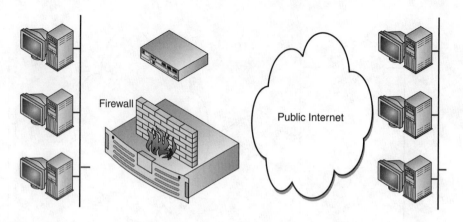

Figure 16-21   Using the Contivity in the network as the firewall

The Serial Menu and CLI

The serial menu and CLI enable users to access and configure a CES through a serial port or Telnet session (see Figure 16-22). The serial menu through the local console port is the only way to configure a CES until an IP address is set up. CLI access through the console port is usually accomplished with a hyperterminal type of program. Settings for the serial (Com) port for the hyperterminal session should be VT-100, 9600 bps, 8 data bits, no parity, and 1 stop bit. The serial connection gives a menu that enables interface configuration, administrative account changes, the capability to create a user control tunnel and restrict management to a tunnel only, to enable or disable HTTP Management, and to enter the CLI submenu. Furthermore, the serial menu and CLI enable for the configuration of shutdown, system boot options, and the configuration of the serial port, as well as restoring the CES to factory defaults. When leaving the serial menu or CLI, it is important to save and invoke the changes.

NOTE   Only CLI can be used to reset a switch to factory default.

NOTE   The serial menu in earlier versions of the software had less options.

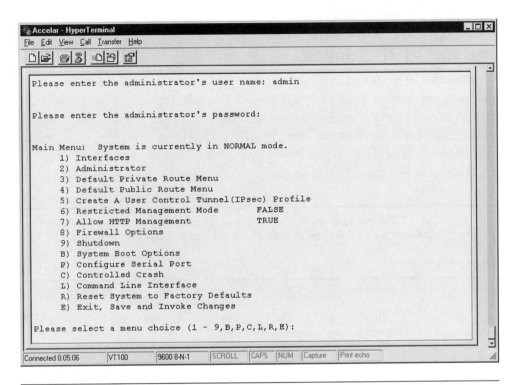

Figure 16-22   The serial menu

Logging into the CES

To log into the CES as the administrator, the default login is admin with a password of setup. There are three command modes available in the CLI submenu. They are user exec mode, privileged exec mode, and global configuration mode.

The user exec mode is the default command mode and the prompt says CES. It can be reached from a standard Telnet session or by typing l from the main menu. It is used to perform pings, show commands, and trace the route to a destination.

The privileged exec mode has the prompt CES#. It can be reached by typing **enable** at the user exec prompt with the administrator's password. It is the mode used to run privileged commands, like kill, reload, and disable/enable.

The global configuration mode with the prompt of CES(config)# is reached by typing **configure terminal**. It can be used to stop the HTTP server, set audible alarms, set the console mode, create control tunnels, use the bulk load command, and create basic SNMP server configuration.

Configuring the CES with the Initial IP Address

Configuration of the initial IP address can be done from a console connection directly attached to the switch. An IP address is necessary for all advanced configuration of the switch. The CLI can be used to create IP addresses for the private and public IP addresses. At minimum a management IP address should be created that can then be used to manage and configure the switch. The management IP address must be in the same subnet as the internal LAN address.

NOTE   The management IP address is a logical address that shares the physical Ethernet port on the system board with the internal LAN private IP address.

If the switch has an address previously configured, it must be zeroed out, and the switch must be restarted before replacing the address.

NOTE   Resetting the switch to factory default does not remove IP addresses configured on the switch. These addresses must be zeroed out first.

It is also possible to assign an IP address to a CES using the IP address configuration utility called *extnetip.exe* (see Figure 16-23).

NOTE   In prior releases this utility was called *baynetip.exe*.

To use the extranetip.exe utility, the workstation must be on the same LAN as the internal LAN interface of the Contivity switch. This utility will go out and search for Contivity switches that have no IP address configured and upon finding one present the administrator with the switch serial number, allowing the switch to be assigned an

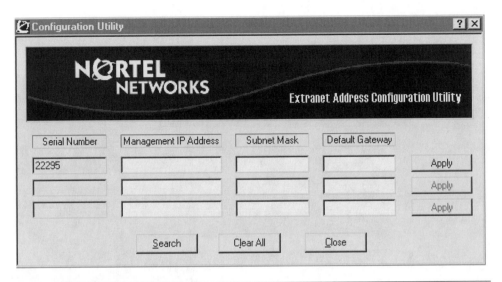

Figure 16-23   Extranet Configuration Utility

IP address. The administrator can then assign an IP address for managing the switch, a subnet mask, and a default gateway.

NOTE   Once a Contivity switch has been assigned an IP address, this utility cannot be used to find it on the LAN. If the IP address of a switch is unknown, it is necessary to connect a serial cable to the switch and use CLI to find the IP address.

Web-Based Management

The switch has an HTTP server that supports web-based management of a single device using a standard browser (Internet Explorer or Netscape). Most of the Contivity configuration is done through the web-based manager. The switch has a Quick Start configuration option to enable an administrator to set up a default configuration with a single management screen in a few minutes. This enables for quick set up of tunnels and the verification of their operation. The next stage of configuration is the *guided configuration*. This option leads an administrator through an entire configuration for the switch with section introductions and online Help (see Figure 16-24).

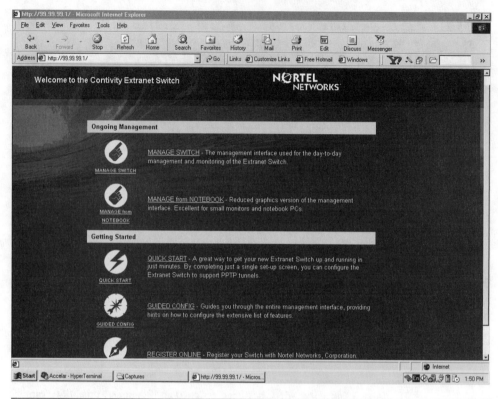

Figure 16-24   Opening a connection to the CES using HTTP

Optivity VPN Manager

A single tool can be used to manage multiple Contivity switches. This utility is Java based and runs on Solaris, NT, HP-UX, and AIX platforms. It includes an add-on for Optivity Network Configuration System (NCS). Optivity also enables bulk configuration and backup capabilities.

II 100/400 Configuration and Management

Configuration for the former II switches differs from the standard Contivity management. To configure the II 100 or II 400 using a TCP/IP connection, the administrator must install the install.exe program on a workstation. Afterwards, the administrator can use the iisetup.exe program to configure the II 100/400 with a private IP address, registration information, name and password for the switch, DNS information, and a public address for the switch.

NOTE   When using a dual Ethernet configuration for the II 100/400, the IP address of a router must be configured.

CES Management

Most management of the Contivity switch is done through web-based management. There are many important steps to managing the CES to ensure network security and proper operability.

Configuring the Administrator Account

The administrator account is configured by default as was mentioned before (see Figure 16-25). To change the default configuration, the Administrator screen enables changes to the user ID and password. This can also be accomplished using CLI.

GUI > ADMIN >Administrator

NOTE   The administrator user ID and password is saved in Flash. Changes to this screen only take effect upon reboot. Do not lose or forget the password once the switch has been configured. Losing or forgetting the password requires returning the switch to Nortel Networks for reconfiguration to default settings. All settings and backups are lost. There is no way to access the system without the primary administrator password.

Safe Mode Configuration

The switch can be booted in one of the two system modes: safe mode or normal mode (see Figure 16-26). Each mode has its own software image, configuration files, and LDAP database. To enable safe mode in the GUI, go to

GUI > System > Settings—changes only take effect after a reboot

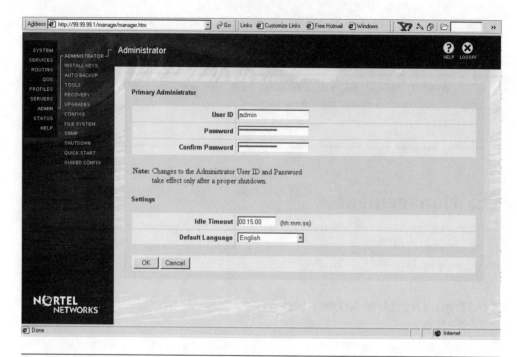

Figure 16-25 Using the HTTP configuration utility to change the administrator account information

NOTE The serial port can also be configured here.

A system booted in safe mode is only allowed to accept secure management tunnel establishment. After the secured management tunnel is established, Telnet, HTTP, and FTP traffic are allowed to come into the switch; no other VPN traffic is enabled through the secured management tunnel or the switch. A configuration must be chosen in **GUI** > Admin > Configs for safe mode configuration once safe mode is enabled.

In normal mode, the system operates with the normal software and configuration and transports both VPN traffic and management traffic.

Upgrading the CES

To upgrade the firmware for an II 100 or 400, the administrator runs the iisetup.exe program and chooses the level of software to upgrade or downgrade the switch.

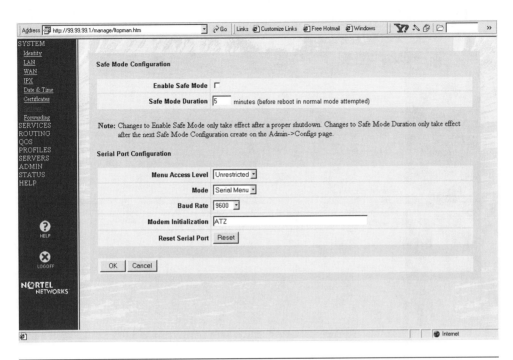

Figure 16-26   System settings for safe mode and serial port configuration

To upgrade a standard CES, the administrator uses an FTP server to load the code onto the Contivity (see Figure 16-27). It will be easier to do the upgrade if the folder containing the Contivity code is located directly in the default FTP directory.

> **NOTE**   Not every FTP server works properly with the CES. The Windows 95 FTP server that is available with the Personal Web server is one of the FTP servers that is recommended.

The upgrade process is performed from the web browser.

GUI > ADMIN > Upgrades

To upgrade, first enter the IP address of the PC that is serving as the FTP server. As long as the folder with the Contivity code is located in the default FTP directory, no path will be necessary. It will be necessary to specify the version for the upgrade, which should be the name of the folder containing the Contivity code on the FTP server. The administrator will need to add a username and password that is valid on the FTP server

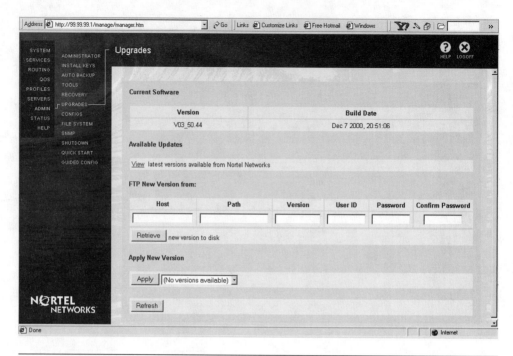

Figure 16-27   Administrator upgrades

for downloading the code. Once all the parameters are filled in, the administrator will use the Retrieve button to begin the upgrade. The browser will prompt the user about the fact that upgrading takes time, and the user will have to agree to continue the upgrade process.

When the new version is loaded, it will be available on the pull-down menu as an option. Select the correct version that was uploaded from the FTP server and choose Apply. The process of applying the new software takes a few minutes after which the switch reboots.

NOTE   If the version of code was not downloaded correctly from the FTP server, it will appear as a choice in the Software Apply Level menu; however, the administrator will get an error message after choosing apply. This prevents the switch from applying incomplete or incorrect software loads.

A maximum of four versions of code is supported on the Contivity VPN switch system disk. If four versions exist in the Web menu, then one must be deleted from the file system before the switch will be able to accept an FTP download of another release.

NOTE Upgrading switch software cannot be done through a branch office tunnel that is using dynamic NAT.

File System

Navigating through the switch file system is available in the HTTP configuration tool (see Figure 16-28).

GUI > Admin > File System

The administrator then selects the appropriate hard drive and clicks Display to see the contents of the hard drive.

This file system tool lists the devices (drives) and directories. This provides flexibility in viewing details of a file or directory, and it enables the deletion of unnecessary files or versions of the operating system that may no longer be necessary. This tool is very

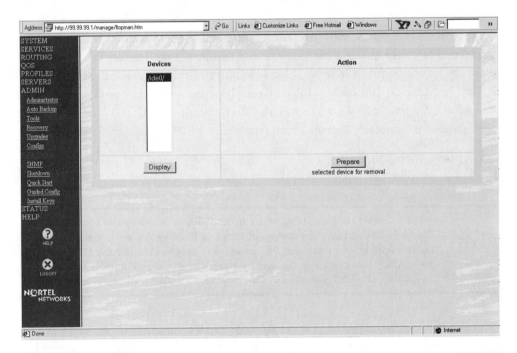

Figure 16-28 Viewing the file system for the CES

useful for deleting versions of the operating system in cases where the files did not download properly.

Contivity Backup and Recovery Process

Backup of the CES is essential for recovery from a failure. Backups should be done to an FTP server at regular intervals to ensure that essential configurations are not lost if something happens to the switch or the network.

It is possible to configure the II 100/400 to automatically back up by using the iisetup.exe.

GUI > File > Backup to Disk

Automatic Backup of the Contivity Switch

The switch checks at regular intervals to see whether system file changes have been made. When there are changes, they are written to each of the backup servers. All of the system files are backed up the first time; thereafter, only the files that have changed are backed up. Backups are performed using the File Transfer Protocol (FTP). Files are transferred from the switch's hard disk to the designated path under the default FTP directory on the backup file server. The administrator must provide the backup host servers' IP address, path, backup interval, user ID, password, and password confirmation on the Automatic Backup screen. This information is stored in flash memory and appears on the Automatic Backup screen (see Figure 16-29).

GUI >Admin > Auto Backup

NOTE Backing up the configuration of the CES here backs up the configuration files only. This includes the backup of interface IP addresses and subnet masks, backup host IP addresses, and DNS names, but does not include the LDAP database, which contains the group and user profiles, filters, and more. It is essential to back up the LDAP database in GUI > Servers > LDAP (refer to Figure 16-15).

The switch enables the administrator to configure regular intervals when the system files are saved to designated host backup file servers. Up to three backup fileservers can

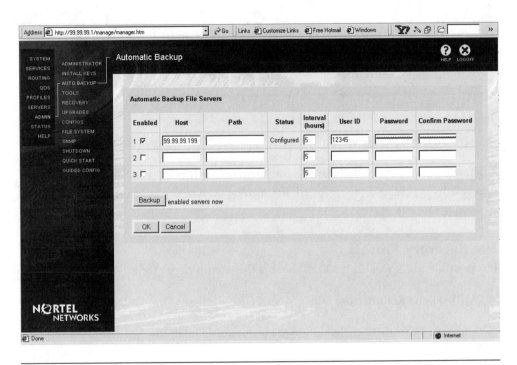

Figure 16-29　Auto backup

be designated. The same backup server can be used for multiple switches. Each switch creates a unique directory based on its serial number by default backup the backup is created as C:/software/backup/v101/serial number, with the serial number being used to uniquely identify each switch's backup data. The serial number will then be used to identify backup configurations from multiple switches that are saved on the same backup server.

The process can be monitored through the **GUI** > Status >Event Log screen. The event log will show an entry indicating the FTP backup and update complete. The **GUI** > Status > Health Check screens can also be used to show the time and date the last backup was completed.

The Recovery Diskette

It is not enough to merely back up a CES. It is also essential to create a recovery disk. Without a recovery disk the CES cannot be restored in the event of a major system failure. A recovery disk can be made even after a failure, providing the client has access to another CES of the same hardware and preferably software level.

NOTE In most cases the recovery disk from an identical switch will work even if the software level is different as long as the dead switch is not a much older software revision than the switch being used to create the recovery disk.

GUI >ADMIN > Recovery

The Recovery screen enables an administrator to format a diskette that is in the floppy drive, or create a recovery disk that can be used in the event of a hard disk crash (see Figure 16-30).

The Recovery Process

It is possible to recover an II 100/400 using the iisetup.exe as well.

GUI > File > Restore from Disk

To recover a Contivity switch, place the restore diskette in the switch and power it on.

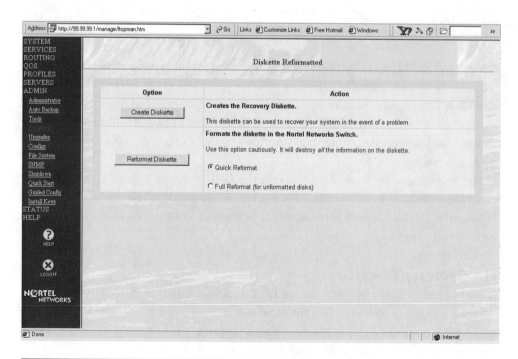

Figure 16-30 Formatting and creating a recovery floppy diskette

> **NOTE** Some models of the Contivity switches need to have the front cover removed to gain access to the diskette drive.

The recovery diskette supplies the switch with a minimal configuration utility that enables the administrator to view the switch from a web browser and perform some system recovery options. All recovery utilities that are available are being read from the diskette (see Figure 16-31).

> **NOTE** Booting to the recovery diskette is very slow as is using the web browser throughout the recovery process because the recovery process is wholly dependent on reading information from a diskette.

The recovery menu options include the capability to restore a factory configuration.

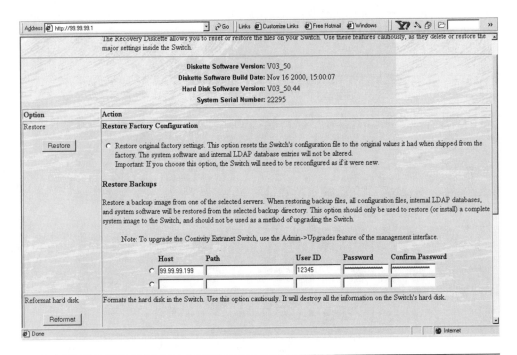

Figure 16-31 Recovery menu options of a switch booted with the recovery diskette

NOTE Selecting the option to restore the diskette to factory configuration requires rebuilding the entire switch configuration again from scratch.

Alternatively, an administrator may choose to reformat the switch's hard drive. This may be necessary in the event of a major system crash.

CAUTION Selecting the reformat option completely wipes out anything that was stored on the hard disk.

The recovery diskette may also be used to restore the switch from a backup (by supplying the backup location's FTP address and directory name) or to replace the current operating system that failed with a new factory default software image and file system. To use these options the administrator should specify the name or address and path of the network file server onto which the software from the Nortel Networks CD has been installed (see Figure 16-32).

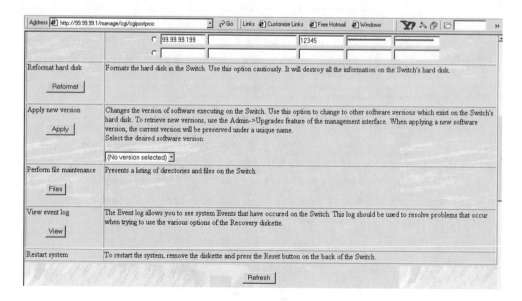

Figure 16-32 Other options for the recovery process include applying a new version of the operating system and performing file maintenance.

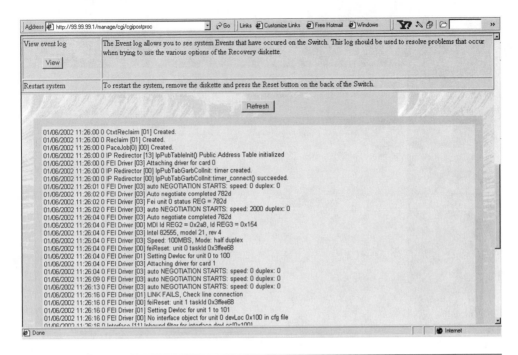

Figure 16-33 Viewing the recovery event log

Finally, the recovery process enables the administrator to view the event log (see Figure 16-33).

CES Configuration

It is important to configure the extranet switch so that it can function in the network. The CES switch is not ready to be used until interfaces, user accounts, groups, and tunnels are configured.

Creating IP Addresses for Private and Public Interfaces

It is important to define all the IP addresses for each interface that will be used in the CES. The HTTP manager can be used to configure LAN interfaces as well as WAN interfaces, depending on what is supported on the switch (see Figure 16-34).

GUI > System > LAN (or WAN) > Click the interface > Add IP

Figure 16-34 Adding interfaces to the Contivity switch using the HTTP utility

NOTE The LAN interface *must* be on the same network (same network mask) as the management interface because they share a single physical Ethernet port.

Groups

GUI > Profiles > Groups > Choose the parent group > Add

Group names can be up to 64 characters long. Groups can also contain subgroups that inherit the attributes of the parent groups (see Figure 16-35).

Figure 16-35 shows the creation of a group named Mygroup that is a member of the VPNusers parent group. This group could have been part of the Base group directly, but because it is part of the VPNusers group, it will gain permissions from that parent group (see Figure 16-36).

The Edit option enables the administrator to review the group information, and the Configure option enables the administrator to change attributes of the group. Attrib-

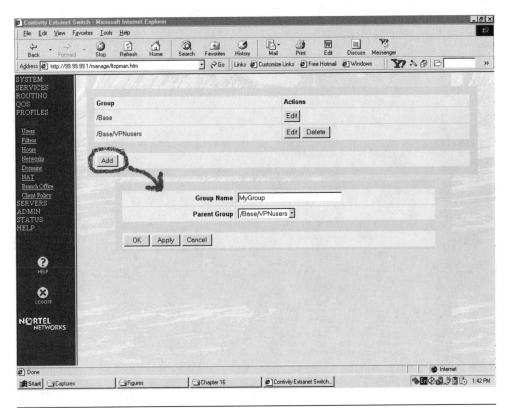

Figure 16-35   Creating subgroups

utes of a group that can be changed include connectivity and tunneling information. A group's unique attributes must be explicitly configured to override inheritance.

> **NOTE**   Because connectivity is a feature of group-level permissions, all tunnels that are created based on a common group will share connectivity parameters.

Users

Users are added to groups. First display the users in a current group by choosing the group by going to **GUI** > Profiles > Users > Group screen and clicking the Display tab. Then add a user by going to **GUI** > Profiles > Users > Add user (see Figure 16-37).

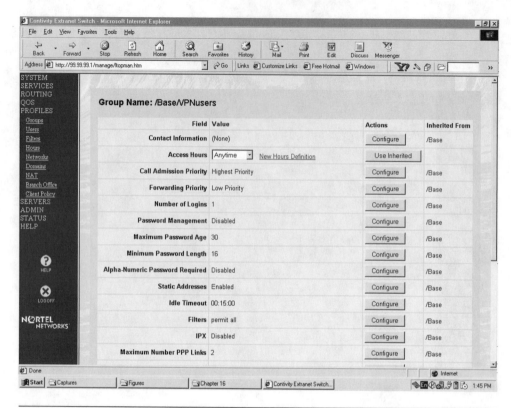

Figure 16-36 Configuring explicit permissions for a group's (VPNusers) connectivity and specifically their access hours

Users need a first name and last name, as well as a user ID and password. In Figure 16-37, the user Mordy Gholian has an IPSec user ID of Mgholian. If an administrator wants to force a user to have a specific IP address, that IP address can be assigned here in the user properties. Figure 16-37 shows that user Mordy has been assigned the IP address of 10.6.6.104. A static address assigned for a user takes precedence over any other address assignment and insures that a user can only log on once because only that address is available to him.

Users can be assigned administrative permissions in the Users screen. Users can also belong to multiple groups but require a different user ID and password for each group membership.

Tunnels

Tunneling, as we said before, is the technology that enables the underlying Internet structure to be hidden from the user and VPN application. Tunneling uses PPTP, L2TP,

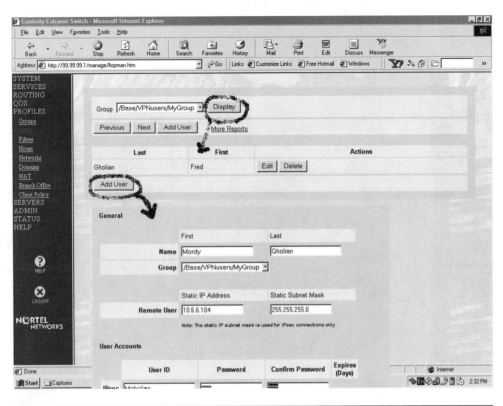

Figure 16-37 Adding a user to the Base\VPNusers\Mygroup group

L2F, and IPSec for security. Tunneling protocols enable the encapsulation of other protocol traffic inside their packets.

To use tunnels, they must be enabled on the CES (see Figure 16-38).

GUI > System > Forwarding

All tunneling protocols are enabled on the public and private networks by default. Because data in tunnels is encrypted, the default setting guarantees that all interactions with the switch are private. To prevent tunnel connections of a particular type (for all users, including administrators), simply disable the tunnel type.

To use IPSec as the only public tunneling protocol, disable the public selection for PPTP, L2TP, and L2F. By leaving IPSec, PPTP, L2TP, and L2F enabled on the private side, tunneled connections can be established to the switch using any of the tunnel types from within the corporate network.

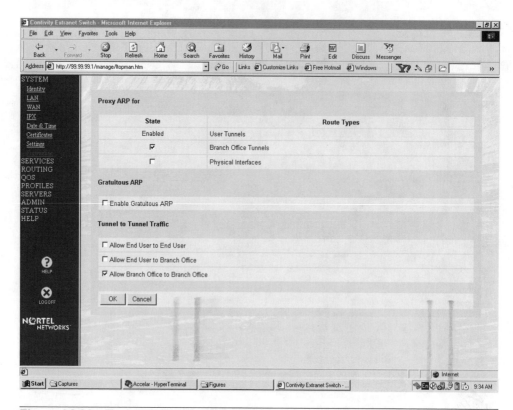

Figure 16-38   Tunnel-to-tunnel traffic is disabled by default. This administrator has enabled branch office tunnels.

User Tunnels   User tunnels are implemented by enabling user tunnels to the switch (refer to Figure 16-38), choosing switch protocols, creating a user, and adding the user to a group that has tunneling permissions.

Branch Office Tunnels   Branch office tunnels are used to create a secure intranet using the Internet and WAN connectivity to remote offices. The branch office feature is used to configure a secure tunnel connection between two private networks. Typically, one private network is behind a locally configured switch, while the other is behind a remote switch. Branch office tunnels are created on demand and are routed between branches of a corporation as necessary. Branch office configuration supports the configuration of accessible subnetworks behind each switch. The configuration also contains the information that is necessary to set up the connection, such as the switch's IP addresses, encryption types, and authentication methods. Local policy restrictions, such as access hours, filter sets, and call admission priorities, can be applied to limit connectivity into local subnetworks. When an administrator configures a branch office, he or she can specify the attributes of the switches that are participating in the connection and set up network parameters for the connection, such as addresses and the tunnel type.

A branch office connection is associated with a group. The branch office connection then inherits the attributes of that group. One can associate multiple branch office connections with the same group, saving setup time and increasing management efficiency. To create branch office tunnels, use the HTTP utility (see Figure 16-39).

GUI > Profiles > Branch offices > Choose group to be associated with the tunnel > Define Connection > New branch office tunnel

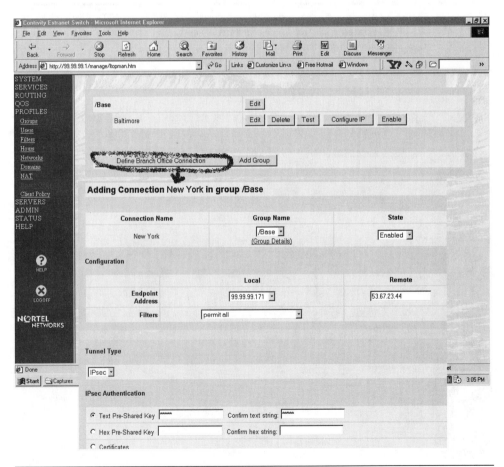

Figure 16-39   Adding the New York branch office connection

NOTE Access hours, bandwidth policies, RIP and OSPF, IPSec encryption, and key exchange are all part of group policies that affect the branch office connection.

Define local end points and remote end points for the tunnel (see Figure 16-40). Additionally, define the filter type, authentication, and if certificates will be used or not. If using IPSec or L2TP, make sure to define the key.

To define a local end point for a tunnel, the subnet must first be defined under **GUI** > Profiles > Networks.

NOTE End points, filters, accessible networks, NAT, PPTP, and L2TP properties are all associated with the specific branch office tunnel connection, not a condition of group policies (see Figure 16-41).

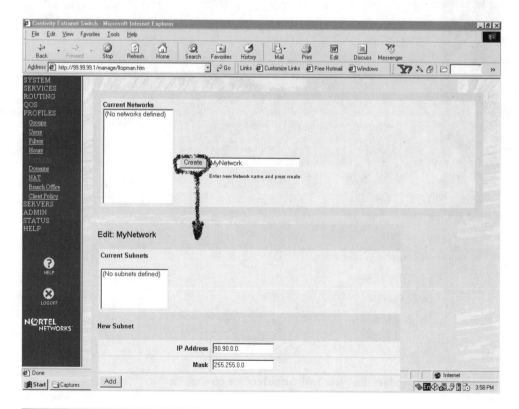

Figure 16-40 Creating the networks for the local end points of a tunnel

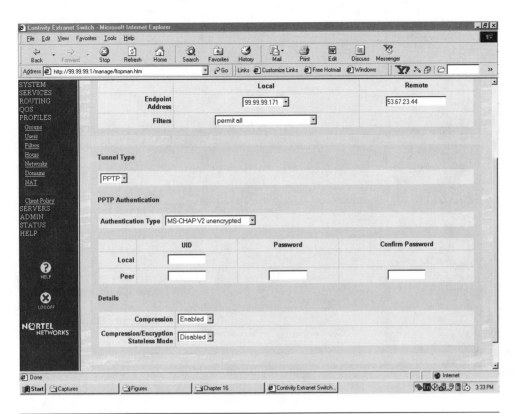

Figure 16-41 Configuring PPTP for branch office tunnels

Routing must be defined for a branch office tunnel. Static, RIP, or OSPF are all available. If static routing is chosen, a local IP subnet must be defined as well as a remote network. Choose whether NAT will be preformed or not. To review IP setup and authentication options, choose Configure IP for the branch office tunnel (see Figure 16-42).

Once the tunnel is defined on both the local and remote ends, it can be tested using the Test tab in the **GUI** > Profiles > Branch Office screen (see Figure 16-43). The event log can be cleared prior to testing the tunnel connection and then examined after the test is run.

IPSec Tunneling Between the II 100/400 and the CES
To configure IPSec tunneling between the II 100/400 and the CES, the II 100/400 must be running the software code level 7.0 or higher. The Contivity switch must be running 2.50 or higher software. Compression is not supported for tunneling between the two switches, and neither is RIP. When setting up the branch office connection on the CES, disable compression and create a static routing entry for the branch office tunnel.

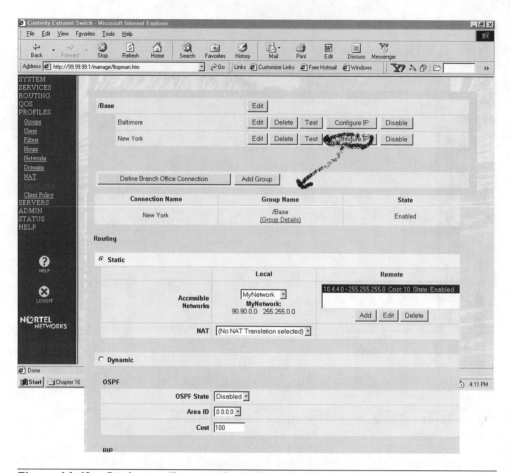

Figure 16-42   Configuring IP routing for the branch office tunnel

NOTE   Branch office tunnels are also known as the *main mode* for the II 100/400 because both end points for the tunnel are known and defined.

On the II 100/400 use the iisetup.exe and add the IPSec support and tunnel. This configuration does not support 40-bit encryption and certificates. DES is used for negotiating the tunnels between the switches.

Control Tunnels   Control tunnels are special tunnels that enable the secure management of a Contivity VPN switch over the Internet. They are created primarily for

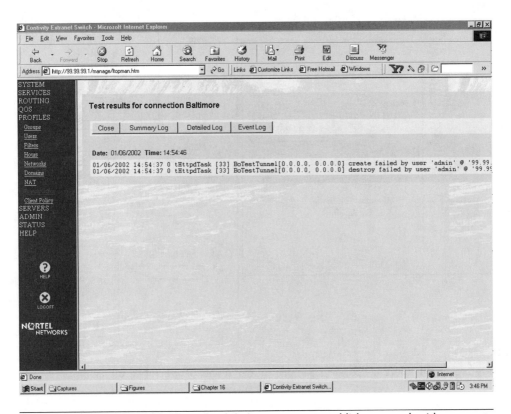

Figure 16-43   Viewing the log of a failed attempt to establish a tunnel with a remote branch office

enabling remote management while providing assurance of intranet data integrity. Control tunnels enable configuring secure tunnels to any switch for management anywhere in the world through an encrypted tunnel to a customer's switch. Through that tunnel an administrator can perform all the necessary management tasks, such as HTTP, FTP, SNMP, and Telnet. DHCP, RADIUS, and DNS servers can be accessed from the switch through the control tunnel. Control tunnels also guarantee that no data from the network behind that customer's switch is accessible through the control tunnel for access by the people on the network that are managing the switch. The traffic inside the tunnels is limited to the switch's management IP address only, which is unique to control tunnels.

There are two types of control tunnels: a branch office control tunnel and a user control tunnel. Both tunnel types enable the establishment of a secure IPSec tunnel to a system for management.

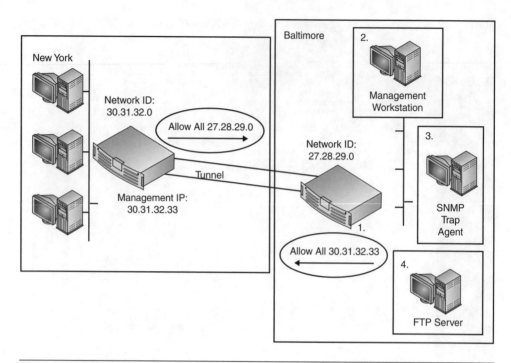

Figure 16-44   Setting up a management control tunnel between NY and Baltimore

On one end of the control tunnel (the switch under management), access is always restricted to the management address only. On the management side of the tunnel more network IP addresses should be accessible to the managed side.

Access to the New York network is limited to the NY Contivity switch only (Figure 16-44). The Baltimore end of the tunnel, in contrast, has allowed access to its entire private network. This enables multiple systems in the Baltimore Network Operations Center (NOC) to communicate with the management address only of the New York switch, or for the New York switch to use remote servers (FTP, DHCP, RADIUS, and DNS servers) on the New York private network.

Branch Office/Management Control Tunnels   Branch office control tunnels enable anyone on the configured network to communicate with a CES being managed. This configuration supports switch communication with various systems within a company's NOC or corporate headquarters. Branch office tunnels are configurable through the GUI and CLI (see Figure 16-45).

> **GUI** > Profiles > Branch offices > Define Branch Office Connection (brings up the
> screen to create a branch office) > Check the Control Tunnel box

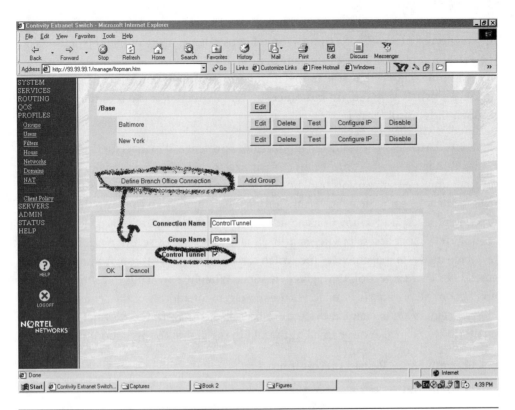

Figure 16-45 Creating a control tunnel with the HTTP manager

The tunnel should be set up like a regular tunnel except extra care should be taken to carefully select which IP network the service provider needs to have access to.

NOTE Make control tunnels as restrictive as possible.

User Control Tunnel User control tunnels enable the Contivity Extranet Access Client to communicate with a switch that is being managed. A user control tunnel is configured so that a remote user can establish a control tunnel when using the IPSec client. These are special tunnels specifically for remote management. This enables network management personnel from anywhere in the world to access the management tasks. A user control tunnel is configurable through the CLI or the serial menu.

In the Serial menu, Option 5: Create a User Control Tunnel (IPSec) Profile enables the creation of a user ID for a control tunnel. A username, password, and IP address are required for the creation of a user control tunnel.

An administrator can use the tunnel features to minimally configure the control tunnel on the switch, ship it to the customer site, and then set up the rest of the parameters through the control tunnel.

Restricted Mode   The restricted mode feature prevents all management of the switch except through a secure control tunnel. Using restricted mode enables the administrator to enforce tighter controls on who can manage the switch. This limits the scope of management to someone who has the proper credentials both to set up the tunnel (if it is an end user) and to log in as an administrator (administrative access privileges). Having the proper access privileges in itself acts as a level of security. Additionally, in restricted mode, management of the switch can only take place through a tunnel, which guarantees data protection through encryption. When the switch is in restricted mode, no user on the private side can access the management address of the switch.

Restricted mode is enabled through the serial menu Option 6: Restricted Management Mode. It can also be enabled in the CLI in the global configuration mode.

CLI command: Restrict on confirm

CLI command: Restrict off confirm

CLI command: Restrict show

In restricted mode, an administrator can perform the key management functions through the control tunnel, including HTTP, FTP, SNMP, and Telnet. All other attempts to perform these actions outside of the control tunnel will fail.

NOTE   The administrator cannot place the switch into restricted mode unless there is an active control tunnel. This ensures there is a mechanism to manage the switch in restricted mode.

Nailed-up Control Tunnels   Typically, branch office tunnels are brought up only when network traffic is destined to go through it. However, if an administrator wants the tunnel up all of the time, the tunnel can be nailed up. This configuration enables some control tunnels to be up even when there is no user traffic traversing the control tunnel; however, for the tunnel to remain up, there must be some traffic over the tunnel. The best way to nail up a tunnel is to create a script that will ping the management interface from the management workstation at appropriate intervals. This will maintain the up state of the control tunnel.

Aggressive Mode

Aggressive mode enables the Contivity to accept tunnel traffic from an unknown device, in this case any IP address that the II may have received via DHCP. This mode is generally used in the CES for accepting tunnel requests from clients that can have any IP address as assigned to them by their ISP. To configure aggressive mode between the II and the Contivity, the CES must be configured with software level 2.6 or higher and II version 7.10 or higher. In this configuration the II will act like a non-Contivity client with the public interface set for DHCP. Configure the II 100/400 using iisetup.exe and create a non-IPSec tunnel that is set for aggressive mode. Additionally, ensure that IP Forwarding is set for the II. The CES that will tunnel with the II must be set up with a tunnel that uses a group that accepts non-Contivity clients using DHCP and is configured for split tunneling (see Figure 16-61).

Saving the System Configuration

Saving the current system configuration or deleting existing system configuration files is done through the **GUI** > Admin > Config screen. An administrator can also use this screen to select one of the previously named configurations and restore it as the current configuration (see Figure 16-46).

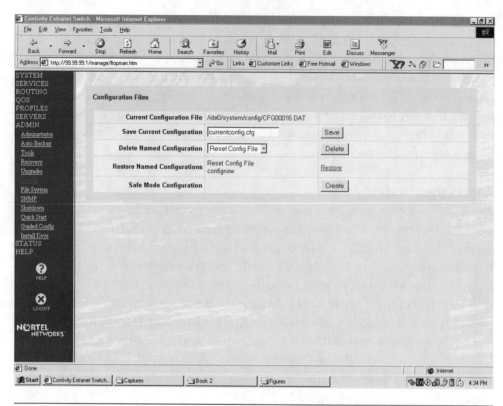

Figure 16-46   Saving the configuration file as currentconfig.cfg

Network Address Translation (NAT)

NAT was discussed extensively in Chapter 4. To review, NAT is the translation of one network IP address that is used within a LAN to a different IP address that is used outside the LAN. NAT is a result of huge growth in Internet usage, more demand of IPv4 address space, and always-on technologies, all of which resulted in companies being unable to get a large block of consecutive registered addresses. NAT enables a system to be identified by one address on its own network, yet be identified by a totally different address to systems on a different network. NAT is also used to increase security, as private addresses schemes using NAT cannot receive an incoming IP connection from the outside network unless it is specifically allowed. NAT is available for branch office connections as well and enables branch office connections to eliminate problems with overlapping addresses on both sides of the connection and to enable the hiding of LAN addresses.

As mentioned in Chapter 3, there are three types of NAT available. They are static, port, and pooled NAT. They are used to hide private network IP addresses and eliminate issues over overlapping addresses in branch office connections. NAT works with IP header modifications, changing the source address for outbound packets and the destination address for inbound packets as well as the IP checksum (see Figure 16-47).

GUI > Profiles > NAT > Create > Provide a name > Add Rule

Static NAT (as seen in Figure 16-47) uses a defined scope of numbers for the internal addresses and the exact number of external addresses, calculated based on the external start address. Remember from Chapter 3 that there is a one-to-one correlation between

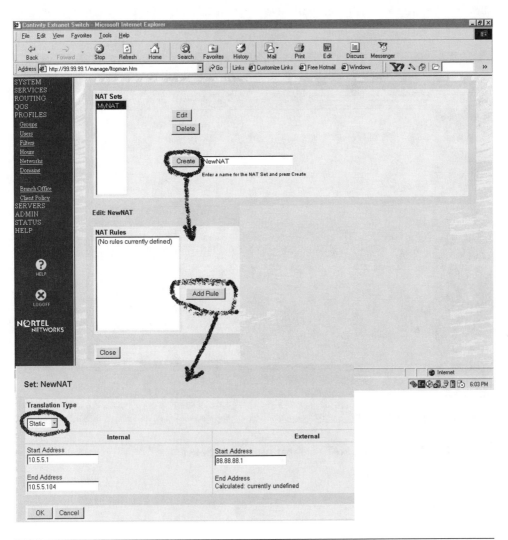

Figure 16-47   Creating a new NAT set using static NAT

internal addresses and external addresses. This is the only type of NAT that enables bi-directional communication.

Pooled NAT uses a defined range of internal addresses as well as external addresses. As seen in Figure 16-48, there can be fewer external addresses than internal addresses. This limits the number of users that are able to get an external address at the same time and connect to external resources. Additionally, communication is only unidirectional; users internally can initiate sessions with external resources, but external workstations cannot initiate sessions with internal servers.

Port NAT uses a defined range of internal addresses with a single external address, as shown in Figure 16-49. All users will have the same address for external communication

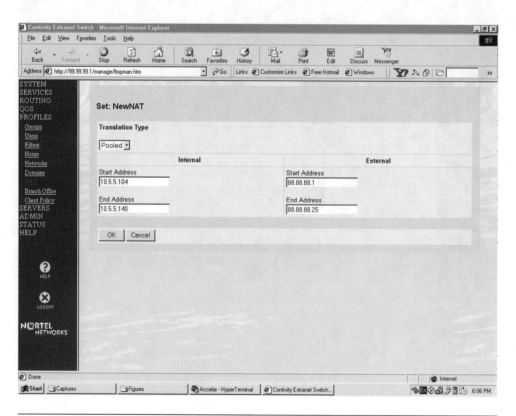

Figure 16-48   Creating a NAT rule that uses pooled NAT

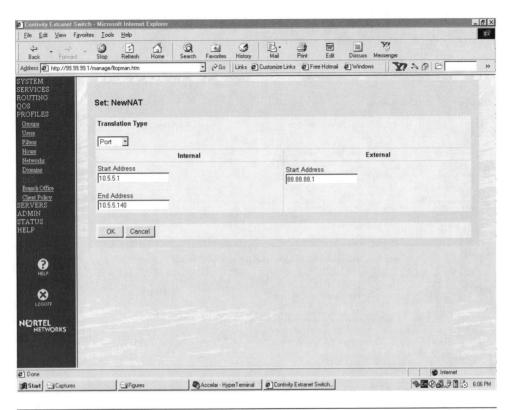

Figure 16-49 Creating a NAT rule that uses port NAT

mapped to a different port on the NAT server. This type of NAT also only enables unidirectional communication initiated from the internal network to external resources.

GUI > Service > Firewall/NAT > Interface NAT > Choose a NAT set

NOTE NAT requires a Contivity firewall to be enabled (Figure 16-50).

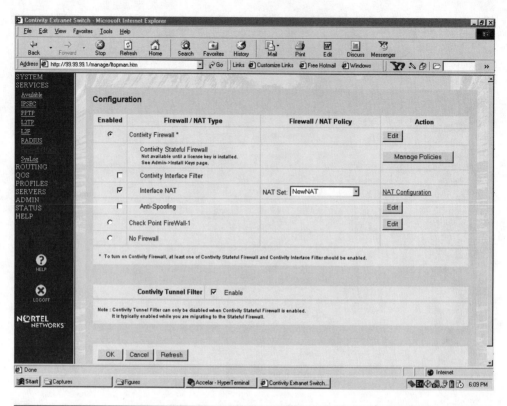

Figure 16-50 Enabling NAT and using the NAT set NewNAT created in Figure 16-47

System Monitoring

System monitoring provides feedback regarding the status of the system, such as the number of active sessions and the system resources in use.

Health Check

The Health Check screen on the switch provides an overall summary of the current state of the switch's hardware and software components (see Figure 16-51).

> **GUI** > Status > Health Check

Colored status indicators on the Health Check screen help to evaluate individual component status. Associated hyperlinks enable the administrator to go to screens for corrective action (see Figure 16-52).

> **GUI** > Health Check > Memory Usage > Hyperlink

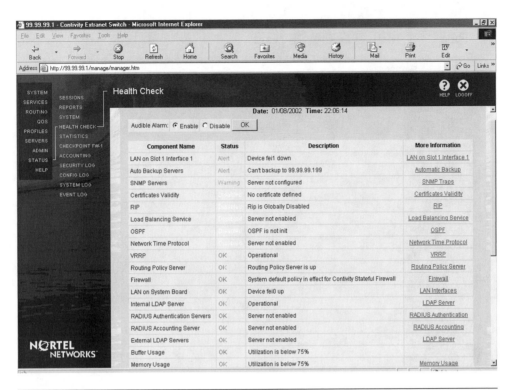

Figure 16-51   The Health Check screen on the CES

Statistics

The statistics available for viewing on the CES include Interfaces, Hardware, Resources, Network, Routing, Admin, and Security (see Figure 16-53). Each category contains many tabs for viewing additional information. Most of the information is specifically designed for Nortel Networks customer support personnel to assist them in diagnosing problems. Some screens, however, such as the LAN Counters, Interfaces, and the WAN Status, can provide useful traffic information.

GUI > Status > Statistics

As shown in Figure 16-53, the Statistics Resources Memory screen shows how the switch allocates memory, including the current free and allocated memory and the cumulative memory.

Status Report

The Status Report screen enables the viewing of system and performance data in text or graphical format. It can be used to generate current or historical graphs of valuable

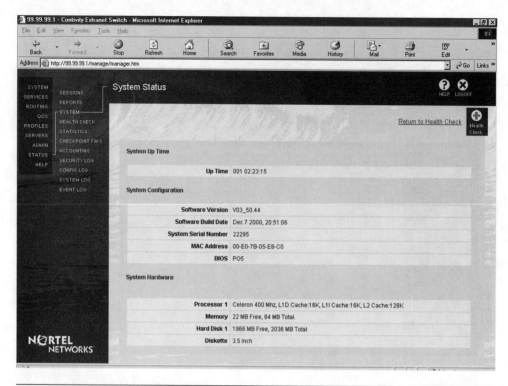

Figure 16-52 Viewing this system information can also be done through the **GUI** > Status > System menu option.

system data. The Reports feature provides a comprehensive screen or downloadable reports on user activity. The following report types are available:

- **Administrators** Lists users with administrator privileges.

- **Users** Lists users and the system database groups that they are in.

- **System** Lists basic system information.

- **Sessions** Lists session information.

- **Failed authorization** Lists failed authorization information.

- **Expired password** Lists users with expired passwords.

- **RADIUS diagnostics** Lists various RADIUS reports that show whether the switch settings are synchronized with the RADIUS server settings.

Figure 16-53 The Statistics screen provides many subscreens that enable the administrator to view details of the CES system.

The Log Files

Log files are very important in maintaining the proper functionality of a Contivity switch. Log files will tell the administrator of problems that are occurring on the system and many other significant events. Administrators should take the time to access logs on a consistent basis to verify the CES's configuration and activities. Log files are directly available from the management interface, and they can be exported to other applications for additional processing. The switch supports both internal storage and backup external storage. Automatic backup and archiving of the logs assure the administrator that the logs are available when necessary.

The System Log The system log contains all system events that are considered significant enough to be written to disk, including those displayed in the configuration and security logs (see Figure 16-54). Events that would appear in the system log include LDAP activity, configuration activity, and server authentication and authorization requests. The system log shows all log events for a given date when it is selected for dis-

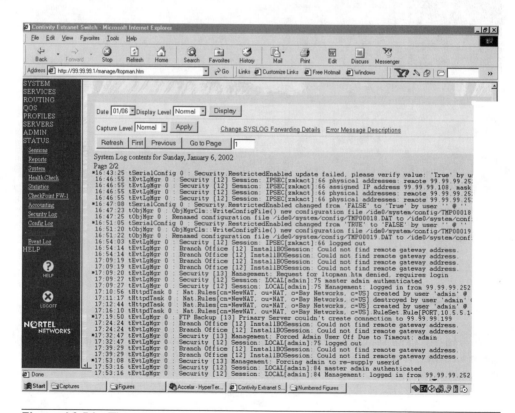

Figure 16-54 The system log

play. Events are stored for 61 days. The event types available for viewing are normal, urgent, detailed, or all recorded. Urgent events are shown with asterisks.

GUI > Status > System Log

The Event Log   The event log is a detailed recording of all events that take place on the system (see Figure 16-55). The event log includes information on tunneling, security, backups, debugging, hardware, security, daemon processes, software drivers, interface card driver events, and packet activity. It can be used to see IP or IPX packets that have been filtered or dropped. This log is displayed in real time and can hold up to 2,000 entries, but is not saved like the system log. As new entries are added to the event log's memory, older entries are overwritten.

GUI > Status > Event Log

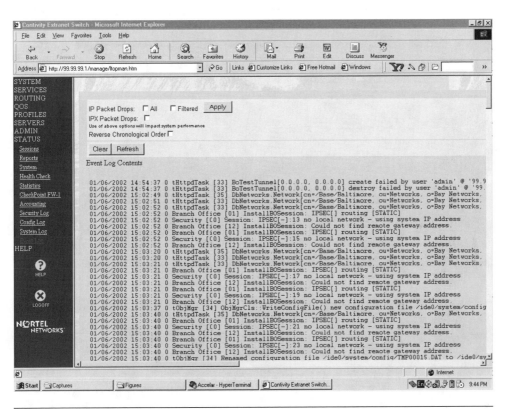

Figure 16-55   The event log

NOTE An option for reverse chronological order is to review newest events first.

The Security Log The security log records all activity about system or user security (see Figure 16-56). The security log lists all security events, both failures and successes. The events can include

- Authentication and authorization

- Tunnel or administration requests

- Encryption, authentication, or compression

- Hours of access

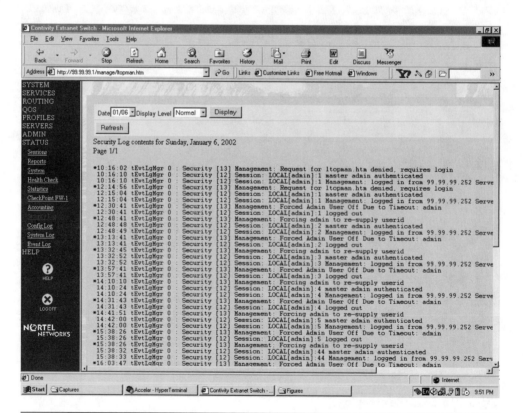

Figure 16-56 The security log

- Number of session violations

- Communication with servers

- LDAP

- RADIUS

GUI > Status > Security Log

The Configuration Log   The configuration log records all configuration changes (see Figure 16-57). For example, it tracks adding, modifying, or deleting configuration parameters like group or user profiles, LAN or WAN interfaces, changes to system access hours, filters, additions of shutdown or startup policies, and file maintenance or backup policies.

GUI > Status > Config Log

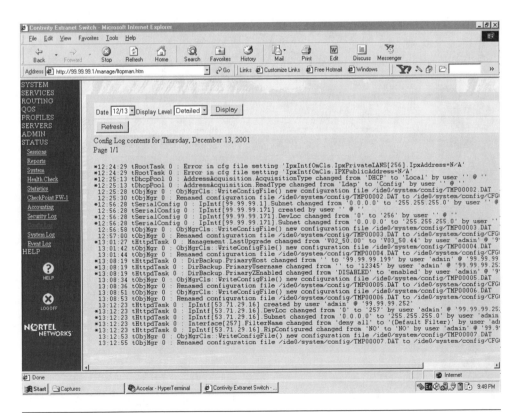

Figure 16-57   The config log

NOTE Only an administrator can clear the log.

Syslog

Utilizing the Syslog utility to enable logging from the Contivity to remote stations is also available. Syslog should be installed on the client that will be receiving the logs from the CES. Syslog must also be enabled from the web manager on the CES log (see Figure 16-58).

GUI > Services > Syslog > Fill out the IP address of the server that the daemon is on and enable the logging

The Syslog host will see anything that goes into the system log on the Contivity switch. To change the amount of data sent, change the message level.

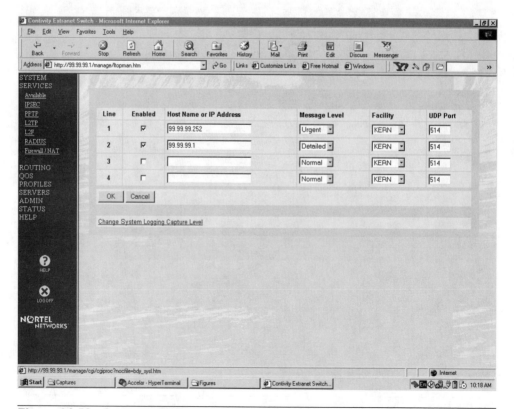

Figure 16-58 Setting up Syslog

Logging is enabled for the II 100/400 through the iisetup.exe utility.

GUI > Support > Advanced TCP/IP Settings—Add the ipsec log 1 command to the
TCP/IP settings listed

Accounting

Accounting is another log file component of the switch. The accounting log provides
information about user sessions. The log provides last and first names, user IDs, the
tunnel type, session start and end dates, and the number of packets and bytes transferred. The log can be searched according to most of these fields (Figure 16-59).

GUI > Status > Accounting

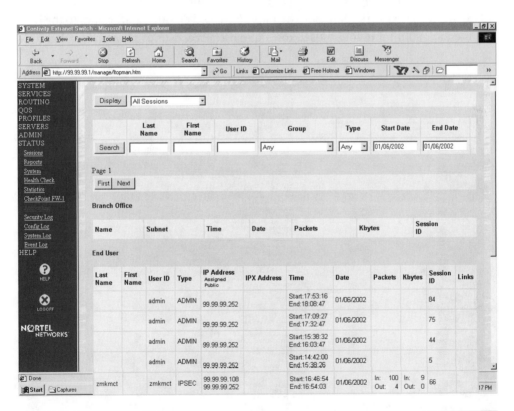

Figure 16-59   Viewing all sessions that were created on the Contivity switch

Client Features

Clients can dial in with the extranet client or Microsoft client. Tunneling is available through PPTP or IPSec. IPSec tunneling, most commonly used with the extranet client, offers many additional client features (see Figure 16-60).

GUI > Profiles > Groups > Select the group > Edit > IPSec

Split Tunneling

All IPSec client traffic is tunneled through the switch by default. Split tunneling enables client data to travel either through a tunnel to the enterprise network or directly to the Internet. Split tunneling works by configuring network routes that are downloaded to the client. These network routes are then tunneled; and all other traffic goes to the local PC interface. Split tunneling is used to enable users access to print and use other local

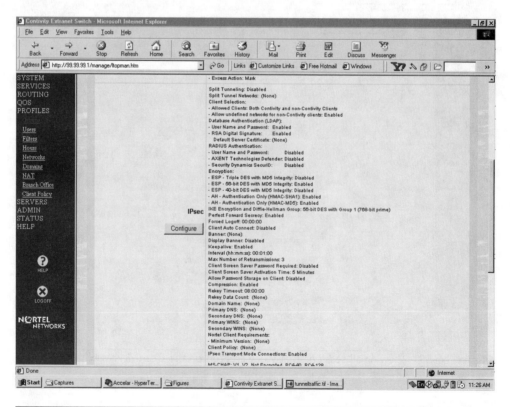

Figure 16-60 Features available for clients using IPSec tunneling

resources without going through the CES, even if they are tunneled into the switch at the same time (see Figure 16-61).

NOTE   Split tunneling is disabled by default.

GUI >Profile > Group > Choose group > IPSec > Edit > Split tunneling field

Although a powerful feature, split tunneling could potentially enable an application on the client to maliciously forward packets from the Internet to the enterprise

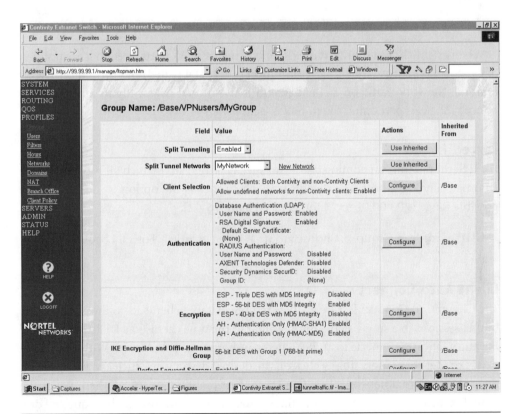

Figure 16-61   Configuring a client for split tunneling and choosing local networks for the client

network. Administrators may want to implement client policies to make the client more secure when using split tunneling.

GUI > Profiles > Client Policies Create tab > Add permitted applications

Client policies enable the administrator to determine which network applications and associated protocols and ports a remote user can have active on a workstation while tunneled into the switch. Limiting certain types of network applications from executing while using the split-tunneling feature can help to eliminate some security threats.

 CAUTION Be careful when choosing the list of network ports that clients can use while using split tunneling because it might prevent acceptable applications from running.

When establishing a tunnel, if the client has any network ports open that are not part of the client policy list, the tunnel connection is not established, and the remote user is notified. Network traffic on a client system is monitored constantly to make sure no policy violations occur after the tunnel is established as well.

Forced Logoff

For IPSec tunneling, an administrator can specify a time after which all active users are automatically logged off. The default is 0, which means the option is turned off. The possible range is 00:00:01 to 23:59:59 (see Figure 16-62).

GUI >Profile > Group > Choose group > IPSec > Edit > Forced Logoff field

Client Auto Connect

The Client Auto Connect feature enables remote extranet clients to connect their IPSec tunnel sessions in a single step. This is similar to the way Microsoft's Dial-Up Networking automatically connects to an ISP when a web browser is launched. With Auto Connect, extranet client users simply click on the desired destination, such as a web page on the private internal network. This first starts their dialup connection, then makes the tunnel connection to the switch, and finally makes the connection to the requested destination. What has in the past taken three distinct user operations is now accomplished

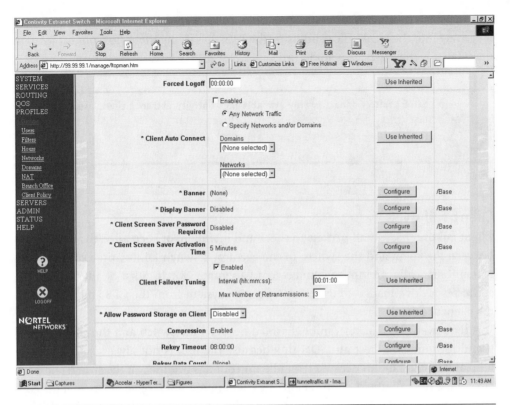

Figure 16-62 Configuring client features for groups in IPSec

by a single action. The Client Auto Connect settings specify those network connections that trigger the extranet Client's Auto Connect feature (see Figure 16-62).

When the extranet client successfully connects to the switch, the switch downloads the list of networks and domains that trigger the Auto Connect feature. This list, which is stored in the extranet client's registry, is used to determine whether a tunnel connection should automatically be started when one is not already active.

GUI >Profile > Group > Choose group> IPSec > Edit > Client Auto Connect

CAUTION After enabling the Client Auto Connect feature, the administrator must reboot the PC on which the extranet client is running and manually make sure the extranet client can connect to the switch.

It may be necessary to temporarily disable the Auto Connect feature for a user who is coming into the local office and using the LAN. Disabling the Auto Connect icon on the taskbar is the easiest way to do this.

> **NOTE** Auto Connect is only available for Contivity extranet client users.

Client Fail-over

Client fail-over uses small packets to check and maintain, or keep alive, the connection between the client and the switch. In the event of a switch failure, the extranet client will automatically attempt to connect to an alternate switch. A list of alternate switch addresses is downloaded to the client operating system from the CES and is stored in the client's registry.

Alternatively, keep alives can be disabled between the switch and the client. This is useful for tunneling over an ISDN link because the link is not always active. Disable keep alives with caution because if an idle timeout has been set on the switch and keep alives have been disabled on the client, the client might not receive notice that the connection has been closed even after the physical connection is no longer active. Because a switch can have an idle timer set to never, the resulting connection could remain established for a long time, which wastes switch resources. Additional trouble occurs if a user is only allowed one login, which is the default. The client will not be able to reconnect by default for about eight hours. In this situation, if the client session drops, it will need to be manually deleted from the switch to enable the user to reconnect.

Banner, Display Banner, Client Screen Saver, and Allow Password Storage on Client

There are many additional useful features for clients using IPSec tunneling. The ones listed previously can only be used with the Contivity extranet client software (see Figures 16-63 and 16-64).

GUI > Profile > Group > Choose group> IPSec > Edit

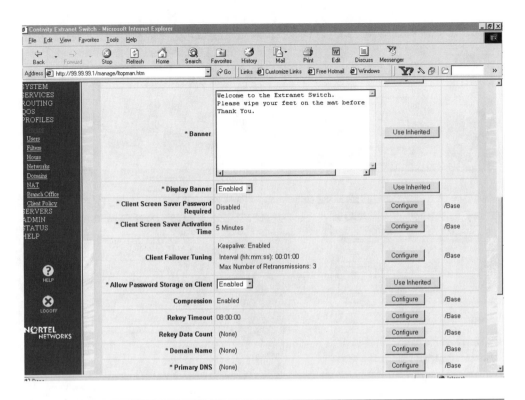

Figure 16-63 Creating a display banner for a client using the Contivity client software and enabling the client to save their password locally

NOTE The first time the client logs on, the Save password feature is disabled. Once the client connects to an extranet switch, the client can save the password locally and it will become available. Figure 16-64 shows this in the second logon in the figure having the password feature available while the first logon does not.

Client Customization

This feature enables a company to insert custom icons in place of the Nortel Networks predefined icons for their clients using the extranet access client. The customizable files are in the \client\custom directory that comes on the Nortel Networks CD. The icons that can be replaced include the corporate icon, (eacapp.ico), the taskbar icons, (blinknone.ico, blinkleft.ico, blinkright.ico, blinkboth.ico) the connection icons (connect1.ico, connect2.ico.), and the extranet connection manager icon (ecmapp.ico).

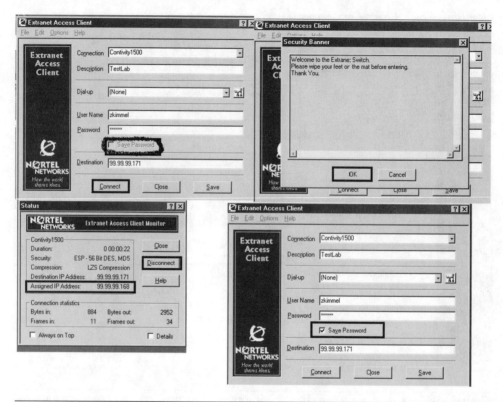

Figure 16-64   Results of the changes made previously in the client

Custom bitmaps can also be created to replace the default (eacdlg.bmp), status (eac-stats.bmp), and connection manager (ecmdlg.bmp) bitmaps.

To replace an icon or bitmap, the user should create a new icon/bitmap and name it with the name of the default icon/bitmap. The icon/bitmap should then be placed into the custom installation directory to be used when installing the extranet access client.

IP Services

User IP Address Assignment

Users can get addresses from many places. An address can be specified in the user properties, as shown in Figure 16-37. Contivity switches can assign a user's addresses from a local address pool created through the switch's internal address pool or from DHCP (see Figure 16-65). Finally, users can also get a static address from the switch's LDAP server or from a RADIUS server.

GUI > Servers > User IP Addr

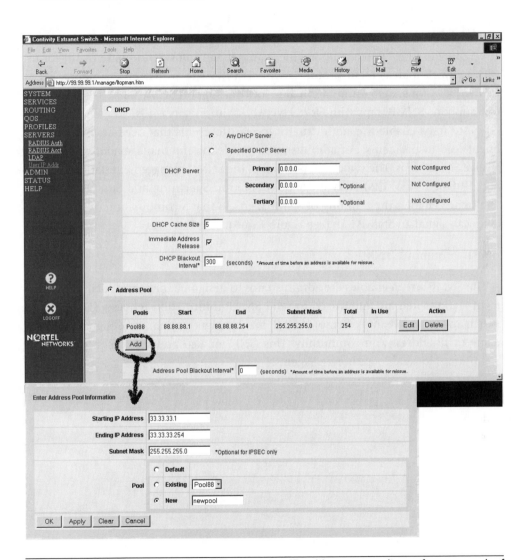

Figure 16-65 Configuring the CES to assign IP addresses to clients from a pool of addresses created by the administrator

Telnet

It is possible to Telnet to the II 100/400 after Telnet has been enabled through iisetup.exe.

GUI > Support > Services

SNMP Traps

The Contivity VPN Switch supports the management information base (MIB) for use with network management protocols with TCP/IP. The switch only supports SNMP GET requests for system information, but does not support SNMP SETs. In addition, the CES supports SNMP traps with Nortel Networks proprietary MIBs.

SNMP traps enable the administrator to react to events that need attention or that might lead to problems. An administrator can define the management stations that receive SNMP traps. The switch supports all of the SNMP management stations, including HP Open View, IBM NetView 6000, Cabletron Spectrum, and Sun Net Manager. The switch enables the scripting of SNMP alerts so that a combination of system variables can signal an SNMP trap (see Figure 16-66).

GUI > Admin > SNMP

The SNMP screen enables the administrator to designate the remote SNMP management stations that are authorized to send SNMP information requests (GETs) to the switch and to receive traps. Remote SNMP management stations are designated by host name or IP address and community. This GUI can also be used to configure which SNMP traps to send to authorized agents.

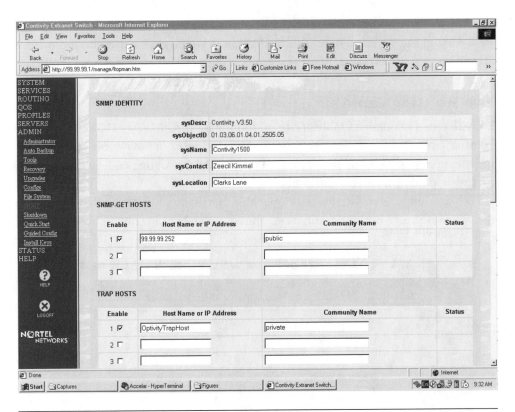

Figure 16-66   SNMP GET and trap configuration screen

Routing (Layer Three)

The switch's routing capabilities include many useful features implemented in most standard layer three routing environments. This switch has additional routing features as well because it is designed to create secure remote access for extranet clients.

Routing features include enabling authorized tunnel traffic to securely flow into and out of the corporation's private network. In addition, the switch can route traffic between two private interfaces and between its public and private interfaces. The switch can also route traffic from its public interfaces to destinations on the Internet. As a result, the switch can be used to connect an organization to the Internet.

To permit traffic to flow between the public and private sides of the network, some type of firewall must be enabled to prevent unauthorized access into the network from the public Internet. (Firewalls will be discussed in the next section.)

With the addition of an integrated firewall, the switch can perform a variety of secure routing functions, depending on how the switch's routing capabilities are set up. The switch can securely route nontunneled traffic from its private interface, through the firewall, and out its public interface. This configuration would enable users on the switch's private network to access the Internet without requiring a separate, dedicated router.

The Routing Table

Every IP router maintains a table of current routing information (see Figure 16-67). The Routing Table Manager (RTM) receives routing updates from the network through the Internet protocols running on the router. Periodically, the routing table manager issues routing updates through the protocols.

Like any router, the switch has a routing table that defines how traffic that comes into the switch is routed onto its destination. The routing table can contain both static and

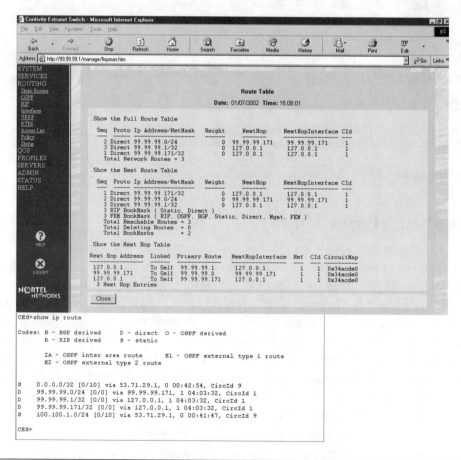

Figure 16-67 The IP routing table as viewed through the HTTP manager and CLI

dynamic routes. Static routes are manually configured routes that do not change. Dynamic routes, however, do change, as they are learned by using the Routing Internet Protocol (RIP) or Open Shortest Path First (OSPF) from a private interface or a branch office tunnel.

CLI Command: show ip route

GUI > Routing > RTM > Route Table

 NOTE The switch does *not* support RIP or OSPF for public interfaces.

Static Routes

The administrator can use static routes to set up routes between switches when no dynamic routing protocol (OSPF or RIP) is enabled. It is possible to use static routes even in a dynamic routing environment to provide stronger security. The switch supports multiple default and static routes. Static routes have a higher precedence; then OSPF or RIP routes. Contivity adds static routes for all interfaces automatically as well as for the branch offices, and it supports multiple static routes to the same location (see Figure 16-68).

To add a static route on an II 100/400 switch, use the iisetup.exe configuration tool.

For the CES, use the HTTP manager: **GUI** > Support > Static Routes. Add the destination address, the subnet mask, the interface for the route, the gateway address, and the metric.

Default Routes

In cases where no specific route is defined, packets are forwarded to the gateway specified as the default route. These default routes can be either private or public static routes. Private routes are always available, but public routes are available only if an integrated firewall is enabled.

 NOTE Private routes are available whether or not a firewall is enabled. Public routes are available only if the firewall is enabled.

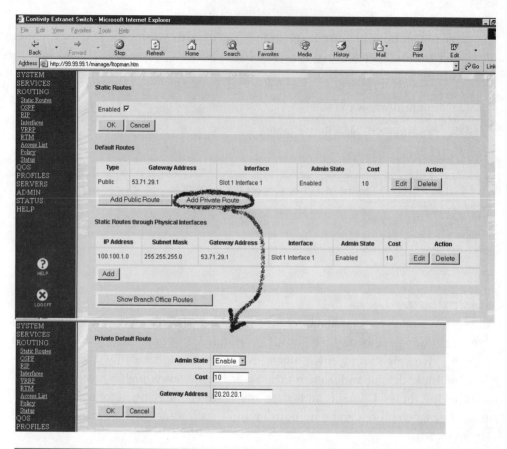

Figure 16-68 Adding a static private route to the Contivity switch

A private default static route is the default route used for traffic that comes into the switch from a private interface. Incoming traffic uses the private default route when there is no public default route defined. If there is no public or private default route, then traffic is dropped. When an administrator adds a private default route, the route table manager adds a new static route to the route table.

A public default static route is the default route used for traffic that comes into the switch from a public interface or through a tunnel. If no public default route is defined, then traffic is dropped. When an administrator adds a public default route, a new static route is added to the route table.

NOTE Multiple default routes can be defined to the same destination network using different gateways.

Add static and default routes by going to **GUI** > Routing > Static Routes, Then add, edit, or delete static routes (refer to Figure 16-68).

Dynamic Routing with RIP1, RIP2, and OSPF

The CES can transmit and receive RIPv1, RIPv2, and OSPF. The transmission and receiving of dynamic RIP or OSPF updates is available for the CES private interfaces or the public-side branch office tunnels only. Branch office tunnels using PPTP, IPSec, or L2TP can all use RIP or OSPF. Dynamic routing protocols can be configured on a per-interface and per-LDAP-group basis. The CES will automatically initialize a branch office tunnel that utilizes RIP or OSPF to manage their routes (see Figures 16-69 and 16-70).

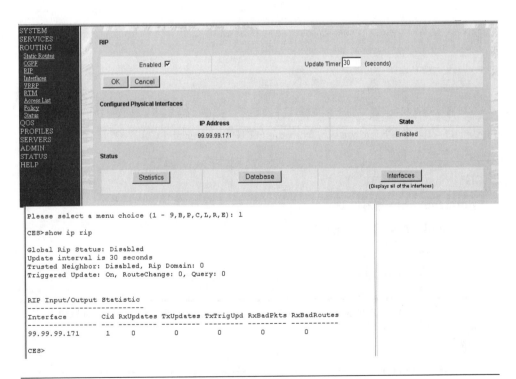

Figure 16-69 GUI and CLI RIP information

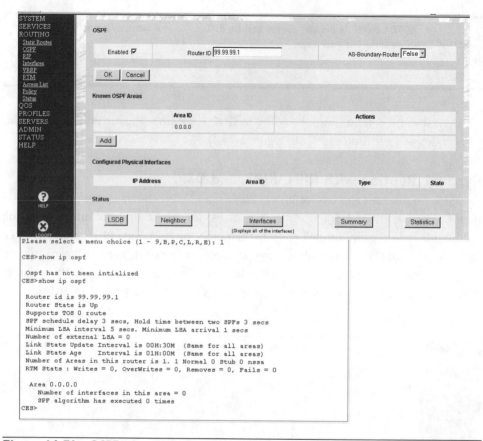

Figure 16-70   OSPF information from the HTTP manager and CLI

GUI > Routing > RIP

Command: show ip rip

Command: show ip ospf

GUI > Routing > OSPF

CAUTION   OSPF is only available once the advanced IP routing key is installed (see Figure 16-75).

Routing Policy Service (RPS)

Contivity enables the creation of route policies to control data flowing into and out of the routing table. We discussed these RIP and OSPF policies in Chapters 6 and 7. These policies are also known as IP accept and announce policies and are used to change the route updates received from other routers or to filter the route updates that are passed on to other routers. In addition to standard RIP and OSPF policies, RPS can use access lists as part of the routing policies. Access lists are created by an administrator using rules and actions to determine whether to drop or enable traffic. RPS will examine each access policy and check for all rules in order to determine which action to take on all packets entering the network. RPS is configured in the **GUI** > Routing > Policy (see Figure 16-71).

An administrator can create access lists that will be associated with any or all policies. This is done through the **GUI** > Routing > Access List. The order of the rules in a policy is very important because as soon as traffic matches a rule, the action specified will be taken. No further rules will be examined (see Figure 16-72).

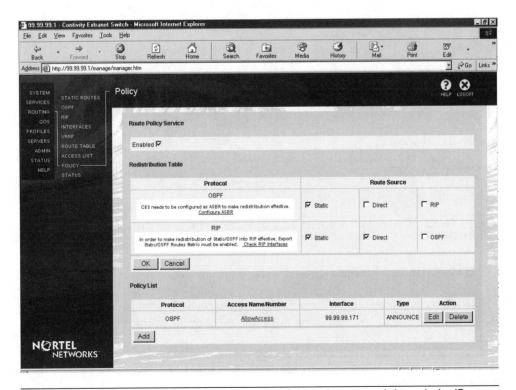

Figure 16-71   Configuring RPS. Notice the use of the policy created through the IP access list in Figure 16-72.

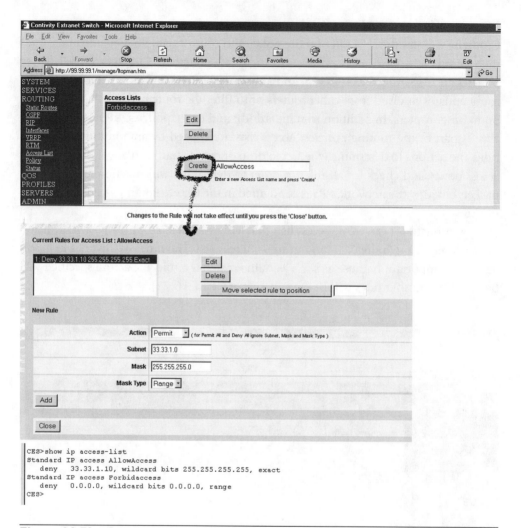

Figure 16-72   Creating an IP access list with HTTP and viewing the access lists in CLI

CLI Command: show ip access-list—shows the created IP access lists

The IP access list created in Figure 16-68 has two rules. The first rule denies access to workstation 33.1.1.10, and the second rule allows all traffic to the 33.1.1.0 network.

CAUTION   Routing policies use the implicit deny all rule unless *allow* is specified.

Virtual Router Redundancy Protocol (VRRP)

VRRP, as we mentioned in Chapter 10, is used to maintain a high state of network availability by ensuring no single point of failure exists with a client's default gateway. With VRRP, multiple CES switches can maintain the same virtual IP address that is used on the user's workstation as the default gateway address. This way if the master router CES switch becomes unavailable, any backup switch configured with the identical virtual IP address can act as the master router and forward network traffic on behalf of workstations (see Figure 16-73).

GUI > Routing > VRRP

CLI Command: `show ip vrrp`

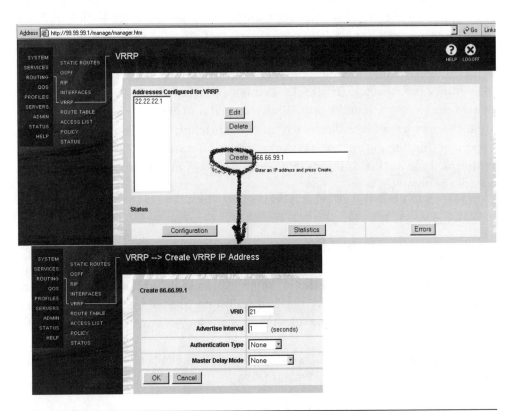

Figure 16-73   Creating a virtual router IP address 66.66.99.1 with a virtual router ID of 21

Packet Security

There are three types of packet security settings that can be implemented on the CES: interface filters, Checkpoint Firewall-1, and Contivity stateful firewall.

Interface Filters

Users can define filters that are applied to an interface or tunnel connection (see Figure 16-74). These filters are created through rules that are applied to every message in a sequence. Actions are applied when a rule is matched. Filters can be applied at the public and/or private interface.

Filters are based on protocol ID, direction, source or destination IP address, source or destination port for TCP and UDP, TCP connection establishment, physical interface, and tunnel identification. Filters are compared to the inner IP header, so filtering takes place after the tunnel headers have been stripped off.

Filters are created through filter profiles. A filter profile consists of a list of rules (one or more outbound rules and one or more inbound rules) that the administrator creates to perform a precise action. Filter rules are built at the TCP or UDP port level with one rule covering a port or range of ports. Each rule field contains a single value. These rules are tested in order until the first match is found; therefore, the order of the rules is very important. The filtering mechanism works such that if no rule matches, then the packet is discarded (denied). This means that no traffic is transmitted or received unless it is specifically permitted.

GUI > Profiles > Filters

Interface filters are limited in their capabilities. They do not have application-level awareness and offer more limited security by only being able to filter on IP network level fields. Performance with interface filters can cause delays and low performance because each and every packet is compared against the rule set. Interface filters are easier to apply, but only offer simple rules that contain single value rule fields and can be applied per interface only.

To enable interface filters the firewall key must be available, and Contivity firewall must be installed (see Figures 16-75 and 16-76).

GUI > Admin > Install Keys—installs the key necessary for firewall activity

GUI > Services > Firewall/NAT—enables the firewall, which supports interface filters

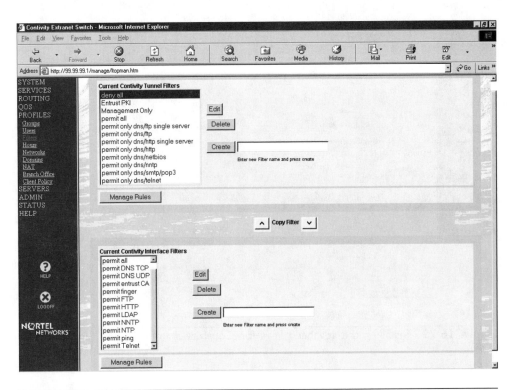

Figure 16-74   Contivity built-in filters

CAUTION   Be very careful not to filter out management traffic to the switch.

Check Point Firewall-1 (FW-1)

For customers who have Check Point FW-1 from Check Point Technologies, the switch offers an optional, separately licensed integrated firewall. FW-1 is available as an added service in software codes 2.50 and above. All rules apply globally to all interfaces. Management station is a separate console. Tunnel traffic does not pass through FW-1. Like the built-in Contivity VPN firewalls, the integrated FW-1 is transparent to both users and applications that access the switch.

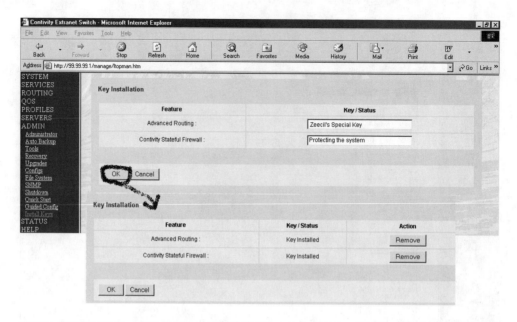

Figure 16-75 Installing the advanced keys for Contivity stateful firewall (and advanced routing)

Contivity Stateful Firewall (CSF)

CSF is available as an added service for software codes 3.5 and above. (It requires an additional key to be installed. Refer to Figure 16-75.) It is not available for the II 100 or 400. CSF provides a full stateful inspection engine, NAT, logging, protection against spoofing through validity checking on source addresses, and protection against denial of service attacks.

CSF works like any other stateful firewall that applies rules to setup messages and uses dynamic state tables. Good performance is ensured because only setup packets are compared to the rule set and subsequent packets have a minimal delay. By using stateful inspection, the CSF provides a high level of security, the fastest run time, and the flexibility to define the rules to fit any environment. The firewall delivers full firewall capabilities, assuring the highest level of network security. To do this, the firewall examines packets in both incoming and outgoing directions running against a common security policy. All service rules are interpreted on IP conversations (not packets) and are fully stateful. Security rules do not filter packets directly, but the firewall services determine how to process them based on the security policy defined.

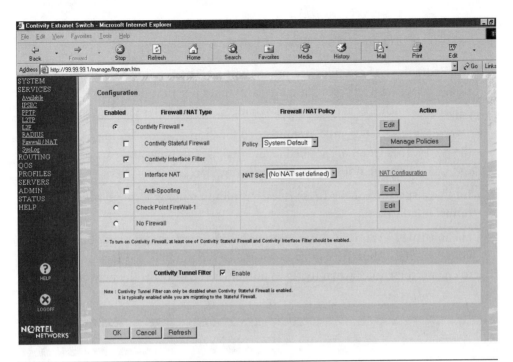

Figure 16-76 Enabling the firewall, which then enables interface filters

CSF offers application-level awareness with very strong security because its firewall comes with prematched filters that work for most applications. Firewall filters are easy to apply and have sophisticated policies with multiple values in each rule field and rules that can be applied switch-wide or per interface. A set of rules defines a specific security policy and determines whether packets should be accepted or rejected based on their source and/or destination. Rules can be created for global use or applied to specific interfaces. Each rule is built at the IP service level; each rule can contain multiple values, and each rule refers to a specific source and destination interface or interface type. Privileges can be based on predefined groups. Rules can even be applied within a tunnel.

Management and logging occur internal to the Contivity. The CSF affects tunnel traffic by default, but tunnel filters can be disabled.

Firewall policies are based on protocol ID, direction, source or destination IP address, source or destination port for TCP and UDP, TCP connection establishment, physical interface, and tunnel identification. Also with CSF, the type of interface (private or public) can be examined for a firewall policy.

Firewall policies are applied at the switch level. Policies can be from one of five rule groups (two are read only). The five groups are

- **Implied rules** These rules are processed first. They enable for tunnel termination, management IP access, and messages that must pass between clients and the Contivity switch. Users cannot make changes to these rules (see Figure 16-77).

- **Override rules** These rules are intended for short-term overriding of the rules in the policy. These rules are applied to an interface grouping: any, trusted, untrusted, or tunnel. They are not applied to specific interfaces.

- **Interface-specific rules** These rules are rules that apply to physical interfaces or tunnel interfaces.

- **Default rules** These rules are also applied to interface groupings and not individual interfaces, but these rules are meant for system-wide use. It is most common to change these rules when trying to implement security for the network.

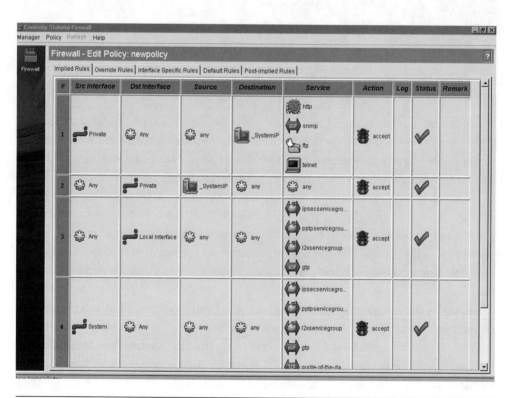

Figure 16-77 Implied rules: Note the first rule enables management access from the private LAN to the system IP address.

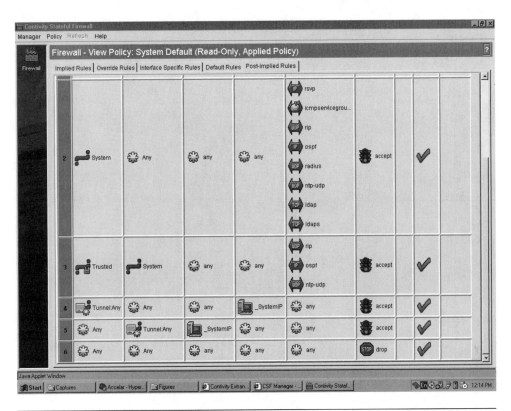

Figure 16-78   Post-implied rules of the default policy. Note the last rule denies everything.

- **Post-implied rules**   These rules are applied at the end and enable RSVP, ICMP, LDAP, RADIUS, and routing protocols (see Figure 16-78). Users cannot change these rules and they contain the cleanup rule of "disallow everything not specifically allowed."

Configuring the CSF   To implement CSF in the network the CSF must be enabled. Go to **GUI** >Admin > Install Keys (refer to Figure 16-75). Next the CSF must be selected in **GUI** > Services > Firewall/NAT. Enabling the firewall will require a reboot. Once the firewall is enabled, the default policy is to deny all. A new policy must be created to reflect the correct network needs. To create a policy, use the CSF manager (see Figure 16-79).

GUI > Services > Firewall/NAT > Choose manage policies > New and give the new policy a name

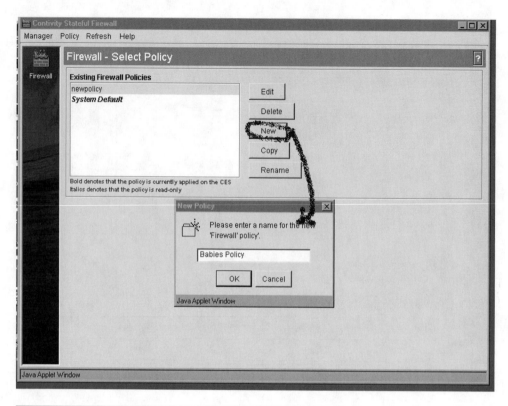

Figure 16-79   CFS manager

Next the administrator must define rules and set the log level for the rule (see Figure 16-80).

> **GUI** > Services > Firewall/NAT > Contivity Stateful Firewall Manage Policies > Choose policy to manage > Default rule > Right-click the number sign > Add rule

Finally, the administrator will want to use the newly created policy. To do so, choose the policy name from the pull-down menu next to the CFS under **GUI** > Services > Firewall/NAT (refer to Figure 16-76).

NOTE   Changing a policy does not require a reboot, but enabling or disabling the firewall does.

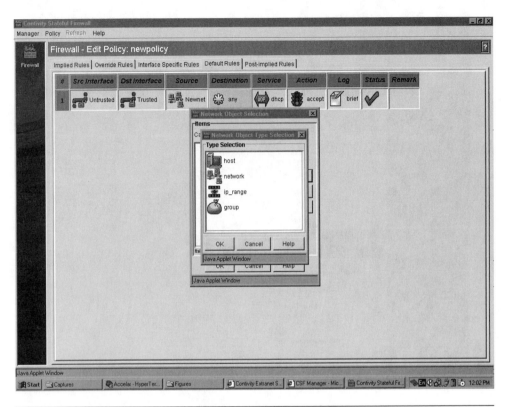

Figure 16-80 Creating a new default rule with the policy manager

QoS

With the switch fully configured and many clients dialing into it, performance and QoS become important (see Figure 16-81). The idea behind QoS is that business-critical applications that require a highly available network without performance degradation get it. Rules must be defined and enforced to afford essential traffic the bandwidth it requires. Part of QoS is classifying the different kinds of traffic so that different levels of service can be applied accordingly. Once traffic is classified, it must then receive the appropriate level of service and bandwidth throughout the network.

Bandwidth Management

Bandwidth management capabilities enable the switch's CPU and interface bandwidth resources to ensure that tunneled sessions get predictable and adequate levels of service. Bandwidth management enables the configuration of switch resources for users,

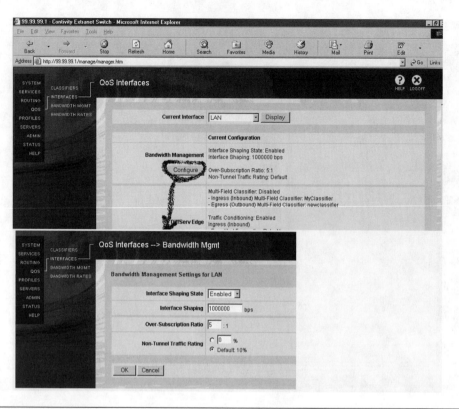

Figure 16-81 Configuring interfaces for QoS

branch offices, and interface-routed traffic. Branch offices and users can be given a minimum guaranteed amount of resources on the CES.

Bandwidth components keep track of and control the level of bandwidth being used on the physical interfaces and the tunnels. Bandwidth management forces tunnels to conform to a set of rates. There are two rates (committed and excess) and two excess actions (mark or drop). Packets are given different drop preferences depending on whether they are below the committed rate (lowest drop preference), between the committed and excess rate (higher drop preference), and above the excess rate (highest drop preference if excess action is marked). When there is congestion on the switch, packets are dropped according to their drop preference. When excess action is dropped, all the packets above the excess rate are dropped.

NOTE To enable bandwidth management, the advanced routing key must be enabled (refer to Figure 16-75).

GUI > QOS > Interfaces > Bandwidth Management Configure tab

In addition to configuring interfaces for bandwidth management, groups should also be configured with bandwidth policies. The administrator should define the committed and excess bandwidth rates using the default rates available or by configuring user-defined rates. Administrators can create rates in the **GUI** > QoS > Bandwidth Rate (see Figure 16-82).

 NOTE Rates are defined in terms of bits per second, so 1 Mbps would be 1,000,000 bits.

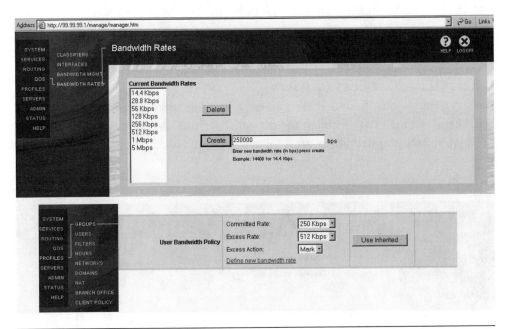

Figure 16-82 Configuring a bandwidth rate and adding it to users' properties

Once a rate is defined, it should be added to the correct group of users. Minimum and maximum bandwidth settings are configurable at a group level.

GUI > Profiles > Groups > Connectivity Edit tab

> **NOTE** The maximum rate is 10 Mbps.

This bandwidth configuration is very useful if, for example, the administrator wants to enable users to have at least 56 Kbps (to accommodate dial-in users) but not allow more than 256 Kbps (to keep cable and DSL users from using all the available bandwidth). In this case, the administrator could set the committed rate to 56 Kbps, the excess rate to 256 Kbps, and the excess action to drop. This will keep the higher bandwidth users limited to between 56 and 256 Kbps, depending upon other traffic activity. When the limits are exceeded, packets are dropped.

Once bandwidth management is configured, it is necessary to enable it in the **GUI** > QoS > Bandwidth Management and set it to Enabled (see Figure 16-83).

Once enabled, the previously set bandwidth limits will now be examined and acted upon.

Differentiated Services (DiffServ)

DiffServ settings classify and mark packets to receive specified per-hop forwarding behavior along their path through the network. Sophisticated classification, marking, policing, and shaping operations are implemented at network boundaries, where traffic

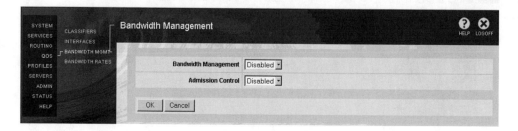

Figure 16-83 Enabling bandwidth management

is lighter. Once traffic is marked at the network boundaries with DiffServ Code Points (DSCPs), all hosts that forward the traffic allocate network resources according to policies that govern how marked traffic is treated. Any DSCPs from marked traffic that are not recognized are forwarded as if marked for the default behavior, Best Effort (BE).

DiffServ classifies traffic according to IP header fields in the packet, including source and destination IP address, protocol ID, and source and destination port. To create classifiers for DiffServ on the CES, go to **GUI** > QOS > Classifiers. Name the classifier and hit the Create tab.

Creating a classifier consists of creating rules that describe the traffic to mark as well as the Per Hop Behavior (PHB) that the traffic will use (see Figure 16-84). The classifier rule is then associated with a classifier.

GUI > QOS > Classifiers > Manage Rules

The CES can act as a DiffServ edge switch and mark packets according to the classifiers created in Figure 16-84. Traffic can also be shaped, and lower-priority traffic can be dropped to ensure that higher-priority traffic gets guaranteed bandwidth (see Figure 16-85). Forwarding priority levels and dropping packets when a queue reaches a preset threshold works with an algorithm called Weighted Random Early Detection (WRED). This algorithm works to detect congestion by keeping an eye on queue size. This controls the percentage of user traffic that will be allowed through under conditions of congestion.

NOTE Without congestion, 100 percent of traffic should be able to pass through.

GUI > QOS > Interfaces > DiffServ Edge > Configure

Reservation Protocol (RSVP)

RSVP signals the network to reserve a portion of the network's bandwidth for a specific connection (see Figure 16-86). RSVP enables two clients in a network to exchange data and obtain reservations that commit to a certain amount of bandwidth for the application session. RSVP works with Token Bucket Depth, which restricts the amount of packets that goes onto the queue. This is designed to shorten the lengths of the packet

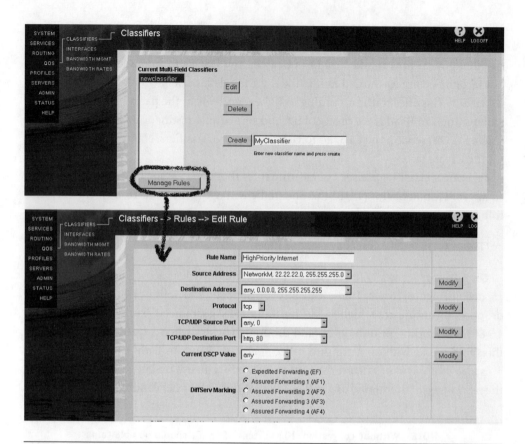

Figure 16-84 Creating a classifier rule to mark all HTTP traffic from network 22.22.22.0 as high-priority traffic

queues to minimize latency for all sessions. Additionally, Token Bucket Rate states the highest average data rate required on the connection.

> **NOTE** RSVP should be enabled with care because it can affect the forwarding and data rate of non-RSVP sessions.

GUI > Profiles > Groups > Connectivity Edit tab > RSVP

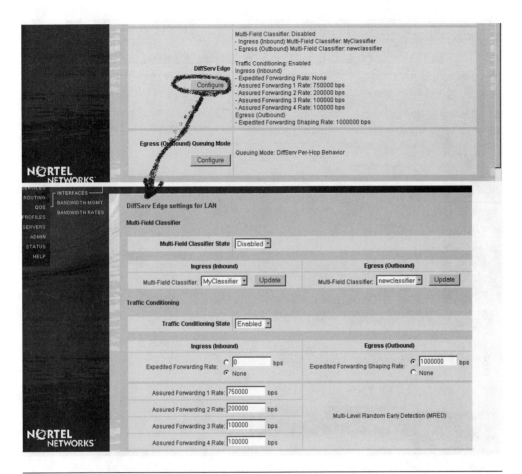

Figure 16-85 Configuring the CES to shape traffic

IPX

The switch supports IPX by encapsulating IPX traffic within IP tunnels.

GUI > System > IPX

NOTE IPX must be enabled for each specific group. Use the Profiles > Groups display to enable IPX for groups that will be using IPX (see Figure 16-87).

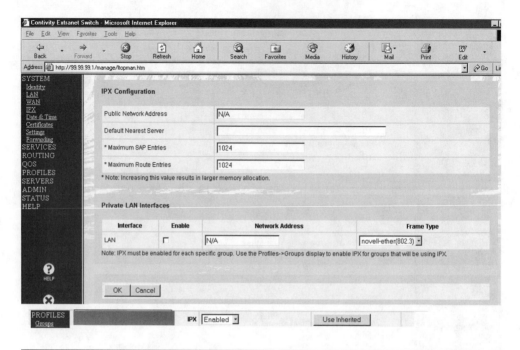

Figure 16-87 IPX configuration for CES

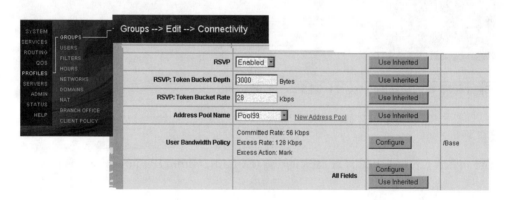

Figure 16-86 Configuring user groups for RSVP

The private interfaces and public interfaces can carry IP and IPX traffic simultaneously over PPTP, L2TP, and L2F. IPSec does not support IPX.

Summary

This chapter covered the features of the II 100 and 400 switches and the Contivity Extranet 1600, 2600, and 4600 switches. In addition, this chapter demonstrated how to configure, manage, and troubleshoot the switches using web-based tools and command line tools.

Review Questions

1. A customer has standardized on an LDAP data store system. All usernames and passwords are stored within this database. They are implementing a Contivity 4500 and a Contivity VPN Client for remote access and want to authenticate users using this existing LDAP data store system. Which authentication method would be configured within the group profile?

   A. External LDAP server

   B. RSA digital signature

   C. Group ID and password

   D. LDAP user name and password

   E. RADIUS username and password

2. Which two are possible reasons for using DES instead of 3DES for a particular application?

   A. Security is a prime consideration.

   B. Data integrity is a prime consideration.

   C. Processing speed is prime consideration.

   D. 3DES is not exportable for your installation.

3. Which statement is true regarding PKI?

   A. PKI makes it possible to deliver private keys securely.

   B. Without PKI, the use of public keys would not be possible.

   C. PKI makes it possible to keep a master list of all root keys.

   D. PKI makes it easier to manage keys, certificates, and security policies.

4. Which two are required to define RADIUS authentication on a Contivity 4500?
   A. Base DN
   B. Server IP address
   C. Server port number
   D. Interim update interval

5. A switch is placed behind a router and in parallel with a firewall. What are two advantages to this configuration?
   A. It requires only a simple policy change to the existing firewall.
   B. The router does not need to be configured to enable tunnel pass-through.
   C. The configuration enables extranet bandwidth without impacting other Internet traffic.
   D. You can retain the existing configuration while still enabling secure extranet connections.
   E. The switch and the firewall can share the existing connection to the PDN.

6. You have assigned a static address to a client. Which statement is true?
   A. Gratuitous ARP must also be enabled.
   B. The user must use the Contivity client.
   C. The user will be allowed only one simultaneous login.
   D. The user will be unable to log in to the remote network.

7. You are configuring a NMS to retrieve statistics via SNMP from a Contivity 2600. Which two must be configured and enabled on the Contivity?
   A. Trap host community name
   B. Trap host name or IP address
   C. SNMP-GET host community name
   D. SNMP-GET host name or IP address

8. A remote user is configuring a PC to use the Contivity VPN Client and Microsoft Dial-up Networking to connect into the corporate Windows domain. Which two need to be set up?
   A. The WINS server must be defined in the Contivity VPN Client profile.
   B. The profile connection name must be the same as the domain name.
   C. The remote user must select the Logon to the Remote Domain option on the client.
   D. The remote user must turn off NetBEUI on the Windows Dial-Up Networking profile.

9. You work for a large insurance company. Several remote sites need access to the corporate LAN. The main site has a Contivity 4500. One remote site has a Contivity 100 and is using DSL in which the ISP will not give them a permanent public registered address. Which two steps are needed to configure the Branch Office connection?
   A. Configure the Alias interface on the host Contivity 4500.
   B. Ensure IP forwarding is enabled on the remote Contivity 100.
   C. Ensure IP forwarding is disabled on the remote Contivity 100.
   D. Add and configure a group for the Dynamic IP clients on the host Contivity 4500.

10. You have configured Auto Connect for your remote users. A remote user has come into the corporate office to work for the day, and when trying to connect to a local corporate server a tunnel opens. How can the user stop Auto Connect on a temporary basis?
    A. Disable Auto Connect on the Contivity.
    B. Disable the Auto Connect icon in the task bar.
    C. Remove Auto Connect entries from the registry.
    D. Disable Auto Connect from the Options menu of the client.

11. What does the Allow All option available with certificates do?
    A. Can only be used for branch office authentication
    B. Prevents the Contivity from checking the CRL
    C. Ensures that a user with a valid user certificate from any CA will be authenticated
    D. Assigns authenticated users to the default group, unless they are otherwise defined in another group

12. Which features require the advanced routing key? (Choose all that apply)
    A. CSF
    B. OSPF
    C. RIP
    D. VRRP

13. Which type of NAT allows for bidirectional session establishment traffic?
    A. Branch office NAT
    B. Satic NAT
    C. Port NAT
    D. Pooled NAT

14. Which technoloy allows an administrator to prioritize traffic?
    A. OSPF
    B. NAT
    C. VPN
    D. QoS

15. Which technology is necessary for securing traffic over the Internet?
    A. Tunneling
    B. NAT
    C. Firewall
    D. Packet security

Answers

1. **E.** This configuration uses RADIUS usernames and passwords because they want to use an existing LDAP data store, and the CES cannot access this external LDAP directly.

2. **C, D.** 3DES provides a very high level of security but at the expense of processing speed. Additionally, because of its strong 168-bit encryption key it cannot be exported.

3. **D.** PKI is a standard that makes it easier to manage keys, certificates, and security policies.

4. **B, D.** To use RADIUS authentication together with the Contivity, the server IP address and port number must be defined.

5. **D, E.**

6. **C.** Because the user is only enabled one static IP address, that will prevent the user from being able to login more than once.

7. **C, D.** Because you are configuring hosts that can retrieve statistics from the CES, you must configure SNMP GET host addresses and community names.

8. **C, D.**

9. **B, D.**

10. **B.**

11. D.

12. **B, D.** CSF does require an additinal key but not the advanced routing key. RIP support is standard with Contivity.

13. B.

14. D.

15. A.

APPENDIX

This CD-ROM contains Total Seminars' Total Tester Software with nine practice exams.

The CD is set up with an autorun function. If your autorun is not turned on, browse the CD and double-click the Launcher.exe file to begin the installation wizard. The wizard allows you to install products or browse the freeware and shareware content.

Installing Total Seminars Test Software

Click the Install Test Software button on the wizard and the installation will proceed automatically.

Once installed, you can open the test program from your Start menu, go to the Program section, click Total Seminars, and then click the All-in-One Nortel Exams to begin the program. You can also start the program with the shortcut the installation places on your desktop.

Navigation

The program allows you to take each of the tests in either Practice or Final mode. Begin by selecting a testing mode and specific test from the menu bar.

Practice Mode

In Practice mode the test includes an assistance window. This gives you access to several study-oriented features. A good way to study and review is by taking each question, checking to see if you answer correctly, and reviewing the explanation and referring to the book for more detailed coverage. At the end of the test you are graded by topic and can review missed questions.

Final Mode

Final mode allows you to test yourself without the ability to see the correct answer. This is a better way to see how well you understand the material and is more like the actual exams you will take. Upon completion you receive a final grade by topic and are able to look over the questions you missed.

Minimum System Requirements
for Total Seminars Software

Pentium 200 MHz, 4x or faster speed CD-ROM, 16MB RAM, 30MB availabe hard disk space, 800×600 resolution at 256 colors, and Windows 9x/2000

Technical Support

For questions regarding the technical content of the exams (questions and answers), please visit *www.osborne.com* or e-mail *customer.service@mcgraw-hill.com*. International customers, please email *international_cs@mcgraw-hill.com*.

For technical problems with the testing software (installation and operation), please visit *www.totalsem.com* or e-mail *techsupport@totalsem.com*.

INDEX

INTERNATIONAL CONTACT INFORMATION

AUSTRALIA
McGraw-Hill Book Company Australia Pty. Ltd.
TEL +61-2-9417-9899
FAX +61-2-9417-5687
http://www.mcgraw-hill.com.au
books-it_sydney@mcgraw-hill.com

CANADA
McGraw-Hill Ryerson Ltd.
TEL +905-430-5000
FAX +905-430-5020
http://www.mcgrawhill.ca

**GREECE, MIDDLE EAST,
NORTHERN AFRICA**
McGraw-Hill Hellas
TEL +30-1-656-0990-3-4
FAX +30-1-654-5525

MEXICO (Also serving Latin America)
McGraw-Hill Interamericana Editores S.A. de C.V.
TEL +525-117-1583
FAX +525-117-1589
http://www.mcgraw-hill.com.mx
fernando_castellanos@mcgraw-hill.com

SINGAPORE (Serving Asia)
McGraw-Hill Book Company
TEL +65-863-1580
FAX +65-862-3354
http://www.mcgraw-hill.com.sg
mghasia@mcgraw-hill.com

SOUTH AFRICA
McGraw-Hill South Africa
TEL +27-11-622-7512
FAX +27-11-622-9045
robyn_swanepoel@mcgraw-hill.com

**UNITED KINGDOM & EUROPE
(Excluding Southern Europe)**
McGraw-Hill Education Europe
TEL +44-1-628-502500
FAX +44-1-628-770224
http://www.mcgraw-hill.co.uk
computing_neurope@mcgraw-hill.com

ALL OTHER INQUIRIES Contact:
Osborne/McGraw-Hill
TEL +1-510-549-6600
FAX +1-510-883-7600
http://www.osborne.com
omg_international@mcgraw-hill.com

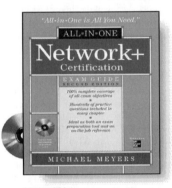

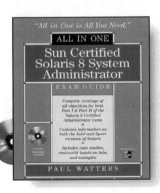

LICENSE AGREEMENT